D1046183

Native American Son

The Life and Sporting Legend of

Jim Thorpe

Kate Buford

UNIVERSITY OF NEBRASKA PRESS · LINCOLN

First Nebraska paperback printing: 2012

Published by arrangement with Alfred A. Knopf, an imprint of The Knopf Doubleday
Publishing Group, a division of Random House, Inc.

Library of Congress Cataloging-in-Publication Data
Buford, Kate.
Native American son: the life and sporting legend of Jim Thorpe / Kate Buford.
p. cm.
Includes bibliographical references and index.
ISBN 978-0-8032-4089-6 (pbk.: alk. paper)
1. Thorpe, Jim, 1887–1953. 2. Athletes—United States—Biography. 3. Indian
athletes—United States—Biography. I. Title.
GV697.T5B84 2012
796.092—dc23
[B] 2011041460

To Lucy and Will

Contents

Prologue

When Jim Thorpe was named the best football player of the half century on January 25, 1950, by an Associated Press poll of 393 national sportswriters and radio broadcasters, there was the usual grousing about comparing "old-timers and new-timers." In response, some who had seen Jim play football in his glory days forty years before spoke up, echoing an earlier, definitive assessment by Kyle Crichton in *Collier's* magazine: "Jim was a man, and the rest are children. I mean that Jim Thorpe was monumental, Brobdingnagian, colossal and perfect; the others are only shadows in his wake."

The next day, when Jesse Owens was named the top track and field athlete with 201 votes and Jim was the runner-up with 74, Jim, sixty-two, spoke at a testimonial dinner in his honor in Carlisle, Pennsylvania. He kept the audience laughing as he reminisced happily about his days at the Carlisle Indian Industrial School. At a sportswriters' banquet in nearby Harrisburg soon thereafter, the crowd rose when he was introduced and applauded him for five minutes. Overcome at the warmth and welcome extended to him by the people who had seen him at his best, he had tears in his eyes. He had been stoic for so long, and the sadness, anger, and helplessness that had been festering for years now flooded over him.

The AP polls continued into February, recognizing the great-est achiever in each major sport, until Sunday, February 12, when sports page headlines across the country announced: "Jim Thorpe Selected as Best Male Athlete of Half Century." He had received 252 first-place votes; Babe Ruth, in second place, had received 86. *New York Times* sportswriter Arthur Daley, ever a Thorpe fan, raved that "[t]he Sac and Fox Indian is almost a legend now. Unlike most legends, though, he never needed any fictional embroidery to add luster to his accomplishments. The truth was breathtaking enough and hard to believe, because it seems inconceivable that any one man could be so overwhelmingly endowed by nature with all the skills and talents the Indian had in superabundance."

The annulment of Thorpe's Olympic performance in 1912 had fueled a grassroots hunger for vindication. He had become a folk hero, one of the last before what Swedish sports historian Leif Yttergren called "the massive media exposure and commercialization" of the celebrity culture that took root in the 1920s. Taciturn, poor, relatively uneducated, clearly ill at ease at public events, the victim of personal tragedy and misfortune self-inflicted and accidental, a man who rarely had peace, Thorpe was someone with whom all people could identify.

While some of his life story is certainly pegged to larger developments in Indian history and U.S. policy, particularly in his early years, it is impossible to fit him into a preconceived pattern. He was sui generis, "not," as his daughter Grace Thorpe once said, "a traditional Indian."* His life is defined in large part by the man people expected him to be, good and bad, as well as the man he really was. His unique fame as the central figure at the dawn of American and international popular sports is clouded by the question of how much he was the victim of prejudice and how much he was his own worst enemy.

A gentle person, intelligent and funny, with many flaws, Jim Thorpe was not a complicated man. But what happened to him was.

---

*The term "Indian" is used in this narrative because it is the word the Thorpe family uses to describe themselves. Similarly, the term "Sac" will be used instead of the more correct "Sauk" because that was the name generally used in written records before and during Jim Thorpe's lifetime.

PART I

The Rules of the Game

This democracy, this land of freedom and equality and pursuit of happiness—it could have worked! There was something to it, after all!! It didn't have to turn into a greedy free-for-all! We didn't have to make a mess of it and the continent and ourselves! . . . For a moment I could imagine the past rewritten, wars unfought, the buffalo and the Indians undestroyed, the prairie unplundered. Maybe history did not absolutely have to turn out the way it did.

—Ian Frazier, *Great Plains*

Black Hawk, prisoner of war at Jefferson Barracks, St. Louis, 1832, by George Catlin

MÚK-A-TAH-MISH-O-KÁH-KAIK, Black Sparrow Hawk—Black Hawk—was the Sac warrior who, in the summer of 1832, just before this portrait was painted, led the last major Indian campaign east of the Mississippi. His defeat and capture meant that the land from the river to the Alleghenies was now safe for the tsunami of white settlement that would follow. Regal and romantic as painted by George Catlin, Black Hawk's face seems to register a dawning awareness that the land war is over. Honored in oral memory as the best runner, jumper, wrestler, and swimmer in the Sac and Fox tribe, he was Jim's warrior model.

CHAPTER ONE

Beginnings · Oklahoma Territory

1887–1904

Contrary to the beliefs of many, there was indeed a past.

— RAY A. YOUNG BEAR, *Black Eagle Child: The Facepaint Narratives*

The path to glory is rough, and many gloomy hours obscure it. May the Great Spirit shed light on yours—and that you may never experience the humility that the power of the American government has reduced me to, is the wish of him, who, in his native forests, was once as proud and bold as yourself.

— BLACK HAWK

In 1885, Father Thomas Bergh, an observant English Benedictine monk, arrived from Ramsgate, the home abbey in Kent, to what was known as the Oklahoma Territory.* Bergh came as a visitator—an emissary and inspector—to the order's Sacred Heart mission church, convent, and day school south of Tecumseh founded in 1876 by Jim's Potawatomi grandfather, Jacob Vieux, and other tribal members. Before returning to England in 1886, Bergh wrote a series of letters

---

*The land between Kansas and the Red River, most of today's Oklahoma, was called "the" Indian Territory from 1830 to 1890, although it was never an official United States territory as defined in the Constitution. In 1890 Oklahoma Territory was created under U.S. law from lands opened by land run and the addition of No Man's Land, today's Oklahoma Panhandle. From 1890 until 1907 and statehood, "the" Indian Territory shrank while Oklahoma Territory grew as subsequent land openings and allotment converted Indian lands to private ownership.

to a Father Swithbert at the abbey that offers his view of the unique environment into which Jim Thorpe would be born a year later.

"There are two sorts of Indians," Bergh noted on arrival, his perspective initially skewed by popular Wild West stereotypes. "Wild Indians with war-paint & scalp knots who dress in a blanket; and Civilized Indians who wear something besides." He noted that although the area was closed to whites, except those who had married into the Potawatomi tribe, "[t]here can be no doubt that the U.S. Government will not be able much longer to restrain the covetousness of the Whites who hover all round the Territory and only wait the chance to rush in and settle." The monk commented on the "slender, failing" Indians, who seemed marked by constant illness. When Bergh paid a pastoral visit to the chief of the Potawatomi—Po-mam-ke-tuck/Peter the Great, Jim's great-great-uncle, who had survived his clan's Trail of Death removal from Indiana to Kansas fifty years before—he found him "not one whit better off than the rest of his tribe" and "with neither bread nor meat." The monk spent the night in the chief's guest hut, "the walls of which are wooden gratings . . . as much as an inch apart." The Oklahoma winter cold was so intense that cutlery froze to the plates in the mission refectory. The constant summer wind whipped the dreaded prairie fires. The Indian boys seemed "always on horseback or up trees," noted Bergh, "irreclaimably averse from study." Their parents were "ever yearning for the old wild life of their ancestors."

Within both the boundaries of the land of the Five Nations (Chickasaw, Choctaw, Seminole, Muscogee [Creek], and Cherokee) to the east and in the Bureau of Indian Affairs–controlled reservations to the west, where the Potawatomi and Sac and Fox lived, U.S. law did not apply, nor did Indian law apply to whites. "In the whole Indian Territory," Bergh wrote, "if a White man commits a crime, he is either lynched; or (should any one care to take the trouble) conveyed [several hundred miles] to Fort Smith in Arkansas, our nearest United States court of Justice." In a series of what he calls "highwayman anecdotes," Bergh recounted to a no doubt rapt Father Swithbert tales of the white "desperadoes" who flocked to the Territory. The James brothers, the Christian brothers, the Younger gang, and the Dalton brothers raided settlements, stealing horses, oxen, and cattle. "How little is thought in . . . the Territory of human life," Bergh wrote. Violent deaths were neither registered nor counted. The word "murder" was not used: "The term 'killing' is more euphonious," the monk explained, "and less likely to be resented as a personal allusion by any of the company present."

Someone in England had snuck a copy of James Fenimore Cooper's *The Pathfinder* into Bergh's things, so he read it. He knew the author had a reputation for idealizing and distorting both Indians and whites, but found instead that the book seemed to him, after months in the Territory, "somehow . . . life-like and true." Bergh mused, as had Cooper, that "[m]odel Indians are not to be found—they are pretty well as scarce as model Whites." By the end of his visit, he was clearly saddened by the injustices done to the Indians he had come to like and respect.

Bergh's descriptions of the moral and legal chaos of Indian Territory not only set the scene of Jim Thorpe's childhood, but also laid out the elements, true and stereotypical, that would form the fractured identity of the boy—and man: outgoing and shy; white and Indian; nurtured and deracinated; "wild" and "civilized."

Jim's parents, Hiram Phillip Thorp* and Charlotte Vieux (also spelled "Vieau" and "View"), met around 1880, most likely at the Sac and Fox Agency, where that tribe, as well as the Kickapoo, Potawatomi, and Shawnee, did business. Hiram belonged to the Sac and Fox, Charlotte to the Potawatomi, with additional French, Menominee, and Kickapoo ancestry. The agency town, near today's Stroud, east of Oklahoma City, was a thriving center of tribal activity with a blacksmith shop, bank, physician's office, post office, cotton gin, cobbler's shop, smokehouse, church, jail, photography studio, hotel, Whistler's Black Hawk Café, the tribal boarding school, and several houses.

Charlotte's father was one of the founders of the Sacred Heart mission, yet she joined with Hiram in an Indian wedding ceremony. Living together constituted Indian marriage, and either party was free to leave the other at any time and enter into another marriage alliance; a separation constituted divorce. Hiram, about twenty-eight, brought

---

*The spelling of the Thorpe family name varied (e.g., Thorp, Tharp), but it was usually spelled without the final "e" until Jim arrived at the Carlisle Indian Industrial School. "Thorpe" will be used throughout except when "Thorp" appears in quoted material or refers to early members of the family.

his bride, about ten years younger, home to his one-room cabin close to the North Canadian River. He had built the house from hickory and cottonwood trees that grew in the rich bottomland along the water. What Jim called the "lazy, flowing" river marked the southern border of what would be for a few months longer the communally held Sac and Fox tribal reservation with no internal boundaries, fences, or roads. The cabin had been home to two previous wives who lived concurrently with Hiram until the day he married Charlotte. With them he had had five children, of whom three survived. Polygamy was not uncommon in the tribe, though white missionaries considered the practice an "evil," along with alcoholism, gambling, "lust," superstition, and "filthiness."

Jim said he was born in the cabin on May 28, 1888. In fact, he was born a year earlier on May 22. His birthplace was registered as Bellemont, a new, tiny crossroads with the nearest post office and store, three miles north. His fraternal twin, Charles, known as Charlie, was named for his mother's brother and formally christened at Sacred Heart as Carolus, the Latin version of his name. James Francis—Jimmie or Jimmy—named for his father's brother, was christened Jacobus Franciscus. Jimmy had pale skin, like the boys' white paternal grandfather. Charlie had the darker skin of their paternal Sac grandmother. The tradition of naming children within the husband's tribal clan—in this case, the Thunder group of Black Hawk—required an Indian name that related to the clan's title. Charlotte gave Jim the name Wa-tha-sko-huk—literally Light After the Lightning, meaning after lightning hit the ground. The simpler version was Bright Path.

Jim was officially Sac and Fox because, as his grandfather Hiram G. Thorp had been a "squawman" (a white man married to an Indian woman), his children had joined his wife's tribe. Such intermarriages produced "half-breed" children, like Jim's father. "I am . . . five-eighths Indian," Jim would say, "three-eighths of that being Potawatomi and the other two-eighths being Sac and Fox." His land rights would be held through the latter. The U.S. government later designated Jim a "mixed-blood."

Both the Sac and Fox and the Potawatomi had been in Oklahoma less than twenty years when Jim was born. Originally tribes of the

Great Lakes—Black Hawk claimed his Sac people originated near Montreal—they were warrior hunters, ethnically and linguistically categorized as Central Algonquian. From the mid-1600s until the Black Hawk War in 1832, both were pushed progressively westward by war with other tribes. The Sac or Sauk called themselves *Asakiwaki,* "people of the outlet" or "they that came forth into the open," and were forced by the Huron to Saginaw Bay, "the place of the Sac" or "(in) Sac country," in today's Michigan. By 1700, the Potawatomi—"people of the place of the fire"—and the Sac had settled in the valley of the Fox River, which flowed from Green Bay in today's Wisconsin. The area was the pivot between the administrative, financial, and hiring headquarters of the French fur trade in Montreal and the wilderness of the Far West, which few, if any, white men had penetrated. A Wisconsin professor, Frederick Jackson Turner, would use this particular history as the paradigm of the white conquest of the continent in his famous 1893 essay, "The Significance of the Frontier in American History."

The Potawatomi, via their trading posts, became essential guides, hunters, and suppliers to the French buyers of beaver, weasel, and other furs or hides. Jim's great-great-grandfather, the six-foot-tall and imposing Jacques Vieau, a Frenchman, is credited with building in 1795 the first structure—his trading post—in what would be the city of Milwaukee; his son-in-law, Solomon Juneau, was one of the founders of the city itself, its first mayor, and publisher of the first newspaper in the Northwest Territory, *The Milwaukee Sentinel.*

French trappers often married into Indian families of influence to secure trading rights with the tribes. Jacques married a Potawatomi-Menominee woman, a granddaughter of chief Ahkenepoweh, and thus functioned as a key liaison between the Indian and white worlds on the expanding frontier; like the many French missionaries and traders acting as intermediaries in tribal disputes and wars, he became indispensable to the Indians. The Potawatomi readily intermarried with the French, hence the prevalence of French surnames and adherence to the Roman Catholic faith. Jacques's son, Louis Vieux (the spelling changed with Louis), married Sha Note/Charlotte Le Great (Jim's mother's namesake), the daughter of a prominent Potawatomi, and continued his father's leadership in the tribe, playing a significant role in the white westward movement before the Civil War. Sacred Heart's founder, Jacob Vieux, was Louis's son.

Forming the allied tribe with which Jim would be identified, the Sac joined in a military alliance in the mid-1700s with the Fox or Mesquakie (*Meskwakihaki*), the Algonquian "red earth people" known, as were the Sac, for their sacred ceremonial runners. For both tribes, athletic feats or games were secular *and* religious, symbolic enactments to call forth desired results—rain, good crops, healthy tribespeople. After forcing out the Illinois, the Sac and Fox built the settlement of Saukenuk on the east bank of the Mississippi, near the site of today's Rock Island, Illinois. It became famous for its rich land, crops, and orderly culture. The tribe raced horses and were known as skilled buffalo hunters. On the open plains across the Mississippi, on playing fields two to three hundred feet long, hundreds of participants massed to play an early form of lacrosse that looked to white observers like a barely organized melee.

When the Louisiana Purchase opened up the continent west of the Mississippi to white American settlers, Thomas Jefferson envisioned a solution to what would soon be known as the "Indian Problem," which Andrew Jackson turned into federal policy with the 1830 Removal Act. Officially implemented to protect Indians from whites, but unofficially designed to free their land for white settlers, the law mandated that the southeastern Five Nations and some Great Lakes tribes be forcibly removed "X the M," Jackson's shorthand for "across the Mississippi." The Black Hawk War two years later was the prototype of Indian wars to come: Indians returning to land they had unwittingly signed away to the U.S. government; spooked whites on the edge of the moving frontier; pursuit by the U.S. Army of the recalcitrant tribe; a misinterpreted attempt at a truce; slaughter of Indian men, women, and children as, in this case, they tried to swim to safety across the Mississippi. Both sides took scalps. Abraham Lincoln and Zachary Taylor took part in the campaign. Lieutenant Jefferson Davis escorted the defeated Black Hawk to Jefferson Barracks in St. Louis.

From 1832 until after the Civil War, the Sac and Fox of the Mississippi, as the tribe was now officially termed by the U.S. government, and the Potawatomi were each "removed"—the official euphemism for dispossession of their lands, followed by forcible transfer to a new location—at least three times in little more than a generation, with some of the long treks marked by bitter cold, hunger, disease, and death. Each time they were promised by treaty the new lands in perpetuity. The Iowa area of the Wisconsin Territory was the first stop for most of both tribes. There, in the area near today's Des Moines, the Sac and Fox population dropped from about 6,000 to 2,500 by 1845. In 1846 Iowa became a state and the tribe, reported the Territory's governor, was "fast progressing toward extermination" because of disappearing game, increased use of whiskey, and a greater reliance on annuities—the payments from the U.S. government to tribes for previous sales of land. The same was said of the Potawatomi. Louis Vieux, though, personally thrived. When his tribe was consolidated after 1846 on a reservation north of the Kansas River, near what is now North Topeka, Kansas, he became one of the principal gatekeepers on the Oregon Trail, outfitting the Donner party, John C. Frémont, and his scout, Kit Carson. By then the Sac and Fox had arrived at their new reservation along the Osage River, about sixty-five miles southwest of today's Kansas City. Most of the Fox, however, later returned to Iowa to settle in Tama, west of Cedar Rapids.

Hiram G. Thorp, Jim's grandfather, was originally from Connecticut and arrived in Kansas around 1845. Though Jim thought he was of Irish descent, there is no indication of a direct connection with Ireland in his ancestry; the surnames of Jim's maternal Thorpe ancestors (e.g., Lamson, Doolittle, Lathrop, Ford, Fenn, Moss) do not indicate an obvious ethnic Irish background either. His great-great-great-great-great-great-grandfather, William Thorp, was of East Anglian origin, and arrived in New England from London in 1637. He came with a group including the Yale family and led by the Reverend John Davenport, a prominent Puritan minister. A year later, Thorp was one of the founders of the theocratic colony of New Haven. In the nine-square town plan—one of the first and most influential in the colonies—his was the lot on square three.

The next two hundred years saw what one genealogist calls the Thorps' "downward slide in social class" and fortune. Jim's grandfather Hiram enlisted in the army in 1837, serving until 1840 with the U.S. Eighth Infantry in the Wisconsin Territory, effecting the removal of the Winnebago tribe to west of the Mississippi. In 1842 he reenlisted, in the U.S. First Infantry, and served in the west until 1844, when he was discharged for disability at Fort Des Moines in Iowa Territory, located near the Sac and Fox reservation. By now he had a taste for frontier life, and he probably met and married the first of his two Sac wives at this time. After the tribe was removed to Kansas in 1845, he was hired by the tribe as a blacksmith and carpenter and married Jim's grandmother, No-ten-o-quah/Wind Before a Rain (or Storm), a tiny birdlike woman born around 1828. Jim referred to her as a niece of the warrior Náh-se-ús-kuk/Whirling Thunder, Black Hawk's eldest son. That is not confirmed by often haphazard early Indian census reports.

Marriage to an Indian not only virtually guaranteed a white man access in this post–Removal Act era to tribal land and annuities, it also promised him more and better land because it was thought he was "competent," the government's term for a person able to manage his affairs and property. Hiram G., five foot seven, with gray eyes and sandy hair, may have decided that Irish descent was a more persuasive and feisty identity to assume on the frontier than his English ancestry: white men with Irish surnames appear in tribal documents, and in the mid-1860s, an Irishman, Henry Donahoe, who had married a Sac woman, was recognized by white authorities as the principal chief of the tribe.

To satisfy incessant demands for land from white settlers and the railroads, an Indian land allotment system was created in Kansas, roughly based on the 1862 Homestead Act. Each Indian was given a piece of reservation land on which to live, farm, and raise livestock (even if an Indian had no interest in doing so) and thus improve himself, like a white. Hiram G. was given a much larger allotment because he was already white. Many of the "competent" Potawatomi, like Vieux, became citizens—Citizen Band Potawatomi—and were given patents to their allotments; four hundred of the tribe's traditionalist Prairie Band refused to apply for citizenship and kept their land in common. The "underutililzed" surplus land—there was always a large surplus—was put up for sale. This method of dispossession would shape federal Indian policy, and the life of Jim's family, for the next forty years.

By the end of the Civil War in 1865, Kansas was a brand-new state with settlers hungry for the Indian allotments. Getting the Indians out was driven by more than a need for land or financial gain; it became, according to H. Craig Miner and William E. Unrau, authors of *The End of Indian Kansas: A Study of Cultural Revolution, 1854–1871*, "a passion, a challenge, a game." The Sac and Fox and the Potawatomi were offered new reservation land in the western half of Indian Territory called Oklahoma (the Choctaw words *okla homma* mean "people" and "red," respectively: "red people"). Partly as punishment for the Five Nations' support of the Confederacy, this western section had been appropriated to provide for both the immediate resettlement of "friendly" Indians like the Potawatomi and the Sac and Fox and the eventual resettlement of the "hostile" tribes of the far western plains and the Southwest. As white squatters circled like vultures in Kansas, the Sac and Fox and Potawatomi signed new removal treaties. Hiram G. opted to sell his allotment and head for Oklahoma. Some of the more affluent, like Louis, chose to stay. Many Potawatomi were forced to sell their allotments for absurdly low prices; eventually much of their land would go to the Santa Fe railroad for $1 per acre.

They became virtual vagrants, without land or money. For those who tried to continue farming, the squatters tore up Indian crops and let animals loose on the land to graze, all in preparation for the Indians' departure. "Everybody knows something of the Sacs and Foxes," wrote *The New York Times* in 1868. "Everybody does not know as much apparently of the leeching and plucking to which this tribe of red men has for years been subject thanks to the Indian Bureau, Indian Agents, & Indian traders." To journalist Horace Greeley, however, speaking for the white majority, it was logical that "[t]hese people must die out, there is no help for them. God has given this earth to those who will subdue it and cultivate it, and it is vain to struggle against His righteous decree."

The new dumping ground of Oklahoma would be the tabula rasa for the latest solution to the Indian Problem: assimilation. More than sixty tribes ended up there eventually, and on every reservation a network of Christian schools and churches, most of them coordinated with the Bureau of Indian Affairs (BIA), was set up to educate, civilize, and convert the Indian (the BIA was also referred to as the Office of Indian Affairs or the Indian Office). Two adjoining reservation tracts east of today's Oklahoma City were chosen for the Sac and Fox and the Potawatomi, though less than 10 percent of the land was suited to agriculture. After a nineteen-day trek from Kansas, young Hiram Phillip, now about seventeen, and his parents, along with about four hundred Sac and Fox, arrived in their new Oklahoma home in December 1869. After 1875, Charlotte and her parents joined in Oklahoma those of the Citizen Band of the Potawatomi who had agreed to resettle. The traditional Prairie Band stayed behind in Mayetta, Kansas, and is there still.

Jim lived the first twenty years of his life in an area that would shortly provide the last and highly dramatic opportunity for white settlers to acquire vast amounts of "free" land. The ensuing disruption perfectly suited Jim's father. Over six feet tall, 235 pounds, a good hunter and athlete, volatile, intelligent, self-sufficient, attractive to women, highly observant, single-minded or feckless as necessary, Hiram Phillip Thorp loved to laugh, had a quick wit, and would easily "desert his plow," said Jim, to plan practical jokes on his fellow tribesmen—all the broader traits of the adult Jim.

He was also an angry man who had seen the Sac and Fox harassed and victimized his whole life. The increasing velocity of change in Oklahoma only added to his frustration. He was credited with killing at least five people and was notorious for raising hell in the "Seven Deadly Saloons" of Keokuk Falls, briefly one of the wildest stops in the West. Local horse thieves would steer clear of his property. Sac and Fox agents reported that he sold liquor on annuity payment days and was "very defiant in the matter."

Hiram looked and dressed like a white, spoke fluent English, and had an Anglo surname; half his blood quantum was white: a half-breed. Yet he very much lived an Indian life on an Indian reservation. He was therefore neither/nor in the eyes of most Indians and whites. Jim, too, would struggle against such stereotypes all his life. He didn't exist between two worlds, but rather within overlapping layers of identity: white, French, English, Sac, Potawatomi; the Catholic faith, the Indian religion; the tribal distrust of the white man's education, Hiram and Charlotte's belief in education; his family's fluency in English and the white man's world those words represented; and the ancient Indian words that so often meant phenomena and feelings impossible to describe in English. A term for an insincere Indian is "apple": red on the outside, white on the inside. To a certain degree, Jim would be the opposite: he looked and spoke like a white but was Indian at the core.

Big-boned, 230 pounds, good-natured, with tough-skinned hands and what Jim described as "a pretty face," Charlotte was the nurturing source of continuity for the large family. She generally put up with her husband, but did not hesitate to move out periodically when his drinking and womanizing went too far. Bergh had noted the strong Christian faith of the Potawatomi, and it was Jim's mother's fierce pride in being Roman Catholic that kept her loyal to Hiram. Charlotte had borne three children before Jim and Charlie arrived, of whom one, George, survived, and in the twenty-odd years after Jim's birth, she had six more children with Hiram: Mary in 1889; Jesse, a boy who died less than a year after he was born, in 1891; Rosetta in 1893 (she died in 1900); Adeline (or Adaline) in 1895; Edward in 1898; and, in late 1901 or early 1902, Henry, who lived three days. Mary ("Big Mary") grew over six feet tall and was legally deaf and able to speak only in a whisper due to an accident that affected her vocal cords. Eventually, as an adult, she assumed Charlotte's role as the caring, responsible head of the family and a strong, reliable presence for Jim.

Family life was simple, plain, and protected for Jim and Charlie. A Sac and Fox neighbor recalled that the Thorpes were considered "not too poor." Hiram was a horse, hog, and cattle rancher who managed between four and five hundred head of cattle for local farmers, as well as his own stock. Like other Sac and Fox, the family raised chickens and planted pumpkins, beans, and fruit, much of which they dried for winter consumption. The terrain was rich in sycamore, cedar, oak, walnut, willow, dogwood, pecan, and locust trees, with clear rivers flowing abundantly. Persimmons, elderberries, strawberries, possum grapes, Chickasaw plums, sassafras, and sumac grew wild. Antelope, prairie hens, turkeys, and fish were plentiful. The residents "worked hard for their living," said one neighbor. "Always had plenty to eat and some to spare for old people. No one was ever hungry." There were frequent droughts. Coyotes and packs of gray timber wolves prowled the open land. Except in the rich bottom soil along the river, the terrain was good only for grazing. Corn grew about two feet high.

Charlotte made the children's clothes with "modern patterns" she bought at the store in Bellemont. Everyone went to bed early and got up with the sun, taking a bath in the river; in the winter, a hole for bathing was cut in the ice. Families living near the damp riverbeds, like the Thorps, were prone to lung infections in the winter and malaria from mosquitoes in the summer. The family seldom used the tribal medicine men because Charlotte's mother, Elizabeth Goslin Vieux, was a specialist in herbal cures. She would search for branches, leaves, and plants in nearby hickory forests and then disappear into her small bark hut near Hiram's house and make the ointments that were used, Jim recalled, for everything from "tired feet to a headache." One day little Jim tried to follow his grandmother, unobserved, on a foraging trek, but she quickly vanished into the forest.

The Christian Thorps were "progressives," as were roughly 15 percent of the tribe. They believed in education and in adapting their habits and attitudes. They consistently dressed in white man's clothing, rather than blankets and buckskin, and spoke English. (In 1890, many Sac men still wore only a breechcloth.) A large number of what white bureaucrats called the "stubborn" traditionalists in the tribe had held on to rites and practices such as face painting, despite BIA directives to stop it. The Thorps did not paint their faces and lived in a log (rather than the traditional elm bark) house year-round, but Charlotte ground flour from corn in a stone dish used by her family since before the removals. Jim's earliest years were thus spent shifting between practices ancient and new.

From Hiram, Jim learned to be competitive, to excel physically in order to earn his father's respect, if not overt affection. Competing with speed and body contact had been the Sac and Fox tradition since the time before Saukenuk. Friends and relatives from nearby cabins and settlements would often gather at the Thorp home in the evenings, after the chores were done, to watch the men play games: broad and high jumping, footraces, swimming in the river, wrestling, and bareback riding. Games were also central to the large Sac and Fox seasonal feasts that drew spectators from all the area's tribes. Every other year, the Sac, Shawnee, and Kickapoo gathered for three days at one of the reservations to race horses and play ballgames at the Festival of Smoking Ponies. The ceremonial practice of the spring midewiwin and the Sacred Bundle Feasts—the objects in the sacred bundles of each clan symbolized supernatural powers—were among the most actively celebrated events. Even for Christian Indians such as the Thorps, the power and magic of the nature-related manitos permeated tribal life and rituals.

Jim described his father as a "marvel," a perennial winner. He was convinced Hiram's skill, endurance, and strength were inspired by

Black Hawk, whose athletic and military feats were a central chapter of the tribe's vivid oral history. Hiram never pushed Jim to excel because the boy didn't need any encouragement. But Hiram paid attention to his son, took the time to teach him vital survival skills and to monitor his progress.

Jim's first sport was swimming. When he was three, his father watched him one day dog-paddling close to the banks of the river. Without taking off his shoes, Hiram waded in and took the boy forty yards into the middle of the rushing river, almost overflowing from spring rains, and returned to the bank to watch his son struggle back to land. When Jim climbed out, Hiram told him, "Don't be afraid of the water, son, and it won't be afraid of you." When Jim began to excel at games and the tribe drew even stronger comparisons between him and Black Hawk, he convinced himself that was why he was his mother's favorite.

The stronger of the twins, Jim had prodigious energy; Charlie was quiet and bookish. They were constant companions, with Jim allowing for his brother's different pace. They were "never in the house when we could be out of it," Jim said, and they "lived in the water." They swung from ropes way out over the river and then dropped in, stuffing their mouths full of the blackberries that grew along the banks as they climbed out. They loved the free-for-all form of lacrosse. They ran and jumped and fought and wrestled. "We didn't have a coach and most of the time we played barefoot," Jim recalled, referring to a rough kind of baseball. "We made our own balls out of whatever was handy, used sticks for bats, flat rocks for bases and made up our own rules." Jim would lead a group of about ten boys in follow-the-leader: swimming the river; scrambling to the top of barn roofs and jumping off; riding horses; wading streams; and climbing a tall hickory or cedar tree, swinging back and forth from a branch at the top before springing to the ground. Hiram cautioned his sons, according to Arthur Wakolee, one of the local boys, to be "clean in all sports, not to cause enemies in other tribes" and, moreover, to "show other races what an Indian can do." The play was arduous, but fair. If an Indian child was too rough, he was warned, twice, and then, upon a third violation, removed from the game to reform his ways.

"The open plain and the river bottoms were my first track fields," Jim said. He let himself be paced by a dog, a jackrabbit, or a colt, and tried to copy what he called the "spirited abandon" of a running horse, "head up and feet coming down" hard. When at his athletic peak, his style was compared to the speed, endurance, and grace of a thoroughbred horse; he would consider it one of the finest compliments he ever received. As he grew bigger and stronger, one of his chores was to chase down Hiram's horses, running and jumping fences in his pursuit. He most loved to catch wild colts from the herds that roamed the range and break them. "He didn't know he had abilities," recalled family friend Cecelia "Ceil" Blanchard, a Shawnee of French descent. "He just grew up doing what came natural to him." He could lasso by the time he was ten and later claimed that, at fifteen, he had "never met a wild [horse] that I could not catch, saddle and ride." This particular training, he said, made him "strong and active and alert . . . [with] quick judgment and decision." On the go all day, he developed an ability, which news reporters would later note, to fall asleep instantly, anywhere.

Visualization—creating a mental image of what you want to achieve, identified almost a century later as a key component of successful athletic performance—was an inherent part of Jim's physical life. When anthropologist Thomas Buckley described the process of visualization among Pueblo runners, there were elements Jim would have known from the ancient Fox/Mesquakie ceremonial runner tradition: "Rather than feeling how your feet hit the ground, emphasis is placed on feeling the ground pushing back up against your feet. Gradually you put more and more trust in the earth, and move into a light trance state when you're no longer interfering in the running." Jim in motion would later look as if he were using the air to propel him.

By the time the twins were six, Hiram was taking them on hunting trips for deer or bear—setting a distance of thirty miles a day—and teaching them forest lore. Hiram "could walk and ride and run for days," Jim wrote, "without showing the least sign of weariness." Jim was the same. Hiram taught the twins how to fish in streams for perch, bass, and catfish with a spear, as their Indian ancestors had, and to shoot, ride horseback, and trap for rabbit, possum, and raccoon. One year they finished with too much game to pack on the backs of their horses, and Hiram slung a buck deer over each shoulder and walked twenty miles home. The feat became a legend in Sac and Fox territory.

The Sac boys—and girls—were routinely taught to be good shots and never to kill more than they needed. Jim and Charlie were given the job of finding small game meat for the family; they shot red and gray squirrels, rabbits, and ducks with an old 12-gauge muzzle-loader shotgun. All his life, Jim's favorite meal would be fried squirrel with cream gravy. Before age ten, he went out alone with an old dog and hunted raccoon, often camping out overnight. He had a preternatural ability to track, to be silent and immobile, to pay attention. Ceil Blanchard went deer hunting with Jim when he was a grown man: "He did it so easily," she said, "even if he hadn't touched a gun in three or four years." The independence and varied challenges of hunting suited him: "I was always of a restless disposition," he said, in the formal locution that sometimes characterized his adult English, happiest when testing himself against a playmate or an animal.

Forest, field, wind, river, rain, darkness, stalking, animals—they were as familiar to Jim as breathing. When the other athletic skills had faded, his early pursuits would evolve into happy constants in Jim's life, his connection with the ancient ways. Sports reporters would routinely ask him to name his favorite sport and be disappointed when he replied, "Hunting and fishing."

This childhood environment, though, was fast disappearing. By the time Jim was taking his first steps, the railroad boom had dramatically increased the frontier chaos Bergh had observed. In what historians would call "aggravated lawlessness," an area largely ignored by whites was now invaded and usurped by them. When the Sac and Fox and the Potawatomi arrived in Oklahoma, the Indian population of the Five Nations' land to the east had been approximately 50,000; by 1900, thirty years later, that number remained the same, but the non-Indian population (whites and blacks) of railroad workers, cowboys, coal miners, and tenant farmers, mostly immigrants not authorized to live on Indian land, had increased 125 times. Although there would be no official frontier left by 1890, as determined by that year's national census, there remained the "Twin Territories" of Oklahoma, promised to and populated by Indians. And whites wanted it.

The relegation of Indians to reservations had initially seemed to make the job of organizing and "civilizing" them easier and more efficient. Riding the waves of the temperance movement, which prohibited liquor on reservations, as well as the public school movement and the women's rights crusade, which pushed coeducation, a broad push of reform movements by self-styled "friends of the Indian" grew. The goal: to save the "aborigine" from both barbarity and certain extinction. A major spur to the policy was the publication in 1881 of Helen Hunt Jackson's landmark exposé, *A Century of Dishonor.* That the Indian was thought to be educable—at least in technical or vocational skills—was an important premise of all these patronizing movements: he could be "saved," with all the meanings given to that word at the time. Most important, the Indian could be saved from himself. The belief that "the only good Indian is a dead Indian," words imputed to General Philip H. Sheridan, gave way to the theory that Indians could be refashioned as white people. The process was named the "vanishing policy." The current term is ethnocide.

By the end of the 1880s, however, frustrated reformers noted that Indians on the reservations were maintaining their old traditions of communal tribal life, work, and ownership. Agents' reports of annuity-based indolence were seen as further proof of a policy failure: because Indians got regular government payments, some of them didn't want to work, i.e., farm. Harking back to the earliest agrarian ideals of the Republic and building on the allotment example of Kansas, the reformers, in the next of a succession of missteps to solve the Indian Problem, decided that individual ownership of land was the key to assimilation. As a thrifty property owner, the Indian would naturally become ambitious, acquisitive, American. "Get the Indian out of the blanket and into trousers," announced Merrill E. Gates, president of Amherst College, at the annual, influential Lake Mohonk Conference of the Friends of the Indian, "and trousers with a pocket in them, and with a *pocket that aches to be filled with dollars!*"

Not all whites got on the bandwagon. A minority report of the House Indian Affairs Committee earlier in the decade had cautioned: "If [allotment] were done in the name of greed it would be bad enough; but to do it in the name of humanity and under the cloak of an ardent desire to promote the Indian's welfare by making him like ourselves, whether he will or not, is infinitely worse." As a tribal people, Indians had lived in a world with a different idea of labor, less defined by acquisition, ownership, exploitation, and wealth; they now lived "in the midst of a society," wrote historian Page Smith, "in which 'work' was only slightly less venerated than 'property.' " To abruptly set up the Indian on an equal and competitive basis with whites was, at best, disingenuous; at worst, corrupt. Oklahoma historian Angie Debo would write, "The general effect of allotment was an orgy of plunder and exploitation probably unparalleled in American history."

Hailed as historically comparable to the Emancipation Proclamation, the General Allotment Act (the Dawes Severalty Act), written and sponsored by Massachusetts senator Henry L. Dawes, a leading "friend of the Indian," was passed by Congress in 1887, the year Jim was born. Theodore Roosevelt described the legislation as "a mighty pulverizing agent to break up the tribal mass." One hundred sixty acres of reservation land were allotted to each family head, with half that amount given to orphans and single persons over eighteen years of age. There was such opposition from Indians to the alien "head of a family" idea—married women and children had property rights in many tribes—that the act was amended to give equal shares to all; Charlotte, for example, would have her own Potawatomi allotment, separate from Hiram's Sac and Fox tract. Each allotment was to be held in trust for twenty-five years by the secretary of the interior, during which time it could not be sold or the title encumbered; at the end of that period, the patent to the land—legal title—would be issued to the owner.

The Sac and Fox and the Potawatomi were very small in number—about 500 and 1,500, respectively. Reducing their large reservations to cookie-cutter individual allotments produced, as it had in Kansas, a generous amount of surplus land to be sold to whites: 80 percent of the Sac and Fox reservation (390,000 acres) and about half of the Potawatomi (275,000 acres). An appropriations bill was added to the Dawes Act that allowed the government to buy, after negotiation, this leftover acreage from the tribes. The Sac and Fox, for example, were paid $1.23 per acre for land that was then sold for as much as $3. The projected new settlement dramatically accelerated Oklahoma statehood, the ultimate goal.

Tribal rhythms were utterly disrupted. Oral histories of Indians alive at the time routinely include the phrases "before allotment" or "after allotment." The reservation, guaranteed in perpetuity less than a quarter century before, ceased to exist. Ignored, as always, was the particular importance of land to the Indian: "more a spiritual than economic resource," in the words of Oklahoma historians W. David Baird and Danny Goble (although how spiritual the land was to someone like Hiram is questionable). Dividing the land into a grid of individually owned sections—much of it dry and good only for "grazing rabbits"—seemed unnatural to the Indian; the Sac and Fox were largely opposed to the policy. To facilitate the bureaucratic challenge of allotment registration on tribal rolls, English names were assigned to most tribal members who did not already have them.

About the time Hiram watched three-year-old Jim crawl out of the river, the western section of the old Indian Territory was designated the official U.S. Territory of Oklahoma. As the allotment process was completed for each reservation, chunks of surplus land emerged for white settlement. While the entire area was marked by rail lines, few if any goods were shipped in or out; there were no towns to speak of, no large farms or factories, no commerce—yet. Mineral resources might lie beneath the virgin soil. Real estate companies in the East advertised for settlers and had no shortage of takers in a nation that had endured a depression in 1873, the strikes of rail workers in 1877 that paralyzed the country, and the Great Plains drought and bust of 1887.

On Easter Sunday, April 21, 1889, the day before the first of a series of government-organized public land runs, this one on the Unassigned Lands west of the Potawatomi and the Sac and Fox, the Very Reverend D. Ignatius Jean, a French Benedictine monk from the Sacred Heart mission, gave a haunting sermon to the white prospective homesteaders massed on the border:

> Tomorrow you will enter into the land for which you have craved so long, and in which you hope to find, I know not how true, rivers flowing with milk and honey. . . . I know the ambition, or rather the providential mission of the United States. I know what its indefatigable people have done during the last century to transform the wilderness. . . . But it is because we love tenderly and sincerely this new fatherland, the great republic of the United States, that we would not see its flag stained with the innocent blood of the Indians. . . . Sitting Bull was right. God is just. . . . Fear to transform this paradise given to you, this new promised land, into a sterile one. Do not forget that a ground naturally fertile becomes sterile by the crimes of its inhabitants.

The reservations of the Sac and Fox, Potawatomi, Iowa, and Shawnee were next. They were divided up into allotments. On September

22, 1891, a few months after Jim's fourth birthday, runs were held on their surplus lands. White settlers lined up for miles along the north bank of the Cimarron River, the northern border of the Sac and Fox reservation. At the sound of the gunfire signal from U.S. marshals at noon, settlers plunged into the water, racing for the roughly 2,300 homesteads available on the other side. Jim no doubt was one of the children who watched frantic wildlife flapping and fleeing and running away just ahead of the rush. Recalled a Sac and Fox onlooker, "Where in the morning there was no one, by nightfall, there [were] families," with tents, claim stakes, and campfires. The tent and wagon metropolis of Shawneetown (later Shawnee) sprang up overnight. Whites classified themselves as Northerners, Southerners—or Sooners, the settlers who had jumped the gun and staked a claim "sooner."

The Sac and Fox began to adjust to the whites' presence, as well as their stores, stagecoaches—and whiskey. The BIA inspector in 1891 reported that while a large number of the tribe had "accepted many of the white mans [sic] ways, it is usually his vices ['hard' drinking, gambling, horse racing, and dancing], seldom . . . his virtues." A later inspector, with a balanced perspective rare then and now, found that the Indians were drinking more, but that the tribe did not use "any more [whiskey] than their white neighbors" and that the alcohol seemed "to have about the same effect upon an Indian that it does upon a white man." The persistence of old customs, such as long hair on tribesmen, was soon expressly forbidden by the Department of the Interior. Short hair was seen as "a great step," insisted the government in a letter to the Sac and Fox agent, to "hasten [the Indians'] progress toward civilization." Indian dances and "so-called Indian feasts" were also prohibited.

All of this obscured the fact that allotment in general—and for the Sac and Fox in particular—was a disaster. From 1887 until the reversal of the Dawes Act under the New Deal in 1934, of the 138 million acres of total Indian land available for allotment, over 60 percent would be sold as surplus. Much of the rest the Indians had received would be lost through fraudulent actions of the U.S. government, business interests, and private citizens. In 1948 the Hoover Commission would look back and conclude that the "rationalization" behind the allotment policy "is so obviously false that it could not have prevailed for so long a time if not supported by the avid demands of others for Indian lands." The avidity had been fueled by more national crises: in 1893, the stock market crashed, about six hundred banks closed, more than 1,500 businesses failed, seventy-four railroads went into receivership, and unemployment rose to unprecedented levels. Oklahoma held great promise for desperate Americans.

In yet another abrupt and devastating change, the U.S. government in 1891, under pressure from white farmers, allowed the general leasing of allotments by Indian owners judged unable to work the land to white tenant farmers—cattlemen from Texas, sharecroppers from the South, hog and wheat farmers from the North—for farming, mineral excavation, lumbering, and cattle grazing. The Department of the Interior would be the custodian of the lease revenues, returning a portion to individual Indians and tribes, but keeping in trust accruing balances. In 1996, a suit brought by Elouise Cobell, a Blackfoot, against the Department of the Interior to account for the lease revenue due Indians since 1891, would reveal fraud of such massive proportions that U.S. District Court Judge Royce C. Lamberth would describe it as "fiscal and governmental irresponsibility in its purest form." A settlement of approximately $4 million would be reached in 2009.

The immediate effect of leasing on the Indians was dramatic. A year before it was approved, the Sac and Fox agent had reported on the productive habits of the tribe, their large herds of cattle, comfortable houses, and the almost total absence of "petty theft." Two years later, as Jim turned five, the agent wrote to his superior in Washington, D.C.: "Should authority be given for the Indians to lease their lands, nearly all would avail themselves of the privilege and their land would be immediately taken up by whites at ridiculously low compensation and the Indian would squander the proceeds and still live an idle, vagabond life."

While the Thorps derived extra income from such arrangements and Jim would receive leasing income money from his allotment for years, the resources of the land were effectively under white control. Having set up an irresistible equation summed up by one inspector as "receiving in the way of rents more for their land than they could by cultivating it," the whites then blamed the Indian, characterizing him as lazy for not working the land himself. New newspapers like *The Stroud Messenger* began to describe the area's Sac and Fox as "dirty," "uncivilized," "beastly intoxicated," "heathenish redskins," and "primitive." The tribe and its clans that had carefully prepared their own food supply and storage and taken care of all the children, elders, and orphans for centuries were now accused of living "day-to-day." Perhaps the worst effect of allotment for Hiram was the diminishment of the wild game he loved to hunt and needed for food. Not only had the local animals fled in front of the settlers in 1891, they were then hunted by the new arrivals. The income Hiram derived from selling raccoon, skunk, and opossum furs was reduced. The streams and rivers were now overfished by the settlers.

The tribe, which had been reported, before allotment, as having better overall health than the other peoples of the region, began to succumb to pneumonia, malaria, cystitis, dropsy (edema), venereal diseases, and meningitis. A smallpox epidemic in 1899–1900 struck the Mo-ko-ho-ko band of the Sac and Fox near Cushing, killing as many as seventy people. For a tribe with, now, less than five hundred total population, this was a huge loss. There was also "a gradual decrease in the number of births," a sign of profound cultural shock. The Sac and Fox of the Mississippi seemed to be heading for extinction. The low point of Indian population within the United States—less than 250,000—was between 1890 and 1910.

For those Indians judged "competent," the Dawes Act's original twenty-five-year waiting period was waived in 1906, allowing them to acquire immediate ownership of their land, which meant they were free to sell it to whites. At about the same time, major oil fields—like the Glenn Pool in 1905—were discovered on Indian land, setting off an oil boom that would last through the 1920s. Oil later found further north under Osage lands between Bartlesville and Ponca City generated—for the benefit of about two thousand Indians—more wealth, according to Baird and Goble, than "all the Old West's famous gold rushes combined." The Sac and Fox, unlike the Osage, did not retain subsurface rights to land they sold, and oil companies profited handsomely after black gold was discovered on Sac and Fox land near Stroud, Cushing, and Drumright. By 1907, Shawnee had several newspapers and banks, more than twenty shoe repair shops, two cotton gins, an opera house, churches, and schools. The railroad depot had an average of forty-two passenger trains and sixty-seven freight trains arriving and departing daily. The nearest new town to the Thorps was tiny Prague, founded by Czech immigrants.

The last hurdle before statehood was the dissolution of the more developed 19.5 million acres of the Five Nations, the remaining eastern half of the Oklahoma landmass given to them by Jackson in 1830. In 1896, the Curtis Act, sponsored by Representative Charles Curtis of Kansas, a Kaw Indian who would enter Jim's life almost forty years later, mandated allotment, division of other property, and the termination of the Five Nations' independent governments.

The move opened a settlement and development opportunity such as had never been seen in the history of Indian exploitation. On November 16, 1907, the eastern Indian Territory was joined to the western Territory of Oklahoma and admitted to the Union as the state of Oklahoma by Proclamation 780, signed with the "pleasedly firm presidential signature" of Theodore Roosevelt. Of the new state's population of almost 1.5 million, 5.3 percent was Indian. Oklahoma was already the nation's leading oil producer.

The Thorp family moved up the North Canadian River one mile to Charlotte's allotment, in the center of the Thorp and Vieux allotments. They settled into what Jim considered an "elaborate home"— a new log-and-timber cabin with two big rooms and a separate sleeping loft.

Up until their sixth birthday, Jim and Charlie were protected from the whites' activity, except for occasional trips into Shawnee. Their isolation ended for good, however, when they were sent during the summer of 1893 to the Sac and Fox Agency School, twenty miles from their home. Jim's parents were anxious to see their children educated. Hiram was one of the thirty tribe members in 1892 who could read and speak English, though he signed his name with an "X." Jim's older brother, George, and his half siblings, Frank and Minnie, had attended the school; Hiram's half sister, Mary, had worked there as a laundress.

The school was part of the network of Indian reservation boarding schools growing across the West. Built in 1872, with later additions, it was "beautifully situated," according to one government report, on a knoll a few miles south of the new town of Stroud, which had replaced the old agency town. Eight buildings made up the complex, including three-story brick-and-frame boys' and girls' dormitories, a school building, a smokehouse, a laundry building, and a barn. A government inspector found "very dirty and filthy" buildings, thirty-four panes of broken glass, and bedding "covered with bed bugs."

The approximately fifty-two boys and thirty-eight girls wore uniforms, and their school day was divided in two parts, with the transition announced by bells. Half of the day was devoted to basic reading, writing, arithmetic, geography, social etiquette, the Christian religion, and history from texts such as the Appleton and McGuffey readers. The afternoons were devoted to vocational skills. The girls were taught cooking, sewing (the uniforms), laundry, and housework. They assisted in the kitchen and dining room and made the beds. The boys learned to cultivate corn and potatoes on a thirty-acre farm, worked the school garden, carried in wood, and did other chores. The school owned two horses, a few milch cows, and hogs. The students' diet was unpredictable. Twelve hundred pounds of cornmeal, received two years earlier, was found by the 1893 inspector to be "full of worms . . . and totally unfit for human food."

The children, with exceptions like Jim and Charlie, arrived unable to speak or understand English, yet were forbidden to use Indian languages. While some of the teachers—Quakers, all white—were competent and kind, others were not. "We got a licking many times when we could not spell a simple word," said one former student. Children with Indian names were given Anglo names; when the school administrators had used up the supply of U.S. presidents' names, they started with the vice presidents and then moved on to the names of otherwise famous people, often religious, such as Calvin, Elijah, Aaron, or Isaac. Not many children finished the full course; some of those who did went on to one of the two main off-reservation Indian boarding schools, the Haskell Institute in Lawrence, Kansas, and the Carlisle Indian Industrial School in Carlisle, Pennsylvania.

The Sac and Fox Agency now also had oversight over Iowa, Kickapoo, Absentee Shawnee, and Potawatomi, and the school served children from all the tribes—if it could get them to come. "The Mo-ko-ho-ko band of the Sac and Fox," the most traditional of the tribe's bands, read an 1894 report, "are opposed to education and civilization; withdrawing the annuities of those who won't send their children to school does not have any effect. [They say] that they will not sell their children." The solution was to round the pupils up. It

was decided that "nothing but force" would work, and the Sac and
Fox agent was given instructions from the commissioner of Indian
affairs to use it. A two-seated spring wagon went the rounds of the
allotments, gathering the children. Often with their parents' consent,
even insistence, children hid in the woods until the school administrator had left.

The twins were sent away as the family was coming apart. In August
1892, the month the new baby, Jesse, died, Charlotte, pregnant with
Rosetta, had filed for divorce under white law. The divorce was never
finalized, but Hiram soon married Fannie Groinhorn McClellan,
under Indian custom. On September 12, 1893, she had a son, William Lasley Thorp, but separated from Hiram when the baby was
not quite a year old. The boy would be known as "Little Jimmie"
because he followed his half brother around like a puppy. Despite the
existence of a strong, extended tribal family web—and Charlotte and
Hiram would reunite off and on for the next several years—it was
a wrenching shift for Jim and Charlie. Jim reacted immediately. A
neighbor recalled that by the time Hiram arrived home in his wagon
after leaving his sons at the school, Jim was already there, having
taken an eighteen-mile shortcut, running the entire way.

Hiram took him back, but the mixture of Jim and school was volatile. He was not "bad," Arthur Wakolee recalled, but "liked some fun
and was always teasing someone." As Jim grew bigger and bolder, he
ran away more frequently, becoming a difficult student; in 1896, he
bolted for two weeks, after which he was duly returned by Hiram.
That same year the school report on the twins, now age nine, judged
Charlie's deportment as "good" and Jim's as "fair." Charlie, at four
feet, two inches tall, sixty pounds, was "a sweet, gentle little boy,"
recalled the Sac and Fox agent's daughter, Harriet Patrick, a teacher.
Jim, a little taller and heavier, was "incorrigible" and "uninterested in
anything except the outdoor life." Patrick observed that Jim was easily distracted in the schoolroom, unfocused. The twins were, nonetheless, inseparable. But for Charlie, Jim would have run away more
often, or permanently.

In early 1897, most of the school's children fell victim to an epidemic of measles, with several cases of typhoid fever and erysipelas (an
acute streptococcus infection). By early March, Patrick was adminis-
tering medicine every hour to so many of the children that when she

finished one round, it was time to start again. The high incidence of illness among the younger children at the school may have been due in part to their being made to take baths in common washtubs in the laundry room and then returning, still wet and in cold weather, to the dormitories. When Charlie contracted pneumonia, Hiram and Charlotte came to help Patrick nurse their son. At 5 a.m. on March 10, Patrick awoke to find the Thorps asleep, exhausted, and their son failing. "I went to him and took him in my arms," she said, "put his little feet in mustard water, and sent for the doctor. But the poor little fellow just lay back and died in my arms."

Now, just short of his tenth birthday, Jim had lost his brother and his best friend. He was what would later be called a "twinless twin," bereft of the other half of a bond considered the closest between two human beings. He mourned Charlie by spending nights in the woods with one of their favorite coon dogs. Hiram sent him back to school for his fourth and last year in fall 1897, but Jim promptly walked home. His father brought him back again. When Hiram returned home this time, Jim was sitting on the doorstep. Jim's half brother Frank and brother George were terrified of their father. Only Jim would stand up to him.

This time, his father said words Jim would repeat throughout his life: "I'm going to send you so far away you'll never find your way back."

The Haskell Institute in Lawrence, Kansas, three hundred miles north of Prague and forty-one miles west of Kansas City, opened as an Indian industrial training boarding school for twenty-two students in 1884. Since Jim's people had been removed from the state after the Civil War, Kansas had gone through what a Haskell school history later described as "rapid and brutal expansion of the railroads and the cattle industry, epidemics of disease . . . the almost constant flow of immigrants from Europe and the ruined South . . . land scandals . . . and weird money deals."

Hiram sent Jim, now eleven, and George, sixteen, to the school in early September 1898. The boys had to travel by wagon and then by two trains to Lawrence. Haskell was run on a military model, with endless bells, an hour-long drill before breakfast, and inspections every Saturday. Otherwise, the school's organization and curriculum were familiar to Jim: boys were taught farming and trades; girls learned housework, cooking, and sewing. Each morning was spent learning English, arithmetic, and history; the afternoons were for learning practical skills and using them to maintain the school plant, grounds, and farm. The boys dug basements and wells, quarried rock, built buildings, sowed and harvested crops. The school was touted by reformers and educators as a cultural finishing school for "stout, hearty, ambitious boys and girls" who would then return to their reservations and bring their people into the new world of productive assimilation. Haskell graduates were creating the core of a new Indian elite, it was hoped, that would be the model for others to follow.

There were early problems recruiting pupils because the school was so far from most reservations, and children had to remain there continuously for three years. Some Sac and Fox parents accused Haskell authorities of transferring children there from home without their "knowledge or consent." The school claimed it was careful not to receive pupils without permission, though it was certainly coercive in some cases. When the Thorp brothers arrived, the school had six hundred students and was limiting enrollment. Within a month, George had run away for good.

"It was in Haskell," Jim later wrote, that "I saw my first football game and developed a love for it." The school offered him an entirely new level of exposure to white games, and he learned to play, after a fashion, all of them, though he was too young for proper teams. Basketball—invented in 1891 by James Naismith in response to those desiring a game with the fast play of football, but without its violence—was played in the winter (Naismith arrived to coach at the University of Kansas in Lawrence the same year Jim arrived at Haskell). Baseball was by far the most popular sport, as it was throughout the country. The school's football team, founded in 1896, played against the University of Denver and Purdue, among others. Jim focused on the team's hero, a big quarterback named Chauncy Archiquette, an Oneida. To emulate Archiquette, Jim organized his classmates into scrub games and played in the backfield after school with a football made of wool yarn or a stocking stuffed with grass and tied at one end.

The games helped Jim adjust to the school. His grades improved and, in a common boyish fantasy, he began to think of sports as a possible future career. Archiquette, an excellent student, left Haskell for the Carlisle Indian boarding school. On Christmas Day 1899, Carlisle beat the University of California, 2–0, in San Francisco, in what was advertised as an "East-West Championship" football game. When the Carlisle team, en route home, stopped in Haskell on January 12, Jim was keenly interested. He saw up close a group that included three "All-America" collegiate players.

Jim continued to thrive at Haskell until the summer of 1901, when he was told by a classmate that Hiram had sent his son a letter telling him he had been shot, probably fatally, in the chest in a hunting accident. Hiram had included the train fare home so Jim could see him before he died, but the school had decided it was not advisable for Jim to leave midterm and had kept the letter from him. According to Jim's many retellings of the story, he jumped onto a freight train just outside Lawrence, only to find it was heading north. He leaped off and then walked and hitched rides on wagons over the next two weeks to get back to Oklahoma. Another classmate, Garland Nevitt, later claimed that Jim was expelled, with several other boys, for drinking; given Hiram's subsequent behavior, Nevitt's story may be correct—or perhaps they both are. Haskell records show only that Jim was "Dropped previous to 10–01–01." In any event, when he arrived home, Hiram, recovered, gave him a severe beating for running away, or for being expelled. Hurt and angry that he'd been greeted violently after traveling so far and after he'd been away for over three years, Jim bolted for the Texas Panhandle. For several months he worked as a ranch hand, repairing fences and helping with horses. There would be stories that he and fellow Oklahoman Will Rogers, part Cherokee and nine years older, met up in Texas. They didn't, though they would later be friends.

Jim recalled that he returned home in time to see his mother, not yet forty, die of blood poisoning shortly after giving birth to her eleventh child. The official probate record has her date of death as January 24, 1902, and the baby's as January 8; Sacred Heart registered both deaths as taking place in November 1901. To ensure that he got Charlotte's spring 1902 annuity payment, Hiram had waited until after the cutoff date of January 1 to alert white authorities of her death. On February 6, he married a white woman, Julia Hardin

Nixon. A son, Ernest, was born on April 10, 1903, and died four months later.

Their mother's death "laid a quiet hand" upon their little community, Jim said, with sad understatement. "We didn't sit in front of the house anymore, watching the games." Jim, fifteen years old, with George's help took over the care of Mary, thirteen, Adeline, seven, and Eddie, three. Charlotte's allotment was divided up, with Hiram selling his inheritance of one-third, fifty acres, for $1,602; her surviving children, including Jim, each got 2/15—about twenty acres each. Life on the former reservation a decade after allotment was quieter, in any case. There was still the occasional theft of a horse or cow, but Jim observed that thieves were "quickly and quietly escorted up into the hickory forests and never returned." Frontier justice was not entirely gone.

For the next three years Jim went to Garden Grove, a new one-room public school a mile from home. Garden Grove was not as well equipped or financed as the Indian agency school—a cause of resentment on the part of local whites. Low salaries made it hard to recruit qualified teachers. Walter White, a brand-new teachers' college graduate, was the school's lone instructor.

White had only been at the job a few weeks when Hiram arrived, Jim in tow. He recalled, fifty years later, the "slender Indian lad who stood aloof, a quizzical expression on his over-wide mouth." Hiram asked, "Can you teach this boy anything?" and told White his son had run away from the agency school repeatedly. White had already encountered Jim while selling homegrown melons off the back of his wagon to a group of Indians. "Will you trade a melon for this knife?" Jim had asked, holding out a small jackknife. White noted he was the only one of the Indians who spoke English. "If that boy ever grows to fit his mouth he will be the biggest Injun in the Sac tribe," said a bystander.

Now, as they stood at Garden Grove, White asked Jim why he had run away. "I don't like it," said the boy. When the teacher asked if he had been punished or hurt, Jim said no, but that the agency school was "not good for Indians." White then asked if he would run away from this school. The question clearly surprised Jim: there would be nowhere to run from a school so close to home. "I will not run away," he said. White, observing the interaction between the boy and his father, concluded that the boy did not want an education, but was simply "choosing the lesser of two evils."

"Jim was handsome, as boys go," White recalled, "with a tendency to legginess. The most striking thing about [him] was the way he handled himself. The easy hip action when he walked marked him as a runner, his movements, cat-like in lightness—yes, even then, one took a second look at Jim Thorpe."

Jim remembered Garden Grove as initially "all book work." There were no organized sports, and he missed playing football. White decided to lay out a track and rigged bars for the high jump and pole vault. One afternoon, as some boys were practicing the high jump, Jim stood by, "seemingly not interested." White asked him to try a jump. "Jim trotted to the bar," recalled White, "and cleared it with apparent ease. The bar was raised and Jim cleared it again. This was repeated till Jim was jumping inches higher than the other, older boys." Soon, Jim was the most "ardent" athlete of all, running, vaulting, jumping, and becoming the best baseball player in the school (White had arranged a box supper to raise money for baseball equipment). There was no question of Jim's bolting now. Indeed, said White, it would have been difficult to keep him away from school.

The next summer White organized baseball games on Saturday afternoons between Garden Grove and small-town teams in the area. The youngest player, Jim was the best at any position he chose, recalled White. Soon people began talking about "the prowess of 'that young Indian.' " Jim moved up to play on the team sponsored by the owner of the Prague movie theater.

Jim had discovered in these rudimentary organized games a pattern of effort his body and mind seemed already to know. When White first mentioned Carlisle, telling him of the sports opportunities it could offer, "Jim shied like a spooked horse." George Sutton, a Prague banker, also encouraged him to go. Jim had been intrigued by the idea since his days at Haskell. Going to Carlisle could be his ticket out of Oklahoma and away from his altered family—especially his father, with whom he now clashed almost daily. But leaving home again, however diminished without his mother, was daunting.

In the end, Jim decided to go to Carlisle. White described Jim's choice as the beginning of a story that would be "like a tale from Homer."

Jim, right, in the Carlisle Indian Industrial School uniform with two classmates, c. 1904

THIS PHOTOGRAPH was most likely taken just after Jim, almost seventeen, arrived at Carlisle in 1904. The neat military uniform jacket is made of blue wool, tight-fitting and uncomfortable. The two boys on the left are clearly Indian. Jim could be almost any northern European nationality.

CHAPTER TWO

Discovery

WINTER 1904–SUMMER 1907

> ... This was the land of our fathers,
> Centuries long to rove—
> Must we be alien and homeless,
> Here on the soil we love?
> No! For the future beckons
> Out of our old alarms
> Out of the tribal fetters,
> Into the nation's arms!

— "Comrades All," a Carlisle Indian Industrial School song

———◆———

Bellmont, OT [Oklahoma Territory]
Dec 13th 1903

U. S. Indian agent
Sac & Fox Agency OT

Dear Sir—I have a boy that I Wish you would Make rangements to
Send of to School Some Ware Caryle or Hampton I dont Care ware
He went to Haskill but I Think it better one of the former plases so
he cannot run a way—he is 14 years old and I Cannot do any thing
with him So plese at your Earlest Convence atend to this for he is
getting worse very day—and I want him to go and make something
of him Self for he cannot do it hear—

Respectfully yours
Hairm Thrope
Bellmont OT

His Name is James Thrope

Captain Richard Henry Pratt, the founder and superintendent of the Carlisle Indian Industrial school, systematically corresponded with as many Indian agents as he could—including W. C. Kohlenberg, the Sac and Fox agent to whom Hiram's letter was addressed—with the goal of attracting students from every tribe. Pratt had other goals as well.

Carlisle had begun playing collegiate football in 1894. Pratt had reluctantly agreed to it, with the proviso that the players set a high example, beat the best football teams in the country, and "if the other fellows slug you will in no case return it." But he quickly saw that if educated, disciplined Indians were offered " 'a fair field and no favor,' " a popular phrase of the time, and beat the whites at their own game, the sporting demonstrations would be an excellent antidote to the falsity of Buffalo Bill's Wild West shows. Ironically, the Carlisle football games would often be seen and reported as re-creations of Indian-white battles for territory. The real Indian had been finally vanquished and relegated to the margins of American life. In his place was built the mythic Indian warrior, the worthy adversary who could be beat again on a football field.

In 1899, Pratt wrote to Sac and Fox agent Lee Patrick what may have been one of the earliest prototypes of the academic recruitment letter: "Incidentally, if you should by chance have a sturdy young man anxious for an education who is especially swift of foot or qualified for athletics, send him and help Carlisle to compete with the great universities." When Kohlenberg, Patrick's successor, aware of Jim's athletic abilities, wrote Carlisle, the school sent him the requisite descriptive statement to fill out, which itemized the new student's tribe, height, weight, age—Jim was actually sixteen—"blood," and family background. Jim put the form in his suitcase and caught the St. Louis and San Francisco railroad at the line's station in Stroud, the first leg of his trip east.

He arrived in the old pre-Revolution frontier town of Carlisle in southern Pennsylvania on February 6, 1904. At five feet, five inches, he was "just a skinny little jigger" for his age, he said. "It's a wonder they ever picked me for Carlisle." There were many Oneida, Chippewa, and Sioux students, but only about ten Sac and Fox. Jim was older than many of them, but needed to be "acclimated to discipline," recalled Albert Exendine, a Cherokee-Delaware and one of the school's greatest athletes. Jim had experienced a similar military schedule at Haskell—

here there was bugle reveille at 6 a.m., academic classes in the morning, vocational classes in the afternoon, competitive drills on the parade ground, taps and room inspection at 9:30 in the evening—but he had been away from any such structure for three years and had to adjust.

A little more than two months after arriving, Jim was told that his father, aged about fifty-four, had died on April 22 of blood poisoning, perhaps from a snake bite. He was not allowed to return to Oklahoma for the funeral. Jim was assigned a legal guardian in Oklahoma, Hiram Holt, to function as liaison with the Sac and Fox agent in all matters concerning his annuity and the rental income from his own allotment. For an adolescent who had once been so attached to his family and Oklahoma terrain, and influenced deeply by his father, whatever their differences, being alone in a big new school farther from home than he'd ever been only deepened his grief and sense of alienation. An orphan, Jim now had no home.

When he became taciturn and withdrawn, the school administration decided to give Jim what it hoped would be a healthy change of scene. The Carlisle Outing Program, termed by Pratt "the Supreme Americanizer," was a method of immersing Indian students in mainstream American life. They were placed with families in homes and farms in the New Jersey or eastern Pennsylvania countryside for anywhere from three summer months to three years. These eastern white families did not have the same prejudice as many westerners who had had more recent conflict with Indians; they were also, at least in the early days of the program, often idealistic Quakers, what Pratt called "thrifty and sympathetic people" eager to help solve the so-called Indian Problem.

The visiting boys did farmwork and the girls learned domestic skills; both were paid for their services (though barely half of what white servants received). Half the students' wages were sent to Carlisle and deposited in interest-bearing accounts, to be paid out to the students when they left the school. The participating families had to compile monthly disciplinary reports for Carlisle, keeping track of cleanliness, use of tobacco, and free time. It was hoped that the participating students who did not speak English would learn the language, as well as the finer nuances of "civilized" behavior, to prepare them for their eventual assimilation into white society. In fact, the program reinforced the lower-class vocational slot to which Indians were usually assigned. If the students stayed through the winter, they attended the local public school. The year before Jim's arrival had been the most successful Outing period, during which almost a thousand boys and girls had been placed.

In late June Jim was sent to live with a Pennsylvania Dutch farmer, A. E. Buckholz, in Summerdale, Pennsylvania. He was, as he later recalled, "anxious to go," and would remain, more or less, away from Carlisle for three years.

Just before Jim arrived at the Buckholz farm, Pratt was fired after twenty-five years as superintendent of Carlisle. The most famous experiment in radical Indian assimilation would now begin to deteriorate. Both the original ideals and their destruction would have a direct impact on Jim.

The creation of an off-reservation eastern boarding school for Indian children had begun as the result of a series of remarkable encounters between Pratt, then an army lieutenant, and some of the most formidable and famous Indian warriors of the Red River War of 1874. Starting in 1867, Pratt had served at Fort Gibson in Indian Territory as an officer commanding the Tenth Cavalry Regiment, made up of units of newly freed slaves and Tonkawa, Choctaw, Cherokee, and Osage scouts. He observed the Indians' "intelligence, civilization and common sense" and found it a "revelation." He trusted them implicitly with dangerous missions and came to believe they were no different from whites in their capacity to learn and function. He became comparatively race-blind, a radical notion. As an earnest, thoughtful, hyperenergetic person, a blend of a soldier and missionary, Pratt then began to reflect on the gross injustice of the Indians' situation: they were not U.S. citizens and were being hounded off their land and segregated onto separate tribal reservations. They were doomed to extinction, he believed, by the relentless momentum of white westward expansion unless some plan could be devised to save them. With characteristic confidence, Pratt believed he was the man to do it.

The opportunity to put his plan in action came when he was assigned responsibility in 1875 for transporting seventy Cheyenne, Arapaho, Kiowa, and Comanche prisoners charged (without trial) with rape, murder, and theft during the Red River War from Fort Sill in Indian Territory to the seventeenth-century Castillo de San Marco, now Fort Marion, in St. Augustine, Florida. Pratt was also put in charge of overseeing their incarceration in this remote eastern fort where Sheridan, now general commander in charge of forcing onto reservations the Indians on the plains between the Rockies and the Mississippi, hoped they would learn the hopelessness of their situation and the futility of any further hostilities. Pratt created a unique environment by removing the prisoners' leg chains and shackles and—risking the loss of his commission—issuing weapons to the Indians, thereby allowing them to police themselves. He created an educational system of English-language instruction, balanced with industrial work and outside employment with local whites, and let the Indians keep the money they earned.

With an aggressive commitment to public relations that would mark his years at Carlisle, Pratt made sure these achievements became known to the public and the members of Congress, which would be his principal source of funding. Inevitably, such reform-minded luminaries as Harriet Beecher Stowe came to sit in on English classes and then wrote about Pratt's innovations. With a rectitude that carried over to his tenure at Carlisle, Pratt insisted that his charges be viewed, treated, and publicized with dignity, as equals.

Pratt's views of the Indian were even more unusual in the context of the racial assumptions of the time. In the 1840s and 1850s there had been a loose convergence of various "scientific" theories about the separate creation and therefore inequality of different races. As creationism was replaced by the theory of evolution in the latter half of the century, what remained common to both was a belief that a culture evolved from primitivism to civilization, from an aboriginal hunter-gatherer society to an agricultural, property-owning political nation. Indians were seen as stuck in the hunter-gatherer stage. A chain of research, historical analysis, and belief was created, looping from early Indian agents and students of Indian customs like Lewis Cass and Henry R. Schoolcraft, to Henry Lewis Morgan's club of amateur ethnologists, to the creation of the Smithsonian Institution's Bureau of American Ethnology, and eventually to the enormously influential scholarship and writing of Francis Parkman and Frederick Jackson Turner.

The last decades of the century were what historian Jacqueline Fear-Segal described as "an era of intense racial debate," with the nation both recovering from slavery and absorbing waves of new immigrants. Ill-defined concepts of race as biological (white, black, "yellow," or "red"), cultural (Anglo-Saxon, Teutonic, Nordic, Gallic, Celtic, and so on), or even national (French, German, Russian) were argued over endlessly. Seeing themselves as the public policy arm of these ideas and developments, and with some of them deeply embedded in the Washington power hierarchy, the reformers were convinced of the "sad uniformity of savage tribal life" and supported the allotment policy of the Dawes Act. Pratt saw the latter as no less isolating than reservations. If Indians were to survive, he insisted, they had to be thrown into white society and totally assimilated.

"Kill the Indian in him and save the man" became Pratt's credo. Indian culture was totally denigrated as a hindrance to assimilation. New immigrants had to adapt to American society; so, insisted Pratt, could Indians. He decided to create not only an exclusive Indian boarding school similar to the one founded for African Americans by Booker T. Washington at Tuskegee, but one located on the East Coast, far from what was seen as the supposedly enervating influence of reservations and the comparatively unstable and hostile white society of the West. Unlike the Hampton Normal and Agricultural Institute in Virginia, formed to acculturate newly freed blacks as well as Indians to subservient roles in post–Civil War life, Pratt's school would seek to prepare Indians to enter white society as equals. In addition to learning English and practical skills, the children from diverse tribes would be formed and homogenized through relentless indoctrination into model, energetic citizens. They would not be allowed to return home for at least five years to ensure that the "civilizing" process took hold.

In 1879, Pratt succeeded in persuading the War Department to approve the creation of a new school at the unused and neatly spare cavalry barracks, surrounded by spacious lawns, in Carlisle, Pennsylvania. The students would be taught practical skills, and some of them prepared to go on to high school and college elsewhere. The first Indians who arrived were from the Dakota Territory, the children of Oglala Sioux chiefs of the Rosebud and Pine Ridge reservations, still considered hostile three years after the Battle of the Little

Big Horn. Pratt had told the chiefs that the tribe's recent loss of land was due, in part, to the fact that they could not read treaties and were therefore ill equipped to deal competently with the white man. By sending their children far from the reservation to learn to read, write, work, and live among whites, Pratt argued, their people would "advance in intelligence and industry."

In the two decades before Jim's arrival, Carlisle became famous for its supposed transformation of savages into acculturated whites. A remarkable series of photographs taken at the time marked the radical physical changes: long-haired Indians in native dress, just off the train from the West, juxtaposed with tidy, shorn Carlisle cadets standing stiffly in military-style blue wool uniforms or girls in long dresses with high collars and fitted waists. The photographs were used for public relations and distributed across the country. As later classes of students arrived already literate in English, literary groups, sports teams, debate societies, and various clubs were formed in the 1890s. Weekly student publications, including *The Indian Helper* and *The Arrow*, inculcated the boys and girls with bromides such as "When you've a task to do, my boys / don't put it off!"

The school was a curious hybrid of a typical nineteenth-century boarding school, complete with awful food and not enough of it, and a vocational institution. The reality behind the photographs and carefully edited publications, as analyzed by Fear-Segal, was lonely and frightening. Significantly, just as automobiles were displacing the horse, the principal products made by Carlisle students were spring buggies and harnesses. Pratt used a minimum of machines in the school's workshops, insisting the students learn to use their hands.

Though Indian students arriving a decade after allotment were, like Jim, older and better educated, their tribes of origin in general continued to show a baffling, to whites, lack of interest in becoming self-supporting farmers. Influenced by agents' reports, such as the ones from Shawnee about the effect of leasing allotments, Congress, reform groups, and Theodore Roosevelt reverted to the idea of Indians as helpless, shiftless wards of the state who needed to be managed. Virulent racism resurfaced, swamping idealistic notions of assimilation and equality and shaping policy that, according to historian Robert F. Berkhofer, Jr., "relegate[d] the Indian to a fixed subordinate position in the economic, political, and intellectual life of the nation." Pratt countered with a steady stream of public attacks on the Bureau of Indian Affairs as a chronically corrupt bureaucracy, rife with political favoritism. He was right: "Nowhere," historian Hazel W. Hertzberg would insist, "was the spoils system more destructive than in the Indian Service."

When Roosevelt became president in 1901, he had already publicly denounced Pratt. He preferred local reservation schools to the twenty-five off-reservation Indian boarding schools as the better mode to prepare students for their future life as "neophyte farmers and stockmen"; he felt that teaching them trades that were useless when they returned to their homelands was a waste of time and taxpayers' money. Indeed, the postgraduation experience of many—but by no means all—Carlisle students affirmed Roosevelt's opinion. Formed by Pratt into quasi-whites, they arrived home to reservation/ allotment cultures that often mistrusted and resented their transformation. When Pratt called for the "complete destruction of the [Indian] Bureau . . . which only [serves] to maintain tribal conditions," Roosevelt fired him.

In March 1905, a year after Jim's arrival at Carlisle and Pratt's dismissal, a battalion of Indian cadets and the Carlisle band marched down Pennsylvania Avenue in Roosevelt's inaugural parade, as they had for every inaugural since 1880. They were behind six mounted chiefs, veterans of the Indian wars, riding abreast. In the center, to whoops of delight from the crowd, was the Chiricahua Apache Geronimo. Everyone in the president's box rose to their feet. When asked why he selected "the greatest single-handed murderer in American history" to march in his parade, the buoyant president—who had also invited what was left of Custer's old Seventh Cavalry and band—answered, "I wanted to give the people a good show." After the Carlisle cadets had passed, the president added, "This is an admirable contrast—first the chiefs, in their native costumes, and then these boys from Carlisle." The Indian wars were truly over, already what one historian would call "as much a part of the nation's collective memory as the Trojan War for the Greeks."

The larger legacy of Pratt, especially as the school gained a certain cachet among some Indian peoples—like a prep school diploma for whites—was what one descendant of a Carlisle student would call a "blank space," a profound break in the continuum of Indian identity. Later generations, inheriting the lost connection, would "try to re-weave what has been like a moth eating a hole." Native scholars describe the cultural destruction as a "soul wound."

Though Jim would look back on Carlisle as the scene of his happiest years, he would also take away the psychic gap between his own sense of self and the model created by Pratt. The successfully assimilated Indian was, in fact, an Indian dead unto himself. Jim Thorpe's unique place within this larger legacy of the school would form what anthropologist Genevieve Bell called "a morality play," the most famous example of "the pitfalls of . . . assimilation."

In spite of his skills and experience with animals, Jim had been initially put to work cleaning the Buckholz house and helping in the kitchen, even cooking on occasion—female chores—for $5 a month. The family insisted he eat in the kitchen instead of in the dining room with them. He reacted angrily, as he usually would when people in authority treated him as somehow inferior, and returned to Carlisle before a year had passed. In March 1905, he was sent to work on another farm and stayed until July. In September he went to a truck farm near Robbinsville, New Jersey, earned $8 a month, ate in the dining room with the family, and was promoted to foreman. After work each day, he ran across fields, he recalled, "hurdling fences and jumping ravines" with the three younger children in the family. Pretending he was a pitcher, he hurled walnuts through a knothole in the fence. In early 1907, he was transferred to a farm in Yardley, Pennsylvania. He said he stayed there only a few weeks before returning to Carlisle in March 1907. School records, however, show that he ran away from both the latter two farms, resuming his old habit of fleeing unhappy situations. But this time, he was running back to school, his only home now. By April he was locked up in the school's stone guardhouse. The oldest building on the campus, built during the Revolutionary War by Hessian soldiers, the guardhouse was used for the "confinement of incorrigible male students."

Jim was then informed by the school authorities that, despite his claim that he had "studied diligently" while on the Outing Program and was ready for the upper grades, he would be required to resume his five-year commitment in the sixth grade. He was angry at an academic demotion that meant he would have to spend an extra two years at the school, graduating in 1911 instead of 1909. He decided to push hard to make an athletic team, do well, and thus make the school's administrators "sorry for having treated me that way." He was solidifying a pattern he would repeat often: anger and resentment at being treated unfairly, followed by a plan to get even by excelling. And once he had a grudge, he kept it. Significantly, given the fact that there were so many permanent runaways from Carlisle and that he was almost twenty years old, with plenty of reasons to leave, Jim chose to stay at the school.

The new superintendent, Captain (later Major) William A. Mercer, had been assigned to the U.S. Seventh Cavalry since 1898, following his service with the U.S. Eighth Infantry in the Apache campaigns of the 1880s and in the care of the injured and the disposal of the dead immediately after Wounded Knee. Mercer was also a football enthusiast. Over objections that the team should be coached by an Indian, preferably one of their own former star players, Mercer had been persuaded by Exendine, the team's captain, to rehire Glenn Scobey "Pop" Warner, the winning Carlisle football coach from 1899 to 1903 (34–18), after Exendine ran into the coach at the 1906 Army–Navy game. Warner, as the new "athletic director," made Exendine, twice an All-American, as well as a track and field standout, his assistant coach, though Exendine would continue to play both sports.

Warner recognized Jim, who was fortunate to have arrived back at Carlisle just as spring athletics were getting under way. He noted that Jim was a lot different from the "scrawny kid" who had arrived from Oklahoma three years earlier, just prior to the coach's departure from the school, and that he "displayed a more grown-up attitude." Jim was now five feet, eight inches tall and weighed 120 pounds. Still, he was not on the coach's sports radar. Late one afternoon, however, after a group of varsity track athletes practicing the high jump had stopped when the bar reached five feet, nine inches, Jim, dressed in overalls, a twill and blue pinstripe hickory shirt, and somebody else's gym shoes, happened to be passing by on his way to a twilight baseball game. He asked if he could try the jump. He cleared the bar on his first attempt and then sauntered away.

The next day, one of the Sioux students, Harry Archambault, told the coach about the student who had cleared the bar "without effort."

Warner immediately sent for Jim and would recount the exchange in his autobiography.

> "You wanted to see me, Coach? Have I done anything wrong?"
> "Son, you've only broken the school record in the high jump. That's all."
> "Pop, I didn't think that very high. I think I can do better in a track suit."

Warner recalled—in his many retellings of this and other Thorpe stories, truth and embellishment were tightly interwoven—that he put his arm around Jim and told him that a tracksuit would be provided because, as of now, he was on the Carlisle track team. The coach told Exendine to "stick with Thorpe. It looks like he might be good material." Fellow Oklahomans, Exendine and Jim got on well. Exendine said he showed Jim "how to shot put, hammer throw and broad jump [the standing long jump] and high jump and [run the] low hurdles and high hurdles." Jim quickly mastered the hurdles. He "knew instinctively," said Exendine, "that time spent in the air was wasted time."

Jim showed a flash of seemingly effortless confidence, talent, and a sense of fun at a Carlisle–Navy meet that season when Warner put Jim in to spur Exendine in a 120-yard high hurdle race. "Every time we took a hurdle," said Exendine, "Jim was right behind me and would say, 'Ex!' At the last hurdle, he said, 'Ex! I've got you licked!' and he jumped a better hurdle and that son of a gun got ahead of me and beat me out!" At Carlisle's Arbor Day contest, Jim won the high jump and the 120-yard high hurdles and came in second in the 220-yard dash. At the last meet of the season, against Bucknell, he placed second in the high jump and high hurdles. Warner was satisfied that his new discovery, though still small and light, was coming along nicely.

By the summer Jim was settled among Warner's athletes and thereby exempt from the three-month Outing requirement. He was assigned to the school paint shop and did well enough to be put in charge of the student workers when the school painter went on a leave of absence. He played in on-campus and locally organized baseball games and noted that several of the varsity football players spent that summer playing baseball for pay: team captain Charles Roy was thought to be playing for the Newark Sailors in the Eastern League;

other teammates played for semipro or minor league teams in Hagerstown, Maryland, and elsewhere.

In early July, Jim wrote to Agent Kohlenberg in Oklahoma:

Dear Sir: I would like you to do me a favor with you and my gardian Mr. Harim Holt. to send me Fifty dollars from my lease money being this is my first letter to you. I hope that you will fill out my request. Well, Mr. Kolenburg I am getting along fine and in good health since I left good old Okla. and to return next summer if nothing happens I hope receive the money in a short time these are the needed articals

suit	$22.00
Pannam hat	$5.00
a watch	$15.00
a pair of shoes	$4.00
spending money	$4.00
	$50.00

Oh yes how is my land getting along and what is the amount received from the land.

Yours Res.
James Thorpe

By mid-August he had not received the money and wrote again. He requested that the money be sent "personaly to me. For you don't I will never see but just a part of it. If you send it through the headquarters here that will be what they will do." School policy prohibited money being sent to students directly, but two annuity checks were sent the following December. Seventy acres of the rich bottomland of his father's old allotment were being rented out for about $160, which was divided among six family members; Jim's own allotment would eventually be leased for crops and grazing at $250 a year. It was a comfortable nest egg, even if he couldn't easily access it.

By the time Jim cleared that first high jump, sports in America had evolved from rural folk activities like boxing, cockfighting, and horse racing in the early nineteenth century to the beginnings of the organized team sports that in the next century would be increasingly embraced by all classes. From the end of the Civil War, what historian S. W. Pope called a "sporting culture" began to grow in the United

States. Baseball and football, as well as the ball fields, stadiums, parks, and playgrounds in which to play them, developed in little more than half a century.

When the 1890 census reported that population density statistics revealed there was no longer an American wilderness—nor the imaginary, constantly westward-moving frontier line that had demarcated it from white civilization since the Revolution—the findings produced a kind of shock. Without the character-forming test of the frontier, at the heart of which was the conquest of the Indian, what kind of physical action could take its place as a means of regenerating the body and the soul of the nation? There emerged an earnest yearning to find a means to re-create in national life the productive, can-do energy of the pioneer. It soon found its most persuasive expression in Roosevelt's promotion of the "strenuous life."

The rise of the modern metropolis, with its overcrowding and social instability, gave rise to the idea of sports as a wholesome activity that could amuse, condition, and stabilize a diverse nation. Urban playgrounds and green baseball fields in the middle of asphalt neighborhoods were built for the masses of new immigrant workers who flooded the eastern cities. The Progressive political movement maintained that a fit, healthy body was manifest proof of a moral man. "Muscular Christianity" became a byword of the era, with suffragist and journalist Frances Willard hailing Pratt as a shining example of the type. The revival of the modern Olympics at the end of the century was based in part on grafting this rediscovery of the body onto the ancient Greek ideal of a "sound mind in a sound body." Sports were not just an antidote, but the means to achieve the ends of individual physical and moral perfection in an industrial age. By 1917, historian Frederic L. Paxson, a disciple of Turner's, would affirm that sports had become the "new safety valve" replacing the frontier.

The old Puritan distrust of "popish and pagan" games came to be seen as effete, even dangerous—an Old World form of stasis. Just as baseball teams began to organize and fans demanded up-to-date news of their games, the telegraph and railroads had created a new information distribution system capable of delivering it. When the game's popularity exploded after the Civil War, a rural, sentimental origin myth was concocted for it. A. G. Spalding, the baseball equipment tycoon, called baseball the "bloodless battle" that had fostered national reconciliation after the war through ritualized conflict. That warlike connection would be eclipsed by football, which was soon to capture the American imagination as a much more explicit territorial conflict, fought yard by yard in a not-so-bloodless battle.

Jim eagerly reported for football practice in fall 1907. Warner thought Jim's chances to make the team slim—he was still too skinny and, in any case, Warner didn't want to see his promising trackman get hurt. The trainer, Wallace Denny, an Oneida, also thought Jim was too light; he wouldn't give him a uniform. Jim pestered both men until he got one that was much too snug. When he appeared on the field, those assembled laughed at what Jim would later call his odd, tramp-like appearance that prefigured Charlie Chaplin.

Warner's credo was "You play the way you practice." Figuring he would take the eager rookie down a peg, Warner handed Jim the ball on one goal line and told him to run, as a tackling practice, through the dozens of players facing him. Jim did as he was told, and Warner later wrote that he made the defenders "look like a bunch of old maids." Those who got close enough to have a decent chance of tackling him were either "bounced off his hard-pumping legs"—a movement that would be a distinctive feature of his running style—"or fell on their faces while grabbing at him."

Jim came running up to the coach with a big grin and tossed him the ball. "You're supposed to let them tackle you, Jim," said an assistant, amused at his apparent misunderstanding of the drill. "You weren't supposed to run through them!" The suspicion that he was being mocked or patronized predictably set Jim off. "Nobody is going to tackle Jim," he said, in what would be another quirk: referring to himself in the third person. Angry at this "display of cockiness," Warner slapped the ball into Jim's chest and said, "Well, let's see if you can do it again, kid!"

Jim ran, dodged, swiveled, and rammed through them all again, and circled back to Warner. He tossed him the ball and said, "Sorry, Pop. Nobody is going to tackle Jim." Furious, Warner swore at Jim and the rest of his varsity defense. He didn't like cockiness and it didn't take much to get him to swear, even when he was impressed. Jim overheard him saying, "He's certainly a wild Indian." To which an assistant replied, "Yeah, untamed and one of a kind." Warner looked back on Jim's performance that afternoon as "an exhibition of athletic talent" in a beginner such as he had never seen and would never see again.

Jim had stepped onto the playing field of a sport that was seen by its elite founders in these, its formative years, as much more than a game. It was a crucible in which American male identity, character, and physical strength were thought to be shaped and honed for success. In the two decades before the First World War, enormously popular and influential football novels and stories in the *Tip Top Weekly* featuring the fictional Yale hero Frank Merriwell glorified a selfless, smart, noble, patrician ideal of college football. Such tales "invested football during these years when relatively few readers of the daily newspapers actually saw any games," wrote Michael Oriard, in *Reading Football: How the Popular Press Created an American Spectacle*, "with the meanings and resonance of heroic myth." When the "romantic" story of an Indian team, stepping onto the field less than twenty years after Wounded Knee, was added to the national character already being invested in sports, the stage was set for Jim Thorpe.

The origins of a game that features kicking a more-or-less round object through a defending force to score a goal—which was very much what football was at the outset—have been traced by some historians to the ancient Greeks, who played a sport called *harpaston*, from the Greek word *harpazein*, to seize, snatch, or carry away. The Romans added a kicking game to make *harpastum*. The leading English public schools in turn developed the game of rugby, but by the end of the 1860s the game played on American campuses most nearly resembled soccer. Harvard then developed a version of football that incorporated the rugby elements of running with the ball and passing it laterally or backward. On November 6, 1869, a game between Princeton and Rutgers on the Rutgers school commons in New Brunswick, New Jersey—played with rules that prohibited running with the ball, but allowed batting it with the fist, butting it with the head, kicking it as in soccer, or even dribbling it—would pass into legend as the first game of American intercollegiate football.

The game developed within a climate of intense fin de siècle scrutiny of the idea of the coach, the captain, the team, and, eventually, the spectator. All were seen as ideally functioning together like a well-oiled machine, the smooth assembly line—the dynamic of American industrial organization. The technological transformation of American society and work in the decades after the Civil War was thought to have been made possible by a stunning national "genius for organization." Teamwork was the defining trait of a nation just starting to step onto the world stage, with victory the common goal. In 1896, Henry Cabot Lodge, speaking at a Harvard commencement dinner, singled out victory, won at the cost of "injuries incurred on the [football] playing field," as "the price which the English-speaking race has paid for being world-conquerors."

The qualities required to win on the collegiate football playing field could be transferred by the nation's future leaders to politics, war, and business. No less a philosopher than William James claimed that football's "fixed machinery of conditions"—its rules and structure of opposing teams working toward a goal—was a playbook of truths applicable to real-life experience. Without perpetuating, through games, the successful model of frontier usurpation and conquest, Americans were in danger of losing what many saw as the unique spirit and energy that made them great. More than a century later, *Time* magazine would describe the game as still "a metaphor for American exceptionalism." That the cult of winning contradicted the growing parallel amateur and aristocratic ideal of playing sport for sport's sake was only one of the hypocrisies that riddled the growing passion for games in general and football in particular.

By 1875, Harvard and Yale were competing essentially with rugby rules, and Harvard vs. Yale became the Big Game. The next year, the Intercollegiate Football Association was formed, including these two schools, plus Princeton and Columbia. Four years later, Walter Camp, a recent Yale football captain and halfback with a passion for the game, would start the career that earned him the moniker Father of American Football. The precision, corporate organization, and Zenlike calm needed for his day job as head of the New Haven Clock Company were brought to bear on football. Over the next forty-five years Camp would exert an unparalleled influence over the nature—and survival—of the game, primarily as a member, and often chairman, of the informal Intercollegiate Rules Committee, as well as author of countless articles explaining and defending the game in influential magazines such as *Collier's Weekly* and *The Outing Magazine*, the leading journalistic voice for the strenuous life.

Camp was also the source of the definitive "All-America" football player designations each December in *Collier's* (the *New York Sun*, the *New York Herald, Leslie's Weekly*, and other publications had competing lists), as well as serving as the technically unpaid advisory coach of the Yale team. As a result, Yale (its record from 1883 to 1910: 285–12–14) served as the incubator for a series of players-turned-coaches who would spread the football gospel to a host of schools eager to master the new game: Carlisle's first four official coaches before Warner were all from Yale. Warner himself would keep up a stream of letters to Camp, full of suggestions for new rules, All-America choices, and pleas to put Carlisle on Yale's fall schedule.

From 1880 until Jim's return to Carlisle in 1907, Camp presided over, and often wrote the language for, a series of key refinements of the game. Each change was fiercely argued about and discussed among enthusiasts from each of the northeastern schools and in the press. In 1880, scrimmage was substituted for the old rugby scrum, opening the way for the creation of an entirely different game based on an orderly, sequenced possession of the ball. Camp designated seven men in the line, a quarterback to receive the ball from a lineman, two halfbacks, and a fullback.

After an 1881 Princeton–Yale game during which one team held the ball without scoring for the first half and the other did the same thing in the second half, Camp devised a method of both controlling undisturbed possession of the ball and balancing the momentum of play between offense and defense: the system of downs (separate attempts to move the ball forward). The team in possession had to gain five yards in three downs, or the ball passed to the opposing team. The field was now marked with lime horizontal lines five yards apart: the "gridiron." In 1883, Camp and his committee put in place a new system of scoring: two points for a touchdown (advancing the ball over the opponent's goal line) and five points for a field goal, or kicking the ball through the posts situated on the goal line. These allocations would be revised multiple times over the next thirty years. When Jim was still an infant in Oklahoma, Camp allowed tackling to knee-level, expanding from the rugby model of tackling at the shoulder or waist. The offensive line was moved shoulder to shoulder. The backs were

pulled in close to the line, eventually leading to the classic T formation. Interference, or what came to be called blocking, was allowed.

In an era when many of the students playing football had learned
Latin and studied ancient battles, military analogies ruled the day. "It
is perhaps the likeness of football to war," Camp wrote, "that so stirs
men's hearts." The passion these educated white Americans had for
the game was based on the oldest models of strategic warfare in Western culture. To Warner and other coaches, a scrimmage was a battle,
the lines were the infantry, and the backs the quick-moving cavalry.
"Engines of attack"—crashing the greatest offensive force through
the weakest part of the defensive line—characterized the game in the
last decade of the century. The most famous and dangerous of the
mass momentum plays was the "flying wedge," a maneuver reportedly
used by Alexander the Great's cavalry to open up a hole in the enemy
line through which the light infantry would guide the phalanxes: the
offense formed into a rushing V, creating a battering ram to enclose and
protect the runner with the ball. Plays were devised with the strategic
elegance of chess, but only those with a deep knowledge of the game
could follow them in the midst of what appeared to be pure mayhem.

The game would change even more rapidly in the early years of
the new century, creating the dynamic environment Jim stepped into.
The "watermelon" ball that began as a copy of the English rugby
ball—fat with blunt ends—and so facilitated the kicking game would
begin to morph into the more spherical shape used today. Leather
helmets evolved from protective earmuffs; the shoes worn were now
high-tops with cleats; shin guards made of hard leather were often
worn under one or two pair of wool socks. Pants were knickers made
of padded canvas or the cotton cloth called moleskin.

The annual Yale–Princeton game at New York City's Polo Grounds
drew crowds of 40,000 to 50,000 in the 1890s. Elite schools with the
best win-loss records now had a powerful recruitment tool to lure the
best players. A whole new culture of paid coaches, alumni boosters,
prep school recruitment, financial inducements, and, somewhat later,
huge collegiate stadiums financed with gate receipts to seat the new
class of passionate spectators began to grow apace.

The new game caused a dramatic increase in player injuries and
deaths. Reaction to the violence churned at the highest circles of the
country's intellectual and political life and would grow into a long,

heated public debate in influential newspapers and magazines over the next two decades. Football's first major and influential critic was Charles W. Eliot, one of Harvard's greatest presidents. The game took time away from academic studies, he insisted, and set the wrong kind of tone with its emphasis on victory, competitiveness, and violence. Princeton professor and rabid football fan Woodrow Wilson vehemently argued against the "football haters" in favor of the "moral training" offered by the game. A precise, obsessive man who glorified victory and had coached the Wesleyan College football team to its most successful season in 1889, Wilson even criticized Harvard's academic curriculum as not rigorous enough to encourage football's disciplined teamwork.

Though flying wedge plays were technically banned in 1894, in the mass of bodies not only was it difficult for officials to see fouls, but uncertainty as to when the ball was actually dead led players to move out from under the pile to gain another yard—only to get stomped on. *The New York Times* thought the sport had disintegrated into little more than glorified pugilism. In 1904, twenty-one players were killed and more than two hundred injured.

Reporters for the rival Pulitzer and Hearst papers had smelled a great, ongoing story in blueblood football violence since William Randolph Hearst bought *The New York Journal* in 1895. *Harper's Weekly, Collier's,* and especially the muckraking *McClure's Magazine* followed all aspects of the controversy. Football's danger to life and limb was elevated to the status of a national issue, and top reporters were assigned to cover collegiate games. When Stephen Crane reported on Harvard's defeat of Carlisle for the *Journal* in 1896, nude and seminude drawings taken from photographs of four of the Carlisle Indian players were printed next to the article to highlight the exotic savage/scientific specimen angle. That the Indian school lost was touted as fresh proof of white frontier superiority. Some white spectators, however, began to root for Carlisle.

In typical yellow-press style, both New York papers hyped the game to such an extent that the term "football hysteria" was coined. Most urban newspapers now offered daily sports coverage, as well as a Sunday sports section. Wire services carried news of the Harvard–Yale and Princeton–Yale games across the continent. *The New York Times* printed coverage of the big football games on the front page above the broadsheet fold. The language, tone, metaphors, and play-by-play style of the big-city reporters in turn influenced local columnists. Without radio, television, or movie newsreels, there were only words, still photographs, and commercial artists' renderings to make football games and players come alive on the page for absent fans.

In 1905, two years before Jim became one of Warner's athletes, the survival of the game seemed in doubt. As much as violence, "commercialism"—money—was seen as spoiling football: "There is something not quite nice," said a *New York Times* editorial on the subject as early as 1897, "in the notion of young gentlemen exhibiting themselves in contests for money." Indeed, there were now so-called vagabond athletes or temporary professionals who played football for whichever college would cover their room, board, and expenses. The *Times* castigated football as the source of the new evil of student gambling. Muckrakers compared it to a form of Darwinian capitalism: winning colleges won generous donations from rich alumni. After the 1904 season, in a development that spun the so-called moral utility of football on its head, a group of Harvard alumni, distressed at their university's inability to win against Camp's Yale powerhouse, had called for a paid coach. Using football as the premier method to build tomorrow's leaders was all well and good, but only if they won. "The object, then, of football is merely to beat Yale," deadpanned *The Nation*.

This elitist approach was based on what sports historian Donald J. Mrozek called a contradictory "genteel sensibility" that questioned first "whether a man of the decent sort could properly be an athlete," and then evolved into the question of whether a man *not* of the decent sort should properly be *allowed* to be an athlete. The dilemma was inherited from the ingrained English upper-class snobbery that considered men who did manual labor as the lower caste, doing work unsuitable for a gentleman. The "amateur" athlete was pure in mind, spirit, and body, "uncorrupted by material considerations." His example served as an inspiration to like young men to give themselves in the service of the larger good of their country and the world, an elite closed circle. Sports were seen as the uncorrupted expression of that ethos. For Caspar Whitney, a leading apologist for amateurism, amateurs were the "virgins of the sporting world"—a compliment.

With only 5 percent of the nation's college-age population attending any institution of higher learning, much less Harvard, Yale, or

Princeton, the scions of the Yankee elite had appropriated to themselves the definition of what it meant to be a man playing college football, this most manly and violent of sports. A mere game had become the touchstone of the nation's larger debate about white male American identity, masculinity, education, leadership, status, and moral character. The subsequent history of football would be, like the social and political history of the country itself, the story of one non-elite group after another breaking in to play with the establishment—starting with Carlisle.

In June and July 1905, *McClure's* published "The College Athlete," a sensational two-part article by Henry Beach Needham. He described a collegiate sporting universe obsessed with the question of amateurism threatened by professionalism—the red-flag issue of the era. Needham cited paid coaches who had "to win at *any* cost"; college athletes who played summer baseball under assumed names (grounds for immediate *demotion* to professional status); the use of inducements by colleges to woo top prep school athletes and the role of alumni boosters in recruiting same; "direct or indirect" subsidies paid to student athletes; and the excessive gate receipts that were funding such projects as the brand-new Harvard stadium, built for more than $250,000. Needham's contrasting "moral" example was "a little colored chap," William Clarence Matthews, "Harvard's best baseball player," who refused to take money from anybody and, instead of playing summer baseball to make extra cash, worked on Pullman sleeping cars.

Needham was a friend of Roosevelt's. The core theme of the articles—the all-American value of fair play, based on rules, and amateur sportsmanship—was squarely in line with the president's thinking: transgressions in the world of sport were sins against a moral code. Though too small, slow, and nearsighted to make the Harvard football team, Roosevelt, like Wilson, was a passionate fan of the game. In a book of essays published in 1897, *American Ideals*, he chose a football metaphor to make his point: "success can only come to the player who 'hits the line hard.' " After the publication of Needham's first article, Roosevelt spoke at Harvard's commencement and linked the shabby state of football with what he saw as the egregious disregard of principle in American industry. When Endicott Peabody, the revered headmaster at Groton prep school, wrote to Roosevelt on behalf of several other eastern schools suggesting a meeting of the Big Three—Harvard, Yale, and Princeton—to resolve the football problem, Roosevelt acted. Riding high after a series of presidential interventions including settling the national coal strike two years earlier and mediating a treaty to end the Russo-Japanese War, he summoned Walter Camp and five other representatives from the three colleges to the White House on October 9, 1905, to fix football.

The general survival of football was not so much in doubt as the kind of game it would be: what Warner later called "the old push-and-pull, close formation game" that hid brutalities from view, or a more open and, thus, it was felt, somewhat safer sport.

William T. Reid, the Harvard coach present at the luncheon, noted in his 1905 diary for that day that Camp was "very slippery" about intentional injuries, as was the Princeton coach, though everyone at the meeting knew they were inflicted routinely. (When Reid's diary was published in 1994, it would reveal as commonplace at Harvard practices such as coaches spying on competing teams, pressuring professors to give star players passing grades, designating which players could cut class to attend practice, and the athletes' gambling, sex, and drinking.)

Roosevelt figured the university presidents could sort out the balance between sport, study, money, and professionalism. His priority was to ensure that the game would retain its new status as the elite's athletic crucible (and that it would survive at his own college, Harvard). He knew safety was the issue everyone could understand. To a public captivated by Progressive politics and muckraking exposés, unnecessary risk, whether from eating meat—Congress would pass the Pure Food and Drug Act in 1906—or playing football, was now intolerable.

The White House meeting was followed by a tumultuous season in which 18 players at all levels were killed and 159 seriously injured. Reform was clearly needed. An intense and intricate power play was triggered between Camp's unofficial rules committee and a new body organized by colleges including West Point and New York University, as well as a few of the formerly excluded "Western universities," to provide a wider base for resolving all the pressing issues. As football historian John Sayle Watterson has described, Harvard brilliantly maneuvered events, with the help of its powerful alumnus, Roosevelt, to bring about a new, less Yale-centered order. Initially called the Intercollegiate Athletic Association, the new group would eventually change its name in 1910 to the National Collegiate Athletic Association (NCAA). A rapid and orderly expansion of collegiate sport beyond the eastern seaboard soon followed, as did needed rule changes.

Warner, in an article published at the beginning of 1905 in *The Illustrated Sporting News*, had in fact suggested most of the changes. The old five yards in three downs—which had encouraged short, conservative gains and "monotonous collisions," which eased the defense's job—was expanded to ten yards to give more scope for daring offensive end runs or trick plays. A minimum of six offensive players had to be on the line of scrimmage, eliminating the opportunity for linemen in the backfield to build up dangerous momentum. The time of a game was reduced from seventy minutes to sixty. A neutral line of scrimmage as wide as the length of the ball was established between the teams to make pushing and shoving (and slugging) before the snap more evident to officials. Though Camp wanted to mandate a wider field to facilitate the open game, Harvard squashed any change to the field width "due to its tremendous investment in a concrete stadium," which could not accommodate such expansion.

The most important innovation, in retrospect, was the legalizing of the forward pass. It was done, Warner wrote, in order to "strengthen the attacking power and scatter the secondary defense" and to keep the game from becoming what he called "a punting and catching contest." The pass was anathema to the old guard like Camp; as late as 1947, Jock Sutherland, coach of the Pittsburgh Steelers after a long, stellar career at the University of Pittsburgh, would complain that only sissies threw the ball. It would take time for the new play to take hold, especially as there were several restrictions on its use, but its introduction marked a radical shift. Though the conventional wisdom is that the brilliant passes by Gus Dorais to Knute Rockne in Notre Dame's upset victory against the Army team in 1913 marked the debut of the modern game, by 1906 the Carlisle Indians were thrilling spectators with their passing mastery.

The new rules would require yet more tweaks almost annually for the next five years to find the right balance of offense and defense. Most coaches struggled to adjust. For an innovator like Warner, however, it was a perfect environment in which to thrive. He saw, among other things, that the use of the forward pass would mean daring, open offensive plays that would create the need for active and speedy backs—like Jim.

The Carlisle Indian Industrial School track team, 1908

A BOYISH, CONFIDENT Jim is in the middle of the front row. He has discovered this season that he is a track star. Albert Exendine is to coach Pop Warner's right; long-distance Hopi marvel Louis Tewanima is second to the left of Jim.

CHAPTER THREE

Warm-up

FALL 1907–SPRING 1909

Part of football's appeal came clearly from the fact that it met two profound American needs: violence and precision. . . . It thus emerged, at last, as the ultimate American game.

— PAGE SMITH

Jim didn't know football," Albert Exendine said of Jim's first practice sessions, "and I taught him how to tackle, how to block, how to be rough." Warner's daylong practice regimen required half an hour of limbering up in the morning, a half-hour strategy discussion, and two hours of strenuous physical workouts. On Sundays, Warner would lead long walks into the countryside to relax the players.

After ten days of practice, Warner told Jim that for the coming season he would be the backup for Albert Payne, the Klamath starting left halfback. Warner's criteria for the position: "fast, strong runner . . . clever in dodging opposing tacklers, skilled in warding them off by the use of the stiff-arm . . . able to hold on to the ball no matter how hard they are tackled or fall . . . quick to think and act, and above all . . . fearless." For the rest of his time at Carlisle, Jim would alternate between right and left halfback on offense; he would be the left halfback on defense. In those days, playing both offense and defense was the norm. He was introduced to the forward pass.

The 1907 team was, in Warner's opinion, a "perfect football machine," the first Carlisle team he considered of true championship caliber. Frank Mt. Pleasant, the five-foot, eight-inch, 140-pound

Tuscarora quarterback, was "formidable"; Little Boy, the Apache center, was "one of the best linemen ever to play for Carlisle"; William Gardner, a Chippewa star of the 1906 team, was paired with Exendine as the ends; Emil Hauser was a large, for Carlisle, talented 173-pound Cheyenne tackle.

Mixing in the new with traditional football, the team's play that season would be marked by their skill with the forward pass. As other early passers were trying to haul the ball up and out with their whole hand, Mt. Pleasant had figured out how to spin it off his fingers, throwing accurate spirals up to forty yards. No coach, insisted Warner, could claim credit for first teaching the spiral pass; the players figured it out for themselves. "How the Indians did take to it!" Warner said. "They shot the ball like a bullet."

Jim watched his teammates practice and play as intently as, in Oklahoma, he'd watched his father compete, or observed the powerful wild horses dash across the open fields until he learned how to catch them. During the early, lopsided victories over Albright, Lebanon Valley, Villanova, and Susquehanna, Jim got limited but productive playing time. He scored two touchdowns against Lebanon Valley and four against Susquehanna. He saw no action against a tough Penn State team and barely played against Syracuse. Against Bucknell, however, Jim "did most of the work carrying the ball," reported *The Arrow*.

The next game was the first big one, against the undefeated University of Pennsylvania, Carlisle's traditional rival. The tension got to Jim. On the way to Philadelphia the day before the game, according to classmate Charlie Wahoo, Jim insisted he needed something to drink. Warner made him promise he would not imbibe until the game was over. Shortly after the team arrived at the hotel, Jim went missing. When he was found, it was clear he'd been drinking. Warner locked Jim in his room, where he was to stay until game time the next day. Sometime later a loud musical noise was heard from Jim's room. When team members entered, they found Jim singing away and beating the railing of the iron bed with his two shoes as accompaniment. Under the bed, teammates found a small zinc tub containing some ten or twelve bottles of beer, packed in ice.

When he was given the ball to carry the next day, before more than 20,000 spectators in suits, hats, and fashionable dresses at Franklin Field, he was still not in control. "I got excited," he said, "and didn't follow my interference." Years later he said he caught a pass and ran seventy-five yards for a touchdown. The record shows he had only two rushes for a total of ten yards in Carlisle's 26–6 win. The fantasy play was the star turn Jim had hoped he'd make.

It was a huge victory for Carlisle, however, as they demonstrated dominance with the forward pass against a major contender. The team employed what Camp called the Carlisle formation—also called the single-wing because its configuration on the field looked like a wing. Warner's invention would become standard for decades in high school, prep, college, and professional games: flanked beyond the defensive tackle on an unbalanced line (two linemen on the left side of the center, four on the right—or the reverse) was a wingback. In the backfield were a fullback, a quarterback, and the tailback, the deepest man in the backfield. This last position, Jim's, was vital because the tailback usually handled the ball from the snap, and because it required someone who could pass, run, and kick with equal skill. The single-wing, wrote Dave Anderson in *The New York Times* in 1980, "turned running backs into legends."

The press coverage of the Penn game reflected the evolving mix of prejudice and admiration regarding the Carlisle team. "With racial savagery and ferocity, the Carlisle Indian eleven grabbed Penn's football scalp and dragged their victim up and down Franklin Field," wrote *The* (Philadelphia) *Press*. "Never has Pennsylvania lost a football game that created greater surprise." A Denver paper, on the other hand, in an article that could have been written by ex-superintendent Pratt, suggested how Carlisle confounded the current assumptions that the Indian was becoming extinct and that football existed primarily to mold and benefit those who had subjugated him: "The race that sends to the gridiron a winning team is not on the downward grade. . . . The Indian on the football field stands in the very front rank. . . . Through all the years of 'mollycoddling' and paternalism on the part of the 'dominant race,' the hereditary trait in the Indian still manifests itself. He can give and take with the best of them in the severest strain that the white man can put him to."

A week after the Penn game, playing at New York City's Polo Grounds on a muddy field, Carlisle lost decisively to Princeton, 16–0, in what would be their only loss of the season. The eastern papers were full of the news, as an example of the big schools closing ranks against Carlisle; it was said that the referee of the Penn game had immediately given all of Carlisle's plays to the Princeton coach. Warner shrugged it off as an indicator that his team was plenty good. The game had brought in a satisfying total of over $9,000 in gate receipts for Carlisle. In early November, Jim sat on the bench for the big game against Harvard, witnessed by 30,000 boisterous, vocal spectators jammed into the stadium at Soldiers Field in Boston. The Harvard players were visibly taller and heavier, but they were baffled by what a Chicago paper called the Indians' "almost weird intuition" for following the ball. The dizzying game, full of "forward passes, double passes, delayed passes, and fakes, crisscrosses, quarterback runs, dives through the tackles, and mad dashes at ends reeled off in bewildering succession," was noted as a demonstration of the "wonderful possibilities of the new game." Carlisle won, 23–15.

Not only was it the first time in twelve years that Carlisle had beat the team from what was considered the finest university in the country, it was also the first time the school had beat two teams of the "Big Four" (Penn was now included) in the same year. Every male student at Carlisle and the fifty-piece school band celebrated on Saturday night with a now-traditional parade through town in their nightshirts and carrying flaming torches. Doing a snake dance—also a victory tradition at Harvard—they accompanied a "corpse," a dummy on a stretcher dressed in a red sweater with a big "H," to the delight of hundreds of spectators. Though interactions between the students and the townspeople were tightly controlled by the school's administration, the local residents were proud of Carlisle and the renown its football victories had brought.

The 1907 season came to an end with a two-week road trip to the Midwest. Pratt had started the tradition, having felt that such journeys on private, first-class Pullman cars were civilizing opportunities. "Few of us," as Jim said, "had traveled very much." Many on the team were excellent musicians, and the players developed a superstition that "a little music before the battle," as Jim described it, made them play better. They stayed at good hotels, and their courteous, quiet behavior made them welcome guests.

Carlisle beat the University of Minnesota in Minneapolis, 12–10. Minnesota's All-America quarterback and a famous dropkicker of the era, George Capron, said their opponents were the "roughest, toughest team" he ever played against. Jim played only briefly. Carlisle's last game of the season was at Chicago's Marshall Field against Amos Alonzo Stagg's University of Chicago, the champions of the Midwest conference. Carlisle pulled another upset, 18–4. In the stands was a young Knute Rockne, who would call Albert Exendine and William Gardner "as great a pair of ends as ever played together on a football team" for their performance that day. In December, Camp named Exendine and Emil Hauser to his second and third 1907 All-America lists, respectively. Warner thought they should have been on the first eleven. He and his team would just have to work harder to overcome Camp's favoritism toward white, elite players.

Though many reporters would seize on Warner's trick plays as the primary—and not quite sportsmanlike—characteristic of his team, the coach insisted that the Indian players won most of their games by good, straight football, just like Yale or Harvard, only better: "faster line charging, good blocking, and deadly tackling." And there was something else, too: "The game of this year owes to them, more than to any other, new developments of the forward pass," said the Yale coach, William F. Knox, to *Harper's Weekly*. A distinctive trait of Warner's teams was their eagerness to try new ideas, new plays like the pass. Jim and his teammates also "dearly loved," said Warner, "to spring surprises."

Carlisle was succeeding while taking a disproportionate pounding. Though Warner maintained Pratt's original injunction against slugging, and Carlisle played a clean game, the players had to endure constant harassment on the field from angry, frustrated opposing players. Carlisle tacklers refrained from falling on a downed Harvard player in one game, but "three or four of the Cambridge team," wrote *The Boston Post*, jumped on every Carlisle man.

Years later, Jim described how his teammates felt about these big games: "[T]he descendents of the losing race came into the east, and . . . played football [against the descendents of their conquerors] with the same . . . fierceness of their ancestors." Though he was writing in his characteristically romantic style, Jim's pride in his own history and ancestors and his satisfaction that he could tip the balance of history on the football field, at least, are clear. Warner was more blunt: "The Indians . . . [had] a real race pride and a fierce determination . . . they believed the armed contests between red man and white had never been waged on equal terms. . . . On the athletic field, where the struggle was man to man, they felt that the Indian had his first even break, and the record proves that they took full advantage of it."

Jim felt he had had a decent first football season with a great, fast, agile, innovative team and a coach who could teach him more. For the first time since leaving Oklahoma, he had a group around him to laugh, eat, and play with on a regular basis. It was like a family.

Jim and Warner began to form a bond of necessity, what would be one of the great symbioses in American sports. To become something other than just another fast Indian from Oklahoma at that time, Jim needed Warner. The coach was as close as Jim ever got to a replacement father figure—as coaches often have been for athletes. Warner was also a white man who could buffer Jim from the perplexing outside world. As for Warner, who was opening up the game of football, giving it "finesse and mobility" after the era of brutal, more boring play, the coach had in Jim an athlete eager to transform these new ideas into action. Each would do wonders for the other. As with many such white-Indian relationships, however, the power and benefits would not be equal.

As an older Cornell freshman in his early twenties, Warner was dubbed "Pop" by his younger football teammates—his barrel-like chest, square head, and stern manner made him seem like a doughty, old-fashioned father—and the nickname stuck. A star left guard, he was persuaded after he graduated with a law degree to stay and play on the 1894 football team. After his playing days, he coached at what is now Iowa State University at Ames and at the University of Georgia, and then returned to Cornell as football coach in 1897 and 1898. In his last season there, his team played against Carlisle and won, 23–6. Warner admired the scrappy losers: "We outscored 'em, but we didn't defeat 'em." Although he would say his move to Carlisle in 1899 was in response to a request from Pratt, he was ready to leave Cornell after a quasi-scandal involving his possibly undue influence on the election of the football team captain.

At Carlisle, Warner was credited with initiating the three-point crouch stance, the body block, and fiber protectors for shoulders and thighs; several of his designs were sold to the A.G. Spalding and Bros. sporting goods company. When Warner realized that the shoes of his Carlisle players were ineffective in muddy weather, he went to the school's shoe trade workshop and designed a sole with longer cleats spaced far apart for better traction. He developed plays such as the "hidden ball" or "hunchback" that became famous. After a Harvard kickoff in 1903, the Carlisle team instantly formed into a huge wedge, the receiving quarterback tucking the ball up under a specially installed elastic band across the back of the sweater of guard Charles Dillon; by the time Harvard realized where the ball was, it was too late to prevent a touchdown. They were called trick plays, but only because no one else had thought of them.

Warner creatively interpreted rules, including possession, until the rules committee adjusted, and banned a play like the hidden ball, for instance. Warner, in turn, took whatever new rules applied as a challenge to his ingenuity. His passion was to experiment, to push the game's limits. Jim and his teammates loved that audacity, even if they never got used to his profanity and aggressive behavior, which they saw as abusive and demeaning. The press would always respect Warner as one of football's greatest coaches and innovators, but they would never adore him as they would Rockne. Warner's accomplishments were best savored by other coaches.

By the time Jim joined the team, Warner already had in place the key elements of his football machine. He created and ran the assembly line and front office that shaped and polished and then spun, amplified, and financed the finished product in the public mind; as sportswriter Jack Newcombe would affirm, he was "light years ahead of his time." Because there were no affluent alumni to make under-the-table payments and phony loans, or fussy professors to object to his crass methods, Warner's genius for improvisation blossomed. Carlisle had no stadium to accommodate a big crowd for home games, so he negotiated top dollar from the elite colleges and universities to have his team on their home schedules. While these colleges typically had one or two "big" games per season, Carlisle sometimes played three of the four top schools (Harvard, Princeton, and Penn), as well as a half dozen of the second-tier schools (among them Syracuse, Brown, and Cornell) in a grueling schedule. As a result, the team was off-campus most weekends and only sporadically in class from September to

Christmas. Some players of multiple sports, like Jim, attended classes less then seventy days during the school year. Warner, with $13,000 from an athletic fund he had created from the game receipts, converted a former hospital building near the football field into special living quarters for the athletes. In their own dining room, the players ate meals prepared in their own kitchen of beef, milk, potatoes, butter, and, occasionally, ginger cake—foods the regular students ate rarely, if ever. Before games, the team was fed soup and crackers.

Warner's "football boys" were allowed much freer access to the town than the weekly outings of the other students, a privilege that would only encourage Jim and the other athletes' taste for whiskey. The players spent evenings out at Halbert's Pool Hall on West High Street, playing for beers, or at Peanut Joe's saloon. Students were required to wear their uniforms off-campus, but the football players were exempt, which allowed them to blend somewhat into the town's after-hours activities. Bootleggers, usually black, provided the Indian boys with liquor. The paler-skinned students, like Jim, could usually get served in one of the many bars in town (selling intoxicating beverages to Indians was a federal offense, a legacy, in part, of a popular stereotype). The players looked forward to the highly popular Indian-themed silent films at the local cinema. D. W. Griffith, among others, often featured doomed, beautiful Indian heroines in his films, as in the 1910 adaptation of *Ramona*. Beleaguered and vanishing chiefs, presented as victims of white immorality, were another favorite narrative. The usually quiet Carlisle students startled townspeople in the audience by yelling and cheering for the celluloid warriors even when they lost.

There were more perks. A special reading room in the football quarters was stocked with Harrisburg, Philadelphia, and Boston newspapers to keep the athletes and Warner up-to-date on the press coverage of their own games. The articles often featured lengthy play-by-play reports, sometimes diagrams, which provided valuable tactical information about opposing teams. Reprinted in *The Arrow*, these chronicles of the team's victories boosted school and town spirit and, further distributed by subscription, spread the word of Carlisle's sports record around the country. As soon as clips featuring Jim started appearing, he began a personal scrapbook that would accompany him his entire life.

The care of the athletes became virtually paternal. Pratt had initiated the custom of giving gifts—a suit of clothes, an overcoat—to successful athletes at the end of the season. Warner refined the system; star players were given charge accounts and made Wardecker's—a store still in Carlisle—their unofficial town hangout, where they could see photographs of themselves on the walls and get a shot of whiskey under the counter. As an added lure, Warner arranged jobs and/or further education for older players. Albert Exendine pursued a law degree at Dickinson College while playing and coaching at Carlisle. Frank Mt. Pleasant was enrolled at a local preparatory school to ready him for entry into Dickinson as a sophomore in 1908; in 1910 he would become the first Indian to graduate from the school.

Because the athletic associations of most colleges and universities were legally incorporated, the Carlisle Indian School Athletic Association, consisting of Warner, the superintendent of the school, a treasurer, and all the varsity athletes, did the same. The association was funded by Carlisle's share of gate receipts for away games, which all of their games were, except for the early season dates against local teams. Warner arranged for either a straight percentage or a guarantee and an option for a percentage of the gate receipts if a game looked likely to bring in significantly more spectators than expected. The 1907 football season earned $58,032 for the athletic fund, from which the players received $9,233 in direct payments and "loans" from the fund; Jim got $500. As other eastern colleges wrestled with the problems of professionalism, money, and—especially after the football crisis in 1905—eligibility requirements, and then started complaining about Carlisle's exemption from any scrutiny, Warner eventually eliminated the direct payments.

The athletic fund was also heavily invested in Northern Pacific and Reading Railroad bonds (a fact not shared with the athletes) and its disbursement controlled by the superintendent, a clerk, and Warner. Sports that lost money, such as lacrosse and track, were subsidized by the fund. Warner also used some of the money to build school structures that were difficult to get funded by Congress—as he had with the athletes' quarters—including a new gym and a two-story house, built by students, for him and his wife. A range of miscellaneous expenses were also covered by the fund, including payments for tutoring, books for the library, remodeling, courtesy donations to the local ministers, and Warner's lucrative financial interest in his hometown Springville (New York) Canning Company, which supplied canned goods to the school.

Having great athletes was only half of Warner's machine. Ensuring that everybody *knew* they were great was the other. Operating out of a building near his home called "the studio," Warner created a formidable publicity and scouting office to "swell the receipts." He built up a syndicate of over 150 newspapers and hired Arthur Martin, editor of *The Carlisle Herald* and a stringer for the Associated Press and *The Philadelphia Evening Telegram*, as a press agent to distribute game reports and "gloomy midweek practice propaganda and misleading injury lists." Warner bet on games, and his publicity system was helpful in influencing the odds. Martin placed ads and "items" in the mainstream press outlets from Philadelphia to Chicago, which were then picked up by papers further west. Press releases were sent out almost daily. A clipping service sent Warner news articles that mentioned Carlisle so that Warner could, as he explained, determine "if anything is being said that is detrimental and untrue" and deny it. Responding to what he described as "the crying demand for advice" as the rules changed by the year, Warner created what would be a successful football correspondence course. A huge number of high school and college coaches subscribed.

At nine o'clock every Monday morning during the season, Warner, Martin, and two scouts would sit down to analyze the past weekend's game. Lighting one Turkish Trophy cigarette from the butt of another, Warner would examine an opposing team's successful plays—"How would you break that up?" he'd ask—and his brain trust would discuss how to counter them. Later, on the field, according to Jim, Warner would "tell us about our opponents, what players were dangerous and needed close watching and what plays were tricky." Defense strategy in hand, Warner worked the team accordingly for the rest of the week. There were also endless drills to sharpen their timing.

His machine—or, rather, its success—inevitably attracted criticism. On November 1, the *New York Herald* complained that "football has been reduced to a science at Carlisle," thanks to "the highest type of professional coaching." Two weeks after the 1907 Chicago game, Warner responded to charges made in a *Chicago Sunday Tribune* article by Dr. Carlos Montezuma, a Yavapai-Apache doctor who had been the school physician at Carlisle toward the end of Pratt's tenure and was emerging as a key spokesman on Indian issues. Montezuma felt that the school had deviated from its proper mission since the departure of Pratt, shifting the balance inordinately from academics to vocational training. He focused on Warner in particular. Claiming that only about a third of the football team were students, Montezuma wrote that Carlisle "might just as well have farmed out its football work to anybody who would take the job." W. G. Thompson, the football manager at Carlisle under Pratt, had catalogued for Montezuma more of Warner's transgressions as coach, including tolerance of athletes' drinking; ignoring their cutting classes and staying out beyond curfew; and payments to athletes on a calibrated scale of performance, which, under collegiate ethics, made them professionals. These more specific charges were not made public; Montezuma chose to focus on the root issue of professionalism's threat to the school's larger mission.

Warner denied the charges in a statement that was reported by *The Washington Post* and other papers. He also wrote privately to Camp. He countered that other than Exendine, Mt. Pleasant, and three others pursuing "off-campus studies," the rest of the fifty-four team members were regular students. In reality, at least one player, Nikifer Shouchuk, attended no classes—he was employed as a janitor and summer cook—and it was thought that Apache lineman Little Boy had been banned from all off-reservation boarding schools, making him ineligible to be at Carlisle. Warner announced that, going forward, Carlisle students would not be allowed to play more than four years and employees of the school would no longer be considered eligible. He lashed out at what he saw as hypocritical prejudice from Carlisle's football competitors. "[N]o institution is compelled to compete with the Indians," he wrote in *The Arrow*, "but when they do compete, and the Indian comes out on top, it is mighty poor sportsmanship for the supporters of beaten institutions and . . . molders of public opinion to come out in the papers and belittle and throw mud at the visitors."

Some of the criticism was indeed sour grapes. "As the Indians are, therefore, not to be classed as a college or university team," said one reporter after the Penn game, "there is less of wounded pride in sustaining a defeat at their hands." And questions about the players and practices could have as appropriately been asked of the Big Four. Harvard's "enormous" football receipts, separately managed, had paid for its lavish stadium in a year when the undergraduate faculty of arts and sciences was operating in the red. At Yale, in the fiscal year ending in September 1904, the athletic association had earnings that almost exactly equaled the university's deficit of $42,000. *The Outing Magazine* had revealed that Walter Camp's secret Yale Financial Union, which managed the sports receipts and expenses of the school's teams, not only ran an annual surplus of more than $100,000 by 1905 (which Camp deposited in secret accounts in New Haven and New York), but paid Camp a salary of $5,000 at a time when full professors were making about $3,500 a year. Yale's 1903 athletic budget, according to sports historian S. W. Pope, equaled the combined salaries of thirty professors.

As Mercer was not the impassioned fund-raiser (or scrupulous administrator) Pratt had been, Warner's ability to raise money had thrown the balance of power in the school to the athletic director. Warner operated virtually free of any oversight. The athletic association was his official employer; he did not work for the Indian Office. He earned $4,000 annually, while the superintendent made $2,650. It was a sweet deal, and it kept Warner at Carlisle. The success of his football machine reinforced the viability of Carlisle in the public mind, but obscured the very real question as to whether there was still justification for an eastern Indian boarding school.

Jim earned a letter for football and one for track at the "leading social function of the [Carlisle] season," the football banquet, on February 27, 1908. The gym was lavishly decorated with banners, electric lights, and red and gold—the school's colors—candles for the event. Warner, paying lip service to the "necessity of strict attention to the education of the mind as well as the body," handed out the letters.

Jim's honors, however, came after he had shown the same self-destructive behavior with which he had started the football season. Before Mercer left the school in January, Jim was caught drunk and disciplined by the superintendent with a stint in the guardhouse. After he came out, Jim said to fellow student Grover C. Long, "I told Mercer that if I was treated that way, I wasn't going to give my honors to Carlisle." Jim, again, was spurred to prove his critics wrong. Like the rest of the students, Long thought of Jim as gifted, but not particularly determined to be an athletic superstar. Later he'd look back on Jim's reaction to Mercer and say of his determination to succeed, "That's what that boy had in his mind, right then, or he wouldn't have said that, would he?"

Football's new rules put a premium on speed and agility, so Warner encouraged Jim—now five feet, ten inches and 150 pounds—Exendine, and Mt. Pleasant to work even harder in track and field. Though Warner had thrown the hammer and put the shot while an undergraduate at Cornell, when he was elevated to Carlisle's director of athletics he had much to learn about the sport. He consulted Michael C. Murphy, the best trainer in the country at the time, and other experts. He learned that many Indians attributed a nonsporting, mystical purpose to running. In "practically every tribe's oral history," according to anthropologist Peter Nabokov, races—"running folklore"—had settled the ancient status of various animals, which formed the origin stories of many clans. More practically, Indians threw objects to catch or snare or kill, necessarily jumping over fences and other obstacles. Jim had run in Oklahoma to catch rabbits or wild horses, and he always wanted to win when he ran competitively. Setting records, however, was for many Carlisle athletes, including Jim, initially an abstract and purposeless exercise.

Warner told Jim that if he could high-jump five feet, ten and a half inches, he would be able to compete against the best at the upcoming Penn Relays in Philadelphia on April 25. At the Relays he high-jumped six feet, earning what he called "my first major medal" and a prize watch. On May 14, in drizzling rain at a dual meet with Syracuse at Elmira, New York, he won the 120-yard and 220-yard hurdles, tied in the high jump, and was second in the shot put; he ended with the highest score of any competitor. Soon afterward, at the first Pennsylvania State Intercollegiate Championship meet in Harrisburg, Carlisle won spectacularly as Jim scored the most individual points, winning the high jump and placing second in the shot put and low hurdles.

The 1908 track season introduced another great Carlisle track athlete, the diminutive Louis Tewanima, a Hopi. He had arrived at Carlisle in 1907 unable to speak, read, or write English. Running was integrated so thoroughly into Hopi life in what is now northern Arizona that Tewanima had thought nothing of running 120 miles, barefoot, to Winslow and back just to see the trains whiz by. He developed so quickly at Carlisle that Warner decided to enter him, along with Mt. Pleasant, Jim, and others, in the June trials in Philadelphia for the fourth Olympic Games, which would take place in London that summer. Mt. Pleasant qualified in the long jump and triple jump and Tewanima for the marathon—a signal feat for Carlisle.

Though he didn't qualify for the Olympics, Jim was clearly now a confident star on the track team. He would clear a final hurdle and look back over his shoulder with a "teasing grin on his face," said Long, "as if to say to the group behind him, 'Come on boys, if you want to make a race of it!' " Jim often just slowly jogged across the finish line when he knew he was the winner. Such behavior was often described as laziness, but mostly it represented a calibrated use of his power and skill once he knew he'd won.

Jim's confidence as an athlete crossed over into the classroom that spring. He got marks of "excellent" for grammar, literature, history, civics, and form and numbers (geometry and fractions), though critics of the school and future historians found it "hard to establish precisely" what students learned at Carlisle academically. Other than writing and recitations in English, they did lots of reading (including *The Pilgrim's Progress* and *The Adventures of Tom Sawyer*). In Jim's industrial major, painting, he received a "good." Miss Wood asked him to take over her freshman academic class for a day and several students reported back that he had been "a fine teacher."

He even wrote a very short story, "Co-Fa-Che-Qul," which was published in *The Arrow*. Such student compositions were often reprinted in newspapers and magazines around the country to promote the achievements of the school. Jim's was a childlike tale of a beautiful Indian maiden, Co-Fa-Che-Qul, the queen of her village, who meets and foils the capture plans of the "bold De Soto" and his Spanish invaders. The soldiers, Jim wrote, "treated the Indians cruelly . . . captured them and made slaves of them; they were compelled to carry their burdens." De Soto found the Mississippi but became "worn and feeble and died." Jim concluded he "was a selfish man. He wanted riches." The most concrete bits of writing by Jim are the references to dogs and horses. He had a romantic, generous nature and

often spoke and wrote in the archaic syntax of the story, like someone who has read more English than he has spoken. The story also
revealed a usually well-hidden awareness of the pain and injustice of
his Indian history.

As he felt more at home, Jim loosened up, settled into himself. He
developed a lighthearted reputation. His new nickname, Libbling,
meant "horsing around." He walked about with apples bulging in
his pockets, in case he got hungry. He carried Richard R. Kaseeta,
the five-year-old Chiricahua Apache "baby of the school," around on
his shoulders. "Everybody was Thorpe's friend," said Arthur Martin,
Warner's press agent. "He was so easygoing." After the Penn Relays,
Jim immediately gave his prize watch away to a Carlisle co-ed. Jim's
class honored his achievements by planting a horse chestnut tree on
the grounds opposite the athletes' quarters on Arbor Day, 1908, and
naming it "Thorpe."

While he could be cautious and reserved with whites—Hyman
Goldstein, the Dickinson quarterback, called him "a loner at heart"—
among Indians Jim was, according to Exendine, "one of the most
talkative. Introverted is not the way I knew him. In comparison with
other whites he might have been. But whites," he added, with deadpan Indian humor, "like to talk a lot." Friends thought Jim quintes-
sentially Indian in his reserve toward those he didn't know, his frank
disdain of those he didn't like, and his readiness to do anything for
someone he considered a friend. He didn't like ambiguities and had
no patience for uncertain, complicated situations off the playing field.
As the attention on him grew, he deflected it. "He didn't talk of his
exploits that I knew of," said his music teacher, Verna Donegan. "He
always felt some of the other boys could have been publicized."

His genial insouciance was in fact largely a façade. Behind it was
a combustible mix of emerging athletic skills, fragile confidence, and
truculence. He knew football was his chance for glory that would live
on in the memories and recountings of those who saw him perform.
He acutely felt the pressure to live up to expectations—not least, his
own. The more his sports skills were ballyhooed, the more tense and
impatient he became: could he do it again?

On the field, he was making steady progress; off the field, he struggled. He wanted to excel so badly he often drank to numb the anxiety,
as he had before his latest stay in the guardhouse. Even Warner had

not yet figured out how to get Jim to channel his energy consistently in his own best interest.

An odd, sinister dissonance flashed out from him at times. "A strange, whimsical fellow," Exendine called him. Both Warner and Exendine noted a tendency in Jim to laugh when angry, as if he could thus detach himself from a situation and then go for the kill. He never looked for a fight, but if he was provoked for no good reason, in his opinion, he'd chuckle, and lash out. "Just before he was about to tear somebody apart," said Exendine, "he always laughed." Warner often felt he was being toyed with by Jim. "It was difficult to know," he told Grantland Rice, one of the most popular and venerated sportswriters until his death in 1954, "if Jim was laughing with you, or at you."

After the 1908 track season, Jim got to play a couple of late-season baseball games for Carlisle, also coached by Warner. The team was undistinguished, but Jim threw a 1–0 shutout against Albright. He was not unmindful that baseball held out more financial potential than any other sport he played.

As summer loomed, he got homesick. He had been away from Oklahoma for four years and was, as he put it, "thinking of my brothers and sisters." He applied to the new superintendent, career educator Moses Friedman, for permission to leave. (Mercer had left after three years, claiming illness, though the more likely reason was the discovery of irregular bookkeeping, and the embezzlement of more than $1,000 by school clerk and former quarterback Frank Hudson.) Friedman allowed Jim to return home with what the administrator thought was the clear verbal understanding that he would return to school in the fall and stay for the additional three years required to get his certificate.

The Oklahoma Jim returned to did not measure up to the childhood memory he had retained. As Jim would realize each time he went home, for the rest of his life, in Oklahoma he was just another Indian, looked down upon, disdained. Carlisle's notion of assimilation didn't apply there, at least as far as Jim could judge. In Shawnee, more than twenty years after allotment, full-bloods and half-breeds, part of the new state's underclass, kept to themselves. His half brother Frank, married to a Shawnee, with four children and a reputation for drinking, was barely making a living from farming thirty acres of cotton and corn near Bellemont. Adeline was about to be sent to the Chilocco Indian Agricultural School near Ponca City, Oklahoma, just south of the Kansas border. (Like Jim years before, she would run away and return home.) His older brother George was married and farming his allotment; Ed, nine, was attending the Sac and Fox boarding school.

Sister Mary had had two disastrous marriages and one child. Intelligent and resourceful, respected by tribal members for her spiritual powers, she had learned to read, write, and read lips, and her siblings could understand her strangulated voice. But her big, formidable stature and odd sounds frightened people and made her the butt of taunts and ridicule. She had decked at least one policeman in Shawnee and fought with two Kickapoo women who had made the mistake of teasing her. Jim admired Mary's survival and strength in the face of adversity. She and Frank, the two most damaged of his siblings, were the ones to whom he felt closest.

He stuck it out through August, hunting, fishing, and riding bareback, waiting until he could return to Carlisle.

When Jim arrived back, the school was abuzz with news of the reception given the U.S. Olympic team by the citizens of New York in August. Though they had not won medals at the Games, Louis Tewanima (ninth in the marathon) and Frank Mt. Pleasant (sixth in both the broad jump and the triple jump) were received by President Roosevelt, who told Tewanima he was "glad to have this country represented by a genuine native American."

For all the enthusiasm, the 1908 Games had left a residue of ill-feeling and resentment among the patrician organizers on both sides of the Atlantic. *The New York Times* called the Games a "deplorable failure" as a means of furthering international goodwill. Americans were criticized for *their* criticism of the conduct of the 400-meter and marathon events and, generally, for what was seen as vulgar New World competitiveness. Americans were angered that there had been no U.S. flag among the other national flags decorating the Shepherd's Bush stadium for the opening ceremonies. The U.S. team's flag bearer responded by refusing to dip the flag as the team passed the royal box during the parade of athletes. The front-runner in the marathon, an Italian, was helped over the finish line by officials after he collapsed and ran the wrong way and was only disqualified after the Americans vehemently objected; the second-place winner, an American, then got the gold medal.

In part as a result of these dramatics and simmering tensions, interest was already keen in the Fifth Olympiad, to be held in Stockholm four years hence.

At Carlisle, the new superintendent turned out to be a nervous, obsessive bureaucrat whose time there would be spent trying to placate both Warner and the politicians and functionaries in Washington. Friedman continued Mercer's emphasis on vocational education and athletics and gave Warner an even broader license to recruit and financially support the kind of athletes that would keep Carlisle at the top of the collegiate athletic hierarchy. By now the football team was the principal source of Carlisle's fame, a recruiting asset as it competed against other Indian schools.

Friedman expanded on Indian commissioner Francis E. Leupp's about-face policy of encouraging the teaching of native arts and crafts so as to ensure that the conquered culture did not die out. In 1904, anthropologist Franz Boas had presented a seminal paper that marked a beginning of a shift from evolutionary models of grades of civilization to a new paradigm, what Boas called "the relative value of all forms of culture." Concurrently, a group of leading Indians began to organize around what would be two key initiatives in the new century—self-determination and sovereignty—and created their own reform group, the Society of American Indians. On the popular level, the Boy Scouts of America and Ernest Thompson Seton's "nostalgic" series of Woodcraft books—such as *Red Book: Or How to Play an Indian*—had begun to ripple out into the minds of white American boys the idea that emulating the hunting, scouting Indian was the most authentic way to develop a strong body and character.

For Jim, who had begun at Carlisle under Pratt, Friedman's changes were baffling. Pratt's goal had been to eradicate the Indian in each student, tribe by tribe, and then homogenize them all into something that passed for white. If Jim—already fragmented by a mixed racial identity, family deaths, and repeated cultural shocks—was no longer being prepared to be a white, then what kind of Indian was he supposed to be? Starting his fifth year at Carlisle, Jim felt as though all he was being adequately prepared to be was an athlete.

With the loss of Exendine and Mt. Pleasant under new eligibility rules, newspaper projections for the 1908 Carlisle football season focused on veterans Michael Balenti, Emil Hauser, and Albert Payne. Carlisle's first game was a 53–0 win over Dickinson Prep. Jim scored one touchdown and four extra points. Carlisle then beat Lebanon Valley, 35–0, and, three days later, Villanova, 10–0, in "a very ragged and rough" game (Villanova had developed an effective defense against Carlisle's forward pass). Jim's three drop-kicked field goals (worth four points each since 1904) during Carlisle's defeat of Penn State, 12–5, on October 3, accounted for all of Carlisle's points. Jim rushed 121 yards, more than four times his 1907 best. In New Haven, Camp cut out a news report for his files that seemed a harbinger of things to come: "The redskins have a drop kicker who will strike terror into the hearts of his opponents once he has passed the midfield chalk mark. It was due to Thorpe's great kicking . . . that Carlisle was able to win."

As "big, heavy" Syracuse had barely missed beating Yale the week before, it was expected Carlisle would lose against them on October 10. Warner fed that expectation by releasing bulletins about Carlisle's injuries. In the event, a record crowd at Buffalo's Baseball Park saw what one reporter hyped as "one of the most spectacular games ever staged on any gridiron," as Carlisle won, 12–0. The team's interference was, according to one reporter, "perfect." Speed was the team's prime characteristic: by comparison, "the Syracuse men," reported *The* (Buffalo) *Express*, "seemed to be walking." The Carlisle style, rhapsodized the paper, was a "thing of beauty." Jim scored all the points.

"There was a man named Thorpe," read one account the next day, "whose clever place kicking and punting spelled victory for the wonderful Carlisle aggregation. Last season Thorpe was practically unknown, but after the game at Buffalo he has jumped into the limelight of football." Observers watched him bound up from "vicious" tackles, "frequently picking his opponents up off the ground with a belt grip, all the while displaying a grin easily discernible from the stands." The fans loved it.

Warner took several of the players to Philadelphia to scout the Penn–Brown game in preparation for their own game against Penn the following week. *The Arrow* reported that "the prospects for a Carlisle victory are not at all reassuring." Penn was "out for revenge," as Jim put it. The star of a team that would have four Camp All-Americans that year was Penn halfback and captain Bill Hollenback. "From the outset," Jim recalled of his first big game as the starting left halfback, "the game was a two-man fight between Hollenback and myself."

As would now be a usual tactic of Carlisle opponents, Penn tried to get Thorpe out of the game early, as the players, Jim said, "clubbed each other like coyotes." Twenty minutes in, Penn scored its only touchdown, still worth five points, and the conversion, for one point. From "the second that big 6 was put up on the scoreboard," reported *The* (Philadelphia) *Press*, "the Indians began to play." Using lateral passes that often led to a forward pass, end runs, and an onside kick—"scarcely a single play [of] straight football from ordinary formations"—Carlisle kept the ball in Penn territory for the rest of the game. The Penn team, joked one observer, was in the air as often as the ball. In the second half, the score still 6–0, Jim took a pass from Michael Balenti for a long touchdown—a "phantom-like flight . . . straight through the whole opposing force," according to *The New York Herald*. He kicked the extra point to even up the score, and that's where it stayed. At the finish, the crowd of 30,000 at Franklin Field exploded, including the more than 300 Carlisle students who had come up on a special train for the only away game to which the school traditionally sent a large contingent of rooters. "Who said the Indian was stoical, unemotional?" asked one reporter. Jim would later call it "the hardest fought game I ever played," collegiate or professional. Penn would win every other game it played that season.

The next week at Annapolis, Jim fumbled the ball on the 12-yard line, allowing previously undefeated Navy to score its only touchdown in a game it lost to Carlisle, 16–6. The score didn't indicate how much Carlisle dominated, scoring all its points on field goals.

On November 7, Carlisle suffered its first defeat of the season, to Harvard, 17–0. Judging from *The Harvard Crimson*, only Jim played well for the losers, kicking, rushing, and receiving in a whirl of motion up and down the field. The game was played in front of 25,000 fans, many of whom were sympathetic to Carlisle. An editorial written in *The Boston Journal* mused that "the hold these up-to-date redskins . . . have upon the followers of the great American college game is altogether remarkable." At this level, at least, Pratt's hope for the persuasive power of a Carlisle football team seemed to be coming true.

During a Pittsburgh snowfall so heavy it was impossible at times to see the players from the stands or for the players to tell each other apart, Carlisle next beat the University of Pittsburgh, 6–0, with Jim kicking the extra point after a touchdown.

On tour in the Midwest, Jim's performance in a 17–0 win against St. Louis University on Thanksgiving Day inspired an editorial writer with a sense of history to recall the treaty signed in that city after Black Hawk's defeat seventy-six years before. "It was St. Louis that made the head men of the Sac and Fox nation drunk and induced them in this condition to sign away the tribal lands. . . . Mr. Thorpe humiliated us nicely, which was just as it should have been. It was coming to us." Two more victories and one loss, to Minnesota, ended the season.

Jim was now a "headline grabber," and Camp named him as a back on his 1908 All-America third team. *The New York Times* summed up Carlisle's 1908 athletic record in all sports as "extremely creditable." The financial results for Carlisle, however, were not nearly as good as the previous year, mainly because there had been no New York or Chicago game on the schedule. The Carlisle Athletic Committee, reacting to the continuing complaints in the press about its "commercialism," discontinued cash bonuses to the athletes and replaced them with "prizes," including gold watches and fobs.

With Jim's growing fame came more free whiskey and beer in local saloons from "loving fans," recalled Warner, as well as bartenders. A Carlisle assistant quartermaster and a school clerk were now also regular suppliers for the athletes. If any of them got drunk, some modest punishment would ensue, but that would not interfere with their playing; Friedman looked the other way. "The football boys," wrote Jack Newcombe, "like all football boys in seasons to come, appeared to indulge more and get away with more." According to Jim's grandson Michael Koehler, with the drinking came the beginning of a certain grandiosity in Jim. He began to feel even more impatient with

restrictions and rules. The alcohol, and encouragement from whoever was buying, also nourished his belief that life off the field, out in
the world, would fall into place as easily as it did on the field.

Jim, feeling his oats as big football man on campus, became even
more mischievous. He persuaded Grover Long to box with him—
once. "I had an idea he'd tried other boys and been too rough with
them," Long recalled, "and they wouldn't box with him." He was
rough with Long, too. "I'd have to say, 'Jim, you've got to slow
down.' " Another day, when Jim saw Long in a brand-new, clean football uniform, he suggested they wrestle on the lawn. "I knew what he
wanted," said Long resignedly. "He wanted to dirty my uniform."
When Jim succeeded, their tussle was over.

The basketball and track and field teams elected Jim captain for
the 1909 spring season. *The Arrow* reported that the 1909 baseball
captain, Michael Balenti, would be joining the Philadelphia Athletics
that summer (from 1911 to 1913 he played for the Cincinnati Reds,
then the St. Louis Browns) and listed other former Carlisle students
who had gone on to organized baseball: the great Philadelphia Athletics pitcher Charles Albert Bender (called "Chief" Bender, in the
stereotypical mode of the time); Frank Jude with the Toledo Mud
Hens, a Class A minor league team, and later with Cincinnati; Louis
LeRoy, with the New York Highlanders (precursors to the Yankees)
of the American League; and Lloyd L. Nephew with several minor
league teams. In a year that had seen 40,000 fans jam into the Polo
Grounds and 50,000 more cling to telegraph poles and elevated tracks
outside to watch the New York Giants lose to the Chicago Cubs for
the National League pennant, baseball gleamed even brighter as the
shining path to sports success.

For Jim, a post-Carlisle future in baseball seemed, in theory, more
probable by the day. An earlier essay in *The Arrow* by Joe Twin, right
fielder for the 1907 Carlisle baseball team, probably with some scout's
encouragement, claimed that the school sent "more men to the major
leagues than any other institution of learning in Pennsylvania." Furthermore, it was a matter of record, he wrote, that "nearly every
school or college ball player who has entered the professional ranks
has risen to the top of the baseball ladder." That wasn't true, but Jim
didn't know that. After a description of the "glad free life" a professional baseball player leads on the road, earning "money enough to

live in elegance from one end of the year to the other," Twin cited names of Carlisle students who had played during the summer in the minor leagues. Though several Carlisle students did so for a summer, very few had a sustained career in the minors, let alone the majors. At least twenty-nine Indians would appear on major league rosters by 1940, according to Indian baseball historian Jeffrey Beck, but "without sufficient coaching and game experience" most of them failed.

During the brief break between football and indoor track season, Jim played basketball and won waltz contests (he was an excellent ballroom dancer). Now at his full adult height of five feet, eleven inches and weighing 185 pounds, Jim initially did well after joining the track team at the end of February. For the first time, Carlisle entered several indoor winter meets. Jim won in the high jump and came in second in the shot put at an event in Trenton, competing against athletes from Yale, Princeton, Penn, and elsewhere. He won the high jump again at the Georgetown University Athletic Association meet in March. At a Johns Hopkins University outdoors meet he won gold medals in the broad jump and shot put, and a silver medal in the 100-yard hurdles.

Then, abruptly, Jim was put on probation by Warner for breaking training. It is thought he left the school twice without permission. On April 12, the team replaced him as captain. But, by April 28, he was off probation, and in the Carlisle class championship he broke the school record in the shot put; equaled the record in the high jump; won the 100-yard dash, the 220-yard dash, the 220-yard hurdles, and the broad jump; and was second in the hammer throw. He performed spectacularly again at a dual meet with Syracuse on May 6, which Carlisle won by one point: he won the 120- and 220-yard hurdles, the shot put (defeating Bill Horr, who had placed sixth in the 1908 Olympics), and the broad jump; tied for first in the high jump; took second place in the 100-yard dash; and placed third in the hammer throw and 220-yard dash.

Before the track season ended in mid-June, in two final meets he established his reputation as one of the most gifted track athletes of the year. At the second Pennsylvania Intercollegiate Meet in Harrisburg on May 29, Jim was "the individual star" and a fan favorite, winning the 220-yard hurdles, high jump, broad jump, and shot put, and coming in second in the 120-yard hurdles. On June 12, in Carlisle's victorious final meet of the season, the Field and Track Meet, held under the auspices of the Atlantic Association of Philadelphia, Jim won the 120- and 220-yard hurdles, high jump, shot put, and broad jump.

In between meets, Jim pitched a couple of shutouts for the baseball team in what would be its last season at Carlisle. The team had rarely had a winning season since the best members of the team, like Jim, were concurrently competing in track and Warner was not a good baseball coach. The coach had finally given in to what Beck calls Warner's self-serving "racial theory of sport": Indians were better suited to the physical prowess of track and field and football than to the comparatively static intricacies of baseball. Warner's lack of commitment to the sport was reinforced by the fact that the expense and effort of maintaining a thirty-game schedule were not offset by the gate receipts. His choice was also pushed by the tightening of eligibility standards, the skepticism about Carlisle's adherence to amateur principles, and, finally, the adamant public protest of the University of Chicago's Amos Alonzo Stagg to undergraduate baseball players "commercializing themselves" and then returning to college to play football, which led to nationwide prohibitions of the practice. Warner would tout his own action of ending baseball at Carlisle as "one of the most advanced steps" taken by any college in the country. In truth, despite the fact that baseball was a favorite sport at Indian schools across the nation, Warner had realized how vulnerable Carlisle was and didn't want a baseball scandal to threaten his football program.

Jim was probably aware that Warner was getting ready to shut down the baseball team because he later claimed he would never have made his next move if he had been able to continue playing ball at Carlisle and developing his talents. He still nursed "the injustice" of having had to restart his school tenure in 1907, making graduation seem like an ever-receding goal. Many times he had told Warner he wanted to play professional baseball and then reluctantly agreed to stay in school and do his duty, as Warner put it, to Carlisle and his people. This time, however, Jim made an emotional—and strategic—decision to quit the school.

As long as he remained at Carlisle Jim could compete only in football and track, neither of which had any career prospects other than coaching. Professional baseball was the only sport that could offer the stability of contracts, decent salaries (at the major league level), and more respectability, if not money, than boxing. ("[T]he only big money," one student recalled, "was in the fight racket.") Jim had gotten just enough of a taste of fame and accolades that school year to think it was time to make his move into the big time, especially as major league games were pulling in more than twice as many fans as they had at the turn of the century.

After Jim, the team's best pitcher and first baseman, pitched his two shutouts, Charlie Kelsner from Albright College, scouting for the minor league Rocky Mount, North Carolina, Railroaders in the Eastern Carolina League, had asked him if he'd like to "go on a little vacation, playing baseball." The Railroaders' season had started off badly and they were looking to upgrade. (Another version of the story had the secretary of the Railroaders asking a friend, Barney Dreyfuss, president of the Pittsburgh Pirates, to help him find some good college players in the Pennsylvania area.) In any case, Jim signed on to be a pitcher. Two other Carlisle players—Joe Libby and Jesse Youngdeer—signed on as well.

Friedman was upset. Jim had promised now to stay two more years in return for his leave of absence to go home the previous summer. An administrative compromise was reached, at least as far as Friedman was concerned. He explained in a letter to agent Kohlenberg that Jim was granted "leave to play ball in the south during the summer months" and was thus considered a "deserter" from the school. He also informed all Indian schools that Jim should not be permitted to enroll in any of them. Warner wrote in his autobiography years later that Jim returned that summer to Oklahoma. "Or," he added, "at least, that is where the school administration at Carlisle thought he had gone to." But Warner knew better.

Joe Libby, Jim, and Jesse Youngdeer, Rocky Mount, North Carolina, 1909

THREE CARLISLE BASEBALL teammates, off to make some money and play ball in the minor leagues.

CHAPTER FOUR

The Minors

SUMMER 1909–SUMMER 1911

*I went to play baseball in North Carolina for a couple of summers and paid
for it for the rest of my life.*

—JIM THORPE

In the *McClure's* pieces that had got the attention of Roosevelt in
1905, Henry Beach Needham reported that "[no] question relating
to the amateur standing of athletes engaged in inter-collegiate sport
has produced more rabid discussion, with opinion greatly divided,
than the propriety of 'summer ball.' " As doping would dominate
sports discussion almost a century later, in 1909 defining what made
an athlete an amateur or a professional was, for the gatekeepers of
sports, the essential question. No period of Jim's life would produce
more controversy than the baseball summers of 1909 and 1910.

Needham had explicitly defined summer baseball as "baseball
played by amateurs, so-called, mainly collegians, on the 'summer
nine'—teams semi-professional in character, not members of any
professional league, which are organized to furnish entertainment for
the visitors at summer resorts," mainly those in the elite mountain
vacation areas of the Adirondacks and northern New England. In
the upper-class society of the eastern seaboard north of Washington,
athletes from Yale, Harvard, Princeton, Brown, and other colleges
had established a tradition of playing where their parents went for the
summer. And they were paid. Teams such as St. Albans in Vermont
recruited top eastern college athletes, who played under assumed

names to protect their amateur status. (In this pre–Social Security era, there was no national system of individual identification; taking a nickname like "Dutch" or a shortened version of one's own name was enough protection.) The colleges readily accepted absurd explanations from returning players. Mike Lynch, a star pitcher at Brown, claimed that his playing ball in the summer of 1903 for the Newport, New Hampshire, team was "accidental and incidental"; he was only a hotel clerk getting $9 a week. After Lynch signed with the National League Pittsburgh Pirates, he told his friends that he actually made $75 a week at Newport, and all his other expenses had been covered.

Michael C. Murphy, the trainer Warner frequently consulted, spoke for many in opposing Needham, insisting that a student had a right to play sports to earn financial help that would allow him to finish college. In fact, summer ball was the least of it: James J. Hogan, the Yale captain and tackle who was on Camp's All-America first team in 1902, 1903, and 1904, got free room and board at Yale, a share of the baseball gate receipts, a suite at Vanderbilt Hall, his meals at the University Club, a commission from the American Tobacco Company on cigarette sales at football games, and a ten-day vacation in Cuba. Hogan was a "poor boy," born in Tipperary, who entered Phillips Exeter prep school when he was twenty-three and Yale four years later.

Needham didn't address playing for a professional minor league team in organized baseball. He didn't need to. Jim's choice to play for the Eastern Carolina League was blatantly professional and would have been seen as such, though many college men played in the minor leagues under assumed names, just as they did in the summer resort leagues. *The Arrow* openly publicized the summer placement of school athletes on professional minor league teams. Jim was fully aware of what he was doing; he was building a career. He had left Carlisle. He saw no need to take an assumed name, no need to protect himself or have anyone protect him. He was on his own.

Jim, Youngdeer, and Libby stepped off the train in Rocky Mount into flat, hot, southern tobacco and cotton country. There weren't many cars or paved roads (Henry Ford's Model T debuted that year). The area dozed in what local reporter and historian Sam T. Mallison would describe as "the languor of an economic Middle Age," isolated from big cities and the sophisticated Northeast: "Except for the export of its farm products and the textile output of the Rocky Mount Mills, the community lived in an economy that was almost self-contained and self-sufficient." White civic boosters, often tobacco and cotton businessmen, many of whom knew little about baseball, funded the teams to enhance the pride, reputation, and commerce of their towns. Spring came early, giving the players plenty of time to get in shape before the season started.

The Rocky Mount Railroaders were a Class D team—the lowest rung of organized baseball. The Eastern Carolina League had been created the previous year with four teams, all but one located along the Atlantic Coast railroad line. Two more teams were added for the 1909 season, one of them the Railroaders. Baseball had become "very popular in the southern states," according to baseball historian Bob McConnell, especially in areas like Rocky Mount where there were not many forms of entertainment—or games to bet on.

North Carolina was the largest state in the country that had never had a professional baseball team. It was thought to lack enough cities to sustain a commercially viable league, the cities and towns that did exist being widely dispersed across the rural state. Without the railroad, baseball leagues would not have been possible. Up until the teens no team or league in the state lasted more than a couple of years. The fate of Jim's teams and others in North Carolina would be rocky indeed.

Without the collegiate moral and ethical freight that affected the development of football, star players in baseball were paid early on. When the Cincinnati Red Stockings, the first professional baseball club in America, played sixty-five games in 1869, winning all of them except for one tie, other teams realized they would have to pay their players if they expected to win. The National League and American Association had been formed by the 1880s. With their teams generally located in larger cities and with the resources to pay higher salaries, they became major leagues. Smaller organizations such as the Northwestern League (composed of Saginaw, Grand Rapids, and other like-sized towns) fell into minor status. An agreement in 1883 set up a basic structure governing contracts and territories, as well as providing an arbitration committee for disputes. Though there were seventeen professional baseball leagues by 1890, a period of economic and interleague instability led to the creation in 1901 of a new agreement and the modern organization that governs minor league baseball, the National Association of Professional Baseball Leagues. The association formalized relations between the major and minor leagues; tightened league classifications, salary, and roster limits; and clarified what had been a chaotic system for drafting players.

By 1901 both major leagues had adopted the foul-strike rule (it's a strike when a batter hits a foul ball unless he already has two strikes against him), perhaps the last rule change in baseball to profoundly impact the way the game is played. The status of minor league teams was further strengthened with the Major-Minor League Agreement in 1903, and the number of minor leagues immediately began to grow. That year there were nineteen leagues; by 1907, there were thirty-six in 244 cities and towns. "Farm teams"—minor league teams officially partnered with designated major league teams to prepare players for the majors—didn't exist as such, though the majors found ways to establish informal if not illegal understandings with minor teams. From 1905 to 1911 a major league team could draft one player per year from a given minor league team, though there was no limit on how many players in total one team could draft from the minors; in 1911, the number would be fixed at eight. A system evolved that allowed a gifted player to advance within organized baseball in a more or less orderly fashion, with graduated payments established at each level. Not until Branch Rickey, manager of the St. Louis Cardinals, bought stakes in a couple of minor league teams in the 1920s would a true farm system emerge and become a consistent, unrivaled source of players.

When Jim arrived in Rocky Mount, minor league baseball thus provided a bona fide chance to get off the farm or out of the city and get scouted for the majors. Class D was not a fabulously lucrative career choice—"Nobody ever thought anything about making money at baseball here in those days," E. J. Johnston, secretary and treasurer of the Railroaders, would recall—but it was adequate. Salaries were guaranteed by the bond that each team posted, and a player's individual pay of between $15 to $25 a week—the same as a family of five, including children, made in the local mill working ten to twelve hours six days a week—could be supplemented, occasionally, with local farmwork. Contracts were short term and could be canceled within days. The players stayed in primitive local hotels and traveled by train, the whole team piling into a private car. Games, sometimes two a day, were played in punishing heat and humidity and were often called on account of train delays, disruptions from the stands, and summer thunderstorms.

The Eastern Carolina League scheduled ninety games in 1909 for each team. *The* (Raleigh) *News and Observer* noted that while there were those who could afford to spend the hot summers at the seashore or the mountains, "the people who cannot leave their business and others who cannot afford prolonged vacations are given a treat" seeing "the cleanest, most enthusiastic and manliest sport" right near home. The paper also gave credit to the other local newspapers for following and keeping up the sport. Playing minor league baseball was not an unnoticed, unreported-on activity in the small towns of North Carolina.

By mid-June the Railroaders were in next-to-last place. All three Carlisle men played their first game on June 15 against Raleigh before a crowd of 650 at the new A & M athletic field in Rocky Mount. The next day, Rocky Mount beat Raleigh, 4–2. Jim's name showed up several times in *The News and Observer*'s account: "The Carlisle Indian and All-American half-back proved to be very effective in the box" (he got two hits). Quickly labeled "Big Chief Thorpe" or "Big Chief 'Bullhead' Thorpe," Jim took to referring to himself as "Chief," the team's batboy, Charles Harris, would recall. It was the stereotypical, dime-novel tag given to Indian athletes, whether they wanted it or not, and Jim was preempting it, with a wink of the eye. On his fifth day with the Railroaders, he hit well and pitched his first professional shutout.

Jim played all positions except catcher and second base. He was one of the best hitters, but on a weak team, and he hit only .253 for the season. As a pitcher he lost more games than he won. His concentration would wander. Baseball was a two-hour game in that era before electric lights, but its comparatively slower pace didn't command his attention like football did. Jim preferred a game in which he was on the move the entire time. He diverted himself by entertaining the spectators with funny commentary. He was often "wild" on the mound and undisciplined as a hitter. Curveballs tormented him; naturally, he saw a steady diet of them. His speed on base, however, remained an asset.

A young reporter for *The Rocky Mount Evening Telegram* at the time, Sam Mallison was assigned to follow Thorpe and "embellish his achievements." He recalled that Thorpe became the "toast of the town" that season. "Small boys, curious adolescents and adult hero worshippers crowded about him on the streets, in the business houses, and Oakland Park whither he usually repaired in the evenings to see an outdoor movie." Part of the initial allure, played up in the newspapers, was the fact that he was supposedly a full-blood Indian, now a rarity along the east coast of the continent. His 1908 All-America football rank heightened the interest and curiosity. Railroader fans felt Thorpe gave them a chance to escape the cellar, and they clung to it all summer.

Mallison's account made no mention of the fact that while Indians were not considered on the same level as blacks in North Carolina, they were not always treated as white either. Depending on the color of their skin, the Indian players could never be sure of their status. Local papers routinely reported on supposed rapes of white southern women by blacks, on lynchings, and on the "nigger" prizefighter Jack Johnson, the first black world heavyweight champion. According to Joe Libby, in Rocky Mount a person of color was not allowed downtown, and if he needed to cross from one side of town to the other, he had to take the "colored road" around the town. Libby sometimes exaggerated when recounting stories about Jim, but this one, told to Jim's son, Jack, sounds credible. One evening Jim, Libby, and Youngdeer—the latter two darker-skinned than Jim—were late heading to the ballfield and decided to take the "shortcut" through town. A policeman stopped them and asked what they were doing downtown. When Jim tried to explain that they were late for the game, the officer started shoving him. Jim knocked the officer out. The three players spent the night in jail. Libby and Youngdeer left the league after a few weeks.

When confronted with prejudice, a biased assumption, or a demand he considered unfair, usually from a person in authority, Jim would often react violently. Alcohol only amplified his sensitivity. In other, sometimes comic, stories, he acted out when he was feeling bored and restless. Libby confessed to Jim's son Jack Thorpe that he was scared of Jim because you never knew from one second to the next what he would do. At a certain primal level, everything was a game to him. "Jim always liked to play," a Rocky Mount teammate recalled, "or that's what he called it."

By early August every umpire in the league had resigned, fed up with harassment from fans. The Railroaders were accusing other teams of doctoring the balls with resin and were themselves accused of throwing games—and they well might have as, at one point, the team lost fourteen in a row. Though none of the subsequent affidavits mentioned Jim, as pitcher and first baseman during the games in question his cooperation would have been required. The league's president called the organization "a laughing stock all over Eastern Carolina."

At the end of the month, the town of Rocky Mount hosted a farewell barbecue for the 27–61 Railroaders. Jim attended, though how welcome he was is questionable. Three days earlier, *The News and Observer* had headlined an article on another Thorpe escapade, this time in Raleigh: " 'Big Chief' on Rampage: Indian Pitcher Thorpe of Rocky Mount Arrested." After getting into a fight in a "near beer" joint with one of his teammates, he threw the police officers who tried to restrain him into a "street barrell" and refused to be arrested until an "umpire" intervened. He spent the night in jail, paid a fine the next morning, and was set free. The season had been thoroughly frustrating.

In early September, the National Baseball Commission made public a list of the major league draft choices for the coming season—"the heaviest draftings upon the minor leagues that have been made within the history of organized baseball," reported *The News and Observer*. Jim was not among them.

Jim left for Oklahoma to stay with his half sister, now Minnie Rider, helping on her farm near Prague. He wrote to Friedman in October, requesting money from his Carlisle account to buy a team, buggy, and feed for him to use on Minnie's property. "He failed to return to school," Friedman wrote of Jim to agent Kohlenberg in response. As a result, and "for the sake of discipline and in order that no precedent be set," Friedman recommended that none of Jim's money be forwarded to him as long as he was not in school. Jim had a balance of $289.75 at Carlisle, part of which was his share of $20,000 recently allocated to the Sac and Fox in lieu of the perpetual annuities that had been paid to the tribe since the Treaty of 1804, when the tribe had ceded all its land east of the Mississippi. That first Sac and Fox treaty—the origin, as Black Hawk said, of all their future troubles—had now been voided.

Kohlenberg wrote the BIA in November to request authorization to approve checks of James Thorpe from his tribal bank account, explaining that the applicant "intends . . . to return to Carlisle in the Spring" and had "enough of practical experience and should be competent to transact this much of his affairs to his best interests." The agent added: "He is the famous football player of the Carlisle team." Jim may have thought claiming a return to Carlisle would give him more credibility with the agent. His application for farm equipment was initially returned because the expenditure had been made without prior approval, meaning Jim, now twenty-two, had simply bought what he needed when he needed it, like any non-Indian would. If Jim had not already begun to develop what would be a lifelong antipathy to the BIA, this paternalistic, bureaucratic runaround no doubt inspired it.

In early November, Friedman wrote again to Kohlenberg: "During the last few months he was here, James was very far from being a desirable student." He suggested that Jim's money remain at the school, earning 3 percent interest, until such time as Jim demonstrated the kind of behavior that would make him "a more desirable element among his people." Friedman wanted Jim held to his 1908 verbal promise to return to Carlisle and graduate, but he didn't "wish him forced back," he wrote. A couple of weeks later he sent a telegram to Kohlenberg insisting that, as Jim had "missed nearly half a year in studies," it did not make sense for him to return to Carlisle until September 1910.

But after a baseball season that had not catapulted him to the majors, Jim now believed and told everyone he was coming back. Carlisle was home, the place where he was known, valued, and admired. He traveled to St. Louis at Thanksgiving to watch Carlisle beat St. Louis University. He ate turkey dinner with his former teammates and Warner. Afterward, Warner spent a few days hunting deer with him in Oklahoma. One can assume they discussed Jim's baseball summer and his future. If he returned to Carlisle to finish out the remaining two years of his term, he would graduate in spring 1912, which would likely make him unable to compete as a Carlisle athlete for the 1912 summer Olympics. Jim had shown promise in 1909 of becoming a great track and field performer. He would later say that he knew in his heart then that he would one day compete in the Olympics. Warner knew Jim was not major league baseball material and that he, Warner, had Jim's fate in his hands.

At Christmas, Jim accompanied a group of new students from Stroud to Carlisle and joined in the familiar feasting and gift-giving holiday rituals at the school. Another Sac and Fox student wrote Kohlenberg that Jim was returning to the school in a month to finish his last two years. But Friedman was firm. Uncertain what he wanted to do, Jim spent the rest of the winter and spring in Oklahoma.

On May 1, 1910, Jim reported back to Rocky Mount as spring training began. After much discussion and dispute, the Eastern Carolina League had finally agreed on salary limits, guarantees, and forfeit fees. Strict rules and fees were necessary to curb the temptation to jack up the bidding for good college players. Without a good quality of play, and prudent management, the teams and the league couldn't survive.

According to Jim, he tore a ligament in his right arm in a preseason game. It is more likely he strained the arm. He pitched often but ineffectively the rest of the season, switching to first base and the outfield at times. He kept performing, often setting "the fans laughing at his little witticisms," wrote *The News and Observer*. On first in the bottom of the ninth of a scoreless game, he raced around the bases when the next batter singled into right field. Twenty-five feet from home plate, he let out "an Indian-like war-whoop," according to the batboy, Charles Harris, and did a flying broad jump, feet aimed at the catcher, who prudently stepped aside as Jim scored.

His stunts were not limited to the field. The morning after a game in Wilmington, when it was light enough to see, Jim jumped out of bed, ran out of the team's boardinghouse and down the boardwalk, and dove into the ocean. The team had been warned not to go in the water, but Jim drifted out with the tide about half a mile. He had no experience of ocean currents or local riptides, no idea of their dangers. Jim "was an impulsive person," his teammate Arthur Dussault said. He was also curious. Maybe he liked testing himself, as Hiram had tested him in the waters of the North Canadian. Jim's teammates gathered on the beach as he struggled to get back. When he finally emerged from the surf, four hours later, it was with no sign of fatigue. He simply walked back to the boardinghouse. "No one ever mentioned it to him," said Dussault. "No one dared."

By mid-July, the league was starting to fall apart. New ownership kept the Railroaders going, and Jim did whatever was asked of him, whatever the position. He had his moments, but not enough for scouts from Philadelphia and Washington who watched him play. *The News and Observer* did report, though, that a nineteen-year-old Eastern League pitcher had been bought for $1,000 by the St. Louis Browns in the American League. "The two big leagues are desperately in search of young blood and, as a consequence, each club, in both leagues, are [sic] competing with each other for the services of promising material." The same week, the great Ty Cobb, leading batter of the American League, received a Chalmers-Detroit car as a reward. "He owns several cars now," said the article in the Raleigh paper. Jim's frustration mounted. The fabulous baseball lifestyle described by Joe Twin's article in *The Arrow* was far beyond his grasp.

In mid-August, Rocky Mount traded Jim and an outfielder to the third-place Fayetteville Highlanders in exchange for another pitcher and an outfielder. Jim worked up another grudge: he felt he had played well enough not to be traded. From the beginning, he clashed with the Fayetteville manager, Charles Clancy, a popular and "resolute Irishman," according to Mallison. Clancy demanded respect and obedience from his players, but Jim became "progressively less responsive to managerial direction," Mallison recalled, becoming "something of a problem child." Clancy later said that Jim "appeared to like a good time too well to be a successful player." Jim's rebellion culminated in a fight with Clancy, according to Mallison. The two soon made up, going fox hunting one afternoon a few weeks later with some team members. Jim wore his Highlanders uniform. Someone took a photo of the group and gave it to Clancy.

Jim's simmering frustration and indecision led to more strange behavior off the field. One night he ambled down the main street of a league town with a gallon jug of liquor, taking a swig every few yards, and then let out a yell heard all over town. One morning on Hay Street in Fayetteville, sitting in a restaurant with an hour to kill before the train left for a game, he bet a friend $5 that he could jump through the glass of the front window with no harm to himself—and even land on his feet. Jim went through the window, letting his back and shoulders take the first impact, and landed feet first. By now a crowd had gathered, and someone bet Jim another $5 he couldn't do it again. He accepted the challenge, and the group moved down the street to Clark's grocery store, which had another big front window. The owner, after trying to warn Jim off, picked up one of the ax handles for sale in his store and stood by the window, waiting. Jim grinned, went to the back of the store, and ran for the window. As he got ready to jump, the store owner hit him on the head, knocking him out. Jim was carried by the crowd to the doctor's office, where eight stitches were required to close the gash. He was just able to make his train.

As the season wound down, Jim was hit twice on the head by the ball during stolen base attempts. After the second incident, reported *The News and Observer*, he "sat down on the bag and laughed." That cut in his head was deep enough to put him in the hospital. Jim wound up hitting .236 for Rocky Mount and .250 for Fayetteville in 1910. There would be claims by locals that Thorpe's performance in the Eastern Carolina League those two summers was better than his statistics indicated. If that had been true, he would have been given a tryout with one of the major league teams (his goal), or at least an offer from a higher minor team. The National Baseball Commission announced that 115 minor league players had been drafted by the major league clubs that year, including two from Fayetteville. Jim was not one of them.

Jim spent the winter of 1910–1911 in Prague with his sister Mary, hunting and fishing. "I knew I stood at a crossroads," he said, "and I was pondering on what I should do." He was clearly not cut out to be a farmer. He began to drift from town to town, looking for work and the odd job. It was time to learn a new skill, he thought, apprentice for a reliable trade he could master and develop, or finish his high school education and continue on to college. But his happy-go-lucky nature had meshed so well with his athletic gifts at Carlisle that any real-world substitute seemed alien and irksome to him. He needed the structure of a team and a coach, and the unique environment of Carlisle had spoiled him. Jim didn't know this yet, if he ever did; he only felt baffled and frightened that life was not going his way. He could only wish, like the Greek heroes he would later be compared with, for a deus ex machina to save him.

In December, Jim closed his account at Carlisle, with a final check sent to Kohlenberg to deposit in Jim's BIA-controlled account. In spring 1911, he signed up with an independent "amateur" baseball team, the Anadarko Champions—as they called themselves—in Anadarko, Oklahoma, about sixty miles southwest of Oklahoma City. Jim was paid to play. In July the manager, according to Jim, found a cheaper player to take his place. His pride and dreams of future glory still alive, Jim told the manager, "You're going to spend a nickel to read about me sometime." He wrote Kohlenberg to tell him he was "not playing ball here anymore" and could the agent please send $35 so he could get home. Meanwhile, Samson Burd, a close friend and captain of the 1911 Carlisle football team, wrote Jim asking him to come back to the school. With six losses in 1910, the team needed help. Jim was twenty-four, had been gone from the school for two years, and had no plans.

Walking down a street in Anadarko that summer, Jim ran into Albert Exendine, who had graduated from law school and was on a visit home from his fall job as football coach at Otterbein College in Ohio.

"What are you doing?" Exendine asked.

"Nothing," said Jim.

"What have you been doing?" asked Exendine.

"Playing baseball," replied Jim.

"Did you graduate from Carlisle?"

"No."

"Why the heck don't you go back there and graduate?" Exendine asked, observing that Jim was a lot bigger and heavier.

"So," Exendine recalled, "I sent a telegram to Pop Warner that Jim Thorpe was here and as big as a mountain. So he sent a telegram and told me to go see the Indian agent [Kohlenberg] and have Jim come to Carlisle. So the agent and Pop Warner got together and the next thing I read was that Jim Thorpe was back at Carlisle."

Jim playing on the Carlisle football team,
c. 1911

ARISTOTLE'S DEFINITION of motion: "The
mode in which the future belongs to the
present . . . the joint presence of potentiality
and actuality." Time, space, action, athlete.
Now. In the top shot, Jim is in Warner's
three-point stance, grinning in anticipation
of the play. In the center, he's running down
the field during a warmup before a game early
in the season. Spectators in shirtsleeves stand
on the sideline. Jim runs low and tight in the
bottom shot, in a crouch to break through the
line, forcing the tackler to grab his hips, rather
than his knees. With a twist, he can throw him
off. He makes his own interference, shifting
the ball from one arm to the other as he runs.

· CHAPTER FIVE ·

Football Phenom

FALL 1911–SPRING 1912

THORPE BEAT HARVARD

> — *The Kansas City Star* headline, November 12, 1911

How could anyone get hurt playing football?

> —JIM THORPE

———◆———

September 24, 1911

Dear Sir:

I would like you to send me or transfer some money here at Carlisle.
I have decided to stay for two years longer. Mr. Kohlenberg have you
seen about my lease and what have you decided on doing. let me hear
from you concerning it for I have some offers . . . our prospects for a
good [football season] is great, and I think we will have a winning team
this fall. We have our first game to-day with Lebon Valley but they
want be any trouble. Well I must close.

Respectfulley Yours
James Thorpe

Lebanon Valley College wasn't any trouble—Carlisle won, 53–0. It
was a taste of things to come.

Jim, as he always pointed out, was only one member of an outstanding team. But even before the 1911 season started, news reports
appeared describing "a young Indian student who promises to become
one of the greatest athletes his race has ever known" and "the world's
greatest all-rounder." Articles with almost identical wording showed

up in myriad papers, suggesting that the source was Warner's busy press office. His most persuasive argument for Jim to return had been that Jim would have a chance, with Louis Tewanima, to make the 1912 U.S. Olympic team as a Carlisle athlete and bring honor to his school, his people, and himself. Jim was aware that he could have also tried out for the U.S. team as a club player. But the sort of athletic clubs that sent athletes to the Olympics were exclusive organizations, not usually open to nonwhites. If Jim tried out from Carlisle, Warner would be his guide, buffer, and trainer. This was Warner's chance, first to consolidate Carlisle's position as the preeminent innovator in football *and* track and field, and then to position himself, approaching forty, as the wizard behind it all.

As Jim resumed his old position of left halfback, he "felt good to be back among my own kind in a football uniform and on the campus of the school I loved." It was the order and regularity of Carlisle that were precious to him after two years floating on his own. There were no more of the juvenile antics that had got him demoted as captain of the track and field team in 1909. He was now happily training, jogging, and exercising for a few hours in the morning in heavy sweat clothes, taking a brief nap, and then going back out and repeating the morning workout in the afternoon. He ate sparsely while getting back into condition. He carefully watched over and trained his roommate, new Chippewa quarterback Gustavus "Gus" Welch, as Exendine had done for him four years before. He befriended William "Lone Star" Dietz, a tackle who claimed to be Oglala Lakota Sioux, but whose origins are a matter of controversy. With Exendine and other former teammates now moving out beyond Carlisle and establishing careers in coaching or other professions, Jim saw that it was possible for a Carlisle athlete to build a successful life afterward.

Two years bumming around in the minors had not fully matured him, however. He could still be moody and unpredictable and chafe under rules and restrictions. Almost twenty-five, he continued to need guidance and protection from himself. But he knew he had come to a dead end in North Carolina and Oklahoma and had to change, make some kind of future for himself. He had left Carlisle in 1909 confident of his emerging athletic skills, only to learn their limitations. Chastened, Jim had to pay attention now, salvage his career.

He returned to a game marked by yet another set of fundamental changes. Prompted by twenty-six fatalities during the 1909 season, new rules had been put in place in 1910 that laid the foundation of the modern game: four fifteen-minute quarters; seven men back again on the scrimmage line; substitutions allowed; elimination once and for all of mass rugbylike scrums pushing the ball carrier forward. The forward pass had a new restriction—it could not go more than twenty yards past the line of scrimmage—that would cut back its use until the rule was eliminated in 1912. Touchdowns were still worth five points, field goals three. In retrospect, the 1910 rules would be seen as not only opening up the game itself, but inspiring its rapid spread south and west. The "Brahmins of the East," Warner would say, started to be supplanted by younger, more progressive coaches and players, eager to junk tradition and try new ideas.

Warner had thoroughly explored the kinks in the new rules. Sophisticated rushing plays were developed to take advantage of the more open game. Similarly, the kicking game, Jim's forte, was even more important to advance the ball. And Jim was now even better at instantly assessing and responding to new situations on the field. He could see the game as clearly as others might see a geometry problem or a game of chess. Warner knew enough to leave Jim alone with his instincts.

In September and early October, Carlisle easily won all its games, against easy opponents. Since Jim had been away from football for two years, reporters wondered if he would show the same "fire and swiftness" he'd shown in the Penn game of 1908. "The sports writers in the East," one reporter wrote, suspected Jim was "something of an in-and-outer—the kind of athlete who now and then has a phenomenal day."

On October 14, against Georgetown, in front of a Washington crowd that included government officials and a large delegation from the Office of Indian Affairs, Jim sped up and down the field with a "deceptive change of pace," according to one report, "the power to pivot as no other player of his time, and a magnificent straight-arm which sent him through the whole Georgetown team for a touchdown." He also scored three extra points and Carlisle won, 28–5. The victory was seen "as something of an upset." Jim Thorpe was back, though some still had doubts that he and his team could hold up to the powerhouses on the rest of its schedule.

Now "the whole East" was primed for Carlisle's game against Pittsburgh at Forbes Field. In a letter to the Cornell football coach, Warner described the Panthers, who had not been scored against in 1910, as a "big heavy team—a lot of bruisers and ringers." When Jim kicked a long high punt into a mass of Pitt players, got down the field in time to catch the ball, and repelled "three or four would-be tacklers," *The Pittsburgh Dispatch* reported he then ran twenty yards for a touchdown. He later caught one of his own punts again, and the avid crowd of football-mad Pennsylvanians roared their approval and delight, "compelled," admitted the *Dispatch*, "to cheer the enemy for its great work." Jim almost doubled his personal rushing best with 235 yards gained, and Carlisle won, 17–0.

He thoroughly enjoyed himself during the game, with a "good-natured smile" throughout. "Next time—left tackle!" he'd shout, for all to hear, across the line of scrimmage, before he smashed through the designated spot. "I never saw him snarl and mostly he just laughed, talked to the other team, and enjoyed himself," Warner said of Jim's newly mature, relaxed style of play. "He had a natural change-of-pace that just floated him past the defense. His reactions were so fast that sometimes you couldn't follow them with the eye. Punishment didn't mean a thing to him. He was fearless and he hit so hard that the other fellow got all the bruises."

The press covering the Pitt game vied for the most enthusiastic, definitive description of Jim's new style and skill. "To say Thorpe is the whole team," said *The Pittsburgh Leader,* "would be fifty percent wrong. . . . His returning of punts, line-bucking, fake plays and other maneuvers [got] him great applause." The *Dispatch* described Jim as "tall and sinewy, as quick as a flash and as powerful as a turbine engine . . . impervious to injury. Kicking from 50 to 70 yards every time his shoe crashed against the ball, he seemed possessed of super-human speed, for wherever the ball alighted, there he was, ready either to grab it or to down the Pitt player who secured it . . . this Sac and Fox shone resplendent—and then some."

Jim injured his right (kicking) leg and sprained the ankle against Lafayette, so he sat out the Penn game, crutches by his side. Carlisle remained undefeated. The stage was now set, public interest "smoking hot," for "the battle of the year," Carlisle versus Harvard. Harvard's coach, the tall, patrician, snobbish, and belligerent Percy Haughton, wrote to Warner before the game warning him that if Carlisle used a Warner trick—sewing half-football patches on the front of the jerseys of the backs—Harvard would cancel the game. Haughton told his second string to suit up to start the game, conserving the varsity's energy for their next games against Dartmouth and Yale, and left for New Haven to scout the Yale–Brown game. As one Carlisle player said, "We pointed to this game because it meant more prestige than any other. On the other hand, Harvard didn't consider us much."

At game time, "Crippled Jimmy Thorpe," as *The Boston Sunday Globe* described Jim, had his still-injured right leg and ankle heavily wrapped with "a basketweave of strapping adhesive plaster running almost from his toe to his knee." This game would set him up as the enduring, punishing model of the iron man who plays regardless of physical handicap. Injuries—he suffered few of them—only made Jim more focused. Revealing a superstitious side to his character, he pointed out that this was the eleventh day of the eleventh month of the eleventh year of the century, and eleven was his lucky number.

The game was epic. "Probably," proclaimed the *Kansas City Star*, "the most spectacular playing ever witnessed." Warner knew Jim was in severe pain, but "not once," he said, "did [Thorpe] ask for a time out," giving "as fine an exhibition of sheer grit as I have ever seen." Harvard had expected him to run with the ball; instead he ran superb interference. Even with a sprained ankle, Jim kicked field goals from Harvard's 13-, then 43-yard lines. At halftime, Harvard led, 9–6.

Refusing to lose to Harvard's second string, Carlisle intensified its game in the third quarter, playing what the *Globe* called an even more aggressive "whirlwind football"—the "slaughter of the substitutes." From the 37-yard line Jim kicked another field goal—like the last one, against the wind. Each kick had such force that it was said that the ball could have sailed through the goal posts from fifteen or twenty yards further back down the field. Disregarding his aching leg and the original game plan, with the score tied 9–9, Jim told quarterback Welch to start feeding him the ball. The Harvard ends and backs were "completely bewildered," said the (Philadelphia) *Public Ledger*, as Jim and Arcasa "ripped off beautiful gains" so constantly and quickly "that no one dared sit down in the stands." Warner heard Jim yell to his interference, "Get out of my way! I mean to do some real running," as he sped with the ball. Powell scored a touchdown, capping a stunning nine-play drive. Carlisle made the extra point.

With twelve minutes left in the game, Carlisle in front 15–9, Harvard sent in its well-rested captain and eight varsity players. Haughton had always planned to send in the first string at the end of the game—a gratuitous slap at Carlisle. The fresh Harvard players broke through the Carlisle defensive line with much greater force and ease. The only way, Jim realized, to beat the Cambridge team was to hold them until the very end and then make another placekick. After Carlisle made a first down and was stopped on the next two plays, at Harvard's 48-yard line, Jim told Arcasa, "Set the ball up. I'll kick it."

The big crowd went quiet. Jim's leg was "pretty sore," he said, but he found the pain "sort of helped me because it made me more deliberate." He knew his team was exhausted. "As long as I live," he would recall, "I will never forget that moment. There I stood in the center of the field, the biggest crowd I had ever seen watching us. . . . I was tired enough so that all my muscles were relaxed. I had confidence, and I wasn't worried. The ball came back square and true, and I swung my leg with all the power and force that I had, and knew, as it left my toe, that it was headed straight for the crossbar and was sure to go over. . . . I got the thrill of that moment. . . . Nothing else mattered." Jim had kicked his fourth field goal—"the most wonderful place kick," said one Boston paper.

He signaled Warner and was carried off the field in the last minutes of play. The crowd jumped to its feet and roared for the great show he had given them. Four minutes later, Harvard scored a final touchdown after a Carlisle fumble. The gun went off, the game was over, the score 18–15, Carlisle.

"When . . . we knew that we had beaten Harvard," Jim said, "a feeling of pride that none of us has ever lost came over all of us. . . . Maybe football victories and athletic championships don't mean very much compared to some of the great accomplishments of famous men, but I'll bet none of them . . . ever got a bigger kick out of winning." "We all played better because of him," said Jim's teammate Henry Roberts. A Harvard lineman came up to congratulate the team with tears running down his face.

Jim was too appreciative of the hard work of his teammates to claim what *The Kansas City Star* ran as its headline: "Thorpe Beat Harvard." But he was proud and self-aware enough to save for his scrapbook Paul E. Shannon's report that day for *The Boston Post*: "If ever defeat was the result of one man's achievements, the downfall of Harvard may be attributed to James Thorpe, the sensational mainstay of Glenn Warner's great team." Warner, never lavish with compliments, described Jim that day as "a one-man wrecking crew." He also noted that the game brought in $10,400 to Carlisle, a new school record.

At a time of minimal national media outlets and a much smaller pool of national celebrities, Jim had become a legend overnight. *The Boston Post* stated that "it was indeed a pleasure to see a man not only live up to a great reputation, but add to it through work beautifully accomplished." Jim was described as Frank Merriwell—the fictional Yale football hero—come to life. Even Haughton admitted, "I realized that here is the theoretical superplayer in flesh and blood," and no doubt regretted he'd missed the game. The loss was his team's last before a four-year undefeated streak. A less rarefied opinion was that "[t]he man on the street was delighted that the refined burghers of Boston had been shown by one redskin why the winning of the West had been so tough." And, implicitly, how the winners had been even tougher to beat such a foe. In 2008, *Sports Illustrated* would point to the 1911 Harvard game as the highlight of a season that would have earned Jim the Heisman Trophy, had it existed then.

Seven days after its tremendous victory, Carlisle lost 12–11 to Syracuse. Both teams splashed around in slush and ankle-deep water that inhibited one of Carlisle's greatest assets, speed: with his highest number of rushes yet—thirty—Jim netted only 133 yards. He later attributed the loss to "overconfidence—that evil which has done more to defeat good teams than any other one thing." That, and the fact that Carlisle had played on successive Saturdays against five of the toughest teams in the country. Jim also didn't like playing in the rain. "What's the fun in that?" he would say to Grantland Rice.

Carlisle won its last two games in impressive fashion, including one against Brown, 12–6. They had scored 298 points overall to their twelve opponents' 49 (half of them didn't score at all). The players elected Jim the captain of the 1912 team. Camp named him as a half-back to his All-America first team, the ultimate football accolade. Newspaper commentators now recalled Jim's track and field performance in 1909 and assessed this unique talent, trying to predict his potential. Jim's power came from his coordination as much as his strength. He was flexible, with easy movements that, combined with a keen, quick intelligence, made for actions and reactions calculated for maximum effect. *The New York Times*, noting his key role in the Harvard and Brown victories, said that "Thorpe is . . . considered America's greatest all-round athlete . . . a revelation in the football world this season." Jim said he simply played with the recklessness that comes from having no fear of getting hurt.

Warner, ever the booster in public, said that Jim was the most natural athlete he had ever seen, born to play football. He'd never seen a player who could penetrate a line like Jim, or run so fast. "He could go skidding through first and second defense," said Warner, "knock off a tackler, stop short and turn past another, ward off still another, and escape the entire pack; or, finally cornered, could go farther with a tackler than any man I ever knew." Jim's ability to concentrate, to observe and act in the moment, sincerely fascinated Warner: "He is . . . always watching for a new motion which will benefit him. . . . It is a splendid sight to see him hurl a football thirty yards on a forward pass with merely an abrupt snap of the wrist, direct to the hands of the receiver, or to see him judge and catch a twisting spiral punt on the dead run."

Privately, Warner called Jim "a lazy Indian" to his face and insisted he only gave about 40 percent of his total capacity. "He didn't like to practice," Warner said, "and he gave his best effort only when he felt like it." When he was "right," the coach admitted, "the sheer joy of playing carried him through; when he wasn't, he showed it." The "lazy" tag was a chronic complaint of Warner's and stuck for the rest of Jim's life, but it was more revelatory of Warner than of Jim. He had a brilliant athlete on his hands who did so much so well, and there would always be a sort of begrudging envy of Jim: Warner wanted to take him down a peg, perhaps to enhance his own role as Jim's supposed Svengali. He needed the obedience of his players, and Jim resisted the idea of obeying anybody.

At the same time, there was some truth to Warner's opinion. The frustration of feeling he'd never seen what Jim might accomplish if he always gave his best got to Warner. Exendine saw it differently: "Sometimes Jim would play a rotten game. But that was against teams he knew he could lick." Against the good teams, "[b]oy, that's when Jim Thorpe showed up." As always, Jim's casual affect masked his inner focus. True to form, he dismissed all the cavils. "I may have had an aversion for work," he said, "but I also had an aversion for getting beat."

With each game in 1911, Jim and his style had further "caught the imagination of the nation," as one writer later said of him. Certainly, Warner's strategic planting of carefully tailored press releases, embellished by newspapers across the country, created an unreal kind of fervor and expectation on the part of the public. Still, Jim remained an outsider, but one who demonstrated by his magnificent performance to blacks, Italians, Irish, Jews, any immigrant or native group, that with only the chance, any one of them might beat the big boys, fair and square. That identification with Jim would have a deep and genuine hold on the popular spirit for decades to come.

Jim was also the subject of a new and more complicated assessment of Indian players. The (Rochester) *Union and Advertiser* looked with pointed irony at the just-concluded World Series, when the Philadelphia Athletics Chippewa pitcher Albert Bender beat the New York Giants with their Cahuilla Mission catcher, John Tortes Meyers (also usually referred to as "Chief" Meyers): "[W]hen the Pilgrims landed on Plymouth Rock they first fell upon their knees, and then fell upon the aborigines. Things have changed. The aborigines now fall upon the whites and make short work of them."

Many of these news articles were already encouraging the idea that the Indian athlete was a "natural" who never trained or even tried very hard: "Thorpe . . . makes no special preparations for his efforts," said one commentator, but "simply meanders carelessly up to his tasks and does them in an unconscious way." That opinion, which would be applied to other minority athletes in years to come, managed to undercut Jim's achievement by attributing it to a kind of brute talent not available to white athletes who were, after all, as they saw it, also bearing the burden of civilization with its more important and learned skills. Jim's skill and supremacy could thus be tolerated—and dismissed—by the elite whites most threatened by them as a freak aberration, like the heart-stopping tricks of an itinerant circus performer. Jim's pride and sly sense of humor led him, in turn, to exaggerate his supposed diffidence for effect: he would not, on principle, appear too eager.

The attitudes of the other Carlisle players were mixed. Thirty years after the founding of the school, about half of them were, like Jim, barely half-Indian. They saw themselves as being nuanced blends of different identities. More important than settling old battlefield scores on the gridiron was the chance the game offered each of them to test and reshape his own sense of power and competence on the open and incontrovertible field of sport—the promise of sports for anyone, anywhere. Because the players were seen as Indians and, in varying degrees, saw themselves as Indians, the elite game was also their symbolic stage on which to venture into the white competitive world. What united them as a team was not only a frank enjoyment of their national fame and their privileges on campus, but a joy in the game of football itself. In this at least the Carlisle players knew they were not any different than their white competitors. As Jim would say, they liked to win.

To Indians beyond Carlisle—fragmented, demoralized, isolated on reservations or trying to eke out a living on tiny allotment lands, with tribes like the Sac and Fox reduced to mere hundreds—Jim, playing at the most famous and most publicized Indian school, was a source of pride and vindication. Through a network of Indian agents and Carlisle graduates, copies of *The Arrow* were mailed out and circulated throughout the reservations, allotments, and other Indian schools. Word of mouth from mainstream news accounts further spread the story of Jim's performance. He reinforced to many Indians that they had an inherent value that had survived all attempts to extinguish it. The Carlisle athletes, who came from tribes all across the country, their new feats of valor and victory won against the best and the brightest of their white peers, were creating a new Pan-Indian story.

Friends noticed that Jim was sunnier and calmer after the 1911 football season. The pressure was off for a while. The goofy "Libbling" kid in him reemerged. He jumped over a normal obstacle, like a gate or wall, instead of walking around it; he dipped the pigtail tips of the girl sitting in front of him in class into his desk inkwell, as if he were fourteen, not twenty-four; he turned a casual walk across the school grounds into a spontaneous race to win. If he expressed anger through physical action, he expressed happiness the same way. He was now comfortable standing up in front of groups such as the Sunday evening meetings of the Catholic students, speaking on subjects like "Athletics in General at Carlisle." He joined the Invincible Debating Society and presented the address before the evening's debate one Friday in January on the topic "Resolved, That Richard III was a worse monarch than Charles II." He threw on clothes in a slapdash fashion. "Jim never liked to dress up," recalled one classmate. "He always went around looking so raggedy. He had an old, long, raggedy coat torn on one side that he always wore, and old, raggedy shoes. He was an old sport; he didn't try to show off, always so happy and jolly."

One unusually perceptive teacher, with a budding interest in sports and athletes, took special note of Jim. When Carlisle's commercial English teacher "suddenly wearied of pedagogy and departed to sell L.C. Smith typewriters" in 1911, as his successor recalled, the school in desperation had hired a local twenty-four-year-old Bryn Mawr graduate with no teaching experience named Marianne Moore. Half a century later, after she had won the Pulitzer Prize for her exquisite, demanding, chimerical poetry, she would readily recall the five years she spent at Carlisle. A passionate Brooklyn Dodgers fan by then, she would particularly remember the athletes, whom she described as having "something Grecian about them."

Jim took her commercial law course, which was designed to teach Carlisle students the rudiments of contracts and other basic legal transactions. The goal was to arm them with the expertise that would prevent their being defrauded when they returned to their reservations and home states. On Decoration Day, after taking her students to tend the graves of the Indian children who had died at the school, Moore led them via a shortcut on the railroad tracks into town to see a visiting circus. Jim and another student walked beside her to be sure their small, gentle teacher didn't stumble on the ties. Jim, who was the same age as Moore, noticed she was carrying what she described as "a man's big cherry-handled cotton umbrella," and he asked, "Miss Moore, may I carry your parasol for you?" She said, "Thank you, James"—she never called him "Jim," though everyone else did—and was "touched by the courtesy of the question" and the quaint word use.

Contrary to the assumptions of many of her white friends, and with the exception of some troubled youths, Moore did not find the Indian students at all frightening. The athletes in her classes were especially helpful. "The Indians had great behavior and ceremony," she recalled, "and were exceedingly chivalrous and decent and cooperative and . . . idealistic." She was particularly "fond" of the "exceedingly generous" Jim. "He was liked by all," she explained, "*liked* in italics, rather than venerated or idolized . . . he was such an all-round phenomenon—'Jim.' He was off-hand, modest, casual about everything in the way of fame or eminence achieved. This modesty, with top performance, was characteristic of him."

She watched Jim in football practice after school and at the spring track and field events. "He had a kind of ease in his gait that is hard to describe," she said. "Equilibrium with no strictures; but crouched in the lineup for football he was the epitome of concentration, wary, with an effect of plenty in reserve. I never saw him irascible, sour, or prized for vengeance." In Moore's classroom, when he was able to show up, Jim was "a little slow—he was a little slow mentally," Moore said to Robert Cantwell, interviewing her for *Sports Illustrated* in 1960. Cantwell interpreted her statement to mean only that Jim "wasn't much at book learning." Moore retained a mental picture of Jim: "head bent earnestly over the paper, [writing] a fine even clerical hand—every character legible, every terminal curving up—consistent and generous."

Moore would later compare Jim with one of her favorite athletes, Willie Mays. Credited with introducing a black "style" of baseball play, with what sportswriter William C. Rhoden called "flair and cool," Mays would seem to be playing "a new game." Jim and the Carlisle team had an Indian style of play—incredible speed, inventiveness, spontaneity, a relaxed sense of fun—that was not only uniquely theirs, but that defined a new type of game as well.

Moore's sympathy for the multiple ironies of her Indian students' lives at Carlisle would have a profound effect on her work. Her lifelong poetic play with the ideas of imposture and protective armor, symbolic and real, suggests an unusual empathy with the existential limbo in which young Indians transplanted to Carlisle lived much of the time. Only recently have scholars suggested that the students at Carlisle directly shaped her "images and rhetorical strategies," offering "a model for a flexible understanding of identity."

Though Elizabeth Walker, an orphaned Tlingit from Sitka, Alaska, described Jim at this stage as someone "all the girls had a crush on," Henry Roberts noticed that Jim "never seemed to bother much about the female sex. . . . He treated all the girls alike." Rose DeNomie, another Carlisle student, said Jim kidded and danced—very well— with all the girls, but that he certainly made no special effort to impress or please them.

If Jim didn't take special notice, one girl enrolled in Moore's typing class had her eye on him. Iva (also called Ivy) Miller was a pretty, smart, well-mannered, and stylish eighteen-year-old with green eyes, thick black hair, and fair creamy skin. With a particularly clear, pleasant speaking voice, she had been chosen as the class elocutionist and was active in school clubs and projects serving as secretary of the girls' debating society and chief justice of a mock city government.

When Jim first met Iva he said, "You're a cute little thing." At a reception held by two student debating clubs, he and Iva led the grand march, a formal dance tradition involving a sequence of "figures" by a group of dancers following the leaders in unison. Jim and Gus Welch had flipped a coin as to who would ask Iva to the Penn game in 1911; Jim won, unaware that Iva had begun to keep a scrapbook of clippings about his games. "A great big book," recalled one student. "She must have idolized him." As Jim's fame grew over the next two years, so would the scrapbook—and the relationship.

Iva Margaret Miller was one of several Carlisle students with dubious or entirely fabricated Indian identities. Six years younger than Jim, she had been born on August 24, 1893, at Pryor Creek, a town north of Fort Gibson on the Missouri, Kansas and Texas Railroad line in the Cherokee section of Indian Territory. "White intruders were more numerous," read one historical account of the area, "than Indians." Her mother, Martha (Mattie) Denton Miller, may have been part Cherokee, though there is no credible evidence to support that claim. Her father, J. (James) Finas Miller, was a white cattleman and sometime hotel keeper whose Scots-Irish ancestors had come from Northern Ireland, settled near Carlisle before the Revolution, and later founded the hamlet of Millersburgh, Kentucky. Iva claimed to be descended from Henry Knox, the nation's first secretary of war, after whom Knoxville, Tennessee, was named.

In 1902, Finas, widowed, put four of his five children, including Iva, in the Chilocco Indian School, a boarding facility. To be eligible for enrollment, students had to be at least one-eighth Indian. Iva and her sister, Grace, were each marked on enrollment as one-fourth Shawnee, which was clearly untrue. But so haphazard were the admissions procedures on the frontier that white children could easily qualify as Indian and readily did to get not only a free education, but one at a boarding school that relieved their parents of the responsibility of raising them. "Many who apply [to Carlisle]," Pratt wrote to the Sac and Fox agent in 1899, "are so nearly white they really do not seem to belong to an Indian school."

Iva, while still at Chilocco, was chosen to be one of a group of almost a hundred of the school's students sent to the 1904 St. Louis World's Fair, a celebration of the centenary of the Louisiana Purchase and America's progress. A section of the fair was devoted to the indigenous peoples whose cultures had been dramatically affected by Thomas Jefferson's acquisition. Various tribes were encamped outside the Indian Territory Building, "as in their original, picturesque environments." Inside the large structure overlooking the fairgrounds, Iva spent eight months singing "The Little Game Called Kissing" and giving recitations of Longfellow's *The Song of Hiawatha*. The star attraction of the fair, Geronimo, took a fancy to Iva. A prisoner of war, he was set up in a special booth under armed guard on the main floor of the building, where he danced and sold photo cards with his signature for a dime each. To the delight of spectators, he regularly asked Iva to dance with him and gave her a dime after her recitations.

Among the distinguished white visitors to the fair was Helen Gould, a daughter of financier Jay Gould. She hosted a large party that featured children supposedly representing every nation in the world and took such a fancy to the "bright little Indian maiden" from

Oklahoma she wanted to adopt her. Finas did not consent, but Iva embraced the ideal of the "sweet" and "beautiful," very rich lady from New York, who wore what Iva described as "simple, elegant gowns." Indian or white, Iva could assume a fresh identity as needed. "Sociable, impressionable—particularly about money—and very feminine," was how her grandson Michael Koehler remembered her. Iva was charming to men all her life, a flirt.

After a year at the St. Louis Convent in Pawhuska, Oklahoma, she applied to Carlisle in 1909 to study nursing and work in the health clinic. In order to be enrolled, she had to be at least one-fourth Indian. Her application claimed that her mother had been a half-blood Cherokee of the "North Carolina Agency" who had left the tribe in 1861. Iva later told one of her daughters that she had no Indian blood and was proud that she had "put one over on the government." Whether she sincerely believed she was not Indian or chose to believe it is still a mystery within her family, as is whether she had any Indian ancestry at all.

Jim, in any case, had no reason to doubt she was mostly Indian, same as him. Plus, she was the prettiest girl in the school, well-mannered, well-spoken, in her own mind a lady. She was also sympathetic and understanding, two irresistible qualities that warmed and nourished Jim. He began to pay more attention to her.

Soon after the end of the football season, Jim was diagnosed with trachoma, popularly called "sore eyes," a highly contagious condition rampant in Indian boarding schools. It was caused by unsanitary conditions, usually dirty towels used on the eyes and forehead. The disease proceeded in stages, beginning much like conjunctivitis. Without treatment, the eyelid became scarred and buckled, forcing the lashes to grow inward and rub on the eye itself. The scarring caused corneal opacity—a condition similar to glaucoma, in which scar tissue prevents light from passing through the cornea, resulting in some loss of vision or blindness. One of Jim's football teammates, Roy Large, would be nearly blind from trachoma by 1914.

Daniel W. White, the Indian Bureau doctor in charge of trachoma patients, was called in to perform the painful surgery on Jim's eyes, which rotated the lashes away from the cornea. Jim was then kept in a darkened room for several days, awaking each morning with his eyes glued together by the fluid oozing from them; Rose DeNomie, assigned to the infirmary, nursed Jim, a lively patient regardless, whom she described as "either mischievous or just ornery." Dr. White wrote later that "a number of sporting editors never knew Jim had any impairment of eye sight." After Carlisle, Jim would never mention trachoma or the operation.

In any case, he jumped right into the 1912 track and field season. As a candidate for the fifth modern Olympic Games, to be staged in Stockholm that summer, Jim was perfectly suited for two events that had been added by the International Olympic Committee (IOC) to test all-around athletic ability: the classic pentathlon that had been performed in ancient Greece (running broad jump, javelin, 200 meters, discus, and 1,500 meters), and the new decathlon (100 meters, running broad jump, shot put, running high jump, 110-meter hurdles, 400 meters, pole vault, discus, javelin, 1,500 meters). For much of the public, track and field were a class apart. "The activities underlying all other sports," according to Craig A. Masback, former CEO of USA Track and Field. "Elemental."

The Carlisle track season was for Jim a warm-up for the Olympic trials later in the spring. Warner and Wallace Denny supervised his track work. Warner recalled "a difficult struggle" initially to keep his star's mind on track that spring. "What's the use in bothering with track?" Jim asked. He was again being tempted by professional baseball, a lucrative possibility compared with spending more time in Carlisle. Finally, Jim settled to the task at hand; later he thanked Warner for keeping him to the "grind." He essentially stopped going to classes and committed to winning the pentathlon and decathlon.

His commitment wasn't only about ego and pride. He hoped to capitalize on the victories to obtain a coaching job at a top college or university. The relationship with Iva had deepened in the months before her graduation in April, though they had successfully kept it secret. On his gold football sweater, with a red C. S. on it, she tied a tiny red-and-gold ribbon. Before she left Carlisle to work for the summer as a boys' matron in the Otoe boarding school in Oklahoma, Jim had promised her that he would get the solid livelihood of a coach's salary before they married. He had to show her family that he could properly provide for her. Iva's brother Earl, living in Inglewood, California, was devoted to her and, with the rest of the Miller family, disapproved of Jim. Though they had been educated among Indians, Earl and Grace looked down on them. They thought Jim, in particular, was uncouth and drank too much to be trusted with their refined Iva.

Jim attended the Catholic meetings on Sunday evenings so he could be with Iva a few last times—and also to distinguish himself before her in a different, less spectacular way. On April 21 he read to the group an article about Father Thomas Byles, a Catholic priest who, after helping third-class passengers onto lifeboats and leading prayers on board for those who were left behind, had gone down with the *Titanic* seven days earlier. Iva, in turn, watched him practice for the Olympics.

Jim had not competed in track and field events since 1909, but proceeded to "great victories" in the broad jump, high jump, and low hurdles, Warner recalled, especially at the annual indoor meet at Trenton. As he trained for the outdoor season that would immediately precede the Olympics, Jim focused on the pole vault, javelin, shot put, and discus. "I trained," Jim said, "as I never trained before—or since." To build his endurance, he rose at dawn and walked and ran fifteen to twenty miles into the Cumberland Valley, taking fellow track team member Sylvester Long as a training partner. Returning to the school at noon for a light lunch of soup and salad, he slept for a couple of hours and then practiced the field events. With an 18-inch neck, 42-inch chest, 32-inch waist, and 24-inch thighs, looking taller than he was because he walked on the balls of his feet, Jim worked himself into the best condition of his life.

To train for the decathlon, he had to strategically decide how much effort he would expend in each event. Some of them were entirely new to him. As winning would be achieved through an accumulation of points, Jim calibrated the relative number awarded for placing in each event and formulated a plan tailored to his strengths and weaknesses. He had never attempted the pole vault because he considered himself too heavy. The ash poles used at the time were brittle; if he fell in practice or at tryouts, an injury might well prevent him from making the Stockholm trip at all. He initially vaulted nine feet, six inches; he knew he could do better but held back, setting a less risky limit for himself, knowing he could excel in the running and jumping events, piling up the points there. He practiced until he could consistently reach at least six feet in the high jump.

Warner took Jim and Tewanima—who was to compete in the marathon and the 10,000 meters—to his Springfield, New York, home for a couple of weeks to work out alone. Since competing in the 1908 London Olympics, Tewanima had dominated several events, including setting a new ten-mile indoor amateur record at Madison Square Garden. Trainer Michael Murphy called him the "best man in America" for either the ten- or fifteen-mile event. The extra practice in Springfield helped Jim win a stack of medals at a series of meets.

For the first time, an organized effort was being made by the American Olympic Committee (AOC) to find athletes from across the country to participate in the Games. The eastern Olympic pentathlon tryouts were held at New York's Celtic Park on May 18. Unaware he was allowed an unlimited run before throwing, Jim took second in the javelin with a throw of 136 feet, 7.5 inches from a standing position. He betrayed "the awkwardness of a novice" in throwing the discus, wrote one reporter, yet won. Ending with three firsts and two seconds, Jim had performed the pentathlon events "in so outstanding a fashion" that the decathlon trial was canceled as superfluous.

Jim had had to learn several of the events—particularly the javelin, discus, and pole vault—with little or no expert training. Warner was not an Olympic-level track and field coach. What training Jim had was certainly not equal to what other Olympic competitors from established athletic clubs or top universities were getting. Abel Kiviat, a New York middle-distance runner at the tryouts, watched Jim put the shot, do everything wrong, and beat the men who were doing it right. He concluded that Warner hadn't taught Jim a thing. Commentators wondered what Thorpe could accomplish with proper training.

As Indian athletes carefully watched others perform before doing an action themselves, and as he had once closely studied the movements of animals, Jim analyzed how stellar athletes went about their preparation and performance. In his head he set up the equivalent of a series of moving-picture shorts, one for each sporting task, and visualized them, over and over, in a sense memorizing them. Some of the other athletes watched him pace out the distance he wanted to reach in the long jump and then sit down and stare at it. What looked to many observers and reporters as passivity or nonchalance was in fact his own method of internal, visual concentration. For the boy who had been dropped into the middle of the North Canadian River and told to swim to shore, failure was not an option. "Like all great athletes," said Jim's grandson Michael Koehler, an athlete himself, "Jim was motivated not so much by the desire to win as by the *refusal* to lose."

It would later become accepted as fact that Jim had never done any of the Olympic events before and simply stepped onto the field and did them, naturally. As Kiviat had noted, to a certain degree that was correct. But hard work brought improvement. In some pre-Olympic news accounts Jim was more accurately described as the latest in a string of remarkable Indian athletes who didn't possess some kind of racial magic inaccessible to whites, but rather were men with "endurance, patience and a world of determination." In mock horror at the performance of Jim, as well as that of two black contenders, Harvard hammer thrower Theodore Cable and 100-yard-dash sprinter Howard Drew (later at USC), the *New York Evening Post* said, "It is plainly time to draw the color line in athletics."

Crowds now showed up at track events primarily to see Jim. Warner kept the publicity spinning. Exaggerations appeared in the press almost daily. A persistent legend, perpetuated by Grantland Rice, among others, was that on May 25 Warner got off the train in Easton, Pennsylvania, with Jim and only Jim for a dual meet between Carlisle and Lafayette, which Carlisle won. In fact, there were eight men on Carlisle's winning team to Lafayette's thirty or more, and Jim took home six firsts.

Jim was again the star on June 12, when a special set of pre-Olympic games were held in New York featuring the U.S. team. Organized as a send-off to the athletes, sailing for Sweden from New York two days later, the event featured Jim in what the *New York American* described as "an exhibition of jumping such as has not been seen in New York for many days." He competed in only one event, the high jump, and defeated, at six feet, five inches, two of the athletes who would win medals for the event in Stockholm.

Not everyone was thrilled with Jim's achievements and future promise. That same day, the new Sac and Fox agent in Oklahoma, Horace Johnson, wrote a letter to Carlisle superintendent Friedman, enclosing a $25 check for Jim. Agent Kohlenberg had been asked by Jim months earlier to forward him $100 for his Olympic expenses: "My chances of going abroad this summer is very bright with the Olympic team. Please send money at once." However, Johnson now insisted that he could not "conscientiously recommend . . . that this be done." His main objection was that Jim was twenty-five years old and "should be perfectly competent to make his own living without depending on trust and lease funds which have cost him no effort to obtain," and "instead of gallivanting around the country, should be at work on his allotment," like his older siblings.

The other athletes on the American team were entirely funded by voluntary contributions raised by the AOC from prominent citizens such as Andrew Carnegie. According to Jim, the AOC informed Carlisle just prior to departure that, due to a shortage of funds, it would not be able to defray the expenses of the Indian athletes. They "would not contest our going," Jim would recall, "if Carlisle would pay the way," adding that Warner had found the money to make up the difference. Much later, Warner would tell a Warner Bros. studio executive that the AOC had covered all expenses of the Carlisle athletes and that the funds raised by the school were used to send Warner to Sweden. Given the BIA bureaucracy and the reflexive snobbery of the AOC, Jim's version is more likely.

In any case, he prepared to sail to Stockholm amid all the hoopla knowing that, in the eyes of the nation he would be representing, he was just an Indian, accountable like a child to the government for every dollar he spent. On that premise, Warner was allowed, regardless of how he financed his travels, to accompany the two Indian athletes to Stockholm.

Rule 6 of the General Regulations for the Olympic Games of 1912, drawn up by the Swedish Olympic Committee, specified that "[n]atural-born or naturalised subjects of a 'nation,' or of a sovereign state of which a 'nation' forms part, are alone eligible to represent that 'nation' as competitors in the Olympic Games." On the entry form for athletics that Jim was required to fill out and send to Sweden before June 6, in the blank labeled "NATION which the competitor represents," he had written "The United States of America." Jim was a ward of the United States of America, not a citizen, certainly not a subject. It was convenient for all concerned to overlook those details, among others.

Jim in the Carlisle track uniform, posed as if on the mark in a track event, 1912

THE STUDIO LIGHTING defines the tensed musculature of Jim, in the peak condition of his life.

CHAPTER SIX

The Most Wonderful Athlete in the World

Summer–Fall 1912

He returned home a hero, to be feted and praised and placed on a pedestal never before occupied by an athlete of this nation, which he had awakened to a new and tremendous pride in its athletic prowess.

— *The* (Carlisle) *Evening Sentinel,* 1953

Thrills were mostly hard work for me.

—Jim Thorpe

The first modern Olympiad in Athens in 1896 revived the Greek athletic tradition after almost 1,500 years. The 1900 games in Paris were a fiasco, the 1904 event in St. Louis considered a failure except by Americans, the well-organized 1906 games in Athens "unofficial," and the London Olympiad in 1908 plagued by political, administrative, and athletic blunders. The 1912 Games in Stockholm were seen as pivotal for the future success—even survival—of the Olympic movement. A record twenty-eight nations entered, with 2,500 athletes, including fifty-seven women. By the end, the Fifth Olympiad would be considered the first smoothly run and truly modern Olympics, the model for all future Games. The 1912 summer weeks in a Stockholm filled with European aristocrats and royalty would also be remembered as "the funeral games of an epoch."

When the Red Star Line SS *Finland* set off from New York for Europe at 9 a.m. on June 14, 1912, the athletes on board were

described in the feverishly patriotic home press as "America's athletic missionaries." They were setting out to demonstrate to the
world, through sports, the growing prominence of the United States.
Roosevelt's speeches extolling the strenuous life, the competitive
posturing by university presidents, new collegiate stadiums, school
and city playgrounds—all had done the job of recasting the national
identity. Against the backdrop of a lively three-way presidential
campaign between Roosevelt, William Howard Taft, and Woodrow
Wilson, the fruit of twenty years of American anxiety and work preparing the country for the end of the frontier and its role in the new
century was thought to be sailing on the *Finland* back to the Old
World.

The incongruity of Jim, Louis Tewanima, and Penobscot long-
distance runner Andrew Sockalexis in that group of American athletes was overlooked in an orgy of national feel-good hyperbole. The
"heterogeneous gathering" on the U.S. team of three Indians and one
black sprinter, Howard P. Drew (who would not have competed at
all in AAU track meets had he lived south of the Mason-Dixon line),
as well as policemen, mechanics, clerks, and several Hawaiian swim-
mers, amid a majority of lawyers, doctors, and "college boys," was
spun as proof that America had successfully assimilated its peoples
generally into one big happy team. "Never in my long life," enthused
former AAU president and founder James E. Sullivan, now the organization's secretary-treasurer and the head of the AOC, "have I seen
its equal." Putting aside realities regarding Americans of color, the
nation wanted to believe in the team for many of the same reasons it
wanted to believe in Jim as proof that the great democratic experiment had come out all right in the end. Now the rest of the world
could learn from America's example.

Newspapers used the phrase "America's Argonauts" to describe the
team, a reference that resonated with the white, educated elite. The
ancient Greeks represented a unity of artistic, athletic, philosophical,
military, and political perfection. To a young country like the United
States, seeking to dignify its rapidly evolving status as a world leader,
Greek models were seen to confer legitimacy. The reference to the
Greek myth of Jason and his band of Argonauts, sailing to recover
the beautiful Golden Fleece, described by Nathaniel Hawthorne as
"the inestimable prize," set a proper tone. Among the original Argo-

nauts was a young Hercules, "the prime example in Greek mythology," Leo Braudy wrote in his history of fame, *The Frenzy of Renown*, "of the human being who by his own efforts became like a god." Hercules' twelve labors, *athloi*, made him the supreme man-god of action. As Roosevelt had claimed for the strenuous life and sports, Hercules used the body to transcend the body. The ten labors of the decathlon were a re-creation of this ancient, Herculean triumph. The athlete who came back with that gold medal, that Golden Fleece, would be a modern Hercules.

The modern Olympics were created by Pierre Frédy, Baron de Coubertin, with the idealistic plan of replacing war with competitive games, while building more vigorous, healthy individual nations. To gather support for his project among the people who were in the position to make it happen, de Coubertin used the concept of amateurism—described by David C. Young as "the fetish of the [fellow] aristocrats whom he regularly courted"—as what de Coubertin called "camouflage." In private, his views were more nuanced. His strategy served both the English upper-class aversion to mixing with the working classes, who couldn't afford to be amateurs anyway, and the American campaign to keep professionalism out of sports. Jim and all the Olympic athletes had to sign an entry form for each event that included a declaration that each was an amateur, "one who has never" competed for money or prize, competed against a professional, taught in any branch of athletics for payment, or "sold, pawned, hired out, or exhibited for payment" any prize.

Amateurism was in fact an invented tradition, based upon a fabrication, a tie with the past that was, *Time* would say in 1992, "completely spurious." The word "amateur" had not existed in ancient Greek, but was a French word derived from the Latin *amare*, to love, i.e., to act out of love, not hope of gain. A misreading of Greek history by Victorian classical scholars became the foundation of the amateur myth that Greek Olympians had played for the pure love of sport and thus received no remuneration. The introduction of professionalism and money into the ancient games, claimed the scholars, was a degeneracy that had doomed Greek civilization. As went Greece, so would go imperial Britain if the games of its upper class were corrupted. Yet the ancient Greek word for athlete "literally meant and always meant," according to a later historian, simply "competitor for a prize," often a lucrative one. De Coubertin's brutally snobbish description of the Greek athlete as "irreproachable personally *and by heredity*, with no blemish either in his own life or *that of his ancestors*" (the italics are de Coubertin's) was a fantasy. An ancient Greek Olympic athlete had only to be a Greek citizen (women and slaves not eligible) to qualify. He played to win and to profit by his victory.

An ambitious Irish American from working-class roots, James Sullivan obtained his ticket to the upper class by translating aristocratic ideals into functioning realities as an administrator. America's "first sports czar," Sullivan was from 1892 until his death in 1914 president of the American Sports Publishing Company in addition to his work with the AAU; he was also editor of the popular and influential Spalding Athletic Library series. Largely thanks to Sullivan's tireless efforts, track and field, the only sport totally under AAU control, became not only the dominant event in the early modern Games but a sport dominated by Americans. Warner described him as "the Walter Camp of the track and field world." Sullivan had also carved out a position of unquestioned dominance of the AOC since heading the small committee that sent American athletes to compete in the first modern Olympic Games in 1896. The AAU, fronted by the AOC, controlled the composition and conduct of the American Olympic team. With the modern Olympics the apogee of sports purely for sports' sake, Sullivan had made himself one of the movement's most powerful men.

What de Coubertin did not anticipate was how quickly the modern Olympics came to shape a nation's idea of itself, of its identity and supremacy on the world stage. Despite his pacifist dream, the Olympics would be seen as directly linked to the belligerent nationalism that culminated in the First World War. The citizens of what historian Mark Dyreson called the American "sporting republic" would consider themselves the natural winners of Olympic Games (and, soon, wars) in part because their New World mongrel mix of races and peoples was believed to be stronger and hardier than those of the tired countries its immigrants had left behind. After what de Coubertin called the "outrageous charade" of the two-day event called Anthropology Days at the 1904 Games in St. Louis (a mock set of games contested among supposedly inferior races such as African Pygmies, Philippine Moros, and American Indians, most of whom had never participated in the sports previously, with the lackluster results used as proof of white athletic supremacy), he predicted, in spite of himself, that "when black men, red men and yellow men learn to run, jump, and throw [they will] leave the white men behind them."

Jim spent hours climbing and crawling around what he described as the "fantastic machinery" of the *Finland*. "I'd never seen a boat as big as that before," he said. The ship had been specially refitted to allow the American team to train onboard: a ninety-yard-long (Sullivan claimed it was one hundred yards) cork running track on the upper deck of the starboard side, weight-throwing pits, swimming tanks, and a gymnasium. On the forward deck was a bicycle trainer on which six men could ride abreast and practice up to three hours a day. The athletes had their own dining room and were forbidden to eat between meals or be in the smoking room during the day. Headed by trainer Michael Murphy, they reported on deck each morning at ten thirty and again at three in the afternoon. At least for Americans, the ship reinforced the idea that their athletes were indeed Argonauts sailing to glory in a magic ship on the high seas. To the British and others, the extravagance was one more indicator that the Americans had an unseemly appetite for victory and a decidedly *professional* approach to training.

A persistent and famous myth would take hold that Jim did not train during the voyage. Ralph Craig, who would win gold medals in the 100-meter and 200-meter dashes at Stockholm, later insisted that Jim did train and that he had a photograph in his personal album to prove it; the two did calisthenics and ran laps every day, each of them challenging the other in sprints. Avery Brundage, a competitor in these Games from the Chicago Athletic Club, also said Jim had trained. Jim, responding in 1930 to what had become a perennial question from sportswriters, said: "I was twenty-four years old [he was twenty-five] at this time, weighed 176 pounds and was in the best condition of my life. I didn't work out strenuously . . . as I felt ready for action and didn't want to become stale or over-trained."

More perceptive reporters saw that behind Jim's apparent ease and naturalness he was "deadly in earnest." Abel Kiviat, who would compete in the 1,500 meters, noticed that while most of the rest of the athletes were nervous, Jim was not. His powers of observation and concentration made him very self-contained. As one of the few outsiders on a ship full of convivial peers—Jim and Kiviat, a New York Jew, were assigned a room in steerage; the college and elite club athletes were in upper-level staterooms—he was wary and put up even more than his usual reserve among whites. His fellow athletes noticed that he wore nothing extraneous, no watch or ring, and carried no wallet.

Privately, Jim was even more focused on his ultimate mission, to prove to Iva and the Millers that he could be a solid, dependable provider, a success. Afraid that he would lose her, Jim had been opposed to a postgraduation visit to her brother Earl in California. His almost daily letters sent to Earl's address during his Olympic trip, in which he would dedicate his various events to her, were, he later found out, not forwarded to Iva in Oklahoma.

When the ship pulled into Stockholm harbor, the American contingent, including Sullivan and Gustavus T. Kirby, AAU president, were greeted by a large, jubilant crowd. Murphy immediately arranged for his athletes to train on the grass practice ground adjacent to the brand-new brick and granite stadium (both had been constructed specially for the Games) before they switched to cinder tracks, to prevent their feet from being sore after two weeks on the ship. Most of the athletes would sleep on board the *Finland*, anchored in front of the royal castle. Jim eventually stayed in quarters on the outskirts of Stockholm, which had been set up after the first week for the long-distance runners.

The inhabitants of the lovely and then-remote city of Stockholm— calling itself the "Venice of the North," with water making up a third of its total area—and the more than four hundred international newspaper reporters assigned to the city for the Games were abuzz at the arrival of the Americans. *The Times* of London special correspondent reported that "the coming triumph of the Stars and Stripes is, indeed, the chief topic wherever the Games are mentioned. It is, perhaps, a pity," he added, in a tone that typified the non-American coverage of these Olympics, "that the Americans talk so much themselves about it." A peculiar feature of American spectators—"rooters," as they called themselves—had been "objectionably conspicuous" at each Olympiad since 1896: their strange yells and chants. Furthermore, claimed *The Times*, a story was circulating in the city that the Americans were boasting they would "[sweep] the boards," which made them not "too popular."

The English observer laid out for his readers the key issues that would roil his countrymen and other non-Americans not only at the 1912 Games but for most of the century. The anticipated "monotonous list of American successes" would be due, he predicted, in no small part to lavish expenditure. The cost of upgrading the *Finland* for the Olympic voyage was a reported £20,000, with at least an equal amount spent on equipment, clothes, and other items. In contrast to the "happy-go-lucky ways" of the British athletes and their trainers, to the extent that the latter existed, was the "thorough and scientific course of training" of the Americans, a result of the nation's "genius for specializing and concentration on whatever may be the immediate thing in hand, whether in sport or in business." Camp would have agreed. He had claimed exactly that for football twenty years earlier.

For a member of the far-flung British Empire, there was also what the London correspondent called the "racial aspect" of the Games. French commentators would make a similar point. The Americans were a "polyglot, many-colored" people, including "Red Indians" like Jim; if Britain, for example, counted its colonial dominions—South Africa, Australia, and Canada—as part of its team, it might be "comfortably in the lead." Chagrin at finding themselves second-class, at best, in international athletic contests alternated in the minds of the British and European elite with an ancient, arrogant class pride that resisted playing by new rules that looked to be heading in a dangerously inclusive direction: should a "Red Indian" be a champion?

Not only the organizing committees but the European teams in the 1912 Olympics were, moreover, conspicuously full of titled athletes: barons, counts, a Russian grand duke, a Prussian prince, and many German and French equestrians with the aristocratic "von" and "de," respectively, attached to their surnames. The atmosphere in Stockholm resembled a family reunion, with teas, dances, receptions, banquets, formal dinners, and royal presentations. Given the amount of inherited wealth underpinning the Games, the "problem" of amateurism, added *The Times*, had an "especial bearing" on the whole equation.

The Swedish Olympic organizers had held hundreds of committee and subcommittee meetings to ensure that everything connected with the Games was smoothly and efficiently run. It was the first Olympiad to be filmed with a motion picture camera and to have a photo finish, as well as the first with a public address system and timing devices that could measure tenths of seconds. After sorting out various nationalism issues (the Irish didn't want to march with the British; the Finns didn't want to be lumped with the Russians; the Czechs succeeded in competing as "Bohemia," though their flag flew with the Austro-Hungarian Empire banner), Sweden put its best foot forward with almost flawless results.

Jim arrived in a city thronged with "sightseers and merrymakers" taking full advantage of the famous short white night of the high northern hemisphere. Interest in the real, live Indians from America was intense. Crowds "looked upon a Redman," he wrote, "as a curiosity of some sort and I didn't want to be the object of their stares." A group of girls stopped him and showed him a picture of an Indian with war paint and a feather headdress. They pointed to his suit and hat, making it clear, though they didn't speak English, "that they doubted I was the genuine article." In a typical burst of humor at his own expense, Jim decided he would live up to their conception of an Indian and "broke out into a war dance with an accompaniment of full-blooded yells." By the time his antics had brought other athletes running to see what was happening, his audience had fled.

The weather was perfect on opening day, Saturday, July 6. The Swedish royal family was seated in the state box as the teams of each of the participating nations paraded into the stadium at 11 a.m. and assembled on the field facing the "middle-aged, respectable-looking" king Gustav V. Many of the non-U.S. athletes were soldiers and marched around the track "with the formal carriage," as the reporter for *Collier's* observed, "of European military tactics." The Germans, in particular, strutted with "protruding chest . . . stiff hands . . . and unnatural step." When the U.S. athletes came into view through the stadium gates, American spectators in the stands began a cheer: "Rah, rah ray! U.S.A.! A-M-E-R-I-C-A!" Dressed in natty blue blazers, white trousers, and straw boater hats, the American team "glided along in any fashion," reported *Collier's*, "their arms and shoulders keeping swing with their walk" with the "loose, springy, natural step of men in perfect control of their bodies and in perfect condition." The reporter, forgetting in his patriotic enthusiasm the Indian athletes, traced the team's style to "the gait of the plainsmen who tamed our wilderness" and concluded that "[h]uman beings were made to walk that way." (John Adams had noted the same marching nonchalance in revolutionary troops.) In a gesture of pointed confidence and in contrast to the defiance of the 1908 games, the team's flag bearer dipped the Stars and Stripes as he passed before the king. All present were asked to join in singing Martin Luther's hymn *"Ein' feste Burg ist unser Gott"* ("A Mighty Fortress Is Our God").

The Games began as the summer heat intensified. Though Sullivan complained that the track surface, electronic timing apparatus for the running events, and photofinish equipment were not up to AAU standards, the games were marked by a new amity and lack of controversy. Women had been previously allowed to compete in decorous sports such as tennis, golf, and archery; in 1912, they were allowed to enter the swimming and diving events (Sullivan did not allow American women to do either). Individual stars quickly emerged as the Games progressed. Craig triumphed in the sprints. Hawaiian swimmer Duke Kahanamoku won the 100-meter freestyle. Abel Kiviat and the other members of the U.S. 3,000-meter cross-country team won gold medals. Louis Tewanima came in second to the first of the famous "Flying Finns," Hannes Kolehmainen, in the 10,000 meters; until Billy Mills, an Oglala Lakota (Sioux) from Pine Ridge, bested Tewanima's silver medal time—32:06.6—for a gold medal in the 1964 Games, it stood as the best by a member of the U.S. team.

The classic pentathlon was held on the second day of the Games. Originally created by the Greeks to showcase "the complete man," the event, according to French track expert Robert Pariente, was meant to "reconcile the irreconcilable: speed and resistance, dynamism and statism, strength and lightness, power and relaxation." The capacity crowd was primed to see a Swede or Englishman triumph.

Jim had gone to the stadium and "looked in a couple of times, just to see what it was like," but had not seen any of the previous events. Now, surrounded by a cluster of Olympic officials dressed in double-breasted dark blazers, ties, white trousers, and straw boaters and clutching score sheets, he stepped onto the sunny stadium field for the five-part event, outfitted in the U.S. Olympic team T-shirt and loose shorts, a thick shock of unruly hair easily visible from the stands.

He took first place in the running broad jump, a test of speed, leaping ability, and accuracy. A still photograph of him in midair shows a strikingly dynamic yet carefree-seeming grace and economy of form, as if he had figured out how to make the air help him fly. He placed a disappointing third in the javelin, a Scandinavian forte, and an event he had taken up only two months before. In one of the most thrilling events of the games, the 200 meters, run in nine three-man heats, Jim finished first. Even with the sun in his eyes, he easily won the discus throw.

There were seven contestants left for the final pentathlon event, the 1,500 meters. (Avery Brundage, who had expected to win the entire event, did not finish this last race.) Jim kept behind the pace until halfway through the second lap, when he started to speed up, coming even with the leader by the beginning of the third lap and passing him by the start of the fourth. To deafening cheers from the capacity crowd, he finished in 4:44.8, nearly five seconds ahead of the second-place finisher. He had won the gold medal—and they were pure gold, for the last time; subsequent Olympiads would award gilded silver medals—with four firsts and one third, for a point-for-place score of seven points out of a perfect five. "What a shock it was," Sullivan crowed, "when Jim Thorpe . . . demolished all theories and calculations." His victory, said Sullivan, "answers the . . . allegation that most of our runners are of foreign parentage for Thorpe is a real American if there ever was one." Jim said he entered this first Olympic contest as he played football for Carlisle—to win.

In the six days before the first decathlon event, Warner maintained Jim's momentum with lesser contests. He placed fifth in the running high jump and, four days later, was seventh in the broad jump. On Saturday, July 13, in a pouring rain, Jim started the grueling decathlon. Because of the large number of entrants, thirty, it was spread out over three days, diminishing the endurance factor; later decathletes such as Bob Mathias and Rafer Johnson would do the event in two days. Scores were calculated by how close an athlete came to the 1908 record in each event, with 10,000 total points (1,000 for each event) for equaling or bettering the record, and the scores descending from there. Though Warner worried the rain would cramp Jim's style and energy, his sturdy frame; powerful chest, biceps, and thighs; and distinctively casual gait became familiar to spectators as he proceeded through the three events of the first day.

He ran the 100 meters, the measure for leg speed, in 11.2 seconds, the same time as Olympic decathlon winner Bob Mathias would run in 1948. After two false starts at the slippery takeoff board, Jim placed third in the broad jump. Now at second place overall, and wanting to end the first day on top, he put the shot, the test of an athlete's arm strength, to take first place. In the dressing room afterward he joked to the soaking-wet Warner that maybe changing into dry warm-up gear for the shot put had helped him win.

The next morning, in beautiful weather, he placed first in the running high jump at 6 feet, 1.6 inches. If it hadn't been for the fact that his "pet shoes" were missing and he had to compete in another pair hastily doctored by Warner, Jim felt he would have jumped the 6 feet, 5 inches he had done only weeks before in New York. His score would keep him among the top high jumpers for decades. In the 400 meters, testing speed and stamina, he came in fourth; he finished third in the discus. With his performance in the last event of the second day, the 110-meter hurdles, designed to measure speed and agility, he brought the crowd to its feet again. His time of 15.6 seconds would also stand as a record for decades (Mathias would place first in the 1948 hurdles with a time of 15.7). Tewanima finished the marathon that day in sixteenth place.

The third and last day of the decathlon, July 15, was also the final day of the Games. Jim had to perform in two of the more technical events he had barely mastered. He "voluntarily quit" the pole vault at third place, as planned. He placed fourth in the javelin, thereby maintaining his point edge going into the final event, the 1,500 meters. Only twelve athletes remained. (Brundage dropped out after the pole vault, and ended in sixteenth place overall.) Though Jim had easily won the 1,500 meters in the pentathlon, observers wondered whether he could repeat the performance after the subsequent days of competition. He had been on the field for five days out of the last nine.

He ran the metric mile in 4 minutes, 40.1 seconds, nearly 5 seconds faster than his pentathlon time. He was faster than Mathias in 1948 and 1952 and nine seconds ahead of Rafer Johnson's time of 4:49.7 in 1960. It wouldn't be until 1972, when Russian Nikolai Avilov ran the distance in 4:22.8, that an Olympic gold medal decathlete beat Jim's 1912 time; in 1976, Bruce Jenner would run an astonishing 4:12.6. Thorpe "ran the distance as good as alone," recorded the official history, "the rest of the field being a long way behind the leader."

He had won the decathlon gold with a point total of 8,412.95 out of a possible 10,000, 688 points ahead of the silver medalist, Hugo Wieslander of Sweden. The spread is still astonishing. In the future, point differentials of less than 100 points between the winning and second-place Olympic decathletes would be more the norm. Jim's score remained a gold standard for years and would have won him a silver medal as late as the 1948 Olympics. His decathlon total would not be beaten until 1932, by American Jim Bausch at the Los Angeles Olympics. In 1998, *USA Today* reported that in a computer study done by Olympic historian Bill Mallon, rating current and past world-record decathlon performances against the individual world records of their respective eras as the fairest way to compare great athletes, Jim emerged as the best. Said Mallon, "It wasn't even close."

The Americans had racked up, not only the highest point total, but also a bounty of medals in track and field, the only part of the Olympics, in their opinion, that counted. Overall, including such events as swimming, shooting, yachting, and equestrian sports, Sweden won the most medals, sixty-three. America was next with sixty-two. America, however, won the top total of twenty-five Olympic gold medals, two more than Sweden and more than twice as many as Great Britain's ten. Mostly thanks to Jim, Carlisle had scored more points than any other American school or college represented on the U.S. team, and was third in number of points scored by the athletes from all the U.S. athletic organizations combined.

When Jim came forward that hot afternoon in his dark suit to have his first laurel (actually oak) wreath placed on his head by the formally dressed king, with top hat and cane, the crowd roared its approval. He received his pentathlon gold medal and a four-foot-high bronze bust of Sweden's great "Lion of the North" soldier-king, Charles XII (1682–1718), given as a challenge trophy by King Gustav V. The 1912 medals were tiny, each about one and one-eighth inches in diameter, and featured two female figures crowning a victor with a wreath on one side and, on the other, a herald proclaiming the Olympic Games standing in front of a bust of Pehr Henrik Ling, the founder of the Swedish system of gymnastics. As Jim walked away, a photographer got a shot of him, wreath back on his head, holding his rolled-brim hat to his chest, eyes to the ground, a small but delighted smile on his face. The heavy bust would be delivered later.

When Jim came back a second time, for the decathlon, he moved with a natural gait and large movements, his jacket unbuttoned and head cocked back. He bowed slightly before the king as he received his second wreath. The king gave him his second gold medal and another challenge trophy, reportedly made by Fabergé and given by Tsar Nicholas II of Russia. It was a "magnificent [sterling] silver vase," according to a note in Warner's autobiography, "of a Viking ship, two feet in length and weighing 30 pounds." As the loudest cheer of the afternoon erupted from the stands, the tall, thin, smiling king said to Jim, in English, "You, sir, are the most wonderful athlete in the world." Jim responded simply, "Thank you." Movie footage (the film of Jim's athletic events does not appear to have survived) shows that he stepped back, bowed to the king with one foot out in front of the other, and walked back to his team. The crowd cheered itself hoarse. The combined European bands struck up John Philip Sousa's "Stars and Stripes Forever," and the crowd started chanting a variation of the American yell: "Rah, Rah, Rah, Ray, Ray, Ray: A-M-E-R-I-C-A!"

It would be claimed that Jim replied, "Thanks, King," as if he knew no better, the story undermining the moment of his greatest triumph. A flippant reply would have been out of character for a man who was highly uncomfortable in public ceremonies and hated to stand out. Jim, and later his family, would insist for years that the trophies were gifts for him to keep. However, as stipulated in Section 16 of the 1912 general regulations, he had signed that day a "guarantee" for each one, promising to return them in "uninjured condition" to the IOC for the next Olympiad in 1916, scheduled to be held in Berlin. Perhaps Jim didn't read the documents carefully in the excitement of his triumph that afternoon.

The athletes went out to celebrate that night in the city's hotels and bars. Jim, with a big grin on his face, drove around the city in a Chalmers 36 automobile with the top down. When the team returned to the ship, Jim, whom Kiviat recalled "would eat and drink anything" when not in training, had clearly had one celebratory glass too many. Warner had observed that throughout the Games Jim's "strength, speed, endurance and competitiveness" were the "topic of most conversations," with the common line being "Isn't he a horse?" This night, Jim paraded around the ship's decks, pushing people aside, saying, "Out of my way! I am a horse. I'm a horse!" The other passengers stood back and applauded with a mixture of admiration, amusement, and shock.

The *Los Angeles Times* and other American newspapers picked up a story from the *London Express* headlined "Yankee Athlete Turns Down King." According to the report, Jim had refused an invitation from the Swedish king for a private audience, saying, "Huh! I don't know much about kings. I guess I won't go." It was another fabrication that would become accepted fact, especially as repeated for years by Grantland Rice and others. According to Jim, the king never extended such an invitation. The false rumor had begun when a group of Swedish naval officers, hosting a party one evening on a nearby ship in port, had asked for Jim to join them. He declined that invitation because, he recalled, "I didn't want to be gazed upon as a curiosity."

Jim was discovering fast that being the first international sports celebrity was confusing, even treacherous. His fame as a comparatively local football hero had been minor compared to the attention he attracted after Stockholm. From now on, his reticence and lack of pretension would often be spun by the press as some kind of aboriginal awkwardness or gracelessness. At the same time, the American press printed headlines such as "Brilliant Performances of Indian . . . Prove Him to Be a Marvel/Personification of Grace," referring more to his physical gifts than his manner. Posed photographs taken of him at Carlisle as a physical specimen, dressed in nothing but a jock strap, were circulated widely. His measurements, previously taken at Dickinson College, were now publicized as a "marvel of physical strength" such as the "world had never seen." The director of physical culture at the University of Michigan made an "anthropological chart" and declared the "aborigine" to be "as near perfection physically as is possible to be in the human being." Little of this seemed strange in an era one historian would describe as "obsessed by genetics" and about to get more so. In 1916, *The Passing of the Great Race*, the eugenics primer extolling the superiority of the "Nordic race" that Adolf Hitler would call his bible, would be a best-seller. Its author, Madison Grant, was a trustee of the American Museum of Natural History and president of the American Zoological Society.

The New York Times pronounced that, generally, Jim's "like has never been seen," and that "his easy method of approaching all of his athletic tasks has been the subject of much comment." *The Philadelphia Inquirer* gushed that "Thorpe is the most marvelous creation fashioned in human likeness that has ever inhabited the earth." Jim Thorpe would have beat Goliath, suggested another paper, because the biblical strongman had lacked speed. Three days after the close of the Games, the *Charlotte Observer* headlined that the now-famous "Thorp" was "Well Remembered in Fayetteville and Eastern Carolina as a Ball Player."

Jim's feats crowned an Olympic triumph seen by Americans as a stunning confirmation. Through sports they had succeeded, with determination and efficiency, in winning for themselves a new kind of status. Across the Atlantic the British, the creators and refiners of so many sporting games, read countless editorials and letters to the editor about the "bitter humiliation felt by England on account of the wretched showing of her athletes." To Americans, sports weren't just for a bit of gentlemanly fun, sniffed *Blackwood's*, but rather to "show that these United States can whip the universe." Others dared to suggest that British sportsmanship was merely a gloss to excuse diffidence and laziness, and sometimes an utter lack of preparation. The *Times* correspondent catalogued all the ways in which the British team was inferior to the "enthusiasm and *esprit de corps*" and training of the Americans, and concluded gloomily: "In the eyes of the world we have lost our supremacy; we have forfeited the reputation so long enjoyed, and are no longer regarded as the men that we were." The French consoled themselves by obsessively insisting that there was no "American" race, though, as a "redskin," Jim Thorpe came close.

When the Olympics resumed in 1920, they would take place on the brink of a decade of remarkable growth in sports. The American Progressive movement, which had found in the strenuous life an optimistic model for a revitalized, postfrontier American identity, did not survive the war. The initial support of American intellectuals, university presidents, and enlightened politicians such as Roosevelt for sport as an agent for social change gradually altered into a distrust of what would soon become only one strain of a new, commercialized mass culture shaped by celebrity and advertising.

The modern Olympics would survive in part because Jim had glamorized them. Every four years the world would wait and hope for another sensation like him. But Jim's achievement was the last of a kind. While the decathlete remained the ultimate athlete—the classic pentathlon was eliminated from Olympic competition after 1924, leaving Jim the only athlete to win both events—achievement in sports in the twentieth century would be increasingly defined by all the factors the Americans were accused of in 1912: specialization, intensive training, equipment, coaches, professionalism, and money.

The authentic Greek ideal of athletic balance and perfection through a sequence of tasks, *athloi*, would be cast aside. Yet the modern world would remember with a particular tenacity and passion the folk hero who came out of nowhere to turn himself into the sports god of his time with the aid of very little but the superb machine of his own body.

Jim decided to remain in Europe for a few weeks, along with several of his teammates, including Abel Kiviat. They agreed to compete in a few meets and, as Kiviat recalled, were the recipients of a lot of free wine and various other gifts. In Reims, in the Champagne region of France, "Mr. Pommery, maker of wines," hosted an exhibition during which Jim raced USC freshman Fred W. Kelly, the 110-meter high hurdles gold medal winner. Kelly gave Jim a two-yard handicap, but in the middle of the event, an airplane flew low down the center of the track before circling to land in the field. Kelly had never seen a plane and, as he told the *Los Angeles Times* in 1930, by the time he figured out what it was, Jim had won. Kelly would go on to be one of the first professional aviators.

In Paris, Jim prowled the streets, eager, he recalled, to learn more about the one-eighth of him that was French. Kiviat watched one night as Jim was the only member of the team to leap and touch a hotel chandelier ten feet above the floor. Each athlete had put a dollar in the pot for the bet. Jim "never had a nickel," said Kiviat. "He just didn't have anything," so the group gave him cash on credit and watched in awe.

Warner, meanwhile, had returned to Carlisle with the trophies and was frantically trying to locate his "wandering athlete" and get him back for the grand celebration the school and town were planning for him and Louis Tewanima. He finally did, after Jim arrived in New York from Cherbourg in early August. The details of the festivities on August 16 were covered by the press nationwide. Carlisle saw it as an event of "international importance" to the Indian people, but no major Washington functionaries attended. After a parade, about seven thousand people gathered at Dickinson to hear speeches that lauded the "conquering heroes." Friedman read various congratulatory letters to Jim from the secretary of the interior and the commissioner of Indian affairs and one from President Taft: "[Y]our victory will serve as an incentive to all," he wrote, "to improve those qualities which characterize the best type of American citizen." Jim would say later, "It was good of everybody to say such kind things."

Warner spoke only a few sentences, with no mention of the two athletes. Jim stood up and said, "All I can say is that you showed me a good time." Tewanima said, "Thank you"—not "Me, too," as would later be reported—and sat down. The coach and the two Olympians were put in a parade carriage and pulled by Carlisle boys through the streets of the town. Students did the snake dance around them, letting out what *The Arrow* called "some pretty blood-curdling yells." The effect, concluded the student newspaper, was "somewhat beautiful, and slightly weird, but surely noisy." A dance in the school gym followed and went on until 1:45 a.m. The school had never seen anything like it and never would again.

Back home, so to speak, Jim enjoyed himself thoroughly. There had been no family to greet him on the dock in New York, "a tinge of sadness," said one news account, added to Jim's story. Attempts to bring any of his siblings in Oklahoma back east for the celebrations had resulted in the terse telegram reply, THORPE'S PARENTS DEAD. To compensate him for not being able to compete in the Games due to illness, Jim gave his quarterback, Gus Welch, the hat he had doffed to the king of Sweden; Welch kept it all his life. The welcome that meant the most to Jim, of course, was from Iva. "I'm glad you're back," she wrote him. "I knew you'd win all the time."

As New York City prepared for its "Monster Parade" on Saturday, August 24 to honor America's Olympic athletes, and Philadelphia did the same for its tribute two days later, across the country news reports and analyses of Jim built in intensity. *The* (Boston) *Traveler* suggested that his likeness be used as the American Indian on the new five-cent coin, to be issued the next year. Amid the patriotic hyperbole, some observers noted the irony of his amazing victories. Though Indians were "threatened with extinction," *The Cincinnati Times-Star* wrote, Jim was proof that there were a few left "who are excellent exemplars of the Greek ideal of what athletes should be!" *The New York Times* printed a bit of doggerel, "Hail to the Chief," cueing off the famous lines of Alexander Pope:

> *Gee Whiz. What is it this is?*
> *Lo, the poor Indian, whose untutored mind,*
> *Seems somewhat defective in falling behind,*
> *Has put it all over the Superior white*
> *And pushed the proud paleface*
> *Plumb out of sight . . .*

The Manhattan parade began at Forty-first Street and Fifth Avenue and headed south through Washington Square to end at City Hall. Business had been suspended along the route. Hundreds of thousands of New Yorkers (some estimates were as high as a million) massed in the streets as "a rain of confetti, streamers and ticker tape" fell down from office windows. Schoolgirls lined up on one side of Fifth Avenue, boys on the other. More than 20,000 people, including mounted police, "athletes, ex-athletes, soldiers, sailors, school children, societies, and more societies . . . athletic clubs and college men" marched or rode in the parade, which was described by one newspaper as "the nearest thing to a Roman triumph" since Admiral Dewey had been welcomed to the city on his return from Manila in 1899.

Drilled by their teachers, the schoolchildren competed to yell loudest the American cheer that had so irritated the non-American spectators in Stockholm. The name of each athlete was added as he passed in an open touring car, a large sign on each car's windshield identifying its occupant for the crowd. The athletes were sequenced alphabetically by last name, with the exception of Jim, whom the president of the New York Athletic Club insisted be placed at the head of the parade line.

The result was headlines like "Red Man, All-Around Champ, Chews Gum and Blushes as He Rides Alone." Jim sat "in embarrassed silence," reported *The Boston Post*, "perhaps the chief attraction in line, but he pulled his panama hat over his eyes, chewed gum, pinched his knees and seldom lifted his face. Piled in front of him were his trophies and above them fluttered the Carlisle pennant." Newspaper photos confirm it. Only once did he show any enthusiasm that day. When his car reached the reviewing stand, he jumped out, removed his hat, and rushed to shake hands with Sullivan. Jim would remember little of it all. "I heard people yelling my name," he said, "and I couldn't realize how one fellow could have so many friends."

Fame was and always would be repellent to Jim. "To be famous, goes the myth," wrote Leo Braudy, "is to rest in solitude, but without aloneness: like Achilles in his tent." To be famous, for Jim, was to feel alone in the middle of a mob. His feelings had been honed sharp by the tribal stories of removals, deaths, bravery, chicanery, and isolation. He recognized that he had shown the outside world something extraordinary: a conquered people could still win. His performance could not be dismissed, ignored, or annulled. The whole world was a witness. By their very public nature, his victories upended the assumptions and stereotypes that had accumulated over centuries. The white culture insisted on parades, speeches, and crowds as a necessary part of fame. Jim didn't need them, didn't want them. Public adulation was antitribal, taking the glory away from others.

In Philadelphia, after a celebration that began at noon and became a parade, at a banquet at the Continental Hotel that was still going at midnight, Jim and Tewanima were surrounded by reporters. It was "some time before either would say anything," said *The Philadelphia Inquirer*. Jim eventually spoke about the team and its showing at the Games. "Not for a moment did he hesitate," continued the article, "until he was asked about the part of the games in which he figured so brilliantly, and there his bashfulness in regard to matters which would tend to place him in the light of a hero returned and he became anxious to talk of other parts of the game." Both athletes continually deferred to Warner. They disclaimed "all credit of their triumph," insisting Warner was "the man who had made them what they are" and he would do all the speechmaking. Jim finally did speak of himself, and eloquently. "The fact that I was able to represent America in such a great thing as an Olympic meet will always be one of the things to which I shall point with pride all my life. And I believe," he added, "that in every thing I say I voice the sentiments of my teammate, Tewanima, here."

Newspaper and magazine articles continued to feed the American public's hunger to know more about Thorpe. "A promoter's dream," Warner called him. A reporter for the *Ohio State Journal* took the train to Carlisle with his two young sons and filed a story describing Jim's "muscular development" as "beautifully smooth," combining "the best attributes of the sprinter and the weight man." Initially stoic, and silent for ten minutes at a time, by the afternoon, after a lunch of two eggs on toast and a cup of tea, Jim became "vibrant," his face "lit up with a perpetual roguish smile . . . as playful and ingenuous as a ten-year-old"—the essential Jim. He later bantered with Warner about beer, cigars, and training, said he liked "plain food . . . steak and potatoes and a lot of vegetables and a big cup of coffee." Then he suddenly said, "I don't care much for celebrations, do I 'Pop'? I like to stand on the sidewalk and see a parade go by. There's something to see, then. But like that Olympic parade the other day in New York that I had to lead, why I was kind of lonesome."

In the press and public opinion, Jim joined New York Giants catcher John Meyers and Philadelphia Athletics pitcher Albert Bender to form a troika of stellar Indian athletes. Their renown seemed to signal a new era of American Indian achievement, with Carlisle leading the way. If Jim's feats stunned the world, in the context of American Indian life in 1912 they gave promise of even greater triumphs over the white man yet to come. The new entertainment medium, the moving picture, temporarily embraced the Indian as its most popular subject, with the release in 1912 of D. W. Griffith's *Iola's Promise*, with Mary Pickford.

In Oklahoma, however, a local newspaper reminded its readers that in the eyes of U.S. law, "Jimmy" Thorpe was technically an "incompetent" Indian, a ward of the government. In order to get any of the lease income from his quarter section of land, he still had to get the approval of the commissioner of Indian affairs. The Sac and Fox agent said that "some day," once Jim had completed his studies at Carlisle, the restrictions would be removed and he would then be "his own boss."

Amid rumors that he would play major league baseball the following year, Jim continued to dominate the sports news into September. On Labor Day he won the annual AAU All-Around Championship in New York's Celtic Park. With only five-minute breaks between each of the ten decathlon events, and all of them performed on one cold and rainy day, he won seven and finished second in the remaining three, winning by more than 3,000 points. He beat the 1900 record of Martin J. Sheridan by 91 points. "In view of conditions," reported *The New York Times*, "Thorpe's performance is little short of remarkable." After the last event, Sheridan was the first to congratulate him. "Jim," he said, "you're the greatest man in the world. I congratulate you." Jim grinned and said, "Thank you, Martin. You were some man yourself."

Before the start of the 1912 football season, he tried to put his financial and family affairs in order. As much as anyone, he was now the head of his fragmented family in Oklahoma, and he felt responsible for them. Not only had his stature changed in the eyes of the world, he saw himself differently. He asked that his brother, Edward, now thirteen, and his sister Adeline, seventeen, be sent to Carlisle, where they could be near him. His request produced a bureaucratic exchange of letters full of both skepticism that Jim would be remaining at Carlisle long enough to make the transfer worthwhile, and condescension toward him, despite what he had achieved. "In fact," wrote agent Horace Johnson, "it is my opinion it is now time he should be out earning his living instead of attending school." A couple of weeks later, John Francis, Jr., chief of the Indian Education Division in Washington, wrote to the commissioner, turning down both applications (Edward would be admitted to Carlisle in January, attend for three years, and become a star cornet player in the school band; Adeline would get married) and stating, "I suggest that you appreciate the fact that you are hinting to the 'world's greatest athlete' that he should close his glorious school days at the age of 26 [Jim was twenty-five]." Francis had written to the commissioner in July to suggest, grudgingly, that some official recognition of Jim's Olympic achievements as an Indian "might not be amiss" since "he has done something to show the stuff that his people are made of, at least physically."

Jim's request for his bank balance of $295.23 inspired another acid reply from Horace Johnson on October 1. After confirming that Jim made $250 per year from his allotment and would get more once his father's estate was finally settled (this process of dividing one plot of land among many heirs would drag on until 1917, typical of the fractionated inheritance legacy of allotment), the agent wrote that, while he had known Jim's "quite notorious" father, he did not know Jim well enough to give a "recommendation"; he had been told that "James Thorp . . . is not a bad fellow, though somewhat inclined to indulge his appetite in intoxicating liquors." Jim got the check, but when he requested that his lease income be sent when collected, Johnson responded: "To the best of my knowledge he has accumulated no property. He is not industrious. His reputation is not good. It is reported that he is addicted to the use of intoxicants, but in view of all of the above he, no doubt, is now as capable of handling this money [$125] and looking after his own affairs as he ever will be."

Jim wrote to his half brother Frank in Oklahoma about his, Jim's, allotment, which needed repairs to fences and ditches. Frank, thirty-one, now leased his own allotment and grew cotton and corn on another plot of land. Jim was closer to Frank, a skilled horse handler and hunter, than he was to his full brother, George. He confided his own hopes and fears, now, almost two months after Stockholm. "Frank, I have the chance to make a bunch of dough after leaving this school," he wrote. "Just started going today. God but its hard to go back again, but it is for my good, so I will make the best of things."

The money on offer was indeed from baseball. On September 9, Richard Adams, the great sachem of the Brotherhood of North American Indians, wrote to the Indian commissioner, outraged at his understanding that "Jim Thorpe has been compelled to get permission of the Government before he can sign a contract with the New York [Giants] baseball team"; he added that Jim was as "competent" to take care of himself as the commissioner was. Other entrepreneurs circled, trying to make a buck out of his international celebrity in an era when the latest phenomenon was instantly taken out on a circuit, any circuit. Jim was inundated with offers from boxing and wrestling promoters and vaudeville impresarios. One hustler wanted to race him against a thoroughbred racehorse, as Jesse Owens would later do as a stunt. C. C. ("Cash & Carry") Pyle, one of the first sports agents, offered Jim $10,000 to go on a baseball tour. Jim turned him down, but the soon-to-be-famous Pyle would reenter his career later.

Moses Friedman explained to the commissioner that while Jim had had offers from several major league baseball teams, he had turned them all down to continue with his schooling. Friedman had told Jim that he should "maintain his amateur standing and not enter the ranks as a professional." He had also "pointed out to him how transient the successes of major league baseball were and how very few Indians had made a success of the game." Friedman told the commissioner that he had advised his most famous pupil to go on to college, maintain his amateur status, and then enter "some profitable legitimate business." Jim's fame as the world's greatest athlete, Friedman concluded, "would be an asset to him in any business he took up."

It was excellent—and self-serving—advice. Friedman and Warner had nurtured and orchestrated something remarkable, with the result that the two men and Carlisle stood poised to enter a new, exciting chapter on the national and international playing field. Warner was there to interpret the bigger world that Jim was now a part of and that wanted a part of him. He also wanted Jim on his 1912 football team to up the gate receipts. Warner persuaded Jim that he would be an even more marketable commodity after another successful football season with Carlisle; the bigger the contract his star player eventually signed, the bigger Warner's take would be as Jim's de facto agent.

Jim had an aversion to being made a public display, but he also earnestly wanted to do what was for his "good," as he had told his brother. He was now a model to Americans and to Indians. Meanwhile, he and Iva had started to make firmer plans: after graduating he would choose the best of the plum jobs that were bound to be offered to him; when his future was secure, they could get married. He had to do this right. For the first time in his life he felt he had real options for success. If he was the best athlete in the whole world, Jim figured he must have more going for him than he'd ever imagined possible.

Warner set four goals for the 1912 football season: beat Syracuse, Pittsburgh, and Army, and have Jim on everybody's All-America lists. The 1912 Carlisle football team would be considered by many, including Warner, one of the school's finest. Warner would later say that it was a team built for Jim.

The sense of anticipation was high, not only among football fans, but in the nation at large. The team that had beat Harvard the year before now saw its star player elevated to the status of world's greatest athlete. And the rules had gone through yet another convulsion. In response to demands from fans for a quicker and more spectacular game, and to make scoring easier, the touchdown was now worth six points (the field goal remained at three) and the extra point was just one point. To accommodate touchdown passes, 10-yard end zones were required after each goal line. But rather than mandate longer fields, the playing length was shortened from 120 to 100 yards to enable teams like Harvard to add the end zones without altering their stadiums. The number of downs a team had to try and make a first down was increased from three to four. The 20-yard restriction on the forward pass was, at Camp's suggestion, eliminated. For the first time, the ball was reduced in size and elongated. There were greater restrictions on and penalties for roughness, coaching—verbal or by signals—from the sidelines, and the flying tackle.

The new rules, said one reporter, made it "easier to gain ground consecutively," allowing longer drives down the field, a perfect opportunity for the Carlisle team to showcase its offensive machine. With tackling moves now more restricted, Jim's running speed and stamina could be used to even better advantage. Warner had his 1911 backfield reinstated, including Arcasa, plus two nineteen-year-old tackles who were destined to be star college and professional players and lifelong friends of Jim's: Pete Calac, a Mission Indian, and Joseph "Joe" Napoleon Guyon, a Chippewa.

Warner began to work out a new formation to capitalize on the more open play: the double-wing, with two wingbacks flanking the ends, which would facilitate a passing attack. He pushed the players even harder in practice so they would stand a better chance of avoiding injury against bigger, heavier players. Defense was not Carlisle's strong point, so Warner emphasized an aggressive offense, taking advantage of the extra down.

Carlisle easily won its first three games. For the fourth, against Villanova, newsmen descended on Harrisburg to watch not only Jim, but the team that seemed to have already mastered the new rules. Jim played only twenty minutes, scoring three touchdowns in a 65–0 rout. He was mobbed by fans and schoolchildren as he left the field.

The next game, against Washington and Jefferson, was full of fumbles and poor teamwork; it ended in an embarrassing 0–0 tie. Jim, ever the hard loser, and Gus Welch headed straight for a Pittsburgh bar during a three-hour delay between trains. As Warner knew well by now, once Jim got started drinking, nothing could stop him. He was "well tanked up," as Warner put it, when the coach arrived and hauled him to a local hotel, where the two men had a loud and very public argument. Jim was eventually persuaded to duck out a back door with Warner to go to the train, but too late—reporters inflated the story into a fistfight, with Warner slamming Jim's head into a wall. A "very penitent" Jim apologized to the team the next day. "His notoriety," Warner said, pinpointing the new dimension of Jim's life as an international celebrity, "got him this negative publicity."

There would be no more such incidents that season. Jim took to heart Warner's reminder that he owed better to his school and the public. He had to "shoulder the responsibility," as his coach put it, for being so famous. It was not an easy task, but he was trying to see himself as a public person. He had to watch himself, be careful in what he did and said. "I cannot quite realize that I have won the greatest honors that can come to any athlete," he told a Baltimore reporter; then he wryly admitted, "I am getting sort of used to this semi-worship of the people."

The tough part of the schedule began on October 12 with Syracuse, which the year before had beaten Carlisle by one point. Jim, still angry over the loss, was determined to win. "Everybody in the town of Syracuse, all the kids," one local resident recalled, "knew that Thorpe was mad." At halftime, Warner blasted him for trying too many end runs on the muddy, slippery field and not using his strength and weight to plunge through the line. For the rest of the game, Jim "tore the Syracuse line into shreds," said Warner, who claimed that from that time on, Jim liked line plays almost as much as end runs. He even had some fun in the muck: stopping short once just as the ends and halfbacks charged up to tackle him, he watched them slide by on the mud and then ran for a big gain. He scored three touchdowns and kicked the three extra points in a 33–0 victory.

Harvard was not on the 1912 schedule because, according to Jim, Haughton did not want to "run the risk of becoming so crippled" they would not beat Yale. Jim personally set his cap on toppling undefeated Pittsburgh. Warner, goading him, told him their coach had boasted that Jim would not be able to repeat his spectacular game against Pitt of the year before. To "rounds of applause, even from the rabid Pitt rooters," Jim scored a touchdown in the first five minutes. He scored another one and six extra points in amassing his best-yet rushing yardage total, 266, as his team trounced Pitt, 45–8. "Thorpe Nearly a Team," ran one headline. The game was marred by Warner's very public berating of the team's left end after the game. Gus Welch, among others, added the incident to a growing list of Warner's inappropriate and destructive actions as their coach.

Before the Georgetown game, Carlisle's key advocate in Congress, Pennsylvania senator and Republican party boss Boies Penrose, promised Jim and Welch that if they won the game and thereby helped the pending Carlisle appropriations bill through Congress, he might make them U.S. citizens. Jim dominated throughout. The Indians won, 34–20. Penrose took no action.

Capitalizing on his team's victories, Warner squeezed in an exhibition game against an aggregation of university rugby players in Toronto. American football rules governed the play in the first half and Canadian rugby rules in the second. It was a lucrative publicity stunt and a sign of Warner's confidence in the game he had done so much to bring to maturity. Jim scored the first touchdown in the first five minutes of play before a sold-out crowd, and scored three more before the end of the first quarter. The final score was 49–1. The Canadians cheered Jim, who stood smiling but stiff.

In a game intensely scrutinized as a preview of Carlisle's upcoming game against Army, Jim "virtually defeated Lehigh," scoring twenty-eight points in Carlisle's 34–14 win. Thirty years later, Kyle

Crichton of *Collier's* would recall watching one of Jim's legendary plays that day. At Carlisle's three-yard line, the Lehigh quarterback took the snap and threw a pass over the line of scrimmage for what he was sure would be a touchdown. Jim intercepted the ball. "Now remember," wrote Crichton, "this pass wasn't out to the side. It was directly over the line of scrimmage, and when Jim caught the ball, he was surrounded by players. But did he touch the ball down [which would have been a touchback, bringing the ball back out to the twenty-yard line]? Not on your life! He started weaving his way out of that mass of humanity. By the time he reached the ten-yard line, he had dodged all tacklers and was in the clear." Then Jim had some fun. He let the quarterback, desperately trying to catch him, get just close enough and then he "gave a little wave of the hand" and accelerated as if his pursuer "were tied down with a load of bricks." He crossed the goal line for a "105-yard" touchdown. (*The Arrow* recorded it as eighty-five yards.)

The 1912 team would be remembered for its humor and pure zest on the field. Jim continued to delight the crowd by calling out the next play. "What about going around right end this time?" he'd yell, and the play would proceed perfectly, despite the fact that the opposing team dutifully massed in force at the designated spot. Giving the plays away only made the game more fun. Shy and embarrassed as a public celebrity, Jim was an extrovert on the field. His team was devoted to Jim in part because he didn't act as if he were anything special. "That 1912 team sure thought a lot of him," Pete Calac said. "We did everything we could to help him."

> *Upon the fields of friendly strife*
> *are sown the seeds that, upon other fields*
> *on other days, will bear the fruits of victory.*

BRIGADIER GENERAL DOUGLAS MACARTHUR,
Superintendent, United States Military Academy, 1919-1922.
Words carved on the stone wall of the West Point gym

The week before the Army game at West Point, Warner grumbled publicly that his team was showing a lack of interest in daily practice and was slacking off, just as they had the year before in the Syracuse game. In fact, he was working the team hard and it was responding.

He and his captain, Jim, had been planning the strategy of this game since Stockholm. Jim was, according to Warner, "primed for that battle" against "the toughest, cleverest team of the season."

In the locker room high on the rocky rampart of the Republic, overlooking the Hudson River, while the world's news chronicled crises in the Balkans, Warner reminded the Carlisle team that they were going out to play against the sons of those who had fought the Indians' fathers a generation before. George Custer was buried in the West Point graveyard. Carlisle had beat Army in 1905 and they could do it again. *These men playing against you today are soldiers,* the coach more or less said, according to several recollections. *You are Indians. Tonight we will know whether or not you are warriors.*

He had left it up to the team to choose which opponent would be the first to face his new double-wing. The formation emphasized deception, with lots of reverses, fake reverses, double reverses, pass options, and speedy sleight-of-hand between the two wingbacks that perfectly suited Carlisle. The team chose Army as their guinea pig. Jim was the left wingback, Arcasa his counterpart on the right. In the cadet backfield were four future World War II generals: Geoffrey Keyes, Leland Hobbs, Vernon Pritchard, and Dwight D. Eisenhower; Omar Bradley, future first chairman of the Joint Chiefs of Staff, was a backup center. Hobbs and Pritchard were in the class of 1915, later known as "the class the stars fell on" because fifty-eight generals would emerge from its 164 members.

Whatever Warner said in the locker room, it worked. "I have never known a team to function more perfectly or throw itself so utterly into the precise mechanism of the game," Jim said later. "They played as one perfect, moving unit." Army scored the first touchdown in the opening quarter and that was it for them. The Army players were like "tissue paper," said the *The New York Times,* "before the Indians." The rhythm of the game seemed to be one Carlisle first down after another: "The rush of men was on in no time after the ball had been snapped," wrote *The* (New York) *Evening Sun* of the Carlisle offensive play. "Each man seemed to be in the right place; there was no wasted effort." The *New York Item* credited Jim's "amazing intelligence" in his runs, fooling "the tacklers by an easy lope that carries him over the ground at remarkable speed without betraying any undue haste." On the bench, Omar Bradley heard his teammates say, "Thorpe runs too fast. We can't keep up with him. Can't get within ten yards of him."

It was a rough game. The cadets were taller and heavier, and they were overconfident, then frustrated. A Carlisle fullback was ejected in the first quarter after a fight with the Army right guard. That incensed Jim. He knew the Army team was "laying" for him, as the *New York American* reported, so he drew as many cadets to him as possible, giving Arcasa a chance to excel as a receiver. At the beginning of the second half, Leland Devore, the six-foot-six, 225-pound Army team captain and All-America tackle, did a running jump onto Joe Guyon, who was sprawled on the field, with such gratuitous force he was benched for the rest of the game. Then Jim was knocked down. His left shoulder "felt funny," he said. The Army team told the officials to waive the regulation two-minute wait. After three minutes, Jim got up. As he walked to his position behind the line, the crowd of about five thousand Army fans, cadets, and Walter Camp gave him a standing ovation.

Meanwhile, Eisenhower and his "particular pal," Charles Benedict, right and left halfback, respectively, had been all over Jim defensively, trying to stop him. In the third quarter they came at him fast, one aiming for Jim's chest, the other for his knees. Just as they got close enough to make contact, Jim swiveled aside, letting the two cadets collide with each other, and then kept on running. "When we got up we staggered a little," Eisenhower said, and they were taken out for the rest of the game. Eisenhower was not seriously injured, though he would be in a later game, after which he never played football again. Nonetheless, it would become an accepted truth that the 1912 game with Jim Thorpe was Eisenhower's last.

In the middle of the second half of Carlisle's "assault on the United States Army," wrote Damon Runyon, "Jim gave out the shrill . . . notes of the enraged Redskin" as, on a punt from Keyes behind his own goal line, he ran forty-five yards, "going through . . . whole companies of soldiers" for a touchdown. The *Times* called the run, which was actually closer to fifty-five yards, "one of the greatest ever seen on the plains" of the academy: "His catch and his start were but one motion. In and out, zigzagging first to one side and then to the other while a flying Cadet went hurling through space, Thorpe wormed his way through the entire Army team." But officials disallowed the play because a Carlisle player had been offside. Arcasa promptly ran the ball for another touchdown that the officials, wrote Runyon, "could not overlook."

Countless retellings of the game, at least one of them from a member of the West Point team and, later, several from *Times* sportswriter Arthur Daley, would claim that Jim also scored the second touchdown. If one terrific run didn't score, the great Jim Thorpe just made another one, went the story. It wasn't enough that his playing *set up* every score; sports reporters had to inflate the story. Eventually, Jim would often be credited with both touchdowns and six points. (Other Carlisle players crossed the goal for Carlisle's four touchdowns; Jim made three extra points.) As the years went on, the Jim Thorpe West Point Touchdown Story became one of the most durable of the Thorpe tales. Jim eventually gave in to the myth. "Ninety-five yards this time," he would say. "That was Jim's biggest thrill." People wanted to believe the fiction so badly, to invest their Bunyanesque hero with prodigious feats, that he let them. By nature, he didn't want to spoil the fun. These tales would become like comfy old grooves, epic tales that everyone knew by heart. In time even Warner would claim that Jim scored all the Carlisle touchdowns that day.

Carlisle won, 27–6. The Indians had "simply outclassed the Cadets," wrote the *Times*, "as they might be expected to outclass a prep school." The score was a shock. It was only Army's fourth loss in nineteen games. The "wards of the nation" had proved themselves to be the best team in the country. Jim called the game a "mighty battle" and gave top marks to his teammates, calling them "charging dynamos [who] could whip their weight in prairie panthers." For Warner it was Jim's day. In 1929 he would compare him with subsequent gridiron stars such as Red Grange, Ernie Nevers, Notre Dame's Four Horsemen, and George Gipp and conclude: "His playing in the Army game alone was enough to give him all-time recognition" as the greatest of them all. After the game, Eisenhower walked the quarter mile back to the gym with Jim, whom he found "very quiet and kind." Army captain Devore told a reporter in the locker room, "That Indian . . . is superhuman, that is all. . . . There is nothing he can't do."

Jim's name dominated the next day's headlines: "Thorpe Plows

Through Army Line and Cadets Are Unable to Check Him"; "Thorpe Alone Defeats Army." *Harper's Weekly* called his performance "simply astonishing." Probably the most definitive of the paeans to his playing came from *The New York Times*:

> The big Indian added more luster to his already brilliant record, and at times the game itself was almost forgotten while the spectators gazed on Thorpe, the individual, to wonder at his prowess. . . . He simply ran wild, while the Cadets tried in vain to stop his progress. It was like trying to clutch a shadow. . . . Thorpe went through the West Point line as if it was an open door; his defensive play was on a par with his attack; and his every move was that of a past master.

Runyon dryly observed that Jim "was so generally present all over the field, that everybody knew who made the plays without asking somebody else."

Winning this game meant for Carlisle that on the symbolic territorial field of football they were as good as the old Army men who had slaughtered their peoples *and* as good as the new men, the future Army generals (who, three decades later, would win the biggest world war in history).

The identification of football as the American crucible of masculine strength, strategic smarts, endurance, and victorious teamwork was now complete. Eisenhower, supreme commander, Allied Expeditionary Force, for the Battle of Normandy in 1944, would say after World War II that he could not recall "ever having to relieve an ex-football player for lack of aggressive leadership, in whatever level of command."

Carlisle threw away the Penn game, 34–26, with what one news report described as play marked by "so many mistakes, due entirely to carelessness." Frustrated and angry, Jim swung at some Penn tacklers piled on top of him and was booed. Playing safety when a long touchdown pass went over his head, Jim, according to Warner, "just stood there." When Warner asked angrily why Jim hadn't intercepted the pass or knocked it down, Jim answered breezily, "I didn't think that the receiver could get to it in time." Warner would always cite that reply as an example of "the one weak trait in Jim's character: Jim was always a little too certain and consequently careless." He "rested content," said the coach, "with his gift." And the gift came through at least once that afternoon as Jim ran for an eighty-yard touchdown, shaking off two gangs of tacklers in a "beautiful . . . piece of open-field running" that Warner would praise for years. But the Penn game was a humiliating loss, and Jim cared more than he had let on because Carlisle had blown its chance for an almost perfect season with the one game. When Penn fans broke from their postgame snake dance to shake his hand, Jim ignored them.

Carlisle won its next game. Two days later, Jim made a surprise announcement. After the Brown game on Thanksgiving, he said, the last game of the season, he would be leaving the "sporting world" and Carlisle. His team had arrived in Worcester, Massachusetts, to practice for two days before heading to Providence. Reporters noted that Jim appeared "somewhat shy" and kept back from the crowd that had gathered at the train station. When asked why the world's greatest athlete was quitting at the top of his form, he answered, in the paraphrase of one newspaper, that it was because of "his abhorrence of the public gaze and the notoriety he has had for his various stunts at the Olympic games and on this side of the water, especially the football."

It was a strange statement and it started a swirl of speculation. Had the pressure of performing and living up to expectations as the world's greatest athlete in each football game that fall taken a toll? Did he want to preempt rumors circulating about his amateur status? Or did something happen that day in Worcester?

The Penn loss had demoralized him: if he'd jumped to intercept that pass, his team might have won. He was tired and battered. He had started to doubt himself. As he headed onto the field in Providence for the Brown game, he felt "something cold . . . grip my heart. I was losing something I would never be able to regain. I felt as though I wanted to fling my arms about the field, the goal posts, and hold them tight."

A crowd of 10,000 fans—the largest seen at a Providence football game—lined up an hour before the game at Andrews Field in what the *Brown Daily Herald* described as a "blinding snowstorm and piercing northwester." Even though extra stands were set up, hundreds had to be turned away. With a wet ball and a lot of fumbles, it was nevertheless a spectacular game. The crowd, most of which stayed to the end, was brought to its freezing feet time after time to watch Jim throw himself into this last collegiate game. At halftime, Warner told the team they owed their captain this victory in return for all he had given them. Jim scored three touchdowns and two extra points. His end runs, passes, run backs of punts, and tackling, plus two fifty-yard runs, made him what *Collier's* would describe almost two decades later as "the whole show, both on the offense and the defense." The final score was 32–0.

Jim's twenty-seventh touchdown—more than any other collegiate player that year—concluded Carlisle's 12–1–1 season. In the twelve games for which a record was kept, Jim scored 224 points, an average of more than 18 a game. In the early 1980s, NCAA researcher Steve Boda would pore through old newspaper accounts and create a de facto, if necessarily incomplete, record of Jim's Carlisle numbers. He scored more than 50 touchdowns and more than 400 points in four years for Carlisle; Walter Payton, as one comparison, registered 66 touchdowns and 464 points at Jackson State by 1974. Jim's 1912 total of 1,869 yards in 191 rushes—with rushing statistics unavailable for two games—tops O. J. Simpson's modern high in 1968 for USC, 355 carries for 1,709 yards and 22 touchdowns. In the absence of rushing statistics for fifteen of Jim's forty-four collegiate games, Boda suggested that he may have been the game's first 2,000-yard rusher.

When Warner became a grand old man of football, he itemized the traits that, in his opinion, made Jim the greatest football player ever: incredible speed (100 yards in ten seconds); enormous power in his high-knee running; a straight arm that could somehow deflect even a pack of tacklers; an uncanny ability to stop, adapt, dodge, and pivot in an instant; remarkable accuracy, consistency, and range as a passer and as a kicker of field goals and punts. "He could come," said Warner, "pretty close to calling his shots." And, he might have added, Jim loved the game. A more impartial critic, John Heisman, the legendary coach at Georgia Tech, said of Jim's 1912 performance: "[He] had everything . . . star punter, a star drop kicker, a star passer. At blocking and end running certainly we've not produced his master."

Carlisle's record for the four years Jim played was 43–5–2, with 1,281 points scored versus 280 for their opponents. The Thorpe years would be assessed by *Sports Illustrated* almost forty years later as "the most remarkable record, all things considered, in the history of the sport." Almost one hundred years later, the magazine suggested Jim would have won his second Heisman Trophy for his performance in 1912. Camp once again named Jim a first-team All-American.

A feeling of pride beyond words, not personal but communal, was Jim's most profound connection to those who had gone before him. Great achievements lived on in the collective memory, like the warrior tale of Black Hawk. Before a celebrity culture forced them to do it, great soldiers and great athletes often had in common a disinclination to explain what they had done, to dwell on it, to take personal pride in what they were taught to see as a group effort. Jim's generous insistence that his teammates also get credit would ensure their respect and lifelong friendship. Though he would not look backward, except when sportswriters demanded it, Jim once summed up his Carlisle career in a terse but revealing style: "I gave little quarter when I played football and never asked for any. I played clean but I played hard."

Questions about Jim's future flew around when Jim returned to Pennsylvania. "Carlisle Indian Reticent While Others Talk" read a headline in the town's *Evening Sentinel.* Most of the rumors suggested that all he wanted to do was go home to Oklahoma.

The Indian Service medical inspector came to measure Jim. This second review of his body since the Olympics was exhaustive and, to a private man like Jim, unbearable. The resulting statistics were then published nationwide, in papers like *The Sunday Herald*: "Today the master athlete of the world, as a type, stands half-way as a physical product, between the sinuous aborigine . . . and the modern product of civilization with specialized muscular development. To *outward* appearance, the resemblance to the aborigine is certainly the more marked." He was found free of the "growths of hair that are the usual accompaniment of tremendous strength." Lumbering, with a slight stoop, awkward, Jim yet had "an agreeable personality" with signs of "marked mental improvement" since entering Carlisle. In a separate box was printed the Anthropometric Table of Thorpe's Measurements, comparing his with those of "average college students" age twenty-four and nineteen. Jim's left elbow, for example, measured 10.5 inches, the college students' 9.8 and 8.8, respectively, and so on.

Jim had "almost overnight changed the image of the Indian in the mind of the [white] public," historian Vine Deloria, Jr., a Sioux, wrote more than fifty years later. Stepping into the vacuum left by Crazy Horse, Chief Joseph, Geronimo, and other great American Indian figures, his super-athlete identity became a new white construct, what Deloria derisively called the "humorous, athletic, subspecies of white man." On the other hand, *The Red Man*, a Carlisle publication, pointed to Jim as proof of Carlisle's mission—Indian equality: "Where undying fame is the chief reward, the name of Jim Thorpe, a Sac and Fox Indian, looms far above all others . . . This real American met the pick of the world's athletes and wrested victory from them."

Jim, as always, remained proud—and wary. When he returned to Oklahoma for Christmas, old friends were greeted by name as if he weren't "the best known on the planet." He was his same old self. There was talk of finding oil on the allotments. With drilling started in Prague, Stroud, and other nearby towns, leases had been taken, reported a local paper, on practically all the Sac and Fox lands. Though this changed nothing in practical terms for Jim's family in Oklahoma, his own future out in the bigger world seemed bright and full of promise. As Warner would later say, life was "juicy fat" for Jim Thorpe.

PART II

The Professional

[T]he college game . . . brings out that something which is lacking in the pro game—I guess you could call it spirit. The college player . . . will willingly sacrifice his leg to gain the necessary yards that spell victory for his team. That's spirit. The professional gridder will play it safe, because he wants to be in condition to earn more money in his next game. That's business.

—JIM THORPE

Jim as a New York Giant

JIM IS ON THE BEST BASEBALL TEAM—the New York Giants—with the toughest, most uncompromising fans in the country. He's put on a few pounds since July 1912, maybe from hanging out with his new, hard-drinking teammates. His face is puffy. The carefree cockiness is gone.

CHAPTER SEVEN

The Public Glare

1913–1914

I always dreamed of winning the Games and hearing the national anthem. But it was bittersweet. It's like learning to play the piano. You sit in front of it for twelve years, and you have a chance to play the most beautiful music in the world, and when it's over you put your hands in your pocket and you never play that music again. I choked up. I started crying. "What am I going to do tomorrow?"

— BRUCE JENNER, gold medal Olympic decathlete, 1976

Toward the end of a Christmas hunting trip, Jim agreed to talk to *The Daily Oklahoman*. Somewhat notorious for being "the most impossible celebrity to be made to grant an interview," whose "absence and silence" had begun "to worry everyone back east," he had just announced in Oklahoma City that he would be returning to Carlisle after all. He said he was "feeling great." He was ready to do his best at whatever Pop Warner wanted him to do. All he'd needed was a vacation and a break from being "the sensation of the football world." When asked if he'd bagged any deer, Jim laughed and said, "Deer? Do you mean deer or dears? The season is closed on one and I can't say about the other." Indeed, Iva was on his mind. Her family was now somewhat more favorably disposed toward him; he *had* made something of himself. It remained to be seen what he would do after graduation in the spring.

He arrived back at Carlisle on January 18, 1913, in time to hear James Sullivan address the school, which was now considered an incubator of superior American athletes. "Young men," he said, "you are the coming stars in the athletic world . . . and we must look to you to uphold the standard of supremacy for the Stars and Stripes. . . . If any of you ever played a game of any kind that was professional I would beg of you never to sign an amateur blank. . . . You are bound to be found out, maybe in a week, maybe in a year, perhaps in ten years." Sullivan may have known more than he let on. Reports had continued to surface that Jim had once played professional baseball. Four days later a front-page article on the subject in *The Worcester Telegram* (Massachusetts) was picked up by newspapers around the world.

The *Telegram*'s baseball reporter, Pat Dowd, was told about Jim's professional interlude by Jesse Burkett, a former major league outfielder, who had managed the Worcester team of the New England League in 1912. Burkett said he had heard about it from someone named "Carney," who was visiting his sister in nearby Southbridge. Dowd told the city editor, who assigned the story to Roy Ruggles Johnson, the county editor.

Johnson wanted to confirm this himself, rather than sending out one of his reporters, and went to Southbridge. After Johnson spent a day trying to track down "Carney," someone realized he was looking for Charles Clancy, the manager of the 1910 Fayetteville Highlanders, who was spending the winter of 1912–13 near Worcester. Clancy proved a "glib talker" all too eager to "reel off" stories about Jim, including his playing professionally for Fayetteville. Johnson took no notes—"the way we got a good many snappy stories in those days," he said. He returned to his office, flipped through his *Reach Baseball Guide*, found a picture of Jim with the Highlanders, and wrote up the story. The managing editor put it on the front page.

Others would later claim credit for the revelation, among them Grantland Rice and a New York sports reporter who had been on the *Finland*, Francis P. Albertani. Joe Libby, one of the Carlisle athletes who had gone with Jim to North Carolina in 1909, said that a local reporter in Rocky Mount had written a demeaning article on Jim, with a photograph of him sitting on a donkey and headlined "Here's Jim Thorpe Sitting on His Ass." Jim had then beat him up, which had prompted the reporter, after the Stockholm games, to reveal Jim's professional hiatus. The reporter was probably Sam T. Mallison, the man assigned by *The Rocky Mount Evening Telegram* to cover Jim in 1909. He later said that when telegrams flooded into the paper's office from all over the country requesting background copy as the scandal broke, all he did was distribute the material, compiled and written up by a staffer, under his byline.

"I signed [Thorpe] as a pitcher," Clancy was quoted as saying in Johnson's article, "but I thought he had a yellow streak in him. He would go along well for seven innings, perhaps, and then he would develop a lame arm. The arm would be all right the next day." Clancy described Jim as a wild drinker, recalled the two jumps through plate glass windows, and said he couldn't hit a curveball. Clancy created a cumulative portrayal of Jim as shifty and dishonest. Johnson made an error in his piece that provided Jim with some wiggle room: Johnson wrote that Jim had played for Clancy on the Winston-Salem team of the Eastern Carolina League. Jim, via Warner, was of course able to deny that forcefully. The accusation that Jim was a coward was generally ridiculed and added credence to the assumption that the story was false or a case of mistaken identity. The nature of Jim's Olympic performance, however, said one report, only "elevate[s] his case into one of international importance."

At first the Associated Press refused to run Johnson's scoop, which ran without a byline, suspecting a fake. The afternoon *Worcester Post* ran a story the next day, featuring a second interview with Clancy, during which he "lied like a gentleman," said Johnson, and insisted he'd given no revelatory interview, didn't know Thorpe. But the genie was out of the bottle.

The New York Times raised an important point. "What surprises the local athletic world, was that if Thorpe did play professional baseball, as alleged, the fact was kept a profound secret for nearly three years," even as his career brought him "before the entire world." *Collier's* figured there must have been two hundred AAU officials in the South, at least one of whom could have cabled the AOC about Jim's baseball summers. Who had the most to gain from going public with the information now?

On January 24, the same day charges challenging Jim's amateur status were filed with James Sullivan at the AAU, Clancy sent Warner a letter in which he made a "complete denial" of his statements quoted in the article, and insisted Jim had never played for him on any team; a few days later he claimed that Johnson had paid him a mere "social call," never told him he was being interviewed for publication, and he then was "made to say things . . . he never would have stood for had he known what was coming." That part was probably true: Clancy would have had nothing to gain by revealing the cozy deception that allowed hundreds of college men to play minor league baseball with no adverse consequences. Warner told a reporter for *The New York Times* who had hustled down to Carlisle for an exclusive "special" that Clancy's letter to him was all Warner knew about the subject and that he had been further assured by Jim that "there is nothing in the story." Warner called Sullivan and told him the same thing. Warner was aggressively bluffing, and so far it was working.

Sullivan launched his own inquiry within three hours of receiving a copy of *The Worcester Telegram* article, amid newspaper speculation that, if guilty, Jim should confess and save the AAU the time and trouble of a full investigation. Meanwhile, the identities of a "Thorpe" who had played for Rocky Mount in 1909 and 1910 and an "A. Thorpe" who had supposedly played for Fayetteville in 1910 were being investigated. The *Times* reported that a B. C. Stewart had claimed he played with Jim; Pete Boyle, the Fayetteville player traded to Rocky Mount in exchange for Jim in 1910, described his playing in detail, complete with batting average. "Reports are being freely circulated," reported the *Times*, "from North Carolina to Massachusetts by individuals professing to give Thorpe's record and his connection with professional baseball."

Jim agonized over what he should do, tramping out into the Cumberland Valley to think it through. It was only a matter of time before the swarm of reporters besieging the Charlotte and Raleigh newspapers for background information would confirm the story. "I had always laid my cards, face up, on the table," he recalled of this, the "biggest ordeal" of his life, and, in the end, that is what he did. He had no advocate, though he thought he did in Warner. By nature, as his wives, children, and friends would all agree, he was a trusting person, too much so, and he trusted Warner. "I don't understand, Pop," he said. "What's . . . baseball got to do with all the jumping and running and field work I did in Stockholm? I never got paid for any of that, did I?"

On January 26, as Washington prepared for the March 4 inauguration of president-elect Woodrow Wilson, Jim signed a letter addressed to Sullivan admitting that he had played professional baseball in North Carolina. Warner (with the assistance of Friedman) wrote the famous letter in which Jim insisted he did "not play for the money . . . but because I liked to play ball. I was not very wise to the ways of the world and did not realize this was wrong. . . . I was simply an Indian schoolboy and did not know all about such things." Jim claimed in the letter that he "never told anyone at the school about it until to-day," that he kept it secret. Warner's truculence—and an implied threat to name names—seeps through in the letter's claims that "several college men from the North" were doing the same thing, but changed their names to protect their amateur status. "I am very sorry, Mr. Sullivan," the letter concluded, "to have it all spoiled in this way, and I hope the Amateur Athletic Union and the people will not be too hard in judging me." Vine Deloria, Jr., would describe the enduring effect of the stereotype Jim's apology reinforced: "[T]he Indian sees himself as an incompetent and childish figure who must have his mistakes forgiven because he is an Indian who does not really understand." Friedman also wrote a letter to Sullivan, stating that the school had done its own "thorough investigation" of Jim's professionalism and assured the AAU secretary that the school and Warner were "without any knowledge of this fact until today."

Someone had to take the fall for the humiliating scandal that tainted the American glory in Stockholm, and it was not going to be the coach, the Carlisle Indian Industrial School, its superintendent, the AAU or the AOC. Sitting in a room somewhere in the school, hunkered down with Warner and Friedman, Jim was made to understand that.

The same day, Sullivan gave his own exclusive interview to *The New York Times*. The Pittsburgh Pirates, he said, had tried to sign Jim in 1912, but Warner had got Sullivan to persuade Jim to stay at Carlisle. Though baseball clearly had nothing to do with track and field, that wasn't the point; Sullivan said that Jim had signed a registration form for the AAU, confirming that he had not broken any amateur rule anywhere, anytime. Furthermore, said Sullivan, "it has been the custom to make pets out of the crack Indian athletes and because of their strange origin nothing back of their Government school careers has ever been delved into."

Warner was informed that the Middle Atlantic Division of the AAU would hold a hearing in Carlisle regarding Jim's status. Warner told Sullivan he would prefer to come to New York to say what he had to say—without Jim. He delivered Jim's letter and Friedman's to Sullivan in his office at 21 Warren Street on January 27. It was no doubt an interesting meeting between two extremely ambitious men who had worked hard to create their places within the new sports hierarchy, now together saving themselves by hanging Jim out to dry. At five that night, the AAU issued a statement insisting that Jim had been chosen for the American Olympic team "without the least suspicion" of any professionalism. Warner was extolled as "a man whose reputation is of the highest and whose accuracy of statement has never been doubted." The document concluded that while Jim was "deserving of the severest condemnation for concealing the fact that he had professionalized himself by receiving money for playing base ball," the AOC and the AAU also felt that, given the wide publicity granted the Olympics and Jim, "those who knew of his professional acts are deserving of still greater censure for their silence." *The Charlotte Observer* retorted with the headline, "Not We Who Were Asleep," and reminded the AAU that "many thousands . . . have known for months of Thorpe's record."

The day after the meeting with Warner, Sullivan received a telegram from Kristian Hellström, the secretary of the Swedish Olympic Committee: IS RUMOR THORPE'S DISQUALIFICATION CORRECT? Sullivan cabled back: YES . . . ALL RECORDS VOID TROPHIES WILL BE RETURNED PUBLIC APOLOGY IS MADE TO SWEDEN AND ALL NATIONS OF THE WORLD ITS SAD AFFAIR LETTER FOLLOWS. SULLIVAN. The return of the prizes, the naming of new winners, and the voiding of Jim's records were all to be done in due course. When Martin Sheridan was told that the amateur all-around championship would now revert to him, he replied that "there wasn't any revert about it; if Thorpe is the best athlete in the world, he is the best athlete in the world and that's all there is to it." There was general agreement with one newspaper's judgment that "in the history of amateur athletics there is no case to parallel the rise to fame of the Sac and Fox Indian and his even more meteoric descent to the ranks of the professionals." It had been less than six months between opening day in Stockholm and Jim's letter to Sullivan.

As the evidence presented by Warner to the AAU was "so vital and convincing," Sullivan and other officers of both the AAU and the AOC determined that no time would be lost "in setting the

United States right before the world." With the *Times* and other papers reporting that Jim had proved how easy it was to be a professional *and* keep it a secret, that one North Carolina summer team had been made up mostly of students from Brown, and that his case was viewed as the "wedge for a more general clean-up of amateur athletics than has been attempted in many years," Sullivan announced he had asked Jim to provide him with a list of other college students who had played with him in North Carolina. (The AAU had been conveniently overlooking athletes who had accepted what was usually called "appearance money" or "a bonus.") Carlisle was ordered by the AAU to return the gold medals and the two royal trophies to New York for shipment back to Sweden. Jim's friend Little Boy told Jim that "some guys went into your room and took all your medals." Jim wasn't trusted to hand them in himself. Five days had elapsed since the newspaper scoop.

The flurry of righteous activity obscured the procedural fact that it was not Sullivan's but the Swedish Olympic Committee's responsibility to adjudicate any challenge to an Olympic event, as far as that process existed in those years, and that the time limit for such challenges was long past. Rule 13 of the general rules of the 1912 Games was clear: "Objections to the qualifications of a competitor must be made in writing . . . to the Swedish Olympic Committee . . . before the lapse of thirty days from the distribution of the prizes." The question of Jim's professionalism had landed in a vacuum between the AAU, the AOC, the Swedish Olympic Committee, and the IOC. "Such a case has not occurred before," the *Revue Olympique* would comment in March, "and a jurisprudence will have to be established."

There was immediate sympathy abroad for Jim. He was seen as a true sportsman being punished for a minor aberration. A Swede, Elis Lindroth, wrote to *Nordiskt Idrottsliv* (*Nordic Sport Life*) voicing the anger that was growing in reaction to what had become an international scandal: "Does anyone believe that the AAU didn't know about Thorpe's 'crime' before the Games?" The American press published reminders from Swedish sportsmen and authorities that the challenge to Jim's medals had technically come too late and, in any case, the rules of amateurship were too severe. Also overlooked was a provision in the 1912 rules for a "Court of Appeal" that specifically dealt not with challenges to the outcome of any event (the judges' decisions were final) but with "the interpretation and application of the rules governing the Games." Such protests had to be made within one hour of the event in question. No one paid any attention. The AAU was directing events, preemptively stripping Jim of his amateur status.

Letters went back and forth in early February between Stockholm and de Coubertin in Gstaad, Switzerland. "The Thorpe affair is maddening, but we have nothing to do with it," wrote Colonel Viktor G. Balck, president of the 1912 Swedish Olympic Committee and one of the founders of the IOC, to de Coubertin on February 4. "The Swedish Committee is waiting calmly for the official advice of the Americans." As the committee could not decide who had the final authority, it would keep Jim's medals and trophies until the IOC met in May in Lausanne and then make the decision on the disposition of the awards and reallocation of points. De Coubertin responded that Jim's letter was "touching in its naïveté" and that the uproar represented "such a lot of blame for a peccadillo!" He insisted, however, that the IOC be the final arbiter regarding the official adjustment of the records. Nothing could be allowed to jeopardize the newly secure and respected position of the modern Olympic Games. By now it had also occurred to a few Swedes that, if Jim's record was eliminated, Sweden would have the gold, silver, *and* bronze winners of the decathlon and be the top gold medal winner of the Games.

American newspapers tracked every turn of the story: " 'Big Injun' Comes Across with Truth: Carlisle in Gloom"; "Thorpe Confesses to Professionalism: Will Be Stripped of All Prizes." *The New York Times* wrote that "Thorpe's deception and subsequent confession deals amateur sport in America the hardest blow it has ever had to take and disarranges the scheme of amateur athletics the world over." The whole apparatus of amateurism came in for withering criticism. The *Los Angeles Times* castigated Sullivan and the AAU in particular as "one of the jokes of the athletic world. . . . It should be plain to any man with an ounce of brains in his head, who has ever had any connections with the AAU, that many of these so-called amateurs are the rankest kind of professionals." As for Jim's achievements, "nothing in the world will efface" them, not even a "pompous little insect" like Sullivan. Damon Runyon agreed. It was "a little thing enough that this great Carlisle star did," he wrote, yet the result would be that "[n]one of his marvelous records will stand. They will be wiped out as completely as if they never had existed, although," he added, presciently, "it is rather doubtful that this summary method will remove them from the memory of the people who follow athletic events."

Popular press opinion and letters to the editor sided with the "gallant," "manly" Jim. He had not tried to "lie his way out of it," he had turned down all post-Olympics offers to professionalize himself, and he had made less in one season of baseball than a white collegian could make from writing one newspaper article. When Jim announced that he would not reveal the names of the college men who had played with him in North Carolina, his stock rose even higher: "Throughout the length and breadth of America . . . only sympathy and praise for the Indian is heard," reported *The Daily Oklahoman.*

There were calls for investigations into the accepted practice of college alumni recruiting athletes, "staking them," said *The Daily Oklahoman,* "to tuition, tobacco money and board." New doubts were raised about Warner. *The Sporting News* insisted, "Glenn Warner must have known—it was his business to know, as one in charge of the government's Indian wards—that Thorpe played professional base ball."

The coverage went on for weeks. The longer it lasted, the more issues it raised. If Jim's performance in Stockholm had provoked a complex reaction, coming to terms with the nation's fall from the pinnacle of amateur grace triggered what amounted to a reevaluation of American sports. The scandal reinforced the previous summer's jibes about American athletes' unseemly hunger for victory at any cost. "The ideals of the gentleman are beyond the comprehension of American athletes," wrote *The Outlook,* "and . . . American sport is thoroughly commercialized." *The Daily Mirror* in London restored some perspective: "Nobody who knows British athletics from the inside, would for a moment imagine that one of our team had not taken payments *sub rosa* in the way of fat expenses."

Ironically, Jim found support among those who saw Indians as inferior. As an Indian, could he be held to "so high a degree of moral accountability as his white competitors?" asked *The State* in Columbia, South Carolina. On the other hand, said the *Buffalo Morning Express,* despite their superior moral education those white competitors still played professional baseball and got away with it. Either Jim was no worse than his white peers or, as an Indian, he was absolved of any moral choice at all.

His claim in the letter that Warner wrote for him that he had played ball because he liked the game endeared him to many. Over time, the fiction would grow that Jim was paid nothing those summers, or only a pittance. His playing minor league ball would be downgraded to his having played "semi-pro baseball." Using his own name proved his virtue: he was too honest and guileless, so the story went, too truly amateur, to play under a false name.

By April popular opinion had hardened in Jim's favor. Even the conservative *Outlook* now thought his punishment was "extraordinarily disproportionate." The *Washington Herald* agreed: nothing about baseball had prepared Jim for, or given him any advantage in, his Olympic events.

The editors of *The Baseball Magazine* presented an analysis of contemporary American sport that laid out why Jim would be remembered as the victim of the most "spectacular [scandal] in the history of sport." Blasting the AAU for clinging to an outmoded amateur code that was rife with hypocrisy, the magazine dismissed the "harebrained, insipid, utterly insufferable idiocy" of professionalizing anyone who had ever accepted any money for any activity related to any sport as a "forlorn relic": professionalism "has come to stay . . . because it is the guiding spirit of the present." As sports had recently exploded in the country, so too had the desire to see the best performance by the best athlete, and the professional was "usually a better performer at his particular specialty" than an amateur. Increased skill in sports should be rewarded with money as determined by the "public demand" (excepting track and field, it was noted, because there was little demand professionally for athletes in that sport), just like anything else. Reform was necessary: an amateur athlete should be required to refrain from professional activity only in his sport.

The magazine summed up the radical nature of what had happened to Jim:

[T]he Indian experienced a more complete and utter reversal of fortune than has fallen to the lot of any other athlete. From the very pinnacle of glory, gained by his unparalleled achievements, he saw himself suddenly hurled beyond the pale. . . . From first to last he has been merely a pawn in the game. . . . His trophies so well won are snatched away; his exploits are erased from the record book as though they did not exist; he is forever barred from further competition in the very lines of sport in which he is acknowledged the master of all time.

In Lausanne, on May 6, the IOC voted to award Jim's trophies and gold medals to the former second-place winners of the pentathlon and decathlon, Ferdinand Bie and Hugo Wieslander, respectively. Jim and others inaccurately claimed for years that the two athletes refused the prizes. Wieslander did write a letter to the AAU saying, "I don't know what your rules are in regard to amateurism, and apparently Thorpe didn't either, but I do know that we met in honest competition and he beat me fairly and decisively. I didn't win the Olympic Decathlon. Jim Thorpe did." The IOC unanimously adopted a British proposal to send congratulations to the AAU for the sportsmanlike manner in which they had handled the affair. The Swedish Olympic Commit-tee issued a meticulous official report of the 1912 Games. Though Jim was not listed as the winner of his two major competitions, his performance in each event was dutifully noted. He was on the final list of competitors, but his results were not included in each official tally. The huge difference between his point totals and those of the silver medal winners made it impossible to ignore him. It was, War-ner admitted, "a brutal business."

The nightmare had begun for Jim. His life was now marked by what *Sports Illustrated* decades later would call "high triumph and bitter despair." He would divide his life into pre- and postscandal eras. The AAU had started asking questions at the time of the Brown game in November, so Jim had been living with dread and uncertainty for months. Though he said that once he made up his mind to "face the world with the truth," he was no longer nervous or worried and "adopted a fatalistic viewpoint" of the scandal, in fact he was in a state of numb confusion. He had worked hard to do amazing things, which were now tossed aside as if they, and he, were worthless. He told a Carlisle friend, Henry Flickinger, "I didn't have too much, and now I don't have the medals."

Nothing in his life had prepared him for worldwide adulation, and now he was alone and abandoned to face all these complications. In a life marked by a series of changes and abrupt transitions from one world to another, this was the most radical. Though Jim had been more assimilated, by white standards, than most of his Carlisle classmates, he had lived embedded in Indian culture, under the protection of family, government, and school. What he did best, sports, had been performed, except for the Olympics, surrounded by a team of fellow Indians, guided by a white coach in a cosseted environment separate from the outside white world. "He had sublimated his personal, social and intellectual development," said his grandson Michael Koehler.

Jim's hope of a coaching job was gone. His plans to marry Iva had to be put aside. She reassured him she was still his girl and would wait. But "branded a professional," he recalled, "and now free to accept money . . . offers poured in." Harry Edwards, a Philadelphia fight promoter, offered him $50,000 to become a professional boxer. Vaudeville gigs were again dangled before him, as were movie contracts. "There was nothing I could do on the stage," he said, "except stand and have people stare at me. I didn't care so much for that. Motion pictures were a complete mystery to me, so I did not let offers from that quarter tempt me. I was skeptical of other promoters and their schemes."

Jim thought his options through for himself, but still he needed someone to trust. He turned to the only person he could—Warner. The trust came at a price. The coach knew that the best deal for Jim would be the one with the most money and therefore the biggest cut for Warner. A lucrative, high-profile job for his protégé could also help repair Warner's reputation. He advised Jim that his best option was to revert to his old dream of going professional, to leverage his notoriety while he could get the best value for it.

If Jim wanted to make a decent, somewhat respectable living at professional sports, organized baseball was really his only choice. He knew he had not done well in the Eastern Carolina League, and it was the sport he had played least at Carlisle. If the subsequent eye operation had left any vision impairment, it could be enough to make a game that required hitting and catching a small ball even more challenging. Moreover, attendance at major league games had dropped from more than seven million in 1909 to an average of slightly more than six million from 1910 to 1913. Jim would be entering the major leagues at a difficult time.

On January 29, the *Los Angeles Times* reported that according to "reliable authority" Jim had signed a contract with the Pittsburgh Pirates the previous fall. A few days later the story changed: Jim had merely promised to sign. The team's owner, Barney Dreyfuss, denied any such thing. At least three other major league ball clubs—the Chicago White Sox, the Cincinnati Reds, and the St. Louis Browns—were after Jim in the last days of January, each telegraphing its terms to Warner at Carlisle or sending a representative.

Then another story grabbed the headlines. Jim, it was said, was already under contract to a minor league baseball team in Beaumont, Texas. Its franchise had been bought by Oklahoma City the previous year, and a James C. (also reported as "G.") Thorp was among the players reserved by that club. After some investigation, it was determined that the missing player had signed with Oklahoma City for the 1912 season, but had not shown up. The owner of the Fayetteville club insisted that Jim was its property—although the Eastern Carolina League had dissolved. Abner Davis, the previous owner of the Oklahoma City franchise, claimed that he had made an offer to Jim in 1911 when he was in the state playing with an amateur team, presumably Anadarko, but Jim had turned it down. Dreyfuss then changed his story, saying Jim had promised in 1911 that he would "never sign a professional contract without giving the Pirates a chance at him." When the Olympic scandal broke, Jim offered to come to the Pirates, as promised. Dreyfuss released him from any obligation. Jim had "kept his word," Dreyfuss said, and "acted the part of a 'white man' with me."

On January 28, Jim, or Warner, telegraphed the Cincinnati owner: WILL CONSIDER PROPOSITION AND SIGN WITH CLUB MAKING BEST OFFER. JAMES THORPE. Similar telegrams had gone out to all the major league clubs. Just who was calling the shots at Carlisle is unclear. Jim was "rather unsophisticated," Warner would recall, "so he asked me to look out for his interests." Jim relied on Warner, not a baseball expert, to give him not only the larger context and relative merits of the teams, but also to gauge which environment would best suit his strengths and build up his weaknesses.

The New York Times finally confirmed on January 31, 1913, that

Jim had accepted a contract with the New York Giants. Giants manager John McGraw and Warner were "old friends" going back to the days both of them had lived in upstate New York. Warner told McGraw that, while Jim was not yet a good ballplayer, he could excel if he wanted to. He explained Jim's habit of carefully watching someone perform and then mastering the task. That would be Jim's approach to baseball, he said. Satisfied, McGraw reportedly doubled Cincinnati's offer. Jim said he'd think about it overnight, then called McGraw twice before accepting the offer. "The engaging of Thorpe by McGraw," said the *Times*, "in the face of such strenuous opposition within twenty-four hours is considered by baseball men a master stroke of baseball diplomacy."

On February 2, Jim and Warner went to New York to sign a contract at the offices of John B. Foster, the secretary of the era's most famous and successful team. The press "packed to the doors," as well as "movie men" and photographers, were waiting for them. "No such scene," read one report, "ever attended the signing of a contract by a baseball player." Jim picked up the pen "[w]ith a broad grin," looking "more like a big college student who had just stepped out of a Broadway toggery shop . . . [wearing] a natty blue Norfolk suit topped off with a Fedora hat of purple hue." Clearly, Warner had outfitted him for the big time, and Warner did most of the talking.

After some coaxing Jim finally spoke. "I am pleased to get a chance to play with the Giants," he said. "Whether I will make good I cannot say. I am going to try my best." He said he didn't care which position he played, though he enjoyed pitching. "I had a lot of speed," he said of his minor league summers, "but I depended mostly on my curve. I had pretty good control of it, too. I don't know whether I had what you writers call a 'jump' on my fastball or not. I guess if I have that there will be no questions about my being a pitcher."

Looking to the *Los Angeles Times* reporter "as happy as a schoolboy off on some lark," Jim took two hours to "sign" the contract over and over so each photographer could get a shot. It was only when pressed to talk about the discovery of his professionalism that he turned reluctant and shy. "No one knows," he finally said, "how sorry I feel about that." When the prizes, already en route back to Europe, were mentioned, Jim said, "There is nothing more to say about that. The quicker it is dropped the more I will be pleased. It's something I don't want to talk about."

Warner suggested that it was more likely Jim would make an ideal outfielder with his "remarkable throwing arm," speed, and "Indian cunning." When reporters brought up that Jim had "never had any professional advice about batting," Warner called him a natural bats-man who hit the ball with "terrific force." The *Times* loftily suggested that Jim was not a "scientific batter." Jim said he had played too many positions in North Carolina to get really good at any of them.

McGraw was on hand to get his first look at the new acquisition. "If he doesn't make a ball player," he said, "I miss my guess." He brushed aside talk of Jim's minor league seasons: "The Indian was only a youngster then and practically all his athletic development has come since those days." All Jim needed, pronounced McGraw, was "proper instruction." When the players arrived at spring training in Marlin, Texas, three weeks later, he said that Jim would be assigned to pitching coach Wilbert Robinson. "I expect him to show a little speed on the bases," said McGraw, "and you know speed is one of my hob-bies." The running game—especially base stealing—was a key part of McGraw's pre-lively-ball-era strategy.

McGraw wouldn't discuss the terms of Jim's three-year contract. Reporters figured that the overall cost to the Giants was $9,000: a $6,000 annual salary making Jim, according to several reports, "the highest salaried untried major league player in the history of the game"; a $500 signing bonus, and a very generous $2,500 to Warner, more than half his Carlisle salary. The coach denied any such pay-ment. No one believed him.

Bozeman Bulger of *The New York Evening World* expected to find a "childlike" Indian at the signing. Instead, he was impressed that Jim studied his surroundings before commenting, which Bulger saw as a "sure sign of a calculating athlete," as was his explanation for choosing the Giants. "I could have gone to St. Louis," Jim said, "and, according to what the scout told me, could have been a regular. But it occurred to me that I had never seen any startling newspaper stories about what the St. Louis team had done. . . . If [they] were willing to put an untried man like me on the regular team they would likely put other untried men on it, and it wouldn't be much of a team. I think I would rather sit on the bench with a good team than be on the field with a bad one. After seeing what good players do I might be able to do it myself." He added, "I have never heard of a ballplayer who sat on the bench with the Giants turning out badly." Michael Koehler, Jim's grandson, would later identify the truism left unsaid that day: the major leagues were not the place to learn to be a major leaguer.

While the Olympic scandal was still discussed by some, most newsmen shifted their focus to how Jim's athletic prowess might help him on the Giants. They assessed his "marvelous concentrative power," the "steam" he used to throw the discus, his powerful and accurate football throwing arm, his ability to "judge and catch a twisting spiral punt on a dead run," and, of course, his speed. All that was left, it seemed, was for McGraw to teach him how to hit.

The overwhelming consensus among the cognoscenti, however, was that Jim had been grabbed for "the advertising." His popularity was soaring. He was the "cherished prize" in the professional world, said The Sporting News, not because he was expected to be a great ballplayer, but because of the "great publicity his very name would mean." His value was directly linked to the "immediate sympathy which the world of sport almost unanimously felt" for him, which was in turn fed by the public's attitude toward the "ridiculous" system of amateurism. McGraw, once he had been convinced by Warner that "the stories of Jim's dissipation were greatly exaggerated," and that with proper handling "the character of the aborigine should prove exemplary," had decided that Jim would bring in far more at the gate than any amount they would have to pay for him. In New York City the public would always flock to see a celebrity.

The day Jim confirmed he would sign with the Giants, McGraw announced plans for an around-the-world winter baseball tour by the Giants and the Chicago White Sox, a publicity junket cooked up by him and Chicago owner Charles Comiskey a month earlier, when McGraw had passed through Chicago on a fifteen-week tour on the biggest vaudeville network of the day, the Keith circuit. What better global gate attraction than Olympic champion Jim Thorpe?

McGraw had great pride in his ability to transform raw material into fine players. He had also been waiting for a publicity coup to counter the hiring of popular manager Frank Chance by the struggling New York Yankees and the opening of Charles Ebbets's new ballpark in Brooklyn. McGraw, said *The Sporting News*, had landed a "hero," the most lucrative commodity of all.

The experience of Indians in professional baseball was complex and painful. Though Indians were not excluded altogether—as were blacks, dark-skinned Hispanics, and Asian Americans—they "endured an integration experience" in organized baseball that, according to sports historian Jeffrey Beck, at a minimum guaranteed the ignorant nickname "Chief" and at worst subjected them to constant war whoops and such jeers from spectators as "Dog soup" (some Indian tribes had a reputation for eating dogs) and "Back to the reservation!" Indians like the dark-skinned John Meyers, the Giants' catcher, were the first ballplayers of the twentieth century to hear "Nigger!" from major league stands. While the press might have toned down the Wild West rhetoric since the 1890s—with the exception of racist cartoons—the fans had not.

Jim's two Indian baseball peers, John Tortes Meyers and Charles Albert Bender, provided different models of how to handle the big-time arena. Carlisle alumnus Bender was one of the game's great pitchers. In the process of winning over two hundred games in a Hall of Fame career, he won three of the five World Series he pitched for the Philadelphia Athletics, including nine complete World Series games. After leaving the majors in 1917, he had a successful second career as a minor league player and coach into the 1940s. Intense, contained, disciplined, tall, and lean, Bender, who wished to be labeled a pitcher rather than an Indian, later admitted to having been extremely, chronically nervous, only he "couldn't let it out." In the middle of a stream of taunts, Bender would just smile, sometimes tip his cap, in some ways anticipating what *New York Times* sports reporter William C. Rhoden would call the accommodating, "tying oneself in knots" behavior of Jackie Robinson. When Bender did lash back, he called abusive fans "foreigners." His manager, the considerate, soft-spoken Connie Mack, scrupulously addressed Bender by his middle name, Albert, not "Chief."

The big, slow-moving Meyers, by contrast, spoke frankly to the press about being an Indian and how that affected his career on the diamond. One of the great catchers of his era, Meyers, who had attended Dartmouth, told reporters, "This is a strange country to me. I'm a stranger in a strange land." He stood up to John McGraw when necessary, having earned the manager's respect as "the greatest natural hitter" in baseball and an iron man who rarely missed a game. In the 1912 season, which preceded Jim's joining the team, Meyers led the league in on-base percentage and was the first major league catcher to hit for the cycle (a home run, triple, double, and single in the same game). Meyers respected McGraw, wanted to learn from him, and remained grateful that the tough, demanding manager had given him a chance and stuck with him when no one else would.

Both Jim's Indian models adapted to survive and excel, but Indians in the major leagues were usually "not accepted as a member of the team, one of the boys," according to Clifford Kachline, former Baseball Hall of Fame historian. "They were looked on as whites looked on blacks, not of the same class." When blacks and then Hispanics entered the game much later, as Joseph B. Oxendine wrote, there would "quickly [develop] a critical mass" of other such players to provide mutual support. There were few Indians in the majors in 1913, and after the 1920s their numbers would decline significantly. Though his fame and white ancestry would provide a buffer against the worst prejudice, Jim was fortunate to have one fellow Indian on his new team.

"All will now be forgiven and forgotten," said the *Times*, editorializing that Jim now had an "opportunity to become a real hero of the Nation." It wouldn't be easy. He was joining one of the top teams in the major leagues in a town where the press and the fans were infamous for giving no quarter. "[I]t is doubtful," pronounced another New York paper, "that the career of any recruit was ever watched as eagerly as fandom will follow Thorpe's career with the Giants."

Jim knew what the people expected. If he'd done so well in Stockholm, inexperienced as he was in several events, why shouldn't he be a great baseball player? To excel at baseball, wasn't all he needed the best coaching and the best manager? Warner had assured him he'd be in good hands with McGraw. Jim figured he would just master baseball as he had every other sport he played. He trusted his body would do his bidding. He loved teams and being with "the boys." He was used to being liked, appreciated, looked up to. He looked forward to the challenge of playing with the famous Giants stars: Fred

Merkle, Jeff Tesreau, George Wiltse, Fred Snodgrass, Larry Doyle, and Josh Devore. When reporters asked Jim at the contract signing if he'd ever met Meyers, Jim said, "No, I never did. But I guess we'll get along together all right. I always have got along with everybody."

The key person to get along with was his manager. John McGraw personified not only the national pastime but the New York style: tough, fast, big, bad, best. Unlike many managers, he had been an excellent ballplayer himself. His history was baseball's history. The year the American League emerged to challenge the established National League, 1903, was also McGraw's first full season with the Giants and the year of the first World Series between the two major leagues. Before Babe Ruth, McGraw was arguably the most important baseball figure as manager of America's richest and most famous—or infamous—team. Two months after Jim signed with the Giants, *The Baseball Magazine* profiled McGraw as "the greatest manager in organized baseball." From 1899 to 1932, his teams won 2,763 games, the second-highest total to date.

Almost a century later, sportswriter Frank Deford would claim that McGraw and his star pitcher, Christy Mathewson, created modern baseball. Before the Giants, McGraw had been what Deford called "the most famous athlete in America" and the manager of baseball's most colorful team at the time, the Baltimore Orioles. He is credited with developing the squeeze and hit-and-run plays. When the Polo Grounds on the northern edge of Harlem was rebuilt into the nation's largest baseball stadium in 1911, New York, home to three teams, stepped into its long glory days as baseball's mecca. At the center of the nation's media, McGraw was guaranteed exhaustive coverage not only of his team's games but also of his gallivanting in Broadway nightspots with jockeys, fighters, actors, and other Manhattan characters in an era when sportswriters such as Heywood Broun, Grantland Rice, and Damon Runyon were establishing their reputations.

McGraw was nicknamed "Little Napoleon" (for his tactical genius) and "Muggsy" (never said to his face). Five feet, six and one-half inches tall and increasingly chunky, the manager was well-known for his intelligence, consummate understanding of the game and of opposing players, deliberate grandstanding to the home crowd, and his temper. His pugnacious attitude and verbal abuse were legendary. He told Jim that he objected to everything any umpire said because eventually the beleaguered official would give in just to get McGraw off his back. (Jim had much the same approach to football tacklers: knock them hard early and they would be wary for the rest of the game.) "McGraw," said one umpire, "eats gunpowder every morning and washes it down with warm blood."

Equally legendary was his total control of his players on and off the field. McGraw cultivated "awkward, untutored, unskilled" players. He monitored what they ate, insisted on a curfew, and enforced it. He had a predilection for players of "doubtful honesty" and hard drinkers because he felt they needed his direction. And he produced amazing results. In his twenty-nine full seasons with the Giants he led the team to ten National League pennants and three World Series victories, out of nine played. The Giants rarely finished lower than fourth place and were baseball's most financially successful club. McGraw, a "heavy stockholder" in the team, had deep pockets and was more than willing to reach down into them—as he had for Jim—to acquire or trade for talent. Before Babe Ruth, he had baseball's highest salary and was accused of "buying" pennants. "He cares for nothing," wrote *The Baseball Magazine*, "but results." The Giants were probably the most hated team in organized baseball, and McGraw became the model for later tough-guy managers and coaches such as Billy Martin and football's Vince Lombardi.

McGraw was more or less race-blind when it came to baseball talent, but the times required maneuvers. In 1901, hoping to get around the segregation prevalent at the time, he had signed for the Orioles Charlie Grant, an excellent—and light-skinned—second baseman from the all-black Columbia Giants. Taking a name of a creek at random from a hotel map in Hot Springs, Arkansas, the Orioles spring training locale that year, he told Grant: "That's going to be your name from now on, Charlie Tokohama, and you're a full-blooded Cherokee." Clearly, McGraw had no hesitation about having Indians on his team.

Mathewson, considered the first professional athlete as role model for the nation's youth, felt McGraw's system worked only if a player bent "without question, to [his] slightest command." "Every play made by a Giant," said Mathewson, "has been ordered by McGraw," thus creating players who were not trained to innovate or play imaginatively. For an athlete like Jim, this sort of control could be a problem.

McGraw's recent and well-publicized experience with pitcher Rube Marquard, however, may have influenced Jim's decision to put himself in the manager's hands. McGraw had bought Marquard's contract from Indianapolis in 1908 for $11,000, an unheard-of amount for a minor league player. When Marquard started off badly, the press labeled him "the $11,000 lemon." McGraw admitted to Marquard that too much was expected of him too soon and offered reassurance for the long term. It took two years, but Marquard developed into a star. The drinking habits of another talented pitcher, Bugs Raymond, who died in 1912 at the age of thirty, had proved too much even for McGraw. And it was Raymond's example that reporters brought up in their coverage of the Thorpe signing: had McGraw hesitated on Jim because he feared a similar problem?

Jim got off to a rocky start, arriving late for spring training in Marlin, Texas. After competing in a track and field event in Boston, he had returned to Carlisle to collect his uniform and then missed his train connection in Harrisburg. "Thorpe Lost by Giants on the Way to Texas" was a headline the next day. Once he caught up with the team well-wishers deluged him all along the way. In Marlin, he was received by more than the usual number of reporters on site.

Until the 1920s, when it was supplanted by Florida, Texas was the favored destination for major league spring training. Ever since McGraw had seen the dramatic benefits to the Orioles of an eight-week spring training in Macon, Georgia, in 1894 (they won the pennant that year), he was convinced that winners started the season in peak condition. In 1908 he chose this sleepy town of four thousand people, twenty-six miles southeast of Waco, in part because its isolation made it easier for him to exert control over the team. "Considering the large quantities of alcohol imbibed by players of that era," wrote one baseball historian, the spa amenities, as well as the difficulty of buying alcohol in "dry" Texas counties, made spring training also a chance to detoxify. San Antonio, Waco, Fort Worth, and Dallas were accessible by train for exhibition games against Texas League teams in an era when spring training featured barnstorming tours. The Marlin townspeople welcomed the team each year with teas, dinners, fish fries, cotillions, and other entertainments. Once, when Marquard fired a pistol through his hotel window at a billboard across the street and the sheriff tried to arrest him, McGraw reminded the lawman that "the Giants put this town on the map, and the Giants can just as quickly wipe it off by leaving."

The players worked out at Emerson Field after walking four miles south of town down a railroad track. Jim's first day, February 19, elicited the newspaper headline "Thorpe Surprises McGraw." Thorpe "surely is fast for a big man," the manager told reporters. "I can see no reason why he should not hit them on the nose as Chief Meyers does if he chokes his bat and drives the ball with his wrist and forearm." McGraw said that for the present Jim would do utility work and learn the game. Subsequent reports from Marlin continued positive, though Jim was often unable to start practice with the rest of the team because of the eager press corps. "He is afraid to be misunderstood by the public," Meyers said. McGraw was reported as thinking Jim "the brainiest recruit" he'd ever seen and ambitious, though he was not yet convinced the rookie was ready for prime time. Jim appeared both "over-anxious" and "over-confident." After ten days, in the first practice game, Jim was nervous and struck out. Glaring at the umpire, Jim took exception to the call—not always a wise thing for a rookie to do.

The first week in March, *The Sporting News* reported that McGraw had in Jim "all that a ball player should be." In a game between the first and second teams in Marlin a week later, Jim hit a long home run off Mathewson. McGraw, reported *The New York Times*, "cried out [it] was the longest hit in the world." The team doctor, meanwhile, was awestruck by Jim's consumption of food, especially breakfast: "This is a sample of his order: Grapefruit, cereal, half a dozen fried eggs, with ham, a sirloin steak with onions, two orders of fried potatoes, country sausage, wheat cakes, rolls and a pot of coffee. This was at 10 in the morning. By 12:30 Jim was always ready to tackle the menu again."

Jim was going through the motions, but emotionally he was struggling. "I remember, very late one night Jim came in and woke me up," recalled Meyers, his roommate in Marlin that spring. "He was crying and tears were rolling down his cheeks. 'You know, Chief,' he

Hiram G. Thorp,
Jim's white grandfather from
Connecticut (*Jim Thorpe Home,
Oklahoma Historical Society*)

No-ten-o-quah/Wind
Before a Rain (or Storm),
Jim's Sac grandmother
(*Jim Thorpe Home,
Oklahoma Historical Society*)

Hiram Phillip Thorp,
Jim's volatile, violent father
*(Cumberland County Historical Society,
Carlisle, Pennsylvania)*

Charlotte Vieux Thorp,
Jim's staunch
Potawatomi-French mother
(Jim Thorpe Association)

Jim, on the left, and his beloved twin, Charlie *(Jim Thorpe Home, Oklahoma Historical Society)*

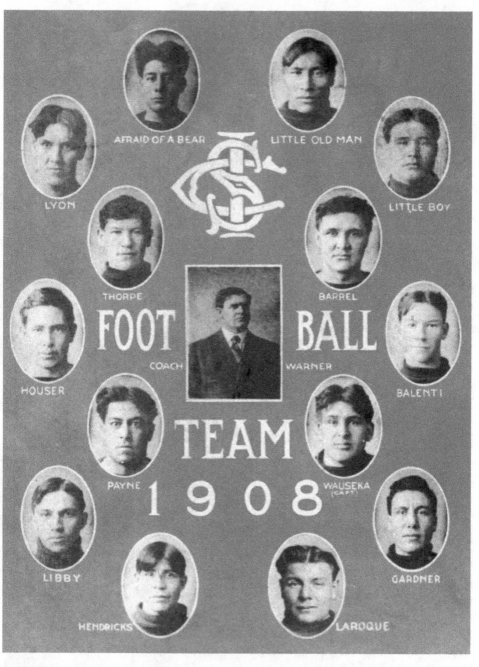

Carlisle Indian Industrial School 1908 football team *(Cumberland County Historical Society, Carlisle, Pennsylvania)*

Glenn Scobey "Pop" Warner,
the brilliant, opportunistic
Carlisle football coach,
1899–1903 and 1907–1914
*(Cumberland County Historical
Society, Carlisle, Pennsylvania)*

The idealized Carlisle Indian
football player; drawing by
William "Lone Star" Dietz
and originally printed
as a small poster
*(Cumberland County Historical
Society, Carlisle, Pennsylvania)*

The buildings and spacious grounds of the Carlisle Indian Industrial School, c. 1884, preserved today at the Army War College as a national landmark *(Cumberland County Historical Society, Carlisle, Pennsylvania)*

Marianne Moore, the future poet and Jim's favorite teacher at Carlisle *(Cumberland County Historical Society, Carlisle, Pennsylvania)*

Jim, far left, leading in the 120-yard hurdles at a state track meet, Harrisburg, Pennsylvania, c. 1909 *(Cumberland County Historical Society, Carlisle, Pennsylvania)*

Celtic Park, New York City: Jim at the 1912 pentathlon Olympic trials *(Robert W. Wheeler Collection)*

The running broad jump, the first event of Jim's gold medal pentathlon performance at the 1912 Olympics in Stockholm *(Robert W. Wheeler Collection)*

Putting the shot, the third event of Jim's gold medal decathlon performance at the Olympics *(Cumberland County Historical Society, Carlisle, Pennsylvania)*

Jim, wearing a victor's wreath, after being presented with his pentathlon gold medal and
the challenge trophy—a bronze bust of Sweden's soldier-king, Charles XII *(Cumberland
County Historical Society, Carlisle, Pennsylvania)*

Pop Warner, Louis Tewanima, and a reluctant Jim on the grandstand at Biddle Field, Carlisle, Pennsylvania, at the celebration honoring the athletes' return from Stockholm, August 16, 1912 *(Cumberland County Historical Society, Carlisle, Pennsylvania)*

Rear view of Jim in an athletic supporter, c. 1912. His body measurements were taken and publicized after the Olympics like those of a prize specimen. *(Cumberland County Historical Society, Carlisle, Pennsylvania)*

A typical newspaper cartoon at the time of the Olympic scandal in January 1913; the "Amateur Athletic Union" is about to commit the sacrifice. *(Library of Congress)*

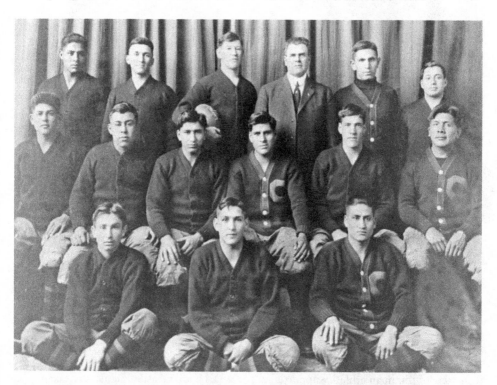

Captain Jim and the 1912 Carlisle football team. Alex Arcasa: front row, far right; Pete Calac: middle row, far left; Joe Guyon: middle row, second from right; Gus Welch: back row, second from left *(Cumberland County Historical Society, Carlisle, Pennsylvania)*

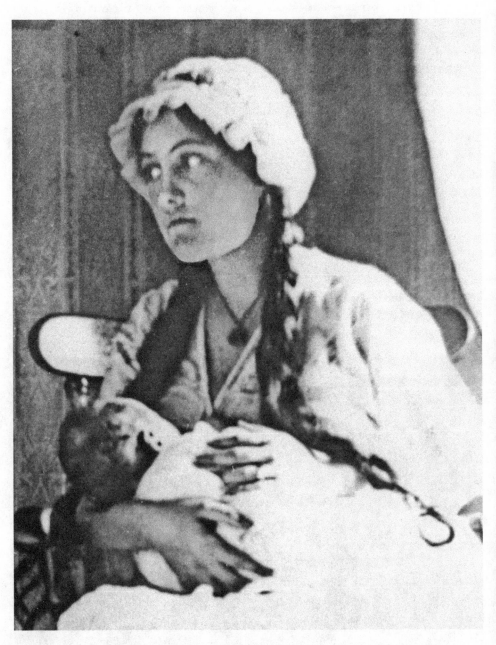

Jim's first wife, Iva Miller Thorpe, with their first child, James Francis Thorpe, Jr., c. 1915 *(Robert W. Wheeler Collection)*

RECEIVED AT

273P RB 11.COLLECT

L CARLISLE PA. JAN 28 13

AUGUST HERMAN   CINTI EXHIBIT CO.

CINTI.O

WILL CONSIDER PROPOSITION AND SIGN WITH CLUB MAKING BEST

OFFER

JAMES THORPE

4 45P

Telegram from Jim to August Herrmann, owner of the Cincinnati Reds baseball team, as major league offers flooded into Carlisle in early 1913 *(National Baseball Hall of Fame Library, Cooperstown, New York)*

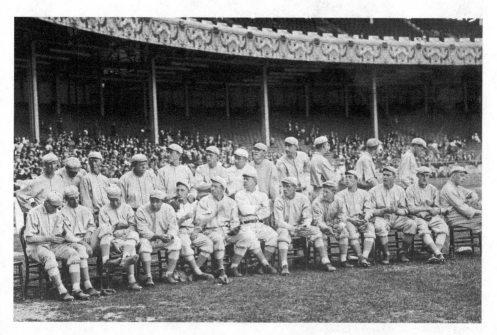

The 1913 New York Giants at the Polo Grounds, New York City. Rookie Jim is fifth from right in the back row. Manager John McGraw is seventh from right in the front row; pitcher Christy Mathewson to his right. *(Library of Congress)*

John "Muggsy" McGraw, the brilliant, tough manager of the New York Giants *(National Baseball Hall of Fame Library, Cooperstown, New York)*

Bloomington: Jim as assistant football
coach, Indiana University, 1915
*(Courtesy: Indiana University Archives
{1916 Arbutus})*

said, 'the King of Sweden gave me those trophies, he gave them to me. But they took them away from me, even though the guy who finished second refused to take them. They're mine, Chief, I won them fair and square.' It broke his heart and he never really recovered." Jim knew the trophies were not his to keep, and that the runners-up had not refused the medals. But he felt pain and humiliation just the same. A vital self-possession had been undermined.

The hype and premature optimism of spring training soon gave way. It was said McGraw didn't have enough time to develop Jim for the 1913 season. He was quoted as describing the rookie as "the rawest recruit" he had ever seen. *The Sporting News* suggested with cruel sarcasm that everybody "share" Thorpe: no circuit would pay twice to see him play, so why not "pass him on" in turn through the two major leagues, down the high minors, and on through the "entire classification" until, late in the season, he might "pull some struggling Class D organization out of the financial hole"?

As the Giants left Marlin in early April, in a "bristling interview" McGraw admitted Jim was green but insisted he had displayed "real, bed-rock ability which will develop." Mathewson praised Jim's potential, saying he had the "athletic instinct." He said Jim showed "great discrimination" at the plate, though he struggled badly with the curveball, and real promise playing first base. Mathewson predicted that in a year Jim would be a .300 hitter.

Throughout the season, rumors were floated about Jim's being traded. McGraw responded by citing Jim's improvement in practice at hitting a curve, or praised his remarkable speed, which led now to McGraw trying him in the outfield. When Jim connected, he hit the ball harder than any other player on the team. His problem was consistency. In the field, he had trouble judging long fly balls. And he still was unable to capitalize on his speed in running the bases.

Jim made his major league debut on opening day, April 14, as a pinch hitter. His first full game as a Giant was not until September 29, when the season was drawing to a close, against the Boston Braves. The Giants had already won the pennant, so McGraw put together a makeshift team to play a doubleheader that day. Jim hit a home run. In total, Jim played in nineteen games in the 1913 season, with only thirty-five times at bat—not enough. William J. "Lord"

Byron, the National League "singing umpire" known for making up little songs at the plate, taunted Jim after he let a third strike sail by:

You'll have to learn, Jim, before you're older
You can't hit the ball with the bat on your shoulder.

Jim's batting average was a paltry .143.

Three days before the World Series began between the Giants and the Athletics, in the second game of a double-header that day against the Phillies, McGraw started Jim in center field and put him at the top of the batting order. "The minute [Jim] stepped from the dugout," said one reporter, the infamous New York "grandstand managers" started their jeers: " 'Pick a bat that hasn't a hole in it!' " Jim struck out twice and hit two weak grounders at Grover Cleveland Alexander, a great pitcher. "Each time Thorpe came to bat," the reporter continued, "there was a repetition of the grim humor in the grandstand, and each time he started back for the bench, there followed the jeers, and by the facial expression and actions Thorpe showed how keenly it hurt him."

The day before the first game of the Series, during a "field day" at the Polo Grounds, Hans Lobert, a lightning-fast third baseman for the Phillies, ran a 100-yard dash against Jim at the Polo Grounds and won. McGraw lost a $100 bet. The Giants went on to lose the series.

Whether Jim had the makings or not of a good player became almost a side issue. Jim had had so little playing time during his first major league season not because he was a rookie—benching a newcomer for a while was common with McGraw—but because the world's finest athlete and its greatest baseball manager had not clicked, upbeat press announcements to the contrary. Despite Jim's publicity value, McGraw came to resent the celebrity attention he attracted. Jim had "a terrific personal appeal to people and was just like a big overgrown kid," said sometime teammate Al Schacht, "in the same mold as Babe Ruth." He had joined the Giants as a star; he didn't need the manager to make him one. The old stories about Jim's supposed lackadaisical attitude started to surface again, however, fed by McGraw, who had begun drinking more, which only made him more touchy.

McGraw's insistence on total obedience grated on Jim from the beginning. Warner had allowed Jim to let loose from time to time; he knew how far to push him and, in any case, Jim excelled so easily at track and football that Warner had had, by comparison, relatively little to do. McGraw hovered. "His way of telling me when to swing and when to take one—all that McGraw stuff," Jim said, "bothered" him. He wasn't the only one bothered. "What kind of league is this where the manager can tell you what bat to use?" future Hall of Famer Edd Roush would complain in 1916. McGraw secretly designated Meyers to read Jim's mail, and when Jim discovered a letter from Iva, opened, in Meyers's locker, he "exploded."

Reports were also circulating that Jim—on a team he would describe as "the wildest, fightingest, most bloodthirsty bunch" of players he'd known—stayed out late drinking during spring training, barely making it to practice the next morning. When McGraw advised Jim to avoid alcohol because no Indian knew how to drink, Jim shot back, "What about the Irish?" McGraw bristled. "Don't get smart with me," he said. When Jim showed up at the ballpark only five minutes before a game, McGraw was enraged. In May, after the Giants lost a close game, Jim asked McGraw why he was being kept on the team since he never got a chance to play. Jim said he didn't need to be berated to be a good player and that McGraw was just a little blowhard. The manager went for him, saying, "Why, you Indian . . ." Jim started to go for McGraw; luckily, his teammates held him back.

McGraw defended Jim when teammates gave him a hard time, but was less understanding when Jim's pranks jeopardized players. One night Jim dangled teammate Schacht, later to become known as the "Clown Prince of Baseball," out a fourteenth-floor hotel room by his heels. Another time, Jim and pitcher Jeff Tesreau were in the outfield in a friendly scuffle, when Jim pinned Tesreau with an armlock. The next day Tesreau had a sore arm and couldn't pitch. McGraw blew up, called Jim in, and threatened to fine him if he roughhoused with any of the other players. "I said that was all right with me," recalled Jim, "because I didn't want to roughhouse with them anyway, but they were always challenging me."

McGraw couldn't resist pushing "the world's greatest athlete," *especially* when he showed improvement. Jim was too old to easily tolerate such treatment and not mature enough to know he had to.

.   .   .

In early September 1913, newspapers across the country announced that Jim Thorpe, twenty-six, was engaged to be married to the "beautiful Cherokee Indian maiden" Iva Margaret Miller, twenty. The wedding would take place in Carlisle as soon as the World Series was over. Their honeymoon would be the world tour of the Giants and White Sox, scheduled to start in Cincinnati on October 18. Photographs showed Iva's dark hair parted down the middle and pulled back in a chignon at the nape of her neck, a reserved smile on her face; Jim wore a high-collared shirt, tie, and suit jacket, his hair slicked down. He smiled warmly, as happy a man as he'd ever been.

The *Los Angeles Times* and other papers reported that Jim's friends were "astounded" by the news of the engagement. Jim had been so "close-mouthed" that even his close friend Rose Roberts was flabbergasted. "It must have all come from the other side, from Iva," she said. Iva would tell her daughters that but for a flip of a coin in 1911 she would have married Jim's friend and quarterback, Gus Welch. But by 1913, Jim had proved himself to her and she, by her steadfast support, to him.

Because both of Iva's parents were dead and she was underage, Moses Friedman agreed to be appointed by the court as Iva's guardian—and to escort her down the aisle. She and Jim went to the Cumberland County marriage office, where Iva declared on the license that her "color" was "Red," her father's was "white," and her mother's "white Red"; she had just told Jim, however, that her Indian heritage was a pretense. Jim listed himself and both his parents as "Red."

Crowds lined the streets near the church as the couple was married the next day, October 14, at St. Patrick's Catholic Church, which Jim and Iva had attended as students. Welch was Jim's best man. Teammates Joe Guyon and Pete Calac and Jim's brother, Ed Thorpe, were among the ushers. After the "formal and elaborate" ceremony in the church, filled with uniformed Carlisle cadets and female students, there was a wedding breakfast and a reception at the superintendent's house, newly and lavishly renovated by the athletic fund. The 1914 football team was out in force to celebrate. The school band played on the central lawn, and later there was a dance in the gym to honor the bride and groom. Their favorite song, played frequently that night, was the 1899 waltz "You Tell Me Your Dream and I'll Tell You Mine":

> *I had a dream, dear*
> *You had one, too.*
> *Mine was the best dream*
> *Because it was of you.*

The newlyweds left Carlisle for what promised to be an epic honeymoon. The world tour had been conceived of by McGraw and Comiskey to mark the twenty-fifth anniversary of the first and only such previous tour, led in 1889–90 by Albert G. Spalding and his Chicago White Stockings. And it couldn't hurt to expose more of the world to America's pastime.

The two organizers were an unlikely pair. Comiskey, owner of the White Sox—and the ballpark named for him—was reportedly both the richest man and the biggest tightwad in baseball. His stingy payment of his players would be a contributory factor in the 1919 Black Sox game-fixing scandal. McGraw, in contrast, freely spent his own money to finance his half of the tour. But the two men agreed that together they could enhance the reputations of their teams and make a lot of money. The American leg of the tour would finance the globe-trotting second leg, with exhibition game stops scheduled in Tokyo, Shanghai, Hong Kong, Manila, Brisbane, Sydney, Melbourne, Colombo, Cairo, Rome, Nice, Paris, and London.

Members of other teams were added to the rosters. The umpire was the National League's Bill Klem, the incorruptible future Hall of Famer McGraw most loved to hate. A filmmaker and a cameraman were with the group to make the first full-length sports documentary, *Giants–White Sox World Tour.* Reporters from *The New York Times* and the *Chicago Record-Herald* covered what *The Baseball Magazine* called a "landmark in baseball history." McGraw would telegraph stories back to the *Times* as well.

From the opening game on October 18 at Redland Field in Cincinnati, until November 19, when the teams boarded the RMS *Empress of Japan* in Victoria, British Columbia, the tour traveled on a luxurious chartered train through cities including Peoria, Tulsa, Dallas, Houston, Marlin, Abilene, Los Angeles, San Francisco, Sacramento, and Seattle. At virtually every stop, local Indians came out in force to see Jim and Meyers. The population of tiny towns like Blue Rapids, Kansas, quadrupled on game day. More than 10,000 fans showed up for one of three games played in San Francisco. The tour had taken in about $100,000 long before it reached Seattle. Though most of the more noteworthy players had not signed on for the foreign part of the tour, Jim had; in fact, he was the international draw, the only player foreign audiences would recognize

Iva kept a diary, "My Trip Abroad." In a clear, even hand, she wrote about each new port after they crossed the Pacific. She and her husband befriended Detroit Tigers outfielder Sam Crawford, a future Hall of Famer, and his wife. The diary entries show frequent affectionate references to Jim, though at one point she worries "if only he would have more confidence in himself." For Christmas he gave her a "lovely gold inlaid tortoise shell dressing table set." She naturally did not attend the stag banquets held for the athletes at each stop, but she would remember the first-class hotels—the Heliopolis Palace in Cairo, the Bristol in Rome, and the St. James D'Albany in Paris—and receptions and special excursions all her life. Sightseeing, shopping, dining, footmen, "golden elevators," maids, butlers, vintage wine, British tea magnate Sir Thomas Lipton in Ceylon, the khedive in Egypt, dukes and counts in Italy, American consuls, George Kessler (the "Champagne King"), the pope, millionaires in Paris, King George V—the trip was fabulous.

Melbourne's lovely parks captivated Iva, as did Jim's performance in right field; he "did some dandy good playing alright," she wrote. She soon developed a casual attitude toward her husband's fame. When they went swimming near Brisbane, a large crowd gathered around the pool. "Pshaw," Iva wrote. "Why should we worry—never see them again, and if we did wouldn't remember them or they us." Jim bought her a canary and drolly named it "Oh, Sing." He taught his bride some tango steps. As the ship neared Fremantle, Jim audaciously kissed Comiskey, to his surprise, in a game of follow-the-leader, and then hugged "this and that one," wrote Iva, adding, "[Of] course we had to do the same."

On January 14, the bride noted that she and her husband had been married three months, "and we are still living together, and as happy as can be." Jim didn't keep a diary, but after the anguish of the last year and his fundamental loneliness since losing both his parents and living so far from home, to find himself married and traveling around the world with a doting and attractive wife must have felt wonderful. His social awkwardness was smoothed over by Iva's ease and graciousness. She enjoyed being the wife of a famous person; he relaxed and enjoyed his status, too. Iva's charm helped him navigate the constant social pressure of talking, dining, playing, and traveling with a group that was more sophisticated than he was.

By February, the last month of the tour, Jim and his bride were thoroughly domesticated. The teams played underneath the Pyramids, where Spalding's White Stockings had played twenty-five years before. As the ship crossed the Mediterranean for Italy, Iva did the laundry, studied French with Jim to prepare for Paris, and wrote that she wanted "very badly" to see the ruins of Pompeii (which she did, the next day). The Catholics in the group had an audience at the Vatican with Pope Pius X, who blessed them. The papal secretary of state also received the party and was, reported *The Baseball Magazine*, "especially interested in Jim Thorpe, and congratulated him on his wonderful success at Stockholm." Iva was thoroughly impressed: "Everyone very anxious to meet" Jim, she wrote, "and they seem to know all about him." Her family—her brothers Earl and Clyde and her sister Grace—could hardly think she'd made a mistake now.

G. W. Axelson, who had been sending back a stream of coverage to the *Chicago Record-Herald*, wrote: "It does not often fall to the lot of an ordinary human being to leave a trail of hero worship some 35,000 miles long." Jim was "apparently known wherever dwell people who can read," he wrote. "He is pointed out in the hotels, on the fields and on the streets. . . . His career is an open book in Japan, in the English possessions, and of course the Philippines. He is no stranger to China." The unanimous opinion around the world was "that an injustice had been done to him." Jim was everywhere praised for his unassuming manner and his pretty, vivacious wife with the "fascinating smile." Their foreign hosts were startled to find that neither of the Thorpes had dark skin, indeed didn't look particularly Indian,

and revised their idea of the "noble redman." Away from the pressure
of New York City, Jim's stardom didn't seem to bother him as much,
no doubt because Iva was at his side to deflect some of the attention.

The tour made its final stops in Nice, Paris, and London, where
Jim and Iva continued to be mobbed. On February 28, the players
and their entourage boarded the *Lusitania* in Liverpool for the final
leg home. The Giants who didn't make the foreign tour had already
started spring training in Marlin for the 1914 season. The big story of
the spring was the new, cash-rich Federal League, busy both at home
and along the tour trying to poach players. As the ship docked in New
York harbor on March 6, Federal League representatives were in the
crowd, handing out cards to coveted world tour players. The line of
automobiles taking the players to the Imperial Hotel turned into a
de facto parade through the snowy Manhattan streets, and the tour
concluded with a dinner at the Biltmore Hotel.

Only two tour players defected to the new league. Jim wasn't interested; besides, he still had two seasons on his contract. With more
playing time on the tour, Jim's game had markedly improved. "Jim
Thorpe has developed into a corking player," McGraw was quoted
as saying in *The Sporting News*, "both from a hitting standpoint and
as a fielder." Personal animosities wouldn't matter if Jim could help
the team. Axelson had been so impressed by Jim's improvements he
wrote that Jim promised to be "the most sensational baseball player of
1914." Jim was now feeling like a real Giant. The next day, March 7,
in Fayetteville, George Herman "Babe" Ruth, a rookie in spring
training with his first professional team, the minor league Baltimore
Orioles, hit a long home run into a cornfield; it sailed past the white
post that had been placed to mark a homer Jim had hit from the same
diamond a few years before.

While Jim and Iva were on tour, matters at their old school had
come to a crisis point. On January 7, 1914, Gus Welch, student body
president, handed a petition to Pennsylvania congressman Arthur R.
Rupley at his home in Carlisle. The document, addressed to Commissioner of Indian Affairs Cato Sells, was signed by 276 male students,
including fifty-five athletes, and requested a government investigation
of their school. The situation—an erratic superintendent, lax disci-

pline, egregious behavior by teachers and other adults in charge—had become so intolerable that both the girls and the boys had embraced the idea of a petition that would make its way to the desk of the secretary of the interior. An official report would describe that "an open break and rebellion" was imminent. Anger at the way Jim had been treated by Warner and Friedman also prompted several of the students to act. Gus Welch had spearheaded the petition, and the varsity football players would be the key witnesses against Warner.

At about the same time, Sells received a letter from the Indian Rights Association. "There are rumors afloat," it read, "reflecting seriously upon the moral atmosphere of the [Carlisle] school. . . . Let the school once acquire a bad name, and its future usefulness is problematical."

Rumors of an investigation had been circulating for some time. Western senators and congressmen regularly challenged the school's annual appropriation, seeing no point now in shipping Indian students east. There had always been resentment of the nebulous status of the school, especially when it beat schools like Harvard. Many suspected that the Olympic scandal had finally tipped the scale; certainly the scrutiny it brought to the institution had not helped.

On January 19, Interior Secretary Franklin K. Lane dispatched an inspector to Carlisle with instructions to make a preliminary investigation specifically of the athletic fund and individual student accounts, and generally of the dormitories, industrial shops, the farm, and every activity of the school. The inspector stayed for two weeks, talking to employees, department heads, administrators, and students. He then presented his findings in a report to the Joint Congressional Commission to Investigate Indian Affairs in Washington. On February 6, two senators and two congressmen on the eight-man commission arrived in Carlisle, unannounced, and met at the local YMCA for two days of closed hearings. When they left, the commission had heard from sixty-one witnesses and compiled 692 pages of typewritten transcript and commentary.

Their findings revealed a cesspool of deceit, cruelty, and deprivation. The inspector's report cited "lack of discipline, morals, lack of interest and proper management in practically every department of said school, lack of sufficient food for the student body . . . disrespect and contempt in which Supt. Friedman is held by the student body, as also by a majority of the employees." Boys were beaten with baseball bats and, in the most egregious example, a Potawatomi girl was hit by a teacher and the matron behind closed doors more than forty times with a piece of wood. Concealed by the administration from the outside world, drinking among the student body, sex among some students, illegitimate children, and gangs had developed since Pratt's departure in 1904. The school "misrepresented" itself by claiming it offered nonexistent courses and did not keep the students in the shops long enough to learn any trades. The original principle of the Outing Program had been "lost"; students were not placed with an appropriate family, but were simply hired hands. The school farm produced eggs, milk, and pork, but the students—except for the football players—ate only gravy, tea, and occasionally bread.

The investigators uncovered a scheme in which the school had been submitting receipts to the government for fictitious student railway tickets, with the reimbursement going to the superintendent. The report on the athletic fund was even more damning. "[It] has caused more to disrupt, to disorganize said school and create a bad feeling and a feeling of unrest and injustice among the student body than all else combined. Everything," the report affirmed, "has been made subservient to football and athletics." Hundreds of checks had been made out to athletes. The slush fund was totally controlled by Warner, who, concluded the commissioners, might as well have been the real superintendent of Carlisle, an employee accountable to no one but himself. The commission noted that, in addition to his $4,000 salary, Warner was "furnished with a comfortable house, heat, light, fuel, and water" and had all his other expenses paid. The commission chair, Arkansas senator Joe T. Robinson, got Warner to testify that, in fact, all the money in the athletic fund—$25,000—belonged to "the boys who compose the team."

The most severe portion in the report was reserved for Warner's behavior as coach. Members of the varsity football team, including Jim's close friends Joe Guyon and Pete Calac, testified either in person or by affidavit against their coach. They said that Warner habitually called players "a son of a bitch" or "you God damn bone head," often in front of other students and spectators. He had nothing to do with his players after they stopped playing football. He kept them in the dark about how much money they earned. Warner hit players for making minor mistakes. He beefed up the team with nonstudent players: Henry Roberts was paid $75 a month to play football for the 1911 season and did not attend any classes. Warner sold tickets in hotel lobbies prior to games and pocketed the money. He was thought to be participating in some kind of "rake-off" with the athletic moneys because the accounts had been so concealed. Gus Welch considered him "a man of no principle . . . no man for the place he holds." The affidavits of Welch and another player stated that Warner—and Friedman, Welch said—had written the "confession" for Jim to copy that was sent to the AAU in January 1913. They wanted it clear who had abandoned their teammate when he needed their help.

The commission recommended that Friedman and Warner be dismissed. Friedman was fired, but Warner, an employee of the incorporated athletic association, couldn't be expelled by those with oversight in Washington. He accepted a coaching offer from the University of Pittsburgh before the end of the school year. He denied all charges, claiming in his testimony and for the rest of his life they were part of a vendetta created by a disaffected minority. The $25,000, he later said, was turned over to the Indian Bureau and he never knew what became of it. If there was more drunkenness and less discipline at Carlisle now than in former years, it was because the boys were "not so easy to manage as they used to be," he told the commissioners. He did not say for the record that such behavior and shady practices on the part of coaches were common at Harvard, Yale, and Princeton, private universities immune from congressional investigation.

Warner went on to build his career as though nothing had happened. His Pitt team was undefeated for four years. Later, from 1924 to 1932, his Stanford Indians—the mascot was his idea—went to three Rose Bowls. On New Year's Day 1925, Stanford famously lost, 27–0, to Knute Rockne's Notre Dame and its Four Horsemen backfield. When Stanford later lost five times in a row to Warner's nemesis, USC, he left for Temple University, where he remained until his retirement to Palo Alto in 1938. Over almost fifty years, his NCAA record is 319 wins, 106 losses, and 32 ties. His Carlisle record: 114 wins, 42 losses, 8 ties.

The highly articulate passion and anger of the students who led the protest against Warner and the other guilty parties were noteworthy. They had learned Pratt's lessons of pride, leadership, self-sufficiency, and survival well, if they had needed to learn them at all. Carlisle was their school; they wanted to be proud of it. They, who were supposed to be in need of civilization from whites, were instead horrified at the behavior and corruption they saw. The game that Welch and his cohorts had mastered had indeed produced independent-thinking, strategic leaders, as its founders had hoped; but no one had expected a group of brilliant Indian athletes to demand the ouster of their game-winning white coach. "Are [the students] proud of the institution?" one of the commission members asked a student. "I do not know," was the reply. "I cannot speak for the rest of them, for myself I would be ashamed to take my diploma away from here . . . because the public are getting the impression we are not a good kind of people."

The students had wanted to save their school, but in the end their initiative helped to kill it. In 1918, the Carlisle barracks were requisitioned for use as a military hospital and the school was closed. The victorious 1912 football season, following on the attention Jim's Olympic triumphs had brought to Carlisle, ironically helped seal the school's demise. The uppity little school had got out of hand. By 1917, the Carlisle football team would lose (to Heisman's Georgia Tech) by its worst score ever, 98–0.

When people asked where were the new Thorpes, Mt. Pleasants, Calacs, Exendines, and Guyons, part of the answer was in the numbers. The 1920 U.S. Census figures show a Native American population of less than a quarter million people compared to more than ten million African Americans and ninety-four million whites. The Carlisle Indian Industrial School had functioned as a concentrated training ground for a very talented but small minority. At its best it made possible a series of remarkable achievements. The focus may have been on athletics, but fine work was done by many students in academics, the arts, and music; several students joined John Philip Sousa's famous band. Carlisle's worst legacy is revealed in the empathic pain evident in the tears and withdrawal of many Indian students today who visit the student graveyard and the Carlisle school campus, preserved as a historic site on the grounds of what is now the Army War College.

The closing of Carlisle largely erased the white memory of it. No alumni newsletters or reunions would perpetuate the Carlisle story. Instead, graduates would remember the school orally, in the Indian manner. "The stories of the school itself," said alumna Laura Mangold, "like all of the heroes, like Thorpe . . . their successes were told in little stories and handed down to each other . . . like a legend that gets carried on and on." When the public had forgotten the details of Carlisle, the names of its other great athletes, the brilliant plays, it would remember Jim Thorpe. He was the brightest distillation of a conveniently forgotten past.

Jim never spoke ill of Carlisle and, along with many others, retained a fondness for the school. Of course, as an athlete, he hadn't experienced the worst of it. Yet he missed not only a chance to be a part of a remarkable event in American Indian history, but also an opportunity to step back with his teammates and assess Carlisle and Warner.

By the 1930s, nearly half of all Indian children attending school would be enrolled in off-reservation boarding schools or boarding and day schools on reservations. Native scholars have now begun to trace the effect of what University of Michigan psychology professor Joseph Gone, a Gros Ventre, called the "unmonitored and unchecked physical and sexual aggression perpetrated by [boarding] school officials against a vulnerable and institutionalized population" on the alcoholism, violence, and sexual abuse in twenty-first-century Indian communities.

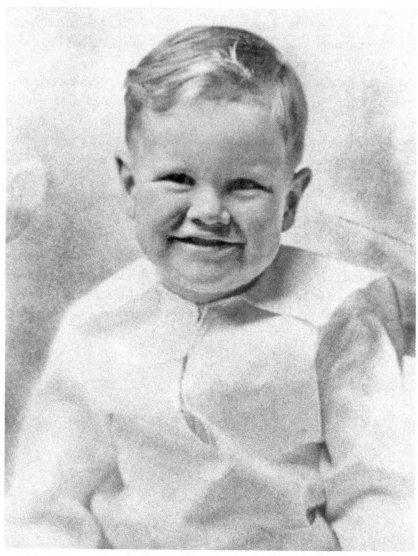

James Francis Thorpe, Jr., c. 1916

JIM AND IVA's first child and son, "Junior." He and his father were of a kind—laughing, playing, teasing, like twins.

CHAPTER EIGHT

The Majors and Ohio

1915–1919

Son, never take your eyes off the wingback.

—JIM THORPE

Jim returned from the world tour to a changed baseball landscape. In 1914, team rosters were reduced from twenty-five to twenty-one as competition from the Federal League, the looming war, and the shift of the public's leisure dollars to the automobile, movies, and other sports, including golf, all contributed to a fall in minor and major league baseball attendance.

Despite his performance on the tour, the 1914 season was a step down for Jim. He played thirty games, was at bat only thirty-one times (even fewer than the previous year), and hit .194. It was impossible to learn and improve with so few plate appearances. "I felt like a sitting hen," Jim complained, "not a ball player." When someone asked what his tribal name was, he answered, "Bench Warmer." The team did not win a pennant for the first time in four years.

In mid-March 1915, the *Los Angeles Times* reported from Marlin that Jim was slated to start in right field, beginning with an exhibition game in San Antonio. Sitting around the dinner table in Waco one night with a bunch of "Giants camp followers," as Damon Runyon described them in his column that week, one remarked on a curveball that Jim had "chased a block." McGraw piped up, playing the press: "Would you fellows be surprised if Jim got into my outfield and hit about .325 this season?" According to Runyon, the group responded skeptically. "All right then," said McGraw, "this is the year Jim gets his real chance to show what he can do. . . . He can hit with anybody. . . . Moreover, he can field. His main weakness is running the bases. In spite of his wonderful speed, he does not get the proper break. . . . I never saw a man so desperately anxious to succeed, and that's the kind I like to help along." Whatever McGraw's animosity for Jim, he was showing belief in him long after others had given up. Presumably, Jim had come to spring training with a new attitude and was showing McGraw some concrete improvement. Of course, McGraw also wanted fans to keep coming to the Polo Grounds in the hope of seeing Jim Thorpe finally play well.

But 1915 was not the year for Jim to shine, or the Giants. Meyers, Marquard, Snodgrass, and Mathewson were not what they had been. After what *The Baseball Magazine* called a "gorgeous start" came "one of the most stunning things of recent baseball history . . . the thorough downfall of the Giants." For the first and only time when McGraw managed for a full season, the Giants wound up last.

On May 12, Jim was shipped across the Hudson to play for the AA (the highest minor league classification at the time) International League Jersey City Skeeters. On July 24, to fill in for a player who had broken his leg, he was shifted again to the same league's Harrisburg Senators, who had just moved from Newark. "Add another to the passing of the red man," one reporter wrote. "Thorpe did well at the start . . . until the pitchers got on to his weakness—curve balls. From that moment on, the poor Indian never looked at anything else." It was now being said that Jim didn't have the mental capacity to outguess pitchers. On September 1, he was back with the Giants in his usual role as pinch hitter amid reports that he had been let go by the Skeeters for unruly conduct—generally, for being a "disturbing influence" on the Jersey City team. McGraw had to take him back. A Pittsburgh paper printed a poem, "O, the Poor Injun!" about Jim's contract. It concluded with the lines "All I want's an iron-clad contract / To just sit around like Thorpe."

Whatever his conduct off the field, Jim worked hard that summer in the minors. In ninety-six games, with 370 at bats, he hit a combined .303. The day after he rejoined the Giants, he played spectacularly in a game against the Phillies. With two singles and a double, scoring two runs, he "put the Giants on their feet," said *The New York Times*, as they won, 6–5. The paper suggested the entire New York team should have been farmed out to Harrisburg.

Nineteen fifteen brought Jim an entirely new kind of happiness that had nothing to do with sports. On May 8, Iva gave birth to James Francis Thorpe, Jr., in New York. The "husky little fellow," as Jim called him, was baptized on May 30 at St. Aloysius Roman Catholic Church on West 132nd Street, just south of the Thorpes' apartment near the Polo Grounds on West 157th Street. "Junior" had his "first outing," as Iva wrote in his baby book, in Mrs. McGraw's car. In August, Iva brought the three-month-old to a game, his first of many. When Junior learned to walk, Iva told Jim she had a "terrific time" keeping him from running onto the diamond to see his father. Jim bought him a baseball uniform and spent hours pitching the ball to the toddler, dubbing him "the little Giant." Eventually, Junior would learn to catch and throw and bat "surprisingly well," according to his father. In his son, Jim felt he was "building my own monument," something private and enduring.

Off-season, Jim and his family stayed in Ponca, Oklahoma, near Iva's family, or in Oklahoma City. He had renewed the leasing of the property in 1913 for an annual income of $400 and continued to receive money from the Sac and Fox tribal trust funds. Jim felt flush enough to forgo the lease income and live one winter on his allotment, where he introduced his son to hunting and fishing, just as Hiram had done for him twenty years earlier. In October 1914, agent Horace Johnson was favorably enough disposed toward him to describe his "excellent character and reputation" and recommend that Jim's request for unrestricted use of his leasing money be approved. When the Indian Office refused to enroll Junior as a Sac and Fox, claiming Jim was white, Johnson backed Jim: how could the office possibly draw that conclusion, he asked, of a man who was a Sac and Fox and owned an allotment? The chief clerk of the Department of the Interior would end the matter in April 1916, writing to Johnson that because Jim was a citizen—he was not, yet—and because the child was born away from Sac and Fox lands and had never lived among Indians, Junior was not entitled to be enrolled.

A few months later, in September, Jim was brought back to the sport he loved best and had been away from for three years. Clarence C. Childs, the football coach at Indiana University in Bloomington, wanted Jim as an assistant backfield coach. Childs was a fellow 1912 Olympian who had won a bronze medal in the hammer throw. Jim asked for a $1,000 salary and accommodation for his family at the Hotel Bowles, in Bloomington. The university president, William Lowe Bryan, approved the deal. Jim would start that fall as soon as the Giants' season was over.

His arrival in Bloomington created what the university yearbook of 1916 described as the "wildest enthusiasm," with the town schoolboys "more in their glory than when a circus comes to town." One of those boys, Herbert H. Skirvin, later the editor of the *Bloomington Daily Telephone*, went with his brothers to Jordan Field one day after school to watch football practice. Jim was conducting kicking tryouts, with the applicants kicking the ball about forty yards. Jim offered some guidance, then kicked the ball even farther. When someone asked what had been his longest kick, Jim took the ball at the goal line and it sailed seventy-five yards through the air and then bounced and rolled over the far goal line. "Everyone watching, except me, gasped," said Skirvin. "I was only six—I didn't understand what had happened. My oldest brother, nine, explained: 'He kicked the ball 100 yards!' "

Called Jim by everybody, he was immediately liked and welcomed and applied himself to his job. He traveled by train to scout the teams coming up on the schedule. When Childs persuaded him to give punting exhibitions during halftimes, "Men came from distances," the yearbook recorded, to see Jim perform, with his "easy nonchalance that seemed almost uncanny." After one game, a boy ran up to the man carrying the ball off the field. The boy reached out, touched the ball, and then ran back to tell his pals: "Jim Thorpe touched that ball and so did I!" Such scenes and homage would occur countless times in the decades to come. Jim's "hearty smile," reported the yearbook, "livened up the gloom that reigned often on Jordan Field." No wonder: Indiana lost its big game, and Jim's first on the job, to the University of Chicago, 13–7, and ended the season with only one win.

Meanwhile, in Canton, Ohio, Jack Cusack, twenty-five, an employee of the East Ohio Gas Company, had been working to beef up the local professional football team. Canton was a bustling town of 59,000, with more than fifty car dealerships and several railroad lines; trains came through filled with immigrants coming to work in the iron bridge works or farm machinery factory. Its most notable resident had been William McKinley, who had conducted his "front porch" presidential campaign from his home in Canton and was buried there after his assassination in 1901. Cusack had been the local team's manager since 1912, when the newly revived team's name had been changed from the Bulldogs to the Professionals in an attempt to distance itself from the enduring legacy of a messy scandal in 1906. Since neighboring Massillon, Canton's archrival, about ten miles to the west, had revived its local Tigers, the young Cusack—an early, essential, passionate advocate of professional football—saw his chance to improve both the national status of the game and the local gate receipts.

Collegiate football had developed under intense public scrutiny, but the professional game evolved comparatively unobserved. It first thrived in the Pittsburgh area. By 1900 there were sixty-seven millionaires in that city alone, wealthy backers and gambling men who founded not only athletic clubs but football teams made up of workers in their factories, mills, and plants. The clubs became exclusive havens of "amateurism" as more and more college graduates played for them. The amateurism was a sham. In 1892 an All-America guard for Yale, William W. "Pudge" Heffelfinger, was paid a $500 "performance bonus," plus expenses, to play for the Allegheny Athletic Association, a leading Pennsylvania club. He was the "first certifiable professional," though he denied the payment for the rest of his life.

The shift of the professional game's center one hundred miles west of Pittsburgh to Stark County, Ohio, occurred when the new Massillon team took its first step toward professionalism in 1903 by hiring an Akron tackle to ensure a victory over Canton. Other Ohio teams followed suit. Local rivalries escalated as eager boosters invested their money and egos in winning local championships. Company-sponsored football teams such as the Columbus Panhandles and the Toledo Overlands also took hold as businessmen saw a means to create a happier workplace (and head off unions). Such worker teams encouraged strong local loyalty, though they were also derided as "welfare capitalism" in that Progressive era.

Players did not have contracts; there were squabbles over the fairness of teams hiring players from beyond the municipal borderline. Both issues prompted intermittent talk of forming a league. It quickly became apparent, according to football historian Marc Maltby, that team managers' "intense desire for victory more often than not undermined their financial stability." These ragtag professional teams scrambled to keep up with the shifting rules of the game without the institutional stability of the northeastern colleges and universities.

By 1905, Canton and Massillon were the best professional football organizations in Ohio, and therefore in the entire country. There wasn't much competition because no one else was willing to pay as much for players, which left the two teams with no equals to play against except each other. The Stark County rivalry quickly became one of the most intense of American sports history, "teem[ing] with romance and rancor." Before their first 1906 game, Grantland Rice, then a young reporter at *The Atlanta Journal*, and destined to become the so-called dean of American sportswriters, penned one of his signature bits of doggerel:

> *In days of old, when knights were bold,*
> *And barons held their way—*
> *The atmosphere was rife, I hear,*
> *With war cries day by day.*
> *From morn to night they'd scrap and fight*
> *With battle ax and mace—*
> *While seas of blood poured like a flood*
> *About the market place.*
> *But no fight ever fought before beneath the shining sun*
> *Will be like that when Canton's team lines up with Massillon.*

Pop Warner said that as much as a million dollars was bet on games between the two towns; Rice pared it down to $100,000. A Massillon player boasted that "the Roman amphitheater was kindergarten stuff" compared to the brutality of professional football—a common opinion. But when accusations of game-throwing, professional gambling, and ringers quickly followed the second game between the two rivals, the sport, already considered chancy, if not downright corrupt, was blackened. By the end of the year, *The* (Cleveland) *Plain Dealer* had concluded that the Canton–Massillon scandal was only what could be expected of the professional game and that the sport would never become popular, nor would a proposed league ever take shape. As went Ohio, so went professional football.

With a few exceptions, outside the state no one paid much attention to the professional game until what football historian Bob Carroll would call the "small football explosion" of 1915. Notre Dame's stunning 1913 defeat of West Point had put the small, Catholic midwestern school on the sporting map, adding significant allure to hiring its players as ringers. The United States was not yet involved in World War I, but the Midwest was a major beneficiary of the post-1914 supply of American food and matériel that was bought and sent to Europe. More money was available to invest in local teams, which, in turn, like the Eastern Carolina minor league of 1909 and 1910, became popular with businesses and civic organizations as a way to boost the pride, identity, and economy of small towns and cities across the region.

In Ohio and beyond, stronger teams began to develop. The Detroit Heralds, Evanston North Ends, Toledo Maroons, and Dayton Triangles had all started out as neighborhood clubs, but now they hired professional talent and set up a schedule of games. Gambling grew apace, putting an added premium on winning, which required better players. The spiral of competitive, escalating salaries to obtain such players was to be covered, it was hoped, by the gambling profits. To protect their slim profit margins, a secret 1914 nontampering agreement among Ohio team managers stipulated that they would not raid one another's talent; it was ignored, especially by Massillon. After America's entry into the war in Europe in 1917, local chauvinism and the hunger for hometown "championships" would only escalate.

By the start of the 1915 season, everybody was importing collegiate or postcollegiate players. The quality of play, the gate receipts, and the odds ratcheted up, depending on which team lured the best players. In November, the two Stark County teams—with Canton now the Bulldogs again—were to compete in two games for what they liked to call the football championship. Massillon made it known that it was hiring top undergraduate collegiate talent, playing under assumed names, and recent graduates such as Notre Dame's star quarterback from 1910 to 1913 and the school's first All-American, Gus Dorais.

Jack Cusack then made a strategic decision that would be seen as pivotal in the history of the professional game. When he realized that he had on his team one of Jim Thorpe's former Carlisle teammates, William Gardner, and that Jim was now less than three hundred miles away in Indiana for the season, Cusack asked Gardner to approach America's most famous athlete with a very attractive offer: if he would play the two Massillon games for Canton in November, he would be paid $250 for each, a princely amount at the time, at least $100 more than the top going rate. Cusack's backers were less than thrilled; the team had already almost gone bankrupt in 1906. But Jim agreed. The Indiana season would be almost over by then, and the money would help support his new family. It was also a welcome opportunity to play again the game he loved. After three disappointing baseball seasons, he had to show the world, Iva, and himself that he could still excel at something.

Jim played the first professional football game of his life at Massillon's Driving Park on Sunday, November 14. The coach, jealous of Jim's fee and resentful that he had not practiced with the team, largely kept Jim on the bench. Canton lost, 16–0. Cusack, furious, fired the coach and brought in Jim as the replacement for the upcoming second game, in which he would also play. Cusack also hired three All-Americans, including a tackle, Gideon "Charlie" Smith, from Michigan Agricultural College, now Michigan State, one of the few early black professional players. Jim was not only a draw for spectators, he was the bait to lure such top players, offering them the chance to play beside him. Cusack was gratified that 6,000 spectators had shown up for the first game, since the usual attendance was about 1,200. Star power worked. Betting was "sky high" for the second game—in favor of Massillon.

As the *Canton Daily News* debated whether the 1915 All-America coach should be Warner, in his first year at Pitt, Harvard's Percy Haughton, or Chicago's Amos Alonzo Stagg, Jim agreed to play a November 25 Thanksgiving Day game in Indiana for the Pine Village Athletic Club against the University All-Stars, a team made up mostly of players from Purdue in West Lafayette, twenty miles west of the hamlet of Pine Village. Lafayette and West Lafayette, across the Wabash River, were at the center of an entrenched semiprofessional football circuit (as opposed to a more organized league) that included teams in Pine Village, Fort Wayne, Hammond and Wabash. Pine Village, which claimed more than one hundred consecutive wins, had in 1915 just re-formed as a professional team. Before a crowd of 3,000 from Indiana and eastern Illinois, Pine Village won. The Lafayette *Journal and Courier* was struck by Jim's size and speed— he "ran like a deer," gaining about 150 yards. The rest of that week before the second Massillon game, "to make [the practice] interesting for himself," as the Indiana University student paper reported, Jim played as a one-man team against an Indiana eleven and won several scrimmages, to the delight of onlookers. "Whenever one of those high balls went sailing over the goal posts," the yearbook said, "that laugh . . . could be heard from one end of the field to the other." The football warrior was back.

On Sunday, November 28, an incredible 8,000 fans showed up at Canton's League Park. Cusack sold standing-room and end zone tickets to accommodate them all. Anticipating problems with spectators so close to the play, both clubs agreed that "any player crossing the goal line into the crowd must be in possession of the ball when he emerge[s] from the crowd." After two of Jim's field goals made the score 6–0, with only a few minutes left, a Massillon receiver caught a pass and charged over the goal line into the crowd for what he thought was the tying touchdown. Seconds later the ball jumped out onto the field and a Canton player got it. The Massillon player, apoplectic, insisted the ball had been kicked out of his hands by a uniformed policeman with brass buttons on his coat. But Canton policemen did not wear uniforms. "A lengthy argument ensued," reported *The Plain Dealer*, "in the fast nearing darkness." The play was eventually ruled a touchback, no score, giving the victory to Canton. Years later, Cusack was told by a Canton man that he, a brass-buttoned streetcar conductor, had kicked the ball out of the receiver's hands. He had $30 riding on Canton. This play, in the last of the games that launched Jim Thorpe into professional football, would become one of the tall but true tales of the fledgling sport's crazy early days.

No certain champion emerged in the 1915 Ohio season, but it was clear the professional game had evolved. Winning players now came increasingly out of the training programs of the colleges and universities, rather than primarily from factory, club, and other non-academic teams. If a team wanted to stay at the top, attract the biggest crowds, as well as the betting action, and make the most money, it needed those players—and they were expensive. The vigorous bidding war that began with Cusack's $250 per game offer to Jim would fundamentally change the sport over the next few years. During what Cusack called the sandlot era of the game, from 1912 to 1914, player salaries had averaged $25 per game. After Jim's entry in 1915, the average tripled to $75. Jim's unparalleled reputation and his skills made him the unique attraction professional football needed to mature; Cusack said he had "hit the jackpot" by hiring Jim. He quit his day job at the gas company to devote himself full-time to managing the Bulldogs.

On December 1, Jim, Iva, and Junior left Bloomington for Oklahoma. There was speculation at Indiana University that Jim would be hired for a year-round position in football, track, and baseball, but Cusack's offer to coach and play for the Bulldogs won out. Jim would never coach football at the collegiate level again.

Jim continued to play baseball, starting the pattern that marked his years as a professional: picking up one sport when another one's season was completed. On April 2, 1916, it was announced Jim was joining the American Association's high minor league Milwaukee Brewers: "Even Thorpe's best friends among the Giants hardly hope that he will ever get out of the minors," reported *The New York Times*. "He can field and run bases, but he seems no further advanced as a hitter than he was two years ago." Respect for the man, however, remained strong. "Jim Thorpe has left a warm place in the hearts of the men who played with him," reported the *Los Angeles Times*, "on account of the gameness with which he tried to conquer his weakness against curve balls and the way he accepted his defeat without a whimper."

John McGraw was actively rebuilding the Giants, or trying to. As the war in Europe dragged on and America's involvement in it looked certain, organized baseball settled into difficult and unsettled years. The Federal League had collapsed, releasing its players back into the two older leagues. The quality of the game in 1916 was expected to be better as a result, but the added competition made Jim's chances of obtaining a permanent place in the majors that much more difficult.

Though Jim had made a good showing during spring training, it wasn't enough. McGraw had tried to convert him to bat left-handed—he batted and threw right-handed—to take better advantage of his speed, but by the time he arrived in Milwaukee he was back to batting right-handed. The consensus was that he couldn't hit major league pitching either way. Many believed that Jim would quit baseball, especially now that his professional services were "in great demand," said *The New York Times*, as a football coach.

His arrival in Milwaukee was seen as a big boost to a team that had finished third from the bottom in 1915. Iva brought Junior, now one year old, in a basket to the opening game in May and wrote in his baby book that the sunny, blond boy was "a marvel of a baby." In 143 games for the Brewers Jim had 573 at bats, the most he would ever have in any one season of organized baseball. He ended the season leading the American Association in stolen bases, forty-eight, and tied for fourth place in home runs and triples. But the Brewers came in last. Jim's batting average was an unglamorous .274. He lacked "strike zone discipline," leading the league with 117 strikeouts. He remained an inadequate fielder—fast, but with poor instincts. No matter how well they hit, such fielders usually ended up in the minors.

That summer, Jim filed a $10,000 libel suit against a Jersey City newspaper. According to *The Sporting Life*, the paper had published a story a year earlier about an "alleged row" in a Jersey City saloon, during which a certain Edward La Forge was knocked unconscious by Jim. Jim claimed the story was malicious, harmed his reputation, "depreciated the value of his services," and had caused him loss of employment. The paper countered that it had "some interesting data on Thorpe's career when he first took up professional ball in North Carolina," probably a reference to the glass window incidents in Fayetteville years earlier. The case came to nothing; Jim may have dropped the charges when he realized that the lawsuit could mean more damning headlines.

For the 1916 football season Cusack put together the first of the stellar Canton teams that would dominate the Ohio League and professional football until the end of the decade. It took a month for him to agree to Jim's terms, which included, in addition to coaching and playing, being given responsibility for "[e]very playing detail and the handling of players." While Iva prepared their ground-floor apartment on Canton's Cleveland Avenue, Jim finished out his baseball season in Milwaukee, missing the Bulldogs' first two games.

Cusack, meanwhile, had recruited, with Jim's approval, what he claimed were more All-America college stars than any other team, ever, including former Georgetown quarterback Harry Costello, a pal of Jim's since Carlisle beat Georgetown in 1912. Cusack kept adding top players throughout the season as the Bulldogs won against the Buffalo All-Stars, with former Carlisle star Frank Mt. Pleasant, as well as the Columbus Panhandles and Youngstown. The first game against Massillon ended in a scoreless tie before a crowd said to be 15,000 strong. As Massillon itself had a population of only 16,000, the attendance claims were probably inflated. But if they were only close, these were incredible numbers for professional football. Warner showed up and told Jim that his Pitt team could whip the Bulldogs.

Just in time for the second game against Massillon on the Sunday after Thanksgiving, Jim's Carlisle teammate, Pete Calac, joined Canton as fullback. The betting was frantic, as rumors of fresh ringers and other lineup changes flew around Stark County. Grifters tried to lure players into throwing games, which only added more fizz to the gambling hysteria. Before the game Jim told a crowd at the Courtland Hotel that his team would trounce Massillon, which led to an *Evening Repository* story on December 4, claiming Jim had bet a Massillon man $2,500 that Canton would win their second game. Another story said Jim had a standing offer to pay $1,000 to any team that could confine him to less than ten yards in four downs. "He simply wasn't the type," retorted Cusack, "to do a foolish thing like that," adding that Jim never had any money to bet anyway because Cusack paid him only at the end of the season. But skeptics found it hard to believe that Jim hadn't bet on his team when he announced that he would not be playing in a specific game—and then came in to save the day in the final quarter. "The player who, in his prime, had the greatest effect on the odds," said an early professional player, "was Jim Thorpe."

Massillon's roster again included Gus Dorais—this time with his old Notre Dame teammate Knute Rockne, now assistant coach at their alma mater, but often moonlighting on Sundays. Rockne's photograph had appeared mostly in South Bend newspapers, leaving him free to play elsewhere as "Jones" or some other assumed name. Managers readily credited pregame rumors that "Smith" or "Jones" was really the latest All-America phenom coming to moonlight. The ruse worked both ways: Rockne may have used a stand-in for one of the 1916 Stark County games, with fans none the wiser.

Despite Massillon's best efforts, Canton won on a soggy day at the Canton ballpark and proclaimed itself the season's champion. Excepting one tie, the Bulldogs had won all their 1916 games. Hiring Jim was paying off, in terms of superior football as well as crowds. "Thorpe sidestepped adversaries and left disaster in his wake," reported the *Canton Daily News* of this second game. "Thorpe, by sheer strength, shook off rivals like the wind blows leaves to the ground."

The crowds sometimes turned ugly that season. When Jim, who had hoped to nurse a sore ankle until the Massillon game, limped onto the field against Youngstown, fell twice, and finally exited with an additional hip injury, the Youngstown spectators booed and jeered: "Kill Thorpe," "Get the Indian," "He's yellow," and "He's a quitter!" The next day the paper castigated the town's citizens for screaming with "wild enthusiasm" as Jim lay injured on the field. He had only agreed to play, claimed the paper, because he "figured, in his own modest way, that a part of the large crowd was interested in seeing him in action." The paper was right.

Jim was luring not only former Carlisle teammates but the cream of the region's collegiate players to Canton. As college football took hold in the Midwest, the pool of collegiate talent had deepened; the other Ohio teams also grew stronger as a result, their players eager to test themselves against Jim or, at the very least, to watch him up close in action. He was forming around him what would be seen as the cadre of players, then coaches, that built the foundation of American professional football.

The Evening Repository in Canton noted—with some exaggeration—that the 1916 Canton–Massillon games were Ohio's answer to the Harvard–Yale and Army–Navy rivalries. The major midwestern papers, a few with national circulation, now provided regular coverage of the Canton games. Money, however, was still a problem. Teams raided one another's rosters, encouraging players to jump from team to team, requesting higher and higher salaries. The bidding war for talent sucked up gate receipts despite the increased crowds. Massillon, like most of the other Ohio teams, ended the 1916 season in the red. Canton was barely profitable. Nevertheless, professional football was starting to build a critical mass.

In 1929, Warner would tell Olympic sprinter-turned-sportswriter Charley Paddock that all Jim learned at Carlisle, he enlarged upon in Ohio. "While he may have lacked some of his old-time fire and recklessness," said Warner, "he more than made up for it with his skill and smoothness." He was older, smarter, more strategic, more disciplined. His combination of speed and power made him a more versatile runner than later professional stars such as Chicago Bears fullback Bronko Nagurski or Red Grange—or even, some Carlisle teammates would insist, 1950s and 1960s college and professional legend Jim Brown.

In 1916 Jim weighed 185 pounds stripped, ten pounds more suited up. His muscles were long and lithe, not bulky. His chest was huge. Running in the open field, he loved to lower his shoulder, charge straight at a defender, and, at the moment of impact, "lift and 'peel back' " the player to predictable effect. On defense he was considered a rough player, but fair. Some professionals gouged eyes, kneed players, and didn't hesitate to "outright slug" time and again. Jim just wore longer cleats, the better to "start kicking his way out of the pile." Warner had taught his backs what he called the "unexpected contact" tactic, which Jim had turned into his signature. "You try to stop a man stopped," Guyon explained, "not charging at you. Then, wham, you hit him with the hip or stiff arm. Sometimes you have to fake him to make him stop, then crush him." Jim rarely tackled the ball carrier. When he had a receiver trapped, he'd launch his body in a kind of cross-body block that almost always forced a fumble. His weakness was his pass defense. As Warner had learned, if Jim didn't think a receiver would catch the ball, he'd make no effort to cover him. "Jim was always saving Jim," said Wilbur F. "Fats" or "Pete" Henry, another Bulldog destined for the professional football Hall of Fame.

On offense, he was usually the team's best passer—he could accurately throw the ball fifty to sixty yards. He was also a good receiver, even if he had few opportunities to exhibit that skill. He still ran with knees churning up high, making it almost impossible to tackle him at the waist. When all these skills eventually faded, he would still be a formidable place- and dropkicker well into his forties. Other players would surpass Jim in these individual skills, but it would be argued for the rest of the century that no one combined all of them to the same degree of perfection.

Cusack believed Jim was "a fierce competitor, absolutely fearless," whose heart was in playing, not coaching. Jim hated practice and rarely bothered to learn the signals. Alfred Earle "Greasy" Neale, an early Bulldog, later the coach of the Philadelphia Eagles and another player recruited by Jim who would end up in the Hall of Fame, said the team didn't see Jim or each other for practice until the day of the game, when he would give them "three or four long plays" and then ask each man how long he thought he could play that day. He didn't like to be told how to play football and assumed they didn't either. Indeed, Cusack saw that Jim was reluctant to replace a player on the field. He was also generous and gave unexpected bonuses when a player had done particularly well.

Off the field, Cusack found Jim "a loveable fellow, bighearted, with a good sense of humor." The morning before a game, Jim would tease Cusack, saying, "I think I'll eat a couple of raw steaks so I can go out there and kill them." Then he would laugh and add: "Aw, Jack, I don't need steaks to do *that*." The two men became close. Jim called Cusack "Buddy," and in 1917 Cusack spent two weeks of his honeymoon with Jim and Iva in Oklahoma. "I loved him and I say that from the heart," Cusack would say in 1972. "He'd give you the shirt off his back and that was what was wrong with him. If he had $500 and somebody he knew, maybe another Indian, asked him, he'd give him half of it." Cusack had the sensitivity to see that Jim was essentially an introvert, a "reticent fellow who didn't need, or want, the publicity." He had a lot of "friends," but few intimate bonds. He once told Cusack that he wished he were in South America, where nobody knew him.

Cusack understood that his star needed "a lot of looking after." Jim's nature, most of the time, was trusting, whimsical, generous, and funny. Cusack would later insist, in response to the chronic questions about Jim and alcohol, that Jim drank to cover his shyness and could not hold that much—"four drinks and he was gone. He'd get sick and want to die." Others felt Jim could drink far, far more. In any case, Jim never drank the night before or the day of a game.

Canton teammate Isaac Roy "Ike" Martin remembered that Jim

"took a terrible beating" physically during these years, yet was so sportsmanlike and delighted with the game that when an opponent finessed him with a good play, he would "grin that big grin." That spirit was infectious. "I can still hear that deep-throated laugh of his," said "Fats" Henry, "as he crashed through, flattening everything in sight." At the same time, if he or a teammate was the target of an intentional foul, Jim retaliated, though usually not right away. "There was nothing dirty about Jim," said Cusack, "unless someone did it to him first. Then he'd spend the rest of the game getting even." During a wintry game in Detroit, Jim was on the bench with the flu and ordered by Cusack to stay there. He watched as Calac was tackled but not brought to the ground by an opponent whom Cusack remembered only as Riley. Even after the whistle blew twice, Riley kept wrestling Calac until the latter fell, with a concussion. "Jim threw off his blanket," recalled Cusack, who couldn't stop him, "and went out on the field. He'd had no food all day. We took the ball on our own forty and he called himself on almost every play. Then he got loose on the sideline. Riley was back toward the middle of the field and couldn't catch him. Jim could have kept going for a touchdown, but he cut back. He turned and went to Riley and hit him head-on. They took Riley off on a stretcher to the hospital."

Football had saved Jim. On the gridiron, he was supreme. The Canton setup suited him, with the Courtland Hotel bar as football headquarters. He had enough time to occasionally help Warner with coaching and drills at Pitt. And he was happy. Not unlike his time at Carlisle, he was with a band of like-minded men building a new sport. Cusack, though, puzzled over why Jim never talked about the future.

Jim, Iva, and Junior went back once again to Oklahoma at the end of the season. Jim was eager, said the *Repository*, for an "outdoor life devoid of care and worry" and to hunt birds before he returned to baseball and his Giants contract. Shortly after the family arrived, Jim received a letter from Sac and Fox agent Johnson, dated December 15, 1916. It informed him that the U.S. government had decided he now qualified to be a United States citizen. Also enclosed was the deed ("fee simple patent"), signed by President Wilson, for his allotment acres. The twenty-five-year waiting period stipulated by the Dawes allotment act when the reservation was divided in 1891 was over. Jim had finally been judged competent to manage his own affairs—up to a point. The new citizen was now subject to white civil, criminal, and inheritance law, but did not necessarily enjoy the same civil rights as whites. The right to vote, for example, was controlled by individual states and would not become truly universal until the late 1940s. In general, annuity, lease, and oil incomes were still overseen by the BIA.

"He has a good education," the Patent in Fee Report read, "and is probably the greatest athlete of his time." Johnson had confirmed that he was "able-bodied, intelligent." It was noted that his property was leased out, largely under cultivation, fenced, and included a "fairly good 3-room house" and box barn. Coming under separate cover were the three talismans of Indian citizenship, an arrow, purse, and "emblem." The arrow, read the letter, "will be to you a symbol of your noble race and of the pride you feel that you come from the first of all Americans." The small purse was to remind him that the money he earned "must be wisely kept." He was advised to wear the emblem, a badge featuring an eagle and the colors of the American flag, in the buttonhole of his coat always. "[M]ay the eagle that is on it never see you do aught of which the flag will not be proud."

The patent document was delivered to Yale, Oklahoma, where Jim and Iva had bought a house on East Boston Street, one block off the main road. The town, which would have a population of only two thousand almost a century later, was a hundred miles north of Oklahoma City. It was a very small one-story house, with five rooms. There was gray clapboard with white trim outside and oak woodwork inside. The rooms were cozy and dark, in the style of the time. A generous yard stretched out behind the kitchen at the back of the house. Next door lived Grace, Iva's sister, and her husband, Charles Morris. Proper and neat, it was the permanent home Jim wanted and the only one he ever owned.

During spring training, Giants teammates enjoyed watching Jim and his little son play on the Marlin hotel lawn. Junior's favorite game was to scramble up one of his father's arms, across his shoulders, and down the other arm, as if Jim were a big tree, both of them laughing each time as if it were the first. When the Giants stopped in Muskogee, Oklahoma, on a post-training tour in early 1917, Carlisle friends Henry and Rose Roberts welcomed Jim, Iva, and Junior into their own new home. "Everything indicated that they were a happy married couple and they were very loving to their little son," recalled Henry.

Early in the 1917 baseball season, on April 24, a deal inaccurately described as "without precedent" was announced: Jim had been lent to the Cincinnati Reds, while the Giants would "retain the privilege of recalling Thorpe in the Fall." The arrangement had been made quickly when Edd Roush, Cincinnati's star outfielder and top batter, was injured in a game against Chicago. Christy Mathewson, now the Reds manager, had wired McGraw for help.

Mathewson's arrival as manager the previous year, along with Giants teammate Roush, turned what *Sport* would call the team's "dull and monotonous plateau of slight accomplishment" into a fourth-place finish in 1917. The next year Cincinnati would climb to third. Jim had been sent to a strong team. Matthewson was expected to "accelerate [Jim's] development as a big leaguer."

Baseball was minor news in a month that saw Congress vote, five days before the opening of the baseball season, to declare war on Germany. In May, Congress passed the Selective Service Act, and the nation was shocked to learn how many young working-class men were physically unqualified for military service. The benefits of sports had only filtered down to a select few. Two hundred fifty-five ballplayers would enlist, including Mathewson and Ty Cobb. According to the War Department, between 20 and 30 percent of all adult Indian men served, compared to approximately 15 percent of the general population; among them were at least two hundred former Carlisle students. The enthusiasm to serve was due in part to the warrior tradition, even if it was in the service of the U.S. Army; there was also the lure of a steady salary. Noncitizen Indians as well as married men with children ("parental dependency"), such as Jim, were not obligated to serve. Jim stayed home. His son Jack was later told that his father did not enlist on McGraw's advice that, with an international renown, he could be a target.

Organized baseball, according to McGraw's biographer Charles C. Alexander, continued as if the war "was taking place on another planet." In contrast to the rapid mobilization that would characterize the American response after Pearl Harbor, in 1917, the nation organized its manpower and resources slowly. On May 2, Jim was featured in a remarkable game at Wrigley Field. Reds pitcher Fred Toney and the Chicago Cubs' Jim "Hippo" Vaughn had just pitched what remains the only double no-hit regulation nine innings in major league history. In the tenth, Jim came to the plate with two outs, Larry Kopf on third, and Hal Chase on second (each pitcher had walked two batters). Jim nicked the ball toward third. Vaughn pounced on the ball, didn't throw to first because of Jim's speed, and tossed to his catcher instead. But not before Kopf slid home. Toney finished with a no-hitter and the Reds won, 1–0.

Nine days later, Jim scored the Reds' two runs as they lost to the Giants at the Polo Grounds. He singled, stole a base, and hit an inside-the-park home run, showcasing his speed. "Yesterday," crowed the *Times*, "[Thorpe] had a chance to run, and don't you think he didn't. He burned around the base paths so fast that the edges of the lawn were scorched."

On June 8, in the bottom of the ninth against the Giants, his single drove in the winning run for the Reds. On June 24, Jim went four for five. He stayed with Cincinnati until August, batting .247 in seventy-seven games. He then returned to the Giants. He made a brief appearance in the World Series, in which the Giants lost to the White Sox, and it was left to his teammates to decide if he would share in the series gate receipts. The vote to include Jim was almost unanimous, the one "nay" a good-natured tease. Jim received an extension on his contract through 1918.

At last, it had been a solid baseball year for Jim Thorpe.

Amid rumors of a new professional football league and a drastic falling-off in attendance, Canton easily retained its world football championship in a 1917 season where few teams were left with a full roster or a healthy bank balance. With ringers in short supply, their cost went up. The use of assumed names was flagrant as awareness of professional football grew apace in midwestern colleges and high schools. Pete Calac, now at West Virginia Wesleyan College, played as "Anderson" and his coach, Greasy Neale, played as "Foster" or "Fisher." Players and coaches were both moonlighting and generally hid it to avoid the taint of professionalism.

Tensions ran high. It was no time to sacrifice a game for any principle, even racial prejudice. When a Syracuse team came to Canton for a
late October game, Neale taunted its halfback, one of the best-known
black professional players of this early era, Henry McDonald: "Black
is black and white is white where I come from and the two don't mix."
McDonald, an experienced boxer, was about to respond when Jim
stepped in. "We're here to play football," he told Neale, and that was
the end of it. "Thorpe's word," said McDonald, "was the law on that
field."

After Canton's loss to Massillon in its last game of the season, and
the announcement of Carlisle's closing, Jim suddenly said he was
leaving baseball, football, and any other "personal indulgence in professional athletics." In the last year he'd found it more difficult to
control his temper on the field. He'd been restrained by his teammates in one game from beating up Massillon's best kicker. The general uncertainties of both sports that year may have influenced him
as well. Moreover, he was now the father of two—Gail Margaret was
born on October 31. Jim wanted a more stable future for what he
called "my little family," around which "all my dreams of a lifetime
now clustered." However, he soon changed his mind, deciding to
keep doing what he knew how to do.

He was an affectionate father who took great delight in returning
to his house in Yale, especially now that Iva could not travel easily
with him and he missed her. He bought a spitz puppy and gently
threw it in the air to the children's delight and stayed up all night
crying over a dying coon dog—his favorite type of hunting hound
trained to track and tree raccoons and possums. Junior's sturdy little
body and his happy nature were for Jim an affirmation that he had
one part of his life absolutely right. For the first time, Oklahoma was
the center of a calm domestic routine. He could hardly believe his
good fortune.

Yet friction was beginning to emerge. Jim's drinking was no more
excessive than that of many of his sporting peers, but it had become
"absolutely abhorrent" to Iva. Oklahoma had been dry since statehood and would remain so until 1959, but liquor was readily available. Yale had plenty of bootleggers selling to the oil workers. Jim
enjoyed playing billiards and drinking at one of the hangouts on
Yale's Main Street. When Calac came to visit, he and Jim would stay

out all night hunting and arrive back in the morning ravenous. As Iva fed them what seemed inordinate amounts of bacon and eggs, she wondered why they were so hungry. Later, she discovered in a closet empty bottles of the whiskey the men had consumed all night. She had been raised a teetotaling Methodist before becoming a Catholic; she also considered herself a lady, which, by the definition of the time, precluded associating with people who drank and smoked to excess. She asked the local priest to talk to Jim and told her husband she would "put up with him until he really fell by the wayside." Several years gone from the protected environment of Carlisle and coarsened by the tough, nomadic life of professional sports, Jim could seem very different from the genial, happy-go-lucky campus star she had known.

Iva's sister Grace encouraged Iva to look down on Jim as an Indian. "She was very strict," said Gail Thorpe of her aunt, "and influenced Mom." Iva would sustain close Indian friends her whole life, but she found it now all too easy to fall in with the prejudice Grace and the rest of the Miller family had always had for Jim. Post-statehood Oklahoma relegated Indians to the lower rungs on its social ladder, a snobbery to which the susceptible Iva also reacted. She reclaimed a romanticized idea of her spurious Indian descent when it suited her, but it was always important for her to distance herself from the common or ordinary.

The tension grew, but Jim retained his sense of humor. As he would most of his life, he kept hunting dogs in a backyard kennel. He named one of the females Grace. Each morning he was home, he'd call the dogs for feeding, yelling loud enough for his sister-in-law to hear: "Come here, Grace, you old bitch!"

He returned for his sixth season in major league baseball playing for the Giants. Major league club owners decided to go ahead with a full 154-game schedule in 1918 after President Wilson announced in April that the country "needed its athletics now more than ever." Yet after Secretary of War Newton D. Baker issued the "work-in-essential-industries-or-fight" order in July, the exodus of players to serve in the military or take jobs in munitions factories and shipyards accelerated. By the time the baseball season halted prematurely on

Labor Day, McGraw's team was a "patched-together outfit." Giants' attendance that year, about 265,000, was the lowest since McGraw arrived from Baltimore. Although McGraw played Jim in the field against left-handed hitters, Jim played only fifty-eight games, batting .248. There were a few flashes of brilliance. He "saved the day," headlined the June 6 *New York Tribune*, scoring two runs against the Pirates; one of his hits, just inside the first base line, was missed by right fielder Casey Stengel. On July 9, Jim hit a high, soaring home run into the left field bleachers against the Chicago Cubs that cinched the game for the Giants, 7–6. Up-and-comer Babe Ruth hit .300 that year, with a .555 slugging percentage and a league-leading eleven home runs for the Boston Red Sox.

Iva had brought the children to New York. As the family headed back to Yale together, Jim noticed that something was wrong with his son: his ankles were swelling and he was listless. When they arrived in Yale, Jim called in doctors. The boy had contracted inflammatory rheumatism, with severe joint pain and a high fever. At four o'clock in the morning, September 23, Junior died in his father's arms in front of the living room fireplace. The doctor had almost to pry the body from him. Jim called Secretary Foster of the Giants to give him the news. "The little Indian lad," reported *The New York Times*, "was a favorite at the Giants' training camp at Marlin, Texas, last Spring and was a familiar figure to Polo Ground fans." After the funeral, he and Iva, Jim said, "packed up the little fellow's baseball suit, bat, balls and toys" and buried their son in Cushing, a town near Yale.

The death of his son, his first child, was of course a catastrophe. Giving up the gold medals and trophies meant nothing compared to this. They were the past; the boy, "the most precious trophy I had ever been awarded," had been his future. Giants teammate Al Schacht said that after the death, "Jim was never the same." He loved children, but from now on he would be guarded around them, aloof, even harsh. He would never mention his first son. The man even close friends thought enigmatic became even more so.

Their son's death pushed Jim and Iva further apart. Iva hid her grief better than Jim, but she was equally devastated (her last words before dying in California in 1981 were about Junior; at her request, her ashes were buried next to him in Cushing). Jim became inaccessible to his wife. "He was brokenhearted," Iva said. "His drinking problem increased after that." The mornings after grew harder. Gail went into his bedroom one day in Canton, where he lay with the window shades down. Iva quickly whisked her out, explaining that Jim was "very sick." Gail would later surmise, "I'm sure it must have been drinking because I'm sure he wasn't sick." He started going out to find alcohol from bootleggers and drinking straight whiskey for hours on end. He was now more prone to crying. "Nothing much mattered," he said.

Two months after Junior's death, the grieving couple mortgaged Jim's allotment property for $350. There had been no 1918 football season for Canton, resulting in a significant loss of income for Jim, who was now used to earning about $15,000 a year. Despite the nation's exuberance as war ended on November 11, it was the beginning of a grim, sad time for the Thorpes.

Jim showed up late in Gainesville, Florida, for spring training in March 1919. He made it into the Giants' starting lineup on April 19, against the Washington Senators, and got hits in his two times at bat. The next day, he went two for five off the great Walter "Big Train" Johnson to lead the team to a 5–3 win.

It was an excellent showing—and his last game for the Giants. Jim and McGraw had come to the end of their touchy alliance. McGraw had put up, barely, with Jim's shortcomings during the past two years of wartime player shortage. Once, when Jim missed a signal while running the bases, costing the team a run, McGraw, furious, had called him "a dumb Indian." Jim took off after the manager and "[i]t took half the team to stop him," Al Schacht recalled. During another game, when Jim felt he had done well enough to be starting, McGraw played someone else. When McGraw told Jim to pinch-hit later in the game, Jim swung wildly three times deliberately and resumed his seat on the bench. McGraw, apoplectic, jumped up and screamed epithets at him and said he was finished with the team. McGraw had swallowed his anger again, but when the war ended and the player pool expanded, he no longer had to tolerate such behavior.

The controlling shares of the Giants had been sold to a new owner in early 1919, but McGraw remained as vice president and manager; he sold Jim to the Boston Braves on May 21. The Braves uniform featured a small Indian head patch on the sleeve, and on the front an Indian head with a full Plains headdress in profile. Braves manager George Stallings was not thrilled to get McGraw's castoff and used him initially only as a pinch hitter.

But the change of scenery galvanized Jim, and he moved to the top end of the batting order. He would start thirty-eight games for the Braves and rarely hit lower than fifth in the lineup—indicating Stallings considered him one of the best hitters on the team. On July 16, the *Los Angeles Times* sports page headlined "Thorpe Leads Batting List." Jim was the leading batter in the National League, with an average of .411 in twenty-two games. A week later, as it appeared Babe Ruth was likely to establish a new home run record, Jim was still the league leader at .373, with Shoeless Joe Jackson leading the American League at .354. By the end of the month, Ty Cobb at .350, and Jim—with thirty-three hits in thirty-four games—at .375 were at the top of their respective leagues. He had learned to hit more consistently, even off right-handed pitchers who, knowing his alleged weakness, threw him a lot of curveballs. When the ever-vocal Boston fans started yelling for Thorpe, he asked for more money and got it.

On August 3, at .366, he was still leading both leagues. But a leg injury, probably incurred running the bases during a game against the Giants, had finally started to tell—or so ran the official story. In actuality, a "certain unpleasantness" had emerged between Jim and his new manager, perhaps because Jim had become a partner in the juvenile pranks of Walter James Vincent "Rabbit" Maranville, the unpredictable, fast, and diminutive Braves shortstop. Jim ended the season hitting .327 but had played in only 60 games for the Braves (prior to 1920, players had to play in 60 percent of their scheduled games to qualify for the batting championship). Edd Roush played in 133 games, enough to qualify for the National League batting title, which he won with an average of .321 (Cobb topped the American League with .384). To the lifelong claim that he couldn't hit a curveball, Jim would point to the 1919 season and say, "I must have hit a few curves." That year he hit well off both left-handed (.333) and right-handed (.316) pitchers, indicating that he had indeed mastered the curve. Sports had come easy to him—except for baseball. He had applied himself to something difficult, complicated to learn, requiring practice and effort, and he'd done it. But it was too late—at least for the majors. The rest of life had caught up with him. "The Redskin looked good at times," admitted *The Sporting News*, "but he never could get going like a star."

Why that was true would bedevil fans and sportswriters for decades. They debated what would have happened if he'd had more and different managers. His personal demons, plucky independence, pride, and stubbornness were all topics of debate, as well as his being Indian and simple bad luck. Jim would later insist that his love of personal independence and "freedom from restraint" were characteristic of his "race," and that influenced his play. His abrupt transition from the familiar, supportive Indian world of Carlisle to the harshly competitive white world of the major leagues had deeply affected him. He had never fully made the switch, persevering like an exile who is never sure what he is supposed to do next.

But it was more his early superstardom that sabotaged Jim. He had gotten used to being given lots of leeway, with little interference. By the time he'd learned to bat, he was less patient, more adversarial and reckless, than the player McGraw signed in 1913.

Jim left the majors just as the lively ball and Babe Ruth were changing the game forever. Eventually, he would even be nostalgic for the old, fractious baseball, when McGraw, the players, and the umpires expected at least one good fight to perk up a game, before "rowdyism" was officially discouraged. "I must be old-fashioned," Jim mused in 1940, when asked about the old days in the major leagues, "or a little rough, even to this day, or a sadist. But . . . times have changed."

On September 16, while Jim was in St. Louis with the Braves, Iva gave birth in Boston to their second daughter, Charlotte Marie, named for Jim's mother. Coming almost one year after Junior's death, it was happy news for Jim. The struggle to maintain a marriage and family and career had only gotten harder, but a new baby gave him and Iva hope that they might make it work after all. The next day he sent a telegram to his wife: DEAR GIRL JUST RECEIVED WONDERFUL NEWS LOVE AND KISSES TO GALE'S [*sic*] NEW LITTLE SISTER AND THE MOST WONDERFUL WIFE AND MOTHER IN THE WORLD.

As soon as the baby could travel, Iva and their two daughters met Jim in Cleveland, and they all drove to Canton for the first football season in two years. There were doubts the Ohio League could be made viable again, and people were looking to Jim as a potential savior. Now thirty-two, he seemed indestructible.

The war effort itself had contributed to a changed sports environment. Army and navy athletic programs had kept soldiers amused and fit. A visitor to a military camp reported seeing almost fifty different games of football, with each camp itself fielding a team. Most important for the professional game, thousands of young men who had had no opportunity to play the game in a top college or prep school learned to love it. The National Committee on Physical Education, set up before the war ended, now required physical education in public schools. Wartime round-the-clock factory production had broken down many of the laws forbidding sporting events on Sundays. Such restrictions had already been discarded in Ohio—the Bulldogs played on Sundays—but the opportunity to schedule professional games elsewhere on the day of rest, no longer competing with collegiate games on Saturdays, dramatically enhanced the game's chances to catch on.

On July 13, 1919, *The New York Times* had announced that "wartime rumors to the contrary," Jim was now "considering the managership of a Canton team of professionals." Jack Cusack had decided to pursue his fortune in the Oklahoma oil fields and turned over the running of the team to Ralph E. Hay, a successful Canton Hupmobile and Pierce-Arrow car dealer who was on friendly terms with both Cusack and Jim. Hay lured Jim with a part interest in the team, and in early August he and the Massillon and Akron team managers met with Jim at the Pittsburgh Athletic Club for a brainstorming session while he was in town with the Braves, who were playing the Pirates.

It was agreed that the core issues of scheduling, player retention, and escalating salaries desperately needed to be organized, as in baseball, if the professional sport was to continue. Betting threatened to keep professional football the disreputable "reptile of the sport." Rockne, as one example of player flexibility, though coaching at Notre Dame, had reportedly moonlighted on five different opposing teams in one season. The up-and-coming Hammond All-Stars in Indiana announced they would pay a total of $20,000 for players and signed Canton's former quarterback, Milton Ghee, and former University of Illinois right end George Halas. The Hammond team would play in Cubs' Park in Chicago, a big-city ballpark—and one out of Ohio. Canton was in danger of being left behind.

Ironically, John McGraw sent a representative to the Pittsburgh meeting. Assuming that the lifting of New York's ban on Sunday baseball applied to football as well, McGraw was starting a professional football team—also called the New York Giants—to play on Sundays at the Polo Grounds, and he wanted the managers assembled at Pittsburgh to put New York on their schedules. McGraw, always with his eye on the gate, had even asked Jim to be his team's coach. Jim said no. Canton and Massillon signed on. When, two months later, it turned out that the new Sunday law applied only to baseball, McGraw quickly folded, but he would be back two years later.

As sports fans were absorbed in the 1919 World Series, Jim brought back to the Bulldogs Calac and another Carlisle teammate, Joe Guyon, 1917 All-America Georgia Tech tackle. Two of the men who had joined to bring down Pop Warner and, they hoped, save their school, were thus reunited with each other and with their school star. Their Carlisle connection was enough to encourage the backers and fans of the Ohio League that their regional sport just might survive. For the game against the Akron Indians, a crowd of almost 10,000 showed up at Canton's Lakeside Park. The bleachers were so full they began to "creak and creak," and a rope was stretched around the playing field to keep the crowd back. When Jim wasn't on the field soon enough, the crowd chanted "Thorpe! Thorpe!"

Jim's 1919 season of nine wins and one tie certainly didn't hurt the game's profile. Hammond's George Halas—later coach and player of the Decatur Staley Starch Workers and storied coach and owner for decades of its successor, the Chicago Bears—loved recounting a game when Jim kicked the ball from Canton's end zone to Hammond's twenty. (Guyon said he kicked it even farther.) Halas also told how in the same game Jim used his special body block to knock a fullback three feet into the air and how, when he landed flat on his back with a loud "Whoos-sh-h-h," it could be heard throughout the stadium. "Jim had a fierce pride in his own strength," said Halas. He "loved to feel the crunch of flesh against flesh." After the game, which Canton won, Halas thanked Jim for not throwing his knees into Halas's ribs after one tackle, which many other players would have done. "Jim," he recalled, "brushed off my gratitude." Iva, showing support and encouragement for Jim, was in the stands with the three-month-old Charlotte and wrote in the baby book: "Daddy stars as usual."

The first Canton–Massillon game of 1919 yielded what became known among Thorpe chroniclers as the Knute Rockne Story, told as often by the Notre Dame coach in 1920s after-dinner speeches as by anyone. Coaching the Irish to a 9–0 season and playing end for Massillon, Rockne successfully tackled Jim. "You shouldn't do that, Sonny," Jim told Rockne, in one version of the story. "All these people came to watch old Jim run." According to Guyon, Jim asked Calac, "a tremendous blocker," to purposely miss Rockne on the next play so he would come through to Jim. "Then Jim gave Rockne the hip," said Guyon, "and knocked him stone cold, laid him out on the field." When they finally brought Rockne to, Jim leaned over him and said, "That's good, Sonny. You let old Jim run." Canton won, 23–0. The Canton quarterback, Mark H. "Devvie" Devlin, Jr., wrote the local paper back home in Lawrence, Massachusetts, "It's the prettiest thing in the world to see Thorpe run through a man that's waiting to tackle him."

A large contingent of Warner's stellar 1916 Pitt team was signed by Massillon for its second game with Canton, including All-American Jock Sutherland, who was soon to succeed Warner at Pitt. *The Evening Repository* joked that somebody should page Warner so he could see his team lose to Jim on Canton's home field. Playing with a dislocated vertebra and with a strong wind at his back—in July, Hay had quietly changed the orientation of the Bulldog field from north–south to east–west, to channel the wind in Canton's favor—Jim kicked a field goal in the third quarter to win, 3–0. Only afterward did he agree to go to the hospital. Canton had again won the championship, Jim's fourth, including the disputed 1915 title.

That last Massillon game of 1919 marked the end of what would be called the Jim Thorpe era of professional football. He would return to Canton, but he would never again play at such a high level and with teammates at the top of their game. There remained, however, a "romance" attached to the star player of the Carlisle Indian team that had once beat Harvard and West Point. "Thorpe didn't put pro football on the map as much as he put himself on the map," said football historian Jim Campbell. "People wanted to read about Thorpe, not necessarily pro football as a whole. Thorpe was truly a drawing card."

Another historian added, "Thorpe put the sport on the front pages because he was bigger than the game itself."

Canton's 28–2–2 record between Jim's arrival in 1915 and 1919 became legend among these early great players of the sport. He had led the pioneers of the game who would end up in the Hall of Fame—located in Canton, with a statue of Jim dominating the foyer—and they never forgot him. For decades, when a group of sportswriters and athletes old enough to have played with or watched Jim got together, the conversation would inevitably turn to Thorpe anecdotes from this era. Young men listened and memorized. The favorite tales focused on Jim's sly sense of humor and delight in sizing up the opposition and then playing with it, like a large cat with an unsuspecting mouse. In the end, for every story of a curveball or saloon brawl, there were two of his football supremacy.

Jim's performance on Ohio's fields had organized a disorganized game, given it credence and logic in an era when even baseball was struggling. But, as Professional Football Researchers Association (PFRA) historian Bob Carroll would point out at the end of the century, "greatness needs numbers." America's greatest early football player played his finest games when the Elias Sports Bureau did not officially track the yardage gained, passes completed, length of kicks of this preleague sport. The scores of the games themselves—and the conflicting newspaper accounts and anecdotal evidence—have to tell the story. Though Thorpe's exploits tended to "increase by ten yards every ten years," his spectacular Olympic performance reinforced the unrecorded claims. Even the wildest tall tales about Jim Thorpe were credible at their core.

CHAPTER NINE

Out of the Public Glare

1920–1929

These are athletes who reached the end of their ability but lived and played on—because they wanted to compete, because they did not want to work in a factory, because, in the end, there is only the game.

—RICH COHEN

Liquor was medicine for the anger . . . for the pain of the loss . . . He was beginning to feel a comfortable place inside himself, close to his own beating heart, near his own warm belly; he crawled inside and watched the storm swirling on the outside and he was safe there; the winds of rage could not touch him.

—LESLIE MARMON SILKO, *Ceremony*

The Canton Bulldogs were the champs, but there wasn't time to celebrate. Several professional football teams in Ohio disbanded entirely at the end of 1919. Even Canton lost money. Except for a few big games, there were not enough spectators to cover expenses; a player roster could cost $2,000 per game. "Some athletes played one team manager against another," said one account, "better than they played their positions." The prevailing powers in the hugely popular college game were more determined to squelch the professionals: in 1920, the Western Conference (Big Ten) would rule that undergraduates would lose their varsity letters if they played in a professional game; a year later, the American Football Coaches' Association would unanimously affirm that the professional game was "detrimental to the best interests of American football and American youth." Fans were frustrated, too; it was hard to stay loyal to a team whose roster changed each week. It seemed a perfect time to leverage Jim's fame and Canton's record for the greater good of the professional sport.

On August 20, 1920, Ralph Hay called a meeting in his Hupmobile offices in Canton with the explicit purpose of forming a professional football league. He and Jim were there for Canton; representatives from Akron, Cleveland, and Dayton also attended. Letters of intent had been received from Rochester, Hammond, and Buffalo. The American Professional Football Conference was formed that day; a month later it became the American Professional Football Association. Financial terms for players were capped and the recruitment of college undergraduates was forbidden. Hay said he would contact the other leading professional teams in Ohio, the Midwest, and western New York with the purpose of standardizing those rules. Their representatives were invited to a second meeting in Canton.

On September 17 so many team representatives—fourteen, for ten teams—showed up that Hay had to hold the meeting in his auto showroom. Two-quart galvanized metal buckets of Prohibition beer hung from car fenders, and the men sat on wide Hupmobile running boards. Among those present was George Halas, who had recently agreed to organize the Staley Starch team, as well as managers or interested businessmen from the Akron Professionals, the Cleveland Tigers, the Dayton Triangles, the Rochester Jeffersons, the Hammond team (now called the Hammond Pros), the Rock Island (Illinois) Independents, the Racine Cardinals (a Chicago team named for that city's Racine Avenue), and the Muncie (Indiana) Flyers. The motion for a $100 membership fee in the APFA was approved, though Halas later doubted if there was "a hundred bucks in the room."

One order of business was electing a league president, one who was well-known outside of Ohio and whose name added credibility to the sport. There was no doubt who that person should be. "Our minds turned to Jim Thorpe," Halas recalled, "the biggest name in sport." He was elected unanimously. His first duty was to appoint a committee to draft a constitution, bylaws, and rules, after which the meeting adjourned. The next day *The Evening Repository* covered the news: "Thorpe Named President of Professional Grid Circuit; Won't

Go After Collegians." Newspapers around the country followed suit. Hay and Jim had laid the cornerstone: in 1922, the APFA would be renamed the National Football League (NFL).

Some great players took the field that fall of 1920: Guy Chamberlin, George Halas, Wilbur Henry, Al Nesser, George Trafton, Paddy Driscoll, Paul Robeson, and another black player, Frederick Douglass "Fritz" Pollard. To showcase the new league, Canton played the Buffalo All-Americans at the Polo Grounds in December. The Manhattan media were out in force. Twelve thousand spectators was a respectable showing for the professional game. The reporters present were surprised by the quality of play. Their assumption that "former stars of the college world loaf through the [professional] game" was quickly disproved, wrote *The New York Times:* "For men who have not been carried through weeks of preparation at a training table, the stamina of the players was remarkable. The tackling was about as hard as two teams ever crowded into one game, but the pros were up and smiling almost as soon as they hit pay dirt." Jim played the entire game in a losing effort, 7–3. "We had the better team," he said, coming off the field. "I have no comment to make other than that, no alibis to give, no players to blame." Canton ended the 1920 season with a 6–3–1 record. The franchise had a $3,000 payroll deficit, but professional football had a higher profile.

League representatives met again in Akron in April 1921. The structure of the league became more detailed. Clear distinctions were to be made between league and nonleague games. Records would be kept, though official league statistics would not be maintained until 1932. It was agreed that Jim had served his purpose as a figurehead president; a real administrator was needed. A former sportswriter from Columbus, Joseph F. Carr, was elected the league's second president. He would keep the title until his death in 1939 and create a stable franchise system that migrated from small cities like Canton into the major urban centers of New York, Chicago, and Philadelphia.

In November, Grantland Rice asked three of the top college coaches, including Pop Warner, and one player to choose among thirty-one nominees from thirteen colleges, including the recently defunct Carlisle, for their "All-Time All-America" collegiate football teams. They voted unanimously and "by acclamation" to put Jim in the backfield of their teams. He was the only player to get all four votes. The branding, as a later generation would say, of the Thorpe legend had begun.

For many, the golden age of American sports began in 1920, when the colt Man o' War won eleven races, Bill Tilden won both the U.S. amateur and Wimbledon tennis championships, and Babe Ruth became a full-time outfielder for the New York Yankees and hit fifty-four home runs. That same year, a new invention, the radio, broadcast Jack Dempsey knocking out Billy Miske in three rounds. In 1921 radio transmitted its first collegiate football game, as well as the Dempsey–Georges Carpentier heavyweight title fight and the World Series. By mid-decade, major games were listened to across the country as college football became part of the exploding national sporting culture (network radio would not cover the NFL, or its championship game, until 1940). Movies ushered in the era of the sports newsreel, with weekly collegiate game highlights of Rockne's Fighting Irish or Warner's Stanford Indians. Attendance at collegiate games increased to more than ten million by 1929, larger than that garnered by major league baseball. It would be nearly three decades after the beginning of the Roaring Twenties, however, that movie newsreels began to cover professional football on a weekly basis.

Newspaper sports coverage had more than doubled in the century's first two decades and more than doubled again in the 1920s. The written word was pumped up to compete with the seductive flicker of moving images and live sound. In sportswriting, "garish embellishment . . . superlatives and breathless adjectives"—what baseball analyst Bill James called "hero journalism in American sports"—became the prevalent style. There had always been exaggeration about yardage gained and length of kicks, but now "a fifteen-yard run," said football historian Jim Campbell, "took five pages to describe."

What most fundamentally set apart the stars of the 1920s, though, was money. The new realms of advertising, public relations, and media outlets found a bonanza in the postwar hunger for fresh heroes. Dempsey would earn over $2.5 million in the ring and another million, he claimed, in endorsement deals and personal appearances. Ruth was eventually paid a salary of $80,000 a year. "It was not simply that they earned more money than their predecessors (or their contemporaries)," wrote Roger Kahn of the decade's golden boys, "the scale of their earning changed the dimensions of American sport." Dempsey and Ruth were great athletes, but they were also celebrities. Fame now translated into cash.

As these other stars rose, Jim's dimmed. He was able to make the professional football league's first Canton meeting in August 1920 because he was playing minor league baseball in nearby Akron for a new team, the Buckeyes, in the AA International League. Despite his excellent batting average with the Braves, his fielding was simply not good enough to keep him in the majors.

He went to Akron reluctantly, though he was to be paid $4,000 a year—perhaps more than any other minor leaguer. It "rankled" Jim, said *The Sporting News*, that "a man who murdered left-hand pitching and rapped .329 [sic] last summer, should be shunted to the minors." The *News* admitted, in the rollicking language of the time, that while Jim could now "[whale] the ball like everything"—curves and all— when he couldn't hit it was because "he forgets to go to bed o' nights." He was reported missing when needed at too many games. Someone like Branch Rickey, the St. Louis Cardinals manager who had transformed "hard case" Ferdie Schupp, the paper speculated, could tame Jim Thorpe.

After seven years of falling baseball attendance and the Black Sox scandal, team owners were thrilled when Ruth hit those fifty-four home runs. Fans were electrified and flocked to the ballparks. The change was, Bill James later said, "the most sudden and dramatic" of the century. The old contest of strategy, bunting, and stolen bases was replaced by a power game. The 1920s would become good years for the minors, too. There were about thirty leagues each season and though several might fail, there were always new backers to launch more. After organized baseball's first commissioner, Judge Kenesaw Mountain Landis, was elected in November 1920, all teams signed a new national agreement, reinstituting the draft. Salaries for minor league players shot up and would remain high for the next ten years. Rickey began the farm system, training new players in the minors for use in the majors.

Jim did well with Akron, batting .360 in 128 games, including sixteen home runs. "The Indian can still hit and he can still play football," said *The Sporting News*. "Just think of a man 34 years old [33, in fact] playing like a whirlwind on the gridiron. Thorpe is undoubtedly the athletic wonder of the age."

Obviously, though, one day the string would run out, and he had no alternate plans. His frustration increasingly showed on and off the field. When a sports editor accused Jim of loafing in the outfield, Jim beat him up. His football days were growing short, he told the *Los Angeles Times*, and there was an increasing risk of injury as he aged. He had turned down an offer to coach football out west because he "did not care to make football his life study," and then bragged that it would have increased his income by about $5,000. This occasional and uncharacteristic arrogance was another sign of his frustration.

His son's death, the humiliation of being demoted from the majors, and the end of his great days in Canton pushed him into a chronic depression. His moods alternated unpredictably between anger and sadness. Increasingly he just let his feelings out, ignoring the consequences. He was playing in Akron but he was adrift. Iva witnessed the changes and loyally worked to support and nurture her husband. She joined Jim when she could, bringing their two girls to be with their father. Charlotte's first birthday was celebrated in Akron with a proper party noted in the baby book. Iva was determined to maintain a family record of normalcy.

Despite his good performance, "[e]verything that could go wrong with Akron did," said minor league historian Robert Hoie. "The payroll was too high, too many players, the revenues too low, perhaps in part because the rubber market collapsed in 1920, with big repercussions in Akron." The club was sold to a new set of local owners eager to trim overhead before eventually selling the franchise to Newark. On January 14, 1921, *The New York Times* reported that Jim had been bought for $1,500 by the Toledo Mud Hens, another quality minor team in the American Association. Three days later it was revealed that Jim had first been sold to the Detroit Tigers, but that was probably no more than a device to circumvent waivers. Jim had an excellent season with the Mud Hens: in 133 games he hit .358. When Toledo played the Kansas City Blues, his family joined him. Iva was pregnant again.

For the 1921 fall season, Jim organized a new football team in Cleveland with his former Bulldogs manager, Jack Cusack, providing the financial backing. Jim was to play, coach, manage, and promote. The Cleveland club was popularly called the "Indians" because the Carlisle trio of Jim, Guyon, and Calac was in the backfield. Jim was out from late October through November with broken ribs and the gate reflected that. On December 3, 1921, the Cleveland Indians "deep in the red," Jim played at the Polo Grounds against McGraw's revived APFA New York Giants. Jim kicked a field goal and an extra point in a 17–0 victory. The team, however, ended the season with a 3–5–0 record. According to the *Los Angeles Times*, Jim experienced "heavy financial losses," losing "most of his earthly goods." Cusack would later say he felt Jim was finished as a football player by 1921.

On December 10, Iva gave birth at home in Yale to a third daughter, Grace Frances, named for Iva's sister.

In March 1922, the Portland Beavers, a club in the Pacific Coast League (PCL), gave Jim a generous contract. It was primarily for pinch hitting and his name because the team already had excellent outfielders. The PCL featured a high level of play; it would produce great players such as Joe DiMaggio and Ted Williams. Jim was to be paid a dazzling $1,000 a month, and it was rumored that the club had paid another $5,000 in purchase money. That made him, said the *Los Angeles Times*, "an $11,000 asset or liability."

Jim arrived in Pasadena in March for spring training. The local media were waiting for him. *Los Angeles Times* sportswriter Harry A. Williams described Jim in terms that had rarely been used since his days at Carlisle. "Jim is a redman," Williams wrote, "except that he isn't. He's as white as the average white guy, who has been out in the sun. But high cheek bones, and expansive face and rather flat nose betray his Indian origin." Williams said Jim had brought along a hunting dog, a gun, and fishing tackle, which he intended to use on his days off. "Thorpe's tepee," he added, "has not yet arrived."

Despite such banalities, after watching Jim for a month Williams provided a sharp, fresh look at Jim's athletic style and a detailed analysis of how his football skills and style failed to translate to baseball. In the absence of film footage, it is a vivid record of Jim in motion, even in these last years of his athletic career:

> Thorpe's football origin shows in his stride particularly and in half a
> dozen other little movements and traits . . . While his muscles are well

co-ordinated through all-around development, at times he seems to lack the elastic freedom of the natural baseball player. Also, his stride, despite its length, seems rather heavy.

But it was not until Thorpe ran out a triple near the end of the series that his football form became so plain that it seemed to hit you right in the face. Running with his head somewhat down and a pronounced drive to each step, as though to force his body through some sudden resistance which might rise up to bar the way, and his balance that of a football player who at the last moment would dive headforemost along the ground to gain that extra yard or two . . .

When he made the turn at first and second it was with the calculating, almost hesitating stride, not of the sprinter, but the backfield man about to shift with his feet or make a sudden twist with his body and elude an impending tackler or shake off one which had already struck. . . .

Like every good open-field runner, Thorpe does not throw everything into his stride and give it complete freedom. He keeps something in reserve for defense.

In the middle of May, *The San Francisco Call and Post* interviewed Jim just as it was announced that Pop Warner was coming to coach at Stanford. Jim lauded him as the greatest coach ever. When asked if the professional or college game was better, Jim said: "Well, now, I'm a professional football player and I'm not going to knock my own game, am I? I believe the professional players [are] more artists in their line than collegians, because of the fact they have had more experience and . . . play a more technically perfect game than the collegians." He compared football to baseball, to the latter's detriment:

> Football always will have something that baseball lacks . . . Suppose you strike out. You don't get another chance to get back your lost reputation for perhaps a half hour. Not so in football. If you make a mistake, you're liable to have a chance on the very next play to rise to glory. You're always on edge. You have to be. You don't have time to think about what's just happened: you have to worry about what is going to happen.

The element of chance in baseball, the surprise play that thrills fans, and the orderly progress of a player around the bases did not have sufficient appeal for Jim's strategic appetite. He wanted, as Vince Lombardi would later say, to "run to daylight," powerfully, forcefully, one quick, brutal down after another. The football didn't just need to be thrown and caught, it had to be *possessed*, gripped, protected, carried to safety.

It was all personal to Jim. *New York Times* sportswriter Harvey Araton eight decades later would write of "the champion's enduring insecurity, the dread of being ordinary." Jim played to be extraordinary. To the game that gave him the most chances to excel, he gave his best.

Jim lasted barely a month in chilly Portland. He hit .308 in thirty-five games but was let go by the team in an economy move. After turning down an offer from the Salt Lake City Bees because, reportedly, they wouldn't give him a signing bonus, on June 6 he was picked up by the Hartford (Connecticut) Senators of the A-level Eastern League, the next tier down the baseball hierarchy from Portland.

Iva made the announcement of Jim's move to reporters in Portland as Jim boarded his train east. Married life had become even more unpredictable and haphazard. She had made the long trip west to settle in for the summer with their three daughters, one of them a six-month-old baby. Now she would pack up again and take them back to Yale. She was left to ponder how much longer Jim would be able to play baseball. And what she could do about his increased drinking.

"Hartford welcomes this doughty Sac and Fox, whose arena had been the athletic fields of many countries," hailed *The Hartford Daily Times* for Jim's debut game on June 14. The honeymoon did not last long. Something had snapped in Jim. For a doubleheader against the New Haven Indians, the stands packed with fans who'd come to see him, he showed up at the park drunk. On the field, reported *The New York Times*, he gave "imitations of a wooden Indian chasing flies." Cheers for Jim from the stands turned to what *The Sporting News* called "hoots and howls." Jim made an early exit to the clubhouse and, "partly dressed," he charged into the stands to find the hecklers. Only when several police subdued him did he agree to leave.

It was a horrible performance. Jim had dropped to a lower level of minor league baseball and he was anguished and scared. Like his father, Jim often tried to right personal wrongs with physical action, no matter how self-destructive. He needed an opportunity to reclaim his glory and he decided he wasn't going to get that in Hartford.

A *Sporting News* editorial ten days later described him as having gone "on one of those rampages for which he has been notorious." He was blasted for having "deliberately and knowing full well the consequences from previous sad experience, seriously damaged if not destroyed his usefulness to his club." The editorial quoted one of the local Hartford papers saying Jim was "full to the gills with the stuff that ruined so many of his forefathers." The incident was indicative of a new problem: athletes drinking Prohibition hooch and wood alcohol, which produced much more bizarre behavior than a couple of beers. Jim was fined $50 by the Senators' management and suspended for four games. The Eastern League fined him another $50.

During a game against the Waterbury Brasscos in August, Jim let several fly balls drop near him. Years later, a reporter who covered that game said that Waterbury had advertised, without Jim's permission, that he would race against its manager in a series of track events that day and that Jim had balked at taking part unless he was paid and then retaliated in the outfield. The crowd, unaware of the circumstances, booed him. He got drunk and was suspended again. On August 15, a wry headline in *The New York Times* reported the next development: "Hartford Turns Jim Thorpe Over to Worcester as a Gift." He played center field and ended the 1922 season a leader in the Eastern League with a .344 average in ninety-six games.

It didn't matter. He was released by Worcester at season's end. No team picked him up. He could hit successfully at that level, but his bizarre personal behavior scared everyone off. He was finished in organized baseball.

Jim had made very good money up through the Hartford debacle but had saved or invested little of it. Now he had three children to provide for. Irresponsibly, he continued to lend money to friends and strangers: he was what one teammate called "big-hearted," but what others might call an easy touch. The alcoholic's attraction to grandiose acts of generosity became stronger as the money dwindled. He did not mature; rather, he was extending his adolescence. He was "always a likeable chap," said Warner, "and never changed." Many of his Carlisle teammates had gone on to lead productive and mostly anonymous lives after sports. Jim's fame kept his mishaps in the public glare.

.   .   .

Toward the end of the 1921 season with the Cleveland football team, Jim and Calac had joined Airedale dog breeder and Canton fan Walter Lingo for a hunting trip in LaRue, Ohio. Lingo soon discovered that not only did Jim enjoy hunting more than anything else, he had a way with hunting dogs; for him they weren't pets, they were partners. Lingo revered the idea of the noble Indian hunter and believed there was a mystical bond between animals and Indians. A short, rather chubby entrepreneur with a taste for celebrities, the right side of his face so disfigured by surgery he would walk about the town only late at night, Lingo had perfected a combination of the British Airedale— itself a mix, he claimed, of the old English sheepdog, black and tan terrier, otter hound, and bulldog—and the champion Crompton Oorang Airedale. The Oorang had a broader head, stronger jaw, more muscular build, and greater stamina than the traditional Airedale, characteristics that aided it in hunting bears, mountain lions, and other big game, as well as stream-side creatures like otters and raccoons. The standard Airedale already had an enthusiastic following. Theodore Roosevelt was an early fan. During World War I, the Germans chose the breed over the German shepherd for use as guard dogs and messengers; the British made them their first official war dog; the Americans used them to retrieve wounded soldiers from no-man's-land. For most of the 1920s, standard Airedales were the most popular dog breed in America. Even Jim called himself an "American Airedale," a mixed breed.

Lingo's kennels had grown into a big, profitable mail-order enterprise after the war. Oorang studs were bred to bitches leased to local farmers. Hunters took the adult dogs, trained them in the field, and returned them to be sold. By the early 1920s, Lingo had 1,000 brood bitches producing about 15,000 dogs a year. The animals were shipped by train from LaRue, where Lingo had his business, to their new owners. Lingo was a natural promoter and orchestrated publicity-filled presentations of free, trained dogs to athletes like Jack Dempsey and Ty Cobb; Gary Cooper's Oorang was named Rusty. Satisfied celebrity owners often came to LaRue to hunt with the Airedale breeder.

Lingo made Jim an offer. He would sponsor and manage a LaRue-based all-Indian football team, to be called the Oorang Indians, if Jim would coach and work as a kennel supervisor for $500 a week. Jim could play in any game, at his own discretion. Lingo thought Jim's fame would attract fans and that Jim could recruit players from his web of Indian connections. Lingo felt he could make money with the team, but its primary purpose was to publicize the kennels. In the postwar decade captivated with the potential of advertising, the project made oddball sense. For Jim it was an ideal combination—football *and* hunting—and he agreed. Lingo paid the franchise fee to the newly named NFL.

Green Bay, Wisconsin, whose new NFL franchise was funded by the Acme Packing Company, was small; LaRue was smaller, its population about eight hundred. With six or seven grocery stores, three car dealers, and four churches, LaRue was the tiniest community the NFL would ever count among its members. But the new league could not be fussy. As teams folded, it needed new blood. Of its eighteen teams for the 1922 season, eight were brand-new franchises.

Jim arrived in LaRue from Worcester in late September 1922. The village was about fifteen miles from Marion, hometown of Lingo's friend President Warren G. Harding, and site of the team's home field. Jim had recruited about a dozen former Carlisle players as part of his twenty-six-man roster. Pete Calac, as well as the last Carlisle All-Americans, Elmer Busch and Joe Guyon, were among the remembered names from the school's glory days. Most of the players had or had assumed "colorful" names like White Cloud, War Eagle, Long Time Sleep, Xavier Downwind, and Red Fox. Tribes represented on the team included Chippewa, Cherokee, Winnebago, Wyandot, and Mohawk.

Jim instituted four-hour afternoon practices south of town on a playing field adjacent to the Scioto River. The field, shared with the local high school team, was approximately a half mile from the Coon Paw Inn, a boardinghouse where some of the team lived. After showers, rubdowns, and dinner, the team was required to hunt raccoons until midnight. One visitor thought the cacophony of noises coming from the various animals out in the woods—a pet coyote, hound dogs, Airedales, and Queen Mary, Lingo's 375-pound Mexican black bear used to train the dogs to tree their prey—as well as "war whoops," college cheers, and football signals from the players sounded like a circus.

On the road, the pregame and halftime shows sapped the team's strength and concentration. As he would do almost all his athletic life, Jim demonstrated drop-kicking before the game. He would start at the thirty- or thirty-five-yard line and work back to the middle of the field, almost invariably kicking the ball through the goalposts. At the fifty-yard line, he would kick the ball through one goalpost and then do the same through the other. The crowd went wild every time.

At halftime Lingo's dogs demonstrated trailing and treeing (chasing Queen Mary up a tree). There were shooting exhibitions, as well as knife, tomahawk, and lariat throwing, and Indian dances. The climax was a reenactment of the part Red Cross Oorangs had played in the recent war by bringing medicine to wounded soldiers in the trenches. The Indians then came forward to testify that the Oorang Airedale was loyal and true, and could kill a bear, wolf, or deer with a single bite.

It was a strange, sad Wild West show. "Rig [an Indian] out in feathers and war paint and give him a pack of dogs," Lingo said, "and he is sure to attract attention." The headlines in the *Marion Star* reinforced the dime novel connection: "Jim Thorpe Has Been Whetting Scalping Knife . . . Palefaces from Columbus Will Be Burned Alive!" Lingo boasted that his veterinarian controlled the diet of both the dogs and the Indians.

On the playing field, things weren't much better. Lingo's team ended the season 3–6. Two of the losses were routs of 62–0 and 36–0. Jim didn't play until the second half of the seventh game. Only once did his presence make a difference. Against the Buffalo All-Americans, he "electrified the crowd," according to a history of the Oorang Indians, with his long runs, plunges through the line, and accurate passing, which led to a 19–7 win. His performance reminded spectators and sportswriters of what he had been. "Athletes come and athletes go," wrote Chicago columnist Bert Collyer, "but apparently Thorpe stays on forever."

His fame matured into a different kind of sports folktale—the star athlete beaten but not bowed. To a later generation the stories could seem apocryphal at best. But most of them were essentially true, like origin stories passed down and embellished until they became a kind of lingua franca of the sports world. Milwaukee Badgers quarterback-coach Jimmy Conzelman, later a Hall of Fame coach of the Chicago Cardinals, once successfully faked Jim and gained sixty yards. When Conzelman tried it again, with a knock from his hip Jim sent him flying out of bounds. Conzelman had grown a mustache, though facial hair was not generally tolerated by players or coaches. When he came to and looked up, there was Jim. " 'Cut that damn thing off!' " Jim ordered, and Conzelman promptly did. "For some reason," he would tell Arthur Daley years later, "the mustache made him mad as hell." Conzelman was also the source of what came to be known as the Jim Thorpe Bear Story. When Lingo's bear wouldn't budge into an adjoining compartment so her keeper could clean out the mess, Jim stepped into the cage and "shouldered" her in, said Conzelman, the "same way he shouldered tacklers."

With the LaRue kennels shipping out over a hundred dogs daily, Lingo decided he could fund the team for another year, despite their poor performance. To drum up interest, from April 1923 to the following spring, each month in *The Athletic World*—a "manly" magazine, initially titled *Football World*, started by J. D. Fetzer in 1921 to capitalize on the postwar "sport mania"—he wrote a chapter of Jim's life story. The first installment featured a photograph of Jim in "full Indian regalia": Plains Indian feathered headdress and fringed buckskins. On the magazine's cover was a more realistic shot of Jim crouched down on one knee, Airedale at his side, shotgun cradled under his right arm—athlete *and* sportsman. Jim's name also showed up on sports pages when charges of professionalism were raised against a member of the team recently picked for the 1924 Olympic Games. "There has been quite an effort," said *The Sporting News*, "to hush up the disclosures just as the facts about Jim Thorpe were hushed up."

Jim put together his 1923 Oorang team while playing summer baseball with a local club in Bucyrus, a town roughly midway between LaRue and Canton. Despite the addition of more Carlisle veterans, the Oorang football season was disastrous. The team didn't score a touchdown until its seventh game. It won only once, and its most spectacular loss (Jim played the entire game), 57–0, was to the Buffalo team he had triumphed against the previous year. Two weeks later at Chicago's Cubs Park, George Halas picked up a Thorpe fumble at the Bears' two-yard line and ran ninety-eight yards for a touchdown, with Jim chasing him and roaring the entire way. Halas's run set a record that was not beaten until 1972.

The players' behavior couldn't have helped matters. Chicago Bears guard Ed Healy said the Oorang players knew football wasn't important to Lingo so "they just partied all the time." The night before a Chicago game, the team went out on the town, drinking until dawn. In St. Louis, after leaving a bar late at night, the players picked up a trolley and turned it around on the tracks. Another time, when a driver behind Jim at a red light started impatiently honking his horn, Jim got out, opened the other car's hood, disconnected the horn, got back in his car, and drove away. Local police began to meet the Oorang Indian train at the station to set ground rules for acceptable behavior. Lingo negotiated with them to let any offenders sleep off their spree with a night in jail and no fine. "White people . . . thought we were all wild men," said Chippewa quarterback Leon Boutwell, "even though almost all of us had been to college and were generally more civilized than they were. . . . Since we were Indians, we could get away with things and whites couldn't. Don't think we didn't take advantage of it."

It was also generally agreed that Jim was not a good coach. He had trouble teaching what came naturally to him, and he was dealing with, unlike his Canton teams, a mixed bag of talent. "A few of the players were good," said Pete Calac, "but most of them were just big Indians." Lingo's son, Bob Lingo, later said that the game was like "sandlot football," with the plays made up as the team went along. Jim himself was starting to feel his thirty-six years: "I couldn't breathe so good," he said. Lingo decided not to support another season.

With four NFL victories in two seasons, the Oorang Indians had ended up as only a sideshow. If spectators had been brought to their games in part by a kind of Wild West nostalgia, the Indian players brought their own complicated feelings. Lingo was financing a circuslike exploitation of their Indian identity, but the players saw a chance to play the game they loved—with each other. Jim wanted to provide, as he said, "bread and butter and babies' boots" for his family, as well as jobs for his Indian friends. If being Indian and playing football was bankable, he would use it. Later analysts such as Philip J. Deloria would examine the revisionist idea of agency and suggest that such experiences of Indians playing Indians in this era, though limiting and debasing, also "ironically . . . offered a certain power to native people who could find and push the right cultural buttons." The Oorang Indians remain the only all-Indian team to play in a major professional sport league.

Jim and Lingo remained close. They were associate editors and publishers of *The Athletic World*'s successor, *Athlete and Sportsman*. In 1926, after the bottom fell out of the Airedale market, Lingo went bankrupt, the kennels were closed, and several hundred puppies had to be put down. Lingo eventually resumed breeding the dogs, but on a much smaller scale. In the years to come, Jim often came to visit the family in LaRue, sleeping on the living room floor. Mrs. Lingo would get up "at the crack of dawn" to make breakfast for her guest. "I never saw anybody," said her son of Jim, "who could eat so much bacon and eggs in my life."

For Jim, the rewards of the Oorang experience in Ohio had little to do with football. Rather, it was about seeing the first light of morning after a long night of hunting—cold, mud, darkness, scufflings, squeaks and cries, the dogs baying at the base of a tree, raccoon staring down from high branches, rifle shots. Some of his happiest times were spent earning the tired, satisfied pleasure of sitting on a car running board at dawn, dog at his feet. Raccoon and deer were Jim's prey of choice. To find them, one had to track and observe. Sitting in a duck blind or up in a deer stand didn't interest him: he wanted to meet the animals on somewhat equal terms.

Out at night, pacing down a trail, he re-created the earliest joys he had ever known, of his Oklahoma youth. It was a protected place, where the child knew the boundaries of his territory and how to find all the creatures that lived therein.

Iva and the three girls had lived with Jim at the Coon Paw Inn. Her initial efforts to maintain the rituals of respectable middle-class life in the midst of bears, dogs, raccoons, a football team, and a husband who was often out on the town were poignant. By the end of the 1923 season, "the thread of my marital happiness snapped," Jim recalled. He and Iva sat down and agreed that "incompatibility stared us in the face."

Sports were partly to blame for the gulf between them: playing two sports took up ten months of the year; he was constantly on the road, not around to be a father and husband. According to Grace Thorpe's recollections, her mother had also developed an even more pronounced antipathy toward Indians, especially those who behaved as if they had gone, as Iva put it, "back to the blanket." She had had to fetch Jim home, drunk, too many times, and his public humiliations, especially when covered in the press, were excruciating for her. Jim later claimed that it was at this point Iva told him she was not Indian: she had "cheated," he said, and that was why they had separated. The story was a self-serving fiction, but it contained an emotional truth: how could Iva know what it felt like to be him if she were not Indian? She had been happy, when her husband's Indian identity was an asset, to claim Indian blood when it added to her romantic allure. "I sure loved him when I married him," she would tell Grace. And she sure didn't now. She took the girls back to Yale and proceeded to cut Jim's image out of many of her photos of them together.

Iva's anger was also fueled by the emergence of a rival, Freeda Kirkpatrick, a petite, pretty, red-haired high school student working at the kennels, whose father managed the Marion Golf Club. A relationship that began with casual chats in 1922 was, by early 1924, after Iva had left, an intense and passionate romance. Freeda was eighteen years younger than Jim. She was thoroughly caught up in being loved by a famous man who traveled and who had lots of famous friends. A shy person, Freeda was also attracted to Jim's low-key but friendly and easygoing personality. "He could draw ladies around pretty easy," Jim's son Bill would later say. Jim told Freeda that even though he was still married, he and she were engaged, and he began the process of divorcing Iva.

As the Eighth Olympiad was taking place in Paris, Jim became even more of a journeyman athlete. The Boston Twilight League—so called because games began at 5:45 p.m., allowing mill workers to attend after work—took him on to play baseball for the Independents in Lawrence, Massachusetts. The semiprofessional league was composed of solid teams from Boston and suburban towns like South Boston, North Cambridge, and Reading. The welcoming crowds applauded each time Jim came to bat. He swam hours on end in the local lake and didn't touch a drop of alcohol. By late May he was leading the team in hits and had a batting average of .455; he would remain in top form for the rest of the season. On June 6, he hit the longest home run in the history of the local O'Sullivan Park. "The crowd went wild as Jim Thorpe strode to the plate and begged for a home run," wrote the *Lawrence Telegram*. "And Thorpe came through."

Besotted with Freeda, he wrote to her in LaRue almost every day. The letters, which Freeda kept all her life, provide an incomparable surviving record, the most personal, immediate access to Jim. "Honey talk about being lonely I miss you so much," he wrote on June 29, just after she had made a visit to Lawrence, "and I can hear you talking at times which only makes things worst for me." He writes about her parents' opposition to the relationship, about his concern that they not read his letters, about how he is keeping in good condition only for her. Lawrence won the first half of the split league pennant race in early July, Jim leading the team in hitting with twelve home runs, and he told Freeda he was getting "plenty of [newspaper] write ups." When a game got rained out, he spent the day "watching the drunks put on their stuff . . . and refused every one that tried to give me a drink." When they told him he was a "big stiff and no good for not drinking with them," Jim "only laughed and had a good time 'kidding' them. Don't you think me fine," he wrote. "Honey dear you're the world to me and am doing all this for you. My love is too great that's all."

Jim was in his own version of heaven: playing ball, mostly beautiful weather, companionship in the form of his friend Little Twig, along for the summer, and steady money. Photographs of him in the *Telegram* show a flat-stomached, lean, healthy man. The letters are full of lovesick pleas for the only thing missing. "Yes, Libby [his nickname for Freeda, perhaps a riff off his old Carlisle nickname, Libbling]," he wrote, "I would love and love you so much that I'm afraid you would get tired of me just go off to sleep and me still hanging on to you. Freeda dear if you only knew how I need and want you." He made several references to their "second honeymoon," which suggests the relationship was already sexual. "You say you're never taking a bath since you left here," he wrote after another visit from LaRue. "Better look out they will be planting potatoes or making garden around your neck and ears. Ha!"

"Honey I had a wonderful dream of you last night," he wrote. "Heard you laugh and call to me. You should of seen me get out of bed. One hop and I was on the floor looking around for you [even?] thought you had hidden and looked. Turned on the lights. Lonesome now." He wrote in the same letter, "Oh yes had another dream of you. Seems we were living in some home where we had a great big fire place and you were sitting where the red fire glow would show you up and in your lap was a baby." In another was a "small snake": Jim "played and had a great time with it. And then took it to the Lake, where I lost it in the water. Some dream. Don't think this was of you." Some of the dreams made him laugh, but others made him "fear some thing the unseen as it may be." He cautioned her: "Honey don't pay to much attention to dreams for lots and lots of them never come true."

There was no mention of his daughters, only complaints about his divorce from Iva, who seemed to be having second thoughts. "I have written to Mrs. T," he wrote on July 8, "and am still looking for a wanted answer. . . . She is wanting to come East but nothing doing as I wrote her that I didn't want to live near or with her, so this should stop all proceedings of wanting to come. I wants my Honey and 'Krazy Kitten' that's all." He was hoping to arrange the split "without giving up everything or if I can clear things up to good advantage."

If Jim needed a reminder of how precarious the bush leagues could be, he got one as the second half of the Boston Twilight season came to a close in mid-August. The North Cambridge team contested the decision of an umpire to forfeit a game in June to the Lawrence team because of bad language from their pitcher, which had given Lawrence the first half championship. The league president confirmed the forfeit, and five teams threatened to quit the league if he relented to the constant pressure from the North Cambridge manager. Rumors circulated about players throwing games. Jim was accused of getting "purposely . . . caught off second." Nothing came of it as the season ended in fairly typical semiprofessional disarray. Jim, one of only nine players left on the team, stuck it out until mid-September. He ended the year batting .427.

It was a sorry end to a great season, and there were no lucrative opportunities left for him in baseball. He went back to football, signing with the NFL Rock Island Independents in Illinois for the 1924 season. The *Telegram* noted that he would be paid $500 per game, yielding in ten games more money than he got for playing baseball in Lawrence all season. Jim played fairly well at age thirty-seven, but only in short spurts. Oklahoman Steve Owen, later coach of the New York Giants, was starting his professional career fresh out of college with the Kansas City Blues. The game against Rock Island provided him with his own favorite Thorpe tale. On Owen's first play as left tackle, Jim, the wingback at right half, didn't block him. The same thing happened on the second play. Owen assumed "Jim had gotten old and didn't care for this blocking business anymore," as he told Arthur Daley in 1943. By the third play, Jim still hadn't made a move so Owen ignored him altogether. "Well, sir," he said to Daley, "I landed exactly on top of my head and didn't know where I was or what had happened." Jim pulled Owen to his feet and said, "Son, never take your eyes off the wingback."

As Jim peeled off the Rock Island Indian players—"Thorpe's All-Stars"—for a postseason football tour of "easy wins and middling crowds" in Texas, the 1924 Indian Citizenship Act was passed. The Society of American Indians had begun to push for citizenship at the beginning of the decade, pointing out that while Indians had fought in the Civil War fifty years earlier to free the slaves, they were not rewarded with their own complete freedom. Jim and his "combination of muscle and intellect" was cited by the society as an example that Indians had "assimilated more readily" than blacks. The secretary of the interior was authorized to issue certificates of citizenship to Indians born in the U.S. and not already citizens. Individual states still retained control over enfranchisement, and it took court action to enforce the law in several states. Indians remained wards of the nation, but the act marked the beginning of a shift in national attitude. Reformers such as John Collier—though there was no one quite like that passionate, controversial, aggressive crusader—formed the American Indian Defense Association. Its mission was, in part, to promote the Indian communal way of life, thought by its advocates to be more authentic and virtuous because it was based on a connection with nature and the supernatural. D. H. Lawrence, living in Taos, where his neighbor Collier had his original, transformative epiphany about the spiritual wisdom of indigenous Americans, observed that the passionate white enthusiast might be "setting the claws of his own benevolent volition into [the Indians]."

Sympathy for Indians and reform was reinforced by the scandal that had rocked the White House. When oil was found on the Navajo reservation in New Mexico, Harding's secretary of the interior and friend, Albert B. Fall, facilitated the leasing of millions of acres to private oil companies. Fall was ultimately found guilty of taking bribes connected to the Teapot Dome and shipped off to prison; Harding died suddenly in office the year before the Citizenship Act was passed. As even more fabulous amounts of oil were discovered in eastern Oklahoma, Indians there faced yet another wave of graft, fraud, and frantic boom-or-bust settlement. Jim's life would have been no more secure if he'd headed home.

Iva, meanwhile, was "in bad circumstances" at the end of 1924, according to the Sac and Fox superintendent. She requested that the balance of the mortgage on the Yale house be paid off with part of the tribal trust fund moneys credited to the three girls, amounting to $1,750. The house was deeded over to them, and Iva went to Tulsa in search of a job, temporarily putting her daughters in a local convent. Eventually she found work as a mail clerk in the Tulsa Hotel and moved into a one-bedroom apartment with an old Carlisle girlfriend. The daughters were sent back to Yale to live with their aunt Grace and her husband. When their aunt and uncle moved to Oklahoma City, the Thorpe house was leased and the girls sent to St. Mary's Academy, the boarding school at the Benedictine compound founded by their great-grandfather.

Iva, calling herself Cherokee, sued for divorce in Tulsa on April 6, 1925, on the grounds of desertion. The divorce decree and property settlement agreement were issued on April 17. Iva won custody of the children and ownership of their only possessions of any potential value—Jim's Carlisle medals and trophies. Jim agreed to pay $125 a month in child support. Iva tried to arrange the payments through the superintendent of the Shawnee Agency, but the Indian Bureau ruled that as they were "educated competent Indians living away from the reservation" there was no reason the couple could not manage their own affairs. The superintendent knew that Iva, familiar with Jim's habits, was trying to ensure regular payments.

The girls, ranging in age from six to ten, were sent to the Haskell Institute, where their father had gone more than twenty-five years before, in fall 1927. An executive with the Prairie Oil and Gas Company in Kansas, Fred S. Cook, who frequently stayed in the Tulsa Hotel, had pulled the strings necessary to get the girls into the school, describing Iva in a letter to an Oklahoma congressman as "a very high class lady" carrying "quite a responsibility . . . all alone." Jim was "very dilatory," wrote Cook, and "for sometime past has paid no alimony." As the 1928 school term was starting, Iva sent a frantic telegram to the BIA commissioner telling him that Haskell had abolished the fourth and fifth grades, and that Gail, age ten, would have to leave. Iva did not want to separate the girls, so all three were transferred to the Indian school at Chilocco, near Tulsa, which Iva had attended. The girls would stay there for most of their childhoods, even after Iva remarried in 1931. Her new husband was an oil executive, Harrison Gray Davies, a kind, well-mannered man who had worked his way up from the oil fields to become president of his own company, Superior Oil. His office was located in the Tulsa Hotel, and it was there that he met Iva. When Davies bought too much stock on margin—putting a small amount of cash down on the value of a stock and borrowing the rest against an anticipated rise in value, a common investment in the 1920s—and lost the company in the crash, he and Iva moved to Chicago, where Davies began another career with the Socony Vacuum Paint Products company.

Though Iva continued to denigrate all things Indian, she also continued to benefit from Indian boarding schools. She told the Chilocco officials that she lived in Oklahoma, a prerequisite for enrollment. The only time the girls left Chilocco was for the summer. When Iva visited, Davies would stay in their "great big Packard car with chrome all around" while Iva entered the dormitory to visit briefly with her children. When she left, Charlotte wrote that she cried her eyes out. They continued to love and admire their beautiful mother but had been virtually abandoned. From their father they sought recognition and affection, but when Jim made a visit to Haskell, his daughter Grace didn't know who he was. He called Charlotte "daughter" and she wondered if he knew her name. "It was like the big hero coming to visit everybody," Gail said of his rare visits to Chilocco. "It wasn't like the father coming to visit the children."

When Charlotte tried to run away from Chilocco in 1931, in the ensuing investigation it was revealed that Iva no longer resided in Oklahoma. The three girls were forced to move to the Davieses' one-bedroom apartment in Chicago. Iva and her husband slept in a Murphy bed in the living room and the girls in the bedroom. Charlotte felt her mother blamed her for the inconvenience, and, though Davies had not adopted the girls, Iva insisted they use his surname in Chicago. Charlotte suspected her mother was still bitter about the divorce and did not want anyone to know who their real father was. Iva was also embarrassed by the bad grammar the girls had picked up in Indian schools. In the apartment storage area, however, Iva had kept all of Jim's medals and memorabilia, trunks and trunks of them.

At the end of October 1925, sports page readers read some version of this small headline: "Jim Thorpe Fades from Sports Scene." A month earlier Jim had been released by Rock Island and had signed with the New York Giants. The brand-new football franchise had been bought by bookmaker Tim Mara, a big step for the NFL: a stable New York team, it was hoped, would get the unparalleled publicity of the city's press. Jim was envisioned as a major draw, to be paid $200 a game to play no more than thirty minutes until he got back in shape. Jim wired the team's coach, Bob Folwell, that he was "in fine physical condition and anxious to be back at the Polo Grounds." But after barely three weeks, he was let go for failing "to show anything like his old form." An injured left knee had not responded to treatment, and a summer spent playing baseball in Ohio for the Zanesville Greys— western novelist Zane Grey was born in the town—a semipro team with seven former major leaguers, hadn't helped. "Observers see the end," said one report, "of [Thorpe's] spectacular athletic career."

On October 23, little more than a month after Freeda turned twenty, Jim, thirty-eight, "signed another contract—in matrimony— and is now honeymooning on his way West," reported *The New York Times*. DEAR FOLKS, read the couple's telegram to Freeda's parents in Ohio, after the marriage in New York on October 23, HAVE JOINED OUR HANDS AS ONE SHALL WRITE LATER GIVING EVERYTHING IN DETAIL HOWS EVERYBODY AT HOME LOVE FREEDA AND JIM. "She came into my life," he would say, "after my best deeds had been done. . . . She brought hope and confidence and an encouragement which made possible my dreams of beginning again." The couple returned to Marion to live, and Jim finished the season with Rock Island. After a mid-November game against the Kansas City team, the Rock Island *Argus* described Jim and teammate Rube Ursella as having "too many years on their veteran legs."

Undeterred, Jim then rounded up some teammates, including Ursella, to join him in Florida in December, primarily to cash in on the Chicago Bears' tour featuring their new star, Harold "Red" Grange. A redheaded running back from Wheaton, Illinois, Grange was dubbed "the Galloping Ghost" for his slippery but relentless style as an open field runner for the University of Illinois. Stories of his hauling ice during summers to earn money further enhanced his popular clean-cut college boy image. Grange had shocked the collegiate world by signing with Halas on November 22 to finish the season with the Bears. He wasn't even going to graduate. "I'd have been more popular," Grange later said, "if I had joined Capone's mob in Chicago."

His timing was perfect. Two years earlier the *Los Angeles Times* had analyzed the emerging trifecta of money, college players, and professional football. With the game still largely concentrated in the East, the NFL's "first problem," it said, "will be to educate the public" in the rest of the country. The league's plan was to build each professional team around at least one college star. Jim was held up as the example of a "really famous" and well-paid—for professional football—player. But even if Jim earned $1,000 a game for ten contests per season, $10,000 was not a "fabulous sum" compared to top boxers, and it was "rather an ordinary salary" for a major league baseball player. For considerably less money, concluded the newspaper, Jim "probably expends more energy and braves more hazards than a fighter does in the average championship contest."

Professional football needed glamour, and the Galloping Ghost was happy to oblige. Movie newsreels featuring his collegiate games had created a national fan base. Halas and Grange's new agent, the colorful C. C. Pyle, the vaudeville trickster known as "Cash and Carry" Pyle who had tried to land Jim after the 1912 Olympics, organized a postseason tour. Cities from the Midwest to the Northeast, down to Florida and New Orleans and across to California, quickly put together star-filled teams to play against Grange. On New Year's Day in Tampa, the Bears were up against Jim and his Florida team— one of its ever-changing names was the Tampa Cardinals—in a game that had been widely hyped up north.

En route south, Jim wrote Freeda from the Grand Hotel in Cincinnati. His handwriting was sprawling and rushed. His life had changed since the halcyon summer of 1924. "I certainly have had my share of hard luck this fall," he wrote, referring to his quick exit from the Giants. He told her he was being dunned for $300, probably for expenses incurred in putting together the Florida team, and that the first money he received would go to pay debt. "I didn't rest any to well," he wrote, "was thinking of everything in the world." Two days later he wrote from the Hotel Tampa Terrace in Florida: "Shall try to get your expenses paid, so you can come down." He added that he had to wire the Rock Island manager for more money. Florida was unexpectedly familiar. "Rushing, hustling, grafting like that of the old days in Oklahoma," he wrote, "when the oil fields first opened up. Can expect most anything here. One has to be mighty careful what he does." The newlyweds were spending Christmas apart.

Less than a week before the game, advance sales were so low that the local promoters tried to get Pyle to agree to a percentage of the take rather than the guaranteed $5,000. Pyle headed for the train; the Tampa promoters relented. Jim, meanwhile, was now confident and focused. On a duck hunt a few nights earlier, his companions were so drunk that one of them fell overboard and Jim had to fish him out. "This don't mean that I was the same way," he reassured Freeda. "For I am sure going to show that Red Grange has nothing on me in the line of football." He badly wanted to win. Otherwise his team would have little chance of luring crowds for any further games they could put together. Two days before the game, he tore a muscle in his right calf during practice. "Want to be right for this game so bad," he wrote his wife that night, afraid he had been working too hard. The night before the game, he claimed his leg was healed and he was ready to show Grange "the time of his young life."

The Bears won, 17–3. "Jim was old, fat and slow," Grange would recall in 1932, "yet he could still hit hard. He smacked me once and I still remember it." Sportswriter Manning Vaughan agreed about Jim's power, stubbornly loyal, like many, to Jim's glory days: "They rave about Grange, but we doubt whether the mighty Red will ever measure up to the standard set by [the] wonderful Indian." The Bears' last game on the Florida circuit was against the instantly assembled Jacksonville All-Stars, featuring Ernie Nevers, Pop Warner's star fullback who had played in the Rose Bowl for Stanford a year before. Nevers was reportedly paid the unlikely sum of $50,000.

Jim appeared stoic, resigned, but underneath was the rarely articulated anger. Grange's contract and tour would earn him around $100,000, an incredible amount for the time. Before he burned through most of the money, he would buy twenty-five suits, eighteen cars, and a house for his father. He was so overwhelmed by the sudden change from the "genteel poverty of amateurism," as he called it, that he walked around, stunned, with his first check for $25,000 in his pocket. The deals came flooding in: a Grange candy bar contract for $10,000 and a percentage of sales; a line of sporting goods trademarked for $3,500; an outboard motor testimonial for $500; a $50,000 cash advance for a movie; Red Grange dolls and sweaters, endorsements for cars, shoes, ginger ale, tobacco—although he didn't smoke—and malted milk.

Not only did the highly publicized flow of money rankle Jim, so did the recognition and excitement accorded Grange, which was at an entirely new level thanks to the altered sports universe of the 1920s. Runyon described the Grange phenomenon as a combination of Dempsey, Ruth, Al Jolson, Paavo Nurmi, and Man o' War. Fourteen years earlier, there had been no such array of comparables to put up against Jim. Grange's stop at the Los Angeles Coliseum later that January drew an estimated 73,000 fans, said by local papers to be the biggest crowd ever to view a professional game. Almost as many had shown up in New York to see Grange play the Giants. Grange had an agent, a handler. Without Pyle, Grange would have got, according to Bears center George Trafton, "a couple bags of peanuts and a nickel or two and [been told] to go to the movies." Instead, the agent pushed Halas to give Grange 50 percent of each game's take. Though the hoopla accorded Grange was mostly 1920s celebrity mania, part of the thrill was seeing a respectable college boy cross over to the dark side of professional sports.

Inspired by Grange, and confirming the worst fears of college football programs that a lucrative professional game would lure away their best players, the other great collegiate star of the decade, the blond, handsome Ernie Nevers, defected a year later. The NCAA promptly prohibited anyone connected in any way with professional football from being a college coach or trainer. The NFL, working to upgrade its image, countered by passing a rule that college players were ineligible for the professional league until their class had graduated. Nevers's deal with the NFL Duluth Eskimos was aided by his collegiate coach, Pop Warner, who was hyping Nevers as a greater player than Jim. "Ernie gave me sixty minutes of himself in every game," said Warner. "I rarely got more than twenty minutes from the Indian." But Pudge Heffelfinger, the first documented college player to accept money, would tell sportswriter John McCallum in 1954 that "deep in his heart, Pop knew the Indian was the better man."

The publicity model set by Grange inspired, according to *Total Football: The Official Encyclopedia of the National Football League*, "the wildest barnstorming trips in pro football history," as each of the newly professional athletes set out in the fall of 1926 to introduce the game across the country. No doubt it occurred to Jim and to Warner that the Carlisle team had been the first national barnstormers. No one knew better than Jim that crowds only came out to see a big star, and they stayed home when his luster was shown to have faded. For now, the burden on a star in the NFL was huge. By the end of the Bears' first barnstorming tour, Guy Chamberlin, current coach of the Canton Bulldogs, would say that Grange "broke down mentally and physically because more was asked of him than any human being could perform." Jim could relate to that.

Grange went on to have a Hall of Fame football career. He proved, as Mara said, "that pro football didn't have to be a losing proposition." A major gate attraction from 1926 to 1934, he aided the NFL in its transition to a big-city league. Eastern and Chicago sportswriters began to seriously and consistently report on "the post-graduate game" for the first time, and their stories were picked up by newspapers nationwide. By 1931, *The New York Times* would note, "Numbers of ball enthusiasts prefer the economical skill, the mature precision, the finesse, and the art of the professional game to the comparatively bungling college match."

Some years after the Florida game, when all the ballyhoo had faded, Thorpe and Grange got to know and like each other. Grange, speaking to *New York Times* sportswriter Ira Berkow, called Jim "a wonderful guy . . . and a friend of mine." Once, they were at a Hollywood party with Pyle when the agent decided to perform one of his old vaudeville magic tricks. He asked Jim, surreptitiously, to make a slit in an apple and slip a quarter into it. With the party guests watching, Pyle would show them an identical coin and make as if he had made it disappear into the apple and then "retrieved" it. But when he went to pull out the quarter, there were two dimes and a nickel. "Oh, was he mad," Grange told Berkow. "He shouted, 'I'll kill that [Thorpe]!' "

Some of Jim's teammates stayed on with him in Florida to play a few more games after the Grange entourage continued west. Jim confessed to Freeda, who was still in Ohio, lonely and strapped for money, that he was "undecided" as to his future plans. "Honey dear," he wrote her, "I intend staying here in the south at least until spring please dear don't think me selfish. . . . Think I can send you Fifty dollars in my next letter." His handwriting was almost unrecognizable. "I know I make a lot of promises," he explained. "My ententions are good. But something always turns up."

Prior to a game at St. Petersburg with his latest assembled team, Jim publicly announced he was quitting the sport. "I have really played for the love of competition," he said. "Now I have a yearning to hunt and fish back with my people." His team then played the Haven Villas, of Winter Haven, to a scoreless tie. Fewer than three hundred people showed up. After playing again before a very small crowd, he retracted, probably because no job offers came in response to his retirement announcement. "I'll never quit athletics until I'm pushing up the daisies and am dead for sure," he said. "If athletics were taken away from me, I might as well be dead." Said one reporter of the almost forty-year-old Jim: "The people see something of romance in the way the veteran goes on, year after year."

Jim was putting on a brave face, but he wrote to Freeda after the St. Petersburg game, "Life . . . certainly is a blue one at present. The game played today a hard fought battle. . . . The split of gate was $160.00 giving each man $13.30 as his share. Nearly kills my heart to think how I worked in the advertising end and paid out twice as much of my money thinking it would be a knock-out. Well such is life. . . . I guess I should never look for the best as things have sure gone wrong in last few years." He couldn't get enough cash to stay solvent, much less send her any. Trying to line up more games and look for a job, he sounded more and more frantic.

He also worried that his new bride, with her parents nearby in Marion still expressing their doubts about him, was losing faith in him. "Do you believe in me," he wrote, "or has some one been telling you wrong. Have been real good but may break out I don't here from you soon." In mid-February he wrote again from Tampa. His luck had turned even worse. A check from the Winter Haven team had bounced. "God honey I'm here with a weeks hotel bill and nothing to pay out with I am the world over to find money. Don't I have a great time trying to stay out of jail? I am a good man too. Makes a man feel like going on a big drunk. Honey if you ever hear of me getting drunk, just take out papers for a divorce. . . . Never never again dear."

Rock Island still owed him for four games of the five-game guarantee he'd contracted for when the Giants fired him, and he intended to collect in person. "A man is a fool with easy money," he continued, "and that I've had. Now let's look for real happiness. Love first of all and the rest will come. Don't you think sweet heart? I am sorry that things didn't go through, but dear there is lots of time. I thought that athletics, base ball, football was out of my life. But I guess that is what I am made for." He wanted to see his old Giants teammate Rube Marquard, now manager of the Eastern League's Providence Rubes, about a job playing and possibly coaching in Rhode Island. "I will come out on top yet," he wrote, "and little woman don't never weaken for my heart and soul is in you."

Just before leaving Florida in February, he wrote Freeda from Tampa that while there was "plenty to do" there, it was not the work he wanted. Neither did he want to return to Shawnee, though Pottawatomie County was in the middle of the oil boom; he had become estranged, through neglect, from his siblings and extended family, and they would not make him welcome. A car company had approached him about being a salesman, which might make him enough money to get back to Ohio. "Want you to write me a good letter," he pleaded, knowing the marriage had hardly gotten off to a promising start, "telling me that you are still in love with me. I know

Honey that it was all my fault." He had wired Rock Island for $500 and the Prague, Oklahoma, bank for the money earned by renting out the small farm property he owned, but hadn't heard back. "I'll get by some way," he promised. "Sure in one h—— of hole at present but these happenings I figure will put me on my feet. When times are better shall know how to take care of things."

It was a refrain Freeda would hear often and a credo Jim sincerely believed. Someday, somehow, things would get better.

An Associated Press wire from Shelby, Montana, in April 1926 alerted the sports world that "another famous red man may make his 'last stand' here this summer, or at least his last athletic stand." Jim had signed as an outfielder with the Shelby Drillers of the Northern Montana League. It was one of the commodity-rich state's "copper loop" or oil teams to which the Pacific Coast League farmed out what the *Los Angeles Times* called "young hopefuls" for further seasoning. "Thorpe has run the gamut of athletics on the diamond and gridiron that has at last landed him in what sport scribes are wont to call the 'bushes,'" wrote the AP. Just below the Canadian border, Shelby was about as remote as one could get and still be in the lower forty-eight, and happy to get even a minor celebrity: in one of the more extreme sports fiascos of the decade, the town had almost bankrupted itself by hosting the Jack Dempsey–Tommy Gibbons world heavyweight boxing title in 1923. Jim took Freeda with him to the west, and ended up playing for the Havre team, but by August was back in Ohio playing for the Oorang Indian Base Ball Club, though how often he showed up is uncertain. By September, Freeda was pregnant.

A month later, Jim rejoined the Canton Bulldogs. The team's schedule had expanded well beyond Ohio to take on the Los Angeles Californians and the St. Louis Colonels, among others. As one mark of the greater attention professional football was getting back east, the *Hartford Courant* in Connecticut headlined an October 10 game between Jim's Bulldogs and Fritz Pollard's Akron Indians as "Fritz Pollard and Jim Thorpe Shine." In fact, Jim appeared only in the second quarter, "to please the fans," and neither player made much difference in the scoreless tie. Two days after the game Akron fired

Pollard, the NFL's first black head coach. Pollard had endured years of terrible treatment on the field, especially from white southern players. In September, the Buffalo Rangers, largely made up of Texans, had refused to play if Pollard was in the Akron lineup. When told there would be no game without him, the Buffalo coach said, "Okay, but my boys will kill him," and the Rangers won, 7–0. The abuse had worn Pollard down. He would form the first all-black professional football team, the Chicago Black Hawks, in 1928.

Jim got a chance to play against Ernie Nevers in the latter's first professional NFL season. Reaching up for a pass during the game, the twenty-three-year-old Nevers was suddenly flattened by Jim. "The Indian hit me in the chest with his shoulder," said Nevers. "I felt as if I'd been pile-driven three feet into the ground. Never before or since have I been hit as hard."

"You all right, young fellow?" said Jim, extending his hand to help him. "Sure Jim," Nevers remembered saying, his head still spinning. "But I'm glad I wasn't playing against you when you were in your prime."

One of Jim's teammates, Guy T. "Zeke" Roberts, described him, in this, his last season playing for Canton, as a "rather quiet self-contained individual, but temperamental at times." He was more cautious now. Before one game, Roberts watched him put some kind of stiff material under his sweater to protect his ribs. But he still had the wherewithal to get even. In one game, Jim said to Roberts, "Let me carry the ball." He took the snap and "ran like a wild horse at [the other team's] defensive end," running over him "like a bowling ball." The end had said something Jim didn't like.

Canton, Akron, and Dayton, three of professional football's "cradle" teams, were eliminated after the 1926 season. The league was now consolidating its emphasis onto larger cities with bigger fan bases and the facilities for expansion. The next year, there would be twelve teams, down from twenty-two. The NFL was maturing.

In December, Jim—who had played decent basketball at Carlisle, but mainly as a time filler between football and track and field—signed to coach an all-Indian team, the World Famous Indians. "WFI" was stitched on the front of their jerseys in big, white letters, above an Indian head in profile. Based in LaRue, with Jim as center and coach, the team featured many Indian players who had been basketball stars at Haskell. The season was long and tough, starting in mid-December in Indianapolis and continuing with daily games throughout Indiana. After Christmas, the team headed east to West Virginia to play college teams. After fifteen consecutive wins, they returned to LaRue to begin another tour, this time to Michigan. In March 1927, WFI played an exhibition game in Carlisle. More than 4,000 people showed up at the town's railroad station to greet Jim and his team. "I thought they had forgotten all about me," he said, "and the presence of this huge gathering of old friends and admirers made me swell up inside." The WFI season ended with a reported fifty-one wins out of sixty-two games in five states.

The basketball tickets and publicity stills featured a full-length photograph of a player dressed in the WFI basketball shorts and jersey, with a feathered headdress. Like the Oorang Indians, the WFI offered "war dances" between halves. The enterprise was hokey, but the team played good basketball, won games, and earned its players a living. The sport was simpler for Jim to manage and execute than football: it was played indoors in the winter and had fewer men to transport, feed, and pay. The sport was gentler on his aging body, too, yet gave him the opportunity, always important to him, to showcase gifted Indian athletes. Most important, basketball provided money for his growing second family: Carl Phillip—named after Jim's friend Carl Hoffmire in Mount Gilead, near Marion, and Jim's father, whose middle name was Phillip—was born on May 1.

Jim turned forty that month, and for the first and only time in his life would end a year, 1927, having played full seasons in three sports. The basketball season over, he organized a baseball team. Thorpe's Collegians—also called Ford's Collegians, after a sponsoring Ford car dealership in Columbus, Ohio—were a poignant collection of over-the-hill athletes, including the great Ohio State halfback Charles W. "Chic" Harley, who had moonlighted for Thorpe's 1919 Bulldogs and inspired the construction in 1922 of the huge Ohio State stadium. He had fallen on hard times and Jim gave him a break. Picking up games at random throughout Ohio, Jim called his team "gypsies" and described himself, with typical self-deprecation, as "eking a living from those who paid their admission to see Thorpe in his unheralded farewell tour."

He wasn't ready for the goodbyes just yet. As the Yankees swept the Pittsburgh Pirates in four straight World Series games, capping the season in which Babe Ruth hit his legendary sixty home runs, Jim signed on to play football. Jack Creasy, the director of public services for the city of Portsmouth, just across the Ohio River from Kentucky, had been busy that summer convincing some of the city's more than a dozen shoe factories, principally the Selby Shoe Company, and the Whitaker-Glessner steel mill to sponsor a semiprofessional team. The collapse of the NFL teams in Dayton, Akron, and Canton had inspired a string of such teams touted as "the new Ohio State League." A team name contest in Portsmouth came up, unsurprisingly, with the "Shoe-Steels." The proud, blue-collar city of 40,000 badly wanted to beat the rival Ironton Tanks, based about thirty miles upriver. Creasy approached Jim with an offer to be player-coach and Jim accepted. He wanted to go out a winner in the game he loved best.

Freeda and baby Phil joined him from Marion. Jim started a program of intensive nightly team workouts: conditioning drills, two-hour scrimmages, and practice sessions of the single-wing. The work paid off: the Shoe-Steels won four of their first five games, with Jim playing in all but one. "Now what are you fellows going to do?" he barked at his team before a game. "Are you going to show some fight or are you just going to play?" The question was noted in the press as "the first time the usually silent Thorpe has become even slightly talkative."

Jim and Creasy recruited players who had played at major colleges such as Ohio State and on professional teams with offers of $50 a game and promises of day jobs. Five thousand fans showed up at Redland Field in Cincinnati—reportedly the biggest crowd the city had ever seen at a professional football game—to watch the Shoe-Steels lose to the National Guards. A local headline read: "Thorpe Slowed Up, but Memories of Great Past Draw Crowd to See Him." For the Ironton game, Jim packed his team with even more new recruits and played a bit less than half the game. The Shoe-Steels lost. For the rematch two weeks later, Jim again beefed up the team with new professional and collegiate ringers. His team won, and Jim was hailed as the coach who had, at long last, beat the Tanks.

When Creasy set up a final, eleventh game of the season, Jim said he would neither coach nor play. His contract was for ten games, he said, not more. Though Creasy offered him a salary increase, Jim refused. Once again, he felt he was being used unfairly, though the Portsmouth manager and backers had clearly thrown themselves enthusiastically into building a winning team and were proud of their famous coach. Once he got a grudge in his head, he was too proud or too stubborn to act rationally. He left for Marion with Freeda—pregnant again—and the baby.

Two days after Christmas, Jim rounded up the World Famous Indians in Ohio for a basketball game in Marion. But the greatest athlete of all time, reported the Marion paper, would not play the next season: "The years are leaving their mark on the famous redman and now he leaves the basketball game to younger and more nimble bodies."

Nineteen twenty-seven had been a remarkable year of sustained physical effort by an athlete on the brink of middle age. However, in what Frederick Lewis Allen would call "the ballyhoo year" of car radios and Charles Lindbergh, his accomplishments went largely unnoticed.

In 2005 a six-inch-long ticket to a March 1, 1927, World Famous Indians exhibition game in Warren, Pennsylvania, would be found at a book sale. Stuck in a 1920s dime novel, *Jesse James and His Greatest Haul*, and in pristine condition, the ticket had presumably been there since the game. The discovery was greeted with nationwide media coverage: who knew Jim Thorpe had played basketball professionally, much less organized an all-Indian team? Moreover, said one report, "artifacts of Thorpe's career . . . are rare and valuable."

Jim returned to stay in Ohio in 1928, playing baseball in Marion for the independent Ohio Pennsylvania League. He had been desperate enough to telegraph the Waterbury club, asking for a job, but was turned down. Newspaper reports said, "Thorpe is considered done now." On August 16, Freeda gave birth to a second son, William "Bill" Kendall Thorpe.

When Jim and Freeda returned to Marion from Chicago, Jim was "pretty blue." His young wife did not see him as he used to be. If he could no longer rely on his body, what was he left with? Job prospects of any kind grew even grimmer.

Three months after Bill's birth, Jim agreed to suit up for football one last time. The Chicago Cardinals were at the end of their third losing season and hired him for the charity benefit Thanksgiving game against the Chicago Bears. "Jim Thorpe . . . played a few minutes . . . but was unable to get anywhere," reported *The New York Times.* "[O]ld and muscle-bound, Thorpe was a mere shadow of his former self."

The year of Jim's last humiliating football game also saw the release of the Meriam Report, officially "The Problem of Indian Administration," one of the most influential examinations of American Indian life since the 1887 Dawes allotment act. The report was commissioned by the secretary of the interior in response to the demands of groups such as John Collier's American Indian Defense Association. The findings were grim: inadequate schooling, housing, and employment, and abysmal health care—trachoma was still rampant on many reservations. The boarding schools in particular disrupted family life and alienated the students from their own culture and kin. The American Indians, stated the report, "wish to remain Indians, to preserve what they have inherited from their fathers"—just like anyone else. Though assimilation of the "retarded race" was still valued, the report set goals, such as reinforcement of tribal family and community life, that would be the foundation of true reform four years later.

Meanwhile, the dapper, energetic C. C. Pyle entered Jim's life for the first time since his vaudeville offer almost twenty years earlier. He asked Jim to be master of ceremonies for the second half of the C. C. Pyle International Marathon Run, dubbed the Bunion Derby in the press. The freakish event began in New York in late March 1929 and ended in Los Angeles in July. Jim joined the American, English, Italian, and Australian runners in Springfield, Missouri, on April 29. To help Pyle finance this stage of the derby, Lon Scott, director of publicity for the U.S. 66 Highway Association, put out a press release on the AP wire that Jim was reapplying to the AAU for reinstatement as an amateur so that he could get his Olympic medals and trophies back. After Jim's "long professional career," however, the amateur body saw no grounds for any reinstatement. In May, Buddy Howard, the national amateur heavyweight boxing champion, had been stripped of his honors and amateur status for professionalism. The decision was considered the organization's most drastic since the

Thorpe scandal. It would be a "trifle fantastic," suggested the AP sports editor, for the AAU to rehabilitate Jim now. After the repercussions in newspapers around the world went on for days, garnering lots of publicity for the derby, the ploy was dismissed by the AAU as "just a little ballyhoo."

The notoriety didn't benefit Jim, who was dead broke. When the runners passed through Odessa, Texas, Jack Cusack met up with him and gave him $100.

Days before the stock market crash in October 1929, the second dominant thread of Jim's life—sports—was also the subject of a reform-minded exposé: "American College Athletics," the Carnegie Foundation report on professionalism in college sports. In part a reaction against Grange's defection and prepared at the request of the NCAA, a team of investigators visited 130 universities in the U.S. and Canada and found only 28 schools that did not in some way subsidize their athletes. Professionalism, recruiting, training tables, secret alumni funds, the game's inherent brutality—all the contentious factors of Jim's days at Carlisle—were revealed by the Carnegie Report to be, if anything, more deeply entrenched in the greatly expanded world of postwar collegiate sports. So was the hypocrisy that denied it.

The stock market disaster would distract the public and the government from sports, but also reinforce the belief that the intercollegiate game had been corrupted by the financial excesses of the decade. From 1929 to 1933 attendance at college football games would shrink by 25 percent. Harvard's new president, James Bryant Conant, announced a deemphasis on the "vicious" connection between gate receipts and the viability of the school's athletic program. But football had nurtured a new structure and system of support for college athletics that would survive the Depression and flourish. Once amateurism was discarded, the new model would cement openly accepted athletic scholarships and proactive recruiting, with NCAA restrictions on the most egregious practices.

Sports had gone through a remarkable metamorphosis in the seventeen years since Jim had given the country and the world a preview of the thrills in store for them.

PART III

Life After Sports

Hollywood: Tom Mix and Jim between takes on *My Pal, the King,* 1932

ONE OF JIM's first Hollywood movies, *My Pal, the King* is for Tom Mix, the cowboy superstar of 1920s silent westerns, one of the last. Between the two men is the movie camera that transfers the dime novel into the century's most persuasive medium, the moving picture. In front of its lens, cowboys are more than they were and Indians are less.

CHAPTER TEN

Hollywood

1930–1939

*I was a kid on the reservation . . . [Jim Thorpe] was a hero to the
people . . . And there [he] was, playing Indians in Western movies for a
livin . . . He was probly the greatest jockstrap this country ever had . . . Well,
could you see me wearin buckskin pants and warpaint and a big old feather
bonnet? Running around yelling with a tommyhawk? Well, neither could I.
I'd feel like a goddam ass . . . I'd feel ashamed.*

—JAMES JONES, *From Here to Eternity*

*They thought I was the Indian I was only pretending to be. After a while,
I started believing it, too. How could I not? They wanted me to be a certain
kind of Indian, and when I acted like that kind of Indian . . . those white
people loved me.*

—SHERMAN ALEXIE, *Ten Little Indians*

I'm working with the paint crew for Standard Oil," Jim told a Los
Angeles sportswriter in March 1930. "Yep, had to go to work at
most anything. Can't keep the wife and the kids in food on ancient
glory." He was painting everything from gas stations to trucks in the
greater Los Angeles area, and no one on the job ever recognized him.

Jim had had to sue C. C. Pyle to get paid, but the Bunion Derby
junket had one lasting benefit: it brought him to Los Angeles, where
he discovered that his reputation still meant something. After organizing a six-day foot race in July 1929, featuring the Bunion Derby
runners at the American Legion Speedway, he was the official greeter
of visiting newspapermen at the national amateur golf champion-

ship in August at Pebble Beach. A week later, he was doing some drop-kicking and punting before an exhibition golf match at the Rancho Golf Club in Los Angeles. He was asked to join other former baseball players onstage in Hollywood at Grauman's Chinese Theatre in September for a comedy program, "At the Ball Game," featuring the Metro-Goldwyn-Mayer (MGM) baseball team. The following day, former New York Giant Mike Donlin, who had been with Jim on the 1913–14 world tour, persuaded him to be on a team of former major league players playing against MGM. He even got some very minor movie work.

The attention flattered and encouraged Jim. He just might be on his way back into the big time. In this sunny place, everything seemed possible.

At the end of December, he wrote to Sylvester Long, the old Carlisle classmate who had run with him to train for the Olympics. Long was now calling himself Chief Buffalo Child Long Lance and living as a member at the exclusive Explorers Club in New York. "The Jack [money] received and sure was a help," Jim wrote, concerning a loan from Long, who had parlayed an ever more exotic, though ersatz, Indian past into one of the most fabulous frauds of the decade. "This is sure one tuff country to make ends meet." Jim, like many others, was in Las Vegas in search of work connected to the imminent construction of the engineering marvel of the decade, the Boulder Dam—later renamed for President Herbert Hoover—which would divert the Colorado River. With the local legalization of gambling in 1931, the population of Las Vegas would quickly quintuple to 25,000. The dam, completed in 1936, would provide the electricity for the lights of the city's famed Glitter Gulch.

"I dropped down here looking for some thing to do," Jim wrote to Long,

> but things are not ready as the plans for the [dam] have not been passed on, from Washington. Every body here expects the good news most any time and then athletic club would be in the makings, still it takes money to handle these things . . . have been running the country over trying to locate a coaching position looks good at Loyola Univ a catholic college in Los Angeles . . . but can't as you know, touch firewater might be a good thing for me would rather land a job where

I could have a little fun. . . . I want to thank you from the very bottom of my heart in what you have done for me, wish you would come out and we can do some writting [writing] together, believe me could cash in a plenty. . . . Your old Injun friend, Jim Thorpe.

A few days later, he wrote again to "Pal Chief." He had not signed the check he sent Long as repayment. "Your letter rec'd and shall sign the check and return at once," he wrote. "I returned from Las Vegas last night . . . there sure is a great chance for some one to make plenty of Jack, the towns wide open. I shall return the Hundred when I get the check on balance or what ever I get. You've been a real friend and want to thank you again for Mrs. Thorpe Injuns and self."

Nothing developed in Las Vegas, and Jim returned to Los Angeles. Then what Michael Oriard would call Jim Thorpe's "canonization as the greatest athlete of all time" began with the publication in *Collier's* of "Chief Bright Path," a four-part article by Charley Paddock about Jim's life. It was the first major retrospective that, with recurring polls, profiles, and comparisons over the next two decades, would maintain Jim's reputation as one who had achieved the gold standard of athletic performance. Paddock quoted Pop Warner as saying that someday another athlete would come along to overshadow Jim, "but in my heart of hearts, I will never admit it." Paddock described Jim as "a giant figure of a man in his forties, who seems to be waiting for something that never happens."

Jim, meanwhile, was enjoying being a celebrity in Southern California. As a result of this newest publicity, all sorts of people wanted him to do things—or said they did. But the work turned out to be sporadic. So Jim took the job at Standard Oil, based in El Segundo, using the painting skills learned at Carlisle. By August 1930, he had some money, felt he was back in shape, and sent for Freeda and the boys. The family rented a small house in what Jim described as "the interesting suburb" of Hawthorne, southwest of Los Angeles and facing what was then an open prairie. Jim could "gaze across the sloping plain and see the sun go down" and chase jackrabbits with his greyhounds, Don and Beezer, just as he had as a child in Oklahoma. "It is the best training I know," he insisted to one of the first of the Los Angeles reporters who, for the rest of his life, would ring the doorbell, wanting to update his life story.

When the Thorpes arrived in Hawthorne—the name chosen by the developer's daughter because she shared a birthday with Nathaniel Hawthorne—more than 6,500 people had settled there to raise poultry or work in one of the small factories near the town. Most of the citizens were renters from the Dust Bowl, and by the middle of the 1930s 45 percent would be on relief, with repossessed plots of land rented to squatters in shacks for $5. Homes could be rented for $10 a month. For amusement, townspeople with extra cash took the Red Car trolley to Redondo Beach or stepped out to Hawthorne Hall, famous for its marathon dances. A young Frankie Laine won the grand prize there after dancing continuously for six days. Later, Norma Jean Baker would temporarily live with her grandmother on Rhode Island Street, one the Thorpes also lived on.

Jim chose Hawthorne to be near his old friend from Shawnee, Ceil, who was married to another Oklahoma Indian, Lee Blanchard. Ceil would tell people she couldn't remember when she hadn't known Jim, a man she described as being "natural as a fresh stream of water." Ceil was petite, smart, tough, and quick, an able rider and shot. Her Indian name was Eagle Woman/Mah-ka-thea-quah, which she explained as meaning "high, looking over, watching down, watching over: insight." The Blanchards had been married about eighteen months when Jim arrived, and had already broken into the movies as extras and bit players. Several Carlisle graduates were working in the business and doing well. Lee was also a skilled rider and Indian costume maker; during his Hollywood career he would sew over eighty Plains headdresses. The two families lived about eight blocks apart. Freeda and Ceil became close; Lee and Jim went hunting together. Ceil was "concerned and heartbroken, like everyone else," about Jim's setbacks since Carlisle and would be a staunch friend.

Jim gathered the Blanchards and other displaced Indians from around the country who had settled in Hawthorne around open campfires in his backyard. He was the most famous among them, his sports deeds and genial personality commanding respect and affection. The Indians could share their common identity and predicaments and outdo each other with dry, deadpan commentary on their new world of Southern California.

Jim left Standard Oil in October 1930 to return to Haskell for an Indian pageant and homecoming football game, featuring a halftime exhibition of his drop-kicking. The Kansas boarding school had replaced Carlisle as the incubator of fine Indian athletes and had nationally famous track and football teams. After his return to Southern California, Jim briefly and unsuccessfully sold oil leases in Venice and other beach towns, trying to find a bankable skill other than athletics. In January 1931, he announced plans for a Pacific Coast professional football conference. "California is ripe for pro football," he said. "For years the doors have been virtually locked to the pros because of amateurism's stranglehold on the football public. But highly exploited and commercialized university gigantics have only paved the way for the pros. The gate is now open." He claimed to have approached "baseball magnates" of the Pacific Coast League about using their parks and to have got "several financiers" interested. But 1931 was not a good year for speculative ventures and his went nowhere.

When told he might gain access to job opportunities in the local forestry or recreation departments if he first worked for the county, Jim picked up a shovel in March and started loading dirt onto trucks at the excavation site for the new Los Angeles County hospital. Listed on the payroll as "J. Thorpe" and making $4 a day, he remained anonymous to the crew for a few weeks.

Then some enterprising reporters found him. One photographed him with the shovel and a sad, angry expression on his face. The shot was picked up across the country as the story that the once-great Jim Thorpe was now digging ditches hit the wires. "I guess it's an old story," Jim told the AP. "I liked to be a good fellow with the boys. But I'll come out of this, and I'll do some saving when I do. . . . I'm not through." Another journalist followed him home and took a photograph of Jim sitting on a sofa, his scrapbook of old clippings on his lap. His two sons sat on either side of him, "properly awed," said *The New York Times*, "as though understanding it all." Boxing promoters and sporting goods companies now deluged him with offers. Jim said he was considering coaching jobs at Dickinson College and Mississippi A & M. The *Los Angeles Times* commended him for "swallow[ing] his pride without a gulp." *The Outlook* resurrected the old stories about his laziness, saying that but for Warner "cracking the whip" Jim would have loafed his entire life away. It was as if everything Jim achieved on his own since Carlisle had never taken place.

But in one of the grimmest years of the Depression, most readers could identify not only with the fallen hero, but with the one who had missed out on the sports bonanza of the 1920s. A local studio executive said that Jim "arrived twenty years too soon." Bobby Jones had just been signed by Warner Bros. for $250,000 to do a golf series; Bill Tilden had received a "fabulous sum" from MGM to do the same for tennis. It was estimated Jim could have raked in well over half a million dollars for a movie deal if he'd won his gold medals a decade later.

The Men's Varsity Club of Whittier, among other organizations, rushed to honor Jim and try to find him more respectable and lucrative work. The *Los Angeles Examiner*, taking a dubious press release at face value, falsely reported that Jim was now president of a newly organized Jim Thorpe Petroleum Syndicate. A few days later Jack Daro, a local wrestling promoter, contacted Jim to try to set up some matches. Most promisingly, a member of a school board outside Oklahoma City persuaded the board to offer Jim the directorship of athletics for their high school; until the job started in the fall, Jim would work as a clerk at a local sand and gravel company and settle his family. "I hold it a great pleasure to be able to take over the work," Jim wrote in an acceptance letter. He planned to arrive in ten days.

He never made it. On reflection, going back home to Oklahoma, taking a job offered by respectful, admiring people, seemed claustrophobic, boring, predictable. He'd rather chase a dream, chase anything, than settle down. And there was a deeper aversion. In 1918, when he was refused a beer in Shawnee in one of the quasi-underground establishments that thrived in "dry" Oklahoma, Jim had exploded with rage; the police were called in, roped him up, and threw him in jail. When he and his brother Frank went down a Shawnee alley another night to share a bottle of liquor, a couple of police followed, hitting Frank on the head with a billy club. Jim pummeled the policemen. Thereafter, anytime Jim came back to town—and the visits were rare—he was jumped by the police. In Oklahoma, for the most part, he was just another Indian.

He stayed in Tinseltown, where being an Indian added to his athletic fame and gave him a competitive edge he couldn't get anywhere else. The dream-makers at Universal Studios took note of the ditch-digging publicity and three months later, on June 6, 1931, announced that Jim Thorpe would play Chief Black Crow of the "Swift Arrow tribe" in a twelve-part talkie serial, *Battling with Buffalo Bill*. The project reunited a slew of silent-movie cowboys, including Francis Ford, elder brother of John. It was very loosely based on William F. Cody's book *The Great West That Was*, whose chapter titles included "Captured by Redskins" and "The Savage Horde." Filming started June 29 and ended July 31.

Stills of Jim, costumed in a feather headdress, were released to the press by mid-July. "[H]e sidles modestly into a room," wrote Grace Kingsley of the *Los Angeles Times*, "and is as easy as an old shoe. Plain spoken, matter of fact, with a keen gaze that somehow reminds you of Will Rogers." Rogers, beloved humorist and social commentator, who was part Cherokee, was the most successful Indian actor in Hollywood. "Running true to form," Kingsley noted, "the producers have decided to bring westerns back, now that the West itself is practically dead." She was skeptical that the "professional picture cowboys," who offscreen "throw their leg over nothing more pastoral than the gear of a Rolls-Royce," would be convincing.

Jim was not alone as a once-famous personality relocated to Hollywood in hopes of finding paying work. Talkies were revolutionizing the movie business as the rest of the economy slid sickeningly downward. The result was what *The New York Times* described as constant arrivals of "men and women whose names have appeared in newspaper headlines in various parts of the world." Casting offices eagerly signed up flying aces, war veterans, Russian aristocrats, former Miss Americas, and, perhaps more than any other single group, sports stars. The movies needed people who knew how to move, and that's what athletes did. Some could do stunts. Probably even more important to studio executives was the publicity value of well-known athletes. Even if Jim was cast only as an extra, his name alone could be splashed across the newspaper ads and theater posters and mentioned on radio spots.

There were more former athletes in the Los Angeles area than in any other American city. Perhaps the most notable crossover into starring roles, so far, was swimmer Johnny Weissmuller, winner of three gold medals in the 1924 Olympics and two more four years later. He was appearing in *Tarzan, the Ape Man*. Eddie Rickenbacker, Red Grange, Jack Dempsey, Babe Ruth, Charley Paddock, and boxer

Max Schmeling were also in the competitive pool of talent. Though Grange's stay in Hollywood was brief, he was credited with starting the westward rush of football players: first John Mack Brown, star for Alabama in the 1926 Rose Bowl, then Randolph Scott from Georgia Tech; by the mid-1930s, more than a hundred gridiron veterans were in Hollywood. The busiest was former USC star Marion "Duke" Morrison, working under the name John Wayne. One studio head quipped that every time a college star ran down the field with a ball under his arm "he's humming, 'You ought to be in pictures.' "

What would be called the "celluloid Indian," "pretend Indian," or the "white man's Indian" was firmly in place when Jim arrived in Hollywood. The movies were maintaining the pattern of Black Hawk, Sitting Bull, Geronimo, and others as Indians showcased to perform what film historian Beverly R. Singer described as "humiliating demonstrations that reenacted the cultural genocide they had fought to prevent." Thomas Edison's first penny arcade peep shows in the 1890s featured Indian dances; his 1894 single-scene movie, *Sioux Ghost Dance*, was made in his New Jersey studio four years after Wounded Knee. The week that Jim became the world's most famous athlete in Stockholm, a one-reel silent movie, *The Fall of Black Hawk*, was released by the American Film Manufacturing Company; *Moving Picture World* summed it up as a depiction of "those stirring events which led to the wanton slaughter of countless white settlers." Later that year, *Indian Massacre* portrayed the glorious quest of the white settlers for land in the West and the sad plight of the Indians as a result. The last scene was of a silhouetted Indian mother praying by her child's grave, a symbolic farewell to the dying race. Two years later, Cecil B. DeMille had directed *The Squaw Man*, the first feature movie made in Hollywood, in an old barn on the corner of Sunset and Vine. D. W. Griffith would make more than thirty Indian-themed movies.

There had been a quick backlash. In the December 1911 issue of the Carlisle School publication *The Red Man*, Jim would have read a protest against "the untrue and libelous brand of moving pictures of Indian life. The majority of these pictures are not only without foundation in fact, but do not even have Indians to pose for them . . . White men or Mexicans usually pose as Indians with blackened faces, wigs and Indian costume; their actions and gestures are absurdly grotesque, and exaggerated." In reaction to *Lo, the Poor Indian*, a delegation of

Chippewa went to Washington, D.C., to demand that President Taft curb the movies' distortion of Indians. A group of western Cheyenne, Shoshone, and Arapaho especially objected to *The Curse of the Red Man*, in which an Indian boarding school graduate and football player returns home to his people in a suit and tie, only to be shunned. He turns to drink and is finally killed by a white posse.

The persistence of the western suggested, at the least, an old unease about the Indian. A significant number of silent films portrayed Indians as noble, and vanishing, victims of white oppression, notably Griffith's 1910 *Ramona*, based on the Helen Hunt Jackson novel. When the movie business permanently shifted from the East Coast to California in the 1910s, directors and their producers actively recruited Indians from both the Wild West shows and the reservations as technical advisers, stunt persons, and actors—but not as directors or stars. Except for a few movies such as *The Vanishing American* in 1925, by the end of the 1920s the western was largely a predictable, minor genre that glorified the conquest of the land and indigenous peoples of the West. After 1929, with the advent of the talkies, sound further enhanced Indian attacks with thunking arrows, crackling rifle shots, and what historian William Savage called a "screaming savage . . . burning, pillaging, raping, scalping, and generally being picturesque." Indians now had predominantly become the bad guys, and producers and casting directors gave little thought to authenticity in the race to turn out product to meet the renewed demand for westerns.

Buckskin, feathers, moccasins, a bow and arrow, a tomahawk, a rifle, and a pony—an entire people was frozen on film as Plains Indians in the so-called Indian wars of the last half of the nineteenth century. No other American minority, as American literature and culture scholar Donald L. Kaufmann would suggest, "has had to pay such a high price as a caretaker of a national dream, of having a deprived present, of being, not people, but a figment of history always in the making and never coming to an ethnic rest." Indians were depicted as communicating with grunts, a made-up "Indian language," and pidgin English. They scowled and had rigid, statuelike bodies. The camera was positioned to look down, not up, at the inferior who always lost.

The talkie western was largely relegated to the "B" (budget) level

of Hollywood output, the lower half of the double bill. With exceptions, that would be Jim's product level. The pictures were made
cheap and fast on "Poverty Row," so called for the strip of studios
on Sunset Boulevard—including Republic, Monogram, and RKO—
that churned out quickie westerns, serials, and adventure flicks from
the 1920s until the mid-1940s. Its offscreen center was the corner of
Sunset and Gower known in the industry as Gower Gulch because
the costumed cowboy and Indian extras congregated there, either
between set calls or hoping for a job. So did Emmett Dalton, of the
Oklahoma Dalton gang, Wyatt Earp, and Jack Johnson—each well
past his prime, but still bankable. The "drugstore cowboys"—though
many of them were real and carried loaded pistols—lounged in the
sunshine on the benches in front of the Columbia drugstore, ate
breakfast at the Copper Skillet, or drank, played poker, and picked up
women in the jam-packed bar on the other side of the street. They
fought over anything from screen credits, money, and jobs to imagined slights: in 1940, one extra would shoot and kill another in broad
daylight.

It was a volatile, competitive, close-knit community, into which
Jim fit comfortably. He had been a nomad for much of the last decade
and a half. His fellow extras were a sort of new team playing together
on the sandlot set of the movies.

Indians streamed into Gower Gulch from all over the country, the
fakery an attractive alternative for many to the poverty and prejudice
beyond the orange groves. The celluloid distortions produced what
later analysts would call "infrapolitics"—a resistance to the dominant
culture that works quietly, transcending "traditional political organization and means of protest." The industry's wage discrimination—
Indian extras earned an average of $5.50 a day, half what non-Indians
made—and denigration of their image produced in many of them a
distinctive unity and response. They worked, both individually and
through various Indian organizations formed in the 1920s and 1930s,
to rectify the pay differences and to encourage more accurate por-
trayals of Indians on-screen, though with very limited success.

Many Indians also found, ironically, that playing fake Indians
awakened in themselves their authentic Indian identities and cultures.
Jim would come to feel more Indian than he had since leaving Carlisle. The most talented and enterprising of the Hollywood Indians,

including Jim, capitalized on the attention and celebrity and developed powwows, lecture tours, and performances focused on Indian culture. Some of this entertainment and pedagogy was just as clichéd and stereotypical as the worst western serials. But the best of it was thoughtful, accurate, and sincere and helped create an early foundation for later, more activist, Indian groups from the 1940s to the Red Power movement of the 1960s and 1970s. Concurrent efforts by the Hollywood Indians to teach their languages, ceremonies, and rituals to their children also anticipated by decades much more organized and widespread efforts to reweave the hole left by centuries of wars, removals, cultural identity theft, denigration, and ignorance.

Jim saw both a career advantage and a personal satisfaction in using his famous name and Indian identity to help his people. He had few illusions about his movie career. While Chief Red Fox, a nephew of Crazy Horse and an early Carlisle student, would describe his feelings about his Hollywood career with raw frankness—"I wanted to go down to a clean stream and wash away my duplicity"—Jim summed up his on-screen performances with terse humor: "I always lost."

Having made his big-screen western debut in *Battling with Buffalo Bill*, Jim headed to Palo Alto to make some educational football shorts, also for Universal, with Pop Warner. Wallace Denny, Jim's Carlisle trainer, was still with the coach, and it felt like old times, or so Jim told reporters. For two weeks he demonstrated the Warner system to Stanford undergraduates and felt he did pretty well. He still could punt the ball seventy-five yards.

At an All-America football dinner in Los Angeles toward the end of the year, as *Collier's* was publishing a six-part series by Warner in which he harked back to Carlisle, Jim, and the grand old formative days of the sport, Pop was less generous. He once again insisted Ernie Nevers was a greater football player than Jim, provoking a lively argument in the sports pages. William Gardner, Jim's Carlisle teammate who had lured him to Canton and was now one of Elliot Ness's "Untouchables" in Chicago, said in response that Nevers "never saw the day" when he could touch Jim as a football player. Grantland Rice pronounced Jim the best all-around football player who ever lived. Rockne concurred in "Rockne Recalls," a multipart life story he'd prepared before his death in a plane crash in March. Paul Lowry, sports columnist at the *Los Angeles Times*, reminded readers that, when asked who was the world's greatest all-around athlete, ninety-nine out of every one hundred people answered "Jim Thorpe."

Jim was fast distancing himself from the ditch-digger image. MGM announced in November that it had bought *Red Son of Carlisle*, a treatment of Jim's life story. It had been written by Jim with Russell J. Birdwell, a flamboyant publicist at the beginning of a long and successful career that would include spearheading the search for the role of Scarlett O'Hara in *Gone with the Wind*. He and Jim were paid $5,000, of which Birdwell got two-thirds. Jim had high hopes for the project—Clark Gable was slated to star—but there were plenty of Hollywood sports projects in play, including one from six-time Kentucky Derby–winning jockey Steve Donaghue; *Red Son* would sit in the MGM development pile for almost twenty years.

But the deal was good publicity for the November opening of *Touchdown*, a collegiate tale written by a former Rockne aide, with Jim in a bit part, along with several other football "notables." Jim was also increasingly tapped, as one of the athletic diaspora in Hollywood, for public sports appearances. He visited John McGraw's Giants at Wrigley Field in Los Angeles during their 1932 spring training. He played in the annual All-Stars baseball game, and was an honorary guest when NFL teams came through town or at innumerable dinners hosted by local athletic clubs.

Like older Hollywood Indian performers Richard Davis Thunderbird and Luther Standing Bear, both in Carlisle's first class, Jim was called on to speak up for local Indian events and causes. He had publicly protested a California bill to segregate Indian and Mexican children from whites in the public school system. He was again in the news when he presided over a meeting open to all Indians living in the Los Angeles area to hear a report on Indian lawsuits involving the return of more than $300 million to the Five Nations. Under his leadership, more than 250 Indians gathered for a powwow in June to protest the use of blacks and Mexicans as Indians in movie roles.

In the spring of 1932, Jim was drawn into one of the most sensational Indian stories of the era: the death of his Carlisle friend, the impostor Sylvester Long. Long's had been a strange and tortured life. Actually black, from North Carolina, with a trace of Lumbee ancestry, Long passed for Indian. When he sent money to Jim in Las Vegas in December 1929, Long's identity as the decade's spectacular Indian—birth as a Blackfoot in Montana, adoption by the Cherokee in North Carolina, glory as a football player at Carlisle, attendance at West Point, tribal status as a chief, and the moniker Chief Buffalo Child Long Lance, all false—was finally starting to fall apart.

On the basis of his best-selling 1928 book, *Long Lance: The Autobiography of a Blackfoot Indian Chief*, and his stunning, chiseled good looks and physique, Long had been cast in the scrupulously researched 1930 silent movie *The Silent Enemy* as the great hunter who saves his dwindling Ojibwa (Chippewa) tribe from starvation. His authenticity was key to the movie's credibility and both the BIA and the nervous Paramount distributors preparing the 1930 release were on the trail of a growing number of rumors. Humphrey Bogart, for one, always suspected Chief Long Lance was a fake. Jim knew Sylvester Long's newer identity was fabricated but didn't care. Long was a famous and useful friend.

On March 20, in the library of the luxurious Rancho Santa Anita, east of Los Angeles in the town of Arcadia, Long was found dead from a shot to the head, an apparent suicide. The circumstances of his death and the evidence presented for suicide looked suspiciously like a cover-up to protect Anita Baldwin, a wealthy and eccentric heiress, who had let Long, her lover, into her ranch house shortly before his death. Like many of Long's friends and associates, Jim was highly skeptical that Long had taken his own life. In mid-March, Long had sent him a letter in which, *The New York Times* reported, there had been "no indication of worry or despondency." Jim and several other prominent local Indians insisted on an inquest. Jim was called to give testimony. When the final verdict came down as suicide, "a number of Indians present," including Jim, reported the *Los Angeles Times*, were dissatisfied and angry, especially as Baldwin, "on the advice of her physician," had not attended the inquest. Her father had been Elias J. "Lucky" Baldwin, one of California's best-known entrepreneurs and founder of the Santa Anita racetrack, for which she was named; in 1932, Anita reportedly paid half of Arcadia's annual tax revenue. No official who valued his job was going to look into the connection between a Baldwin and the death of an Indian who might actually be black. An Indian, even a famous one, was as expendable to power in Los Angeles as anywhere else, as Jim would soon discover.

Hosting the 1932 Olympic Games was a huge coup for Los Angeles, the western city still seen by many as a mere movie capital. An Olympiad had not been held in the United States since 1904. Moreover, the Games were taking place in the midst of the Depression and a pivotal presidential campaign. As one of the most famous Olympians in the area, Jim was called on for a series of events in the frenzy leading up to opening day, July 30. On May 11, he hosted a radio presentation, "Heroes of the Olympics." He and collaborator Thomas F. Collison had written a book, *Jim Thorpe's History of the Olympics*, with a foreword by Lawson Robertson, the assistant coach for the Olympic team in 1912 and 1920 and head U.S. coach at each Olympics since. Throughout July, Jim did book signings around town, including at the upscale Robinson's department store and in the auditorium of the Broadway Department Store, where he was joined by several of his Indian friends, in costume. Jim was photographed in buckskins and headdress in the hot California sunshine, standing on a landing strip next to champion swimmer Josephine McKim perched in a bathing suit on a biplane; the pair were slated to drop flyers from the plane before the Games. The local Breakfast Club welcomed Jim as their guest of honor. Two days before the start of the Games, he joined a venerable group, including Warner, former heavyweight boxing champs Dempsey, Jess Willard, and Jim Jeffries, and swimmer Duke Kahanamoku, Jim's fellow champion in Stockholm, for the Junior Chamber of Commerce "Old Champions" night at the Los Angeles Athletic Club. Hanging on the walls of the gym were photographs of the champs in their prime. It was a thrilling time to be a famous athlete in California.

On Saturday, July 30, spectators showed their $3 tickets and hustled into the Los Angeles Coliseum for the opening ceremonies. No one had reserved a ticket for Jim, much less a pass to the Games. He hadn't been asked to sit with any of his fellow athletes or the businessmen who had recently honored him. He knew Dempsey, Warner, and other sports luminaries were not paying for their admission.

At the last minute, he was given a pass to the press box. He watched Vice President Charles Curtis, the Kaw Indian whose 1896 Curtis Act had terminated the independent governments of the Five Nations, press a silver button to light the Olympic torch and start the opening parade, distinguished by what reporters described as the popular Fascist Italian team and the "smartly attired" Germans, the "most impressive delegations" of the day. As in 1912, the American team was "strangely reluctant" to march in step; "[a]pparently," decided one reporter, "we are not a nation of trained marchers." When the more than 100,000 spectators stood to hear a 2,000-person chorus sing the national anthem and the American athletes dipped their flag before Curtis, Jim openly cried. The *Los Angeles Times* had made an editorial decision to put a "sob story" in the paper each day of their daily coverage of the Games. The next morning, July 31, Jim's tears were front-page news: "Jim Thorpe Denied One Little Ticket; Weeps as Huge Parade Passes."

On the Republican ticket with President Herbert Hoover for the coming November presidential election, Curtis was the guest of honor the next day at a reception at the home of Louis B. Mayer, head of MGM and vice chairman of the Republican State Central Committee. The governor, the mayor, politicians, judges, socialites, and important movie people were among the guests. When Mayer, who had befriended Jim and relied on him as a contact person for Indian extras, told Curtis about Jim being overlooked, Curtis asked to see a copy of the *Times* and read the story on the spot. He then asked Mayer to get Jim a pass to the Games in his name. "I was not only surprised," Curtis told a reporter, who described the vice president's reaction as "astounded," "I actually felt almost tearful when I read that story. If I had known Jim Thorpe was here and had not been made an honored guest at the Games, I'd have invited him to ride to the stadium with me yesterday and sit right next to me throughout the opening ceremony. . . . Jim Thorpe is the greatest athlete the world has ever seen, and I'm proud to think that he and I are descended from the American Indian race."

At the Games, nine minutes of applause followed after showman Sid Grauman, owner of Grauman's Chinese Theatre, mentioned Jim during what the *Los Angeles Times* called one of his "famed prologues" (before screening top releases at his theater he presented themed live shows with his own colorful commentary). By that time, Kansan Jim Bausch had broken Jim's decathlon record of 8,412.95 points with a total of 8,462.23.

A couple of days after Curtis set things right, Jim said that personally he didn't mind being snubbed by the American Olympic Committee. He'd suffered worse from them. He resented the humiliation as an insult to Indians. "It had to be another Indian," he said, "who finally got me the invitation."

The AOC chairman since 1929 had been Avery Brundage. He was also president of the AAU and, since 1930, vice president of the International Amateur Athletic Foundation (IAAF). In 1928, the AAU had unanimously approved an amendment to its constitution with a new definition of amateurs: "those who engage in sport solely for the pleasure and physical, mental or social benefits they derive therefrom and to whom sport is nothing more than an avocation." On the eve of the 1932 games, the International Olympic Committee had stunned the world by disqualifying Finnish runner Paavo Nurmi, winner of nine Olympic gold medals in the 1920s, because he had been overcompensated for his travel expenses at a meet in Germany.

With the burgeoning of professional sports, Brundage was circling the wagons. He would become famous for what the *Chicago Daily News* called an "old-fashioned idealism" about sports amateurs. "In a spiritual way," he told a reporter in 1930, "there is a vast gulf separating the two classes [professional and amateur] which will never be bridged." In his own daily professional life, Brundage had virtually rebuilt Chicago with bridges, factories, office buildings, and apartment towers along Lake Michigan; on a single day in 1926, there were seven Brundage buildings and a bridge going up in Chicago at the same time. He was not only a successful, self-made man, but an obsessive, officious executive. As the new defender of amateurism, it would have been anathema for him to flout the decision of nineteen years earlier by allowing Jim official recognition as an Olympic champion. On a personal level, as a losing competitor to Jim in an Olympic event he had been favored to win, he "proudly claimed and zealously guarded" his adjusted fifth-place in the 1912 pentathlon and his fifteenth place in the decathlon, which he had not even finished. He would never admit it, but Brundage bore a lasting grudge against Jim. As long as Brundage was in charge, Jim would remain an outcast.

When the athletes had all gone home, Los Angeles congratulated itself on hosting a well-run, successful Olympiad, the first to make a profit. Brundage was honored with a luncheon at the University Club. Jim was not invited.

With Freeda pregnant for the third time, Jim kept busy with a steady stream of movie work in 1932, often as an uncredited extra. In May he finished *My Pal, the King* with Tom Mix, a real cowboy who had spent a lot of time in the old Indian Territory about the time Jim left it for Carlisle (and who hated John Wayne, considering him "a fake"). Jim drew a paycheck the next month for his role as a coach in RKO's *Hold 'Em Jail,* a weak football satire featuring Betty Grable. It was competing with the great *Horse Feathers,* another football spoof with the Marx Brothers. In *The Dark Horse,* an election-year political satire starring Bette Davis, Jim played an uncredited Blackfoot Indian chief. In a baseball comedy short, *Off His Base,* he was cast as himself.

In August, he was thrown by a wild pony while filming Paramount's *Wild Horse Mesa,* a Zane Grey story starring Randolph Scott, with Jim as an Indian chief. The movie was a "barbed wire" western, one in which the plot devolves from the introduction of the fencing material that doomed large-scale, open-range ranches. Jim's brief hospitalization delayed by a couple of days an appearance at what was described as the "official welcoming to Los Angeles of giant television." From an improvised studio set up in a window of the May Company department store, Jim, the city's mayor, a violinist, some comedians, and other musicians were filmed, their "fullscale visions" broadcast to an audience in the store's auditorium.

Air Mail, Jim's first movie directed by John Ford, opened in October; he and his son Bill were credited at the bottom of the cast list, along with Enrico Caruso. Released five years after Charles Lindbergh's *Spirit of St. Louis* crossed the Atlantic, the project was dedicated to the airmail service, the hazardous and solitary job done by pilots like Jim's Olympic friend Fred Kelly. Footage from Ford's 1924 *The Iron Horse* was recycled into Jim's next job in Fox's forgettable *The Golden West.* His screen persona was especially ironic as he had not lived the western life for almost three decades

In between movies, Jim kept up his civic work, profiting from the

publicity related to the Olympic ticket brouhaha. He chaired a meeting at Trinity Church, at Twelfth and Flower streets, to discuss ways
to relieve the economic distress of Indians in the Los Angeles area.
On October 23, just before the presidential election, a national radio
special was broadcast, mobilizing "an army of sports stars"—including Jim, "Babe" Didrikson, Johnny Weissmuller, and Lou Gehrig—
to make an appeal for national relief. A six-day bike marathon at the
Winter Garden Velodrome featured Jim as official starter and Jimmy
Durante as the entertainer. When Curly Lambeau brought his Green
Bay Packers, now three-time NFL champs, to play a team of mostly
former USC all-stars, Jim was the field judge. Jess Orndorff, former catcher for the Boston Braves, organized the Old-Timers Baseball Club to play exhibition games, and Jim was among those who
signed on.

It was a busy, productive time as Jim hustled to support his growing
family: Richard "Dickie" Allen was born December 19, 1932. Freeda,
twenty-eight, now had three boys under the age of six to care for. Her
husband almost never saw his children from his first marriage, now
living with Iva in Chicago.

But the rush of movie work abruptly dried up in Depression-stunned
1933. "Glad to see you at work again, Jim," Lionel Barrymore told
Jim one day on the RKO set of *Sweepings*. "What are you playing,
an Indian?" "Naw," joked Jim dryly. "I can't play an Indian in this
Depression. They only pay me half as much as they used to. I can't
play an Indian on half pay. Half pay, half breed. Full-blooded Indian,
full pay."

But one of his pictures released that year was a huge success, playing to more than 50,000 viewers in New York the first day alone.
King Kong would be subjected to endless analyses of its possible
meanings—"monstrous eroticism," rape fantasy, racial parable, a
"symbolic dream of world domination." Its director, Merian C. Cooper, would always insist the movie was "never intended to be anything
but the best damn adventure picture ever made." Jim was cast as one
of the native dancers who live outside the ancient wall that has kept
the huge gorilla Kong contained. The actors wore shaggy wigs, grass
skirts, and one infamous coconut bra; most were black, including
Etta McDaniel, Hattie's sister. The village sequences were shot on

the back lot of the RKO Pathé studio in Culver City, using sets left over from DeMille's *King of Kings*.

Jim's movie work cannot be said to have a true iconography, but there are works that bear an eerie relevance to his life. It was grotesque enough to play a cartoon native in *King Kong*. But the symbolic parallels to the film's lead are haunting. Like Kong, Jim was capable of incredible feats—but he was no match for reporters' flashbulbs. What was Jim to segments of the public if not a superhuman brute, civilization's captive? Paraded, scowling, down the streets of New York in 1912; measured and photographed in his jock strap; shown off and then dumped by Warner; hired by McGraw for his publicity value; jeered at by baseball fans; kept behind a wall higher and thicker than Kong's to prevent him from being admitted to the Tenth Olympiad.

The Thorpes' next-door neighbors on Hawthorne's Raymond Avenue were Iva's brother Clyde Miller and his wife, Emza. They had moved to California years earlier to join Iva's other brother, Earl. Like the rest of the Miller family, they had all also once held an antipathy toward Jim. After her second husband, Harrison Davies, died in 1957, Iva would also move to Hawthorne and live down the street from Freeda; relations between the two women would be civil, but not cordial. The odd group of Thorpes and Millers, each distant from his or her place of origin, formed a different kind of loose family unit. With Jim often gone on movie shoots or hunting trips, Freeda and her sons turned to the childless Millers next door. The kindly Emza became the boys' babysitter and befriended Freeda, taking pity on the young mother with three lively boys who was far away from any kin. Emza ran a stationery and book store, and Freeda worked for her before setting up her own shop in Los Angeles, featuring her handmade children's dresses. Dickie was a special favorite of Emza's: he once crawled from his house in his diapers, down the sidewalk, and into the Miller house, looking for his "aunt."

Jim frequently got Phil, Bill, and Freeda cast in crowd or Indian family gathering scenes—Freeda wore a dark wig when she needed to look Indian—as well as the Blanchards. All were charter members of the Screen Actors Guild and the Screen Extras Guild. On the set, between takes, the two older boys listened in on their father's bull sessions with stars and watched him hand wrestling and "joshing with the guys," as Bill recalled. Occasionally he would bring his movie friends, including such stars as Tom Mix and Buck Jones, home for dinner. Wallace Beery was a particular favorite of the boys. "A big, friendly guy," Phil said. "He and my dad would tip a few and there'd be this big, noisy ruckus in the house at 2 or 3 a.m." when they came home. His sons thought the two beefy, sometimes obstreperous men were very alike.

The boxing promoter Stephen "Suey" Welch brought fighters to the Thorpe home for spaghetti dinners. Welch and Jim had known each other since 1917, when Welch and a partner had bought the Akron professional football team and renamed it the Akron Pros. Welch had then switched sports and would end up in the World Boxing Hall of Fame.

Jim was not at this time a daily drinker. Iron Eyes Cody, an Italian American who claimed all his life to be Cherokee and told equally exaggerated tales of his years as a Hollywood actor, said Jim's drinking, at least in Gower Gulch, "never appeared to become a problem." Jim did indeed tip a few with friends—the promise to Freeda had been long broken—but not alone. One problem was that people liked being with him and he didn't like being alone, unless he was hunting or fishing. "Jim was so likeable, he was his own worst enemy" in that respect, said Earl Miller. People would buy him drinks and then claim Jim as a friend. When he needed them, they would disappear.

At a poker game one night at Cody's home, Jim drank too much whiskey and became "dour and withdrawn." He started in on the Olympic medals, saying, according to Cody, "I'm still the best! They can't take that away from me." When one of the other players told him to shut up and play, they were sick of hearing about the 1912 Games, Jim broke the man's jaw. Like someone coming out of a daze, he snapped to and apologized to Cody's wife, then helped get the bleeding man to a hospital.

Jim would often be taunted, pushed too far, get swung at, feel compelled to respond, and thereby perpetuate the popular idea of him as an Indian drunk. Though a good fighter, with power in either hand, he "didn't like that stuff," recalled Garland Nevitt, a Haskell schoolmate. "But, if somebody was trying to push something over on him . . . he soon as kill you as to look at you. He was pushed around so many times . . . He would run away from trouble as far as I'm concerned. But if he ever got into it, he was a bad man." Jim's daughter Charlotte, grown up and in town once for a visit, witnessed a scene at Hollywood's Palm Grove bar when the hard-drinking actor W. C. Fields provoked Jim to drink, setting him up to arm-wrestle with "local bully boys" or jump over chairs in a barroom track meet. Some were sickened by the antics. Jim crushed a beer glass in his hands as he tried to control himself.

He could go for long periods without drinking at all. He didn't keep alcohol in the house. He was what one relative called a "periodic drinker," who would get drunk and stay that way for days and then not touch alcohol for long stretches, once for two years. "Many, many times we were with him, hunting and fishing for days," Bill said, "and he didn't drink. About the only time he overindulged was around a bunch of people." When he did go on a binge, Freeda inevitably was called to pick him up; she usually told the caller to put him in jail and let him sleep it off. Drunk, he was stubborn and did not like being touched by police, or told to move along; he would sit on the curb and refuse to move, just as he had during the Raleigh "rampage" long before.

The boys found that their father was much more approachable under the influence. "When he was drinking was the only time he'd really talk to us," Phil said. "He'd say, 'I really screwed up my life drinking. Don't ever drink.' He'd say it so many times, so many ways. . . . I guess it was his way of apologizing for not spending more time with us, but he was never one to apologize for anything." The rest of the time their father was "strict. Awful strict," said Phil. "He'd have that switch out in a minute. One thing he hated worse even than lying and stealing was bragging." Bill called discipline one of his father's favorite sports. "He bopped me over the head with a stool once and put blisters on my bottom with a belt," said Bill. "You know, I don't begrudge that at all. I had it coming." A few decades later, Bill said quietly, "Dad was one mean son of a gun." Jack was more blunt: "As a father, he wasn't worth a shit."

When Grace bolted from Iva's Chicago apartment and came to

live with her father, she was treated differently, most of the time. Her father was gentle to her, she said, "so graceful, very quiet . . . pretty calm and simple in his pleasures." But his mood could change quickly, especially when Grace started "running around wild," as one of her half brothers recalled. Once, when she took the car "tooting around town," Jim took out the switch, pulled down her pants, and gave her a beating. Her father never got drunk at home, she observed, but when he did drink, it was "a sad thing" to see him lose his physical grace and slur his words. Everywhere they went, people recognized him. "It bothered him," she said. "I remember once we stopped at a diner and ordered sandwiches . . . A man [walked] up to us and [said] to my dad, 'Aren't you Jim Thorpe?' And I looked at my dad and I knew he wanted to say, 'No, I'm not.' " But his pride never wavered, either. When Grace once used his name to gain some advantage, he said, "Don't use my name like that. *I* earned the name."

He never bragged or even talked about his exploits with his children; he never talked much at all. But every once in a while the boys would get a private glimpse of his remarkable athletic skills. One afternoon the boys were in their backyard, which was bordered on one side by a stucco wall about five and a half feet high. Phil kept pestering his father, who was lying on a hammock, to jump over it until, with "one move," Phil said, "he just jumped off the hammock and went over [the wall]. It was so smooth, he looked like he just stepped over. I can still see that big leg of his going over."

When Jim was home, Bill recalled, he played ball with his children. Bill remembers being backed against the garage door with a catcher's mitt and told "Either catch it, or get hit." Jim took the boys fishing off the pier in Redondo Beach or at the end of the old Hyperion pier near El Segundo. He would sit, "staring off and relaxing," silently. "We're here to fish," he'd say, "not to debate." But Jim once set Phil and Bill a challenge very like the one his father had set for him years before. The boys started bragging about how they could swim all the way to Catalina Island, more than twenty miles away. Jim suddenly threw them off the pier. "Actually," Phil said, "we couldn't swim worth a damn." Another fisherman offered to use his halibut net to fish them out, but Jim said no. The boys started yelling, "Dad, save us!" But Jim just pointed and said, "The beach is that way." With a large crowd watching, Phil and Bill made it, barely, to the sand.

Fishing, raccoon hunting, and his favorite current greyhounds, Sonny Boy, Beezer, and Bolger, were the pleasures that sustained Jim. He cooked food for the animals—at one point he had eighteen dogs in the Hawthorne backyard—putting it in special copper buckets. He sat under a tree with a short bow, aiming for squirrels. Close observation of animals was the earliest skill he had learned, and he shared it with his sons, teaching them to read tracks. This was how he saw his role as a father—passing down the manly Indian skills he had learned from Hiram. He would take the boys out on a drive and let the dogs loose—they "ran as fast as jackrabbits," said Ceil—while they stayed out until two in the morning. If the boys tired, Jim would say, "The car's that way. You've got your flashlight. Hit the road, climb in the car and go to sleep." For a few early years, his sons were getting their own form of an Oklahoma childhood on the outskirts of Los Angeles.

In 1933, John Collier, President Franklin D. Roosevelt's New Deal Indian commissioner, and his friend Harold Ickes, secretary of the interior, were bringing a fresh and overtly sympathetic approach to the Indian Problem. The Depression had shocked many Americans into a radical reassessment of their nation. The almost-exterminated Indians now seemed to represent what Collier called an "integrated, inwardly-seeking life and art." They were an authentic, colorful national treasure. After attempts at annihilation and assimilation, there was an effort at preservation based on yet another wave of well-intentioned nostalgia. Twentieth-century Indians looked on with varying degrees of hope, hostility, wariness, and amusement.

Collier, aware that such popular sympathy could be fleeting, set out to overturn the government's Indian policy. The Wheeler-Howard Act, or the Indian Reorganization Act (IRA), the Indian New Deal, was passed in 1934 to rebuild tribes and tribal culture, authorize funds for the purchase of land, and institute a measure of self-government, among other initiatives (because of the complexity of applying the law in a state with so many Indians and tribes, the IRA did not, except in some minor details, initially apply to Oklahoma). Collier wanted to shift power to the Indians, but Congress restricted many of the original bill's provisions, especially those pertaining to tribal lands, allotments, and the bloodline threshold for tribal membership. The progressive language encouraging self-determination was eliminated. Collier's legacy would be controversial and complicated, with opposition from conservative whites who opposed increased "privileges" for Indians, Indians who resented the law as yet more governmental interference, and other Indians who felt it did not go far enough. Ultimately, despite its shortcomings, it would be seen as a high-water mark of the government's policy regarding native autonomy and Indian interests.

Jim felt that at least now Washington was more sympathetic. If something was wrong, unjust, or unfair, the new team in the nation's capital might be able to fix it.

With studio work dried up, he returned to Oklahoma a month after *King Kong* opened to manage an amateur baseball team. The backer of the Harjo Oklahoma Indian Base Ball Club was Ben Harjo, a full-blooded Creek, living in Holdenville and married to Susey Walker Harjo, a wealthy Seminole. Oil had been struck on Susey's allotment land in 1927; in 1929, she had a balance in her government account of a quarter of a million dollars, with monthly earnings of over $9,000. As an "incompetent" Indian, she was allowed to use about $1,000 a month. Conforming to the stereotype at the time of the fabulously oil-rich Oklahoma Indian, Susey owned three cars, her notoriety attracting a flood of requests for handouts, investment schemes, and donations. Her husband had no money of his own, but lots of baseball ideas—ideas that required infusions of Susey's money.

As Indians were entering the new Civilian Conservation Corps—85,000 by 1942—and then organizing baseball teams, Ben Harjo's plan in 1933 to partner with Jim to put together an all-Indian baseball club was timely. Jim was to play, do publicity, and, Jim later claimed, be the team's manager and administrator. The two men signed a contract with a local lawyer, and by the end of May reports were appearing in national newspapers that the Harjo club's tour was drawing good crowds in Kansas, Colorado, and Nebraska. On August 10, the Indians played the Lowell Lauriers, a new Massachusetts minor league team. In packed stands, A. Grant Carrow, a young fan brought to the game by his father, thought Jim looked like Babe Ruth, with his "very well-pronounced bulging waistline." But when Jim put himself in the game in the eighth inning as a pinch hitter, he lined a ball into

right field and with what Carrow remembered as a "beautifully executed fade-away slide," evaded the tag at second base, jumped to his
feet, and smiled at a "chagrined" right fielder, who had nonchalanted
the ball. Carrow's father nudged him: they had just seen "the hands
of time turned back." Jim was forty-six.

Four months later, the season over, the Five Nations agent in
Muskogee refused Susey Harjo's request for $10,000 to pay the team,
its manager, and other debts. Ben had incurred the debts and signed
the contract with Jim without prior approval from the BIA; there was
no legitimate claim to withdraw the money from Susey's restricted
funds.

Jim, stranded in Oklahoma with no money, started a dogged campaign to get his due. He first fired off a telegram to Collier in Washington insisting that "the need for this money is acute." Three days
later he sent a letter to California senator William Gibbs McAdoo: "I
am from California and wish to return there to my family. . . . Please
use your influence through Com. Collier of the Indian Affairs there.
Action must be immediate to keep from trouble." He signed the letter, "Jim Thorpe, Athletic Fame." Susey also wrote Collier, explaining that if the money was not forthcoming, the Indian players would
be "upon the Red Cross." Meanwhile, she concluded, those who were
owed money were "hounding us to death."

To get rid of Jim, Susey gave him $500 of the $2,050 he was
demanding—while insisting she and Ben didn't owe him anything—
and he returned to California. Gus Welch, now a football coach at
Haskell, aware of Jim's money problems, asked him in early November to help prepare his Indian team for a game against Grinnell
College. Welch got his old friend to do some exhibition kicking at
halftime, too, to lure fans. In early January 1934, Jim wrote again to
Collier to say he had an opportunity to buy a house in California for
a "real bargain" and asked if the money matter could be cleared up.
He also asked the commissioner if there was "some kind of opening
for field work, say Health Inspector can give talks on all branches of
sports." The request was denied.

A year later, Jim wrote President Roosevelt that he was still owed
"$1465.00 Dollars," and ended his appeal by stating, "I've stood for
the Indian and represented him before the world in the Olympic

Games and stand very high in the public opinion. All I want is justice and pay for my endeavor. Yours very truly, Jim Thorpe." He then wrote to E. W. Marland, governor of Oklahoma, who had run on the slogan "Bring the New Deal to Oklahoma." Jim enclosed the contract he had signed with Ben Harjo and said that he had "borrowed money on several occasions while in the east to carry the Ball club, this to protect my name and reputation." The letter ended with another plea: "I am in need of this money the worst kind and detaining me from making a deal to advantage."

Jim's letter to Roosevelt was forwarded to the agent in Muskogee, who wrote to Collier. He suggested that if Jim reduced the amount, Susey might pay it. "The business affairs of the team," the agent concluded, "were very poorly managed and they have no record of payments made or any other information on which settlement can be based." After the matter had dragged on for yet another year, the Interior Department finally agreed to give Susey money to pay Jim, only to be told in February 1936 that she and Ben refused to pay Jim anything. The $500 already paid him had been given to him because, Susey said, he "claimed to be without sufficient funds to return to his home." The agent told Collier there was nothing further to be done and the matter was closed.

But not for Jim. He needed the cash, desperately. Yet another year later, on May 31, 1937, now living in a rented house on South Washington Street in Hawthorne and working as a photo processor at Acme News Pictures in Los Angeles, and with Freeda pregnant with Jack, their last child, he wrote to Roosevelt again. "Your Excellency," Jim begged, "This trespass upon your time is prompted by necessity and the demands of simple justice. . . . I would like to ask your Excellency," he continued, "whether or not I as the aggrieved party should seek redress through Congress, or whether it is possible to obtain some measure of justice through the Indian Department. I am in need of these funds and considering our circumstances, it is my duty to fight this matter out." He ended breezily: "Please accept my best wishes for your Administration and trust that you will be able to go over the goal line when the final whistle blows."

No reply from the president to Jim has been found, and it is unlikely that he wrote one. In Washington, Jim's case was a minor matter during years filled with unprecedented crises. But to Jim it was talismanic. Continuing to pester then plead with people like Marland and Roosevelt for five years showed a proud but deluded belief in the enduring power of his reputation. He never got the rest of the money.

On September 4, 1934, the "Grid Gossip" sports column in the *Los Angeles Times* announced that "Jim Thorpe . . . is working in the movies again." Shooting for *College Rhythm*, Paramount's annual "grid picture," was taking place at the Coliseum, with most of the USC varsity joining Jim as extras. The project featured the first night game on-screen, and the plot was, ironically, about a college football hero who has difficulty finding lucrative work after graduation.

The NFL, meanwhile, had recently reorganized itself into two divisions, with an annual championship game between the respective winners. At the end of the year the AP would vote the growth of professional football the major trend in sports of 1934. Pop Warner, who had just left Stanford to coach at Temple, began his season with his latest spin, pronouncing that Temple player Dave Smukler was now "the outstanding fullback of the country, greater than Nevers or Thorpe."

Before starting work on *College Rhythm*, Jim intensified his involvement in his other parallel tracks of sports and Hollywood Indian life. He attended the opening ceremonies for the City League high school baseball season and an Indian thanksgiving rain rite with about twenty tribes in Montrose. The Blanchards and Thorpes continued to perform the traditional Eagle Dance and Feather Dance at area recreational facilities, parks, and country clubs. On the Fourth of July, Jim dressed in feather headdress, buckskin tunic, beads, and moccasins to appear with former outlaw Emmett Dalton, a former Indian fighter, a Blackfoot chief from Montana, a pardoned train robber, and a Texas Indian scout in an event dubbed "Famous Redskins and Characters of the Old West."

The 1935 California Pacific International Exposition the following summer in San Diego was even more incongruous. Jim put on his regalia to join about 150 local Indians from twenty tribes in the exposition's facsimile Indian village called "End of the Trail." Rug and basket weaving and arrow making were on display, as well as dance performances with tom-toms. The Indians had to "thump pretty heftily," said one reporter, to compete with the nearby motion picture hall of fame, featuring Chaplin's tramp's shoes and Mary Pickford's curls, Standard Oil's Tower to the Sun "Aztec masterpiece," and the Midget Village and Farm, where little people brought from around the world went about an ordinary farm life.

Jim announced in mid-July that he had set up a casting agency. Being an Indian in and of itself wasn't a clear enough advantage—studio casting offices still refused to differentiate between Indians, Chinese, Japanese, Mexicans, or some blacks. But leveraging his athletic fame against his Indian identity, Jim saw an opportunity to reinvent himself and to get work for himself and other Indians. He would do what he could to see that the Indians on-screen were real. His job, as described in the *Los Angeles Times*, was "collecting his tribesmen in the numbers demanded by the studios." He made it his business to know which Indians had which skills, so he soon became the go-to guy for studio casting directors when they needed Indians who could authentically ride, shoot a bow and arrow or rifle, rope a horse, or fall convincingly off one galloping away from the cavalry.

Ceil Blanchard, unlike most of Jim's Indian network, had a telephone, so she took the calls from the studios. Jim negotiated and finalized contracts. Ceil kept the records and call sheets, with available Indians listed by tribe and relevant skills. "They were a commodity," she said bluntly, "for sale to the studios." She and Jim were in touch with Indians all over the country, but Oklahoma in particular was well equipped with full-bloods who, often being less assimilated, were more likely to have retained the skills needed by the studios. At the same time, they needed to be rehearsed and prepared by Jim for Hollywood. In general, a major part of Jim's work was ensuring that his Indians showed up on time. On the set, the challenge often was to teach them to follow orders in the "hurry up and wait" production rhythm of Hollywood.

"Jim was accepted almost as a fullblood," Ceil said. "He was welcomed with open arms by Indians." The Indians got work and Jim gained a reputation as a man who could deliver reliable talent. He was also contacted for projects such as the construction of the Hollywood Park racetrack, which opened in 1938, or for work at Standard Oil. "We all shared in the bean pot," said Ceil. An ironic drawback, however, as Ceil noticed, was that Jim's fame could work against him: he was *too* well-known. Casting directors feared he might insist on the more expensive options of a screen credit or the use of his name in the publicity. Ceil often saw him waiting long days for a call from a studio.

Hollywood casting during the Depression was cutthroat, and only made worse by the lack of concern for racial or ethnic authenticity. "The redskins have been having quite a time deciding just who is a legitimate Indian and who is not," reported the *Los Angeles Times* on the several emerging groups, including "one led by Jim Thorpe." The problem was not confined to Indians. MGM was starting to cast the screen adaptation of *The Good Earth*, Pearl Buck's Pulitzer Prize–winning novel about village life in China. Their requirement: "atmospheric people." Chinese actors appealed to the Chinese consul and the Chinese government emissary for help in ensuring the jobs would go to real Chinese. The studio announced they didn't care where the actors came from as long as they were "the right types." MGM wanted the principal parts filled by actors who could speak perfect English. It was difficult to find Chinese at the time whose accents were not too pronounced. Older Chinese in San Francisco who spoke English well were mostly prosperous businessmen and not interested. James Wong Howe, in the early stages of a distinguished career as a cinematographer, was reportedly "in hiding" at MGM so he wouldn't be forced to go in front of a camera. MGM announced that not until "all sources of Chinese talent are exhausted" would it cast whites in the principal roles. But in the end, white actors played all the main characters, with Chinese in supporting roles. Paul Muni, a Jewish immigrant from what is now Ukraine, and Luise Rainer, a German, both played the principal Chinese roles. At least one Indian, Molly Spotted Elk, made it into the movie.

Jim's involvement in Indian life deepened. In August, he was a guest at another "Thanksgiving for Rainfall" ceremony held by representatives from numerous tribes at Indian Springs. Following the example of Standing Bear and others, in September Jim organized Hawthorne's first annual powwow, a three-day event featuring daily parades with Indians and cowboys on horseback, decorated vehicles, and floats depicting pioneer scenes. Jim led 120 visitors representing one hundred tribes, his appearance at such an event now routinely covered by the area newspapers. He tried to teach his sons some of the Sac language, but stopped when their teachers in school insisted they speak only English. The boys were outfitted in traditional buckskin regalia and headdresses and taught Sac and Fox dances to perform at powwows. Jim told them to take pride in their part-Indian ancestry. The boys, in turn, observed that their father was, Bill said, "very proud to be an Indian."

Within a few months he had gone from performing in a crude Hollywood version of an Indian village to a real powwow, run by the Indians themselves. Even with a few cowboys and pioneers, the event demonstrated with flair that there was a vital, authentic Indian culture in Los Angeles—and one that had nothing to do with the movies.

Nineteen thirty-five would prove to be the peak of Jim's Hollywood career. He appeared in at least seventeen movies that year. From January to March, he was at work as "Chief Scarface" in *Rustlers of Red Dog*, a twelve-part western serial for Universal. The individual titles were a dime-novel history of the western movement: *Hostile Redskins!*, *Flaming Arrows!*, *Flames of Vengeance*, *Law and Order*. In June, from the set of John Ford's *Steamboat Round the Bend*, Will Rogers, who was performing in the movie, wrote in his nationally syndicated column: "Funny thing, on the picture with us is Jim Thorpe, our greatest all-around athlete of all time." Rogers would "secretly burn up," he wrote, when younger cast members approached him to ask why he admired Jim so much: Who was he? What had he done? they asked. Two months later, Rogers, the man considered by many to be the most popular star in Hollywood, who "boasted and gloried" in being part Cherokee, died in an Alaska plane crash with Oklahoma aviator Wiley Post. *Steamboat Round the Bend* was released after his death.

In February, as Jim was appealing to Roosevelt for the first time about the Harjo money, Fox released *Under Pressure*, starring Victor McLaglen and Charles Bickford as rival sandhogs, each digging from opposite directions on the Fulton Street tunnel between

Shipped down to the minors: Jim
with the Toledo Mud Hens, 1921
*(Cumberland County Historical Society,
Carlisle, Pennsylvania)*

The NFL Oorang Indians, based in LaRue, Ohio, 1923 *(Cumberland County Historical Society, Carlisle, Pennsylvania)*

Jim and Bud Clark, manager of the Oorang Airedale dog kennels, after a night of successful raccoon hunting, c. 1922 *(Cumberland County Historical Society, Carlisle, Pennsylvania)*

Jim's second family. From the left: Dick, Freeda, Bill, Jim, and Phil Thorpe in Hawthorne, California, 1934 *(Cumberland County Historical Society, Carlisle, Pennsylvania)*

The "ditch digger" image published by newspapers across the country in March 1931
(Hulton Archive / Getty Images)

Jim petitioned FDR to get paid for managing the Depression-era traveling Harjo's Oklahoma Indian Base Ball Club (photo c. 1933). *(Courtesy of Jack Thorpe)*

Jim's third wife, Patsy, with Jim and their dog, Butch, c. 1950 *(Photofest)*

Bob Hope, Jim, and Bing Crosby in 1946 on the set of *Road to Utopia*. Hope was a friend who also lent money to Jim. *(Watson Family Photo Archive)*

Jim and Hedda Hopper, the Hollywood gossip columnist who spearheaded a national fund-raising campaign for him in 1951 *(Robert W. Wheeler Collection)*

· R·F·K ·

Dear Sirs,

I wanted you to know how disturbed I, and all those with whom I have talked of the matter, were at your disgraceful treatment of Jim Thorpe. So related in the nation's newspapers and magazines, and commented on particularly by Arthur Daley in the "New York Times" we feel that your monetary arrangements with Mr Thorpe were as an extreme case of exploitation as

we have ever heard. To put it bluntly — It is disgusting

We feel your company is a national disgrace and we are urging all our friends to boycott your movies.

Robert F Kennedy

3330 N St N.W.
Washington, D.C.

One of the earliest examples of a protest by Robert F. Kennedy (then about twenty-five), writing to Warner Bros. against what he believed was an injustice toward Jim, c. 1950
(Courtesy of the Robert F. Kennedy Family / Warner Bros. Collection)

The Thorpe children, except Phil, shortly after Jim's death in 1953: back row, left to right, Jack, Dick, and Bill; front row, Charlotte, Gail, and Grace *(Robert W. Wheeler Collection)*

The Jim Thorpe grave site in the Pennsylvania town of Jim Thorpe, formerly the two municipalities of Mauch Chunk and East Mauch Chunk. There are some family members who would like his remains moved to his native Oklahoma. *(The U.S. Army Military History Institute)*

Brooklyn and Manhattan. Jim played a "mucker"; he was paid $75 a week. This time it was the Irish who protested, even before the script was finished. Already angry over a drunken, noisy wake portrayed in Raoul Walsh's *Manlock*, the *Gaelic American* in 1934 had warned against making "another vile picture caricaturing the Irish." Screenwriter Borden Chase assured Fox that, since he had worked for ten years in river tunnels with crews that were "85 percent Irish" and his "few friends" were all sandhogs, it was unreasonable to think he would offend any of them. But Billy Wilder, Phillip Dunne, and Finley Peter Dunne, Jr., were all called in for revisions, as the producers hastened to remove any offending scenes.

One of Jim and Ceil's more successful casting assignments was for United Artists' 1935 gold rush feature, *Barbary Coast*. Jim, cast as an uncredited extra, brought in fifty Indians with him. In Jim's scene, Joel McCrea tells what one review termed the "slightly soiled but intrinsically 'good' " heroine, Mary Rutledge, played by Miriam Hopkins, "There is something inside of people that can't be touched. They can stand in mud up to their necks but that thing inside stays bright and shiny." To which Hopkins replies, "Do you think I'm still Mary Rutledge? Do you think I'm still a white woman?" The camera cuts to Jim, with dark braids and a headband, a janitor walking up the stairs in the background carrying a mop and bucket.

Jim was an Indian chief extra with the star, Sylvia Sidney, playing the "Indian girl" in Paramount's *Behold My Wife! Variety* called it "[f]rank melodrama of the hokiest sort." The plot was slightly progressive: Sidney remains an Indian to the end, even after her marriage to a wealthy white.

Jim's announcement in July that he'd set up his casting agency was timed to coincide with the opening of *She*, a movie *The New York Times* summed up as "a gaudy, spectacular and generally fantastic photoplay." It featured Jim in his first and only important, credited speaking part. Based on the famous H. Rider Haggard adventure novel of fifty years earlier and transposed from Africa to the Arctic, the RKO project was produced by *King Kong*'s Merian C. Cooper. It debuted Helen Gahagan as the seven-hundred-year-old Princess of Kor, so sinister and beautiful that Walt Disney modeled Snow White's evil stepmother on her. Jim played the queen's captain of the guard, strutting about in a cape, ordering his men around in a gruff, clipped voice. There were plenty of natives dressed in loincloths with wild, stringy hair, but he wasn't one of them. Intended by Cooper to be a surreal romantic tale of a lost kingdom under the frozen earth, the movie was pure Hollywood kitsch.

Jim then went to Paramount to make *Wanderer of the Waste-land*, a western with a long cast of "former rodeo singers [and] vaude stooges." He spent seventeen days with Ann Sheridan, Andy Devine, and some former football greats making *Fighting Youth*, a movie *Variety* decided was an unlikely "weave of radicalism and campus football." The plot revolved around the efforts of Communist student Sheridan to persuade a college halfback to throw games, undermining the "big business" of football in which players are only pawns for profit. Jim played the "old grad" who returns to his alma mater as an assistant coach. The movie's climax, what *Variety* called a "corker" of a game, was actually played before 75,000 spectators in the Coliseum.

In a feature about the Erie Canal that *Variety* backhandedly suggested should do well "in towns where there is or had been a canal," Jim appeared with a young Henry Fonda in the movie adaptation of *The Farmer Takes a Wife* (Fonda had starred in the hit play). Jim, uncredited, played an Indian. In *One-Run Elmer*, a short starring Buster Keaton, Jim, in a long, black wig, played outfield to Keaton's batter on a scrubby diamond in the middle of nowhere. In November, Jim was among the "sundry athletes" at Paramount making *Klondike Annie* with Mae West.

His heady Hollywood year ended with a bravura finale as a tubby pirate in *Captain Blood*, released in time for Christmas. Starring Errol Flynn in his breakthrough role as an exuberant sixteenth-century Caribbean pirate—sixty years later *The New Yorker* would say the movie was still a "stirring and ebullient swashbuckler"—*Captain Blood* marked a new era of stylish, romantic costume pictures. Flynn and Jim became drinking buddies who would appear in a few pictures together, including the 1941 Custer biopic, *They Died with Their Boots On*, in which Flynn played Custer.

Captain Blood also aided the career of Michael Curtiz, who would become the most prolific Warner Bros. director, creating such hits as *Yankee Doodle Dandy* and *Casablanca*. The Hungarian-born Curtiz claimed to have been a member of his country's fencing team in the

Stockholm Olympics—although, according to IOC archives, he was not. But, like an athlete, Curtiz had an eye for efficient movement, which he used to make swiftly paced action sequences. Fifteen years later he and Jim would work together on another movie and it would be all about sports.

In 1936, Jim would be lucky to get bit parts of short duration. He contracted with Fox in the new year to appear for a mere $50 a week in *Under Two Flags*, a legionnaire drama with a star-studded cast, including Ronald Coleman and Claudette Colbert. His contract stipulated that he provide his own clothes, shoes, socks, and underwear. When *Klondike Annie* opened, the Legion of Decency and William Randolph Hearst attacked the film, calling it lewd. Hearst ordered his newspaper chain not to print Mae West's name in copy or advertising, the first time he had ever issued such a command. His campaign drove record numbers of viewers to theaters. The story of old San Francisco, which featured West murdering a Chinese lover and speaking lines such as "Give a man a free hand and he tries to put it all over you," was considered by some to be responsible for Hollywood's new censorship drive. Victor McLaglen, the ship captain who wins West, had won an Oscar the year before in the John Ford–directed *The Informer*, and had once fought Jack Johnson in an exhibition match. He was haughty and overbearing toward Jim, who steered clear of him.

Wildcat Trooper, a "northwestern yarn" about two rival fur-trapping outfits, opened in May, with Jim as an Indian. He appeared a month later as Chief Red Smoke in *Treachery Rides the Range*. The third in a series starring Dick Foran, one of the era's popular singing cowboys, the movie "brim[med] with horsemanship and gunplay" and had been shot in twenty days. Jim had a speaking part, sort of: the script indicates that he is to grunt and speak "Cheyenne," which frontiersman Pawnee Pete translates:

CHIEF RED SMOKE: (He expounds with much eloquence in Cheyenne.)
BARTON: (interrupting) What's he saying?
PAWNEE PETE: He says he'll send his two sons with something from the medicine man . . .

Treachery Rides the Range "presents the Indians in a thoroughly sympathetic light," read a studio synopsis draft, "and not just as unreasoning savages. In other words, it adheres closely to genuine history." Studio head Jack Warner was *un*sympathetic when he saw the dailies: "[W]e do not want to make again any WESTERN PICTURES with Indians," he wrote in a memo to producer Bryan "Brynie" Foy, known as "the Keeper of the B's." "In other words, we want to make Western pictures. I didn't know that this was an Indian story or I would never have agreed to make it, so let your writers start thinking on western ranges . . . and hard riding . . . As soon as you get Indians into the picture, you take your audience back to 1851–1849 [*sic*], and that makes the picture look old-fashioned and hokey."

It is unlikely Warner read a seminal article, "The Hollywooden Indian," published that year in the *Southwest Review*. Historian Walter Campbell, writing under the pseudonym Stanley Vestal, castigated the movie industry for inaccuracies in depicting Indian costume, camps, manners, and customs, as well as "an almost complete ignorance of Indian strategy and tactics in warfare." The misuse of Indian talent by directors was "bad business": even for western fans, the "grotesque" Indian was too much. "[F]or misrepresentation, sensationalism, and all-around falsity," Campbell wrote, "Indian pictures are in a class by themselves."

So were the 1936 Summer Olympics, held that summer in Berlin. Amid the raging controversy as to whether the American team should compete in anti-Semitic, racist Nazi Germany, Jim was asked if, twenty years younger and fifty pounds lighter, he could have run faster than track and field star Jesse Owens. "Yes, sir, I sure would and I tell you why," he answered. "That boy is a marvelous athlete, but he's a specialist. I never specialized, I tried everything." He lamented, "There's no fun in it . . . anymore. . . . If a fellow can run high hurdles, he runs high hurdles and nothing else. No other track events, and you bet they don't let him play football."

Jim thought the American team should go to Berlin, despite the protests. "Taking the competitors' standpoint," he said, "it wouldn't be fair to the American boys, who have trained and perfected themselves for a chance to test their ability against the world's best." Jim also had his mind on the black athletes. "They must go and do their best," he later told a reporter, "and ignore any slurs or insults the

Nazi people hurled at them. . . . The Negro had to go to prove he was a real man." He sounded like Carlisle superintendent Richard Pratt exhorting Indian athletes to excel and realized that "it was history all over again."

In June, a month before the Olympics began and the same month Max Schmeling knocked out the unbeaten Joe Louis, a *Los Angeles Times* reporter came out to Hawthorne to check on the former Olympian and his family. "It is a house," he wrote, "by the side of the road . . . [T]he seeds grow high and the vines cling to the warped wood hiding its ugly, unpainted finish." The reporter found the forty-nine-year-old Jim to be shaggy and with an "inflated paunch." The family was photographed eating dinner at a small table with a bright white cloth; Jim was seen watering the lawn with two of his greyhounds watching. When the topic of the 1912 Olympic trophies came up, he produced two battered engraved silver mugs, the only mementoes left to him, and spilled from them a collection of safety pins, collar buttons, and other miscellaneous articles. "We use 'em to put trash in now," said Jim. He posed for a *Times* photographer in a Plains headdress, holding the mugs. To the reporter, Jim was vehement: "[Amateurism] is purely commercialism," he said, "nothing more."

Brundage, a new member of the IOC, was equally emphatic on arrival in Germany in late July: the Berlin Olympiad would be "the greatest Olympic Games ever held." He immediately established his own bona fides by disqualifying American backstroke champion Eleanor Holm Jarrett for drinking Champagne on the ship in violation of training rules—a draconian action that prompted journalists to hark back to the treatment of Jim in 1913.

In his 1936 year-end sports roundup, *Los Angeles Times* columnist Braven Dyer noted that Jim Thorpe had "rather soured on the world." Jim was making no appearances without payment, with the exception of Indian matters. It was increasingly difficult for him to show up before he'd had a few drinks at events like the annual USC homecoming banquet and look lively on the dais with successful sports luminaries like Warner.

He willingly chaired, however, a meeting of about sixty Sac and

Fox at his house in Hawthorne to discuss a rumor that John Collier planned to strike from tribal rolls all Indians not living in Oklahoma. The perceived threat, derived from congressional battles to define Indian eligibility under the IRA, came to naught: persons not living on a reservation but descended from a member of a recognized Indian tribe and persons who were at least half-Indian by blood quantum generally qualified for IRA benefits. But anxiety on the part of Hollywood Indians remained. Popular sympathy for the Indian, as Collier had feared, was being eclipsed by the public's and the government's more immediate economic concerns.

The Indian community in Hollywood watched movie opportunities shrink even more rapidly and formed, in response, the Los Angeles Indian Center as a meeting place and welfare agency. Victor Daniels (aka Chief Thundercloud, Tonto in the movie versions of *The Lone Ranger*) and Harold Jay Smith (aka Jay Silverheels, a Mohawk, who was later cast as Tonto in TV's *The Lone Ranger*) were among the handful of Indians in Hollywood who made a viable living in the movies. By the end of the 1930s, Daniels, who claimed to be Oklahoma Cherokee, though that has been questioned, would unsuccessfully file a petition with the BIA in Washington for official recognition of the expatriate Hollywood Indian colony as a tribe. Tongue-in-cheek, they called themselves the "DeMille Indians."

Jim redoubled his efforts. "Jim Thorpe Takes Warpath: Fake Indians Taking Film Work from Real Ones, He Complains" headlined a 1936 article about Jim's visit to the U.S. Attorney in Los Angeles to protest. With the Department of Labor, he had been checking casting lists to see if Mexicans and Italians were claiming to be Indian, and said that less than 50 percent of Indian extras were bona fide. "It is unfair to the Indian," he said. "There are only a few pictures each year that we can work in and when they use white men it just means we can't make a living." Indians were even underbidding each other to get the scant movie work. His recommendation: hire only Thorpe-certified Indians. But by then Jim had serious competition from one of his own. Carlisle's Luther Standing Bear, now one of the most distinguished Indian actors, author of four books on Indian history and culture, and a teacher at the University of California, Los Angeles, formed the nonprofit Indian Actors Association (IAA) in 1936. He would lead it until his death in 1939, when another Carlisle alumnus, William Hazlett, took over the operation. The IAA objected to screen Indians being made to "talk and grunt like morons" and the unequal pay. Eventually the salary discrepancy was adjusted, if not eliminated.

Jim's own legal campaign suffered a setback when the U.S. attorney confirmed that there was no federal law against impersonating Indians. Cecil B. DeMille chimed in, saying that he had always used Indians wherever possible, and that they should be, as the *Los Angeles Times* paraphrased his remarks, "given all the breaks." He had sent an entire unit out to the Cheyenne Lame Deer Reservation in Montana for his latest movie, *The Plainsman*, and two white actors were cast in Indian parts only after "scores of redskins" were tested and found "incapable." DeMille promised to support Jim in keeping "the phoney Indians out of Hollywood." Jim, however, was furious that the director had paid $200,000 to the local Cheyenne when he could have hired work-starved, trained Hollywood Indians, such as the ones Jim had recently provided for RKO's *Annie Oakley*. "I wanted Indians that looked like real Indians, not the Hollywood variety," retorted DeMille, whose casting signaled the shift to shooting westerns on location and hiring extras from a nearby reservation at minimal pay. Jim ignored the director and wrote Roosevelt another letter.

The Cherokee Indian Women's Club in Los Angeles took up Jim's cause, unanimously adopting a resolution against the hiring of non-Indians in Indian roles. They appealed to Mrs. Robert Lawson, the president of the General Federation of Women's Clubs— and a Cherokee—to promote federal legislation against the practice. A copy of the local resolution was sent to John Collier and to Will Hays, the president of the Motion Picture Producers' Association. Jim addressed the federation, testifying that even when Indians were cast, their portrayal in the movies was "in many instances a wholly false picture and quite grotesque." It was one of his last high-profile appearances as an Indian advocate. By the end of the decade, the IAA was affiliated with the Screen Actors' Guild and superseded Jim's group in importance and effectiveness. As with his presidency of the NFL, Jim's initial influence and ability to attract publicity by virtue of his name was significant, but his ability to administer a growing organization was limited.

Throughout, Ceil Blanchard remained loyal to Jim professionally and personally. She felt few people ever understood him. "Too many people wanted to capitalize on him as a 'colorful' person," she said, and they would brag, falsely, to have known or played sports with him. When he needed them, however, they ignored him. She saw Jim take people off the street to help them. "Nobody ever publicized the good he did. All they called him was a drunken Indian." Jim, she said, "would take you at your word, give you that first chance."

He didn't like to be bothered, she insisted. He was a true individualist. He loved his fishing, his hunting, and "conversing one-on-one." He placed great value on friendship. She saw the spiritual dimension in Jim's "inner thinking," the basic layer beneath all that he had accumulated. His religion manifested as a stolid serenity: he would not die, but "move over." "He didn't know where it started," said Ceil, "and where it ended," but he told her "we come with life and we leave with life."

Despite his many sorrows, Ceil thought his Indian name, Bright Path, was descriptive of his core being. The Thunder Clan's swirl of wind and clouds and the violent lightning that burst out of them were symbolic of life's turmoil: "nothing stays the same." She saw Jim's life as a constant churning, a splintering of triumphs, reversals and tragedies. He had had, in Ceil's words, to "adapt from one extreme to another." "The average person," she said, "doesn't get to the eye of the storm." But Jim had. As an Indian and as someone who had known him for so long, Ceil understood Jim's absences and drinking as consequences of that storm. He was damaged. She didn't condone his faults, but neither did she blame him for being unable consistently to manage the tumult of his life.

Jim knew that sports and Hollywood were what he called "pretend worlds." He had survived, and he was more empathic for it. "I've got more pity than guts," he'd tell her, and Ceil knew what he meant. He'd rather help someone than fight him.

Articles by prominent journalists such as Grantland Rice and Kyle Crichton continued to perpetuate Jim's standing as a giant among sports legends, but he was making $200 a week at best, sometimes as little as $50. Most often he did daily work: $7.50 for "atmosphere" or $25 if he spoke a line of dialogue. None of the work was steady. He was no longer a novelty in Los Angeles, though he still played the annual Old Timers' baseball game in June and was invited to each year's USC homecoming banquet. Occasionally he was called home for tribal matters or publicity appearances, with the tribe or host organization footing the travel costs.

The unending scramble for work was getting to him. He economized by reviving his Carlisle tailoring skills to mend the boys' clothing and his own. Grace watched him work under a lamp at the kitchen table, peering over his glasses, mending his pants. A photo of him with Chicago Bears running back Bronko Nagurski in the late 1930s shows a portly man in a suit and tie, his eyes and smile three genial slits in his fleshy face.

He contacted the W. Colston Leigh talent management agency, with offices in New York and Chicago, to arrange paid speaking engagements for him. As a "lecturer to our American youth," he developed four topics, which could be adapted for schoolchildren or adult audiences: "Jim Thorpe Views the Sports Season," with analysis of football in the winter and baseball in the summer; "Until Now or Thirty Years an Athlete," Jim's story of his career; "The American Indian Today," presented in costume, a survey of the Indian in contemporary America, plus legends and ancient culture; and "An Hour with Jim Thorpe," an inspirational talk on sports in modern life and the meaning of sportsmanship, designed for young audiences and father-son banquets. A brochure featured a handsome, benign-looking Jim on the front; to the left was a small cutout shot of him in his Hollywood Plains regalia. Instruction sheets were typed up for school principals, suggesting that the school's coach introduce Jim. A summary of the highlights of his career was provided. According to a coach at Washington High School in Los Angeles who had booked him, Jim was paid $25.

Though he presented well and persuasively, with an easy humor in a soft, modulated voice, he didn't like public speaking. Freeda was surprised that someone who was by nature introverted could do "really a nice job" of holding an audience's attention. Jim told Grace he wished he could speak as easily as she, a happy extrovert, did. But he simply got on with it and took engagements all over the country, sometimes as many as four a day. He drank to dull the stage fright often enough that the agency sometimes stipulated that Freeda join him on the road to ensure he showed up and had someone to take him home. "I said," Freeda later recalled, " 'if you think my being with Jim is going to keep him from drinking, you've got another guess coming. Because, whatever he wants to do, he does it. And my telling him no is not going to stop him.' But they wouldn't give him the job unless I went. So, there I was . . . living out of the car, driving all over the United States," leaving the children in the care of Emza. Freeda could remember only one occasion when Jim got so drunk that he was unable to hold his own. She noticed that even in the country's most desolate locations, Jim knew where they were without consulting a map. One night, she drove with the car's top down and Jim lay in the back seat, telling her which direction to go. "How do you know where we are going?" Freeda asked, and he told her he was reading the stars.

If alone, he drove his big solid Packard for hours and hours, night and day, with lecture notes piled in the front seat, dogs in the back, and his shotgun in the trunk. Once he showed up in Chicago at the apartment of daughter Gail, now in her twenties, married to Joseph McShane; by 1940 they would have two daughters. Jim held up a rabbit he'd shot. "What am I supposed to do with *that*?" Gail asked. "Well, you just skin it and eat it," said her long-delinquent father.

Jim often stayed with old Carlisle friends such as Pete Calac, now a policeman in Canton, or Gus Welch, at the summer camp he owned near Bedford, Virginia. Welch was always willing to lend—or give—Jim money when he was strapped. Once he paid a hotel bill of Jim's of almost $1,000. But Jim's favorite refuge was in the area around LaRue, Ohio. Walter Lingo and "Doc" Hoopes, the Oorang kennel veterinarian, were always glad to see him. At the home in nearby Mount Gilead, Ohio, of Carl Hoffmire and his wife, Luella, he'd play with their children, sitting at the piano, one on either side, pounding a bass note as if it were a drum and showing them how to do war whoops. Luella wondered if he missed his sons.

Even in such seemingly friendly places Jim was always on his guard. One night in 1936, at the Mount Gilead Fraternal Order of the Eagles Club, where Jim was the only Indian member, a young man walked up to him and, after confirming he was talking with "big

Jim Thorpe," hit him hard on the chin, knocking him slightly back on his heels. "Angered," said Luella, "Jim hit him with the full force of his right elbow [and] . . . knocked the young man over two tables." When the man was unable to work the next day, Jim paid him a full day's wages to avoid the publicity. "I can't have it in the paper that some farmer behind a corn stalk clipped me on the chin," he told his friends. Jack Thorpe once watched his father, after being harassed by a man in a bar, put a hundred-dollar bill on the counter, tell the man that if he couldn't knock Jim down, Jim would get his own punch and another $100. Jim took the punch, returned it, and took the money.

He didn't need confrontations to attract attention. In Atlantic City, Jim repeated the strange stunt he'd pulled in Wilmington, North Carolina, in 1910. After "one too many beers," he told the Hoffmires, he went swimming in the ocean and floated so far out he could barely see the lights of the boardwalk. Eventually he swam back to shore, some distance from a large crowd of tourists, police, and Coast Guard personnel at the water's edge. When he walked over to find out what was going on, a policeman told him, "The famous athlete, Jim Thorpe, went swimming a couple of hours ago, and he hasn't been seen yet!"

Other old friends found a newer, sadder Jim on their doorsteps. One such was Montreville Yuda, an Oneida classmate who had come back to work in Carlisle after heading a five-hundred-Indian shipbuilding unit during World War I at Hog Island in Philadelphia, at the time said to be the largest shipyard in the world. Yuda's young son George recalled returning home after school and seeing Jim, "a big, husky fellow," at the dining room table with his father, talking about the old days at Carlisle. "Dad had a sad feeling about Jim," said George. "He felt really badly about how he had turned out. The school [Carlisle] was not here anymore. There was no one to counsel him, to help him. Jim had no problems at Carlisle, but out in the world, that's where the problems began. He was away from the clutches of the school, a lost person. He won all the medals and then lost them. What do you do when you're let down? Used to have a lot of friends and now not? Depression went with it, but in those days what did you do about depression? People don't want to have anything to do with a drunk. His personal problems got worse. He went down, down." When Jim showed up, he usually asked for money.

Jim's tale was echoed in a football story, "Uptown Boy," published in *Collier's* in 1938. It created a new stereotype: the professional football bum. The arc of this and other such fictional stories depended on the down-and-out hero—a former All-American, too fond of alcohol, lamenting his lost fame, playing for Podunk teams—finally coming to terms with being an adult who can no longer play young people's games, like football. Fans now had the *former* athlete to consider and analyze. There were clearly many parallels to Jim's story, but to his old friends such comparisons forced Jim into a mold that didn't fit. He was not ever, Ceil Blanchard observed, allowed to be an individual. "There have been too many negative things said about the man," she said. "Derogatory remarks have come in from people that couldn't get anything out of him and complimentary remarks from people that he had promised to do something for. There was a lot laid on Jim's steps." Jim knew he could count on teammates and old friends. They almost all felt about him as Ceil and Yuda did.

Jim applied for one of the new Social Security cards on March 27, 1937, listing his residence as the Hotel Taylor on Pasadena's Colorado Street. The hotel was his base during the week while he worked down the street as a car salesman. The lecture circuit was sparse during the winter, so in between being a featured guest at a January Bears–Packers game in Los Angeles and a round of radio sports spots, he made do. He and many other former baseball players applied for jobs as umpires in the Pacific Coast League that spring, but the jobs did not pan out. By August he was working in construction, building an addition to a Goodyear plant. At least he was not back in Oklahoma where, as Oklahoma senator Elmer Thomas, chairman of the Indian Affairs Committee, wired Roosevelt, many of the state's Indians had "raised nothing and are unable to collect rentals on allotments because the lessee tenants have likewise suffered complete crop failures."

At the end of the year, Jim did return there briefly for a tribal battle typical of many being fought in response to the Indian Recovery Act. Senator Thomas had held a series of hearings across Oklahoma, occasionally with John Collier present, to explain the new law to the state's Indians. Out of the feedback came the Thomas-Rogers

Oklahoma Indian Welfare Act of 1936, which adapted the policies of the IRA to Oklahoma, home to one-third of the nation's Indians. One of the primary features of Collier's so-called Indian New Deal was encouraging a form of tribal self-governance through formal constitutions. Congress, however, had stipulated that to receive IRA funding, individual tribes, after first voting to accept the IRA, were required to hold an election to adopt, by a majority of all adult tribal members, their new constitution, as approved by the secretary of the interior from a general template. The Sac and Fox, like many tribes, already had a government structure in place. Their reaction divided into the usual camps: the progressives, who ultimately supported and staffed the new tribal governments; and the traditional bands who adamantly opposed the constitution as government interference and control. Even with a constitution, most major tribal decisions—disbursement of trust moneys, business ventures—would still have to be approved by Washington.

Jim was recruited as the spokesman for the tribe's conservative group. He arrived in Shawnee on December 5, 1937, two days before the date of the tribal vote to approve the new constitution. He promptly announced that the act was "an attempt to drive the Indian back to the reservation . . . back to the blanket days"—a final threat to what remained of his tribe's integrity. "Outnumbered one hundred to one by whites on what had once been their reservation," wrote a historian of the Sac and Fox, William T. Hagan, the tribe had "lost all semblance of tribal unity." In fact, there was an intact tribal tradition, but ceremonial activities were held privately by tribal elders and often concealed from Hagan and other outsiders. The Sac and Fox ratified their constitution, despite Jim's best efforts, joining the approximately 50 percent of tribes that did so, accepting the IRA and organizing new governments. Jim immediately tried, unsuccessfully, to convince his tribe to rescind the vote. On the day after Christmas, *The New York Times* printed a wire service release from Oklahoma City reporting that Jim "fat and fiftyish . . . waddles his 235 pounds in and out of the offices of local bigwigs, quotes theories and impressive-sounding figures, and tosses off jokes like a professional baby-kisser."

Jim had remained in some ways a Carlisle product: like the school's founder, Richard Pratt, he thought the BIA should be abolished and

Indians should not be treated like inferior beings who need government help to survive. Unlike Pratt, he felt they should be allowed to
keep traditional customs, with no interference, well-intentioned or
not. A childhood as an "up-to-date" Indian who spoke English and
wore modern clothes and an adult life spent among whites had given
him a more stringent view than many in his tribe: "The government
insists on special legislation for the Indian," he explained. "So it is all
done under the guise of helping him out, of offering protection. But
that's a lot of hooey. There are poor, down-and-out Indians. Sure
there are. But there are poor, down-and-out Irishmen, Scotchmen
and Germans, too, aren't there? And there is no special legislation set
up for them. And listen," he continued, "there hasn't been a single
poor Indian helped by any of this legislation. . . . We are trying to
keep our tribe free from government meddling, to give the Indian a
chance to stand on his own."

In late January 1938, he objected that the New Deal forced the
Indian into "Communistic cooperatives" and that the government,
from Collier to local BIA agents, had built a "perpetual guardianship." The Indian, he said, "should be permitted to shed his inferior-
ity complex and live like a normal American citizen." He now headed
a new group of 460 Sac and Fox, the "Ah-tha-kee-way Mes-qua-kee
[Sac Fox] Association." A photograph appeared in newspapers across
the country of Jim holding tribal documents, looking solemnly at the
camera, dressed in a conventional dark suit, white button-down shirt,
and tie.

His efforts were unsuccessful, though the Sac and Fox constitution would adjust the codes and laws to fit the tribe's traditional ways.
The document's balance of respect for social customs and rituals with
the creation of a practical business committee to deal with legislation, and with a court system to mediate between the two, would be
emulated by many other tribes. But it would be another fifty years,
according to Jim's son Jack, eventually a chief of the tribe, before they
"were able to use the right of self-government that the Act was supposed to be able to do for Indian tribes. Even then the Sac and Fox
went through eleven major law suits to exercise our right to control
our destiny. We are still in court battles." In 1992, Robert H. Henry,
Tenth Circuit U.S. Court of Appeals judge and Oklahoman, would

affirm that "the full sweep of tribal and state regulatory jurisdiction is still unclear."

At the end of the decade, Jim found his burly shape in some demand for a new, to him, genre—gangster pictures. "Only tough guys wanted!" read one MGM casting call. *Big City*'s finale featured what *Daily Variety* in 1937 called "a glorious fistic melee" with a roundup of sports celebrities beating up the other side in a taxi war on the New York waterfront: heavyweight champs Dempsey and Jeffries and other boxers, wrestlers Man Mountain Dean and Bull Montana, and Jim. In *Racket Busters*, starring Humphrey Bogart and based on New York district attorney Thomas Dewey's famous corruption cleanup campaigns, Jim was part of the so-called Wrecking Crew, made up of former prizefighters, playing the racketeers and truck drivers who trash the trucks of their rivals. There were still the occasional sports flicks. When the 1937 football season rolled around, Columbia released *Start Cheering*, a football musical full of former collegiate gridiron stars, including Jim as head linesman and Notre Dame's Nick Lukats as quarterback. Comic relief was provided by Jimmy Durante and the Three Stooges. The football sequences were filmed in Pasadena's Rose Bowl.

In May 1938, MGM held an unusual screen test at the Hermosa Beach Municipal Pier for a Myrna Loy and Clark Gable picture, *Too Hot to Handle*. Between five hundred and six hundred extras were needed for a scene fourteen miles offshore, where a gambling barge catches fire and sinks while fully clothed actors tread water for an hour. Jim showed up. After assuring the casting directors that they knew how to swim, the would-be extras were required to swim a half mile around the pier in sixty-degree water. Only 308 passed. When it became apparent that many were at risk from exhaustion, thirty guards on surfboards and dories picked them up. "A dangerous bluff for jobs," said the *Hollywood Citizen-News* of the fiasco. The next day's front-page headline in the *Los Angeles Times*: "Guards Save 180 Actors from Death." Jim, fifty-one, was one of them; he said his leg had cramped.

Personal press coverage grew ever more invasive, as reporters or editors recycled the soap opera aspects of Jim's life. Many nights, just as the family was sitting down to dinner, there would be a knock at the door. A place at the table was found for the intrusive reporter; Freeda always had extra food on the stove for her hungry boys and husband. Jim also often invited people home for dinner and forgot to tell Freeda. Like most housewives of the time, she wanted some notice so she could put her house in order before a guest arrived. One reporter showed up, unannounced, at the Hawthorne house on Freeda's washing day. A hardworking, meticulous housekeeper, she was in old clothes and had "all this laundry piled up all around," she said, "and the washing machine going and it looked like disarray . . . worse than our situation really was." The reporter persisted, and she talked to him, "not knowing," she said, "what I know now." The article ran, focusing on "how destitute the family of Jim Thorpe was." Freeda never forgave the reporter, who she later found out was Ernie Pyle, famous for a syndicated column about unusual people he found around the country and later one of the great World War II correspondents.

As the years went on, Jim was home less and less. Increasingly alone, Freeda found life with four boys overwhelming. "We were wild as hares," said Bill. "If one wasn't in trouble, the other one was. Mom couldn't get sick . . . Every night she would sit on the back porch and cry." Jim was unable to keep or save money; for Freeda, brought up in a prudent Methodist family, managing money was important. There wasn't even enough of it to give all the children shoes; they went barefoot in the summer. Freeda literally patched their clothes together to make them last. When Jim was home, there were fights. Bill watched her chase Jim around the house, with a frying pan or a baseball bat in her hand. She was no longer the shy child he had married and her life was being built out of hard memories. "When the boys saw Jim," Freeda told Robert L. Whitman in 1984, "he was usually going through town and they were happy to see their father, a kiss on the cheek, a throw in the air, maybe a new shiny quarter and he was gone." Jim's two older boys would agree that after the early 1930s the "[o]ne thing we never had much of was family life."

.   .   .

Despite Jim's earlier casting objections, the 1937 release of DeMille's *The Plainsman* was such a box office success that the western was solidly reborn in big-budget, top-of-the-bill form. Jim profited from the genre's comeback. He appeared in a bit part in *Born to the West (Hell Town)*, a 1938 quickie lasting less than an hour and starring John Wayne. *Variety* dismissed the singing cowboy feature *Cattle Raiders*, in which Jim played a juror: "Nothing distinguishes [it] from run-of-the-mill cow country drama." *Frontier Scout*, released by Grand National as the first of its Fine Arts westerns, had Jim as an uncredited extra in a Wild Bill Hickok drama. That iconic hero of the West, observed *Variety*, "has run the gamut in Hollywood: he has been colossaled [DeMille], serialed [Columbia] and now, quickied. . . . *Frontier Scout* will take its place among the rank and file westerns which pour from poverty row and the California landscape in generous quantities." More poured forth in 1939, as Jim appeared in *Henry Goes to Arizona, Man from Texas*, the fifteen-part serial *The Oregon Trail*, and *Man of Conquest*, based on Sam Houston and the birth of Texas.

Man of Conquest marked a provocative point in Jim's movie career. "To what extent was the attempted removal of the Cherokees to the Bad Lands of Oklahoma characteristic of American policy with regard to the weaker groups in her midst?" asked *The Guide to the Critical Appreciation of the Photoplay*, referring to the movie's depiction of Houston's defense of the Cherokee in defiance of Andrew Jackson and his Removal Act. "Have we treated the Indians fairly?" the guide asked. *The New York Times* review of the movie answered in the negative, recalling "the bilking of the Cherokees and the scrapping of their treaties." The *Daily Worker*, on the other hand, praised the movie as "exceptional in its honesty in dealing with Houston's stubborn defense of the Five Nations." The Indian Actors Association successfully appealed to the Screen Actors' Guild when the producers refused to pay the Indian actors the same rate for sign language as they paid for speaking parts.

By late 1939, more big-budget A-westerns, including *Jesse James* and Curtiz's *Dodge City*, also with Errol Flynn, confirmed the genre's new popularity at the box office. John Ford's *Stagecoach*, released that year, marked a new apotheosis: masterful black-and-white cinematography, thrilling editing, Apaches threatening the white passengers in the stagecoach, and the fresh, thoroughly anti-Indian John Wayne, in the role that made him a star. The old Apache warrior showcased by Theodore Roosevelt at his 1905 inaugural parade was resurrected in 1939's *Geronimo*. Playing the title role, Victor Daniels was made to serve as a timely parallel to the devious, evil Nazi: Manifest Destiny now served the hopes and fears of an audience watching the offscreen threat to their civilization. In the next two years, the Hollywood balance would shift to what one movie historian called "racial unity." Indians would need to cross the seas again as soldiers, as they had in the previous war, to be seen as part of the team.

In August 1938, Hans von Tschammer und Osten, the Nazi Reichssportführer, wrote a letter to Avery Brundage with welcome news. Karl Ritter von Halt, a German IOC member who had competed against Jim in the 1912 pentathlon, had forwarded to the Nazi official a letter from Brundage, in which he had asked if his Chicago firm could help build the new German embassy in Washington, D.C. "Having brought your proven record of your friendly attitude toward German sports before the responsible authorities," wrote the Reichssportführer to Brundage, "I can happily tell you that both the German foreign minister as well as General Building Inspector [Albert] Speer have declared to me that you take part." A few months later, the project on hold due to world events, Brundage described in a letter to von Halt "the overwhelming proportion of Jewish advertising" that had filled "our papers . . . with anti-Nazi propaganda." When, despite protests, the IOC persisted in 1939 with its decision to award the 1940 Summer Games to Tokyo, Brundage issued a statement maintaining that the American Olympic Committee could "do nothing to stop the present conflict in the orient" and, in any case, was "concerned solely with amateur sport."

In early 1940, *Chicago Herald-American* reporter Edward W. Cochrane appealed in his column to Brundage to have the 1912 Olympic trophies returned to Jim. Brundage replied in a letter he knew would be published. "I agree with your idea that he was penalized enough," he wrote. "Thorpe, in my opinion, was really an amateur at heart." Jim's transgression was "venial"; he was not dishonest; amateurism was a "thing of the spirit," so difficult to express in words. He thought the trophies had gone to subsequent winners of Jim's events, but he would contact the authorities in Sweden to find out. And there the matter ended. The letter was a public relations exercise: Brundage knew the trophies were perpetual, not intended to be kept by one athlete. With time, such appeals by fans and sportswriters to get Jim what they saw as his due would only increase, and Brundage's response would get more obdurate and uncompromising.

Jim as a guard at Ford Motor Company's River Rouge factory, Dearborn, Michigan, 1942

As the Ford factory cranks out Jeeps and B-54 bombers, Jim checks the ID papers of incoming workers and visitors. In a publicity coup for Henry Ford, the man once—and still, for so many—the greatest athlete in the world now guards the main gate of one of the key hubs of President Roosevelt's "arsenal of democracy."

CHAPTER ELEVEN

Divorce, World War, and River Rouge

1939–1945

Since his football days, Jim has had a whirl at several careers, being by turn a movie actor, a lecturer and a laborer. He is now . . . around Detroit as a guard. Saboteurs, spies and general nuisances would do well to keep clear of the old gent.

—KYLE CRICHTON, 1942

Though Jim claimed to be in his forties, he turned fifty-two in 1939. Like everybody else in Hollywood he shaved a few years off his age.

He had avoided the ring, a last refuge of many athletes, despite earlier attempts to get him to fight, but at the end of the year he agreed to manage Choctaw professional wrestler and former boxer Theodore Roebuck. "Tiny Roebuck, the giant [six feet, six inches and 270 pounds] Indian now managed by Jim Thorpe is out to scalp Pantaleon Manlapig, the Filipino heavyweight," read a news bulletin covering the Jack Daro wrestling carnival held at the Olympic Auditorium in downtown Los Angeles. The Oklahoma-born Roebuck had been a star tackle on the 1926 Haskell football team and, after an early string of knockout wins as a professional heavyweight, had worked his way to the West Coast for fights at the Hollywood Legion Stadium. Like Jim, he went on to appear in several movies, including *Robinson Crusoe of Clipper Island*, a 1936 Republic serial. Two years later, Roebuck had switched to wrestling.

Jim's managership was considered "a new lease on life" for the thirty-three-year-old Roebuck, but the arrangement didn't last long.

Managing required Jim to be an aggressive hustler, and he was getting too old for that. A few weeks after the Manlapig match, he wrote
to Carl Hoffmire in Ohio to thank him for his hospitality during a
recent visit and to tell him that he had "some thing in mind and if the
two [leads] turn out to my advantage you'll be seeing the old redskin
again." One of the plans involved a Chautauqua lecture tour of the
East and Midwest over the course of a year and a half. He closed
the letter with Christmas and New Year's wishes, adding that "Mrs.
Thorpe joins me."

That last was wishful thinking. At thirty-six, Freeda was no longer
so tolerant of Jim's long absences, his drinking, and, she suspected,
the trysts so common in Hollywood. She'd become feisty and outspo-
ken, unafraid to stand her ground. She had also taken her artistic bent
(she had produced endless crocheted doilies and afghans, as well as
quilts, and had designed and sewn all of her own clothes) to another
level with oil painting. Eventually Freeda would sell her canvases for
as much as $500 apiece. The constant worries about money had worn
her down, but now she had confidence she would be able to support
herself. Jim, in response, threw himself into the task of saving his
marriage—and image.

A big, three-photo spread—"Indian Jim Thorpe's Life Just Beginning at 50"—appeared on the February 2, 1940, *Los Angeles Times*
sports page. Jim was shown in an open-collared, pin-striped shirt,
wearing glasses perched on his nose, reviewing a pile of papers. An
upbeat list of plans was said to be in the works: an autobiography,
"in which several publishers have shown more than passing interest";
another lecture series to schoolchildren that would take him from
Annapolis to Rochester to New York City; an offer from Australia for
three months of personal appearances; and a possible coaching job.
"Sure, he hasn't made a moving picture in six months," one of Jim's
friends was quoted as saying. "Sometimes he works and sometimes he
doesn't. What of it?"

In May, the *Los Angeles Times Sunday Magazine* ran another multi-
photo spread, reporting that Jim was a member of a group organizing
a "new tribe of culture-preserving Hollywood Indians." Its purpose,
prompted by a dying wish of Luther Standing Bear, was to save
"intertribal sign language" and "the fast-vanishing knowledge of pic-
tographic writing," as well as to "study and gravely act out ancient

mysteries, ceremonials and dances." Tribal members were to be at least one-fourth Indian, meetings were to be entirely private, and all were to use the English translation of their Indian names. Jim had not used his, Bright Path, in decades. A few months later, most of the tribe—including Jim, as a charter member—joined the Native Red Men, yet another group of Indian actors formed to improve working conditions for their members, and to "teach the younger Indian something of old Indian life."

The movie business picked up as the economy improved. Jim moved into top-of-the-bill features, though his roles remained minor. In Frank Capra's *Meet John Doe*, shooting that summer in Hollywood with Barbara Stanwyck and Gary Cooper, Jim played an unshaven hobo. Ceil, among others, revered Capra as a "godsend to Indians," with a "sense of serenity about him" that made him loved and respected. By September, Jim was at work on *Hudson's Bay*, an epic chronicling the seventeenth-century Canadian fur trade, with Paul Muni and Gene Tierney. He appeared, briefly, in four movies released in the fall of 1940. He played the Indian surrogate father of Tex Ritter's character, who is passing for Indian, in *Arizona Frontier*; an uncredited extra in *Mexican Spitfire Out West*; and Chief Sancho in yet another Wild Bill thriller, *Prairie Schooners* ("Plot does the redskins dirt," said *Variety* of the last, its review an example of a shift in attitude since the early talkie westerns. "Maybe the Indians . . . at the time were that dumb, but it hardly is conceivable. . . . Another quaint twist is the failure of the Indians to come out victorious although outnumbering the white settlers about two to one"). The other film, *Northwest Passage*, a King Vidor blockbuster based on the Kenneth Roberts novel of the French and Indian War, would later be cited as a prime example of the "ominous and racist" connection in 1940 between killing Indians and gearing up to defeat the Germans and Japanese. Spencer Tracy played the leader of a guerrilla group, affiliated with the British, that wipes out an Abenaki village with horrific violence for 1940 Hollywood. Jim was again an uncredited extra. Between takes while shooting in Idaho, Bill Frawley (later Fred Mertz of television's *I Love Lucy*) bet that a fifty-odd-year-old, unknown except to Frawley as Jim Thorpe, could beat the other extras, many of them college athletes, in a standing broad jump. Jim jumped ten feet, eight inches, six inches less than the world's record, and won.

In *Knute Rockne*, Jim, a greater player than Notre Dame's George Gipp, led by a more creative coach than Rockne, had a minor role as an umpire (his sons Phil and Bill appeared in early sandlot scenes) in the movie that elevated both Fighting Irish to sports sainthood. The biopic represented that the forward pass was used for the first time and most effectively by Notre Dame to beat Army in 1913. (Pop Warner continued to insist that his Indians had mastered the pass years earlier.) *The New York Post* thought that Rockne's justification for football in the film—that it channeled the "combative instinct of youth" much better than the "recurrent wars which trouble football-less Europe"—sounded more like a 1940 afterthought. But cameos by Warner and Amos Alonzo Stagg reinforced the character-building origins of football. Watching the movie in what Winston Churchill would soon call "the dark days of 1940," the audience was made to feel that the game fulfilled the hopes once pinned on it by the nation's elite. The vigor, discipline, and adaptability instilled by football would seem to its true believers to have shaped the warriors who would save the world and the generals who would lead them.

Freeda was not encouraged by this rush of activities. In April, Jim was arrested for speeding and told the judge, "I guess I still like speed too much, Your Honor." In September, a month before *Knute Rockne* premiered, the couple separated. Jim went to live with the Blanchards. Freeda sued for divorce in Los Angeles Superior Court on March 30, 1941, after fifteen years of marriage, on grounds of "physical and mental cruelty to an extreme degree."

She would later admit that Jim never physically abused her. He just was not a responsible person. He wasn't a mean drunk—she called him a "good time Charlie"—but his drinking and financial uncertainty were the big factors in her wanting to end the marriage. Years later, during an interview, Freeda suddenly said, "I often wondered why Jim drank so much. Do you think he had more problems than he could handle? Do you think it was me and the kids? I just don't know why he drank so much." She would also later admit she never understood her husband. "It was like the problems a person from one nationality would have whenever he or she married someone from another nationality," she told *Sports Illustrated* in 1982. Looking back, Jack wondered if his father might have been better suited to life with another Indian, a woman more conditioned to understand—or tolerate—him. Yet the fact that many of Jim's Carlisle teammates led very different lives from his suggests that his "Indian" lack of interest in money, possessions, or staying very long around home is more of an excuse than an explanation. Jim was never taken advantage of because he was an Indian, Freeda felt, but rather because of "his happy-go-lucky nature."

On October 29, 1941, in a smart hat and suit, Freeda appeared before Los Angeles Superior Court judge John Gee Clark; Jim was on a lecture tour in New Jersey. She testified that he "used liquor to excess for some time before our separation. And he stayed away from home for long periods of time." Her attorney asked her about her husband's attitude to their children. "He was very indifferent," she said. "He didn't seem to care how we got along. It's now more than a year since he left home the last time." Freeda was granted the divorce and custody of the four boys: Phil, thirteen; Bill, twelve; Dick, eight, and Jack, three. The headline in the next day's *Los Angeles Times* read "Jim Thorpe Divorced on Firewater Charges."

Jim did not contest the split. He had indeed been out of town on the Chautauqua speaking tour for some time. On August 6, in Shady Nook, Pennsylvania, he had written to a friend: "Left Newark Thursday evening—had to check out of Hotel because lack of funds to pay up or give some toward account, so thought it best to take off—had 5 spot to my name, but was enough to get me on Jersey Shore, where I am staying with a friend on the dear old farm . . . I really don't know just what I should do as you know cash is scarce as hens teeth . . . Wonder if you wouldn't loan me a ten spot for awhile." Lonely, he stopped to see daughter Charlotte, now married, when he was passing through Chicago. They sat for hours in a bar, drinking orange blossom specials of gin and orange juice. Jim expected his daughter to pay. She didn't see him again for years.

He hit a new low of public humiliation to earn cash. New York attorney Bill Shea, whose name would be more closely associated with baseball, had started a football team. He hired Jim to be a novelty attraction during the games. Based in Huntington, New York, the Long Island Indians were not affiliated with the NFL and only lasted a few wartime years. Shea's daughter, Kathy Shea Alfuso, recalled that Jim, all dressed up in his Indian clothes out on the field, "was like a freak sideshow. He could have been in a circus, people would have stared at him just the same. Think about the 1940s and here's this guy who was a phenomenal athlete and got propelled into prominence. Now he was making these appearances. He was not a weak man, but a man that was beaten."

Gary Stevens, later a nationally syndicated newspaper columnist and executive with Warner Bros., was fresh out of college in New York City. One day he walked into Hubert's Museum, "a swill-type, broken down place" on Forty-second Street, west of Broadway. The main attraction was a flea circus. The other draw was the "washed-up athletes." There was Jim, in full Indian dress, next to Grover Cleveland Alexander and Jack Johnson, "hired to be stared at," recalled Stevens, "by fathers and kids." The ringmaster called out to Stevens: "Want to ask any questions of Jim Thorpe?" Stevens said nothing.

When Henry Ford's River Rouge factory in Dearborn, Michigan, opened in 1927, it was the largest industrial complex in the world, sprawling over a thousand acres. Sand, iron ore, and coal came down the Rouge River on enormous freighters and were used to build Model A's, tractors, and, eventually, airplanes. Ford's introduction of the Model T in 1908 had given Americans the motor vehicle in which they could take off and enjoy the continent. In 1913, as Jim signed with the Giants, Ford and his engineers in Highland Park were revolutionizing mass production.

As Brundage was angling for the German embassy project in 1938, Ford had accepted the Nazi government's special award for noteworthy non-Germans, the Grand Cross of the German Eagle. He was recognized as what Douglas Brinkley called the "ideal industrialist," whose Model T was the inspiration for Hitler's Volkswagen. Ford, Brundage, and Charles Lindbergh would be members of the isolationist America First Committee, formed in 1940. Nevertheless, in an example of what River Rouge historian Joseph Cabadas called Henry Ford's contradictory "fighting pacifism," the Ford Motor Company had signed a contract in 1938 to manufacture forty aircraft engines a day for the B-26 bomber, adding for the purpose a new plant at River Rouge in less than eight months. In August 1941, the company

started to build another new facility—Willow Run, near Ann Arbor—
to meet the huge military assignment of producing B-24 bombers.
After the Japanese bombing of Pearl Harbor at the end of the year,
the United States at war on two fronts, the Ford Motor Company
shifted into a continuous defense work schedule of ten-hour shifts.
Lindbergh was hired to help with the aviation program and moved
his family to Detroit. On February 10, 1942, the last peacetime Ford
sedan rolled off the famous 950-foot assembly line, followed by an
Army Jeep.

Exactly a month later, while passing through Dearborn on a speaking tour, Jim was hired by the Ford Service Department. He had
attracted the attention of Stanley Fay, former quarterback and captain of the 1933 University of Michigan champions and now executive secretary to Harry H. Bennett, Ford's personnel director. (From
1915 to 1918 the company had hired sixty-eight Carlisle students,
including Pete Calac, as Outing Program apprentices to work on
the Highland Park factory floor.) "Mr. Ford's personal man," Bennett was, most notoriously, the head of the Service Department, an
in-house gang of three hundred men referred to by *The American
Mercury* in 1940 as "the most powerful private police force in the
world." Counting his contacts around the country, Bennett had an
estimated three thousand goons working for him. Henry Ford was
known to be an absolute dictator in his automotive kingdom, and a
virulently anti-Semitic and anti-Catholic one. That made Bennett,
according to the *Mercury*, "roughly equivalent" to Heinrich Himmler.
Roosevelt's new National Labor Relations Board described Bennett's
Service Department as upholding "a rule of terror and repression."

Bennett was fifty when he hired Jim, though he looked ten years
younger, and was angling to succeed the aged Ford. The "Little Fella"
or the "Little Giant," as the press called him, was five feet, five inches
tall, wiry, handsome, tattooed, graceful as a cat in his movements;
he always wore a bow tie, reportedly so nobody could choke him
with a regular one. His autobiography, *We Never Called Him Henry*,
is engaging, intelligent, funny, and thoroughly unreliable. He had no
bank account and drew no regular salary. A crack shot, when bored at
work he'd shoot the tips off pencils on his desk. After leaving school
in the eighth grade, he had been a lightweight champion in the navy,
and retained a fondness for athletes in general, especially ones well

past their prime. "I was attracted," he said, "to the man who could do what I couldn't." He liked to brag about the former prizefighters, wrestlers, and football players on his personal team and recite their stats. Bennett also made a point of hiring ex-convicts, to "rehabilitate" them, and "former policemen discharged by trial boards."

Not surprisingly, his employees were passionately devoted to Bennett and willing to do whatever he wanted. What he wanted was to know everything going on at the Ford plant. The company had agreed to unionize in 1941 only after notoriously bitter and bloody opposition, organized by Bennett. A year later, his Service Department team was focused on frustrating further solidarity in the workforce. About 10 percent of his men were thought to be spies and informers, assigned to roam the assembly line to listen and observe, or to work at machines and lure a fellow employee to vent, quietly— employees were forbidden to talk or sit down—about his frustrations at Ford; the consequences were intimidation or dismissal. The rest of the force were thugs sent out locally to beat up union organizers and perform any other investigation of interest to Bennett. He freely handed out new cars to celebrities. Babe Ruth got a Lincoln Continental, the biggest and most expensive car of the time.

Jim was an irresistible prize, a symbol, said Brinkley, of "hyper-masculinity." Bennett was just the kind of charismatic sociopath to know how to entice Jim "to help win the war" by joining his big, happy family at Ford. For the men now working double and triple time, Jim was an ideal morale booster. They could say they had America's greatest athlete on-site and get him to sign autographs. But he evidently took some persuading. Ford employee records show that he stayed only about two weeks in March, living at the Dearborn Hotel, and was paid a base salary of $180 a month to work in "Plant Protection." Then he took off for Mount Gilead to see his old hunting pals, but by May 5, he was back in Dearborn, rehired at $225 a month—hardly lavish, but secure—as an assistant foreman and gate guard and assigned the eight-to-four day shift at Gate 4, the main entrance to River Rouge. His duties, verifying the Ford badge and other identification of all persons entering the plant, were essential during wartime. Hiring him was also a smart strategic move for a company eager to deflect public memory from Henry Ford's earlier isolationism.

A steady paycheck, in one fixed location, was a good deal for Jim, too. Working for Bennett was the first daily job in Jim's life. A man used to working out of doors, even in the movies, he was now punching a clock in a huge, ceaselessly swarming hive of men and women Lindbergh called a "creation of Faustian man." He settled in a rented house at 5267 Glenis Street in Romulus and sent for his four sons. Freeda had custody, but after seventeen years of marriage and motherhood, she wanted a clean break to start a new life. Jim would later tell an Oklahoma friend that Freeda "did not care" for the boys, so he had to take over. Another family member, when asked how a mother could send her young children to stay in a strange city thousands of miles from home with the man she had just divorced and whom she thought irresponsible, replied, "Survival." Whatever the reasons, to the adults in charge of them, Jim's children were expendable.

Phil, fifteen, enrolled in trade school. As Jim had to be at River Rouge by eight each morning, it was left to Bill, fourteen, to feed his brothers and get them off to school. If either was sick and had to stay home, Bill stayed home, too. The result was what he would feel was a crippling gap in his education as he was entering high school. After school, the boys were unsupervised, and neighbors became convinced the Thorpe ménage were "wild Indians" and inappropriate as playmates for their children. Before joining the Women's Army Corps (WAC) in the spring of 1943, Grace also worked at the Ford plant. In July, she started basic training at Fort Oglethorpe and was assigned to recruiting duty in the Ninth Service Command at Fort Douglas. After serving for more than two years in New Guinea, she would be selected as a member of General Douglas MacArthur's staff at his command headquarters in Japan after the war.

Jim became very close to Bennett and one of his henchmen, Harry Kipke, an All-America back on the 1922 Michigan team, head coach at his alma mater from 1930 to 1937, and credited, at least in Michigan, with the phrase "a great defense is a great offense." When Kipke was fired in 1937 after a string of unsuccessful seasons, Bennett promptly hired him. According to Garland Nevitt, Jim's Haskell friend who was now living in Dearborn, Jim also worked with Kipke at Bennett's home as a bodyguard. Bennett had built a castle overlooking the Huron River Valley, with two towers, electric gates, armed guard patrols with dogs, banks of floodlights, a Roman bath, underground

tunnels, lion and tiger dens—Bennett raised the big cats as a hobby—
a "Secret Room," and many secret panels. The castle was often the
site of parties for politicians and other influential people, a "veritable
nightclub," with Bennett's athletes keeping order or doing whatever
else their boss wanted them to do.

Nevitt watched Jim get into what he described as a "bad crowd"
in Dearborn, drinking heavily. In the end, Bennett, known for his
protective care of his personal men, stepped in to help. But if Jim
drank heavily at this time, it was not on the job. He had an excellent work record in a key security job at a major military plant in
wartime amid fears of Nazi spies and infiltration. Though Bennett
was obsessed with athletic feats, Jim never talked about his, or about
anything unless he was asked first. He was, one Ford employee who
worked with him at Gate 4 recalled, "very quiet. Everybody liked
him. He was a good man."

He also did Bennett's dirty work on the job. On July 17, 1942, a "Personal and Confidential" letter went out from the "Detroit-Michigan"
FBI office, notifying the bureau's director, J. Edgar Hoover, that Gerald L. K. Smith, the virulently anti-Semitic, pro-Fascist member of
the America First Committee and soon to become the leader of the
even more isolationist America First Party, was continuing to work
closely with Bennett on Smith's campaign for a Michigan U.S. Senate
seat. The FBI office reported that "Smith has had considerable assistance in getting his nominating petitions filled from employees of the
Ford Motor Company. The former football player, JIM THORPE,
filled one complete petition during one eight-hour shift." Smith lost
in the primary.

On February 12, 1943, newspapers across the country carried the
news that Jim was in Henry Ford Hospital following a heart attack at
Gate 4. A week later he was discharged in satisfactory condition and
sent to Oklahoma to recuperate. *Los Angeles Times* sports columnist
Braven Dyer suggested that his readers cheer Jim up by writing him
a letter and provided the address: Shawnee, Oklahoma. In reply to
similar pleas across the country, letters poured in. One, from Ben
Templeton in Raleigh, North Carolina, captures not only the admiration still felt for Jim, but also how his memory was handed down from

one generation to another. In a time of war and mounting American casualties, the thought of such an athlete's brush with death was chilling:

> Mr. Thorpe, Knute Rockne once said that you couldn't be stopped, but that now you were almost stopped. You can't die, Mr. Thorpe! You will always live in my memory.
>
> I have never seen you perform, but I have heard so much about you that I have begun to like you very much. I am only a boy of 15, but I like sports, and I like to play them. As one sports lover to another, please, Mr. Thorpe, get well.
>
> If you get well sports will mean more to me and millions of other American boys like to know [sic] that a true sportsman can pull through anything, that they have guts enough to face death in the face and defeat death.
>
> So, Mr. Thorpe, *please, please* get well soon . . .
>
> P.S. I know that you have never heard of me and don't know me, but I know you are the greatest sportsman that ever lived.

With Jim's name back in the news, it took only a few weeks for an Oklahoma legislator, Dan M. Madrano, to introduce a resolution in the state house of representatives to petition the AAU for the return of Jim's Olympic medals and trophies and the restoration of his name to the official records. The resolution passed, and on April 2 legislators sent copies to the AAU. It was turned down for the usual reasons. When Arthur Daley at *The New York Times* asked Leon Miller, a Carlisle schoolmate of Jim's and now lacrosse coach at New York's City College, what he thought of the appeal, Miller replied angrily: "Something should be done for Jim because he's been kicked around long enough. . . . He's been punished enough. And for what?" Lon Scott, the publicity director who had helped C. C. Pyle with the 1929 Bunion Derby, read about Jim's heart attack and wrote to Bennett from his home in Tulsa to ask for Jim's address. "[T]he old Injun is feeling great," Jim, back in Dearborn, replied to Scott's letter. "Only needed some rest. being a father, mother, nurse, cook and House Keeper for my 4 boys takes up alot of a mans time. so with a cold-flu and nerves shot, had to take the rest cure . . . would sure like to be out there if only had the right set up—if you know what I mean."

Inspired by the idea that Oklahoma should take care of one of its own, and eager to do his part in rectifying the injustice done to Jim, over the next eighteen months Scott would spend untold hours typing letters, making phone calls, sending telegrams, and calling on some of the state's most influential people—trying to find a job for Jim in his native state and place his boys in Indian boarding schools. Their correspondence, largely on Scott's side, gives painful insight into why so many who tried to help Jim grew frustrated. No one could have done more for Jim, but only rarely in his letters to Scott are there any thanks or acknowledgment of efforts made on his behalf. Jim neglected to follow up on job offers or contact schools that were very interested and eager to take in his sons as time ran short before the September start of term. Concurrently, Jim kept asking Scott to call one more person, check on one more school, chase another job opening. He was distracted and incapable of organizing his life, not to mention four dependent children. The Depression, divorce, his heart attack, and constant dislocation had damaged him further. Scott, now the Oklahoma technologist for scale and corrosion consultants D. W. Haering & Co., Inc., in Chicago, was a busy, thoughtful, and highly organized man; it was not easy for him to take Jim on, much less stick with him. But he did, hoping he and Jim could partner in a hat manufacturing company after the war. "Swell looking, great big, cowboy type western hats," he wrote, "which we will call the JIM THORPE hat."

Scott had set up contacts with the educational supervisor of the Five Nations in Muskogee; the superintendent of the Shawnee Agency; the superintendent of the Thomas Gilcrease Foundation in Tulsa, which ran a school for Indian orphans; the head of the Oklahoma Ordnance Works; and Governor Robert S. Kerr, who told Scott he was sure a job as a guard or guide in the Capitol Building, as well as schooling for the boys, would be appropriate and easily arranged. Because of the war, there were vacancies at nearly all the boarding schools. Jim followed up with none of them, leaving Scott to handle the admissions paperwork, make apologies, and push Jim to make up his mind whether he was returning to Oklahoma. "You had better let me know 'Injun' what your plans are," he wrote Jim, "so I can stop bothering some of these good Oklahoma folks if you do not plan to come back here soon."

Jim continued on at Ford six days a week, hoping to stay there another couple of months before he went south. His car was out of commission, and money was tight. And there was the usual problem of getting the boys into Oklahoma Indian schools if he did not live in the state. As Freeda had legal custody, the schools insisted Jim get the court order changed to give him responsibility for them; Jim said he had not heard from her in over a year. In early August, Burton Logan, the Gilcrease school superintendent, went to Shawnee to see Jim's sister Mary, hoping to establish some family contact. "He did not find her," Scott recorded in a memo to himself, "but heard she had turned deaf and dumb. He finally found where one of Jim's brothers, George, lived in a shack on the river but he was gone. His wife told Logan they thought Jim was still living in Detroit, didn't know he was divorced from a second wife in Los Angeles or even had any children."

On leave from Ford, Jim finally drove down to Oklahoma with his sons, arriving on September 17. En route they stopped in Claremore to see the Will Rogers memorial and Jim wept, telling his sons, "That was my friend." In Shawnee, photographers snapped shots of four handsome, sturdy, smiling boys posed on the hood of the car, "tow-haired Jackie's feet" resting on the Michigan license plate. The Gilcrease school offered to take Jack, as the youngest, at no cost to Jim, but he was instead placed in the Pawnee Indian school with Bill and Dick; Phil went to Chilocco, where Iva and his half sisters had gone.

Jim was vague to reporters about whether he would stay in Oklahoma. He could always go back to Bennett, but Ford was a tenuous place—Edsel Ford had died in May, with the mentally and physically frail Henry Ford reassuming control of the company. To be alone in Dearborn without his sons seemed bleak. There was a chance Hollywood would finally make a movie of his life, he said, with him "naturally cast in the leading role"—an absurd idea given his age and physical state. He applied for a job with the Douglas Aircraft Company, then took some time to fish and hunt squirrels while he stayed with Mary in Shawnee. Scott inquired about jobs with the Sinclair Refining Company and, unaware of Jim's mistrust of it, the Shawnee police department. Scott telephoned the governor, again, and wrote Jim that Governor Kerr would "give you a job anytime you asked for it as long as he is governor."

In early October Jim wrote to Scott. "I have nothing definate as to a job and is worrying me somewhat. Can't live with out paying my way. Thinking of returning to Detroit. Hated to leave boys behind. . . . They're getting along fine." Douglas Aircraft thought they might find something for Jim in their New Executives' Club, but Jim was not enthused. He stopped in Tulsa and Scott bought him a suit. In mid-November, Scott wrote Jim that the governor was offering him a job as a speaker in schools and civic clubs, and would he please provide Scott with a current address. Only days earlier Kerr had been quoted calling Jim "one of the most romantic figures Oklahoma has produced." Scott then read in the newspaper that Jim was back in California.

"I know you'll be rather surprised to know I'm out here and working in Pictures again," Jim breezily wrote Scott from his new address, the Blanchards' home at 1140 1/4 West Seventh Street in Los Angeles. "Getting $125 per week with all expenses . . . as for work there, wanted to stay and be near boys [but] I needed ready cash and a job. . . . There's been no publicity as to my being here and which I'm glad of. . . . When I move just go and friends hear of me later. Will write again." Scott covered up for Jim, writing to the governor so that he "would not get the wrong impression of you." There were evidently no hard feelings on Scott's part.

Before Jim attended the annual *Los Angeles Times* National Sports Awards Dinner at the Biltmore Bowl on December 27, joining Bob Hope, Bing Crosby, Amos Alonzo Stagg, Pop Warner, Joe DiMaggio, Babe Didrikson, and others, he wrote to Scott in an expansive mood.

Well Xmas is over thank God and had just a little "Cheer" handled it better than former years Hope you had a real good day. . . . I honestly believe my life story is going to be made, but every Tim, Dick and Harry wants the story for nothing. Have had propositions running around the 20 Grand mark, but feel that it is my last stand and would enjoy the Flowers now and not after my death. . . . So I am setting tight signing nothing, until the right time and plenty of dough behind the deal. Now after the picture is made, want to come back there, buy a good ranch. Where hunting, fishing and the "Moon is Pale" [a reference to a fictitious Indian maiden he fantasized about, someone to take care of him]. I want to take life easy, enjoy books, old friends and a real fire-place to look at.

That was the lifestyle he ached for now. All he needed was the big break.

He also told Scott that Phil had taken leave from school to stay with his aunt Mary. She lived in a little house on a hill, with a windmill, no electricity or running water, an outhouse, a hand water pump, a woodstove, kerosene lamps, two changes of clothing. Her property was near where Jim was born, and it became a refuge for her nephews. Like her Potawatomi grandmother, Mary had become a medicine woman. One stormy summer night Jack watched her build a medicine fire, heat an ax blade, place it back on its handle, stick the blade in the ground toward the coming storm, put tobacco on the ground, and pray to the spirit world to send the storm away from them and not harm her growing corn. The storm split around the corn. Jack, an impressionable five-year-old, was profoundly affected by Mary's seeming powers. Of all Jim's children, Jack would most thoroughly claim his Indian nature. After a period of drug and alcohol abuse, he would "return to my tribe and traditional ways" and find peace of mind—a peace, he knew, that had eluded his father.

Jim assured Scott that the local BIA agent, on his instructions, had got Phil returned to school safe and sound. "Dear Jackie has the flu," he continued, and asked Scott to check on him, adding that "one of the best hospitals in the state is there." The memory of Junior's sudden death from influenza more than twenty years before haunted him: Jack, already prone to asthma attacks, made worse with a cold or the flu, had almost died a few months before. Too ill to get up, he had defecated in his bed. When an older boy at the school, assigned to take care of the younger ones, saw the mess, he got a razor strap and started hitting Jack, then dragged him into the showers and turned on the cold water. At the hospital, Jack was diagnosed with double bronchial pneumonia. By the time he got to eighth grade, at a different Indian boarding school, he would have a "leather butt" from beatings.

Judging from these letters to Scott and despite reports that the boys were doing well, with their grades "much better," Jim felt guilty and frustrated about the choice between caring for his sons and making a living: "Can't do nothing when they are around must look after them." Freeda's help was out of the question. "Their mother is re-married," he wrote Scott, "and they would cause a lot of trouble wanting to see her. Which I understand is impossible she wrote them to that effect. I might as well start the Guardianship of the boys . . . believe they would rather stay with their Dad. It's up to me to look after them and see through until they are capable of doing so for them selves." He asked Scott to thank Governor Kerr for his help and finally apologized for leaving Oklahoma so abruptly. He said he was being considered for a job as head of recreation for the state of California, but did not elaborate or mention it ever again.

In Hollywood, there was indeed talk of a biopic. "Eventually somebody will produce a motion picture based on the life of Jim Thorpe," wrote Braven Dyer in the *Los Angeles Times* in January 1944. "I don't recall any other athlete in American sports history whose name has been kept before the public with such prominence over a period of 35 years." But the timing wasn't right, and the project went back on the MGM development pile. Undeterred, Jim plunged into movie work and war bond drives in Los Angeles, Detroit, and Chicago, as well as other local fund-raisers. "Saw Ann Sheridan yesterday," he wrote Scott, of the decade's "Oomph Girl," "and sorta made my heart go around a little. I knew her when she was in my class [a reference to the fact they had both arrived in Hollywood in the early 1930s]. Said Hello Jimmie where have you been all these long years. She's sweet and a fine gal."

He was in at least four pictures in 1944, his first onscreen appearances since 1941: *Outlaw Trail*, a "hoss opera geared for the duals" [the bottom half of a double feature]; *Outlaws of Santa Fe*, an adaptation of the O. Henry short story "Alias Jimmy Valentine"; *Beyond the Pecos*, with Jim as a cowboy extra; and *Can't Help Singing*, a Deanna Durbin musical set during the California gold rush. Publicity for the last claimed that Jim was playing his 147th Indian role. If anywhere near accurate, that number suggests that he appeared, uncredited, in many more movies than were recorded or for which records survive—not unusual for Hollywood extras of the time. He wrote Scott in March that he was doing publicity for *Buffalo Bill*, and news clips from 1944 report Jim working on "Pilebuck," eventually *The Jolson Story*, and on *The Black Arrow*, a serial. He appeared in *Queen of the Nile (Sudan)*. None of these titles show up on existing lists of his film work.

One anecdote encapsulated what American servicemen fighting far from home in a world war had made of him in their minds and memories. In mid-September 1944, *The New York News* printed a story from the Marine Corps newspaper, *Chevron*, about a marine unit aboard an LST—"landing ship, tank"—an amphibious vessel designed to land battle-ready tanks. Just prior to the July Allied invasion of Guam, to take their minds off what was ahead of them, the men took a poll to decide "the greatest athlete the world ever produced." Jim won. The *News* reporter noted that most of the men had not been born during Jim's heyday. "If Jim was half as good as my dad said he was," said one marine, "he would be able to broad jump from our L.S.T. over the reef to Guam. He'd pick up a bushel of hand grenades and throw them like a football, 50 or 60 yards. If any pillboxes barred the path, he would pole vault over them. And whatever Japs he could find, he would drop kick them into the ocean."

Jim was arrested on October 4 for drunk driving on the Imperial Highway in Southern California. Giving him a suspended sentence a month later, with a fine of $50, the judge chastised Jim with words that must have been bitter to hear: "You are probably the greatest athlete this country has ever known and as such are a legend to American youth. It is a pity that a situation like this should have occurred."

Jim at the Carlisle, Pennsylvania, premiere of *Jim Thorpe—All American*, 1951

JIM AT SIXTY-FOUR, in August 1951, tipping his summer hat to the crowd massed on the sidewalks of Carlisle to see him passing by.

CHAPTER TWELVE

Rediscovery

1945–1953

He was a symbol for things beyond mortal possibility.

—GERALD ESKENAZI, sportswriter

Heartache does something to a man . . . many of the things I did would have been done differently . . . but I didn't know what I know now. No one ever told me . . . no one ever guided me . . . I just did things from day to day . . . hour to hour . . . Sometimes I didn't know I was doing them.

—JIM THORPE

On June 3, 1945, Jim woke up in a Tijuana hotel room next to a woman he knew, but not that well.

"Why are you here?" he asked her.

"We got married yesterday," replied Patricia (Patsy) Gladys Askew. "Don't you remember?" A quick marriage in Tijuana had bypassed California's three-day waiting period.

Jim's third wife was a petite, angular, artificially dark-haired woman of forty-six—she would turn forty-seven on December 23—with looks one friend described as "death-warmed-over-pale." She was born in Missouri, but always said she was from Louisville, Kentucky, where she may have lived for a time with a husband with the surname Askew. She had two grown daughters. She also said she had graduated from Vassar, but there is no record of that. She was a good cocktail bar piano player and claimed she had played piano in one of Al Capone's

Chicago speakeasies. She had her own orchestra, the Patricians, for a while, always signing off an evening with "Good Night, Sweetheart." She said she first met Jim, briefly, after a Rock Island Independents football game in the 1920s. C. E. "Slim" Harrison, a barkeeper living in San Pedro, California, insisted he had introduced the two. Jim said Patsy had renewed the acquaintance through a chance meeting in Lomita, California, a town near Hawthorne.

Intelligent, witty, and observant, Patsy was also an alcoholic, manipulative, mercurial, predatory, and sometimes cruel and unbalanced. Jim's sons and most of his daughters were convinced that she had married their father solely to exploit him. Bill called her a "nut case," the marriage "the worst thing Dad could have done." Patsy didn't care. "They all hate me and think I am a hellcat," she wrote Charlotte. "And that is all right with me." Charlotte felt her stepmother was sincere in her attempts to get Jim to make something of his life.

Married or not, Jim had his own plans. Eleven days after his marriage, he was onboard a Merchant Marine cargo ship, the SS *Southwestern Victory*, as it rounded Catalina Island, bound for Melbourne, Calcutta, Colombo, Suez, Port Said, and New York. He had tried to enlist in one of the armed services after the 1941 bombing of Pearl Harbor—Phil Thorpe, now eighteen, had just enlisted in the army—and do his part for the war effort, but was turned down as too old. Ernie Nevers was a captain in the Marines and even Gene Tunney was in the service; their examples spurred Jim on. Indians had eagerly signed up to serve, announced the Indian Office: 18,000 by 1943. Jim was accepted as a ship's carpenter.

Even though the war in Europe ended in May 1945, the Pacific campaign was continuing. The Merchant Marine delivered food, fuel, medicine, war matériel, tanks, trucks, guns, bombs, and more to the troops anywhere in the world. They were not part of the military, and the seamen were paid civilian wages. Nevertheless, the service had one of the highest casualty rates of the war, since the ships were ideal targets for enemy torpedoes. Loaded on the *Southwestern Victory* was a cargo of 100-octane aviation gasoline and five-hundred-pound bombs. Another "Victory ship," the SS *Walter Camp*, was torpedoed and sunk in the Indian Ocean in 1944; others were named for Knute Rockne, Christy Mathewson, and George Gipp.

It had been thirty-two years since Jim sailed across the Pacific with John McGraw, the Giants, and the White Sox. He managed to keep a low profile until a reporter from the military newspaper *Stars & Stripes* came onboard to interview him. On arriving in Calcutta for a two-week cargo loading in late July, the ship's captain, Carl J. Carlson, received a request from the port commander, Brigadier General Robert R. Neyland, to see their famous carpenter. A 1916 graduate of West Point who had been a freshman cadet in the crowd watching the 1912 Carlisle–Army game, Neyland had served as an aide to Douglas MacArthur when he was superintendent of West Point and had gone on to be a great coach at the University of Tennessee, using his revered seven "game maxims" of football. (Number 1: the team that makes the fewest mistakes will win.) At the end of the century, *Sports Illustrated* would name him defensive coordinator of its all-century college football team. Neyland accorded Jim the full courtesies usually shown to the top brass, asking him to appear before the troops as his guest of honor and giving him personal tours of the local military installations.

After the *Stars & Stripes* article appeared, Jim was persuaded to tell his story to the crew. "He asked that all questions be held until he finished," the captain later recalled, concluding that Jim had memorized his lecture circuit speech. "If interrupted, he went back to [the talk's] beginning." Ralph Starr, a nineteen-year-old oiler in the engine room, said Jim "never bragged about anything. He was Pop to all of us." He would sit in the mess hall after dinner or out on a hatch cover during the long, monotonous nights for bull sessions with the deck crew and off-duty Navy Armed Guard, "talking for hours," said Starr, "about how he ran down rabbits until they lay down and then he'd pick them up. Carlisle, Ohio, Rock Island, baseball, stunt work for the movies, Errol Flynn, the West Point game with Eisenhower, how he always wanted to be a coach, always wanted to start a junior Olympics." He didn't talk about his family. George Hermanson, one of the navy gunners listening, thought Jim, underneath it all, was "a bitter man" who "felt bad" about his life.

On August 6, the Allies dropped the atomic bomb on Hiroshima. Clarkson was ordered to discharge the ship's cargo in Bombay and proceed home. They arrived in New York on September 3. Ralph Starr remembered seeing the captain of one of the tugboats sent to guide the ship look up, see Jim standing at the rail, and hail him: "Hi, Jim!"

Patsy wrote to Lon Scott in Tulsa on V-J Day to introduce herself and to explore Jim's postwar future. "Now that the war is over," she explained, "it is my earnest wish to have something worth while 'lined up' for him, upon his return. I have several 'irons in the fire' . . . to bring him back into the public eye with constructive publicity. It would be most fitting for Oklahoma to offer something so as to re-locate their native son." Scott's many earlier efforts went unacknowledged as she rattled off plans for a syndicated cartoon strip on Jim's life and one more football game. "Fantastic as it sounds," she wrote, "Jim is forty-seven years of age!" He was, in fact, fifty-eight. "Do you still entertain the hat manufacturing plan?" she asked. "As I have Jim's power of attorney and I am his 'self-designated' business manager, I should like very much hearing from you."

At the suggestion of columnist Dorothy Kilgallen, Patsy started to charge $500, sometimes $1,000, plus expenses, for any Jim Thorpe appearance after Jim returned to Los Angeles. "Patsy was a very shrewd, harsh business lady," said Slim Harrison, "and she took care of the financial end of things." She had worked in public relations at some point and certainly managed her new client with an iron hand. "She wouldn't let him go out and mess up," said Harrison.

With the money he'd saved from the Merchant Marine, Jim bought a bar called the Bank Café on the San Pedro waterfront. The building had once been a bank and the teller cages were turned into booths, with the liquor stored in the vault. Jim was the rough, seedy dive's main attraction, although Harrison, its bartender, also hired prostitutes to convince male customers to buy drinks. Soon, Jim sold his interest to Harrison. He and Patsy bought a trailer, where they would live for the next few years. Jim joked that he had knots all over his head from bumping into the ceiling. Patsy claimed the mobile home was a deliberate choice, not the last refuge of itinerant ne'er-do-wells: Jim liked to be on the move, she said, and didn't want to be tied down. In fact, they didn't have the money to buy a house. What money Jim earned was spent quickly.

Jim made the peripatetic arrangement work for him. If he saw a good fishing place while they were on the road, he'd halt and there they'd stay; early in the morning he'd head out on foot with a string, hook, and sinker, settle down for a nap, and wake up when he felt a nibble. At times, Patsy found him too taciturn. She would call people on a telephone just "to hear the sound of a human voice." Jim was comfortable with Indians, according to Patsy, but not at home in contemporary society. He couldn't "acclimate to his greatness," she said; he didn't think what he'd done was that remarkable. She often felt, too, that he was trying to hang on to something that had been lost. Jim was overwhelmed by her strong personality and referred to his life before Patsy as "B.P." His earlier dreams of settling in one place to hunt, fish, and gaze into a blazing fireplace disappeared.

On November 9, Jim sent a telegram to Lon Scott: LAND IN OKLA CITY MONDAY BY TRAILER AVAILABLE FOR PERSONAL APPEERENCE FIFTY DOLLARS CONSIDERATION. PER PROGRAM. REGARDS WILL CALL. JIM THORPE. Five-hundred-dollar paydays had never materialized. Patsy was, however, trying to capitalize on Jim's war service and his appearance in two movies released in 1945: a satire of the movie business, *Road to Utopia*, with Bob Hope and Bing Crosby, and *Vampire's Ghost*, a horror quickie the *Hollywood Reporter* dismissed as "a horror, all right," in which Jim played a gambler.

By the end of January 1946, the newlyweds had arrived in Florida with the trailer. Planning to start a school "to teach youngsters the sports that made Jim famous," they settled in Hollywood, next to a bar on the main drag to Miami. The *Miami Daily News* ran a multipart series on Jim's life after dogged prompting by Patsy. Freeda, who had reassumed custody of the boys when Jim left, decided to send fourteen-year-old Dick to live with his father. The year before, she had had Mary drive Dick and Jack from Oklahoma back to California, where Dick joined Phil at the Sherman Institute, an Indian boarding school in Riverside. Jack was placed with a family who "tried to take the heathen" out of him, as he put it later. Freeda put Dick on a bus in Los Angeles with no change of clothes, no money, and no food. The other passengers took turns feeding him as they crossed the country. In Arkansas, the boy lost his ticket and the bus company issued him another one. When he arrived in Florida, he squeezed into the trailer with Jim, Patsy, and their dog, Butch.

Florida did not work out as planned. The couple bought a hotel in Charleston, South Carolina, and quickly sold it. They moved to New York with Dick, where they briefly lived near Madison Square

Garden. For the next two years they traveled around the country, to wherever speaking events could be arranged. At Patsy's instigation, Jim tried to position himself as a spokesperson for physical fitness and a national Junior Olympics. George Halas included Jim with Red Grange, Bronko Nagurski, and other "greatest players of all time" as guests at a game between his Bears and the New York Giants on September 1, 1946, at Chicago's Wrigley Field, to benefit servicemen— the first of the annual armed forces games that would continue for twenty-five years. Early each fall for the next few years Leon Miller brought his old Carlisle friend Jim to give a pep talk to the City College of New York (CCNY) lacrosse team during the practice sessions that preceded the intercollegiate season. One player would recall Jim as a big physical presence, a handsome man, well-dressed in a camel hair coat.

His name now came up repeatedly, in a positive way, at home and around the world. A 1946 poll was taken of 132 sportswriters to name the "Outstanding Sports Events of the Last One Hundred Years." The heavyweight championship fight between Jack Dempsey and Luis Firpo in 1923 came in first. Second was the 1927 Dempsey–Gene Tunney heavyweight "long count" fight, and third was Bobby Jones's 1930 golf grand slam. Fourth was Jim Thorpe's "entire career."

When Jackie Robinson joined the Brooklyn Dodgers in 1947, integrating major league baseball, sportswriters went back thirty-five years to find, in Jim, a player comparable to Robinson. The parallels were hardly exact, but the instinct was right. Both were outsiders who changed the face of sports by incontrovertibly outstanding performance. UCLA football coach Henry "Red" Sanders, for whom Robinson had not played, said Jim was probably a better football player, but did not come near Robinson's skill in baseball or basketball. In track and field, Sanders also favored Robinson, an NCAA broad jump champion. USC's coach Jeff Cravath added that Robinson's success had come when competition was much tougher. Responding as he had in 1936 to similar queries about Jesse Owens, Jim insisted that, in his prime, he was just as good an athlete as Robinson. He did not mention that, unlike McGraw in 1913, Dodgers manager Branch Rickey had carefully warmed up Robinson in 1946 by a solid season in the minors.

Jim took a job in May 1948 as track coach and assistant to the general supervisor of physical activities with the Chicago park district, working in youth programs such as the Junior Olympics, and touring city parks to teach children running, jumping, putting the shot, and discus throwing. As Olympic trials were held in June for the 1948 London Games, comparisons started to appear between Jim and a seventeen-year-old California track and field star, Bob Mathias. In July, when the Freedom Train, a cross-country rolling exhibit promoted by President Harry Truman to remind Americans of their common ground of liberty, came through Chicago, bearing more than one hundred original documents such as the Mayflower Compact, one of the original copies of the Constitution, and the Emancipation Proclamation, Jim's picture appeared in the *Chicago Tribune*, leading a group of children in the Freedom Pledge: "I am an American. A free American." At an Old Timers baseball game at Wrigley Field, he hit a 384-foot home run. At a mid-September luncheon at Toots Shor's in midtown Manhattan, Haim Glovinsky, the president of the Israel Football Association, announced that Jim had been hired as Olympic trainer for the Israeli national soccer team, scheduled to play at the Polo Grounds later in the month. "Our country," said Glovinsky of the new nation in the middle of the 1948 Arab-Israeli War, "when its troubles are over, will accent sports . . . The people of Israel are happy to have Jim Thorpe as the trainer for their team."

Whatever fees Jim received, Phil noticed, were spent on jewelry and furs for Patsy. Bill would recall that she "drank up the profits." Gail watched her latest stepmother publicly berate her father. Jim took it silently. She wondered why they had ever gotten married. Jim was always short of money. Stopping in Cleveland, he was invited to dinner by Arthur Dussault, the Rocky Mount teammate who saw Jim jump into the ocean in Wilmington in 1910. When he was leaving, Jim told Dussault that he had only seven cents in his pocket.

At the end of the year, Jim, Patsy, and Dick headed back toward Los Angeles, towing the trailer, arguing all the way. Their life together had settled into a toxic routine of Patsy playing the piano and drinking at bars and then badgering Jim, who by now had lost patience and would get angry and, sometimes, slap her, something he had never done with Iva or Freeda. His first two wives had been gentle women;

Patsy was not. Her insults were vicious; Jim would endure them for about a week and then take off to drink for three or four days. When they reached Oklahoma, the couple decided they didn't want to continue to Los Angeles with Dick, now sixteen. They put him on a train in Holdenville to take him to the Indian school in Pawnee; the superintendent of the school, who had not been informed of Dick's pending arrival, put him back on the train to Holdenville. Upon arrival, Dick called his aunt Emza, collect, in Hawthorne, and told her he was stranded. She arranged for him to take a bus to his mother's home in California.

Freeda promptly handed off Dick, along with Jack, to Jim and Patsy in their newly rented apartment at 5162 Melrose Avenue in Hollywood. The boys went to a parochial school until Jack arrived home one day with hands swollen from being smacked with a ruler. Jim asked what had happened. Jack replied, "The nuns." Jim stormed into the school and straight into the office of the mother superior. "I will not have my children beat on," he hollered. "No excuse!" When the nun told the school's coach to throw Jim out, Jim threw *him* out into the hallway. At Patsy's behest, the boys were soon sent to Chemawa Indian School in Oregon.

Jim jumped back into the movie business and was cast in December as an assistant football coach in *Yes Sir, That's My Baby*, a timely spoof on GI Bill veterans going back to college—and football—with babies and wives. Two days after the movie wrapped, Jim joined several other football greats, including the 1925 Four Horsemen of Notre Dame, to honor Grantland Rice on the NBC radio show *This Is Your Life*. Later that evening, Jim was once again at the annual *Los Angeles Times* National Sports Awards dinner, this time at the Ambassador Hotel, with Danny Thomas hosting and entertainment by the former Hawthorne marathon dance champ, Frankie Laine, and Peggy Lee. The "most dramatic moment" of the evening, according to the *Times*, was when Bob Mathias, who had won the Olympic decathlon in London, was introduced to Jim, the 1912 decathlete "18 years before the incredible youngster was born." Mathias said it was a great honor to meet his "boyhood hero," who had outperformed him thirty-six years earlier in four decathlon events and tied him in one. Cameras flashed iconic shots of the lean, dark-haired, intense Mathias next to a genial, portly Jim.

At another sports dinner about a month later, Dick Hyland, sports columnist for the *Los Angeles Times*, was seated between Jim and Grover Cleveland Alexander, two of his own boyhood heroes. Hyland recalled the seventh inning of the seventh game of the 1926 World Series, bases loaded and two outs, when an aging and hungover Alexander, recently sent to the St. Louis Cardinals by the Chicago Cubs because of his drunkenness and other unruly behavior, came to the mound and struck out Tony Lazzeri of the Yankees with three pitches. Jim recounted to Hyland his own "greatest thrill"—the 1911 Harvard game, when he intercepted a kick from behind the Crimson goal line for a touchdown that was discounted because a teammate had been offside, after which he ran it again and scored. The play didn't happen at the Harvard game. It didn't happen at West Point the next year, the game usually credited for the mythical play. It didn't ever happen. All the games were starting to run together, though nobody noticed.

Riding a wave of enthusiasm for softball inspired by the All-American Girls' Baseball League in the Midwest, Jim started a new local girls' team, the Thunderbirds, in the spring of 1949. Patsy was convinced that streams of fans would come to see Jim coach third base. To judge by the size of the crowd, one sportswriter suggested after the opening game on Jim's birthday, the public was not going to find "softball gals in shorts irresistible." Jim quit and took a job as assistant sales manager for a Hudson car dealership.

As talk circulated that a movie of his life might finally be in the works at MGM, Jim was hired to work evenings at the Sports Club, a restaurant and bar in downtown Los Angeles on Hill Street, run by his old Akron football and boxing friend Suey Welch. "He's Here to Meet and Greet You Personally!" read the newspaper ads. Car salesmanship had not worked out, movie work was sporadic, and even with his picture regularly in the paper associated with one sports banquet after another, cash was as scarce as ever. "Seems I'll have to keep going a while longer before I can take it easy," said Jim. The Sports Club was the kind of bar where jockeys, promoters, athletes, their fans, and sports announcers hung out. In the absence of West Coast major league baseball, the minor league Hollywood Stars and the Los Angeles Angels were the local sports figures. So were boxers:

Los Angeles was a big fight town, and its scene thrived in a seedy splendor divorced from the studios. Fighters headed for places like the Sports Club to meet promoters like Welch, who had launched black fighter Gorilla Jones, a former middleweight champ who eventually quit boxing to be Mae West's bodyguard. Jim rode a bus two hours to get to the job, and two hours back.

One evening shortly after Welch hired Jim, Al Stump, a journalist for *Sport* magazine, launched in 1945, interviewed "the timeless national symbol of unmatched power and precision" at Welch's club, and left with a haunting portrait:

> The place is a small, dimly-lit bar and grill on a noise-ridden street in . . . Los Angeles shadowed by teeming Pershing Square. It is easily missed . . . By 10 p.m. the place is usually packed. Most of the customers come . . . because one man makes the Sports Club unique among the taprooms of the world. In a clean, white shirt, thick arms passively folded on the table, he sits in a booth against the wall and silently watches the shifting crowd. He makes little conversation. . . . Even when a well-dressed, middle-aged man, obviously gripped by emotion, approaches to murmur, "This is a big moment for me—I've wanted to meet you since I was a kid," he sits stolidly unmoved. "Thanks," says Jim Thorpe, automatically. "Thanks."

"He's not just on exhibition, like a freak," wrote Stump. "The big, old guy is earning his money." Throughout the interview, fans came up to Jim, asking the same old questions, repeated like a catechism:

> "Those AAU no-goods took away your trophies, Jim, after you won 'em fair and square. When will you get them back?"
> "Hey, Jim, what about the time you beat Army all by yourself?"
> "Where did McGraw get off saying you couldn't hit a curve ball? Wasn't true, was it?"
> "What was the best day you ever had, Jim?"
> "Don't know about that," said Jim, "I was in a lot of games in a lot of places."

Stump was clearly a fan, but an honest one. "Jim Thorpe is not a complex man," he wrote. "He was weak, pliable, irresponsible, and sometimes unruly, and he contributed to his own downfall."

He was also "the most idolized, publicized, dramatic figure and the most picturesque, too, of any sports century. Kids of future generations . . . may not know that he was the embodiment of this country's eternal treatment of the vanishing Indian, that he was underpaid, exploited, stripped of his medals, his records and his pride." Stump said that although Jim weighed 215 pounds—he was closer to 235—his "graceful body still moves with a certain effortless spring." But when he ran for a trolley, he easily got out of breath. "Nope, the old warhorse is all through," Jim said grinning. "One of these days, they'll take me out and shoot me."

Half a century later, *Sports Illustrated* would describe a very different sports "culture of nostalgia," in which "no onetime superstar athlete need ever be poor as long as he can sign his name."

Jim's face was soon beaming from movie screens in Jimmy Cagney's gangster comeback, *White Heat.* He was cast as one of the line of prison inmates at the mess hall table who pass word to Cagney's Cody Jarrett that his mother is dead.

Wagon Master, one of director John Ford's favorite films, was Jim's last. Shot in Moab, Utah, in late 1949, it is a poetic, lyrical, ambling narrative of one Mormon wagon train's trek to a Utah valley "reserved to us by the Lord," says one traveler, "so we can plow it and seed it and make it fruitful in His eyes." Jim plays a Navajo in a credited, though minimal, part. In the cast was Ford's older brother, Francis, who had been in one of Jim's first movies, *Battling with Buffalo Bill,* in 1931. The coproducer was Merian C. Cooper. *Wagon Master* was released the same year as *Broken Arrow,* the breakthrough movie that presented an Indian, the Apache Cochise—played by a white man, Jeff Chandler—as intelligent, competent, and human. Ford's Indians in *Wagon Master* were, observed one reviewer, "in the current Hollywood manner . . . amenable to reason."

Some critics would consider *Wagon Master* the pinnacle of Ford's westerns, spare, unpretentious, gently ironic, without John Wayne and not as pessimistic and ambiguous as his later work, notably *The Searchers.* Beginning with *Stagecoach* in 1939, Ford, more than any other director, defined the "classical" western movie by reinventing the tired genre into a more romantic, morally complex, even tragic, form. Deeply nostalgic, irresistibly manipulative, Ford's movie ends with a knowing twist. When the hard-bitten pioneers—so realistic, as one reviewer joked, they would have made Sergei Eisenstein happy—finally arrive at their yearned-for valley, the audience sees only their faces, reacting to the sight. Ford had positioned the camera looking east from the ever-receding horizon that lured the white man west.

Wagon Master is the amber in which the popular, enduring, and false image of the American Indian is preserved. The movie is in part a cinematic distillation of the forces that buffeted Black Hawk, Jacques Vieux in Wisconsin, Louis Vieux at the Oregon Trail crossing in Kansas, the Potawatomi on the Trail of Death from Indiana, Hiram G. Thorp arriving in Kansas from Connecticut, Jim's father trading whiskey in Oklahoma, Senator Dawes, innumerable Indian agents, and Benedictine monks—the ghosts of the frontier past who made Jim the child he started out as in 1887.

MGM had indeed, after eighteen years, started talking seriously about making a movie of Jim's life. *Los Angeles Examiner* sportswriter Vincent X. Flaherty had been gathering material on Jim for years, intending to write a book. He mentioned the idea of a movie to MGM's head, Louis B. Mayer, already favorably disposed to Jim. Mayer took an interest and hired Flaherty and a screenwriter. *The Saturday Evening Post* asked Flaherty to do five articles on Jim's life, and he offered to give the Thorpes half of what he was paid. "I conscientiously wanted to help Jim," he later wrote Jack Warner. "He needed it." Patsy insisted he sign a contract to that effect, Flaherty told Warner, a "little slip of paper," which he did. David O. Selznick read an article on Jim in *Reader's Digest* and also took the idea of a biopic to MGM's new production chief, Dore Schary, who agreed to take a meeting with Jim. The appearance of the man who walked into his office, one of his "boyhood's supermen," he would recall in his autobiography, *Heyday*, shocked him. "Puffy, stomach sagged over his trousers belt. There was no spring in his movements—disappointment, age and booze had battered him down. It was like seeing a reflection of his young self in a trick mirror in an amusement park."

When the studio expressed an interest in putting all four Thorpe sons in the movie, Jim and Patsy took Freeda to court, gained custody of the two youngest boys, and brought them home from Chemewa when summer break started. They were abruptly shipped back in the middle of the summer when Patsy demanded more money for them than the studio was willing to pay. When Flaherty got back to Hollywood, he found out that Patsy had amended the contract to include anything he wrote, including the movie story, and had had it notarized. "The ramifications were terrific," he wrote to Warner. "Mrs. Thorpe came to MGM and heaped abuse upon the executives. She threatened to sue them and threatened to tell all of the syndicated newspaper columnists that a big movie studio was taking advantage of a poor Indian." When Mayer learned of Patsy's behavior, he promptly dropped the Thorpe project. It wasn't worth the unfavorable publicity. MGM then sold the property to Flaherty for $8,000, who sold it to Warner Bros. for $35,000. On January 10, 1950, Hedda Hopper announced in her column that the hot new postwar star Burt Lancaster would play Jim. The studio confirmed that the movie, *Jim Thorpe—All American*, would be produced by Everett Freeman, veteran Hollywood screenwriter, and directed by Michael Curtiz. Shooting would start later that year.

In January 1950, there were a lot of newspaper mentions of Jim. After Freeman and Grantland Rice had each approached the AAU in unsuccessful attempts to get Jim's Olympic medals restored, it was reported that Jim had called Avery Brundage a "stuffed shirt." Patsy issued a correction: *she* had called Brundage a stuffed shirt, and, moreover, he still was one. In Sweden, Hugo Wieslander, who had just given his decathlon gold medal to the Swedish Sports Museum, said that though he would abide by whatever the museum director decided regarding its disposal, he was genuinely sorry for Jim. The museum's director said the medal would stay in Sweden. In mid-January, Jim announced in Philadelphia that he was working on a campaign to collect $456,760,000 from the federal government for the remaining 460 Sac and Fox. "Here's the story," he told reporters. "In 1814 the government purchased 70,000 acres from my tribe. . . . That money was deposited in a St. Louis bank for the Indians." The compound interest, he claimed, was now worth almost half a billion dollars. A spokesman for the First National Bank in St. Louis dismissed the story as "ridiculous." In light of later revelations about the mishandling of Indian moneys by the federal government, Jim's claim may well have been valid. Not reported in the headlines was a telephone call Jim made to Freeman on January 23 asking for a $500 advance. "Apparently," wrote Freeman to studio production head Steve Trilling, "the combination of his wife and his trip East ran him out of funds."

On January 24, thirty-seven years to the day after he wrote his confession to Sullivan, Jim was named the greatest football player of the century by a poll of 391 Associated Press sportswriters and radio broadcasters. Jim got 170 votes; second-place Grange got 138. *The New York Times* looked back to his 1911 and 1912 Carlisle seasons as "two of the greatest football years ever enjoyed by any athlete." The Harvard game of 1911 was recalled in mythic but true terms: "with his legs encased in bandages . . . Thorpe kicked four field goals and plunged 70 yards in nine plays for a touchdown that brought the Indians an 18-to-15 victory. The decisive field goal was booted from the 48-yard line."

On February 11, Jim was given the ultimate half-century sports accolade: greatest male athlete. As with his Olympic records, the disparity between his score and those of the runners-up was dramatic. "The storied Indian lapped them going and coming," reported the *Times*. It was generally agreed that Jim won so decisively thanks to his feats in college football and track and field, but that he had "cemented his claim to immortality" by going on to dominate professional football *and* play major and minor league baseball for another sixteen years.

A reporter for Ohio's *Marion Star* wondered if Jim had a mysterious secret responsible for sports success and figured Walter Lingo might know. "Many sportswriters, in fact almost all of them," said Jim's Oorang Indians pal, "have said that Jim was lazy. They are wrong. I used to train dogs with Jim and I know he wasn't lazy. No man is lazy when he can stay out without sleep in the worst weather for 16 and 24 hours at a stretch. No, what made Jim appear lazy was the secret of his success. He knew three things—how to completely relax, how to avoid tension under the most trying conditions, and when to stop training to keep from going stale. . . . Jim never worried about anything he couldn't do anything about. . . . It may sound easy, but try it."

·   ·   ·

Since September, Patsy had demanded what Warner Bros. described as an "astronomical" amount for Jim's services and threatened to sue if the studio's story deviated from the one sold to MGM in 1931. Freeman complained to Steve Trilling, "I am hamstrung if I have to follow structurally what Metro couldn't lick for seventeen years." For the next year, Patsy would harass and threaten Freeman to such an extent that he, too, almost canceled the project. Jim's previous wives posed no problem: Iva, according to Charlotte, refused to accept any money; Freeda, like Patsy, was not in the script. Patsy decided that Phil Thorpe should play the lead, while Jim wanted his Sac and Fox tribesmen to appear in the movie, performing traditional dances and songs in full regalia. Both ideas were nixed by Freeman, the latter as not feasible while telling a long story efficiently. Pop Warner, "aware of the troublesome nature of the current Mrs. Thorpe," had offered to contact Jim and "advise him to play ball with us on our terms and forget his wife's fantastic notions of remuneration." Warner thought the movie was the best thing that had ever happened to Jim.

Having booked Jim into speaking dates up and down the East Coast, Patsy traveled around the country to obtain name and identity releases from Wallace Denny, Warner's assistant at Carlisle and Stanford; former Carlisle superintendent Moses Friedman; Louis Tewanima; Gus Welch; and Frank Mt. Pleasant. She wrote a stream of letters on hotel stationery to the patient, measured Freeman, telling him that Jim was expecting $1 million from the government for a reason she didn't specify; that speaking requests were coming in from all over the country; that he had been offered a job by the Philadelphia Eagles; that she was suing *Sport* magazine for $100,000; that she was leaving for Chicago, where Jim had four appearances; and that if Freeman did not tell her when production was going to start, she would leak to the press the "cheap details" of the contract with Jim.

Freeman handled Patsy carefully, even gently, his eyes on the bigger prize: Jim. Patsy, typing in capital letters, berated Freeman for using high-salaried writers for the script, rather than consulting with "the expert himself." When Gus Welch expressed some reservations about his release, Patsy told Freeman he was "suspicious of all legal documents, as all Indians are . . . stubborn and afraid"; when she learned that Welch had trained as a lawyer, she wrote that he "[m]aybe isn't so stupid after all." Tewanima, living at Shungopavi

Village, Arizona, refused to sign the release. He was happy with his sheep, beans, melons, peaches, and a signed photograph of Warner. Patsy ascribed *his* reluctance to his "primitive intelligence" and said his involvement was Jim's idea, anyway. She dunned Freeman for more money. An aunt had withdrawn all financial help, she claimed, implying the aunt had been at least partially supporting the couple. "I have never been broke before in my entire life," Patsy complained, "& believe me when I state, *I do not like it.*" She also claimed Jim had been borrowing money, unbeknownst to her, then told Freeman that Jim was going to be installed as head of the NFL. Meanwhile, she had "exactly $22 and 95 cents!" and needed money "*now.*"

In between speaking engagements, Jim was managing popular wrestler Suni Warcloud for $750 a week, plus expenses. Suni—born Sonny or Joseph Vance Chorre—and his sister Marie Chorre had appeared in the 1936 version of *Ramona*. Chorre claimed to be a Mission Indian and often did an Indian rain dance in the ring before knocking out his opponent—which he did most of the time at Buffalo's War Memorial Auditorium from March to June. Once in Buffalo, Jim got together with his son Bill, who was in town on a sales job. Bill was taken aback at his father's appearance: older, fatter, wrinkled, slower.

Jim picked up another hefty check endorsing Lucky Strike cigarettes, though he "doesn't smoke a package of cigarettes a month," Patsy wrote Freeman. She had come up with an idea for a half-hour television show, with Jim as host to guest athletes and children. Budweiser, she said, was willing to be the sponsor, but she preferred to try for Borden's or Kellogg's as more wholesome brands for young viewers. Freeman told her the show idea didn't quite work. As her comments to the press became more strident, Freeman cautioned Patsy that statements like "anybody who wants Jim will have to pay through the nose" hurt more than they helped. "It is not dignified for either of you," he wrote in March. "Remember you are playing a big game now and, when the picture is released, you will be playing an even bigger game. Don't let anything you say now hurt your chances later. . . . Jim is a beautiful figure in America and I want to keep him that way." Patsy ignored him and gave an interview to the *Los Angeles Examiner* during which she boasted that Jim was the world's greatest athlete. Freeman shot off another letter to her at the Statler Hotel in Buffalo. "Frankly," he wrote, "there is no need for this type of statement coming from you or Jim. The fact that Jim is great is conclusively proved . . . by the sports writers' poll. . . . These things appearing in print do not tally with the character we are trying to portray on the screen."

Freeman's concerns were indicative of the script's biggest challenge: how to positively spin the story of a person who was not only still alive, but who had also peaked early and, in the popular mind, at least, slid downward since. Screenwriter Douglas Morrow set out the dilemma in a memo to Trilling. "You said something yesterday about Jim still being a bum," he wrote. "Maybe he is. I don't know. All I know is that . . . I have tried to keep as uncynical about Jim as possible and have kept my mind free of the thought that he might still be a bum. The audience doesn't know what we know concerning his intimate personal life; they will know only what we tell them. And we can only tell them something effectively if we ourselves assume, even temporarily, a greater sincerity of feeling regarding the fictitious construction in the second part [post-1912] of the story. We must make ourselves believe it if we have any hope of making the audience believe it. After all," he wrote, resignedly, "we are making a motion picture, not writing history."

Whatever the truth, Jim still had millions of admirers. Letters came into the studio, including one from a seventeen-year-old serviceman: "[A]t one time [Jim Thorpe] was the ideal of all. . . . He is to football what Babe Ruth is to baseball. An ideal to the kids of our nation." Given such sentiments, Warner Bros. could not risk seeming to further humiliate the people's hero. Freeman assured Patsy that the script did not overemphasize Jim's drinking, indeed showed "Jim's great moral fiber" when he overcomes the death of his first son. Pop Warner was sent a copy of the script in Palo Alto, where he had retired. He told Freeman he was pleased with "the very nice way my part in the story has been handled." He was to be portrayed on-screen by Charles Bickford, a craggy, avuncular Hollywood pro, in his first role since his Oscar nomination for *Johnny Belinda*.

Patsy's behavior and wild statements to the press continued to undercut the studio's prerelease campaign to make the real Jim tally with the character they were presenting on the screen. Her last battle with the studio concerned the starting date and Jim's contract. Freeman told Jim that shooting would start in mid-July. Patsy retorted that Jim was supposed to start with the Eagles on August 1—although there was no further mention of the deal, which suggests that Patsy made it up to use for leverage or had killed it with her demands. In the contract, characterized to the press by Patsy as much less remunerative than it actually was, Warner Bros. had agreed to pay Jim, as a technical adviser, $250 a week for five weeks during preparation of the script. He was also to receive $5,000 up front and $5,000 upon completion of the movie. The studio had an option on Jim's services for five additional weeks at a higher fee, but only if it proceeded with the actual production. In all, he could be paid over $15,000. While Jim was in New York appearing in a "Jim Thorpe Night" at Madison Square Garden, Patsy continued to insist on better terms. Freeman wrote to her in San Bernadino, "I am now at the limit of my patience."

Jim finally stopped into the studio in mid-June to see Freeman. Jim "was very pleasant and cooperative," Freeman wrote Trilling, "and suggested wryly that he really ought to have a look at the screenplay we have prepared of his life." Freeman agreed. Peculiarly for Jim, this movie would fix selected parts of his life on celluloid while he was alive to see it. He was still often uncomfortable with fame and the public glare: when the studio scheduled a pre-publicity-tour face-lift for him, he showed up for the surgery and then abruptly left. He didn't see any point in changing himself now.

Patsy then threatened the studio with litigation for not paying Jim's expenses for moving from Chicago to California to become technical adviser. She claimed her health had been wrecked, she had to care for the two boys—of whom she was "extremely fond"—during summer vacation, and so on. By the time production started on July 15, Patsy was out of the picture, literally. "My efforts in the behalf of Jim Thorpe are at an end," she wrote to Freeman. "You stated *you* would take care of Jim. He is *all* yours. . . . You at Warner Bros. will not be hearing from me again. . . . Now—*you* keep him sober, cleaned up & support him. I have resigned . . . I shall *rest* after five years of beating myself to death."

Jim, meanwhile, had been quietly doing research on the facts of his own life to help the screenwriters. For several weeks he rode a bus from Redondo Beach to the Helms Athletic Foundation in Culver City, where he used its extensive sports history collection to verify dates, locations, and records. Paul Hoy Helms, a successful

Los Angeles businessman, created the foundation in 1936 to support the ideals of the Olympic movement and to house his growing collection of sports memorabilia. Helms Hall, where Jim went to do research, housed the executive headquarters of the foundation, a hall of fame, the Olympic rooms, and a library. Before most sports halls of fame existed, the Helms Athletic Foundation was a shrine for fans, a major repository of sports history, and a gathering place for the many coaches, athletes, and former athletes in the Los Angeles area. The beautiful building and its welcoming staff were for Jim a frequent haven and an escape from Patsy. He talked with whoever was there. He was respected for what he had done, not for what he could do for someone else. The foundation had even unearthed his Olympic records and published them as a "public service."

The managing director and cofounder of Helms Hall and the foundation was Willrich R. "Bill" Schroeder, a former Hollywood High School baseball player, manager of the semiprofessional football Hollywood Bears, and a generous, outgoing man with a sense of humor and a soft spot for down-and-out athletes. He knew the majority of the major sports figures of his time, and had first met and liked Jim in 1938. His wallet was always open for those who had fallen on hard times, especially Jim. When Jim wanted to fact-check his life story, Schroeder asked his secretary, Margaret Farnum, to help him. "Jim was really nice, very quiet," Farnum recalled. He wanted to do his own research and liked the privacy he was given. Farnum gave him a tablet of paper and he worked for a few months, until he was satisfied. When he left, he brought her a box of chocolates. He was shy around women, Farnum noticed, more at ease with other men and athletes. Though clearly not wealthy, and despite his sixty-three years and weight gain, he was, she thought, "well-kempt" and very erect, an older version of the athlete he'd been. Sometimes he walked slowly, with effort. The lines on his face were, to her, those of a disappointed person. "He was the kindest man," Farnum would recall in 2002, "a hard worker, a humble person."

After all the preproduction hassles, shooting on the biopic went smoothly. Locations all over Los Angeles were used for the sports sequences: Griffith Park; the Rose Bowl; North Hollywood Playground, as the Carlisle football field; Los Angeles High School for a Penn game; and the Los Angeles Coliseum for the 1912 Olympics.

Lancaster had trained for weeks to simulate on-screen the greatest athlete ever, a formidable task, even for a former circus acrobat who kept himself in prime physical shape. Former coaches from USC and UCLA were hired as technical advisers, and players from the rival teams were rounded up to perform in the football sequences. When the players were told they would be wearing the minimal uniforms of Jim's Carlisle years, they were aghast: "No padding? What do you think we are, stunt men?" An ex-USC fullback told a reporter: "Football is a more slashing and faster game today. Players hit very hard." Jim, who had routinely knocked players out cold, was standing nearby and mildly interjected: "We hit pretty hard in those days." The collegians were told that Lancaster, whose legs had been insured for $1 million, wouldn't be wearing any padding, either. In fact, claimed the press releases, he'd be suited up with the same measurements as Jim's old Carlisle gear. The Rawlings Manufacturing Company in St. Louis still had the record of Jim's Carlisle measurements, which the studio claimed fit Lancaster perfectly: 44-inch shirt, 31-inch pants, size 10 shoe, and size 7⅜ headgear.

The Carlisle sequences were filmed during a month spent at Balcone College, an Indian high school and junior college just outside Muskogee, Oklahoma. The architecture of the Indian schools in Oregon, California, and Arizona was too western to pass for the eastern barracks style of Carlisle. Furthermore, according to *The New York Times*, when Warner Bros. tried to cast Hollywood Indians, it "discovered less than 200 much-used, middle-aged or older redskins" in the available pool, the residue of Jim's prewar network. The BIA suggested Balcone, not only because it looked historically correct, but also because it came with a supply of authentic extras. Curtiz, however, discovered that the Balcone students were paler-skinned than those in the Carlisle-era photographs he had used to cue makeup for the white actors, like Lancaster, and the faces and hands of the real Indians also had to be darkened. The female students complained that their feet hurt in moccasins. Suni Warcloud was cast as Warner's assistant coach, Wallace Denny. The real Denny had signed his Warner Bros. release with an "X." Jim's contract did not cover location work so he stayed behind in California.

Jim Thorpe—All American was the first mainstream movie made about a modern Indian, as opposed to historical treatments like *Bro-*

ken Arrow. The BIA sent representatives to Oklahoma to observe the filming and assess the movie's potential impact on Indian populations. The town of Muskogee, population 35,000, responded enthusiastically to Hollywood's arrival. Townspeople stopped at the hotel where the stars stayed to chat on the house phone or join them in the dining room. Camera dollies, cranes, quick costume changes for hundreds of extras, overnight construction of sets—the Balcone students and locals couldn't get enough of it. Before they headed home the technicians pooled their money to fund two scholarships for the Indian school that had made them feel so welcome. The Hollywood group returned to California in mid-September, and production wrapped on March 11, 1951.

Though Jim was initially angry that other coaches were also on hand as experts, he adjusted and even gave Lancaster, who had never played football and needed fourteen takes for one scene, a few pointers on punting the ball. Watching Lancaster, Jim said, "I get a funny feeling, sitting here watching Burt doing the things I did. . . . I don't think I was ever that handsome." According to *New York Times* sportswriter Gerald Eskenazi, Jim was "overbearing" with the star, coming on the set to correct him. For his part, Lancaster found Thorpe's efforts to teach him touching. "His life had gone to pot," he would recall thirty years later. Otherwise, Jim stayed in the background, quiet. "If he's asked a question," said one observer, "he gives a straight answer, but no more."

Jim announced that he was suspending his campaign to help get the half billion dollars for the Sac and Fox. The Korean War had started in June—his son Bill would be drafted in 1951—and "until Uncle Sam doesn't need the money for defense," he said, he'd hold off. When five hundred of California's top sports names were organized to support Governor Earl Warren's reelection campaign in the fall, Jim headed the list. "The greatest group of sportsmen ever gathered together to back any candidate for public office, state or national," said the chair of the Warren campaign's sports division, and he was probably right. Warren was also the first candidate to use television adroitly. Its "power . . . was never emphasized more vividly than at the Gov. Warren sports dinner," reported Braven Dyer of the October event, "when 100 champions literally walked into the living rooms of Southland [Southern California] voters as they paid their

respects to California's chief executive." Jim and his Giants teammate John Tortes Meyers were among those selected to greet Warren
individually on camera. Dyer was surprised at the governor's intimate
knowledge of each athlete who shook his hand.

Four coaching offers had reportedly come in for Jim since the
beginning of the movie's production, but Patsy put their Warner Bros.
money into a bar and restaurant on the south side of Los Angeles after
establishing that Jim, as a competent and independent Indian, and not
a full-blood, could legally have a California liquor license. The Jim
Thorpe All-American Supper Club's attraction was, of course, Jim.
The studio did not approve of a bar named for the movie, according
to Lancaster. It "went crazy and bought [Patsy] out."

In late 1945, after the Merchant Marine, Jim had made a new friend.
The relationship would have been unusual anywhere but in Hollywood, where broken stars, athletes, and celebrities of any kind met a
ready supply of starstruck young sycophants. People recalled 1931's *The
Champ*, with Wallace Beery in an Academy Award performance as the
aging boxer and child star Jackie Cooper as the kid, when they saw Jim
with the ruggedly handsome William Thourlby, soon to be known as
Buddy Thorpe. Thourlby was twenty-one, about the same age as Jim's
eldest son, Phil, when he first met Jim in the San Pedro bar. "How's
business?" asked the six-foot, four-inch ex-serviceman, the "drifting
offspring," as he put it, of a wealthy Michigan industrialist. There was
a "For Sale" sign in the front window and the place was empty, except
for Jim and the bartender. "Not much of it," said Jim, with a wry smile.

Thus began the relationship. Thourlby would later play Jayne
Mansfield's husband on Broadway in *Will Success Spoil Rock Hunter?*,
appear with Alfred Lunt and Lynn Fontanne in *The Visit*, and be cast
in more than 250 television shows, first-run movies such as *The Man-
churian Candidate*, and B titles like *Bloodlust* and *The Creeping Terror*, a classic of horror sci-fi. He would also be one of the country's
top models, own two men's clothing stores, be a wardrobe consultant
for three U.S. presidents, write a syndicated newspaper column, and
author books with titles like *You Are What You Wear* and *Passport to
Power*. However, Thourlby's biggest claim to fame is as the first Marl-
boro Man. When Camel cigarettes were king, and Marlboros a mild

women's cigarette with red filter tips to hide lipstick stains, a 1954 ad campaign plastering bare-chested Thourlby on billboards across the country would increase sales by 5,000 percent in eight months.

But all that came later. Thourlby had a small stake of money and impulsively bought another bar for Jim and called it the Champ. "Something," he would later say, "neither of us needed: one of us who didn't drink and one of us who couldn't." Down-and-out athletes, of which there were many in Los Angeles, came in begging a free meal and a drink. Jim would give it to them. "It wasn't long," Thourlby said, "before we were closed down."

One day Thourlby was with Jim when he visited Bob Hope at Paramount. Hope had lent Jim some money. They arrived at Hope's bungalow and talked for a while with him and his entourage. Hope then said to Jim that he wanted to discuss something and they went into a back room. "Bob was classy that way," recalls Thourlby, meaning that Hope wouldn't embarrass Jim by talking about the loan in front of other people. As they left, Hope said to Thourlby, "Buddy, take care of this guy. He's the best." When Thourlby asked Jim what he'd talked to Hope about, Jim said, "He helped us out a little. Bob is one of the good guys."

After their visit, they ran into some grips who had worked with Jim. "This is my boy, Buddy," Jim said, introducing Thourlby. "He's a *great* athlete." (Thourlby had played a little college football and sandlot baseball.) "The Los Angeles Rams want him," added Jim, "but he wants to be an actor." The grips, impressed, said director Arthur Lubin was casting a new project, *Rhubarb*, about a feral cat and baseball. Jim said, "Buddy has just finished a big picture at Metro." (Thourlby had worked for one day at MGM, enough to get his SAG card.) The two men continued on to Lubin, who asked Thourlby if he could play baseball? Pitch? Thourlby said sure, figuring Jim would teach him. He signed a contract on the spot for an uncredited part as a ballplayer. It was only as they were leaving the studio that Thourlby noticed the name on the document was Buddy Thorpe. Jim smiled. "Good," he said, "from now on that's what it will be." Thourlby would be listed as "Buddy Thorpe" in two movies besides *Rhubarb*— *Fixed Bayonets* in 1951 and *The Joe Louis Story* in 1953, where he made a brief appearance as Max Schmeling.

The two men and Patsy made up a new family. Thourlby called

Patsy "Mom"; Jim called her "Mother" or "the Missus." When he had work as an actor, Thourlby gave her his check for the three of them. Patsy was a dynamo who was "on the phone all the time," he said, blasting people, including the two men. "You are two kids going nowhere," she'd say, "with all your lives to get there." Unlike just about everyone else, Thourlby liked Patsy and claimed to understand her abrasive personality. "She had a husband she loved," he said. "Nobody wanted to give him a day's work, he was being pushed around. She fought for him like a lion. I loved her. She was the only one standing up for us."

When Thourlby was in Los Angeles, he would pick Jim up in the morning at his apartment off Highland and Sunset and they'd drive around looking for something to do. "We were both lonely," said Thourlby. "I was twenty-three going on twelve and Jim was sixty going on nineteen." The two could go for hours in companionable silence. Jim rarely talked about his former glory days—"The word 'I' was not in his vocabulary," said Thourlby. When Thourlby asked him about playing Eisenhower in 1912, Jim, whose memory came and went more than ever, said he didn't remember "the kid" at all.

In late 1950, Jim had started to make some money appearing at sportsmen trade shows in the East. Thourlby was getting stage jobs on Broadway, so the men rented a cold-water flat on West Fifty-eighth Street in Manhattan for $19.85 a month; Patsy did not join them. There were three rooms, a toilet in the hall, a door to put over the bathtub in the kitchen to make a table. If they could find a television, Jim loved to watch old westerns. "But Dad," said Thourlby, "the Indians always lose." Jim would just smile.

Jim at this late stage was not drinking, according to Thourlby. He knew he could handle no more than a couple of drinks before his knees went weak. He was, however, generous to a fault. One day when Thourlby got an unemployment check in New York, he told Jim to meet him at Lindy's restaurant to celebrate with Jim's favorite dish, bacon and eggs. Thourlby arrived as Jim was saying goodbye to a scruffy character outside the entrance. "Poor guy was broke," said Jim. "So?" Thourlby asked. "I had to loan him ten bucks," Jim explained. "You don't have ten bucks, Dad," said Thourlby. "I didn't have it," Jim admitted, "but I borrowed five." His pride, as much as anything else, led him to lend when he had nothing.

Thourlby seems to have genuinely loved Jim for this generosity as well as for his "incredible capacity to treat everyone exactly the same," whether it was Frank Sinatra, begging to shake Jim's hand, or a nameless indigent. Jim's strength and grace amazed his young friend. One night as the "family" was coming out of a restaurant in Los Angeles, a man on the sidewalk made a remark about Patsy. "Like a ballet dancer," said Thourlby, Jim lowered his fist to the street and brought it up with a turn to hit the man in the crotch and neck, flattening him. Then he winked. The peculiar relationship was idealized, on both sides. The younger man admired Jim's stoicism. He watched as one person after another promised Jim a job or a deal and did not come through. "He'd been brought up in a world of trust," recalled Thourlby, "and betrayed by people he put his trust in." The press accepted Thourlby—as an adopted son, a stepson, or even a real son of Jim's. However, when Thourlby started being referred to as Billy or Bill Thorpe and credited as such on a few minor movies, the real Bill threatened to sue Patsy, the supposed mastermind of that particular name switch.

> *The Lone Oklahoma Indian Whose Fighting Courage*
> *Brought Him Love, Fame And The Title*
> *"GREATEST ATHLETE OF OUR TIME"!*
> *His Battle Back To A Nation's Cheers . . . And One Cheer More!*
> *Everybody's Hero And One Woman's IDOL . . . !*
> *Silver Anniversary Of Talking Pictures!*
>
> —ADVERTISEMENT FOR *Jim Thorpe—All American*, 1951

Jim Thorpe—All American had a double premiere in Oklahoma City and Carlisle on August 23, 1951. Jim appeared in Carlisle, where a large stone testimonial to him in Carlisle's courthouse square was unveiled. One of the dedication ceremony's musicians, Paul A. Brehm, was sitting at the base of the platform when he saw someone grab Jim as he "staggered and nearly toppled." He had been drunk at the screening, and was drunk again. Brehm recalled that the only time during the visit that Jim seemed to be sober was on the stage of the high school, for a program featuring visiting sports celebrities. Five hundred people—including Pennsylvania's governor; actress

Phyllis Thaxter, who played Iva in the movie; and Carlisle sports greats Pete Calac, Lone Star Dietz, Leon Miller, and Gus Welch— came to Dickinson College's gym to honor him. The Philadelphia Eagles' new coach, Bo McMillan, made the trip and told the old story of Jim tackling Rockne. Pop Warner had been invited, but could not attend. Phil was there, now twenty-two and an army corporal stationed at the Carlisle Barracks. Reporters thought he looked exactly as his father had.

Jim was as close to home as he ever got. The emotions churned up by the homecoming were deep and strong. Being back in Carlisle *and* seeing a Hollywood version of himself and his life on the big screen for everyone to compare with the real life and the real person was intolerable. The public glare was still too much. He couldn't live up to it and took refuge in the numbing buzz of alcohol.

A week later, a special gala preview took place at Warner Bros.' Hollywood Theater. Four members of Jim's Olympic team, including aviator Fred Kelly and high jumper Alma Richards, were among the sports invitees. Johnny Weissmuller, other Olympic winners, and a group of USC and Notre Dame football stars were added to the guest list, as the event became the talk of the town. Irene Dunne, Rhonda Fleming, Charles Coburn, Nancy Davis, Roy Rogers, Dale Evans, Virginia Mayo, Roddy McDowall, and many more Hollywood celebrities jammed into the theater. Newspaper accounts did not mention Jim as one of the attendees.

Jim Thorpe—All American opened to generally good reviews and attendance figures. "It is a story recognizable from former film performances," said *The New York Times*, "and not from the unique Thorpe's life." *Time* caught the dilemma of the screenwriters and of their subject: "The film . . . seems unable to decide whether Thorpe was unstable by nature or embittered by circumstances." Later film analysts would track how Curtiz visualized this fundamental conflict by using deep-focus photography to show Jim's active, happy expressive self on the field, running toward his goal and the camera. Dark close-up interior shots mimicked Jim's sense of frustration and entrapment. The football sequences, which the studio's research department had painstakingly vetted for anachronisms, were described as thrilling. Lancaster was credited for not only looking more than plausible as a world-class athlete, but also for giving the scenes of

Jim's disintegration after the loss of the medals and his first son an authentic passion. It was "the sullen and frustrated Thorpe," said the *Times*, "who gives this drama its class." Indeed, the role set up Lancaster for more ambitious character parts in *Come Back, Little Sheba; The Rose Tattoo;* and *Sweet Smell of Success.* Some reviewers regretted that the movie overly conformed to the upbeat biopic formula, avoiding "the excitement inherent in such a colorful existence"—although Everett Freeman would have countered that the life was *too* colorful for a 1951 audience. The movie was learned by heart, however, by impressionable boys and girls, among them future track star and USA Track & Field CEO Craig A. Masback. "*Jim Thorpe—All American* had such an impact," said Masback, who as an adult would run thirty sub-four-minute miles. "It was an important part of my childhood."

While the movie played in theaters throughout the fall, Jim and Patsy burned through the money Jim had earned. They started yet another venture, Jim Thorpe's All-America Thunderbirds, an Indian nightclub tour featuring about six Indian singers and dancers. The show opened in Philadelphia in October, kicking off what was to be a nationwide tour. But on November 9, the news broke that Jim Thorpe had undergone surgery at Philadelphia's Lankenau Hospital for removal of a cancerous growth on his right lower lip. His lower jaw was taped shut, and he was forbidden to talk. Even bigger news: he was a charity case. Patsy wept at a news conference, reported *The New York Times*, as she thanked the surgeon for refusing any money. "We're broke," she told *Time*. "Jim has nothing but his name and his memories. He has spent money on his own people and has given it away." Both she and Jim claimed that Warner Bros. had paid him nothing, or a pittance.

The news, coming so soon after the movie's release, stirred up the old fervor for the great man wronged. People had assumed that Jim was now financially set for the rest of his life and were outraged to think he was destitute. An Indian group in New York formed a committee to raise funds. Henry Modell, the son of the founder of Modell's Sporting Goods in New York, started a Committee for Fair Play for Jim Thorpe, composed of other prominent businessmen and former Olympic athletes, with the purpose of making the "twilight days" of the former champion secure. At a Friars Club dinner in Los Angeles honoring New York Giants manager Leo Durocher, he and the manager of the local Hollywood Stars scheduled a benefit base-ball game for Jim for the following spring. When Hedda Hopper alerted the readers of her Hollywood gossip column that Jim was having a hard time of it, a young man came to her office and gave her $5 to start a Jim Thorpe fund. The contributions flooded in. James Leggett, a bellhop at the Laguna Hotel, sent a check, writing Hopper that he'd been watching the sports columns "in hopes of some big Sportsman starting and Heading a fund." A woman sent in money in honor of her father, "one of Dartmouth's great athletes." Each donor received a personal letter from Hopper. "I had no idea that one small item in my column about Jim Thorpe would bring the large number of responses from people in all walks of life," she wrote. "As he gave of himself to the public, now the public is giving, in part only, back to him."

Warner Bros. also got letters, like the one from a Mr. Van Sickle on New York's Fifth Avenue, saying that had he not been so moved by *Jim Thorpe—All American*, he would not now be so "saddened and terribly shocked" by Jim's condition. Jim could hardly be blamed, for he was an Indian. "[T]hough educated," Van Sickle explained, "[he] thinks differently from us." Jim was an old man, "friendless and hopeless." Why couldn't Warner Bros. hire him as a gatekeeper? The studio let it be known that it had paid Jim $15,000, but even so, Mort Blumenstock, head of publicity, donated $2,500 toward an annuity fund for Jim.

One of the most irate letters to the studio was handwritten from 3330 N Street, N.W., in Washington, D.C., on paper with the mono-gram RFK:

Dear Sirs:
I wanted you to know how shocked I, and all those with whom I have talked of the matter, were at your disrespectful treatment of Jim Thorpe as related in the nation's newspapers and magazines, and commented on particularly by Arthur Daley in "The New York Times." We feel that your monetary arrangements were as an [*sic*] extreme case of exploitation as we have ever heard. To put it bluntly—it is <u>disgusting</u>.
    We feel your company is a national disgrace and we are urging all our friends to boycott your movies.

Robert F. Kennedy

Maxwell Taylor Kennedy, Bobby's son, would later say that the letter may be the earliest example—Bobby was twenty-five at the time and recently graduated from law school—of his father's public advocacy on behalf of someone he felt had been wronged.

The donations kept pouring in. A radio broadcaster in Dallas got $500 from listeners. When Jim appeared on television on December 4, Ben T. Stillman of Uniontown, Pennsylvania, offered to give him a four-room house and a stipend to cover his expenses for the rest of his life. Western Pennsylvania sports fans gave Jim a check for $1,993.50. *American Weekly* ran an article on Jim and was inundated with letters, telegrams, and gifts for him, including pennies from children. The Green Bay Packers organized a committee of the town's mayor, former players, and others to raise a lifetime income fund for Jim; the General Tire and Rubber Company in Akron launched a similar campaign. George Trautman, the president of the National Association of Professional Baseball Leagues, said that gifts were coming from all over the country in response to his appeal: from Ohio State's 1916–1917 football team; Alaskans who had always been thrilled with Jim's feats; several Indians; an Illinois army private and his wife, who were given a lift by Jim when they were hitchhiking; and what *The New York Times* called a "host of plain, everyday fans." Trautman presented the checks, amounting to more than $2,000, to Jim with Thourlby standing between the two men, his arms on their shoulders. After three weeks, the donations reportedly totaled about $15,000. "Everybody has been so nice to me since my operation," said Jim, "it makes me feel warm and thankful for the many kind and thoughtful people who exist."

He was out of the hospital and in New York by November 20. He was wearing a small patch on his lip, but looked otherwise well to Arthur Daley. Jim told Daley the fiction that he had "received nothing" for his life story since the $1,700 from MGM in 1931, and had had to pay 65 cents at a movie box office to see it. Daley asked him how he'd ended up broke. Jim "shook his head sadly." Further downtown, at a sportsmen's trade show, where Jim was put on display on a raised platform, "I felt sadness," remembered Arthur Einhorn, a young man interested in Indian culture and history, who had come to the show to see Jim, "at the image of a great athlete reduced to signing autographs." Another reporter, Jerry Izenberg, later a sports

columnist at *The Star-Ledger* in Newark, spotted Jim and "Buddy" at
the opening of a New Jersey sporting goods store. A wide piece of
adhesive tape across his lower lip, Jim spoke "slowly, haltingly and far
too sadly," said Izenberg, and blinked as flashbulbs snapped. Buddy
talked about his "father," telling apocryphal stories of his youth as the
son of a famous athlete.

Ted Williams, the great, irascible Boston Red Sox star, was dem-
onstrating fly casting at a New York sportsmen's show that featured
Jim and was immediately struck with his size and presence. This was
a man he admired for, among other things, once hitting a triple off
a fence with "that old dead ball" against pitcher Grover Cleveland
Alexander. "Boy," Williams told John Underwood in *My Turn at Bat*,
"just one look and you knew he had it . . . I was so impressed with
how quiet and attentive he was, how he would listen to people. Here's
Jim Thorpe, all-time, all-time, and he'd listen to anybody. He'd
smile and he'd laugh and he'd listen." Williams asked Jim how good
a hitter he'd been in the major leagues. Jim said he'd hit .327 one
year—1919—even though the press said he couldn't hit a curveball.
One writer had written that he wasn't a team player. Williams could
tell that Jim was deeply bothered by that even thirty-odd years later.
"Well, if you ever met Jim Thorpe," he said, "you would realize that
if he was upset a little bit, he was *upset*." After telling Williams how to
get along with reporters—Williams was well-known for his problems
with the press and taunting fans—Jim admitted he had gone up to the
reporter who had maligned him, asked him what he'd do if someone
wrote such a thing about *him*, and when the reporter said he'd punch
him in the nose, Jim "punched him in the nose, and down he went."
Williams said he and Jim "both laughed like hell."

At another sportsmen's show in Boston, Jim was introduced to the
reporter who in 1913 had revealed that Jim was not a true amateur,
Roy Ruggles Johnson, now a sportswriter for *The Boston Globe*. Johnson, who had always thought the AAU was too strict with Jim, said,
"Jim, I'm proud to shake your hand. I always thought you were the
greatest athlete that ever lived." Jim, smiling the broad smile he usually put on for such occasions, replied, "You were only doing your
job." Johnson's son would later say that his father had indeed felt it
was his job as a newspaperman to write the story—but he had not
written, boasted, or talked about it since.

Patsy launched another campaign to get Jim's Olympic awards returned. Her husband should be allowed to go to the happy hunting ground, she said, knowing he had been vindicated. Though Grantland Rice's personal appeal to the AOC had been turned down, she wanted to use the momentum created by the movie to try again. "I'd be the happiest man in the world if I could just get my medals back," Jim dutifully told reporters. He also threatened to sue unless the two trophies were returned to him by the AAU and said that if Warner had backed him in 1913, he wouldn't have had to send them back. Branch Rickey, then general manager of the Pittsburgh Pirates, had already started a movement to get the medals restored, but on December 1, the AAU again refused to change its 1913 decision, saying that no facts had been presented to justify a reversal. Ferdinand Bie, the designated 1912 pentathlon winner and a doctor in Kristiansand, Norway, told the Associated Press that if the IOC and the Norwegian Sports Association approved, he would be glad to let Jim have the medal. On December 4, IOC president Sigfrid Edström wrote to the organization's headquarters in Lausanne, cautioning the personnel not to answer any telegrams or queries about Jim. "He is a great swindler," he wrote, "and bothered me to death before I could get rid of him."

Al Clark, columnist of *The Patriot-News* in Harrisburg, Pennsylvania, invited Jim to his home to talk after the AAU's announcement. Though Patsy tried to get him to sound more positive, Jim, "cracking the knuckles of his huge ham-like hands," as Clark wrote, quietly insisted there was nothing he could do or say now that could matter anymore. "The white man hurt me most," he said, "because he didn't understand me . . . because I couldn't understand him." His only real friends were the men he had played with and Pop Warner. Vance C. McCormick, the Yale All-American who was Carlisle's first official football coach, had tried to set him straight. "Vance called me a 'smart Indian but a dumb white man,' " he told Clark, explaining that McCormick meant Jim couldn't do the things that a white man does, like drinking, because he couldn't stop doing them. "I should have listened," said Jim, "but I didn't. I regret now that I didn't. But now it's too late." If the medals came back after he was dead, he wanted them brought to Carlisle. "I was happy there, for a little while."

So many people wanted tickets to a testimonial benefit dinner organized by Rickey in Jim's honor in Canton, Ohio, on January 30, 1952, that extra tables were set up outside the Onesto Hotel's ballroom banquet hall. The mayor claimed the gathering was the largest and most distinguished in the history of the city. With old friends like Pete Calac looking on, Jim was presented with an engraved wristwatch and a check for $1,000; he would receive more money later. There were many speeches, but Rickey's was perhaps the most impassioned and ornate. He referred to King Gustav V's praise in 1912 and then said:

> [T]he world's conscience is continuously pricked with a profound sense of obligation to give belated recognition to the greatest athlete in the world. Many years ago our distant forebears discovered a new race on this continent, a copper-colored race. That race gave us a gladsome and generous welcome. We have pushed them back and further back. I regret that history may have the chance . . . to point back to the prudery of this present day when America cap-sheathed its injustice by stripping the race's foremost athletic representative of his Olympic medals.

Ohio governor Frank J. Lausche was overwhelmed by the applause given to Jim that night. "I think there is a lesson to be learned about the fearless and gallant conduct of this great athlete," he said, then turned to Jim. "Since you've been out of sports, Jim," he ended, "you've taken everything like a champion." He had often not, but this was a night for generous hyperbole.

Throughout the long evening Jim just sat quietly. The man who had "rocked the cradle of professional football," said *The New York Times*, was "characteristically nonplussed by the ovation given to him." When he finally got up to speak, he was quick and concise. "I can see I'm not a forgotten man," he said. "I appreciate the kindness shown me tonight. It has been wonderful to come back tonight, to see so many of my friends, to see the fellows I played with and against. I love Canton."

The fuss finally began to abate. Brundage was named the first American president of the IOC in 1952, when Edström retired. Jim was still hoping for the return of the trophies. Meanwhile, he drank and continued to do bizarre things when he did. Forest "Forrie" Hopkins, the flamboyant editor of the *North East Star* in North East, Pennsylvania, and owner of the local Concord Hotel, was an admirer and frequently let Jim stay there for free if he had a lecture or sports show in the area. On the shores of Lake Erie, between Buffalo and Cleveland, North East was tiny and known, if at all, for grapes, wineries, and Welch's grape juice. One night, according to Hopkins, after they had both had a few drinks, Jim offered to sell his body to him. The editor was flabbergasted. "Think about it," Jim said. "For only $300, you can bury me here in North East and my grave will be a tourist attraction for years to come." The idea had a certain appeal to someone who loved his town and sports, but the next morning Hopkins gently told Jim that he should be buried in a place that was important to him, and gave him $300 to go home.

Jim and Patsy decided to try the bar business again despite previous failures, this time in Pittman, Nevada, a tiny town on the Boulder Highway, south of Las Vegas. In April, Jim leased a Quonset hut called the Hut Club on the north side of the highway and opened it on May 28, six days after his sixty-fifth birthday, as Jim Thorpe's All-American Supper Club and Casino. Local residents were uncertain why the Thorpes had chosen their town. Most days Jim sat silently at one end of the bar with a beer, while Patsy and the manager served the few customers.

On June 22, a week before the Republican National Convention that would nominate Dwight D. Eisenhower as the party's presidential candidate, Ike came to McCarran Field in Las Vegas. Jim was present and the two men shook hands, embraced, and compared memories of their one football game together in 1912. When told later that the president remembered the game "only hazily," Jim would say, with a grin and clear recall, "I guess so. I think he was not in his head after a few plays." After Eisenhower was elected president in November, it was claimed that he took pride in the fact he'd once tackled the great Jim Thorpe. He hadn't and insisted he never had. He'd only *tried* to take Jim out of the game.

At the Fourth of July American Legion Junior Baseball game for Boulder City's Jamboree celebration, Jim staggered as he walked to the pitcher's mound to throw the first ball. When asked afterward about his medals, he said he only wanted his Olympic records restored for the sake of his children. On the morning of July 22, he was asleep in the passenger seat of a friend's pickup truck when it crashed into the rear end of a state highway truck at a stoplight in South San Gabriel, California. No one was seriously hurt, but Jim had a broken nose and lacerations and was hospitalized briefly. On August 8, in Nevada, he collapsed and was brought to the hospital in Henderson, unconscious, at 2:50 in the afternoon. He was placed in an oxygen tent and improved rapidly enough to be released by August 11. The doctors ordered him to take things easy; he had had another heart attack. There were no reporters waiting outside the hospital to ask him what he thought of Bob Mathias's second decathlon gold medal, won by a huge margin in Helsinki at the recently concluded 1952 Summer Olympics. He had beat every one of Jim's 1912 scores except one, the 1,500-meter race.

When the Hut Club's manager died in a car crash, Jim and Patsy sold the business and moved back to Los Angeles. They settled in September into a trailer park at 2442 Pacific Coast Highway in Lomita, the little town between Hawthorne and Long Beach where Jim remembered renewing his acquaintance with Patsy. Or at least Jim settled there. Syd Kronenthal, Culver City parks and recreation director, Bill Schroeder's right-hand volunteer and friend at the Helms Foundation, would say, years later, that Patsy had kicked Jim out. Jim had come to the end of his usefulness, as far as she was concerned. She moved into an apartment on McFarland Avenue in Wilmington, several blocks north of the Long Beach U.S. Navy complex, and went back to running what Slim Harrison called "a little beer joint" she had briefly managed in 1951. Jim stayed with Kronenthal for a couple of nights until Schroeder found the trailer park for him; Ted Williams had provided the trailer. At this point Jim was, said Kronenthal, a "pathetic figure," with clothes that looked like they had come from the Salvation Army and then been slept in. Though only in his sixties, he looked as if he were ninety. Schroeder took Jim to the local men's clothes shop and bought him a pair of trousers and a shirt, as he often did for other indigent athletes.

Kronenthal would admit that he didn't fully appreciate at the time the irony and sadness of Jim's situation. "He was a mutation of his time," he recalled, "not equipped to face the world that adored him." A "sweet guy," Jim was also, according to Kronenthal, "pretty hard to handle." Thunderbird wine, dreadful but cheap, fortified at 17.5 percent alcohol, was now Jim's drink of choice. It was also the favorite of, and deliberately marketed to, winos, migrant workers, Indians, and skid row drunks. When Jim had too much of it, he "wouldn't move," said Kronenthal.

Jim managed to get back to New York briefly to see Thourlby, as well as his daughter Grace, in Pearl River. She was now the former Mrs. Fred Seeley, divorced in 1950 from the husband she had met in New Guinea, and the mother of two children born in Japan, Dagmar and Paul. At the end of the visit, after dropping her father off in front of the local movie theater to catch a bus back to Manhattan, she glanced back and saw that the marquee letters spelled out "Jim Thorpe—All American." Her father stood there, she said, wearing a cowboy hat, a fringed suede jacket, and holding his beat-up leather luggage, "just waiting for the bus." It was her last sight of him.

Seamy indignities kept befalling him. Jim and Patsy were together, at Patsy's insistence, in the Wilmington bar on the evening of February 10, 1953, when police officers arrested them for labor law violations. An employee, Thomas F. Murray, had filed a claim in 1951 for $335.50 in salary due him. The couple was booked at the San Pedro jail and released on bail of $200 each. Patsy promptly collapsed. Jim said he had flown home from New York the day before their arrest when he learned his wife was ill, adding that he had financed the trip by making a "personal appearance in New York." On February 17, Murray made a written request that the charges be dropped, and they were. "Jim gave me his word he would pay," he said, adding, "anyway, it's Brotherhood Week." Jim called Thourlby in New York on March 27 to say he was heading east and would see him soon.

By Monday, March 30, Thourlby and most of Jim's children had heard on the radio or read in the newspapers that Jim was dead, less than two months shy of his sixty-sixth birthday. He had died on the afternoon of Saturday, March 28, in his trailer in Lomita, of coronary sclerosis. In the back of his old car was his Carlisle football helmet.

Epilogue

1953–1983

There is no myth more plaintive, and beloved by men, than the fall of the gifted athlete.

—ALESSANDRA STANLEY, *The New York Times*, 2009

The coroner didn't sign Jim's death certificate until two days after the body was found. Bill Schroeder's notes, later consulted by his daughter, Jan Schroeder Iverson, record that at about midnight on March 28 he got a phone call at his home from the United Press Association to tell him Jim had died. "The mortician won't touch Thorpe's body because Jim's wife has no money," said the reporter. Schroeder said he would see what he could do.

Early the next morning he and Kronenthal drove to the trailer court. "Jim's gnarled hands were purple," said Kronenthal. No one had claimed the body. Patsy wanted nothing to do with her husband and refused to discuss the matter. The two men managed to have the body taken temporarily to the A. M. Gamby Mortuary in Lomita. Then Schroeder called David Malloy, the owner of Malloy and Malloy Mortuary at 1717 South Flower Street in downtown Los Angeles. A "devout baseball fan," according to Jan Iverson, Malloy offered to pick up the body and handle all arrangements and expenses. A few days earlier, Schroeder had chaired a testimonial dinner for the sports editor of the *Los Angeles Herald-Examiner* and there was $700 left over. The committee members agreed to use the money to buy a coffin to hold Jim's body.

Meanwhile, on the front pages of newspapers across the country, Americans read that Jim had been eating dinner with his wife in the trailer when he suffered a heart attack. "Mrs. Thorpe's screams" alerted a neighbor, who administered artificial respiration for nearly half an hour. A county fire rescue squad temporarily revived Jim. Last rites of the Catholic church were administered by the Reverend John V. Hegarty of St. Margaret Mary Church in Lomita. Other reports claimed that an ambulance driver said Jim had died about 4:02, after reviving at 4:00, and that his wife, "Mildred," collapsed at his death and was put under the care of a physician. In fact, Patsy was there but her screams were at the rescue squad, accusing them of killing Jim as they tried to revive him. Myths were part of his death as they were part of his life. The death certificate has the time of death as 3:25. Like millions of American boys, Schroeder had followed Jim's career since childhood. He was as aware as anyone of Jim's importance to American sports and the unique loyalty and passion his story inspired. When Jim needed a friend, Schroeder had taken care of him. He did so now, crafting a dignified send-off and memorial for Jim.

On Monday, "all hell broke loose," said Kronenthal. "Everybody jumped in," including Patsy, once she realized that Jim's death was an opportunity. She tapped Slim Harrison to take charge of the funeral services, all subsequent press releases, and, as he said, "blasting it on all the radio stations." She also started a campaign to get the 1912 trophies "recovered" so, she claimed, Jim could "have them with him throughout eternity." The Red Cross was trying to locate Phil and Bill in Korea, Grace in Pearl River, and Dick, a seaman first class in the Navy Air Corps at San Pedro, to bring them home. Charlotte (married for the second time and now Mrs. Earl Koehler; Michael, her son by her first husband, would take his stepfather's surname) and Gail, divorced, still lived in Chicago. Jack had heard the news on the radio in Oregon, at the Chemawa Indian School.

Pennsylvania politicians and business executives, the dean of Dickinson Law School, the commandant of the Army War College—now based at the former Carlisle Indian School quarters—and Carlisle town officials released a statement saying that Jim's body should be brought back to the site of his school, to be buried in the old Indian cemetery where other Carlisle students had been interred. The

American Indian Hall of Fame in Anadarko offered to take the body. Jim's half brother Frank approached Shawnee oilman Ross Porter, a friend of Jim's, and told him the family would like to bring the body to Oklahoma, but they didn't have the money. Porter immediately started a local campaign to bring the body and family back to Oklahoma for the funeral. He also persuaded state legislators to push a bill providing seed money for a Thorpe memorial in Shawnee that would exceed the Will Rogers Claremore site in size and tourism appeal. The Shawnee Chamber of Commerce wired Patsy, offering to pay for all funeral expenses and round-trip train tickets to Oklahoma. She said she would not release her husband's body to Oklahoma or anywhere else unless a "separate special memorial" was definitely to be built there. Anadarko would not be getting the body; she was considering Carlisle. Privately, she wrote to a Carlisle resident that "Jim was rather well fed up on Oklahoma . . . he did not care if he ever saw the state again," and that morticians had assured her that, if necessary, "Jim will remain just as beautiful as he is for from eighteen months to two years." Grantland Rice commented that "Thorpe's body has been more in demand than it ever was during the last 20 years of his life. . . . Looking down on it all, old Jim must be chuckling an ironic chuckle."

Obituaries, tributes, multipart series on his life, letters to the editor, Jim Thorpe stories, editorials, and updates on the body's whereabouts and ultimate destination filled newspaper pages across the country. "To a whole generation of American sport-lovers 'the greatest athlete of them all' is gone with the passing of Jim Thorpe," said an editorial in *The New York Times*. "Most, if not all, of his track and field records have since been surpassed, but no one has equaled the hold that he had on the imagination of all who saw him in action. . . . He had all the strength, speed and coordination of the finest players, plus an incredible stamina. . . . His memory should be kept for what it deserves—that of the greatest all-around athlete of our time." Arthur Daley noted that "Jim never retaliated. He was one of the cleanest players ever to pull on a cleat." Of course, Jim did retaliate, but he was not a dirty player. The *Chicago Daily News* printed a comparison of Jim's 1912 decathlon record with that of Mathias the previous summer in Helsinki, but only after somebody in the newsroom cautioned the editor not to run the piece if it "makes Jim look bad."

Reporters immediately showed up on Pop Warner's doorstep in Palo Alto. Eighty-two and crippled by arthritis, he said Jim's death was a "shock" and, though they hadn't seen much of each other recently, he had always thought of him as one of his closest friends.

One of the best of the new crop of sportswriters, Red Smith, wrote a farewell to Jim, "a burly, simple wonderful gent," that would be anthologized as one of his finest pieces. "He was the greatest athlete of his time," Smith wrote, "maybe the greatest of any time in any land and he needed no gilded geegaws to prove it. . . . No one who ever saw him on a football field could ever forget the wild glory of that indestructible Indian."

Other commentators wondered why no one ever came forward to guide him after the glory days; the story was so much more melodramatic if Jim was cast as the helpless pawn at the mercy of predators he couldn't control or escape from. It was left to Vincent Flaherty, who had bought Jim's story from MGM and sold it to Warner Bros., to score his life with the extreme highs and lows of an all-American opera.

> Let historians decide whether or not James Francis Thorpe was the greatest athlete of all time. Certainly Thorpe . . . was at least the greatest of an impressionable generation. . . .
>
> The story of Jim Thorpe should be a compulsory study for every athlete—his to digest, in all of its depressing nuances, his to retain and evaluate as a bitter object lesson.
>
> Thorpe had a running start in life. The sun shone upon him with a spectacular radiance such as few young men, of any era, have ever known. He was enriched with greater physical attributes than any athlete of his time . . .
>
> His every classic movement was a museum show piece of coordination—an incredible communion of mind and muscle so acutely perfect as to become one and the same.

Ernie Nevers sent this telegram to Patsy: HAIL AND FAREWELL TO THE GREATEST ATHLETE OF ALL.

On April 3, Elmer Kenison, the secretary of the Shawnee Chamber of Commerce, announced that the body would arrive in Oklahoma on Thursday, April 9. The family had taken a vote and decided on Shawnee for the burial. Carlisle and the Army War College, which had got permission from government officials to bury the body in what had been the Carlisle football field, were told of the decision. During the week before its removal to Oklahoma, the body was available for viewing at Malloy and Malloy. More than three thousand mourners, many of them schoolchildren, came to pay their respects. The casket was open but, as specified by Patsy, under glass, the body dressed in a buckskin jacket and moccasins, Jim's lecture outfit. In his hands were a Catholic rosary and an Indian testament. On the day before the body was shipped to Shawnee, a delegation of Indians from Riverside County, an area southeast of Los Angeles heavily populated by Indians, was the first to pass the bier; by early afternoon, more than three hundred people had filed by, many of them, reported *The New York Times*, "weeping unashamedly." That evening four hundred more people came for a recital of the rosary, including Jim Donahue and Alma Richards from the 1912 U.S. Olympic team, John Meyers, Vic Kelley (a Choctaw student who had taken over as coach at Carlisle when Warner was fired), Suey Welch, and Joe Stydahar, coach of the Chicago Cardinals and future Hall of Famer. Jim's children, all of whom, except Phil, were there, were upset that the glass prevented them from touching their father.

The next morning Patsy and Grace boarded the train to Oklahoma with the body. In Shawnee it took nine men to lift the coffin, encased in a rough crate, out of the baggage car and into the hearse. Under police motorcycle escort, the body was taken to the mortuary, where it was to lie in state again; after the funerals, until $100,000 for a memorial to Jim was raised, the body would stay in another mausoleum, Fairview Cemetery, north of town. When Patsy arrived at her hotel, she received a telegram from the president of the United States. "I learned with sorrow," said Eisenhower, "of the death of my old friend, Jim Thorpe. I am delighted that, as a tribute to his achievements and to his warm personality, a fitting memorial is to be erected in his memory. . . . As one who played against him in football more than forty years ago, I personally feel that no other athlete has possessed his all-around abilities in games and sports."

The Sac and Fox Thunder Clan and Potawatomi family members gathered for the tribal funeral late on Sunday afternoon at a farm less than ten miles from where Jim was born. Fires were built to create the smoke that would carry prayers for Jim's spirit to the Creator. The feasting, praying, and singing took place in the traditional tribal wickiup, a structure of bent, domed branches covered, for this ceremony, with canvas rather than bark. Tobacco and medicine were placed in the coffin; all debts were forgiven. A new pair of moccasins was placed next to the body for Jim's journey. The ritual was to go on all night, releasing the dead man's spirit after sunrise to travel to its final resting place in the west, beyond the setting sun. Although such occasions are usually private, one reporter—a respectful, observant one, from the *Oklahoma City Times*—was allowed to attend. Family and friends drove up in cars, bringing pots filled with beef, venison, chicken, and corn. Former teammates Albert Exendine and Joe Guyon and the immediate family—with the exception of Patsy—were there. Family members told stories of the old days in Wisconsin, Illinois, Iowa, and Kansas, of Hiram and Charlotte, of Jim and Charlie as little boys playing along the North Canadian. Most of the talk was in English, with an occasional Sauk word or phrase.

Suddenly, Patsy burst in and announced that it was "too cold" for Jim to stay any longer. She was backed up by policemen she had insisted accompany her. The casket was hoisted up, put back into the hearse, and taken away. The group was dumbstruck. The ceremony wasn't finished: Jim's spirit had not been released and put to rest.

Late the following morning, several hundred people came to St. Benedict's Roman Catholic Church in Shawnee for a requiem high mass. Leaving the mausoleum, Patsy cried out, "Goodbye, dear! I've brought you back home." A little more than a week later, Oklahoma governor Bill "Alfalfa" Murray signed a bill creating the Jim Thorpe memorial commission; in mid-June, facing a revenue deficit, he vetoed the appropriation to fund it. The tiny family graveyard, where Hiram was buried, was in Garden Grove, near the school Jim attended before Carlisle. But Jim's body, deprived of its memorial, lingered without burial in Shawnee, at Patsy's wish. In July, she threatened to take the body to California unless more progress was made, and quickly, on an alternate fund-raising plan organized by Ross Porter. Carlisle was also back in the running, but John B. Fowler, a town leader, told *Sports Illustrated* in 1983 that "Pat just wanted too much money. . . . We felt we were getting into a bidding war." Later there were claims that she had asked the town to change its name to Jim Thorpe.

In August, Patsy suddenly showed up with a trailer at night at Fairview Cemetery. "Where's Jim?" she asked. "Over there," said the attendant. "Pick him up and put him in that trailer," she said, and took the body a hundred miles north to Tulsa's Rose Hill Memorial Park mausoleum. She now thought Tulsa would properly honor Jim, but the city wasn't interested. Jim's children were livid. Bill urged Governor Murray to "intercede and hold any further action until we are notified of procedure that is being taken." Murray did nothing, saying, "I don't see what authority I have to enter into any family squabble."

The tiny Pennsylvania towns of Mauch Chunk (Machk Tschunk/ Bear Mountain or Mountain of the Sleeping Bear)—which included Upper Mauch Chunk—and East Mauch Chunk had faced each other across a deep bend in the Lehigh River gorge at the base of Bear Mountain since around 1818, when they became a hub of anthracite coal transport. The towns boomed when the railroads arrived later in the century and were known as the "Switzerland of America." Second only to Niagara Falls as a tourist destination, the Chunks were home to thirteen millionaires, ornate Victorian mansions, and seven grand hotels. Asa Packer, one of the millionaires and reportedly the third-richest man in the country, founded Lehigh University and created and built the Lehigh Valley Railroad as a more efficient means than barges to transport the coal. Five U.S. presidents—Grant, Garfield, Cleveland, McKinley, and Teddy Roosevelt—stayed at the local Mansion Hotel. Charles Riley, Jesse Owens's junior high school coach, grew up in Mauch Chunk.

By the early 1950s, the towns were dying, with no jobs for local youth. Anthracite production was dwindling as oil supplanted it. Each town—their combined population was barely 6,000—had its own public school system, its own Catholic school, ethnic origin—Mauch Chunk, Irish; East Mauch Chunk, German—churches, municipal services, and antagonisms. "They hated each other," said Richard Dugan, whose family owns Dugan's Store, the oldest business in Mauch Chunk.

In response to the crisis, Joseph L. Boyle, the publisher and editor of the *Mauch Chunk Times-News*, started a nickel-a-week fund. Each family was asked to donate a nickel a week for five years; the funds would be used to construct a factory building with which to lure a new industry to save the Chunks. Boyle's other plan was to get the two towns to consolidate, but neither wanted to give up its identity or name. A television producer from the ABC affiliate in Philadelphia heard about the nickel campaign and thought it was a "great story," recalled Dugan. "Like 'The little town pulling itself up by its bootstraps, phoenix-like.'" A camera crew came to town, and a news documentary about the Chunks and their predicament was aired on Channel 3 in Philadelphia on its six o'clock news one night in September 1953.

Patsy, in Philadelphia to see NFL commissioner Bert Bell at the league's headquarters, was sitting in her room at the Bellevue Stratford hotel watching Channel 3 the night of the Chunks story. She decided the towns might be receptive to taking Jim off her hands. That Jim had never set foot in the towns, which were nearly a hundred miles from Carlisle, was unimportant. A few days later she walked into the Mauch Chunk National Bank carrying her Pekingese dog and asked a teller where she could find Joseph Boyle. He happened to be at the next window. Patsy made her pitch: if the towns changed their name to Jim Thorpe, they could have the body. Boyle, by all accounts a generous, kind man, was at first taken aback. But as he reflected on the seemingly bizarre idea he started to believe it made some sense: the name change would force the towns to unify. He was desperate to save his town, recalled his daughter, Rita Boyle Huggler, and was willing by this point "to do *anything*."

By November, the plans had been considerably enhanced: not only would there be a memorial, there would also be a mausoleum, a football shrine, the Jim Thorpe Museum, the Jim Thorpe Memorial Heart and Cancer Foundation, the five-hundred-bed Jim Thorpe Hospital, a $10 million cancer center, an Olympic stadium, and a sporting goods factory with a Jim Thorpe trademark. The Fraternal Order of the Eagles, in recognition of Jim's long fondness for the Mount Gilead aerie and of its historical commitment to covering funeral expenses for indigent members, agreed to pay for the memorial. Commissioner Bell would work to see that the towns got the bid to have the Pro Football Hall of Fame. Patsy thought she might open a hotel for all the new tourists who would be coming and call it Jim Thorpe's Teepees.

The two town councils approved the idea. Patsy agreed to bring the body up from Tulsa to show her good faith. On Monday, February 8, 1954, eleven months after Jim's death, the body arrived. It was placed in a crypt, its sixth resting place. On May 18, the voters approved a town consolidation and the new name by a ten-to-one margin.

The next day, Patsy and five officials of the new municipality signed what the *Inquirer Magazine* in Philadelphia would later describe as "a remarkable contract in which the only real property was a corpse." Patsy agreed that neither she nor any of her heirs would remove the body, but only for so long as the towns "are officially known and designated as 'Jim Thorpe.' " The question of whether Patsy received money for Jim's body has never been settled definitively. There was no such language in the formal agreement. *Sports Illustrated* later reported that Bob Knappenberger, a Mauch Chunk Bank employee, had turned over a check to Patsy to cement the deal for an amount he wouldn't disclose. Boyle said she was paid about $500 for her expenses. In 1996, the Knight-Ridder/Tribune News Service would report that Knappenberger still refused to name the amount. In 2001, Knappenberger would deny the stories as "pure fiction" in the *Pittsburgh Post-Gazette*. So would most everybody else in Jim Thorpe, Pennsylvania. The town had no money to spare in 1953, making it more likely that after trying to extract a payment for the body Patsy had to be satisfied with a check for her expenses.

In the next three years, the deadline for the fulfillment of the stipulated promises, there were unexpected setbacks. The Fraternal Order of Eagles backed out of financing the mausoleum. Some of the money raised by the nickel campaign for a factory building had to be used instead. When one of the pallbearers said the coffin was so heavy, it could only have been filled with rocks, Boyle got local morticians to open the coffin. "There was a plastic bag over the head," he told the the *Inquirer Magazine*. "We removed it. There was no doubt it was Jim." Another group of disgruntled locals tried to pry the coffin out of the crypt with the intent of dumping it on Boyle's front porch in protest, but they couldn't budge it. A few scholars and Sac and Fox recalled that not long after Black Hawk's death in 1838 his remains—placed sitting erect in a small mausoleum of logs in Iowa—were stolen, then retrieved and put on display in a museum that burned down in 1855.

Nine days after the deadline passed, on Memorial Day, May 30, 1957, the town of Jim Thorpe held a grand dedication ceremony. A quiet, grottolike site up a steep hill had been chosen a short distance out of town. It would purposely not be commercialized, and no admission would be charged. The twenty-ton austere red marble Jim Thorpe Memorial Mausoleum featured medallion images of an athlete hurdling, jumping, and running; a baseball player at bat; a gridiron warrior heading off a tackle; and an Indian in feathered headdress sitting on a horse. Etched into the stone, Jim's birth date was off by one year. Soil from Oklahoma, the Stockholm stadium (gathered by 1912 decathlete Wieslander), the Polo Grounds, and Carlisle's Indian Field was distributed around the base. Escorted by police cruisers, Indian maidens, Nickel Bearers (marchers representing the nickel-a-week campaign), a Miss Jim Thorpe float, scout troops, veterans, National Guard troops, Rotarians and Knights of Columbus, a Central Railroad of New Jersey float, and some of Jim's family and friends, the body was finally buried. Jim had been dead four years and two months.

By the mid-1960s, the citizens of Jim Thorpe felt like suckers. Not only had none of the grand projects materialized, virtually no one was coming to the town to see the Thorpe memorial; local undertakers used it as a drop-off for used funeral wreaths. Johnny H. Otto, chairman of the County Water and Sewer Authority, told *The New York Times*, "You mention you're from Jim Thorpe and nobody knows what you're talking about." He also famously said to *Sports Illustrated*, "All we got was a dead Indian," and initiated two referenda that sought to rename the two original towns under one of the old names, Mauch Chunk.

Feelings ran high. A month before the first referendum on November 3, 1964, vandals smashed the mausoleum with 123—a reporter counted them—blows from a hammer, defacing the letters of Jim's name and the engravings. The referendum was defeated by a slim margin. A year later, a second referendum was also defeated, and more decisively, by 1,418 to 810. The old-timers were dying off.

Anyone born after 1954 had known the town only as Jim Thorpe. But whenever the movie *Jim Thorpe—All American* was shown on local television, few old Chunkers could bring themselves to watch it.

Many attempts had been made since the 1940s to restore Jim's official Olympic standing and records, but it was not until the 1970s that momentum began to build. In 1973, the AAU board of governors voted unanimously to restore retroactively Jim's amateur eligibility for the period covering 1909–1912, the necessary first step to an Olympic reinstatement. *The Wall Street Journal* pointed out that while Jim's professionalism, as judged by the AAU in 1913, was "beyond dispute," the feeling persisted that Jim had been a "scapegoat." Pressure mounted from a new movement of militant and moderate Indian groups. Over the next decade there would emerge an array of Jim Thorpe committees, initiatives, and campaigns, each organized around one or more of the following causes: reinstatement of Jim's 1912 Olympic records in the decathlon and pentathlon individual events and point totals; return of the original two gold medals, or replicas, to his family; the "return" of the two lavish trophies; and the return of Jim's remains to Oklahoma, so he could be buried where he came from and with his people.

Aside from the issue of whether Jim's actions were right or wrong, the essential question regarding the Olympic records was who had the authority to reinstate Jim. What were the necessary steps, the process, needed to bring the issue before whoever had that authority? A key obstacle was removed when Brundage resigned as head of the IOC after the 1972 Olympics in Munich. He could no longer hold on to any kind of relevance or power. Brundage's successor, the Irish Lord Killanin, was himself replaced in 1980 by Juan Antonio Samaranch. With the United States—Los Angeles—the site of the 1984 Games, and the time optimum for the tattered Olympic movement and the IOC to be positioned in a more modern, less elitist light, redressing the wrong done to the American Indian athlete Jim Thorpe looked like the smart and right thing to do.

To persuade what was still a snobbish organization to revisit a pesky cause took a fresh approach with the right presentation. The U.S. Olympic Committee (USOC) and the IOC would respond only to an appeal that was impossible to refuse and that was made by individuals they deemed worthy of respect. In 1982, Thorpe biographer Robert Wheeler and his wife, sociologist Florence Ridlon, sister of Syracuse University and Dallas Cowboys All-Pro Jim Ridlon, formed yet another Jim Thorpe organization, the Jim Thorpe Foundation. It was unofficially headquartered at Danker's restaurant, a popular haunt of Capitol Hill lawmakers. Their board was composed of one-third politicians, one-third Indians, and one-third "sports immortals," and included Democrat Thomas P. "Tip" O'Neill, Jr., Speaker of the House; Republican Robert H. Michel, House minority leader; basketball star and senator Bill Bradley; decathlete Rafer Johnson; and former sports greats Sonny Jurgensen, John Brodie, and Sam Huff. Billy Mills, who had won the gold medal in the 10,000-meter race in a stunning surprise finish at the 1964 Olympics, joined; he frequently said how important Jim's example had been to him growing up on the Pine Ridge reservation when, despite the Native Americans who had played at the higher levels of sports in the twentieth century, the only ones most Americans saw were "mascots." Building on the many previous and dogged efforts of Charlotte, Grace, Gail, Phil, Bill, Dick, Jack, and others, Wheeler and Ridlon got more than 100,000 names on a new batch of petitions to restore Jim's Olympic status. Congressional Resolution 364, calling for the restoration of Jim's medals, passed on October 1. And after years of administrative dodging among the USOC, the International Association of Athletic Federations (IAFF), and the IOC, Wheeler and Ridlon finally connected with the person who was both willing and influential enough to strong-arm Jim's reinstatement through the IOC.

William E. Simon, previously treasury secretary in the Nixon and Ford administrations and, concurrently, director of the Federal Energy Office during the 1970s oil crisis, was a dynamic, generous, principled, very successful businessman, father of seven, a devout Catholic who had worked his way up from a non-elite childhood in Paterson, New Jersey. He became president of the USOC in 1981. That same year, following a gradual broadening of the eligibility rules since Brundage's exit and only after a furious debate, the word "amateur" was deleted from the Olympic charter. Florence Ridlon, meanwhile, had found a copy of the text of the 1912 Swedish rule that specified that challenges or objections must be made within thirty days after an event. The IOC had insisted it did not exist.

After the law firm of Baker & McKenzie agreed to handle, pro bono, any suit brought against the IOC, Wheeler and Ridlon approached Simon in the fall of 1982, shortly before the meeting of the nine-member IOC executive board scheduled for October. They presented two lines of argument in favor of reinstatement, one moral and one legal. Simon said he agreed with the moral grounds but could not do anything concrete with them; the legal argument, based on the original rule, was more persuasive. Though not a member of the IOC, he had enormous influence with the organization. "Simon ran with it," said Robert Wheeler. To win over Samaranch, the new IOC president, he had to "take [him] by the elbow," said Wheeler, and persuade him to be a hero. In Lausanne, Simon told Samaranch, in so many words, that he could rectify an old wrong, burnish the image of the Olympic movement, and get all the credit. After what Emmy Award–winning filmmaker Bud Greenspan would describe as an "impassioned plea" by Simon to the IOC executive board, Jim's 1912 Olympic amateur status was restored on October 13, 1982. New medals would be cast from the original molds and given to the family. (Bie's original medal had been stolen three years earlier, and Wieslander's was believed to be in Stockholm, in a chest with hundreds of other Olympic memorabilia.) Though some of Jim's children persisted in believing that the two trophies rightfully belonged to their father, they didn't, and the matter was dropped. The ironies were rich. James Sullivan, Avery Brundage, and others had buttressed their punishment of Jim with a supposed strict adherence to the rules of amateurism—and now it was the rules that made the matter simple to resolve. President Ronald Reagan sent a letter to Charlotte on October 19 saying, "At long last, we have set the record straight."

It took about a week after the IOC vote for reporters and commentators to find holes in the decision. According to the official IOC press release of October 13, 1982, "the name of James Thorpe will be added to the list of athletes who were crowned Olympic champions of the 1912 Games. However, the official report for these Games will not be modified." That meant the second-place finishers and the others down the line would retain their upgraded status of 1913; their records for each event would stand in the official record book. Jim's scores in the fifteen events of the pentathlon and decathlon and the respective totals would not be listed. It was a classic case of Olympic hypocrisy. If Jim's records were reinstated, the runners-up would logically have to be demoted. There can't be two gold medalists, especially if the record of the real winner makes the other look meager by comparison, as Jim's point lead did. With no official record for Jim, there were now two gold medal winners for the 1912 pentathlon and the decathlon.

"The joy felt by the entire sports world," wrote Greenspan in *The New York Times* on October 31, "is somewhat diluted." *Sports Illustrated* insisted the "co-champion" designation was "in the worst tradition of asterisk record keeping." Without the public records, what did reinstatement mean? There was a whiff of frontier noblesse oblige: give the Indians the shiny trinkets but honor the dominant tradition and maintain the false but official record. "As this country's most famous representative of the Indian people," wrote Wheeler and Ridlon to Samaranch, "it is important that [Jim Thorpe's] tarnished image be refurbished." Jack Thorpe, for one, assumed that the IOC reinstatement meant that his father's records would again be on the official books. On legal grounds, it made no sense to go only halfway. If Jim had been wronged, deprived of due process, then why not fix the whole problem, including the records?

Even with the uproar, Samaranch was adamant that Jim would not be listed as the sole winner and the records would remain unchanged. "This is simply outrageous," Wheeler told the *Los Angeles Times*. "The Olympic Committee has disgraced the Olympic movement. It is a greater disgrace not to list Thorpe as champion than not to give back his medals." He and Ridlon would say that they encouraged the Thorpes not to settle for co-champion status, but, as with any large, fractured family, it would have been difficult to get consensus.

A luncheon and reception to present the replicas to the family were held at the Biltmore Hotel in Los Angeles on January 18, 1983. Burt Lancaster attended and the family dubbed him "Dad," in recognition of the fact he had played their father in the movie thirty-two years earlier. Two sets of gold vermeil replicas had been made from the original molds in the Swedish foundry that had crafted the 1912 medals; one was presented to Gail as the oldest daughter, and the other to Bill, as the oldest son. Seven silver replicas were presented to each of the Thorpe children. One set of the gold medals would later be on permanent display in the rotunda of the state capitol building in Oklahoma City. Though Charlotte had wanted the two trophies to be displayed during the 1984 Games, the IOC found that the solid silver Viking ship, originally given by the Russian tsar, was of "such a high value" that no insurance company was willing to cover the risk of shipping it to and showing it in Los Angeles.

In May, the *Olympic Review*, the official publication of the IOC, with reference to Jim, quoted from one of the last interviews given by Olympic founder de Coubertin before his death in 1937. "Oh, what a stupid old business Olympic amateurism is," he had said. "It is respect in sport which interests me, and not respect for this ridiculous English concept which only allows millionaires to dedicate themselves to sport. That sort of amateurism is not what I wanted."

Jim's body, too, would be left to a middling fate. Some of the family agreed that their father's soul was doomed to wander until the Indian burial ceremony was finished and he was buried in the land where he had been born. "No way," responded Jim Thorpe mayor Mike Hickock. "They can't take the body back." Another local businessman admitted the Thorpe family had a point. In 1983, Jim Thorpe, Pennsylvania, had the look, said *Forbes* magazine, of "an abandoned movie set: dusty, deserted, empty stores, no traffic."

Within the next twenty years, however, the town would become a charming, thriving tourist destination, gateway to the Poconos, a "fabulous story," said Richard Dugan, of a resilient town that "thrived in a part of the state that has continued to have a slow, lingering death." The revival had little to do with the fact that Jim Thorpe was buried there. His grave is still an afterthought for visitors. The average person on the street "doesn't spend time thinking of Jim Thorpe at all," according to Dugan.

There have since been periodic attempts by some of the Thorpe family to bring Jim's remains back to Oklahoma to be buried in the Garden Grove cemetery next to his father. In June 2010 a lawsuit was filed by Jack Thorpe in the U.S. District Court in Scranton, Pennsylvania, under the 1990 Native American Graves Protection and Repatriation Act, to have the remains returned to Oklahoma.

He continues to insist that without a complete Indian burial ceremony, their father's spirit is a restless traveler from one dimension to
another, at home in neither of them. In August 2010, the Jim Thorpe
borough council voted to fight the lawsuit. Civic leaders believe the
town has been loyal and vigorous in its honoring of Jim for the past
half century and his remains should stay in Pennsylvania.

By the 1970s football had replaced baseball as the nation's most
popular spectator sport. In 2010 a *Time* magazine cover featured a
photograph of an old, beat-up NFL football with the headline: "The
Most Dangerous Game." Teddy Roosevelt's White House conference in 1905 was recalled in the article's historical background summary, as was Woodrow Wilson's fervent belief in football's "moral
qualities." The new crisis of the game Jim had played for more than
twenty years was the disturbing prevalence in former football players
of an old boxer's syndrome—CTE, chronic traumatic encephalopa-
thy, a series of concussions that can produce memory loss and depression in middle age. One of the rule changes that was suggested to
encourage more blocking with the arms and hands rather than with
the head: eliminate the three-point stance. That it had been one of
Pop Warner's early innovations was not mentioned.

Two years short of the hundredth anniversary of Jim's spectacular performance in 1912, American Indians make up about 1 percent of the U.S. population but account for only 0.4 percent of the
scholarship athletes at the major college level. "American Indians,"
wrote Selena Roberts in *The New York Times*, "have won less recognition in athletics than most other ethnic or racial groups in the
United States." Despite many state basketball championships and
cross-country titles, which have brought plenty of recognition on a
local and regional level, Indian athletes find the transition to the top
level of American sports difficult. The immediate reasons: ignorance
or indifference on the part of recruiting coaches and reluctance of
the young athletes to leave the reservation. The deeper reasons: lack
of self-confidence out in the white world and fear of becoming no
longer an Indian.

Back where and when Jim began, white surveyors—easily distinguished from other white men in the Territory by their supply wag-

ons and instruments—were mapping a section of land near the Thorp allotments one morning around 1897, ten years after the Dawes allotment act. Jim remembered everything that was about to happen for the rest of his life. Jim, ten, and his father, accompanied by one of Hiram's mongrel hunting dogs, joined a group of other Indians silently watching the process. So this was how the earth got divided up and assigned to individual owners.

One of the surveyors walked by with a bulldog. He cautioned Hiram to keep an eye on his mutt because the bulldog might kill him. "I think my dog," said Jim's father, "can take care of himself." Sure enough, the dogs started fighting and Hiram's mutt sunk his teeth into the bulldog's neck. When the surveyor pleaded with him to restrain his dog, Hiram pulled the dogs apart and "held them aloft in his hands," Jim would recall, "until they cooled down." When he put the dogs back on the ground, the bulldog ran off, whimpering. "Mongrels grow tough in this climate," said Hiram.

The angry surveyor said that the owner of the mongrel couldn't beat the owner of the bulldog. "My father," wrote Jim, "met the challenge with a blow to the man's chin which sent him against his surveying instrument, toppling it to the ground he had just charted." So much for dividing up the land.

Jim and his father walked away, Hiram smiling broadly because he had not only been "invited to participate in the sport at which he excelled," recalled his son, "but one of the sports he enjoyed most."

The fight was more than a game.

Acknowledgments

Many people gave generously of their time and talent in the service of this biography. Many of them are cited in the book and endnotes. Special thanks, however, must be given first and foremost to Jim Thorpe's children. Gail Thorpe and Grace Thorpe provided their memories, file material, photographs, overall help, and delightful company; I wish they had lived to see the book. Bill and his late wife, Robbie, and Richard Thorpe were equally generous and unstinting in their readiness to do whatever they could to help me. Jack Thorpe spent hours driving me around the Shawnee, Oklahoma, environs of his father's birthplace and arranged a Potawatomi ceremony to bless this project on its way. Grace's daughter, Dagmar Seeley Thorpe, provided much helpful material regarding the history of the Thorpe family and reviewed the early chapters. Gail's daughter, Sharon Kossakowski, helped with family photographs. Charlotte's son, Michael Koehler, graciously let me review his research on his grandfather and shared his thoughtful, wise perspective on the Thorpe family.

Robert W. Wheeler, the author of the definitive biography of Thorpe in 1975, gave me copies of the transcripts of all his interviews, made when many of Thorpe's friends and colleagues were still alive, as well as unrestricted access to his collection of photographs. His wife, Dr. Florence Ridlon, helped fill in details of their essential role in the 1982 campaign to have Thorpe's 1912 Olympic status reinstated. This book would not have been possible without their help and support.

Judge Robert H. Henry, a passionate Oklahoman originally from Shawnee and chief justice of the 10th Circuit Court of Appeals, steered me to the works of Oklahoma historian Angie Debo and introduced me to several helpful Oklahomans, including Bob Blackburn, the director of the Oklahoma Historical Society. Lynne Draper, former executive director of the Jim Thorpe Association in Oklahoma City, provided excellent insight into the Thorpe career, as well as material from the association's collection. The association awards the Jim

Thorpe Award for best defensive back in college football each year, as well as sponsoring numerous other awards and activities. James E. Elfers provided essential insight into the 1913–1914 Giants–White Sox world tour.

In Pennsylvania, Barbara Kriete Landis, the Carlisle Indian Industrial School archivist at the Cumberland County Historical Society (CCHS) in Carlisle, was unstinting in her readiness to open all the resources of the society for this project. Her parents, Charles and Dorothy Kriete, hospitably provided bed and board—and many lively discussions of football, biography, and the Carlisle Indian school. The entire staff of the CCHS was invaluable, including Richard Tritt, the photo archivist, who provided many of the photographs for this book. Landis introduced me to Jacqueline Fear-Segal, American studies professor at the University of East Anglia, who graciously took the time to give me a tour of the area of East Anglia near Norwich when I was researching Thorpe's English ancestry. Regarding Jim Thorpe, Pennsylvania, Chunkers Richard Dugan and Rita Boyle Huggler provided helpful insight into the town's history and development.

Jim Campbell, former archivist at the Pro Football Hall of Fame in Canton, Ohio, shared materials from his collection, as well as hours of patient explanation of the intricacies of early football history. At the Hall of Fame, Joe Horrigan, vice president for communications/exhibits, and Saleem Choudry, researcher, were invaluable on both general and arcane points of football lore; Chad Reese, Hall of Fame information systems administrator, researched and copied local newspaper coverage of the Canton Bulldogs team from 1915 to 1920. John Sayle Watterson in Charlottesville, Virginia, reviewed the collegiate football chapters of the manuscript and gave essential suggestions. Bob Gill and the late Bob Carroll at the Professional Football Researchers Association were very helpful in reviewing the details of Jim Thorpe's professional football career. Robert L. Whitman, Oorang football team historian, was generous with his time, research materials, and photographs.

Robert Hoie, acknowledged expert of minor and major league baseball history, was helpful and enthusiastic in both reviewing the manuscript and tolerating many e-mails and phone calls about obscure—to most people—minor league teams. Tim Wiles, director of research at the National Baseball Hall of Fame in Cooperstown, New York, and his staff facilitated many requests and clarifications. Jeffrey Beck reviewed the sections of the manuscript concerning the involvement of Indians in organized baseball.

As with any of these dedicated professionals, any errors in the final book are in spite of their best efforts.

Ned Comstock, revered archivist at the University of Southern California's cinema-television library, took it on himself to send me a list of all the citations referencing Jim Thorpe in the *Los Angeles Times*—the important source of Thorpe's activities from 1929 until his death. Ned also provided other information about Thorpe's Hollywood career from the USC archives.

Ben Cheever first insisted that I pursue this book idea, saying Jim Thorpe was the "mother lode of subjects." His suggestions and opinions over the long process that ensued have been invaluable. The encouragement of the other members of our Westchester writers' group—Marilyn Johnson, Esmeralda Santiago, Terry Bazes, and Larkin Warren—was appreciated, to say the least. Walter Montgomery at Robinson Lerer and Montgomery in New York allowed me to shift to a part-time schedule while I started research on this book. To Brittley Wise Jarrell, my friend and former colleague at RLM: thank you.

When Chris Gavaler and I discovered that we were both living in Lexington, Virginia, and working on projects about the Carlisle Indian Industrial School, it was a delightful surprise: what were the odds? Chris provided me with much helpful information about Thorpe's first wife, Iva Miller, and Sylvester Long from his research for his fictional work about Carlisle, *School for Tricksters*. The scholarship Chris and his wife, Lesley Wheeler, both on the faculty of the University of Washington and Lee, have done on Marianne Moore was essential to an understanding of the importance of the Carlisle school to Moore's later work.

In Irvington-on-Hudson, New York, special thanks to the late Peter Oley, distinguished coach of the Irvington High School track team (and my son's fourth-grade teacher). His wife, Marianne Oley, translated the 1912 Swedish media materials written in "old Swedish," provided to me by Leif Yttergren, the Stockholm sports historian cited herein. Genealogist Anita Lustenberger traced Thorpe's white ancestry back to East Anglia. Ronda Billig and Philip Boffey provided warm hospitality and a guest bed countless times, as did Patricia and John Armstrong across the street. The late Mary Louise Grinnell Bunaes, Lakota Sioux/Prairie Band Potawatomi/French, graciously shared her family's memories of Mayetta, Kansas, the Rosebud Sioux Reservation, and the Haskell Institute.

Special thanks to the research staff at both the "old" Oklahoma Historical Society quarters and at the splendid new Oklahoma History Center—especially research division archivist Jennifer Day—for help navigating the records of that unique state. Archivist Sara Berndt tracked down several Native American records at the National Archives in Washington, D.C. Pamela Strachan, director of the Irvington, New York, Public Library, as well as the staff of the Lexington, Virginia, branch of the Rockbridge Regional Library system, facilitated many interlibrary loan requests. Louise Sandberg, special collections librarian at the Lawrence Public Library in Lawrence, Massachusetts, provided copies of local newspaper coverage of Jim Thorpe's 1924 summer playing ball for the Lawrence Independents. Sarah Snip Stroup photocopied the *Los Angeles Times* articles at Alderman Library at the University of Virginia. Robert W. Reising reviewed the North Carolina chapter and provided much helpful information on Jim's career in general.

In Stockholm, Leif Yttergren, referenced above, researched and made copies of contemporary accounts of the 1912 Olympics in Swedish publications and archives; Wolf Lyberg, Swedish Olympic historian, provided essential guidance and material regarding the actions of the Swedish Olympic Committee, de Coubertin, and the IOC after the revelations in 1913 of Thorpe's prior professionalism. Cindy Slater, manager, library and archives, USOC, Colorado Springs, facilitated the copying of all USOC correspondence relating to the various Jim Thorpe reinstatement campaigns and helped clarify the equivocal nature of Thorpe's current Olympic status.

Thanks, too, to Susan Campbell, Potawatomi, and historian of the tribe; Sara Keckeisen, Kansas State Historical Society; Martha McIntosh, document information officer, Marie Morsia-Villemin, historical archives, and Barbara Schenkel, documentation, IOC, Lausanne; George Yuda, Carlisle, Pennsylvania; Dennis Martin, reference librarian, Hawthorne Library, Hawthorne, California;

W. J. Gobrecht, Harrisburg, Pennsylvania; William Thourlby; Chuck Bednarik; Kathy Shea Alfuso; Paul Wilson, Fairfield, Virginia; George Baron; Margaret Farnum; Jan Schroeder Iverson; Paula Stuart Warren, CG; Richard L. Baker at the U.S. Army Military History Institute; and Kathy Gourley at the State Historical Society of Iowa.

My agent, Sloan Harris at International Creative Management, was, as ever, the sage and calm guide through this long project. At Knopf, Joey McGarvey meticulously reviewed the manuscript and helped turn it into a book; the stellar design and production staff, especially Carol Devine Carson, crafted the handsome product you hold in your hand.

The efforts of my scrupulous and dogged editor, Jonathan Segal, are evident on every page. Thank you, once again.

To family and friends in California, Virginia, Alabama, Oklahoma, Texas, and New York—especially my two children, Lucy and Will: a profound thank you for your love and support.

Notes

BHOF   Jim Thorpe clip file, Baseball Hall of Fame, Cooperstown, N.Y., unless otherwise noted.

CCHS   Cumberland County Historical Society, Carlisle, Pa.

LSC   Lon Scott File. Correspondence between Lon Scott and Jim Thorpe, Lon Scott Correspondence 1943–1945, Jim Thorpe House, Yale, Okla., Oklahoma Historical Society.

LAT   *Los Angeles Times*. After Thorpe's move to California in 1929, the *Los Angeles Times* is the principal source of public information on his activities.

NARA   National Archives and Records Administration, Washington, D.C., and College Park, Md.

NYT   *The New York Times*

OHS   Oklahoma Historical Society, Oklahoma City

PFHOF   Jim Thorpe clip file, Pro Football Hall of Fame, Canton, Ohio, unless otherwise noted.

RG75   Records of the Bureau of Indian Affairs (BIA), Record Group 75, 1793–1989.

RNO   *The* (Raleigh, N.C.) *News and Observer*

RWWC   Robert W. Wheeler Collection (private)

TSN   *The Sporting News*

USC   School of Cinema-Television, University of Southern California

WCC   Walter Camp Collection, Yale University, New Haven, Conn.

All interviews were conducted by the author unless otherwise noted.

As with many ephemeral popular culture records that include early sports materials, documents were not often properly archived initially. A news clip, for example, in a private collection, e.g., the Walter Camp Collection at Yale, or some of the materials gathered unsystematically over a long period of time, such as some from the early years of the twentieth century in the Baseball Hall of Fame or the Pro Football Hall of Fame, had neither date nor name of publication noted on the newspaper or magazine clip when they were first accessed. The author notes such lack of information as "n.d." (no date) and/or the probable date in brackets, and "unattributed" (no name of periodical noted).

PROLOGUE

xi "old-timers and new-timers": Kyle Crichton, "Good King Jim," *Collier's*, Nov. 14, 1942.
xi "Jim was a man": Ibid.
xii "Jim Thorpe Selected as Best Male Athlete": *LAT*, Feb. 12, 1950.
xii He had received 252 first-place votes: The votes were calculated differently from the single-sport polls: each participant was asked to vote his first, second, and third choices, for which points were compiled on a 3-2-1 basis.
xii "[t]he Sac and Fox Indian is almost a legend now": *NYT*, Jan. 29, 1950.
xii "the massive media exposure": Leif Yttergren, interview.
xii "not" . . . "a traditional Indian": Grace Thorpe, interview. All quoted material of Grace Thorpe, unless otherwise noted, is taken from this source. The author had several interviews with the late Ms. Thorpe at her home in Prague, Oklahoma. See also: Grace F. Thorpe, "The Jim Thorpe Family: From Wisconsin to Indian Territory, Part 1," *The Chronicles of Oklahoma*, vol. 59, no. 1 (Spring 1981), and "The Jim Thorpe Family: Part 2," *The Chronicles of Oklahoma*, vol. 59, no. 2 (Summer 1981).

PART I: THE RULES OF THE GAME

1 "This democracy, this land of freedom": Ian Frazier, *Great Plains* (New York: Penguin Books, 1990), 173.
2 Jim's warrior model: Jim Thorpe said that his grandfather, Hiram G. Thorp, "had married a niece" of Black Hawk (Jim Thorpe, with Russell Birdwell, *The Red Son of Carlisle*, unpublished autobiography, Production File, *Jim Thorpe—All American* [1951], Warner Bros. Collection, USC, 4—hereafter cited as *Red Son*). According to Jack Thorpe, Jim's youngest child, Sac and Fox tribal elders believe that Hiram G. Thorp's wife, No-ten-o-quah, was the daughter of Whirling Thunder, Black Hawk's son. Grace Thorpe, Jim's youngest daughter, insisted there was no direct connection. Paula Stuart Warren, CG (Certified Geneologist), specialist in Indian records, says, "In Native American research . . . the stories passed down through the generations are vital knowledge. That said, there can be misstatements made. There could very well be truth in what the elders have said, but it could also be that the terminology of the tribe over time has changed as far as the meaning of relationship terms" (e-mail to author, Nov. 18, 2009).
    A census of the Sac and Fox, taken prior to 1840 in Iowa (http://www.meskwaki .bia.edu/history/MeskinteractiveCD1/Pages/index.htm), lists Whirling Thunder (spelled Nah-she-wah-kuck and identified as a son of Black Hawk) and his family in Book One, page three. No-ten-o-quah, who would have been about twelve, is not among them. Book Two, page thirteen, lists a "Not ten okay" under family group number 86, with the head of household described as "old woman." It is very likely that this Not-ten-okay is Jim's grandmother, who may have been orphaned in the Black Hawk War. Kathy Gourley, who discovered the census while doing research at the State Historical Society in Des Moines, Iowa, says, "The agent would have been writing the names down phonetically, as he heard them. Sauk and Meskwaki [Fox] language had not been written before EuroAmericans entered the picture,

so there was no standardized way to spell any words. Each person wrote what they heard—and sometimes that varied widely! We may never be able to say with absolute certainty that a particular entry is Jim Thorpe's ancestor" (e-mail from Gourley to author, May 12, 2010).

CHAPTER ONE
Beginnings · Oklahoma Territory, *1887–1904*

3 "Contrary to the beliefs of many": Ray A. Young Bear, *Black Eagle Child: The Face-paint Narratives* (Iowa City: University of Iowa Press, 1992), 149.

3 "The path to glory is rough": Múk-a-tah-mish-o-káh-kaik/Black Hawk, *Black Hawk: An Autobiography*, ed. Donald Jackson (Urbana: University of Illinois Press, 1955), 37.

3 the land between Kansas and the Red River: The author thanks Bob L. Blackburn, executive director of the Oklahoma Historical Society, the source of the text of this footnote.

4 "There are two sorts of Indians": Letter from Father Thomas Bergh, OSB, Indian Territory, to Rev. Father Swithbert, Aug. 31, 1885. The Unpublished Letters of Father Thomas Bergh, monk of Ramsgate Abbey, England, Visitator at Sacred Heart from Aug. 15, 1885, to Feb. 8, 1886, written to Father Swithbert at Ramsgate. St. Gregory's Abbey, Shawnee, Oklahoma. The author thanks Benedict McCaffree, who transcribed the letters, for alerting her to their existence.

4 "[t]here can be no doubt": Bergh Letters, Sept. 21, 1885.

4 "slender, failing": Bergh Letters, Oct. 26, 1885.

4 "not one whit better off": Bergh Letters, Sept. 11, 1885.

4 "the walls of which": Ibid.

4 "always on horseback or up trees": Bergh Letters, Sept. 21, 1885.

4 "ever yearning for the old wild life": Bergh Letters, Oct. 26, 1885.

4 "In the whole Indian Territory": Bergh Letters, Sept. 21, 1885.

4 "highwayman anecdotes": Ibid.

4 "How little is thought in": Bergh Letters, Dec. 26, 1885.

5 "The term 'killing' is more euphonious": Bergh Letters, Sept. 21, 1885.

5 "somehow . . . life-like and true.": Ibid.

5 "[m]odel Indians are not to be found": Ibid.

5 yet she joined with Hiram: There was no record of a Roman Catholic marriage at Sacred Heart, though after Hiram's death one relative remembered Hiram and Charlotte referring to such a ceremony: Estate of Hiram Thorp, Ex-Parte Affidavit of Mary McCoy, Dec. 10, 1914, Central Classified Files, 1907–1939, Sac and Fox, Oklahoma: file 136686-1914-350, Box 84, NARA.

5 The spelling of the Thorpe family name: In 1912 the Sac and Fox agent pointed out the discrepancy to Carlisle's superintendent: "I do not know where he [James Thorp] picked up the 'E.' " Letter from Horace J. Johnson, Sac and Fox agent, to Moses Friedman, Superintendent, Carlisle Indian Industrial School, Oct. 22, 1912. Indian Archives Collection, Sac and Fox–Shawnee Agency Records—Carlisle Indian School, Sept. 27, 1880–Dec. 30, 1911, Box 542, folder 5. OHS.

6 "lazy, flowing": *Red Son*, 6.

6 The cabin had been home: To marry his third wife—and to conform to her Catholic

beliefs—Hiram had to break relations with Mary James, a Shawnee he had married, "Indian fashion" (i.e., by mutual agreement), in 1874 and with whom he had four children. He had also married Sarah LaBlanche, a Creek, in the Indian manner. Their daughter was about a year old when Hiram married Charlotte.

6   "evil" . . . "filthiness": Michael Reinschmidt, *Ethnohistory of the Sauk, 1885–1985: A Socio-political Study on Continuity and Change* (Goettingen, Germany: Cuvillier Verlag, 1993), 117.

6   "I am . . . five-eighths Indian": *Red Son*, 5.

7   "people of the outlet" or "they that came forth into the open": Reinschmidt, 21.

7   "(in) Sac country": Gordon Whittaker, *Conversational Sauk: A Practical Guide to the Language of Black Hawk* (Stroud, Okla.: Sac and Fox National Public Library, 1996), ix.

7   Jim's great-great-grandfather: A plaque in Milwaukee's Mitchell Park, near the site of the original cabin, reads, "On this site, the first permanent fur trader JACQUES VIEAU IN 1795 built his cabin, the first house in Milwaukee. Here also was the crossing of the Green Bay–Chicago trail. This tablet was erected under the auspices of the Old Settlers' Club of Milwaukee County 1925." Jacques married Angelique Roy (Roi), in the Green Bay home of her father, Joseph Roy, in 1786; the home is now known as the Roi/Tank cottage and is part of Heritage Hill Park in Green Bay. Jacques and Angelique were both buried in the French Catholic cemetery, later called the Allouez cemetery.

8   ceremonial runners: Truman Michelson, "Notes on the Ceremonial Runners of the Fox Indians," *Contributions to Fox Ethnology*, Washington, D.C.: Bureau of American Ethnology, Bulletin 85, 1927.

8   symbolic enactments: Steward Culin, referred to in Peter Nabokov, *Indian Running: Native American History and Tradition* (Santa Barbara, Calif.: Capra Press, 1981), 68.

8   "X the M": Letter from Andrew Jackson to Major William B. Lewis, Aug. 25, 1830. Marquis James, *The Life of Andrew Jackson* (Indianapolis, Ind.: Bobbs-Merrill, 1938), 550.

9   "fast progressing toward extermination": Robert Lucas, governor, Iowa Territory, quoted in William T. Hagan, *The Sac and Fox Indians* (Norman: University of Oklahoma Press, 1958), 205.

9   When his tribe was consolidated: Louis Vieux ran a toll bridge over the Vermillion River, a campground for wagon trains and military personnel, stables for changing horses, a blacksmith shop, a livestock yard, and a farm that provided the pork, beef, grain, vegetables, and hay sold as provisions. He made numerous trips to Washington, D.C., on his tribe's behalf and became known as "Uncle Louis," his advice sought by both Indians and whites. When he died in 1872, he left a two-hundred-page will listing land holdings (44,000 acres of Kansas land, including half the town of Louisville, most of the town of Belvue, farmlands, and shares in two grist mills).

9   By then the Sac and Fox had arrived: The U.S. government continued to use the "Sac and Fox of the Mississippi" designation.

9   Though Jim thought he was of Irish descent: The word "Thorp/Thorpe" passed into Anglo-Saxon English from Old Norse and originally meant "farmstead" or "settlement." Because it came to England with the Vikings in the eighth century, the name shows up mainly on the eastern side of that country, especially in Northumberland, Yorkshire, and East Anglia, in place-names such as Micklethorpe (small village),

Bridgthorpe (village by the bridge), Thorpe Hamlet, Thorpe Hall, and Thorpe Market. One of the most distinctive features of medieval Yarmouth was the narrow east-west passageways connecting the main streets. One of them was called Thorpe's Row.

9   one of the founders: "William Thorp's name appeared as a free planter (a voting citizen and freeman) who assented to the Fundamental Agreement of the New Haven Colony on June 4, 1639, and in 1641 he had a town lot shown in an early map." E-mail to the author from Anita A. Lustenberger, CG, Aug. 31, 2004. The "Thorpe" family genealogy was prepared for the author by Lustenberger in August 2002. The author also thanks Brad Siegler for generously providing his Thorpe genealogy.

9   "downward slide in social class": "Thorpe" genealogy, 5. Hiram G. Thorp served from Dec. 29, 1837, to Dec. 28, 1840, in the U.S. Eighth Infantry, Company A, when he was discharged after his three-year tour of duty. He reenlisted in the U.S. First Infantry, Company F, and served from January 1842 to Nov. 23, 1844, when he was discharged for disability. Register of Enlistments in the U.S. Army, 1798–1914; (National Archives Microfilm Publication M233, 81 rolls); Records of the Adjutant Generals Office, 1780s–1917, Record Group 94; National Archives, Washington, D.C. Digitized images viewed at Ancestry.com (Ancestry.com. U.S. Army, Register of Enlistments, 1798–1914 [database online]. Provo, UT, USA: Ancestry.com Operations, Inc., 2007.)

10   After the tribe was removed: The 1842 treaty that had removed the tribes from Iowa to Kansas stipulated, as most of these treaties did, that the government provide for blacksmiths. Hiram's name would show up on Indian agent employee reports from 1853 to 1861; in 1859 he was promoted to full blacksmith. When more than three hundred members of the two tribes died in an epidemic of smallpox and flux in 1851, he was also put to work building burial boxes or cribbed frames.

10   "a passion, a challenge, a game": H. Craig Miner and William E. Unrau, *The End of Indian Kansas: A Study of Cultural Revolution, 1854–1871* (Lawrence: University Press of Kansas, 1990), 108n.

11   "Everybody knows something": *NYT*, Dec. 20, 1861, quoted in Miner and Unrau, 74.

11   "[t]hese people must die out": Horace Greeley, *An Overland Journey from New York to San Francisco in the Summer of 1859* (New York: C. M. Saxton, Barker & Co., 1860), 152.

12   "desert his plow": *Red Son*, 5.

12   "very defiant in the matter": Sac and Fox agent Lee Patrick, quoted in Jack Newcombe, *The Best of the Athletic Boys: The White Man's Impact on Jim Thorpe* (Garden City, N.Y.: Doubleday, 1975), 50.

12   He didn't exist: See D'Arcy McNickle's 1936 novel, *The Surrounded*, for a nuanced delineation of the overlapping religious traditions in an Indian family and community similar to Jim's.

12   "a pretty face": *Red Son*, 4.

13   "not too poor": Letter from Arthur Wakolee to Robert W. Wheeler, Nov. 18, 1967, RWWC. All quotations of Wakolee's are taken from this source.

13   "worked hard for their living": Ibid.

13   "modern patterns": *Red Son*, 7.

14   "tired feet to a headache": Ibid., 4.

14   "marvel": Ibid., 5.

15   "Don't be afraid of the water, son": Hiram Thorp, quoted in ibid., 6.

15   "never in the house": Jim Thorpe, quoted in Walter H. Lingo, "The Life Story of
     Jim Thorpe: The World's Greatest Athlete," chapter 2, *Athletic World*, May 1923.

15   "We didn't have a coach": Jim Thorpe, quoted in n.d., unattributed news clip,
     RWWC.

15   "The open plain and the river bottoms": *Red Son*, 5.

16   "spirited abandon": Ibid., 6.

16   "He didn't know he had abilities": Cecelia Blanchard, interview. All subsequent
     quotations of hers are drawn from this source.

16   "never met a wild [horse] that I could not catch": Jim Thorpe, with Maxwell Stiles,
     "This Is My Story," *Sport World*, Sept. 1949.

16   "Rather than feeling how your feet": Thomas Buckley, quoted in Nabokov, 144.

16   "could walk and ride and run for days": *Red Son*, 7.

17   "I was always of a restless disposition": Jim Thorpe, quoted in Lingo, "The Life
     Story of Jim Thorpe," May 1923.

17   "aggravated lawlessness": W. David Baird and Danny Goble, *The Story of Oklahoma*
     (Norman: University of Oklahoma Press, 1994), 193.

18   "the only good Indian": According to Dee Brown, Sheridan actually said, "The only
     good Indians I ever saw were dead." Dee Brown, *Bury My Heart at Wounded Knee:
     An Indian History of the American West* (New York: Henry Holt, 2007), 170.

18   "vanishing policy": Hazel W. Hertzberg, *The Search for an American Indian Identity:
     Modern Pan-Indian Movements* (Syracuse, N.Y.: Syracuse University Press, 1971), 22.

18   "Get the Indian out of the blanket": Merrill E. Gates, quoted in Robert F. Berk-
     hofer, Jr., *The White Man's Indian: Images of the American Indian from Colombus to the
     Present* (New York: Alfred A. Knopf, 1978), 173.

18   "If [allotment] were done in the name of greed": Minority report of the House
     Indian Affairs Committee, as quoted in Angie Debo, *A History of the Indians of the
     United States* (Norman: University of Oklahoma Press, 1970), 300.

18   "in the midst of a society": Page Smith, *The Rise of Industrial America: A People's His-
     tory of the Post-Reconstruction Era*, vol. 6 (New York: McGraw-Hill, 1984), 83.

19   "The general effect of allotment": Angie Debo, *And Still the Waters Run: The Betrayal
     of the Five Civilized Tribes* (Princeton, N.J.: Princeton University Press, 1968), 91.

19   "a mighty pulverizing agent": Theodore Roosevelt, quoted in Berkhofer, 175.

19   "more a spiritual than economic resource": Baird and Goble, 23.

20   "Tomorrow you will enter into the land": The Very Reverend D. Ignatius Jean,
     OSB, quoted in Joseph F. Murphy, *Tenacious Monks: The Oklahoma Benedictines,
     1875–1975; Indian Missionaries, Catholic Founders, Educators, Agriculturalists* (Shaw-
     nee, Okla.: Benedictine Color Press, 1974), 451.

21   "Where in the morning there was no one": Burl McGee, oral history, OHS.

21   "accepted many of the white mans ways": Aug. 3, 1891, (Tinker) Report 6459,
     Records of the Office of the Secretary of the Interior, RG48, Entry 682, Reports of
     Inspections of the Field Jurisdictions, Sac and Fox Agency, Indian Territory, micro-
     film M1070, roll 45, NARA.

21   "any more [whiskey] than their white neighbors": Feb. 26, 1897, (Duncan) Report
     1999, Records of the Office of the Secretary of the Interior, RG48, Entry 682,
     Reports of Inspections of the Field Jurisdictions, 1880–1900, Sac and Fox Miss.
     School and Absentee Shawnee School, Indian Territory, microfilm M1070, roll 45,
     NARA.

21   "a great step": Letter from Department of the Interior to U.S. Indian Agent, Sac

and Fox Agency, Oklahoma, Jan. 9, 1902, Sac and Fox Letter Book, Roll 32, frame 134, OHS.

21 "rationalization": The Indian Task Force of The Commission on the Organization of the Executive Branch of the Government (the Hoover Commission), created by act of Congress July 7, 1947, quoted in Debo, *A History of the Indians of the United States*, 331.

22 In 1996, a suit: U.S. District Judge Royce Lamberth, quoted in *AARP Magazine*, Jan./Feb. 2007.

22 "Should authority be given for the Indians": Sac and Fox agent Samuel L. Patrick, the father of agent Lee Patrick, quoted in Reinschmidt, 72.

22 "receiving in the way of rents": Feb. 26, 1897, (Duncan) Report 1999, Records of the Office of the Secretary of the Interior, RG48, Entry 682, Reports of Inspections of the Field Jurisdictions, 1880–1900, Sac and Fox Miss. School and Absentee Shawnee School, Indian Territory, microfilm M1070, roll 45, NARA.

22 "dirty," "uncivilized," "beastly intoxicated," "heathenish redskins," "primitive": Contemporary news clips quoted in Reinschmidt, 83.

23 "a gradual decrease in the number of births": Ibid., 90.

23 "all the Old West's famous gold rushes combined": Baird and Goble, 368.

24 "pleasedly firm presidential signature": Edmund Morris, *Theodore Rex* (New York: Random House, 2001), 448.

24 "elaborate home": *Red Son*, 2.

24 "beautifully situated": Aug. 2, 1897, (Nesler) Report 5962, Records of the Office of the Secretary of the Interior, RG48, Entry 682, Reports of Inspections of the Field Jurisdictions, 1880–1900, Sac and Fox Agency, Indian Territory, microfilm M1070, roll 45, NARA.

25 "very dirty and filthy": July 18, 1887, (Marcum) Report 3891. Records of the Office of the Secretary of the Interior, RG48, Entry 682, Reports of Inspections of the Field Jurisdictions, 1880–1900, Sac and Fox Agency, Indian Territory, microfilm M1070, roll 45, NARA.

25 "full of worms": April 23, 1887, (Gardner) Report 2375. Records of the Office of the Secretary of the Interior, RG48, Entry 682, Reports of Inspections of the Field Jurisdictions, 1880–1900, Sac and Fox Agency, Indian Territory, microfilm M1070, roll 45, NARA.

25 "We got a licking many times": Wakolee Letter.

25 "The Mo-ko-ho-ko band of the Sac and Fox": Dec. 28, 1894, (Faison) Report 18. Records of the Office of the Secretary of the Interior, RG48, Entry 682, Reports of Inspections of the Field Jurisdictions, 1880–1900, Sac and Fox Agency, Indian Territory, microfilm M1070, roll 45, NARA.

26 "nothing but force": Nov. 5, 1895, (Faison) Report 8121, Records of the Office of the Secretary of the Interior, RG48, Entry 682, Reports of Inspections of the Field Jurisdictions, 1880–1900, Sac and Fox Agency, Indian Territory, microfilm M1070, roll 45, NARA.

26 "good" . . ."fair": Sac and Fox School inspection report, quoted in Newcombe, 44.

27 "I went to him and took him in my arms": Harriet Patrick, quoted in Newcombe, 196.

27 "twinless twin": Jane Gross, "For Twins, a Lost Double and a Missing Half," *NYT*, Nov. 24, 2001.

27 "I'm going to send you so far away": Hiram P. Thorp, quoted in *Red Son*, 11.

27 "rapid and brutal expansion": Writers' Sub-Committee of the 75th Anniversary
    Celebration Committee, *A Brief Collection of Stories* (Lawrence, Kansas: Haskell
    Institute, 1959), RWWC.

28 "stout, hearty, ambitious boys and girls": Letter from Department of Interior,
    Indian School Service, Office of Superintendent, Indian School, Lawrence, Kansas
    to Superintendent Kohlenberg, Sac and Fox Agency, Oklahoma Territory, Aug. 10,
    1905, Indian Archives Collection, Sac and Fox–Shawnee Agency Records—Haskell
    Institute Box 545, folder 1, Oct. 6, 1884–Dec. 3, 1906, document 143, OHS.

28 "knowledge or consent": Letter from Department of Interior, Indian School Ser-
    vice, Office of Superintendent, Indian School, Lawrence, Kansas, to Hon. Ed. L.
    Thomas, U.S. Indian agent, Sac and Fox Agency, Oklahoma Territory, April 12,
    1894, Indian Archives Collection, Sac and Fox–Shawnee Agency Records—Haskell
    Institute Box 545, folder 1, Oct. 6, 1884–Dec. 3, 1906, document 42, OHS.

28 "It was in Haskell": *Red Son*, 12.

29 "Dropped previous to 10-01-01": Jim Thorpe student file, Haskell School, Law-
    rence, Kansas. Haskell records for students during the years Thorpe attended the
    school are often not complete. Thorpe's Haskell file "contains very little documen-
    tation," according to Mark Corriston, director, Records Management Operations,
    NARA—Central Plains Region.

29 Jim recalled that he returned home in time: As recently as 1899 an annuity roll had
    noted that Hiram and Charlotte were "[s]eparated" from each other. They were not
    enrolled together again up to the time of her death, but the documents disposing of
    Hiram's estate in 1914 would note that though no white marriage license had ever
    been issued to Hiram, he "drew the payment due [Charlotte] after her death." (In
    1897 the Act of the Territorial Legislature of Oklahoma had rendered legal exist-
    ing Indian marriages and divorces.) Argument, Estate of Hiram P. Thorp, Dec. 21,
    1914, Indian Archives Collection, Sac and Fox–Shawnee Agency Records—Estates
    Box 162, folder 3, Jan. 2, 1912–Dec. 18, 1912, document 253, OHS.

29 The official probate record: Charlotte's grave marker, near her father's at the Sacred
    Heart mission church still used by the Potawatomi today, has the November death
    date.

30 "laid a quiet hand": *Red Son*, 14.

30 "quickly and quietly escorted": Ibid.

30 "slender Indian lad": Walter White, "The Greatest Athlete," typed manuscript,
    Jim Thorpe Association, Oklahoma City. All quoted material of Walter White, Jim
    Thorpe, and Hiram Thorpe in this Garden Grove section is taken from this source.
    On Oct. 22, 1993, a $28,000 scholarship was presented to East Central State Uni-
    versity in Ada, Oklahoma, for a worthy boy interested in athletics. The scholarship
    is called the Thorpe-White Scholarship and represents 5 percent of Mr. White's
    estate.

CHAPTER TWO
Discovery · *Winter 1904–Summer 1907*

33 "This was the land": "Comrades All," Carlisle School song quoted by Genevieve
    Bell, *Telling Stories Out of School: Remembering the Carlisle Indian Industrial School,
    1879–1918*. Ph.D. dissertation, Department of Anthropology, Stanford University,

June 1998, 58. (Microform edition, UMI Microform Number: 9908713, 1998). Words by Elaine Goodman Eastman, music by Robert Hord Bowers.

33 "Dear Sir—I have a boy": Letter from Hiram Thorp to U.S. Indian Agent [Superintendent W. C. Kohlenberg], Dec. 13, 1903. Indian Archives Collection, Sac and Fox–Shawnee Agency Records—Individual Indian Files Box 285, folder 10, Thorp, James, 244, OHS.

34 Captain Richard Henry Pratt: Pratt was a lieutenant when he started Carlisle in 1879. He was then promoted to captain, major, colonel, and finally, in 1903, to brigadier general. The Carlisle students always called him "Captain Pratt."

34 "if the other fellows slug": Richard H. Pratt, *Battlefield and Classroom, Four Decades with the American Indian, 1876–1904*, ed. Robert M. Utley (Norman: University of Oklahoma Press, 2004), 317.

34 "Incidentally, if you should by chance": Letter from Superintendent R. H. Pratt to Lee Patrick, Indian agent, Sac and Fox, May 5, 1899, Sac and Fox–Shawnee Agency, Carlisle Indian School, Sept. 27, 1880–Dec. 30, 1911, RG75, NARA, OHS.

34 "just a skinny little jigger": Jim Thorpe, quoted in *Sport*, Dec. 1949.

34 "acclimated to discipline": Albert Exendine, oral history, OHS. All quoted material of Exendine's is taken from this source unless otherwise noted. Albert Exendine is in the College Football Hall of Fame as a coach at Georgetown and other schools. He also earned a law degree and worked off-season as a lawyer with the BIA in Oklahoma.

35 A little more than two months: Hiram's wife was pregnant and would give birth to the last of Hiram's children, Roscoe, on July 5. Hiram had had five wives, all but the last by Indian custom, two of them simultaneously, and nineteen recorded children, of whom ten survived to adulthood.

35 "the Supreme Americanizer": Richard H. Pratt, quoted in Linda F. Witmer, *The Indian Industrial School, Carlisle Pennsylvania, 1879–1918* (Carlisle, Pa.: Cumberland County Historical Society, 2000), 35.

35 "thrifty and sympathetic people": Letter from Superintendent Richard H. Pratt to W. C. Kohlenberg, Sac and Fox agent, Aug. 15, 1904, Sac and Fox–Shawnee Agency, Carlisle Indian School, Sept. 27, 1880–Dec. 30, 1911, RG75, NARA, OHS.

36 "anxious to go": *Red Son*, 15.

36 "intelligence, civilization and common sense": Pratt, 5.

38 "an era of intense racial debate": Jacqueline Fear-Segal, *White Man's Club: Schools, Race, and the Struggle of Indian Acculturation* (Lincoln: University of Nebraska Press, 2007), xiii.

38 "sad uniformity of savage tribal life": *Lake Mohonk Conference Proceedings* (Washington, D.C.: Board of Indian Commissioners, 1900), 14.

38 "Kill the Indian in him and save the man": Richard H. Pratt, quoted in David Wallace Adams, *Education for Extinction: American Indians and the Boarding School Experience, 1875–1928* (Lawrence: University Press of Kansas, 1995), 52. The Indian Rights Association (IRA), founded in 1882, became a powerful lobbying group for such Indian school reforms and attracted well-connected leaders such as Francis Leupp, later commissioner of Indian Affairs with a particular interest in Carlisle. He was closely allied with Theodore Roosevelt, who would arrive in Washington in 1889 as the new, reforming civil service commissioner destined to lock horns with Pratt.

39 "advance in intelligence and industry": Pratt, 224.

39 weekly student publication: *The Arrow*, "edited and printed by Indian pupils repre-

senting forty American tribes," was a Carlisle Indian Industrial School weekly publication now archived at the Cumberland County Historical Society. From the first
issue on Aug. 25, 1904, until the issue of June 19, 1908, it was called *The Arrow;* with
the first issue of the 1908 academic year, Sept. 11, 1908, the name changed to *The
Carlisle Arrow.* The publication will be referred to as *The Arrow* throughout this book.

39 "When you've a task to do": *The Indian Helper,* vol. 3, no. 15, Nov. 18, 1887, CCHS.

39 "relegate[d] the Indian to a fixed subordinate position": Berkhofer, 246.

40 "Nowhere . . . was the spoils system": Hertzberg, 5.

40 "neophyte farmers and stockmen": William T. Hagan, *Theodore Roosevelt and Six
Friends of the Indian* (Norman: University of Oklahoma Press, 1997), 23.

40 "complete destruction of the [Indian] Bureau": Richard H. Pratt, quoted in Bell, 73.

40 "the greatest single-handed murderer": Woodworth Clum, quoted in Angie Debo,
Geronimo: The Man, His Time, His Place (Norman: University of Oklahoma Press,
1976), 419.

40 "I wanted to give the people a good show": Theodore Roosevelt, quoted in ibid.

40 "This is an admirable contrast": Theodore Roosevelt, quoted in *The Arrow,* March
9, 1905.

40 "as much a part of the nation's collective memory": Page Smith, 83.

40 "blank space"; "try to re-weave": Brenda Finnicum, interview.

41 "soul wound": Andrea Smith, "Soul Wound: The Legacy of Native American
Schools," *Amnesty Magazine,* www.amnestyusa.org/amnestynow/soulwound.html.

41 "a morality play": Bell, 6.

41 "hurdling fences and jumping ravines": *Red Son,* 18.

41 "confinement of incorrigible male students": Richard H. Pratt, 5, as quoted in Witmer, 23.

42 "sorry for having treated me that way": *Red Son,* 19.

42 Mercer had been persuaded by Exendine: Albert Exendine oral history.

42 "scrawny kid": Glenn S. Warner, *Pop Warner: Football's Greatest Teacher: The Epic
Autobiography of Major College Football's Winningest Coach, Glenn S. (Pop) Warner,* ed.
Michael J. Bynum (Langhorne, Pa.: Gridiron Football Properties, 1993), 119–120.
All quoted material of Warner's relating to the story of Jim Thorpe's initial clearing
of the Carlisle high jump in 1907 is taken from this source.

42 The next day, one of the Sioux students: Warner recalled that Archambault told him
of Jim's high jump skill. Exendine recalled that he told Warner. It's impossible at this
date to confirm which version is correct, though Exendine was usually accurate in
his memories and Warner often wasn't.

43 "knew instinctively": Albert Exendine, quoted in Stump, "Jim Thorpe: Greatest of
Them All," *Sport,* Dec. 1949.

44 "Dear Sir: I would like you": Letter from Jim Thorpe to W. C. Kohlenberg, Sac and
Fox agent, July 5, 1907, Sac and Fox–Shawnee Agency, Carlisle Indian School, Sept.
27, 1880–Dec. 30, 1911, Record Group 75, NARA, OHS.

44 "personaly to me": Letter from Jim Thorpe to W. C. Kohlenberg, Sac and Fox agent,
Aug. 14, 1907, Sac and Fox–Shawnee Agency, Carlisle Indian School, Sept. 27, 1880–
Dec. 30, 1911, Record Group 75, NARA, OHS.

45 "sporting culture": S. W. Pope, *Patriotic Games: Sporting Traditions in the American
Imagination, 1876–1926* (New York: Oxford University Press, 1997), 3.

45 "the strenuous life": Theodore Roosevelt, *The Strenuous Life: Essays and Addresses*
(New York: The Century Co., 1902).

45 "sound mind in a sound body": One translation of the Latin *mens sana in corpore sano*, from Satire X by the Roman poet Juvenal.

45 "new safety valve": Frederic L. Paxson, quoted in Mark Dyreson, *Making the American Team: Sport, Culture, and the Olympic Experience* (Urbana and Chicago: University of Illinois Press, 1998), 76.

45 "popish and pagan": Melvin L. Adelman, *A Sporting Time: New York City and the Rise of Modern Athletics, 1820–1870* (Urbana and Chicago: University of Illinois Press, 1986), 269.

46 "bloodless battle": A. G. Spalding, quoted in Donald J. Mrozek, *Sport and American Mentality, 1880–1910* (Knoxville: University of Tennessee Press, 1983), 173.

46 "You play the way you practice": Glenn S. Warner, quoted in news clip, Nov. 9, 1999, unattributed, provided to the author by Jim Campbell.

46 "look like a bunch of old maids": Warner, *Pop Warner*, 121. Unless otherwise noted, all quoted material regarding Jim's first football practice comes from this source.

47 "invested football during these years": Oriard, 109.

48 "genius for organization": Mrozek, 10.

48 "injuries incurred on the [football] playing field": Henry Cabot Lodge, quoted in Mrozek, 28.

48 "fixed machinery of conditions": William James, quoted in Dyreson, 11.

48 "a metaphor for American exceptionalism": Sean Gregory, "The Problem with Football: Our Favorite Sport Is Too Dangerous. How to Make the Game Safer," *Time*, Feb. 8, 2010.

49 Camp was also the source: "The first list of players presented as an All-American team was selected by [Caspar] Whitney and appeared in *Harper's Weekly* in 1889. Soon after that Whitney and [Walter] Camp collaborated, Camp eventually continuing the annual assignment single-handed, with his All-America team[s] appearing each December in *Collier's*, until the year of his death, 1924." Christy Walsh, "All-America Selections," *Intercollegiate Football: A Complete Pictorial and Statistical Review from 1869 to 1934* (New York: Doubleday, Doran & Company, for Intercollegiate Football, 1934), 11. In 1924, the All-America Board of Football was formed, and it included Pop Warner. It decided to name only eleven players each year, rather than Camp's system of first, second, and third teams, on the theory that there should be only one All-America team.

50 "It is perhaps the likeness of football": Speech by Walter Camp, n.d., Roll 22, Box 33, WCC.

51 "moral training": John Sayle Watterson, *College Football: History, Spectacle, Controversy* (Baltimore: Johns Hopkins University Press, 2000), 26. As president of Princeton, Wilson would enact a unified course of general studies for the first two years of undergraduate study, a declared "major" subject for the final two years, and an honors program for qualified students—the structure used by most U.S. colleges today.

52 "There is something not quite nice": *NYT*, Nov. 10, 1897.

52 "The object, then, of football": *The Nation*, Dec. 29, 1904.

52 "genteel sensibility": Mrozek, xvi.

52 "whether a man of the decent sort": Ibid., xiv.

52 "uncorrupted by material considerations": Richard Espy, *The Politics of the Olympic Games* (Berkeley: University of California Press, 1979), 5.

52 "virgins of the sporting world": Caspar Whitney, quoted in Oriard, 155.

53 "to win at *any* cost": Henry Beach Needham, "The College Athlete: How Commer-

cialism Is Making Him a Professional," *McClure's Magazine*, June 1905, and "The College Athlete: His Amateur Code; Its Evasion and Administration." *McClure's Magazine*, July 1905.

53 "moral" example was "a little colored chap": Needham, *McClure's*, June 1905. William C. Matthews (1876–1928) has been called the "the Jackie Robinson of his time"—except that he wasn't, but perhaps could have been. Booker T. Washington arranged for him to attend Phillips Andover prep school, and at Harvard, Matthews was a star of the varsity baseball team, ending his fourth and last undergraduate year with a .400 batting average. When Fred Tenney, manager of the National League Boston Beaneaters, tried to recruit Matthews to play second base in 1905, assuming that as he was a Harvard man none of the players or fans would object, there was such opposition from white southerners, the offer was dropped. He did play for one season with the Upper Midwest Class D Northern League, then studied law at Harvard and Boston University, passed the bar, and practiced law until 1912. Roosevelt appointed him to the district attorney's office in Boston that year, and subsequently he was legal counsel to Marcus Garvey, worked on the 1924 presidential campaign of Calvin Coolidge, and was appointed assistant U.S. attorney general.

53 "success can only come to the player": Theodore Roosevelt, quoted in Mrozek, 34.

54 "the old push-and-pull": Glenn Scobey Warner, *Football for Coaches and Players* (Stanford University, California: Glenn Scobey Warner, 1927), vii.

54 "very slippery": Ronald A. Smith, ed., *Big-Time Football at Harvard, 1905: The Diary of Coach Bill Reid* (Urbana and Chicago: University of Illinois Press, 1994), 194. Reid's assistant coach for the 1905 season was William H. Lewis, the first black All-America football player.

54 The White House meeting was followed: "The most traumatic injury [of the 1905 season] occurred in a game between New York University and Union College in which a Union player was killed. Immediately President Henry MacCracken of NYU called for a reform conference, which led to a larger conference just after Christmas and the appointment of a reform committee." Note to the author from John Sayle Watterson, April 2009.

55 "monotonous collisions": Glenn S. Warner, "How the Game of Football Should Be Changed," *The Illustrated Sporting News*, Jan. 14, 1905.

55 "due to its tremendous investment": Guy Maxton Lewis, "The American Intercollegiate Football Spectacle, 1869–1917," thesis submitted to the faculty of the Graduate School of the University of Maryland in partial fulfillment of the requirements for the degree of doctor of philosophy, 1964, 248.

55 "strengthen the attacking power": Warner, *Football for Coaches and Players*, vii.

55 "a punting and catching contest": Warner, "How the Game of Football Should Be Changed."

CHAPTER THREE
Warm-up · *Fall 1907–Spring 1909*

57 "Part of football's appeal": Smith, 850.

57 "fast, strong runner": Glenn Scobey Warner, *A Course in Football for Players and Coaches* (Carlisle, Pa., 1912), 70.

57 "perfect . . . football machine": Glenn S. Warner, quoted in Robert W. Wheeler,

Jim Thorpe: World's Greatest Athlete (Norman: University of Oklahoma Press, 1979), 55.

58 "formidable": Warner, *Pop Warner*, 125.

58 "one of the best linemen": Ibid., 124.

58 "How the Indians did take to it!": Glenn S. Warner, quoted in Allison Danzig, ed., *Oh, How They Played the Game: The Early Days of Football and the Heroes Who Made It Great* (New York: Macmillan, 1971), 167.

58 "did most of the work": *The Arrow*, Oct. 25, 1907.

58 On the way to Philadelphia: "Innis Brown Gives Real Info on Jim Thorpe. Famous Athlete Has Been 'Bad Injun' at Times," n.d. [1912], unattributed article, BHOF. All quoted material regarding this anecdote is taken from this source.

58 "I got excited and didn't follow": *Red Son*, 22.

59 "turned running backs": Dave Anderson, "A Position of Respect in N.F.L." *NYT*, Nov. 18, 1980. See also "Old Is New, New Is Old: Back to the Future with the Single Wing," Tim Layden, *Sports Illustrated*, Dec. 1, 2008.

59 "With racial savagery and ferocity": *The* (Philadelphia) *Press*, as quoted in "Victory over 'Pennsy,' " *The Arrow*, Nov. 1, 1907.

59 "The race that sends to the gridiron": *Denver Express*, as quoted in "Indians on the Football Field," *The Arrow*, Nov. 8, 1907.

59 The eastern papers: "W. W. Roper, Head Coach of the Princeton Football Team, Didn't Tip Off Indians' Play," n.d. [1907], unattributed news clip, WCC.

60 "almost weird intuition": "Indians' Speed Beats Harvard," n.d. [1907], unattributed news clip from a Chicago newspaper, WCC. Also partially reprinted in *The Arrow*, Nov. 15, 1907.

60 "forward passes, double passes": Ibid.

60 "wonderful possibilities of the new game": *The Arrow*, Nov. 15, 1907.

60 "Few of us": *Red Son*, 24.

60 "roughest, toughest team": George Capron, quoted in *LAT*, Feb. 7, 1937.

61 "as great a pair of ends": "Rockne Recalls: By the Late Knute Rockne," *LAT*, Sept. 28, 1931.

61 "faster line charging": Glenn S. Warner, "Heap Big Run-Most-Fast," *Collier's*, Oct. 24, 1931.

61 "The game of this year": *Harper's Weekly*, Dec. 7, 1907.

61 "dearly loved": Glenn S. Warner, "The Indian Massacres," *Collier's*, Oct. 17, 1931.

61 "three or four of the Cambridge team": *Boston Post*, as reprinted in *The Arrow*, Jan. 19, 1912.

61 "[T]he descendents of the losing race": Lingo, "The Life Story of Jim Thorpe," Part 10, Jan. 1924.

61 "The Indians . . . [had] a real race pride": "The Indian Massacres."

61 "finesse and mobility": Danzig, 345.

61 "We outscored 'em, but we didn't defeat 'em": Glenn S. Warner, quoted in Stump, "Jim Thorpe: Greatest of Them All."

63 "light years ahead of his time": Jack Newcombe, "Carlisle Was a College Team with a Professional Approach," *NYT*, May 2, 1982.

66 "swell the receipts": Hearings Before the Joint Commission of the Congress of the United States to Investigate Indian Affairs, Carlisle Indian School, Feb. 6–8 and March 25, 1914. 63rd Congress, 2nd Session, Part II (Washington, D.C.: Government Printing Office, 1914), 1227.

66 "gloomy midweek practice propaganda": Newcombe, 112.

66 "if anything is being said that is detrimental": Carlisle Hearings, 1227.

66 "the crying demand for advice": Glenn Scobey Warner, *A Course in Football for Players and Coaches,* 1913 ed. [pamphlet format; no publisher indicated], CCHS.

66 "How would you break that up?": Arthur Martin, interview by Robert W. Wheeler, RWWC.

66 "tell us about our opponents": *Red Son,* 22.

67 "might just as well": "Carlisle's Athletic Policy Criticized by Dr. Montezuma," *Chicago Sunday Tribune,* Nov. 24, 1907.

67 Warner denied the charges: *Washington Post,* Dec. 6, 1907.

67 "[N]o institution is compelled to compete": Glenn S. Warner, quoted in *The Arrow,* Dec. 13, 1907. All quoted material from Warner's circular letter comes from this source. See also: Letter from the Carlisle Indian Athletic Association (G. S. Warner, Prest. [*sic*] and Athletic Director; A. M. Venne, Secretary; W. H. Miller, Treasurer) to Walter Camp, Dec. 12, 1907, WCC.

67 "As the Indians are, therefore, not to be classed": "Penn Was Not Penn in the Carlisle Contest," n.d. [1907], unattributed article, WCC.

68 *The Outing Magazine* had revealed: Pope, 25.

68 "leading social function of the [Carlisle] season": *The Arrow,* Feb. 28, 1908. All quotes referring to the banquet are taken from this source.

68 "I told Mercer": Jim Thorpe, quoted in Grover Long oral history, OHS. All subsequent quoted material of Long's, unless otherwise noted, is taken from this source.

69 "practically every tribe's oral history": Nabokov, 23.

69 "my first major medal": *Red Son,* 25.

70 "hard to establish precisely": Bell, 154.

70 "a fine teacher": Newcombe, 124.

70 "Co-Fa-Che-Qul": *The Arrow,* Oct. 23, 1908. All quoted material is taken from this source.

71 "baby of the school": Richard R. Kaseeta, quoted in n.d. and unattributed news clip by L. J. Fitzpatrick, Jr., Jim Thorpe Drop File, CCHS.

71 "a loner at heart": Hyman Goldstein, quoted in Michael Koehler's unpublished biography of Jim Thorpe.

71 "Introverted is not": Albert Exendine, quoted in Frank Luksa, " 'Bright Path' Still Shines Despite Gloomy Twilight Years," *Fort Worth Star-Telegram,* April 2, 1972.

71 "He didn't talk of his exploits": Mrs. Edward L. (Verna Donegan) Whistler, quoted in L. J. Fitzpatrick, Jr., news clip.

72 "A strange, whimsical fellow": Albert Exendine, quoted in *Washington Times-Herald,* March 26, 1940.

72 "Just before he was about to tear somebody apart": Albert Exendine, quoted in Sally Jenkins, *The Real All-Americans: The Team That Changed a Game, a People, a Nation* (New York: Doubleday, 2007), 263.

72 "It was difficult to know": Glenn S. Warner, quoted in Grantland Rice, *The Tumult and the Shouting: My Life in Sport,* memorial ed. (New York: A. S. Barnes & Company, 1954), 233.

72 "thinking of my brothers and sisters": *Red Son,* 26.

73 "glad to have this country represented": Theodore Roosevelt, quoted in *The Arrow,* Sept. 11, 1908.

73 "deplorable failure": *NYT,* July 26, 1908.

74 "the relative value of all forms of culture": Franz Boas, "The History of Anthropology," *Congress of Arts and Science: Universal Exposition, St. Louis, 1904*, vol. 5, ed. Howard J. Rogers (Boston and New York: Houghton, Mifflin and Company, 1906).

75 "a very ragged and rough": *The Arrow*, Sept. 25, 1908.

75 "The redskins have a drop kicker": "Football Is Still in Chaotic State," n.d., unattributed news clip, [1908], WCC.

75 "big, heavy": *Buffalo Express*, reprinted in *The Arrow*, Oct. 16, 1908.

75 "one of the most spectacular games": "Redskins Humble Syracuse Eleven," n.d., unattributed news clip, [1908], WCC.

75 "perfect": Ibid.

75 "the Syracuse men": *Buffalo Express*.

75 "There was a man named Thorpe": "Redskins Humble Syracuse Eleven."

75 "vicious" . . . "frequently picking his opponents up": Lingo, "The Life Story of Jim Thorpe," chapter 4, July 1923.

75 "the prospects for a Carlisle victory": *The Arrow*, Oct. 23, 1908.

76 "out for revenge": *Red Son*, 27.

76 "From the outset": Ibid. All quotations of Jim Thorpe in this section on the 1908 Penn game are taken from this source.

76 "the second that big 6": *The* (Philadelphia) *Press*, as reprinted in *The Arrow*, Oct. 30, 1908.

76 "scarcely a single play": *Philadelphia Record*, as reprinted in *The Arrow*, Oct. 30, 1908.

76 "phantom-like flight": "Thorpe Makes Long Run," *New York Herald*, Oct. 25, 1908.

76 "Who said the Indian": *The* (Philadelphia) *Press*.

76 The score didn't indicate: The following year, in response to Navy's presentation of the chart of the game—"a lot of long blue lines" for Navy drives "and practically no red ones" for Carlisle's, as a Navy player recalled to Arthur Daley at the *New York Times* in 1943—the Intercollegiate Athletic Association decreased field goals to three points and increased the touchdown point total to six. Arthur Daley, "Jim Thorpe Dominates Another Conversation," *NYT*, March 30, 1943.

76 "the hold these up-to-date redskins": *Boston Journal*, Nov. 9, 1908, as reprinted in *The Arrow*, Nov. 13, 1908.

77 "It was St. Louis that": *St. Louis Post-Dispatch*, Nov. 28, 1908, as cited in David Wallace Adams, "More Than a Game: The Carlisle Indians Take to the Gridiron, 1893–1917," *The Western Historical Quarterly* 32 (Spring, 2001), no. 1.

77 "headline grabber": Warner, *Pop Warner*, 126.

77 "extremely creditable": *NYT*, March 22, 1909.

77 "loving fans": Warner, *Pop Warner*, 126.

77 "The football boys": Newcombe, 137.

78 "more men to the major leagues": Joe Twin, "Baseball: Essay Written by Joe Twin, the 'Foxy' Right Fielder of the Indians," *The Arrow*, May 24, 1907. All quoted material of Twin's is taken from this source.

79 "without sufficient coaching": Jeffrey Powers-Beck, *The American Indian Integration of Baseball* (Lincoln: University of Nebraska Press, 2004), 47.

79 (he was an excellent ballroom dancer): Under Mercer's tenure as superintendent at Carlisle, more social dances were allowed, and they became a popular activity. Friedman restricted the Saturday night dances, but versions of them persisted under the cover of the more formal student clubs and debating societies. One example, citing Jim, from *The Arrow*, Nov. 27, 1908: "On the twelfth of November the Susan

Longstreth Literary Society [one of the school's debating societies] held their annual reception. . . . After a few more dances, came the prize waltz . . . Elmira Jerome and James Thorpe were given the second prize."

79 "the individual star": *The Arrow*, June 4, 1909.

79 "racial theory of sport": Powers-Beck, 44.

79 "commercializing themselves": Amos Alonzo Stagg, quoted in "Colleges Refusing to Lower the Bar," *Washington Post*, July 21, 1909.

79 "one of the most advanced steps": *The Red Man*, Dec. 1912.

79 "the injustice": *Red Son*, 30.

80 "[T]he only big money": Fitzpatrick news clip.

80 "go on a little vacation": *Red Son*, 30.

80 "leave to play ball": Letter from Superintendent Maurice Friedman to Sac and Fox Superintendent W. C. Kohlenberg, Oct. 27, 1909, Sac and Fox–Shawnee Agency, Carlisle Indian School, Sept. 27, 1880–Dec. 30, 1911, Record Group 75, NARA, OHS.

80 "Or . . . at least": Warner, *Pop Warner*, 127.

CHAPTER FOUR

The Minors · *Summer 1909–Summer 1911*

83 "I went to play baseball": Jim Thorpe, quoted in "Indian's Gallant Return," n.d. [1939], unattributed news clip, PFHOF.

83 "[no] question relating to the amateur standing": Needham, *McClure's*, July 1905. All quoted material of Needham's referring to summer baseball is taken from this source.

83 Teams such as St. Albans in Vermont: A team photograph of "Paul Smith's" team around 1902 in the Adirondacks—"a haven for Yale baseball men"—printed in *McClure's* showed eight players wearing either their Yale letter sweater or a Yale baseball uniform.

84 Hogan was a "poor boy": Hogan, who went on to attend Columbia Law School and work at the New York law firm of Simpson, Bartlett and Thatcher, died suddenly of Bright's disease in 1910.

84 "the languor of an economic Middle Age": Sam T. Mallison, *Let's Set a Spell* (Charleston, W.Va.: Education Foundation, 1961), 85. All quoted material of Mallison's is taken from this source.

85 "very popular in the southern states": Telephone interview with Bob McConnell, Professional Football Researchers Association.

86 "Nobody ever thought anything about making money": E. J. Johnston, quoted in "Man Who Paid Thorpe the Fatal $2 Urges Medals Be Returned to Carlisle Indian," unattributed news clip, Feb. 2, 1952, CCHS.

87 "the people who cannot leave": *RNO*, July 14, 1909.

87 "The Carlisle Indian": *RNO*, June 17, 1909.

87 "Big Chief 'Bullhead' Thorpe": *RNO*, Aug. 25, 1909.

88 According to Joe Libby: This anecdote was told to the author by Jim Thorpe's son Jack Thorpe, who had been told it by Joe Libby.

89 "Jim always liked to play": Arthur J. Dussault, quoted in Harold Sauerbrel, "Thorpe Was So Powerful That He Even Beat Tide of Atlantic Ocean, Ex-Teammate Recalls,"

(Cleveland) *Plain Dealer*, March 5, 1950. All subsequent quotes of Dussault, unless otherwise noted, are from this source.

89 "a laughing stock": *RNO*, Aug. 27, 1909.

89 " 'Big Chief' on Rampage": Ibid.

89 "the heaviest draftings": *RNO*, Sept. 3, 1909.

89 Jim was not among them: According to Robert Reising, Jim "was wanted by other clubs of higher classification" (Robert Reising, interview). The author did not find any record of such interest in the local contemporary news coverage.

89 "He failed to return to school": Letter from Superintendent Maurice Friedman to W. C. Kohlenberg, Superintendent, Sac and Fox Agency, Oct. 27, 1909. Indian Archives Collection, Sac and Fox–Shawnee Agency Records—Carlisle Indian School, Box 542, folder 5, Sept. 27, 1880–Dec. 30, 1911, OHS.

90 in lieu of the perpetual annuities: Letter from Superintendent Maurice Friedman to W. C. Kohlenberg, Superintendent, Sac and Fox Agency, March 4, 1909. Indian Archives Collection, Sac and Fox–Shawnee Agency Records—Carlisle Indian School, Box 542, folder 5, Sept. 27, 1880–Dec. 30, 1911, OHS. A consent form was sent to members of the Sac and Fox tribe with reference to commutation of the "permanent" annuity stipulated by the Treaty of Nov. 3, 1804, to be paid to the Sac and Fox of the Mississippi.

90 "intends ... to return to Carlisle in the Spring": Letter from W. C. Kohlenberg, superintendent, Sac and Fox Agency, to Commissioner of Indian Affairs [n.d.; original date of application is referenced by Superintendent Friedman in his Oct. 27, 1909, letter to Kohlenberg as Oct. 18, 1909; two dates of receipt are stamped on Kohlenberg's letter: Oct. 25, 1909 (Office of Indian Affairs) and Nov. 8, 1909 (probably the date the application was returned to the Sac and Fox Agency, having been approved on Nov. 4, 1909)]. Indian Archives Collection, Sac and Fox–Shawnee Agency Records—Carlisle Indian School, Box 543, folder 9, Jan. 12, 1912–Jan. 19, 1919, and undated, OHS.

90 "During the last few months he was here": Letter from Superintendent Maurice Friedman to W. C. Kohlenberg, superintendent, Sac and Fox Agency, Nov. 6, 1909. Indian Archives Collection, Sac and Fox–Shawnee Agency Records—Carlisle Indian School, Box 543, folder 9, Jan. 12, 1912–Jan. 19, 1919, and undated, OHS.

90 "missed nearly half year in studies": Telegram from Superintendent Maurice Friedman to W. C. Kohlenberg, Sac and Fox agent, Nov. 23, 1909. Indian Archives Collection, Sac and Fox–Shawnee Agency Records—Carlisle Indian School, Box 543, folder 9, Jan. 12, 1912–Jan. 19, 1919, and undated, OHS.

91 According to Jim: *Red Son*, 31.

91 "the fans laughing at his little witticisms": *RNO*, June 2, 1910.

91 "an Indian-like war-whoop": Charles Harris, quoted in Robert W. Reising, *Jim Thorpe: Tar Heel* (Rocky Mount, N.C.: Communiqué, 1974), 16.

92 "The two big leagues": *RNO*, Aug. 6, 1910.

92 "appeared to like a good time": Charles Clancy, quoted in "Thorpe with Professional Baseball Team Says Clancy," *Worcester Telegram* (Mass.), Jan. 22, 1913.

93 One morning on Hay Street: The details of this window incident come from Reising, 21. Reising told the author the incident may have taken place in 1909 rather than in 1910. Other stories never made the papers. One of the players in North Carolina for the summer, a Penn undergraduate playing under an assumed name, was Elmer Hess, later a distinguished urologist, founder of the American Board of

Urology, and president of the American Medical Association. According to Miley B. Wesson, a San Francisco doctor, Hess would recount stories of his time with Jim, including one recalled by Wesson in 1949 in a letter to a Warner Bros. studio executive: "On one occasion [Elmer] rescued Jim from a negro house of prostitution where he was spread-eagled on the floor and the negroes were working him over with razors so that he looked like the crust of an apple pie—Jim still carries those scars." Letter from Miley B. Wesson, M.D., to Dr. Harry C. Martin, June 7, 1949, *Jim Thorpe—All American* production file, Warner Bros. Collection, USC.

93 "sat down on the bag": *RNO*, Sept. 4, 1910.

93 Jim wound up hitting .236: Jim Thorpe's pitching average for 1909 Rocky Mount was .474, nine wins, ten losses; for 1910 Rocky Mount .500, ten wins, ten losses.

93 "I knew I stood at a crossroads": *Red Son*, 32.

94 In spring 1911, he signed up: For a description of the 1911 season of the Anadarko Champions, see Bill Crawford, *All American: The Rise and Fall of Jim Thorpe* (Hoboken: John Wiley and Sons, Inc., 2005), 131.

94 "You're going to spend": Jim Thorpe, quoted in Francis L. Fugate and Roberta B. Fugate, *Roadside History of Oklahoma* (Missoula, Mont.: Mountain Press Publishing Co., 1991), 188, as cited by Crawford, 259.

94 "not playing ball here anymore": Letter from Jim Thorpe to W. C. Kohlenberg, Sac and Fox agent, July 25, 1911, Indian Archives Collection, Sac and Fox–Shawnee Agency Records—Carlisle Indian School, Box 542, folder 6, Jan. 18, 1910–Dec. 30, 1911, OHS.

94 "What are you doing?": Albert Exendine oral history.

CHAPTER FIVE

Football Phenom · *Fall 1911–Spring 1912*

96 "the mode in which the future": Aristotle, quoted in Nabokov, 27.

97 "How could anyone get hurt playing football?": Jim Thorpe, quoted in "Good King Jim."

97 "September 24, 1911": Letter from Jim Thorpe to W. C. Kohlenberg, Sac and Fox agent, Sept. 24, 1911, Indian Archives Collection, Sac and Fox–Shawnee Agency Records—Carlisle Indian School, Box 543, folder 6, Jan. 12, 1912–Jan. 19, 1919, and undated. OHS.

97 "a young Indian student": "Thorpe a Great Athlete," (Carlisle) *Evening Sentinel*, n.d. [1911].

98 "felt good to be back": *Red Son*, 33.

98 He befriended: William "Lone Star" Dietz played football with Jim as a tackle in 1911, and was Warner's assistant coach from 1912 to 1914. A superb illustrator and designer, Dietz was called "the coaches' coach" by Damon Runyon and was one of the country's most successful coaches in the period between the two world wars. What may have been a fictitious Indian "origin story" not only got him into Carlisle, but also provided an identity upon which he based his life. When George Preston Marshall changed the name of his NFL franchise from the Boston Braves to the Boston Redskins in 1933, it was ostensibly in honor of Dietz, the team's head coach in 1933 and 1934. When the team moved to the nation's capital in 1936, it became known as the Washington Redskins. Almost sixty years later, with Dietz

long dead, Indian activists began a campaign to get the team to change the disparaging name. The Redskins owners countered that because the name was in honor of their "Indian" coach, it was an "honorific" to all Indians. Whether Dietz was Indian or not is a matter of dispute; see Linda Waggoner, "Reclaiming James One Star," *Indian Country Today*, 2004, five-part series: http://www.indiancountrytoday.com/archive/28175109.html.

99 "Brahmins of the East": Warner, "Battles of Brawn."

99 "fire and swiftness": Ibid.

99 "the sports writers in the East": Charley Paddock, "Chief Bright Path," *Collier's*, Oct. 12, 1929. This is part 2 of a four-part series.

99 "deceptive change of pace": Ibid.

99 "as something of an upset": Ibid.

100 "the whole East": Ibid.

100 "big heavy team": Letter from Glenn S. Warner to "Johnny," Oct. 17, 1911, WCC.

100 "three or four would-be tacklers": *Pittsburgh Dispatch*, as reprinted in *The Arrow*, Nov. 10, 1911.

100 "good-natured smile": Stump, "Jim Thorpe: Greatest of Them All."

100 "Next time—left tackle!": Jim Thorpe, quoted in ibid.

100 "I never saw him snarl": Glenn S. Warner, quoted in ibid.

100 "To say Thorpe is the whole team": *Pittsburgh Leader*, reprinted in *The Arrow*, Nov. 10, 1911.

100 "tall and sinewy": *Pittsburgh Dispatch*, reprinted in ibid.

101 "smoking hot": Stump, "Jim Thorpe: Greatest of Them All."

101 "We pointed to this game": Stansill (also spelled Stancil) "Possum" Powell, quoted in John Parris, "Noah Powell Was Proud of Brother," *Asheville Citizen*, Apr. 6, 1973.

101 "Crippled Jimmy Thorpe": *Boston Sunday Globe*, Nov. 12, 1911. All quoted material regarding this 1911 Carlisle–Harvard game is taken from this source.

101 "Probably the most spectacular": "Thorpe Beat Harvard," *Kansas City Star*, Nov. 12, 1911, WCC.

101 "not once": Warner, *Pop Warner*, 128.

101 "as fine an exhibition of sheer grit": "The Indian Massacres."

101 "completely bewildered": "Carlisle Defeats Harvard 18 to 15," *Public Ledger* (Philadelphia), n.d. [Nov. 12, 1911], WCC.

102 "Get out of my way": Jim Thorpe, quoted in Glenn S. Warner, "Heap Big Run-Most-Fast," *Collier's*, Oct. 24, 1931.

102 "Set the ball up.": Jim Thorpe, quoted in *NYT*, May 27, 1957. See Newcombe, 167–68, for a discussion of this "first era of the dominance of the field goal in college football," including references to Harvard's Charles Brickley and the different size of the ball used in Thorpe's era at Carlisle.

102 "pretty sore"; "sort of helped me": Jim Thorpe, quoted in Paddock, "Chief Bright Path."

102 "As long as I live": Jim Thorpe, quoted in Stump, "Jim Thorpe: Greatest of Them All."

102 "the most wonderful place kick": *Boston Sunday Globe*.

102 "When . . . we knew": Jim Thorpe, quoted in Paddock, "Chief Bright Path."

102 "We all played better": Henry Roberts, quoted in Newcombe, 166.

103 "If ever defeat was the result": Paul H. Shannon, *Boston Herald*, Nov. 12, 1911, quoted in *Red Son*, 35.

103   "a one-man wrecking crew": Warner, *Pop Warner,* 128.

103   "it was indeed a pleasure": *Boston Post,* as reprinted in *The Arrow,* Nov. 24, 1911.

103   "I realized that here": Percy Haughton, quoted in Brad Steiger and Charlotte Thorpe, *Thorpe's Gold* (New York: Quicksilver Books, in association with Dell Publishing, 1984), 157. In 1915, Haughton's team beat both Princeton and Yale, the latter by a score of 41–0.

103   "[t]he man on the street was delighted": Stump, "Jim Thorpe: Greatest of Them All."

103   In 2008, *Sports Illustrated:* Mike Beacom, "Who Would Have Won the Heisman from 1900–1934?" Dec. 12, 2008, special to SI.com. http://www.sportsillustrated .cnn.com.

103   "overconfidence—that evil": *Red Son,* 37.

103   "What's the fun in that?": Jim Thorpe, quoted in Crichton, "Good King Jim."

104   "Thorpe is . . . considered": *NYT,* Dec. 2, 1911.

104   "He could go skidding": Glenn S. Warner, quoted in Walter H. Lingo, "The Life Story of Jim Thorpe," *Athletic World,* July 1923.

104   "He is . . . always watching": Ibid.

104   "a lazy Indian": Glenn S. Warner, quoted in Rice, 233.

104   "He didn't like to practice": Glenn S. Warner, quoted in Stump, "Jim Thorpe: Greatest of Them All."

105   "I may have had an aversion for work": Jim Thorpe, quoted in *Los Angeles Examiner,* April 1, 1953.

105   "caught the imagination": James A. Peterson, *Thorpe of Carlisle,* 1955. Paper "written and compiled" by Peterson for the Nineteenth Annual Hinckley and Schmitt Football Luncheon, Jim Thorpe Drop File, CCHS.

105   "[W]hen the Pilgrims landed on Plymouth Rock": (Rochester) *Union and Advertiser,* as reprinted in *The Arrow,* Dec. 1, 1911.

105   "Thorpe . . . makes no special preparations": *Philadelphia Inquirer,* as quoted in Newcombe, 163.

107   "Resolved, That Richard III": *The Arrow,* Jan. 19, 1912.

107   "Jim never liked to dress up": Rose Roberts in Henry and Rose [DeNomie] Roberts oral history, OHS. All subsequent quotations of Rose or Henry Roberts are taken from this source, unless otherwise noted. Rose DeNomie became Rose Roberts when she married Henry Roberts.

107   "suddenly wearied of pedagogy": Marianne Moore, quoted in Robert Cantwell, "The Poet, the Bums and the Legendary Redmen," *Sports Illustrated,* Feb. 15, 1960.

107   "something Grecian about them": Ibid.

108   "Miss Moore, may I carry": Jim Thorpe, quoted in Marianne Moore, "Ten Answers, Letter from an October Afternoon, Part 2," *Harper's Magazine,* Nov. 1964.

108   "The Indians had great behavior": Marianne Moore, quoted in Cantwell, "The Poet, the Bums and the Legendary Redmen."

108   "fond" . . . "exceedingly generous": Ibid.

108   "He was liked by all": Moore, "Ten Answers."

108   "He had a kind of ease": Moore, quoted in Cantwell, "The Poet, the Bums and the Legendary Redmen."

108   "head bent earnestly": Moore, "Ten Answers."

108   "flair and cool": William C. Rhoden, *$40 Million Slaves: The Rise, Fall and Redemption of the Black Athlete* (New York: Crown Publishers, 2006), 152.

109   "images and rhetorical strategies": Lesley Wheeler and Chris Gavaler, "Imposters

and Chameleons: Marianne Moore and the Carlisle Indian School," *Paideuma*, vol. 33, nos. 2 and 3 (Fall and Winter 2004): 53–82. Wheeler and Gavaler quote James Fenton: "If we want to hold in our minds a single image of the poet Marianne Moore, it should not be the grand old lady of the New York scene so much as the earnest young woman cycling daily to the [Carlisle] Federal Barracks."

109 "all the girls had a crush on": E-mail to author, Oct. 12, 2001, from the Reverend Kurt Neilson. His paternal grandmother was Carlisle student Elizabeth Walker.

109 "You're a cute little thing": Jim Thorpe, quoted in Newcombe, 171.

109 "A great big book": Henry and Rose [DeNomie] Roberts oral history.

109 "White intruders were more numerous": John W. Morris, Charles R. Goins, and Edwin C. McReynolds, *Historical Atlas of Oklahoma*, 3rd ed. (Norman: University of Oklahoma Press, 1986), 36.

110 "Many who apply": Letter from Superintendent R. H. Pratt to Lee Patrick, Indian agent, Sac and Fox, Dec. 4, 1899. Indian Archives Collection, Sac and Fox–Shawnee Agency Records—Carlisle Indian School, Box 543, folder 1, Jan. 12, 1912–Jan. 19, 1919, and undated. OHS.

110 "as in their original": Etha Lawrence, "Mrs. Iva Thorpe Had Lived a Very Picturesque Life," *The American Indian*, Nov. 1926.

110 "bright little Indian maiden": Ibid.

111 "sweet" . . . "beautiful": Ibid.

111 "Sociable, impressionable": Michael Koehler, unpublished biography of Jim Thorpe.

111 "North Carolina Agency": Application for Enrollment in a Nonreservation School, Carlisle, Pa., for Iva Miller, Sept. 17, 1909, RG75, Entry 1327, File 5533, NARA. The author is grateful to Chris Gavaler for providing Chilocco Indian School application materials relating to Iva Miller.

111 "put one over on the government": Gail Thorpe, interview.

111 "sore eyes": There are two sources used here as references to the trachoma surgery performed on Jim at Carlisle. In NARA, RG75, Central Classified Files—General Services, Box 1116, File 15281-1924-737, there is an exchange of letters in 1924 between "Ear Nose Throat Doctors in Tulsa, OK—Doctors White & White" and E. B. Merritt, commissioner of Indian Affairs, in which Dr. Daniel White seeks a copy of his eye exam and surgery on Jim in the Carlisle School records. The second source is the oral history of Rose DeNomie Roberts, previously referenced. She assisted Dr. White during the surgery and took care of Jim while he recovered.

112 "The activities underlying": Telephone interview, Craig A. Masback, former CEO of USA Track & Field (USATF). The late Peter Oley, track coach at Irvington High School in Irvington, New York, suggested that the author contact Mr. Masback.

112 "a difficult struggle": Warner, *Pop Warner*, 130.

112 "What's the use": Jim Thorpe, quoted in ibid.

112 "grind": *Red Son*, 41.

113 "great victories": Warner, *Pop Warner*, 130.

113 "I trained": *Red Son*, 40.

114 "best man in America": Michael C. Murphy, quoted in John Steckbeck (as told to Rusty Cowan), "From Hopi Indian to the Waldorf: The Louis Tewanimi Saga of Footracing," n.d. [1954], unattributed news clip, CCHS.

114 "the awkwardness of a novice": "Jim Thorpe Wins Pentathlon Tryout," unattributed news clip, n.d. [1912], BHOF.

114 "in so outstanding a fashion": James E. Sullivan, quoted in ibid.

115 "Like all great athletes": Koehler, unpublished biography of Jim Thorpe.

115 "endurance, patience and a world of determination": "Indian Race Produces Great Athletic Stars," *St. Louis Republic*, Jan. 14, 1912, reprinted in *The Arrow*, March 1, 1912.

115 "It is plainly time": *New York Evening Post*, quoted in Dyreson, 113; editorial reprinted with commentary in "What's the Matter with White Men?" *The Crisis* 4 (July 1912): 123–24.

115 "an exhibition of jumping": *The Arrow*, July 4, 1912.

116 "My chances of going abroad": Letter from Jim Thorpe to W. C. Kohlenberg, Sac and Fox agent, March 15, 1912, Indian Archives Collection, Sac and Fox–Shawnee Agency Records, Carlisle Indian School, Box 543, Folder 7, Jan. 19, 1912–Jan. 6, 1913, OHS.

116 "conscientiously recommend": Letter from Sac and Fox agent Horace Johnson to Superintendent Maurice Friedman, June 12, 1912. Indian Archives Collection, Sac and Fox–Shawnee Agency Records—Letterpress Books, General Correspondence, Box 652, May 21, 1912–June 24, 1912, p. 344, OHS.

116 "would not contest our going": *Red Son*, 42.

116 "[n]atural-born or naturalized subjects": *Fifth Olympiad, Olympic Games of Stockholm 1912, Programme, Rules and General Regulations* (Stockholm: Swedish Olympic Committee, 1912), 4.

116 On the entry form: Entry Form for Athletics, Fifth Olympiad. LA84 Foundation Sports Library, Los Angeles, Calif.

CHAPTER SIX

The Most Wonderful Athlete in the World · *Summer–Fall 1912*

119 "He returned home a hero": *The* (Carlisle) *Sentinel, n.d.* [1953], Scrapbook, P1 021-004.008, John S. Steckbeck Indian School Collection, CCHS.

119 "Thrills were mostly hard work for me": Jim Thorpe, quoted in Tobin Spirer, "Jim Thorpe: Man and Legend," n.d., unattributed news clip, PFHOF.

119 the well-organized 1906 games in Athens: The Intercalated or Interim Games of 1906 were held by the Greeks as an attempt to hold their own games every four years between the official Olympics. The IOC considered them unofficial.

119 "the funeral games of an epoch": Dyreson, 179.

120 "America's athletic missionaries": Edward Bayard Moss, quoted in Pope, 49.

120 "heterogeneous gathering": Dyreson, 157.

120 "Never in my long life": James E. Sullivan, quoted in ibid.

120 "America's Argonauts": Edward Bayard Moss, quoted in Pope, 49.

120 "the inestimable prize": Nathaniel Hawthorne, "The Golden Fleece," *Tales and Sketches Including Twice-Told Tales, Mosses from an Old Manse, and Their Snow-Image, A Wonder Book for Girls and Boys, Tanglewood Tales for Girls and Boys, Being a Second Wonder Book* (New York: Library Classics of the United States, 1982), 1467.

121 "the prime example in Greek mythology": Leo Braudy, *The Frenzy of Renown: Fame and Its History* (New York: Oxford University Press, 1986), 40.

121 "the fetish of the [fellow] aristocrats": David C. Young, *The Olympic Myth of Greek Amateur Athletics* (Chicago: Areas Publishers, Inc., 1984), 60.

121 "camouflage": Pierre de Coubertin, quoted in Young, 63.

121   "one who has never": Entry Form for Athletics.

121   "completely spurious": *Time*, July 27, 1992.

121   "literally meant and always meant": Young, 7. See Young for a detailed refutation of the claims made by English classical scholars for the basis in ancient Greek Olympic Games for a code of amateurism.

122   "irreproachable personally": Pierre de Coubertin, quoted in Young, 73. From Pierre de Coubertin, *Souvenirs d'Amérique et de Grèce* (Paris: Hachette, 1897).

122   "first sports czar": *Dictionary of American Biography*, quoted by Pope, 31.

122   "the Walter Camp": Warner, *Pop Warner*, 133.

122   "sporting republic": Dyreson, 2.

122   "outrageous charade": Pierre de Coubertin, quoted in the Associated Press and Grolier, *The Olympic Story: Pursuit of Excellence* (Danbury, Conn.: Grolier Enterprises, 1979), 53.

123   "when black men, red men and yellow men": Ibid.

123   "fantastic machinery": Grace Thorpe, quoted in James Hannigan, "Thorpe Restored to Land of Giants," *The Times* (London), Sept. 19, 1999.

123   "I'd never seen a boat": Jim Thorpe, quoted in Newcombe, 183.

123   "I was twenty-four years old": *Red Son*, 43.

123   "deadly in earnest": Unattributed news clip, n.d., copied by Wheeler from Jim Thorpe's scrapbook, RWWC.

124   "the coming triumph of the Stars and Stripes": *The Times* (London), July 3, 1912.

125   "monotonous list of American successes": *The Times* (London), July 9, 1912.

126   "sightseers and merrymakers": *The Times* (London), July 15, 1912.

126   "looked upon a Redman": *Red Son*, 44. All Thorpe's recollections of this incident come from this source.

126   "middle-aged, respectable-looking": Will Irwin, "The Olympic Games: The Dramatic and Picturesque Contest in Which America's Team Won from the Flower of the Athletic World," *Collier's*, Aug. 10, 1912. All the quotations regarding this opening ceremony are taken from this source.

127   "reconcile the irreconcilable": Robert Pariente, "Jim Thorpe: What a Storybook Life!" *Olympic Review*, May 1983.

127   the classic pentathlon: The modern pentathlon was a different event; on the 1912 U.S. team was Lieutenant George S. Patton, Jr., who placed fifth.

127   "looked in a couple of times": *Red Son*, 44.

128   He had won the gold medal: Because Jim Thorpe's 1912 Olympic records are not official, the scores for his events often differ from source to source. The author chooses to use the data in Bill Mallon and Ture Widlund's *The 1912 Olympic Games: Results for All Competitors in All Events, with Commentary* (Jefferson, N.C., and London: McFarland & Company, 2002), 121, checked against the official report of the 1912 Games that listed most of Jim's scores, though they were unofficial by the time the report was published in 1913, as follows: pentathlon events—broad (long) jump, javelin throw, 200 meters, discus throw, and 1,500 meters (7.07 meters, 46.71 meters, 22.9, 35.57 meters, 4:44.8).

128   "What a shock it was": Sullivan, *The Olympic Games Stockholm 1912*, 73.

128   "answers the . . . allegation": James E. Sullivan, quoted in Newcombe, 185.

129   "voluntarily quit": *Red Son*, 45.

130   "ran the distance": *The Fifth Olympiad, The Official Report of the Olympic Games of Stockholm 1912* (Stockholm: Wahlstrom & Widstrand, 1913), 420.

130   He had won the decathlon gold: Mallon and Widlund's decathlon totals, also checked against the official report of the 1912 Games, are as follows for the 100 meters, broad (long) jump, shot put, high jump, 400 meters, discus throw, 110-meter hurdles, pole vault, javelin throw, 1,500 meters: 11.2, 679 centimeters, 12.89 meters, 187 centimeters, 52.2, 36.98 meters, 15.6, 325 centimeters, 45.70 meters, 4:40.1. Mallon and Widlund, *The 1912 Olympic Games*, 119.

130   "It wasn't even close": William Mallon, quoted in *USA Today*, [May 1998]. The exact date of the article is unclear on the clip, from the Thorpe clip file in the PFHOF; it is either May 8 or 10.

130   four-foot-high bronze bust: Although subsequent references to the 1912 pentathlon challenge trophy describe it as a bust of King Gustav V, news accounts at the time and the Programme Général of the 1920 Seventh Olympiad in Antwerp identify it as "Buste de Charles XII, offert par S.M. le Roi de Suède." Comité Exécutif de la VIIme Olympiade, VIIme Olympiade, Jeux Olympiques à Anvers (Belgique) en 1920, Réglements Généraux Comités, Programme Général, Bruxelles, 75.

131   "magnificent [sterling] silver vase": Warner, *Pop Warner*, 135.

131   "You, sir, you are the most": "Thorpe Wonderful Athlete," n.d. [1912], unattributed news clip, WCC; "Three Views of Jim Thorpe, the World's Greatest All-around Athlete," July 20, 1912, [attribution unclear], Riksarkivet, Stockholm; "Thorpe a Wonderful Athlete," *Columbus Advocate*, as reprinted in *The Arrow*, Sept. 27, 1912. Many accounts would tweak King Gustav's words into "the greatest athlete in the world."

131   "Thank you": *Red Son*, 46.

131   "guarantee": Copies of the two guarantees Jim Thorpe signed for the two perpetual trophies are in the LA84 Foundation archives in Los Angeles. In 1920, the IOC would stipulate that all such trophies (and there were several given by monarchs, aristocrats, and sports associations for various events) be kept in the Olympic Museum in Lausanne between Olympiads, to be inscribed with the names of the subsequent winners. Eventually such perpetual trophies were phased out altogether. As of April 1, 2009, according to an e-mail to the author from Joëlle Bertoncini Moret, exhibit project officer, Museology Services, at the IOC in Lausanne, "the Olympic athletics challenge trophy for the decathlon is still in the permanent exhibition of the Olympic Museum in Lausanne, and the Olympic athletics challenge trophy for the pentathlon is for long-term loan for a traveling exhibition called 'Pierre de Coubertin and the Arts' made by the Deutsches Sport & Olympia Museum."

131   "would eat and drink anything": Abel Kiviat, quoted in Lewis H. Carlson and John J. Fogarty, *Tales of Gold: An Oral History of the Summer Olympic Games Told by America's Gold Medal Winners* (Chicago: Contemporary Books, 1987).

132   "strength, speed, endurance": Warner, *Pop Warner*, 135.

132   "Out of my way!": Jim Thorpe, quoted in ibid.

132   The *Los Angeles Times*: *LAT*, July 22, 1912.

132   "I didn't want to be gazed upon": *Red Son*, 47.

132   "Brilliant Performances of Indian": Undated and unattributed news clip, 1912, PFHOF.

132   "marvel of physical strength": *Philadelphia Inquirer*, n.d. [1912], BHOF.

132   "anthropological chart": *Daily Oklahoman*, Jan. 21, 1913.

132   Little of this seemed strange: In 1999, "scientific evidence" would be presented by Jon Entine that black athletes with West African ancestry have a biological

advantage in sprinting and jumping because of various factors, including muscle mass, center of gravity, and testosterone. Robert Lipsyte, "Raising an Old Question About Race, and Ignoring the Real Issue," *NYT,* Nov. 28, 1999.

132 "obsessed by genetics": Page Smith, *America Enters the World: A People's History of the Progressive Era and World War I* (New York: McGraw-Hill, 1985), 137.

133 "like has never been seen": *NYT,* July 21, 1912.

133 "Thorpe is the most marvelous creation": *Philadelphia Inquirer,* undated, [July 1912], BHOF.

133 "Well Remembered in Fayetteville": *Charlotte Observer,* July 18, 1912.

133 "bitter humiliation felt by England": "The 'Scandal of the Swedish Olympic Games,' " *LAT,* Aug. 4, 1912.

133 "show that these United States": *Blackwood's Magazine,* quoted in Dyreson, 164.

133 "enthusiasm and *esprit de corps*": *The Times* (London), July 29, 1912.

134 Kelly had never seen a plane: *LAT,* Nov. 9, 1930.

135 "never had a nickel": Abel Kiviat, quoted in *Tales of Gold,* 9.

135 "wandering athlete": *Red Son,* 48.

135 "international importance": Letter from Maurice Friedman, superintendent, Carlisle Indian Industrial School, to Robert Valentine, commissioner of Indian Affairs, July 22, 1912. RG75, Central Classified Files: Carlisle Indian School, File 71916 (1912), 047, NARA.

135 "conquering heroes": *The Arrow,* Sept. 13, 1912. All quoted material regarding the Carlisle celebration, unless otherwise noted, is taken from this source.

135 "It was good of everybody": *Red Son,* 52.

135 "a tinge of sadness": Clipping, n.d. [1912], from Jim Thorpe scrapbook, RWWC.

135 THORPE'S PARENTS DEAD: Ibid.

136 "I'm glad you're back": Iva Miller Thorpe, quoted in ibid.

136 "Monster Parade": *Charlotte Observer,* July 26, 1912.

136 *The* (Boston) *Traveler:* (Boston) *Traveler,* reprinted in *The Arrow,* Sept. 13, 1912.

136 "threatened with extinction": *Cincinnati Times-Star,* reprinted in *The Arrow,* Sept. 13, 1912.

136 *"Gee Whiz. What is it this is?":* W. J. Lampton, *NYT,* reprinted in *The Arrow,* Sept. 13, 1912.

136 "a rain of confetti, streamers and ticker tape": "Thousands Pay Tribute to Athletes," n.d. [1912], unattributed news clip, RG75, Entry 1327, Folder 1783, NARA.

136 "athletes, ex-athletes, soldiers": "Reception to Olympic Visitors Starts To-night," n.d. [1912], unattributed news clip, RG75, Entry 1327, Folder 1783, NARA.

136 "the nearest thing to a Roman triumph": Ibid.

137 The athletes were sequenced: "Thorpe to Have Place of Honor in Athletes' Parade," *New York Tribune,* n.d. [1912], RG75, Entry 1327, Folder 1783, NARA.

137 "Red Man, All-Around Champ": *Record-Herald,* [no city indicated on news clip], Aug. 25, 1912, RG75, Entry 1327, Folder 1783, NARA.

137 "in embarrassed silence": *Boston Post,* Aug. 25, 1912.

137 any enthusiasm: "Olympic Victors Welcomed by 1,000,000," n.d. [1912], unattributed news clip, RG75, Entry 1327, Folder 1783, NARA.

137 "I heard people yelling my name": Jim Thorpe, quoted in Bob Bernotas, *Jim Thorpe: Sac and Fox Athlete,* North American Indians of Achievement (New York: Chelsea House Publishers, 1992), 21.

137 "To be famous, goes the myth": Braudy, 6.

137 "some time before either would say anything": "Indian Athletes Tell of Victories," *Philadelphia Inquirer*, n.d. [1912], RG75, Entry 1327, Folder 1783, NARA. All quoted material about this interview with reporters in Philadelphia is taken from this source.

138 "A promoter's dream": Warner, *Pop Warner*, 142.

138 "muscular development": Thomas McVeigh, Jr., (Columbus) *Ohio State Journal*, reprinted in "Jim Thorpe at School," *Literary Digest*, Oct. 5, 1912. All quoted material regarding this interview is taken from this source.

138 "incompetent": "Jim Thorp [*sic*] Incompetent in Eyes of Government," *Vinita Weekly Chieftain* (Oklahoma), Aug. 16, 1912. All the quoted material in this paragraph, regarding Jim Thorpe's incompetent status, is taken from this source.

139 "In view of conditions": *NYT*, Sept. 3, 1912.

139 "Jim . . . you're the greatest man": Martin Sheridan, quoted in "Jim Thorpe Shows Athletic Prowess," n.d. [1912], unattributed, BHOF.

139 "In fact . . . it is my opinion": Letter from Supt. Horace J. Johnson of the Sac and Fox School to the Indian Commissioner, Sept. 17, 1912, RG75, Central Classified Files: Carlisle Indian School, File 88975 (1912), 825, NARA.

139 "I suggest that you appreciate": Letter from John Francis, Jr., chief, Education Division, to J. H. Abbott, acting commissioner, Oct. 1, 1912. RG75, Central Classified Files: Carlisle Indian School, File 88975 (1912), 825, NARA.

140 "might not be amiss": Memo to commissioner from John Francis, Jr., chief, Education Division, July 16, 1912. RG75, Central Classified Files: Carlisle Indian School, File 71916 (1912), 047, NARA.

140 "quite notorious": Department of the Interior, United States Indian Service, check request form dated Sept. 17, 1912, signed by Horace J. Johnson, Sac and Fox agent, Indian Archives Collection, Sac and Fox–Shawnee Agency Records—Individual Indian Files, Box 285, Folder 10, Thorp [*sic*], James, 244, OHS.

140 "To the best of my knowledge": Department of the Interior, United States Indian Service, check request form dated Dec. 23, 1912, signed by Horace J. Johnson, Sac and Fox agent; see previous note for location.

140 "Frank, I have the chance": Jim Thorpe, letter to Frank Thorpe, quoted in Newcombe, 193.

140 "Jim Thorpe has been compelled": Letter from Richard Adams, great sachem, Brotherhood of North American Indians, to commissioner of Indian Affairs, Sept. 9, 1912. RG75, Central Classified Files: Carlisle Indian School, File 89680 (1912), 047, NARA.

141 "maintain his amateur standing": Letter from Maurice Friedman, superintendent, Carlisle Indian Industrial School, to commissioner of Indian Affairs, Sept. 25, 1912. RG75, Central Classified Files: Carlisle Indian School, File 89680 (1912), 047, NARA. All quotations of Friedman's in this paragraph are taken from this source.

142 "easier to gain ground consecutively": (Carlisle) *Evening Sentinel*, Sept. 23, 1912.

142 Warner had his 1911 backfield: Pete Calac was Luiseño Rincon Mission. Joseph "Joe" Napoleon Guyon was French-Chippewa.

143 "well tanked up": Warner, *Pop Warner*, 138. All quoted material regarding this incident is taken from this source.

143 "I cannot quite realize": Jim Thorpe, quoted in *The Arrow*, Nov. 1, 1912.

143 "Everybody in the town of Syracuse": Dr. Joseph Alexander, an early professional football player, interview by Robert W. Wheeler, RWWC.

144 "tore the Syracuse line": Glenn S. Warner, "Here Come the Giants!" *Collier's*, Nov. 21, 1931.

144 "run the risk of becoming so crippled": *Red Son*, 56.

144 "rounds of applause": (Carlisle) *Evening Sentinel*, Oct. 21, 1912.

144 "Thorpe Nearly a Team": News clip quoted in Koehler, unpublished biography of Jim Thorpe.

144 "virtually defeated Lehigh": (Carlisle) *Evening Sentinel*, Nov. 4, 1912.

145 "Now remember": Crichton, "Good King Jim."

145 "What about going around": Jim Thorpe, quoted in ibid.

145 "That 1912 team": Pete Calac, interview with Robert L. Wheeler, RWWC.

145 *"Upon the fields of friendly strife"*: The author thanks Dr. Stephen Grove, former U.S. Military Academy historian, for his help in verifying the correct text of this quotation, as well as its location at West Point.

146 "primed for that battle": Paddock, "Chief Bright Path," part 3, *Collier's*, Oct. 19, 1929.

146 "class the stars fell on": Jenkins, 281.

146 "I have never known a team": *Red Son*, 58.

146 "tissue paper": *NYT*, Nov. 10, 1912.

146 "The rush of men was on": (New York) *Evening Sun*, as reprinted in *The Arrow*, Dec. 20, 1912.

146 "amazing intelligence": *New York Item*, as reprinted in *The Arrow*, Dec. 20, 1912.

147 "Thorpe runs too fast": Omar Bradley, quoted in Gary Stevens, interview.

147 "laying": *New York American*, Nov. 24, 1912.

147 "felt funny": Jim Thorpe, "The Day Jim Thorpe Wrecked Army . . . Even Ike Eisenhower Couldn't Stop Him," *Esquire*, Sept. 1952.

147 "particular pal": Dwight D. Eisenhower, interview by Robert W. Wheeler, RWWC.

147 "When we got up": Ibid.

147 "assault on the United States Army": Damon Runyon, "Thorpe Alone Defeats Army," *Louisville Herald*, Nov. 10, 1912. All quoted material of Runyon regarding the 1912 Army–Carlisle game is taken from this source.

147 "one of the greatest": *NYT*, Nov. 10, 1912. All quoted material from the *Times*, unless otherwise noted, is taken from this source.

148 Countless retellings of the game: NCAA, *Football's Finest: The NCAA's Career Statistics to Nearly 3,000 of the Finest Players and Coaches to Be Associated with Collegiate Football* (NCAA, 2002), 72, lists Jim's collegiate statistics. These are based on those compiled by Steve Boda, Jr., NCAA associate director of statistics before his retirement in 1969, in *College Football All-Time Record Book, 1869–1969* (New York: National Collegiate Sports Services, 1969), 81, which credits Jim with two scoring touchdowns in the 1912 game against Army. Thus, the NCAA record, though not official for 1912, still credits Jim with the two touchdowns.

148 "Ninety-five yards this time": Thorpe, "The Day Jim Thorpe Wrecked Army."

148 "mighty battle": *Red Son*, 59.

148 "His playing in the Army game alone": Glenn S. Warner, quoted in Paddock, "Chief Bright Path," *Collier's*, Oct. 19, 1929.

148 "very quiet and kind": Eisenhower interview.

148 "That Indian": Leland Devore, quoted in Wheeler, 132.

148 "Thorpe Plows Through Army Line": *NYT.*

149 "Thorpe Alone Defeats Army": *Louisville Herald*, Nov. 10, 1912.

149 "simply astonishing": Edward Bayard Moss, "The Strain of the Game," *Harper's Weekly*, Nov. 30, 1912.

149 "ever having to relieve an ex-football player": Dwight D. Eisenhower, quoted in Danzig, *Oh, How They Played the Game*, 291.

149 "so many mistakes": *The Arrow*, Nov. 27, 1912.

149 "just stood there": Warner, quoted in *NYT*, Nov. 20, 1947.

149 "I didn't think": Jim Thorpe, quoted in Warner, *Pop Warner*, 139.

150 "the one weak trait": Ibid.

150 "rested content": Warner, "Here Come the Giants!"

150 "beautiful . . . piece of open-field running": Warner, "The Indian Massacres."

150 "sporting world": "Jim Thorpe Says He Will Quit Carlisle and Retire," Unattributed news clip,, Nov. 25, 1912, BHOF. All quoted material regarding Jim's arrival in Providence comes from this source.

150 "somewhat shy": *The Arrow*, Nov. 27, 1912.

150 "something cold . . . grip my heart": *Red Son*, 62.

150 "blinding snowstorm": *Brown Daily Herald*, Nov. 29, 1912.

151 "the whole show": Paddock, "Chief Bright Path," part 4, Oct. 26, 1929.

151 Jim's twenty-seventh touchdown: Steve Boda, Jr., compiled his statistics for collegiate football for the period before 1937, the year uniform reporting and statistical guidelines were implemented. His findings, published in *College Football All-Time Record Book, 1869–1969*, previously referenced, list Jim Thorpe's Carlisle statistics (available for twenty-nine of the forty-four games he appeared in; the actual totals would be significantly higher) on pages 20–27 and 81: career rushing, 433 yards; most yards gained per game, 186.9 (1912); highest average gain per rush for one season, 9.79 (1912); all-purpose running (rushing, pass receiving, and all runbacks), most yards gained in one game, 449 (Carlisle vs. Penn, 1912); most yards gained in one season, 2,447 (1912): 1,869 rushing; 40 pass receiving; 95 interception returns; 259 punt returns; 184 kickoff returns. Jim's (partial) collegiate statistics are also in *NCAA Football's Finest* (Indianapolis, Ind.: National Collegiate Athletic Association, 2002), 72. The author thanks Ellen L. Summers, librarian, NCAA, for providing her with relevant pages from this book.

151 "He could come": Warner, "Here Come the Giants!"

151 "[He] had everything": John Heisman, quoted in *American History*, June 1997.

152 "the most remarkable record": Cantwell, "The Poet, the Bums and the Legendary Redmen."

152 Almost one hundred years later: Beacom, "Who Would Have Won the Heisman from 1900–1934?"

152 "I gave little quarter": *Red Son*, 63.

152 "Carlisle Indian Reticent": (Carlisle) *Evening Sentinel*, Nov. 27, 1912.

152 "Today the master athlete": *Sunday Herald* (Boston), Dec. 29, 1912. All the quoted material concerning Thorpe's measurements are from this source.

153 "almost overnight changed": Vine Deloria, Jr., *Custer Died for Your Sins: An Indian Manifesto* (Norman: University of Oklahoma Press, 1988), 199.

153 "Where undying fame": *The Red Man*, March 1913.

153 "the best known on the planet": "Thorpe Hero in His Own Town," unattributed newsclip, Dec. 20, 1912, BHOF.

153 "juicy fat": Warner, *Pop Warner*, 143.

PART II: THE PROFESSIONAL

155 "[T]he college game": Jim Thorpe, quoted in *San Francisco Call and Post*, May 12, 1922.

CHAPTER SEVEN
The Public Glare · *1913–1914*

157 "I always dreamed of winning the Games": Bruce Jenner, quoted in *NYT, Play*, August 2008.

157 "the most impossible celebrity": *Daily Oklahoman*, Jan. 12, 1913. All the quoted material regarding Jim's visit to Oklahoma comes from this source.

157 "Young men": (New York) *Evening Mail*, Jan. 29, 1913.

158 Four days later: *The Worcester Telegram* (Mass.), Jan. 22, 1913. An article that appeared two days later in the *Providence* (R.I.) *Times* is sometimes cited as the earliest evidence of the news story that broke the Thorpe scandal.

158 "glib talker": Letter from Roy R[uggles]. Johnson to John Steckbeck, Feb. 14, 1952, P1-021-004, John S. Steckbeck Indian School Collection, CCHS. All quoted material regarding the *Telegram* scoop is taken from this source. Parts of the letter also appear in Al Clark's "The Sports Shop" column in the Harrisburg, Pennsylvania, *Sunday Patriot-News*, Apr. 5, 1953.

158 "Here's Jim Thorpe": Koehler, unpublished biography of Jim Thorpe. This story was told to Michael Koehler by Jack Thorpe, who had been told it by Joe Libby.

159 "I signed [Thorpe] as a pitcher": Charles Clancy, quoted in *The Worcester Telegram*. All the quoted material of Clancy's is taken from this source.

159 "elevate[s] his case": Unattributed article, n.d., Jan. 1913, BHOF.

159 "What surprises the local athletic world": *NYT*, Jan. 26, 1913.

159 "complete denial": *Daily Oklahoman*, Jan. 25, 1913.

159 "social call": *Charlotte Observer*, Feb. 1, 1913.

160 for an exclusive "special": *NYT*, Jan. 25, 1913.

160 "Reports are being freely circulated": Ibid.

160 "I had always laid my cards": *Red Son*, 64.

160 "What's . . . baseball got to do": Jim Thorpe, quoted in Glenn S. Warner, "Red Menaces," *Collier's*, Oct. 31, 1931.

161 "not play for the money": Letter from James Thorpe to James E. Sullivan, Jan. 26, 1913, reprinted in AAU 1913 yearbook, 113. Photocopy provided by AAU archives, Lake Buena Vista, Fla.

161 "[T]he Indian sees himself": Vine Deloria, Jr., "The American Indian Image in North America," reprinted in the *Encyclopedia of Indians in the Americas*, vol. 1 (St. Clair Shores, Mich.: Scholarly Press, 1974), 40–44; and in Gretchen M. Bataille and Charles L. P. Silet, *The Pretend Indians: Images of Native Americans in the Movies* (Ames: Iowa State University Press, 1980), 49–54.

161 "thorough investigation": Letter from M. Friedman, superintendent, to James E. Sullivan, Jan. 26, 1913, reprinted in AAU 1913 yearbook, 114.

161 "it has been the custom": *NYT*, Jan. 27, 1913.

162 "without the least suspicion": Statement by the Amateur Athletic Union of the United States in Regard to James Thorpe, Jan. 27, 1913, reprinted in AAU 1913 yearbook, 115.

162 "Not We Who Were Asleep": *Charlotte Observer,* Jan. 29, 1913.

162 IS RUMOR THORPE'S DISQUALIFICATION: Telegram from Kristian Hellström to James E. Sullivan, Jan. 28, 1913. Stockholmsolympiaden 1912, Volym: EIII:5, Korrespondens. Handlingar ang. 'amateurism' haer: James Thorpe's diskvalifikation. Swedish National Archives, Stockholm.

162 "Yes . . . all records void": Telegram from James E. Sullivan to Kristian Hellström, Jan. 29, 1913. Stockholmsolympiaden 1912, Volym: EIII:5, Korrespondens. Handlingar ang. 'amateurism' haer: James Thorpe's diskvalifikation. Swedish National Archives, Stockholm.

162 "there wasn't any revert about it": Martin Sheridan, quoted in *LAT,* Jan. 29, 1913.

162 "in the history of amateur athletics": "A.A.U. Explains Its Position—Loses All His Prizes and Records," n.d. [Jan. 1913], unattributed news clip, BHOF.

162 "so vital and convincing": Ibid.

163 "wedge for a more general clean-up": Ibid.

163 "Objections to the qualifications . . .": *Fifth Olympiad, Olympic Games of Stockholm 1912, Programme, Rules and General Regulations* (Stockholm: Swedish Olympic Committee, 1912), 5.

163 "Such a case": *Revue Olympique,* March 1913. Translation provided by IOC archive, Lausanne, Switzerland.

163 "Does anyone believe": Letter from Elis Lindroth to *Nordiskt Idrottsliv* (*Nordic Sport Life*), July 24, 1913. Translated from Swedish by Mariane Oley.

164 "The Thorpe affair is maddening": Letter from Col. Viktor G. Balck to Pierre de Coubertin, Feb. 4, 1913. IOC Archives, Lausanne. Translation from French by author.

164 "touching in its naiveté": Letter from Pierre de Coubertin to Godefrey X. de Blonay, Feb. 9 [day unclear], 1913, IOC Archives, Lausanne. Translation from French by author.

164 " 'Big Injun' Comes Across with Truth": *Charlotte Observer,* Jan. 28, 1913.

164 "Thorpe Confesses to Professionalism": *Daily Oklahoman,* Jan. 28, 1913.

164 "Thorpe's deception": *NYT,* Jan. 28, 1913.

164 "one of the jokes": *LAT,* Jan. 29, 1913.

164 "a little thing enough": Damon Runyon, quoted in Steiger and Thorpe, 208.

165 "gallant," "manly": *Daily Oklahoman,* Jan. 31, 1913.

165 "lie his way out of it": Ibid.

165 "Throughout the length": *Daily Oklahoman,* Feb. 2, 1913.

165 "staking them": *Daily Oklahoman,* Feb. 3, 1913.

165 "Glenn Warner must have known": *TSN,* Feb. 6, 1913.

165 "The ideals of the gentleman": *Outlook,* Feb. 8, 1913.

165 "Nobody who knows British athletics": *Daily Mirror,* reprinted in *The Literary Digest,* Feb. 8, 1913.

165 "so high a degree": *The State* (Columbia, S.C.), reprinted in *Outlook,* Feb. 15, 1913.

165 On the other hand: *Buffalo Morning Express,* reprinted in ibid.

166 "extraordinarily disproportionate": *Outlook,* Feb. 8, 1913.

166 The *Washington Herald* agreed: *Washington Herald,* quoted in ibid.

166 "spectacular]scandal] in the history of sport": F. C. Lane, "Amateur Athletics Arraigned," *The Baseball Magazine,* April 1913. All quoted material in this analysis is taken from this source.

167 "I don't know what your rules are": Letter from Hugo Wieslander to the AAU, as

quoted in letter from Everett Freeman, Warner Bros., to Grantland Rice, July 27, 1949. *Jim Thorpe—All American* production file, USC.

167 "a brutal business": "Red Menaces."

167 "high triumph and bitter despair": Jack McCallum, "The Regilding of a Legend," *Sports Illustrated*, Oct. 25, 1982.

167 "face the world with the truth": *Red Son*, 65.

167 "adopted a fatalistic viewpoint": Ibid.

167 "I didn't have too much": Jim Thorpe, quoted in Henry Flickinger, oral history, CCHS.

168 "He had sublimated his personal": Michael Koehler, "Jim Thorpe's Grandson on School Athletics," *College Board Review*, Feb. 1995.

168 "branded a professional": *Red Son*, 65.

168 "There was nothing I could do": Ibid.

169 "never sign a professional contract": *TSN*, Feb. 13, 1913.

169 WILL CONSIDER PROPOSITION: Western Union telegram from James Thorpe to August [Garry] Herrmann, Jan. 28, 1913, BHOF.

169 "rather unsophisticated": Warner, *Pop Warner*, 144.

170 "old friends": In 1892 Warner, playing for the Springville, N.Y., local baseball team the summer before he entered Cornell law school, had played against McGraw, already a professional minor leaguer, who was brought in to play one game for nearby Gowanda in "the deciding game of the amateur series." Warner, *Pop Warner: Football's Greatest Teacher*, 40.

170 "The engaging of Thorpe by McGraw": *NYT*, Feb. 1, 1913.

170 "packed to the doors": "John J. McGraw Greets Indian Athlete for the First Time" n.d., unattributed news clip, BHOF.

170 "No such scene": Ibid.

170 "[w]ith a broad grin": *NYT*, Feb. 2, 1913.

170 "I am pleased to get a chance": Ibid.

170 "I had a lot of speed": *Literary Digest*, Feb. 15, 1913.

170 "as happy as a schoolboy": *LAT*, Feb. 2, 1913.

170 "No one knows": *NYT*, Feb. 2, 1913.

170 "There is nothing more to say": *LAT*, Feb. 2, 1913.

171 "remarkable throwing arm," "Indian cunning": *NYT*, Feb. 2, 1913.

171 "never had any professional advice": Ibid.

171 "If he doesn't make a ball player": Ibid.

171 "The Indian was only a youngster then": "John J. McGraw Greets Indian Athlete for the First Time."

171 "I expect him to show": "Thorpe to Wear Uniform of Giants Next Season," n.d. [Jan. 1913], unattributed news clip, BHOF.

171 "the highest salaried": "McGraw Pays $9000 to Sign Jim Thorpe," n.d. [Feb. 1913], unattributed news clip, BHOF.

171 "childlike": *Literary Digest*, Feb. 15, 1913. All quoted material from this interview is taken from this source.

172 "marvelous concentrative power": *Daily Oklahoman*, Feb. 16, 1913.

172 "judge and catch": Ibid.

172 "cherished prize": *TSN*, Feb. 6, 1913. All the quoted material in this paragraph is taken from this source.

173   "endured an integration experience": Powers-Beck, 1.

173   "couldn't let it out": Charles Albert Bender, quoted in ibid., 75.

173   "tying oneself in knots": Rhoden, 101.

174   "This is a strange country": John Tortes Meyer, quoted in Powers-Beck, 77.

174   "the greatest natural hitter": John McGraw, quoted in ibid., 82.

174   "not accepted as a member of the team": Clifford Kaehline telephone interview.

174   "quickly [develop] a critical mass": Joseph B. Oxendine, foreword, Powers-Beck, xii.

174   "All will now be forgiven": NYT, Feb. 2, 1913.

174   "[I]t is doubtful": "Thorpe to Wear Uniform of Giants Next Season," n.d. [Jan. 1913], unattributed news clip, BHOF.

175   "No, I never did": LAT, Feb. 2, 1913.

175   Two months after Jim signed: F. C. Lane, "The Greatest Manager in Organized Baseball," The Baseball Magazine, May 1913.

175   From 1899 to 1932: Connie Mack has the highest number of career victories: 3,731. NYT, June 28, 2009.

175   "the most famous athlete in America": Frank Deford, The Old Ball Game: How John McGraw, Christy Mathewson, and the New York Giants Created Modern Baseball (New York: Atlantic Monthly Press, 2005), 7.

176   "McGraw eats gunpowder": Charles Alexander, John McGraw (New York: Viking Penguin, 1988), 4.

176   "awkward, untutored, unskilled": Lane, "The Greatest Manager."

176   "heavy stockholder": Ibid.

176   "He cares for nothing": F. C. Lane, "John McGraw, the Dominant Figure of the National League," The Baseball Magazine, Nov. 1917.

176   "That's going to be your name": John McGraw, quoted in Patty Loew, "Tinker to Evers to Chief: Baseball from Indian Country," Wisconsin Magazine of History, Spring 2004.

176   "without question": Lane, "The Greatest Manager."

177   "Thorpe Lost by Giants": "Thorpe Lost by Giants on the Way to Texas," n.d. [Feb. 1913], unattributed article, BHOF.

177   "Considering the large quantities": Frank Johnson, "Crossing Red River: Spring Training in Texas," The National Pastime: A Review of Baseball History, Society for American Baseball Research (SABR), vol. 26, 2006.

178   "the Giants put this town": John McGraw, quoted in ibid.

178   "Thorpe Surprises McGraw": NYT, Feb. 20, 1913.

178   "surely is fast for a big man": TSN, Feb. 27, 1913.

178   "He is afraid to be misunderstood": John Tortes Meyers, "Meyers Lauds Jim Thorpe, Olympic Hero," New York American, May 25, 1913.

178   "the brainiest recruit": LAT, Feb. 28, 1913.

178   "over-anxious" and "over-confident": John McGraw, quoted in Poughkeepsie (N.Y.) Eagle, Feb. 28, 1913.

178   "all that a ball player should be": TSN, March 6, 1913.

178   "cried out [it] was the longest hit": NYT, March 12, 1913.

178   "This is a sample": News clip, n.d. [Oct. 1915], unattributed, BHOF.

178   "I remember, very late one night": Meyers, quoted in Lawrence S. Ritter, The Glory of Their Times: The Story of the Early Days of Baseball Told by the Men Who Played It (New York: William Morrow, 1984), 183. Meyers told this story several times.

179   "the rawest recruit": TSN, March 27, 1913.

179 *The Sporting News* suggested: Ibid. All quoted material is taken from this source.

179 "bristling interview": Christy Mathewson, "McGraw Will Retain Jim Thorpe," April 6, 1913, dateline, n.d., unattributed news clip, BHOF.

180 "You'll have to learn, Jim": Jim Thorpe, as told to Irving Wallace, "It's Mister Umpire," *American Legion Magazine*, April 1940.

180 "The minute [Jim] stepped from the dugout": "Thorpe Is Tragic Figure in Series," n.d. [1913], unattributed news clip, PFHOF. All quoted material in this anecdote is taken from this source. See also *NYT*, Oct. 5, 1913.

180 "a terrific personal appeal": Al Schacht, quoted in Wheeler, 158.

181 "His way of telling me": Jim Thorpe, quoted in Jane R. Smith, "Triumph and Tragedy," *American History*, May/June 1997.

181 "What kind of league is this": Edd Roush, quoted in Joseph Durso, *The Days of Mr. McGraw: The Wild, Wacky, Wooly Era of John J. McGraw and His Baseball Giants* (Englewood Cliffs, N.J.: Prentice-Hall, 1969), 103.

181 "exploded": Blanche McGraw, *The Real McGraw*, ed. Arthur Mann (New York: David McKay Co., 1953), 241.

181 "What about the Irish?": Jim Thorpe, quoted in Bozeman Bulger, "Passing of Jim Thorpe Proves Great Athletes Often Fail in Baseball," *Salt Lake* (Utah) *Telegraph*, May 22, 1915.

181 "Why, you Indian": John McGraw, quoted in Gene Schoor, with Henry Gilfond, *Jim Thorpe: America's Greatest Athlete* (New York: Julian Messner, 1951), 129.

181 "I said that was all right": Jim Thorpe, quoted in Frank Graham, Jr., "The Saga of Jim Thorpe," *Sport*, Oct. 1958.

182 "beautiful Cherokee Indian maiden": *LAT*, Sept. 2, 1913.

182 "astounded": Ibid.

182 "close-mouthed": "Moving Pictures to Snap Passing of Thorpe into Happy Bondage," *New York Herald*, n.d. [1913], news clip, RG75, Entry 1327, Folder 1783, NARA.

182 "color": Application for Marriage License, Commonwealth of Pennsylvania, No. 69 22, Oct. 13, 1913, Jim Thorpe drop file, CCHS.

182 "formal and elaborate": "Moving Pictures to Snap Passing of Thorpe into Happy Bondage."

183 "You Tell Me Your Dream": Words: Seymour A. Rice and Albert H. Brown; music: Charles Daniels.

183 A filmmaker and a cameraman: The cameraman was Victor Miller, who later changed his name to Victor Milner and, as a cinematographer, won an Oscar for the 1934 version of *Cleopatra*.

183 "landmark in baseball history.": Frank McGlynn, "Striking Scenes from Around the World," part 1 of a five-part series, *The Baseball Magazine*, Aug. 1913.

184 "if only he would": World Baseball Tour Diary of Iva Thorpe, Jim Thorpe Home, 706 E. Boston Street, Yale, Okla., OHS. All subsequent quotations of Iva Thorpe's regarding the world tour are taken from this source.

184 "golden elevators": Lawrence, "Mrs. Iva Thorpe Has Lived a Very Picturesque Life."

184 George Kessler (the "Champagne King"): Kessler would survive the sinking of the *Lusitania* on May 7, 1915, after having pestered the captain about the absence of evacuation drills for the passengers.

185 "especially interested in Jim Thorpe": Frank McGlynn, "Striking Scenes from Around the World," part 4 of a five-part series, *The Baseball Magazine*, Nov. 1914.

185 "It does not often fall": G. W. Axelson, "Sox and Giants Find Thorpe World Famous," *Chicago Record-Herald*, Feb. 25, 1914.

185 "fascinating smile": Ibid.

186 "Jim Thorpe has developed": John McGraw, quoted in James E. Elfers, *The Tour to End All Tours: The Story of Major League Baseball's 1913–1914 World Tour* (Lincoln: University of Nebraska Press, 2003), 195. See also Joe Farrell, "They May Be Christians but Differ Little from Heathens," *TSN*, March 5, 1914.

186 "the most sensational": G. W. Axelson, "Indian Jim Thorpe Is Promising Star," *Chicago Record-Herald*, April 19, 1914.

187 "an open break and rebellion": Hearings, 1335. Inspector Linnen's report is reprinted in the commission report. All subsequent quotations from the hearings are taken from this source. Friedman was tried in federal court for embezzling and financial malfeasance and acquitted.

187 "There are rumors afloat": M. K. Sniffer, quoted in Bell, 93.

187 On February 6: The Joint Commission comprised eight members: Senators Joe T. Robinson, Arkansas, chairman; Harry Lane, Oregon; Charles E. Townsend, Michigan; and Representatives John T. Stephens, Texas, Charles D. Carter, Oklahoma, and Charles H. Burke, South Dakota. Robinson, Lane, Stephens, and Carter went to Carlisle.

188 Members of the varsity football team: Elmer Busch and Joe Guyon had been named to Camp's 1913 All-America second team, the last time Carlisle football players would be on his lists. In the absence of an official All-America list in the war year of 1917, Camp instead published a "Stars of 1917" list, which included Pete Calac, now at West Virginia Wesleyan, and Guyon, who was on John Heisman's national championship team at Georgia Tech. Guyon was also on the 1918 Camp All-America list.

189 His Carlisle record: Warner's career collegiate coaching record was provided by the NCAA (http://webl.ncaa.org/stats/statssrv/careercoach).

190 "The stories of the school itself": Luana Mangold, oral history, CCHS.

191 "unmonitored and unchecked": Joseph Gone, quoted in Andrea Smith, "Soul Wound: The Legacy of Native American Schools," *Amnesty Magazine*, www.amnestyusa.org/amnestynow/soulwound.html.

CHAPTER EIGHT
The Majors and Ohio · *1915–1919*

193 "Son, never take": Jim Thorpe, quoted by Steve Owen, *NYT*, March 30, 1943.

193 "I felt like a sitting hen": Jim Thorpe, quoted in Newcombe, 215.

193 "Bench Warmer": Jim Thorpe quoted in inter-office memo from Everett Freeman to Douglas Morrow, June 22, 1949, Harry B. Friedman Collection, Folder 20, *Jim Thorpe—All American*, USC.

193 "Giants camp followers": Damon Runyon, "The Mornin's Mornin" column, *New York Morning Telegraph*, datelined March 14 [1914], BHOF. All quoted material regarding Runyon in Texas comes from this source.

194 "gorgeous start,": *Baseball Magazine*, June, 1915.

194 "Add another to the passing": News clip, n.d. [1915], unattributed, BHOF.

194 "disturbing influence": "Jim Thorpe Thrown Back on Giants' Hands," n.d. [1915], unattributed news clip, BHOF.

194 "O, the Poor Injun!": *Pittsburgh Post*, Jan. 30., 1915, BHOF.

195 "put the Giants on their feet,": *NYT*, Sept. 2, 1915.

195 "husky little fellow": *Red Son*, 67.

195 "first outing": Baby book of James Francis Thorpe, Jr., Jim Thorpe Home, 706 E. Boston Street, Yale, Okla., OHS.

195 "terrific time": *Red Son*, 68.

195 "surprisingly well": Ibid

195 "building my own monument": Ibid.

195 "excellent character and reputation": Letter from Horace J. Johnson, Sac and Fox superintendent, to commissioner of Indian Affairs, "Application of James Thorp for his share of tribal trust funds," Oct. 20, 1914, Sac and Fox Letter Book, OHS.

196 "wildest enthusiasm": Louis W. Bonsib, *The 1916 Arbutus: A Motion Picture of the Life and Customs of Indiana University* (Bloomington: The Senior Class of Indiana University, 1916), 70. Unless otherwise noted, all quoted material regarding Thorpe's time at Indiana University is taken from this source.

196 "Everyone watching": Herbert H. Skirvin, "Looking Back: Athlete Jim Thorpe Was an Assistant UI Coach," *Bloomington* (Ind.) *Herald Times*, Nov. 24, 1979. All quoted material about the Skirvin anecdote is taken from this source.

197 "performance bonus": Robert W. Peterson, *Pigskin: The Early Years of Pro Football* (New York: Oxford University Press), 29.

197 "first certifiable professional": Ibid.

198 "intense desire for victory": Marc S. Maltby, "The Origins and Early Development of Professional Football, 1890–1920." Ph.D. dissertation, Ohio University, August 1987, 184.

198 "teem[ing] with romance and rancor": Grantland Rice, "Canton–Massillon Feud Teems with Romance and Rancor," *Atlanta Journal*, n.d. [1906], PFHOF.

198 "*In days of old*": Ibid.

198 "the Roman amphitheater": Warner, "Battles of Brawn."

198 By the end of the year: (Cleveland) *Plain Dealer*, Nov. 21, 1906.

199 "small football explosion": Bob Carroll, and PFRA (Pro Football Researchers Association) Research, *The Ohio League: 1910–1919* (N. Huntingdon, Pa.: PFRA, 1997), 36. Prior to Jim's entry into the tight little world of this new sport, there were interesting overlaps. John McGraw's Christy Mathewson, a former fullback and excellent punter at Bucknell, played for the Pittsburgh Stars football team in 1902; the Stars, according to Robert W. Peterson, were probably funded by baseball's Barney Dreyfuss, who may have originally sent Jim to the Rocky Mount Railroaders, and definitely tried to sign him after the Olympic scandal broke. Also in 1902, the baseball Athletics manager, Connie Mack, was doubling as manager of the Philadelphia (football) Athletics; the team was coached by C. E. "Bondy" Wallace, who would be Canton's coach in the scandalous year of 1906. In late December 1902, while Jim was warming up to sports at Garden Grove School in Oklahoma and starting to think about Carlisle, Warner, back at Cornell as football coach, performed at Madison Square Garden in what would later be called the first football "world series." He and his brother Bill played for pay for the Syracuse (N.Y.) Athletic Club.

201 "ran like a deer": *Lafayette* (Ind.) *Journal and Courier* (1915), quoted in Jack Alkire, "Thorpe and Pine Village Teamed Up Against Purdue," *Lafayette Journal and Courier*, Nov. 24, 1977, RWWC.

201 "to make [the practice] interesting for himself": *Indiana Daily Student*, Nov. 29, 1915.

201 "any player crossing the goal line": Jack Cusack, *Pioneer in Pro Football: Jack Cusack's Own Story of the Period from 1912 to 1917, Inclusive, and the Year 1921* (Fort Worth, Texas: n.p., 1963), 16.

201 After two of Jim's field goals: (Cleveland) *Plain Dealer* reported that Knute Rockne caught the last pass of the game: "Thorpe's Toe Gives Canton Pros Victory," *Plain Dealer*, datelined Nov. 28, 1915, reprinted in *Scrapbook History of Pro Football*, ed. Richard M. Cohen, Jordan A. Deutsch, Roland T. Johnson, and David S. Neft (Indianapolis, Ind.: Bobbs-Merrill, 1976), 17. That claim has subsequently been disputed.

201 uniformed policeman with brass buttons: *The Ohio League: 1910–1919*, 43.

201 "A lengthy argument ensued": "Thorpe's Toe."

202 "hit the jackpot": Cusack, 12.

202 "Jim Thorpe has left": *LAT*, April 3, 1916.

203 "in great demand": *NYT*, April 2, 1916.

203 "a marvel of a baby": James F. Thorpe, Jr., baby book.

203 "strike zone discipline": Robert Hoie, interview. All subsequent quoted material of Hoie's comes from this source.

203 That summer, Jim filed: "Thorpe Sues for Libel: Asks $10,000 from Jersey Paper for Story of Alleged Row," *The Sporting Life*, June 10, 1916.

203 "depreciated the value of his services": Ibid.

203 "some interesting data": "May Open Up Thorpe's Case," June 8, 1916, unattributed news clip, BHOF.

203 "[e]very playing detail": *Canton Daily News*, Oct. 1, 1916.

204 "He simply wasn't the type": Cusack, 31.

204 "The player who, in his prime": Dr. Joseph Alexander interview.

205 "Thorpe sidestepped adversaries": *Canton Daily News*, Dec. 4, 1916.

205 "Kill Thorpe!": Shame on Fans Who Would Besmirch the Fair Name of Indian Jim Thorpe," *The Youngstown [Telegram*? illegible], n.d. [Nov. 1916], PFHOF. All quotations regarding this Youngstown game are taken from this source.

206 In 1929, Warner would tell: Paddock won a total of two gold and two silver medals at the 1920 and 1924 Games.

206 "While he may have lacked": Glenn S. Warner, quoted in Paddock, "Chief Bright Path."

206 "unexpected contact": Glenn S. Warner, quoted by Joseph Guyon in Jim Benagh, "We Remember Jim Thorpe," *Sport*, Dec. 1966.

206 "You try to stop a man": Joseph Guyon, quoted in ibid.

206 "Jim was always saving Jim": Wilbur F. Henry, quoted in *NYT*, March 28, 1943.

207 "a fierce competitor": Jack Cusack, quoted in "Jim Thorpe in Canton," unattributed news clip, n.d., Jim Thorpe clip file, CCHS.

207 "three or four long plays": Albert Earle "Greasy" Neale, as quoted in Gerald Holland, "Greasy Neale: Nothing to Prove, Nothing to Ask," *Sports Illustrated*, Aug. 24, 1964.

207 "a loveable fellow": Jack Cusack, quoted in "Jim Thorpe in Canton."

207 "I think I'll eat": Jim Thorpe, quoted in Benagh, "We Remember Jim Thorpe."

207 "I loved him and I say that": Jack Cusack, quoted in Frank Luksa, "Liquor: Hurdle Thorpe Didn't Clear," *Fort Worth Star-Telegram*, April 6, 1972.

207 "reticent fellow": Jack Cusack, quoted in Benagh, "We Remember Jim Thorpe."

207 "a lot of looking after": Jack Cusack, quoted in ibid.

207 "four drinks and he was gone": Jack Cusack, quoted in Luksa, "Liquor."

208 "took a terrible beating": Isaac Ray Martin, quoted in Wheeler, 267.

208 "grin that big grin": Ibid.

208 "I can still hear": Wilbur F. Henry, quoted in NYT, March 28, 1943.

208 "There was nothing dirty": Jack Cusack, quoted in Frank Luksa, "Power, Finesse
     Blended," Fort Worth Star-Telegram, April 4, 1972. All quoted material of Cusack
     here is taken from this source.

208 "outdoor life devoid of care and worry": Canton Repository, Dec. 14, 1916.

209 "He has a good education": Patent in Fee Report, 1916, RG75, Central Classified
     Files, 1907–1939, Sac and Fox, Oklahoma, File 25389-1916-312, NARA (Jim's Pat-
     ent Number was 548421).

209 "able-bodied, intelligent": Report on Application for a Patent in Fee, 1916, RG75,
     Central Classified Files, 1907–1939, Sac and Fox, Oklahoma, File 25389-1916-312,
     NARA.

209 "will be to you a symbol": Letter from Horace Johnson, superintendent and S.D.A.,
     Sac and Fox Indian School, to James Thorp, Dec. 15, 1916, Sac and Fox Letter
     Book, OHS.

210 "without precedent": "McGraw Loans Jim Thorpe to Matty's Reds," n.d. [April
     1917], unattributed, BHOF.

210 "dull and monotonous plateau": Lee Allen, "The Cincinnati Reds: The Oldest Club
     in Baseball," Sport (Baseball Jubilee Issue), May 1951.

210 "accelerate [Jim's] development": "McGraw Loans Jim Thorpe to Matty's Reds."

210 at least two hundred former Carlisle students: Bell, 365.

210 "was taking place on another planet": Alexander, 195.

211 "Yesterday": NYT, May 12, 1917.

212 "Thorpe's word": Henry McDonald quoted in Joe Horrigan, "Charles Follis Led
     Early Black Pioneers in Pro Football," http://www.profootballhof.com/history/
     release.aspx?release_id=1381. Jan. 18, 2010.

212 "personal indulgence": Dayton Herald, Dec. 14, 1917.

212 "my little family": Red Son, 68.

212 "absolutely abhorrent": Written note from Gail Margaret Thorpe to Michael Koeh-
     ler, quoted in Koehler, unpublished biography of Jim Thorpe.

213 "put up with him": Ibid.

213 "She was very strict": Ibid.

213 "Come here, Grace": Grace Thorpe interview.

213 "needed its athletics": The Baseball Magazine, April 1918.

214 "patched-together outfit": Alexander, 205.

214 Babe Ruth hit: Slugging percentage is a measure of the power of a hitter: total bases
     divided by at bats.

214 "The little Indian lad": NYT, Sept. 29, 1918.

214 "packed up the little fellow's baseball suit": Red Son, 69.

214 "the most precious": Ibid.

214 "Jim was never the same": Al Schacht, quoted in Wheeler, 164.

214 "He was brokenhearted": Iva Thorpe, quoted in Bernotas, 74.

215 "very sick": Gail Thorpe, quoted in Koehler, unpublished biography of Jim Thorpe.

215 "Nothing much mattered": Letter from Patricia Thorpe to Everett Freeman,

n.d. [April 1950], *Jim Thorpe—All American* production file, Warner Bros. Collection, USC.

215 "a dumb Indian": John McGraw, quoted by Schacht in Wheeler, 166.

215 "[i]t took half the team": Al Schacht, quoted in ibid.

216 A week later: *LAT*, July 20, 1919.

216 "certain unpleasantness": Lingo, "The Life Story of Jim Thorpe," chapter 5, Aug. 1923.

216 To the lifelong claim: Thorpe's career statistics for six years in the major leagues are 289 games; 91 runs scored; 82 runs batted in; .252 batting average. Joseph L. Reichler, ed., *The Baseball Encyclopedia: The Complete and Official Record of Major League Baseball*, 5th ed., revised and updated (New York: Macmillan, 1982), 1410.

217 "The Redskin looked good at times": *TSN*, May 29, 1919.

217 "freedom from restraint": Lingo, "The Life Story of Jim Thorpe," chapter 5, Aug. 1923.

217 "I must be old-fashioned": Jim Thorpe, "It's Mister Umpire."

217 DEAR GIRL JUST RECEIVED: Telegram from Jim Thorpe to Iva Thorpe, Sept. 17, 1919, Jim Thorpe Home.

219 "creak and creak": *Canton Repository*, Nov. 3, 1919.

219 "Jim had a fierce pride": George Halas, quoted in *Oh, How They Played*, 304.

219 "Jim," he recalled: George Halas with Gwen Morgan and Arthur Veysey, *Halas by Halas: The Autobiography of George Halas* (Chicago: Bonus Books, 1986), 52.

220 "Daddy stars as usual": Charlotte Thorpe baby book, Jim Thorpe Home.

220 "a tremendous blocker": Joseph Guyon, quoted in Benagh, "We Remember Jim Thorpe." All quoted material regarding the Rockne story comes from this source.

220 "It's the prettiest thing": Mark H. Devlin, Jr., quoted in *Lawrence* (Mass.) *Telegram*, Dec. 5, 1919.

220 Canton had again won: The one tie was another game against Hammond, who used that score to also claim the championship in the free-for-all mode of the time.

220 That last Massillon game: In thirty games from 1916 to 1919 the Bulldogs' defense had allowed a total of forty-three points, "in other words," according to analyst Bob Gill, "nobody was gaining much ground against them." Bob Gill, "A Legend Comes to Life: Jim Thorpe in the Days Before the NFL," *The Coffin Corner*, vol. 12, no. 2 (1990).

220 "Thorpe didn't put pro football": E-mail to author from Jim Campbell, April 30, 2002.

221 "Thorpe put the sport": Bob Carroll and PFRA (Professional Football Researchers Association) Research, *The Ohio League: 1910–1919* (North Huntingdon, Pa.: 1947), 42.

221 "greatness needs numbers": Bob Carroll, "Pro Football History: Passing the Test of Time; Thorpe's Greatness Can't Be Quantified with Statistics," April 22, 1998, www.profootballweekly.com.

CHAPTER NINE
Out of the Public Glare · *1920–1929*

223 "These are athletes": Rich Cohen, "The Boys of Winter: In Praise of the Aging Athlete," *Harper's Magazine*, June 2002.

223 "Liquor was medicine": Leslie Marmon Silko, *Ceremony* (New York: Penguin Books, 1986), 40.

224 "a hundred bucks in the room": George Halas, quoted in Peterson, 70.

224 "Our minds turned to Jim Thorpe": George Halas, 61. Halas recalled in his auto-biography that Jim was absent from the meeting; however, the minutes record that "Mr. Thorpe appointed" the committee: "Minutes of Meeting—September 17th—1920," signed by A. F. Ranney, the newly elected secretary-treasurer, PHFOF.

224 "Thorpe Named President": *Canton Repository*, Sept. 18, 1920. The term "commissioner" would be substituted in the 1940s.

225 "former stars of the college world": *NYT*, as quoted in Jeffrey Miller, "The New Pro League Is a Big Hit in the Big Apple: Buffalo Faces Canton in the Polo Grounds," *The Coffin Corner*, vol. 24, no. 6 (2002).

225 Jim played the entire game: "In this initial game at the Polo Grounds, which helped to legitimize pro football, Jim had a hand in all of the scoring. His third quarter field goal put Canton in the lead 3–0. Later in the same quarter his punt was blocked by [Adolph Frederick] 'Swede' Youngstrom and returned for a touchdown. Consequently, in this bruising defensive spectacle, the world's greatest all-around football player ironically had a hand (foot) in all of the game's points." E-mail to author from Robert Ricca, former head football coach at St. John's University, New York, Dec. 29, 2009.

225 "We had the better team": Jim Thorpe, quoted in *Canton Repository*, Dec. 5, 1920.

225 They voted unanimously: *Canton Repository*, Nov. 6, 1920.

226 "garish embellishment": Michael Oriard, *King Football: Sport and Spectacle in the Golden Age of Radio and Newsreels* (Chapel Hill: University of North Carolina Press, 2001), 28.

226 "hero journalism": James, *The Bill James Historical Baseball Abstract*, 133.

226 "a fifteen-yard run": Campbell interview.

226 "It was not simply": Roger Kahn, *A Flame of Pure Fire: Jack Dempsey and the Roaring '20's* (New York: Harcourt Brace, 1999), 131.

227 "rankled": *TSN*, Jan. 20, 1921.

227 "the most sudden and dramatic": James, 124.

227 Jim did well with Akron: Thirty-six doubles, thirteen triples, 122 runs batted in, nine home runs, and thirty-four stolen bases.

227 "The Indian can still hit": *TSN*, Dec. 16, 1920.

228 Three days later it was revealed: *LAT*, Jan. 18, 1921. The Detroit sale was probably a device to circumvent the waiver that would have been required from other International League teams before Jim could be sold directly to Toledo.

229 "deep in the red": *Bulldogs on Sunday: 1921*, A PFRA (Professional Football Researchers Association) Publication, n.d., n.p.

229 "heavy financial losses": *LAT*, Mar. 24, 1922.

229 "an $11,000 asset or liability": *LAT*, March 11, 1922.

229 "Jim is a redman": *LAT*, March 14, 1922.

229 Thorpe's football origin: *LAT*, April 13, 1922.

230 "Well, now, I'm a professional football player": *San Francisco Call and Post*, May 12, 1922.

230 "run to daylight": Vince Lombardi, *Run to Daylight* (New York: Simon & Schuster, 1963).

231 "the champion's enduring insecurity": Harvey Araton, "Another Positive Test, Another Test of Faith," *NYT*, Aug. 20, 2006.

231 "Hartford welcomes": *The Hartford Daily Times*, June 14, 1922.

231   "imitations of a wooden Indian": *NYT,* July 12, 1922.

231   "hoots and howls": *TSN,* July 20, 1922.

231   "partly dressed": Ibid.

232   "on one of those rampages": Ibid.

232   Years later, a reporter: *The American Weekly,* n.d. [c. 1952], Jim Thorpe Drop File, CCHS.

232   "big-hearted": "I Remember: Ike Martin Remembers Jim Thorpe," n.d., unattributed news clip, PFHOF.

232   "always a likeable chap": Glenn S. Warner, quoted in Danzig, 173.

233   "American Airedale": Herman L. Masin, "Meet Jim Thorpe: Greatest Athlete of Them All," *Senior Scholastic,* May 7, 1952.

234   Pete Calac, as well as: Joe Guyon went on to play outfield in 1925 with the first-place American Association Louisville Colonels, leading the league in batting with .363. He played football the same year for the Rock Island Independents with Jim, and later for the New York Giants. He was elected to the Pro Football Hall of Fame in 1966. Perhaps Jim's closest friend, Calac, after one year with the Buffalo All-Stars, came back to Ohio to play with the Bulldogs in 1925. The following year he joined the Canton police department, where he stayed until his retirement in 1950. Though nominated for the Hall of Fame, Calac was not selected, a decision many disagreed with.

235   "Rig [an Indian] out": Walter Lingo, quoted in *Success,* Feb. 1923.

235   The headlines in the *Marion Star: Marion Star,* Oct. 6, 1922, as quoted in Charles Frueling Springwood, "Playing Football, Playing Indian: A History of the Native Americans Who Were the NFL's Oorang Indians," *Native Athletes in Sport and Society: A Reader,* C. Richard King, ed. (Lincoln: University of Nebraska Press, 2005), 132.

235   Lingo's team ended the season: The Oorang Indians played nine NFL games in 1922: Dayton Triangles, Columbus Panhandles (win), Canton Bulldogs, Akron Pros, Minneapolis Marines, Chicago Bears, Milwaukee Badgers, Buffalo All-Americans (win), and Columbus Panhandles, again (win). They played four nonleague games: Bucyrus (Ohio) Cranes (win), Indianapolis Belmonts (win), Durant (Mich.) All-Stars, and the Baltimore Pros.

235   "electrified the crowd": Robert L. Whitman, *Jim Thorpe and the Oorang Indians: N.F.L.'s Most Colorful Franchise* (Defiance, Ohio: The Hubbard Company, 1984), 60. Also, Bob Braunwart, Bob Carroll, and Joe Horrigan, "Oorang Indians Media Guide, 1922–1923," Professional Football Researchers Association, 1981, 20.

235   "Athletes come and athletes go": Bert Collyer, quoted in *Cape May City Beacon,* May 23, 1927.

236   "Cut that damn thing off!": Jim Thorpe, quoted by Jimmy Conzelman in Benagh, "We Remember Jim Thorpe."

236   "For some reason": Jimmy Conzelman, quoted in *American Record* (Boston), Jan. 8, 1969.

236   "shouldered" her in: Ibid.

236   "sport mania": *Football World,* Oct. 1921

236   "There has been quite an effort": *TSN,* July 5, 1923.

236   Jim put together his 1923 Oorang team: The 1923 Oorang Indians played ten NFL games: Milwaukee Badgers, Toledo Maroons, Minneapolis Marines, Buffalo All-Americans, Cleveland Indians, Chicago Bears, St. Louis All-Stars, Canton Bull-

dogs, Columbus Tigers, Chicago Cardinals, and Louisville Brecks (win). Their one nonleague game was against the Marion Athletic Club (win).

237   "partied all the time": Ed Healy, quoted in www.baron-von-aliff.home.att.net/what's-an-oorang.html. Jan. 18, 2010. Ed Healy was bought by George Halas from the Rock Island Independents in 1922, making him "so far as is known—the first pro football player to be sold." *Great Football Writing: Sports Illustrated, 1954–2006*, ed. Rob Fleder (New York: Sports Illustrated Books, 2006), 18.

237   "White people": Leon Boutwell, quoted in Whitman, 69.

237   "A few of the players": Pete Calac, quoted in "Sport Pickups," Jan. 25, 1968, unattributed news clip, RWWC.

237   "sandlot football": Bob Lingo, quoted in Chris Willis, "Remembering the Oorang Indians, Part 2: An Interview with Bob Lingo," *The Coffin Corner*, vol. 24, no. 4 (2002).

237   "I couldn't breathe so good": Jim Thorpe, quoted in *Bulldogs on Sunday: 1922*, a PFRA (Professional Football Researchers Association) publication, n.d., n.p., 19.

237   "bread and butter and babies' boots": *Red Son*, 72.

238   "ironically . . . offered": Philip Deloria, " 'I Am of the Body': Thoughts on My Grandfather, Culture and Sports," *South Atlantic Quarterly* 95:2 (1996): 321–38. Also quoted in Springwood, "Playing Football, Playing Indian," 139.

238   "at the crack of dawn," "I never saw anybody": Bob Lingo, quoted in Chris Willis, "Remembering the Oorang Indians, Part 2."

238   "the thread of my marital happiness snapped," "incompatibility": *Red Son*, 72.

239   "cheated": Mrs. Harrison Ground, interview with Robert W. Wheeler, RWWC.

239   "I sure loved him": Iva Thorpe, quoted in Grace Thorpe interview.

240   "The crowd went wild": *Lawrence* (Mass.) *Telegram*, June 7, 1924. The author thanks Louise Sandberg, Special Collections, Lawrence Public Library, for providing her with photocopies of Thorpe-related articles from the *Telegram*, April 30–Sept. 22, 1924.

240   "Honey talk about being lonely": Letter from Jim Thorpe to Freeda Kirkpatrick, July 7, 1924. All subsequent quotations of Thorpe in letters to Freeda Kirkpatrick come from the collection of his letters to her written from June 29 to Aug. 3, 1924, and from Dec. 21, 1925, to Feb. 18, 1926, CCHS. The author thanks Bill Thorpe and the late Robbie Thorpe for providing her with photocopies of the letters prior to their sale at Sotheby's in 2007 to the Cumberland County Historical Society.

241   "purposely . . . caught off second": *Lawrence* (Mass.) *Telegram*, Aug. 12, 1924.

241   stuck it out until mid-September: The Independents and the North Cambridge team decided between themselves to hold a "little world series" (*Lawrence* [Mass.] *Telegram*, Sept. 4, 1924) to decide the contested game. The Cambridge team wiped up the Independents in four straight wins after Lawrence won the first game.

242   The *Telegram* noted: *Lawrence* (Mass.) *Telegram*, Sept. 19, 1924.

242   "Jim had gotten old": Jimmy Conzelman, quoted in *NYT*, March 30, 1943.

242   "easy wins and middling crowds": Bob Braunwart and Bob Carroll, "The Rock Island Independents," *The Coffin Corner* vol. 5, no. 3 (1983).

242   the 1924 Indian Citizenship Act: Its authorship was credited to Senator Charles Curtis, who as a Kansas congressman had written the 1898 Curtis Act, extending allotment to the Oklahoma lands of the Five Nations.

242   "combination of muscle and intellect": *LAT*, Nov. 20, 1920.

243   "setting the claws": D. H. Lawrence, quoted in James Wilson, *The Earth Shall Weep: History of Native America* (New York: Grove Press, 2000), 336.

243   "in bad circumstances": Telegram from George V. Labadie to commissioner of Indian Affairs, Department of the Interior, Sept. 10, 1924, RG75, Central Classified Files, Shawnee, 61295-24-311, NARA.

243   "educated competent Indians": Letter from Assistant Commissioner of Indian Affairs to Superintendent A. W. Leech, Shawnee Indian Agency, April 30, 1925, RG75, Central Classified Files 1907–1939, Sac and Fox Oklahoma, Box 46, File 28909-1925-225, NARA.

244   "a very high class lady": Letter from Fred S. Cook, superintendent, Land Department, the Prairie Oil and Gas Company, to Hon. Phil P. Campbell, Sept. 20 ,1927, RG75, Central Classified Files–Haskell File 47676-1928-820, NARA.

244   "great big Packard car": Steiger and Thorpe, *Thorpe's Gold*, 27. All quotations of Charlotte Thorpe in this paragraph are taken from this source.

244   "It was like the big hero": Gail Thorpe, quoted in Koehler, unpublished biography of Jim Thorpe. Gail joined a Catholic Youth Organization basketball team in Chicago and was scouted to play professionally, but got married instead. Later she would earn a B.A. and M.B.A. from Northeastern Oklahoma University.

245   "Jim Thorpe Fades from Sports Scene": *NYT*, Oct. 29, 1925.

245   "in fine physical condition": "Jim Thorpe to Play with N.Y. Gridders," Sept. 29, 1925, unattributed news clip, PFHOF.

245   "to show anything": "Jim Thorpe Gets Release," Oct. 29, 1925, unattributed news clip, PFHOF.

245   "Observers see the end": Ibid.

245   "signed another contract": *NYT*, Oct. 29, 1925.

245   DEAR FOLKS: Telegram from Freeda and Jim Thorpe to Mr. and Mrs. W. L. Fitzpatrick, Oct. 23, 1925, CCHS.

245   "She came into my life": *Red Son*, 74.

246   "too many years": Rock Island *Argus*, n.d. [1924], PFHOF.

246   "I'd have been more popular": Harold "Red" Grange, quoted in Ira Berkow, "A Conversation with the Ghost," in Joseph L. Vecchione, *The New York Times Book of Sports Legends* (New York: Random House, 1991), 86.

246   "first problem": Harry A. Williams, "Sport Shrapnel," *LAT*, Sept. 19, 1923. All quotations of Williams in this section are taken from this source.

247   "I certainly have had my share": Jim Thorpe–Freeda Thorpe letters at CCHS. All subsequent quoted material in these letters is from this source.

247   "Jim was old, fat and slow": Red Grange, "The College Game Is Easier," *Saturday Evening Post*, Nov. 5, 1932.

247   "They rave about Grange": Manning Vaughan, "Jim Thorpe Nears End of Trail," n.d., unattributed clip, PFHOF.

248   "genteel poverty of amateurism": Red Grange, quoted in *LAT*, Dec. 29, 1929.

248   "a couple bags of peanuts": George Trafton, interview by Robert W. Wheeler, RWWC.

249   "Ernie gave me sixty minutes": Glenn S. Warner, quoted in Arthur Daley, " 'Greater than Jim Thorpe,' " *Milwaukee Journal*, May 16, 1965.

249   "deep in his heart": W. W. "Pudge" Heffelfinger, as told to John McCallum, *This Was Football* (New York: A. S. Barnes and Company, 1954), 58. Heffelfinger died in April 1954.

249   "the wildest barnstorming trips": Bob Carroll, Michael Gershman, David Neft, John Thorn, Elias Sports Bureau, David Pietrusza, managing editor, *Total Football:*

The Official Encyclopedia of the National Football League (New York: HarperCollins, 1997), 16.

249 "broke down mentally": Guy Chamberlin (Frankford Yellow Jackets player-coach), quoted in John M. Carroll, "The Impact of Red Grange on Pro Football in 1925," *The Coffin Corner,* vol. 20, 1998.

249 "that pro football didn't": Tim Mara, quoted in John Devaney, "From Rags to Riches: The Story of Professional Football," *The American Legion Magazine,* Oct. 1966.

249 "Numbers of ball enthusiasts": *NYT,* June 15, 1931.

250 "a wonderful guy": Berkow, "A Conversation with the Ghost."

250 "I have really played": *NYT,* Jan. 16, 1926.

250 "I'll never quit athletics": *Columbus Citizen,* Jan. 22, 1926, PFHOF.

250 "The people see something": "Thorpe Is Still a Football Player," Jan. 22, 1926 [illegible attribution], PFHOF.

252 "another famous red man": *LAT,* April 25, 1926.

252 "young hopefuls": Ibid.

252 "Thorpe has run the gamut": Ibid.

252 "Fritz Pollard and Jim Thorpe Shine": Reprint from the *Hartford Courant,* reproduced in *Scrapbook History of Pro Football,* ed. Richard M. Cohen, Jordan A. Deutsch, Roland T. Johnson, and David S. Neft (Indianapolis, Ind.: Bobbs-Merrill, 1976), 37.

252 "to please the fans": *Akron Beacon-Journal,* as quoted in Phil Dietrich, *Down Payments: Professional Football 1896–1930 as Viewed from the Summit; Professional Football in Akron* (N. Huntingdon, Pa.: Professional Football Researchers Association, 1995), 167.

253 "Okay, but my boys": Recollection of Akron Indians player Paul Sheeks, quoted in ibid., 166.

253 "The Indian hit me": Ernie Nevers, quoted in Arthur Daley, " 'Greater Than Jim Thorpe,' " *Milwaukee Journal,* May 16, 1965.

253 "rather quiet self-contained individual": Guy T. "Zeke" Roberts quoted in unattributed news clip, n.d., PFHOF.

254 "I thought they had forgotten": Unattributed news clip, n.d. [1941], Jim Thorpe Scrapbook, CCHS.

254 "eking a living": *Red Son,* 75.

255 "the new Ohio State League.": *Akron Beacon-Journal,* Sept. 13, 1927, quoted in Dietrich, *Down Payments,* 171.

255 "Now what are you fellows": "Coach Thorpe to Start Game Sunday; Tanks Here Nov. 6," n.d. [1927], unattributed news clip, PFHOF.

255 "the first time": Ibid.

255 "Thorpe Slowed Up, But Memories of Great Past Draw Crowd to See Him": News clip, n.d. [1927], unattributed, reproduced in Carl M. Becker, "Jim Thorpe Comes to Portsmouth . . . and Leaves," *Timeline* (a publication of the Ohio Historical Society), Sept.–Oct., 2001.

256 "The years are leaving": "Famous Athletes to Perform Here," reprint of [Dec. 1927] unattributed news article, Marion [Ohio] County Historical Society.

256 "the ballyhoo year": Frederick Lewis Allen, quoted in Kahn, 404.

256 "artifacts of Thorpe's athletic career": Bill Pennington, "Jim Thorpe and a Ticket to Serendipity," *NYT,* Mar. 29, 2005.

256   "Thorpe is considered done now.": News clip, April 13, 1928, unattributed, BHOF.

256   "pretty blue": *Red Son*, 77.

257   "Jim Thorpe . . . played": *NYT*, Nov. 30, 1928.

257   Jim's last humiliating football game: Brookings Institution, Institute for Government Research, "The Problem of Indian Administration: Report of a Survey Made at the Request of Honorable Hubert Work, Secretary of the Interior, and Submitted to Him, February 21, 1928" (Baltimore: Johns Hopkins Press, 1928). Online facsimile: http://www.alaskool.org/native_ed/research_reports/IndianAdmin/Indian_Admin_Problms.html (accessed Dec. 19, 2009).

257   "wish to remain Indians": Meriam Report, quoted in Jacquelyn Kilpatrick, *Celluloid Indians: Native Americans and Film* (Lincoln: University of Nebraska Press, 1999), 40.

257   "retarded race": Meriam Report, quoted in Berkhofer, *The White Man's Indian*, 182.

257   "long professional career": Daniel J. Ferris, secretary of the AAU, quoted in *NYT*, May 2, 1929.

258   "trifle fantastic,": *LAT*, May 3, 1929.

258   "just a little ballyhoo": Daniel J. Ferris, quoted in *NYT*.

258   "American College Athletics": Howard Savage, et al., *Current Developments in American College Athletics, with a Preface by Henry Suzallo, President of the Foundation, Bulletin Number 26* (New York: Carnegie Foundation for the Advancement of Teaching, 1931).

258   "vicious" connection: James Bryant Conant, quoted in *NYT*, May 19, 1935.

PART III: LIFE AFTER SPORTS

CHAPTER TEN
Hollywood · *1930–1939*

261   "I was a kid": James Jones, *From Here to Eternity* (New York: Charles Scribner's Sons, 1951), 468.

261   "They thought I was the Indian": Sherman Alexie, *Ten Little Indians: Stories* (New York: Grove Press, 2003), 42.

261   "I'm working with the paint crew": *LAT*, March 19, 1930.

262   "The Jack [money] received": Letter from Jim Thorpe to Chief Buffalo Long Lance (aka Sylvester Long), Dec. 30, 1929. U.S. Army Military History Institute, Carlisle Barracks Collection, Carlisle Indian School Athletics, U.S. Army War College, Carlisle, Pa. The author photocopied the two letters cited in these endnotes at the Military History Institute (MHI) in 2002. A subsequent attempt in 2010 to confirm the citation, after a thorough search by institute archivists, was unsuccessful: the letters could not be found. The letters were cited by Sylvester Long's biographer Donald Smith (*Chief Buffalo Long Lance: The Glorious Impersonator*, Red Deer, Alberta, Canada: Red Deer Press, 1999, footnote 6, p. 366), and Smith confirmed to the author that he had seen them when researching his book (e-mail from Smith to author, Feb. 19, 2010). John Slonaker, the MHI archivist who assisted Smith in his research, confirmed to the author that the letters were in the collection prior to his retirement in 1999 (e-mail from Slonaker to author, Mar. 3, 2010). The author has given photocopies of the two handwritten letters on "Overland Hotel" stationery from Jim Thorpe cited here to the CCHS, including a photocopy of the stamped

envelope of one of them addressed to "Chief B. C. Long Lance, Explorers Club, New York City, N.Y.," postmarked 1929.

263 "Your letter rec'd": Letter from Thorpe to Long Lance, Jan. 3, 1930, U.S. Army Military History Institute. See previous endnote.

263 "canonization": Oriard, *King Football*, 291.

263 "a giant figure of a man": Charley Paddock, "The Greatest Athlete's Greatest Thrill," *American Magazine*, July 1929.

263 "interesting suburb": *Red Son*, 77.

263 "gaze across the sloping plain": Ibid., 78.

263 "It is the best training": Jim Thorpe, quoted in news clip, Jan. 15, 1930, unattributed, PFHOF.

264 "natural as a fresh": Ceil Blanchard, interview. All quoted material of Blanchard's is from this source.

265 "California is ripe": Jim Thorpe quoted in *LAT*, Jan. 25, 1931.

265 "I guess it's an old story": Jim Thorpe, quoted in *NYT*, March 4, 1931.

265 "properly awed": Ibid.

265 "swallow[ing] his pride": *LAT*, March 4, 1931.

265 "cracking the whip": *Outlook*, March 25, 1931.

266 "arrived twenty years too soon": *LAT*, March 8, 1931.

266 "fabulous sum": Ibid.

266 "I hold it a great pleasure": Jim Thorpe, quoted in "Jim Thorpe to Coach at County School," n.d. [1931], unattributed Oklahoma news clip, Jim Thorpe Association, Oklahoma City.

266 In 1918, when he was refused: "Liquor was available by free delivery 24 hours a day from bootleggers . . . Bootleggers freely distributed business cards bearing their telephone numbers, and many had current price lists on their reverse sides" (http://www.oeta.tv/stateline.html). Will Rogers once said that "Oklahoma would remain dry as long as its voters were sober enough to stagger to the polls." See Jimmie Lewis Franklin, *Born Sober: Prohibition in Oklahoma, 1907–1959* (Norman: University of Oklahoma Press, 1971). The author thanks Robert Henry for the loan of his copy of this book.

266 When he and his brother Frank: Jack Thorpe, interview.

267 "[H]e sidles modestly": *LAT*, June 25, 1931. All quoted material of Grace Kingsley's comes from this source.

267 "men and women whose names": *NYT*, March 20, 1932.

268 "he's humming": *LAT*, Oct. 29, 1935.

268 "humiliating demonstrations": Beverly R. Singer, *Wiping the War Paint Off the Lens: Native American Film and Video* (Minneapolis: University of Minnesota Press, 2001), 22.

268 "those stirring events": Michael Hilger, *The American Indian in Film* (Metuchen, N.J.: Scarecrow Press, 1986), 21.

268 "the untrue and libelous brand": *The Red Man*, December 1911. CCHS.

269 "screaming savage": William W. Savage, Jr., ed. *Indian Life: Transforming an American Myth* (Norman: University of Oklahoma Press, 1977), 9.

269 "has had to pay": Donald L. Kaufmann, "The Indian as Media Hand-Me-Down," in *The Pretend Indians: Images of Native Americans in the Movies*, ed. Gretchen M. Bataille and Charles L. P. Silet (Ames: Iowa State University Press, 1980), 34.

270 "traditional political": Nicholas G. Rosenthal, "Representing Indians: Native

American Actors on Hollywood's Frontier," *The Western Historical Quarterly* 36 (Autumn 2005).

271   "I wanted to go down": Red Fox (Chief), *Memoirs of Chief Red Fox* (New York: McGraw-Hill, 1971), 157.

271   "I always lost": Jim Thorpe, quoted in Ceil Blanchard interview.

271   "never saw the day": William Gardner, quoted in *LAT*, Oct. 25, 1931.

271   "Rockne Recalls": This was an eighteen-part series prepared for exclusive publication in the *Los Angeles Times* before Rockne's death in March 1931 and appeared in the paper after his death. The part that focused on Jim: *LAT*, April 6, 1933.

273   "no indication of worry": *NYT*, March 22, 1932. For a full recounting of Long's life and the circumstances of his death, see Donald B. Smith, *Chief Buffalo Long Lance: The Glorious Impersonator*.

273   "a number of Indians present": *LAT*, March 25, 1932.

275   "smartly attired," "most impressive delegations," "strangely reluctant," "[a]pparently": *LAT*, July 31, 1932.

275   "sob story": *LAT*, Feb. 18, 1960.

275   "I was not only surprised": Charles Curtis, quoted in *LAT*, Aug. 1, 1932.

275   At the Games, nine minutes: *LAT*, July 3, 1941.

276   "It had to be another Indian": Jim Thorpe, quoted in *LAT*, Aug. 2, 1932.

276   "those who engage in sport": Amendment to AAU constitution, quoted in *Kansas City Times*, Nov. 17, 1931.

276   "old-fashioned idealism": *Chicago Daily News*, April 23, 1934.

276   "In a spiritual way": Edgar Munzel, "Brundage's 25 Years with Amateurs," [1930], unattributed news clip, Scrapbook 12A, Record Series 26/20/37, Avery Brundage Collection, University of Illinois at Urbana-Champaign.

276   "proudly claimed and zealously guarded": Young, 83.

277   "official welcoming to Los Angeles": *LAT*, Aug. 12, 1932.

278   "an army of sports stars": *LAT*, Oct. 23, 1932.

278   "Glad to see you at work": Lionel Barrymore, quoted in *LAT*, Dec. 26, 1932. All quoted material relevant to this anecdote is taken from this source.

278   "monstrous eroticism": *Pacific Film Archive*, Nov. 1990.

278   "symbolic dream of world domination": *L.A. Weekly*, Aug. 14, 1998.

278   "never intended to be anything": Merian C. Cooper, quoted in *LAT*, March 24, 1989.

280   "joshing with the guys": Bill Thorpe, interview. All quotations of Bill Thorpe's, unless otherwise noted, are from this source.

280   "A big, friendly guy": Phil Thorpe, quoted in Paul Zimmerman, "Calling Signals," unattributed news clip, Oct. [25? notation on photocopy is unclear], 1974, PFHOF. All quoted material from Phil Thorpe in this section is taken from this source.

280   "never appeared": Iron Eyes Cody [Espera DeCorti], *Iron Eyes: My Life as a Hollywood Indian* (New York: Everest House, 1982), 148.

280   "Jim was so likeable": Earl Miller, quoted in Koehler, unpublished biography of Jim Thorpe.

280   "dour and withdrawn": Cody, 151.

281   "didn't like that stuff": Garland Nevitt, interview by Robert W. Wheeler, RWWC.

281   "local bully boys": Steiger and Thorpe, *Thorpe's Gold*, 222.

281   "periodic drinker": Gail Thorpe, quoted in Koehler, unpublished biography of Jim Thorpe.

281 "Many, many times": Bill Thorpe, quoted in Frank Luksa, "Thorpe Left a Special Legacy to His Son," *Fort Worth Star-Telegram*, undated, c. 1970, PFHOF.

281 "When he was drinking": Phil Thorpe, quoted in Zimmerman, "Calling Signals."

281 "As a father": Jack Thorpe, interview.

282 "so graceful": Grace Thorpe, interview. All quotations of Grace Thorpe's in this section, unless otherwise noted, come from this source.

282 "running around wild": Richard Thorpe, interview. All quotations of Dick Thorpe's, unless otherwise noted, come from this source.

282 "a sad thing," "It bothered him": Bob Greene, "Jim Thorpe Lived Sad Life, His Daughter Recalls," *Columbus Dispatch*, Aug. 10, 1992, PFHOF.

282 "Don't use my name": Jim Thorpe, quoted in Grace Thorpe interview.

282 "one move": Phil Thorpe, quoted in "Calling Signals."

282 "Either catch it": Jim Thorpe, quoted in Bill Thorpe interview.

282 "Actually . . . we couldn't swim": Phil Thorpe, quoted in "Calling Signals."

283 "The car's that way": Jim Thorpe, quoted in Bill Thorpe interview.

283 "integrated, inwardly-seeking": John Collier, quoted in Wilson, 345.

284 Collier's legacy: Berkhofer, 186.

284 "very well-pronounced bulging waistline": A. Grant Carrow, "Remembering a Night When Jim Thorpe Came to Lowell," c. 1991, unattributed news clip, probably a local Lowell newspaper, Jim Thorpe drop file, CCHS. All quotations of Carrow's in this section are taken from this source.

285 "the need for this money": Telegram from Jim Thorpe to Interior Secretary John Collier, Oct. 4, 1933, RG75, Central Classified Files, Seminole 34605-24-306, NARA.

285 "I am from California": Letter from Jim Thorpe to Senator William McAdoo, Oct. 7, 1933, in ibid.

285 "upon the Red Cross": Letter from Susey Harjo to Interior Secretary John Collier, Oct. 10, 1933, in ibid.

285 "real bargain": Letter from Jim Thorpe to Interior Secretary John Collier, Jan. 6, 1934 [Thorpe incorrectly dated the handwritten letter as 1933], in ibid.

285 "$1465.00 Dollars": Letter from Jim Thorpe to President Franklin D. Roosevelt, Feb. 1, 1935, in ibid.

286 "borrowed money on several occasions": Letter from Jim Thorpe to Governor E. W. Marland, Feb. 5, 1935, in ibid.

286 "The business affairs of the team": Letter from superintendent at Muskogee Landman, June 25, 1935, in ibid.

286 "claimed to be without": Letter from field agent in Holdenville to superintendent at Muskogee Landman, Feb. 4, 1936, in ibid.

286 "Your Excellency": Letter from Jim Thorpe to President Franklin D. Roosevelt, May 31, 1937, in ibid.

287 "the outstanding fullback": *LAT*, Nov. 20, 1934.

287 "Famous Redskins and Characters of the Old West Assemble": *LAT*, July 5, 1934.

288 "thump pretty heftily": *LAT*, May 30, 1935.

288 "collecting his tribesmen": *LAT*, July 18, 1935.

289 "The redskins have been": *LAT*, Dec. 1, 1935. All quoted material regarding the casting of *The Good Earth* is taken from this source.

289 "Thanksgiving for Rainfall": *LAT*, Aug. 26, 1935.

290 "Funny thing": *LAT*, June 13, 1935.

290 "boasted and gloried": Abe Kronenberg, quoted in Gray Cutler, "Jim Thorpe: Native American Legend," *Films in Review*, July/August 1996.

291 "another vile picture": Editorial, *Gaelic American*, Aug. 25, 1934, quoted in letter from Edwin P. Kilroe to George F. Wasson, Fox Film Studios, Aug. 30, 1934, *Under Pressure*, FXLR 1006, University of California at Los Angeles.

291 "85 percent Irish," "few friends": Memo letter from Borden Chase to George F. Wasson, Fox Film Studios, n.d., in ibid.

291 "slightly soiled but intrinsically 'good' ": *Hollywood Reporter*, Sept. 20, 1935.

291 "[f]rank melodrama": *Variety*, Feb. 20, 1935.

291 "a gaudy, spectacular": *NYT*, July 26, 1935.

292 "former rodeo singers": *Variety*, Oct. 16, 1935.

292 "weave of radicalism": *Variety*, Nov. 6, 1935.

292 "big business": Press book, *Fighting Youth* production file, Warner Bros. Collection, USC.

292 "corker": *Variety*, Nov. 6, 1935.

292 "in towns where there is": *Variety*, Aug. 14, 1935.

292 "sundry athletes": *LAT*, Nov. 18, 1935.

292 "stirring and ebullient swashbuckler": *The New Yorker*, Dec. 21, 1992.

293 "northwestern yarn": *Variety*, May 26, 1937.

293 "brim[med] with horsemanship and gunplay": *Variety*, June 3, 1936.

294 "presents the Indians": *Treachery Rides the Trail* [an earlier title]; A Warner Bros. First National Picture; "The Story," n.d., *Treachery Rides the Range* Production File, Warner Bros. Collection, USC.

294 "[W]e do not want": Interoffice Communication from J. L. Warner to Bryan Foy, Dec. 12, 1935, *Treachery Rides the Range* Production File, Warner Bros. Collection, USC.

294 "an almost complete ignorance": Stanley Vestal, "The Hollywooden Indian," *Southwest Review* 21 (1936): 418–23, as reprinted in Gretchen M. Bataille and Charles L. P. Silet, eds., *The Pretend Indians: Images of Native Americans in the Movies* (Ames: Iowa State University Press, 1980), 63. All quoted material regarding this article comes from this source.

294 "Yes, sir, I sure would": *Oklahoma City Times*, June 27, 1935.

294 "Taking the competitors' standpoint": *LAT*, Dec. 9, 1935.

294 "They must go and do their best": (Harrisburg) *Patriot-News*, "The Sports Shop" column by sportswriter Al Clark, April 1, 1953.

295 "It is a house": *LAT*, June 8, 1936. All quotations from this interview are taken from this source.

295 "the greatest Olympic Games ever held": *LAT*, July 25, 1936. Brundage remained proud of the 1936 Olympics, going so far as to claim in 1952 that the IOC "was the only organization, not barring the League of Nations, which laid down the law to the Nazis before World War II—and made it stick." Avery Brundage, "My Biggest Olympic Battles," *This Week*, June 29, 1952. All subsequent quoted material is taken from this source.

295 "rather soured on the world": *LAT*, July 9, 1936.

296 "De Mille Indians": *New York Herald Tribune*, Nov. 17, 1940.

296 "Jim Thorpe Takes Warpath": *LAT*, Sept. 24, 1936.

296 "It is unfair to the Indian": Ibid.

297 "talk and grunt like morons": Indian Actors Association, quoted in Angela Aleiss,

Making the White Man's Indian: Native Americans and Hollywood Movies (Westport, Conn.: Praeger Publishers, 2005), 54.

297 "given all the breaks": *LAT*, Sept. 28, 1936. All subsequent quotations regarding DeMille, unless otherwise noted, are taken from this source. These are not direct quotations of DeMille, but rather the *Times* restating his opinions.

297 "I wanted Indians": Cecil B. DeMille, quoted in Aleiss, 57.

297 "in many instances": *LAT*, Oct. 11, 1936.

298 "atmosphere": *Oklahoma City Times*, June 27, 1935.

299 "lecturer to our American youth": Instruction sheet to "The Principal," given to schools hosting Jim Thorpe, n.d., PFHOF.

299 developed four topics: "Jim Thorpe," publicity brochure printed by W. Colston Leigh, Inc., 521 Fifth Ave., New York City, PFHOF. All quoted material regarding Thorpe's lecture topics is taken from this source.

299 "really a nice job": Freeda Thorpe, interview with Robert L. Whitman, 1984. The author thanks Dr. Whitman for graciously allowing her to use this interview. All quotations of Freeda Thorpe's, unless otherwise noted, are taken from this source.

300 "What am I supposed to do": Gail Thorpe, quoted in Koehler, unpublished biography of Jim Thorpe.

300 Luella wondered: Whitman, *Jim Thorpe and the Oorang Indians*, 93.

300 "big Jim Thorpe": Ibid.

301 "Angered," said Luella: Luella Hoffmire Auker, quoted in ibid.

301 "I can't have it": Jim Thorpe, quoted in ibid.

301 Jack Thorpe once watched: Crawford, 228.

301 "one too many beers": Whitman, *Jim Thorpe and the Oorang Indians*, 93.

301 "a big, husky fellow,": George Yuda, interview. All quoted material of Yuda's comes from this source.

302 "raised nothing and are unable": Telegram from Senator Elmer Thomas to President Franklin D. Roosevelt, Sept. 22, 1936, Elmer Thomas Collection, Carl Albert Center, University of Oklahoma.

303 "an attempt to drive": Jim Thorpe, quoted in *LAT*, Dec. 6, 1937.

303 "Outnumbered one hundred to one": Hagan, 262.

303 "fat and fiftyish": *NYT*, Dec. 26, 1937.

304 "The government insists": Jim Thorpe, quoted in ibid.

304 "Communistic cooperatives": *LAT*, Jan. 31, 1938.

304 "were able to use the right": E-mail to author from Jack Thorpe.

305 "the full sweep of tribal": Robert Henry, "Nations Within a Nation: Once They Ruled This Continent. Now They'd Like to Rule Themselves." *Oklahoma Today*, May–June 1992.

305 "Only tough guys wanted!": Press book, *Big City* production file, Warner Bros. Collection, USC.

305 "a glorious fistic melee": *Daily Variety*, Aug. 25, 1937.

305 "Guards Save 180 Actors": *LAT*, May 30, 1938.

305 "A dangerous bluff for jobs": *Hollywood Citizen-News*, n.d. [May 1938].

306 "[o]ne thing we never had much of": Phil Thorpe, quoted in "Calling Signals."

307 "Nothing distinguishes": *Variety*, n.d., [1938], *Cattle Raiders* clip file, Margaret Herrick Library, The Academy of Motion Picture Arts and Sciences.

307 "has run the gamut": *Variety*, n.d. [1938], *Frontier Scout* clip file, Margaret Herrick Library, The Academy of Motion Picture Arts and Sciences.

307 "To what extent": Group Discussion Guide, vol. 4, Series of 1939, no. 3, *Guide to the Critical Appreciation of the Photoplay Dealing with the Career of Sam Houston*, Educational and Recreational Guides, Inc., gen. ed. Max J. Herzberg, *Man of Conquest* clip file, Margaret Herrick Library, The Academy of Motion Picture Arts and Sciences.

307 "the bilking of the Cherokees": *NYT*, April 28, 1939.

307 "exceptional in its honesty": *Daily Worker*, April 29, 1939.

308 "racial unity": Aleiss, 70.

308 "Having brought your proven record": Letter from Reichssportsführer Hans von Tschammer und Osten to Avery Brundage, Aug. 8, 1938, quoted in Robert Lipsyte, "Olympics: Evidence Ties Olympic Taint to 1936 Games," *NYT*, Feb. 21, 1999. Avery Brundage Collection, University of Illinois at Urbana-Champaign.

308 "the overwhelming proportion": Letter from Avery Brundage to Karl Ritter von Halt, quoted in ibid.

308 "do nothing to stop the present conflict": "Olympic Board Regrets Losing Bingham's Help," n.d. [1939], unattributed news clip, Avery Brundage Collection, University of Illinois at Urbana-Champaign.

308 "I agree with your idea": Letter from Avery Brundage to Edward W. Cochrane, March 3, 1940 reprinted in the *Chicago Herald-American*, n.d. [1940], Avery Brundage Collection, University of Illinois at Urbana-Champaign.

CHAPTER ELEVEN
Divorce, World War, and River Rouge · *1939–1945*

310 "arsenal of democracy": Franklin D. Roosevelt, "Fireside Chat" radio broadcast, Dec. 29, 1940. Franklin Delano Roosevelt, *FDR's Fireside Chats*, ed. Russell D. Buhite and David W. Levy (Norman: University of Oklahoma Press, 1992), 164.

311 "Since his football days": Collier, "Good King Jim."

311 "Tiny Roebuck": *LAT*, Dec. 3, 1939.

311 "a new lease on life": *LAT*, Dec. 6, 1939.

312 "some thing in mind": Letter from Jim Thorpe to Carl Hoffmire, Dec. [20? copy unclear], 1939. PFHOF.

312 In May the *Los Angeles Times Sunday Magazine*: Harry MacPherson, "Hollywood Tribe: The Hollywood Indians Are Forming a New Tribe to Preserve Old Customs," *Los Angeles Times Sunday Magazine*, May 5, 1940.

313 "teach the younger Indian": *LAT*, Nov. 12, 1940.

313 "Plot does the redskins dirt": *Variety*, Nov. 13, 1940, *Prairie Schooners* clip file, Margaret Herrick Library, The Academy of Motion Picture Arts and Sciences.

313 "ominous and racist": Hilger, 54.

314 "combative instinct of youth": *New York Post*, Oct. 19, 1940.

314 "the dark days of 1940": Winston Churchill, quoted in *NYT*, Nov. 30, 1944.

314 "I guess I still like speed": *LAT*, April 24, 1940.

314 "physical and mental cruelty": *LAT*, Oct. 30, 1941.

314 "I often wondered": Robert L. Whitman interview with Freeda Thorpe.

314 "It was like the problems": Freeda Thorpe, quoted in *Sports Illustrated*, Oct. 25, 1982.

315 "his happy-go-lucky nature": Frank Luksa, "Thorpe Left Special Legacy to His Son," *Fort Worth Star-Telegram*, n.d. [1971], PFHOF.

315 "used liquor to excess": *LAT*, Oct. 30, 1941. All quoted material of Freeda Thorpe's regarding the divorce ruling is taken from this source.

315 "Left Newark Thursday evening": Letter from Jim Thorpe to "Dear Friend Russell," Aug. 6, 1941, PFHOF.

316 "was like a freak sideshow": Kathy Shea Anfuso, telephone interview.

316 "a swill-type, broken down place": Gary Stevens, telephone interview.

316 "ideal industrialist": Douglas Brinkley, telephone interview.

316 "fighting pacifism": Joseph Cabadas, *River Rouge: Ford's Industrial Colossus* (St. Paul, Minn.: Motorbooks International/MBI Publishing Company, 2004), 82.

317 From 1915 to 1918: For a full discussion of the Ford Motor Company apprenticeship program with Carlisle, see Bell, 198–205.

317 "Mr. Ford's personal man": John McCarten, "The Little Man in Henry Ford's Basement," *American Mercury*, May 1942, vol. 50, no. 197. Vertical File—Harry Bennett, Benson Ford Research Center, Henry Ford Museum & Greenfield Village, Dearborn, Mich.

317 "the most powerful private police force": Ibid.

317 Bennett had an estimated three thousand goons: John H. O'Brien, "Henry Ford's Commander in Chief: Harry Bennett and His Private Army," *Forum*, Feb. 1938. Vertical File—Harry Bennett, Benson Ford Research Center, Henry Ford Museum & Greenfield Village, Dearborn, Mich.

317 "a rule of terror and repression": National Labor Relations Board, quoted in "The Little Man."

318 "I was attracted": Harry Bennett, as told to Paul Marcus, *We Never Called Him Henry* (New York: Fawcett, 1951), 105.

318 "former policemen discharged": "Henry Ford's Commander."

318 "Plant Protection": Letter from Sharon James, request coordinator, Ford Motor Company, to the author, Aug. 13, 2002. All the subsequent information regarding Thorpe's salary, dates of employment, position titles, and addresses comes from this source.

319 "creation of Faustian man": Charles Lindbergh, quoted in Anne Morrow Lindbergh, *War Within and Without: Diaries and Letters of Anne Morrow Lindbergh, 1939–1944* (New York: Harcourt Brace Jovanovich, 1980), 305.

319 "did not care": Memo to files, Lon Scott, Aug. 10, 1943. Lon Scott Correspondence, Jim Thorpe House, Yale, Okla. The author thanks Michael Koehler for informing her about this correspondence and Kathy Dickson, outreach director, Oklahoma Historical Society, for making a copy of it for use in this biography.

319 "wild Indians": Jack Thorpe, interview.

319 "a great defense": Jim Brandstatter, *Tales from Michigan Stadium*, vol. 2 (n.p.: Sports Publishing, 2005), 170.

320 "veritable nightclub": Bennett, 84.

320 "bad crowd": Garland Nevitt, interview. All subsequent quotations of Nevitt's are taken from this source.

320 "very quiet": Luther Bass, a Ford Motor Company employee in the 1940s, interview with Robert W. Wheeler, RWWC.

320 "Personal and Confidential": Letter from Federal Bureau of Investigation, U.S.

Department of Justice, Detroit, Mich., July 17, 1942, to Director, Federal Bureau of Investigation, Washington, D.C., Freedom of Information Act request dated April 4, 2002, U.S. Department of Justice, Office of Information and Privacy.

320 "Smith has had": Ibid.

321 "Mr. Thorpe": Letter from Ben Templeton to Jim Thorpe, reprinted in *LAT*, Jan. 17, 1944.

321 "Something should be done": Leon Miller, quoted in *NYT*, April 20, 1943.

321 "[T]he old Injun is feeling great": Letter to Lon Scott from Jim Thorpe, March 28, 1943, LSC.

322 "Swell looking, great big": Letter to Jim Thorpe from Lon Scott, Oct. 22, 1943, LSC.

322 "You had better let me know": Letter to Jim Thorpe from Lon Scott, Aug. 11, 1943, LSC.

323 "He did not find her": Memorandum from Lon Scott to self, Aug. 10, 1943, LSC.

323 "tow-haired Jackie's feet": *Tulsa Daily World*, Sept. 18, 1943.

323 "naturally cast in the leading role": Ibid.

323 "give you a job": Letter to Jim Thorpe from Lon Scott, Oct. 6, 1945, LSC.

324 "I have nothing definate": Letter to Lon Scott from Jim Thorpe, Oct. 6, 1943, LSC.

324 was not enthused: Memo to files, Lon Scott, Oct. 13, 1943, LSC.

324 "one of the most romantic figures": *Tribune*, Oct. 13, 1943. Clipping in LSC.

324 "I know you'll be": Letter to Lon Scott from Jim Thorpe, Oct. 21, 1943, LSC. The letter is incorrectly dated, as Lon Scott pointed out to Jim. The postmark was Nov. 22 and Jim was not yet in California on Oct. 21.

324 "would not get the wrong impression": Letter from Lon Scott to Jim Thorpe, Nov. 26, 1943, LSC.

324 "Well Xmas is over": Letter from Jim Thorpe to Lon Scott, Dec. 27, 1943, LSC.

325 "return to my tribe": Jack Thorpe, interview.

325 "Dear Jackie has the flu": Letter from Jim Thorpe to Lon Scott, Dec. 27, 1943, LSC.

325 "leather butt": Jack Thorpe, interview.

325 "Can't do nothing": Letter from Jim Thorpe to Lon Scott, March 30, 1944, LSC.

326 "Eventually somebody will produce": *LAT*, Jan. 17, 1944.

326 "Saw Ann Sheridan yesterday": Letter from Jim Thorpe to Lon Scott, March 30, 1944, LSC.

326 "hoss opera geared for the duals": *Variety*, May 10, 1944.

327 "the greatest athlete": *LAT*, Sept. 17, 1944. The story in *The New York News* was reprinted in the *LAT*.

327 "You are probably the greatest athlete": Judge Frank Carrell, Gardena Justice Court, quoted in *LAT*, Nov. 4, 1944.

CHAPTER TWELVE

Rediscovery · *1945–1953*

329 "a symbol for things": Gerald Eskenazi, telephone interview.

329 "Heartache does something to a man": (Harrisburg) *Patriot-News*, "The Sports Shop" column by sportswriter Al Clark, April 1, 1953.

329 "Why are you here?": Patricia Thorpe, quoted in Gail Thorpe interview.

329 "death-warmed-over-pale": William Thourlby, interview. All quotations of Thourlby's, unless otherwise noted, come from this source.

330 "They all hate me": Patricia Thorpe, quoted in Koehler, unpublished biography of
Jim Thorpe.

331 "He asked that all questions": E-mail from John V. Carlson (son of Captain Carl J.
Carlson) to author. All quotations regarding Mr. Carlson's recollections are taken
from this source.

331 "never bragged about anything": Ralph Starr, telephone interview. All quoted material of Starr's comes from this source.

331 "a bitter man": George Hermanson, telephone interview.

331 Clarkson was ordered: Secret log for a U.S. merchant vessel, United States Fleet,
Headquarters of the Commander in Chief, 1943. SS *Southwestern Victory*. No.
29683, NARA—Northeast Region, New York, N.Y.

332 "Now that the war is over": Letter from Patricia Thorpe to Lon Scott, Aug. 15,
1945, LSC.

332 "Patsy was a very shrewd": C. E. "Slim" Harrison, interview with Robert W.
Wheeler, RWWC. All subsequent quotations of Harrison's, unless otherwise noted,
are taken from this source.

333 "to hear the sound": Patricia Thorpe, interview with Robert W. Wheeler, RWWC.
All the quotations of Patricia Thorpe's in this section are taken from this source.

333 LAND IN OKLA CITY MONDAY: Telegram from Jim Thorpe to Lon Scott, Nov. 9,
1945, LSC.

333 "a horror, all right": *Hollywood Reporter*, n.d. [1945], *Vampire's Ghost* clipping file,
Margaret Herrick Library, The Academy of Motion Picture Arts and Sciences.

333 "to teach youngsters": "Modern Day Football Slows Backfield Says Jim Thorpe,"
Jan. 24, 1946, unattributed news clip, Jim Thorpe Drop File, CCHS.

333 Freeda put Dick on a bus: Richard Thorpe, interview. The details of Dick Thorpe's
stay with his father and Patsy are taken from this source.

333 "Outstanding Sports Events": *LAT*, Feb. 24, 1946. "#5—Babe Ruth calling his
home-run shot in the third game of the Yankee–Cub World Series Oct. 1, 1932;
#6—Grover Cleveland Alexander's pitching in the World Series game of Oct. 10,
1926, when he stopped the Yankees by fanning Lazzeri; #7—Red Grange's 'Galloping Ghost' performance, the greatest of his career, in an Illinois–Michigan game;
#8—Fourth game of 1929 World Series when Athletics scored 10 runs in one inning
to win after the Cubs had apparently won the game . . . #10—Dempsey–Willard
fight, 1919 . . . #12—Charlie [*sic*] Paddock winning 100- and 200-meter races at
Inter-Allied Games . . ."

335 "I am an American": "The Freedom Pledge," *Documents on the Freedom Train*,
American Heritage Foundation, 1947 pamphlet. Photograph of Jim Thorpe leading the pledge appeared in the *Albany Park Times*, July 8, 1948. For reproductions
of the pamphlet, the full text of the pledge, a list of the documents, the organizers,
and more, see: http://www.rootsweb.ancestry.com/~miporthu/FreedomTrain.htm.

335 "Our country": Haim Glovinsky, quoted in *NYT*, Sept. 15, 1948.

335 were spent on jewelry and furs: McCallum, "The Regilding of a Legend."

335 "drank up the profits": Jack Thorpe, interview.

336 "I will not have": Jim Thorpe, quoted in Jack Thorpe interview.

336 "most dramatic moment": Jim Thorpe, quoted in *LAT*, Dec. 28, 1948. All quoted
material regarding this awards dinner comes from this source.

337 "greatest thrill": *LAT*, Feb. 2, 1949.

337 "softball gals in shorts": *LAT*, April 24, 1949.

337 "He's Here to Meet": *LAT*, June 12, 1949.

337 "Seems I'll have to keep going": Jim Thorpe, quoted in Stump, "Jim Thorpe: Greatest of Them All." Unless otherwise noted, all subsequent quotations regarding the Sports Club are taken from this source. Though Stump said that Jim was "underpaid," in fact he was well paid as a professional baseball and football player up until 1925.

339 "culture of nostalgia": Richard Hoffer, "The Eternal Muhammad," *Sports Illustrated*, Dec. 21, 2001.

339 "in the current Hollywood manner": *LAT*, April 8, 1950.

340 "I conscientiously wanted": Letter from Vincent X. Flaherty to Jack Warner, Nov. 22, 1950, *Jim Thorpe—All American* production file, Warner Bros. Collection, USC.

340 "boyhood's supermen": Dore Schary, *Heyday: An Autobiography* (Boston: Little, Brown, 1979), 147.

341 "The ramifications": Letter from Flaherty to Warner.

341 "stuffed shirt": *LAT*, Jan. 11, 1950.

341 "Here's the story": Jim Thorpe, quoted in *LAT*, Jan. 13, 1950.

341 "ridiculous": Ibid.

342 "Apparently," wrote Freeman: Warner Bros. interoffice communication from Everett Freeman to Steve Trilling, Jan. 23, 1950, *Jim Thorpe—All American* production file, Warner Bros. Collection, USC.

342 "two of the greatest football years": *NYT*, Jan. 25, 1950.

342 "The storied Indian": *NYT*, Feb. 12, 1950.

342 "cemented his claim to immortality": *LAT*, Feb. 12, 1950.

342 "Many sportswriters": Walter Lingo, quoted in *The Marion Star*, Feb. 20, 1950.

343 "astronomical": Interoffice communication from Everett Freeman to Steve Trilling, Sept. 8, 1949, *Jim Thorpe—All American* production file, Warner Bros. Collection, USC.

343 "I am hamstrung": Ibid.

343 "aware of the troublesome nature": Interoffice communication from Everett Freeman to Steve Trilling, Aug. 3, 1949, *Jim Thorpe—All American* production file, Warner Bros. Collection, USC.

343 "cheap details": Letter from Patricia Thorpe to Everett Freeman, Feb. 9, 1950, *Jim Thorpe—All American* production file, Warner Bros. Collection, USC.

343 "the expert himself": Letter from Patricia Thorpe to Everett Freeman, March 10, 1950, *Jim Thorpe—All American* production file, Warner Bros. Collection, USC.

343 "suspicious of all legal documents": Letter from Patricia Thorpe to Everett Freeman, March 13, 1950, *Jim Thorpe—All American* production file, Warner Bros. Collection, USC.

343 "[m]aybe isn't so stupid after all.": Ibid.

344 "primitive intelligence": Letter from Patricia Thorpe to Everett Freeman, March 23, 1950, *Jim Thorpe—All American* production file, Warner Bros. Collection, USC.

344 "I have never been broke before": Letter from Patricia Thorpe to Everett Freeman, March 17 and 18, 1950, *Jim Thorpe—All American* production file, Warner Bros. Collection, USC.

344 "exactly $22 and 95 cents!": Ibid.

344 In between speaking engagements: As Sonny Chorre, Joseph Vance Chorre appeared in several movies, including *Joe Palooka in the Knockout*, 1947, and *Joe Palooka in the Counterpunch*, 1949, both for Monogram. Gorgeous George was in *Alias the Champ* in 1949 for Republic.

344 "doesn't smoke a package": Letter from Patricia Thorpe to Everett Freeman, March 18, 1950, *Jim Thorpe—All American* production file, Warner Bros. Collection, USC.

344 "anybody who wants Jim": Letter from Everett Freeman to Patricia Thorpe, March 21, 1950, *Jim Thorpe—All American* production file, Warner Bros. Collection, USC.

344 "It is not dignified": Ibid.

344 "Frankly": Letter from Everett Freeman to Patricia Thorpe, March 23, 1950, *Jim Thorpe—All American* production file, Warner Bros. Collection, USC.

345 "You said something yesterday": Warner Bros. interoffice communication from Douglas Morrow to Steve Trilling, Sept. 1, 1950, *Jim Thorpe—All American* production file, Warner Bros. Collection, USC.

345 "[A]t one time": Letter from Jack Welch to Warner Bros., n.d. [1949], Memos and Correspondence File, Warner Bros., *Jim Thorpe—All American*, Warner Bros. Collection, USC.

345 "Jim's great moral fiber": Letter from Everett Freeman to Patricia Thorpe, March 23, 1950, *Jim Thorpe—All American* production file, Warner Bros. Collection, USC.

345 "the very nice way": Letter from Pop Warner to Warner Bros., Oct. 1, 1951, *Jim Thorpe—All American* production file, Warner Bros. Collection, USC.

346 "I am now at the limit": Letter from Everett Freeman to Patricia Thorpe, May 9, 1950, *Jim Thorpe—All American* production file, Warner Bros. Collection, USC.

346 "was very pleasant and cooperative": Warner Bros. interoffice communication from Everett Freeman to Steve Trilling, June 12, 1950, *Jim Thorpe—All American* production file, Warner Bros. Collection, USC.

346 "extremely fond": Letter from Patricia Thorpe to Everett Freeman, May 6, 1950, *Jim Thorpe—All American* production file, Warner Bros. Collection, USC.

346 "My efforts in the behalf": Letter from Patricia Thorpe to Warner Bros., Sunday, a.m., n.d., *Jim Thorpe—All American* production file, Warner Bros. Collection, USC.

346 Paul Hoy Helms: Within a year of starting the Helms Bakery in 1931, Paul Hoy Helms had built a successful business with no storefronts, but three hundred vans that left each morning from headquarters, ringing distinctively like ice cream trucks, to sell fresh bread and doughnuts throughout the greater Los Angeles area. In 1969 a Helms loaf would be the first bread on the moon. An enthusiastic promoter of athletics—his uncle, William "Dummy" Hoy, a deaf major league outfielder from 1888 to 1902, is credited with first insisting umpires use a hand signal for a strike so he would know the call—Helms was instrumental in setting up the first Olympic Village, for the 1932 games, in the area known as Baldwin Hills (named for Anita Baldwin's father) and then arranging for his company to be chosen as the athletes' official bread supplier.

347 "public service": Stump, "Jim Thorpe."

347 "Jim was really nice": Margaret U. Farnum, telephone interview. All subsequent quotations of Farnum's are taken from this source. When the author interviewed Mrs. Farnum in 2002, she was the chief administrative officer of the Los Angeles Memorial Coliseum Commission.

348 "No padding?": Press release, Warner Bros. Studio, n.d. [1951], Clipping File, *Jim Thorpe—All American*, Margaret Herrick Library, The Academy of Motion Picture Arts and Sciences.

348 "Football is a more slashing": Ibid.

348 "discovered less than 200": *NYT*, n.d. [1950], Harry B. Friedman Collection, Folder 20, *Jim Thorpe—All American* production file, Warner Bros. Collection, USC.

349 "I get a funny feeling": Jim Thorpe, quoted in press release, Warner Bros. Studio, n.d. [1951], Clipping File, *Jim Thorpe—All American*, Margaret Herrick Library, The Academy of Motion Picture Arts and Sciences.

349 "overbearing": Eskenazi interview.

349 "His life had gone to pot": Burt Lancaster, quoted in *NYT*, Oct. 15, 1982.

349 "If he's asked a question": Press release, Warner Bros. Studio, n.d. [1951], Clipping File, *Jim Thorpe—All American*, Margaret Herrick Library, The Academy of Motion Picture Arts and Sciences.

349 "until Uncle Sam doesn't need": Harry B. Friedman Collection, Folder 20, *Jim Thorpe—All American* production file, Warner Bros. Collection, USC.

349 "The greatest group of sportsmen": *LAT*, Oct. 1, 1950.

349 "power . . . was never emphasized": *LAT*, Oct. 26, 1950.

350 "went crazy and bought": Burt Lancaster, quoted in *NYT*, Oct. 15, 1982.

350 "How's business?": Jim Thorpe, quoted in William Thourlby interview. The story of how Thourlby was first identified by Jim as his son is also from this interview.

353 "*The Lone Oklahoma Indian*": Advertisement for *Jim Thorpe—All American*, *LAT*, Aug. 29, 1951.

353 "staggered and nearly toppled": Paul A. Brehm, quoted in *Shoppers' Guide* (Carlisle, Pa.), Oct. 10, 1968. U.S. Army Military History Collection, Carlisle Barracks Collection, Carlisle Indian School Athletics, Box 18, Army War College, Carlisle, Pa.

354 "It is a story recognizable": *NYT*, Aug. 25, 1951.

354 "The film . . . seems unable": *Time*, Sept. 24, 1951.

355 "the excitement inherent": *NYT*.

355 "*Jim Thorpe—All American* had such an impact": Masback interview.

355 Patsy wept: *NYT*, Nov. 10, 1951.

355 "We're broke": *Time*, Nov. 19, 1951.

356 a young man: *LAT*, Dec. 1, 1951.

356 "in hopes of some big Sportsman": Letter from James Leggett to Hedda Hopper, Dec. 14, 1951, Hedda Hopper Collection, Jim Thorpe File, Margaret Herrick Library, The Academy of Motion Picture Arts and Sciences.

356 "one of Dartmouth's great athletes": *LAT*, Dec. 11, 1951.

356 "I had no idea": Sample of letter sent to each donor, Dec. 11, 1951, Hedda Hopper Collection, Jim Thorpe File, Margaret Herrick Library, The Academy of Motion Picture Arts and Sciences.

356 "saddened and terribly shocked": Letter from E. R. Van Sickle to Warner Bros., Nov. 12, 1951, *Jim Thorpe—All American* production file, Warner Bros. Collection, USC.

356 "Dear Sirs:": Letter from Robert F. Kennedy to Warner Bros., n.d. [1951], Memos and Correspondence File, *Jim Thorpe—All American*, Warner Bros. Collection, USC. The author is grateful to Maxwell Taylor Kennedy for his help confirming that this letter was written by his father, Robert F. Kennedy, and for the Robert F. Kennedy family's permission to quote it.

357 "host of plain, everyday fans": *NYT*, Dec. 2, 1951.

357 "Everybody has been so nice": Newspaper article, n.d. [late 1951], unattributed, Jim Thorpe Drop File, CCHS.

357 Jim told Daley: *NYT*, Nov. 21, 1951.

357 "I felt sadness": Letter from Arthur Einhorn to author.

358 "slowly, haltingly": Jerry Izenberg, "Jim Thorpe Medals Get 'Polish,' " unattributed [Newark *Star-Ledger*], Dec. 31, 1972, Jim Thorpe Drop File, CCHS.

358 "that old dead ball": Ted Williams, quoted in news clip, n.d., unattributed, PFHOF.

358 "Boy," Williams told: Ted Williams with John Underwood, *My Turn at Bat: The Story of My Life* (New York: Pocket Books, 1970), 8. All quoted material from Williams in this section is taken from this source.

358 "Jim, I'm proud": "Scribe Didn't Regret Thorpe Scoop," n.d. [1973], unattributed, PFHOF.

359 "I'd be the happiest man": "Thorpe Renews Fight for Olympic Medals," n.d. [1951], unattributed news clip, *Jim Thorpe—All American* production file, Warner Bros. Collection, USC.

359 Ferdinand Bie, the designated: It was reported that Wieslander, when told of the medals campaign, said with far less sympathy than before, "Oh, so he wants it back again, eh? Well it isn't the first time. . . . I don't know how many times I have denied the weird rumor that I refused to accept the gold medal. This whole business has been tormenting me during the past 20-odd years." Hugo Wieslander, quoted in unattributed news clip, Dec. 3, 1951, clipping file, *Jim Thorpe—All American*, Margaret Herrick Library, The Academy of Motion Picture Arts and Sciences.

359 "He is a great swindler": Letter from Sigfrid Edström to Otto Mayer, Dec. 4, 1951, Sigfrid Edström Correspondence File, 1951, IOC Archive, IOC, Lausanne.

359 "cracking the knuckles": Al Clark, (Harrisburg) *Patriot-News*, April 1, 1953, Jim Thorpe Drop File, CCHS. All quotations from this interview are taken from this source.

360 "[T]he world's conscience": Branch Rickey, quoted in ibid.

360 "I think there is a lesson": Governor Frank J. Lausche, quoted in ibid.

360 "rocked the cradle": *NYT*, Jan. 31, 1952.

360 "I can see I'm not": (Cleveland) *Plain Dealer*, Jan. 31, 1952.

361 "Think about it": *Erie* (Pa.) *Sunday Times-News*, April 13, 1997.

361 In April, Jim leased: According to the website of the Nevada Department of Cultural Affairs, as of March 2007, the Quonset hut was still on the north side of the Boulder Highway.

361 "only hazily": *Los Angeles Herald*, March 30, 1953.

362 "pathetic figure": Syd Kronenthal, telephone interview. All subsequent quotations of Kronenthal's are taken from this source. In 1952 the energetic, outgoing Kronenthal was at the beginning of a distinguished career that would include the position of Parks and Recreation director, later director of Human Services, of the City of Culver City and the AAU national vice chairman of the Long Distance Running Committee. One of his first projects after the Second World War was to revive the Culver City marathon at a time when, outside of Boston, marathons were considered unhealthy, "crazy," as he put it, events. In 1992, a park in Culver City was renamed in Kronenthal's honor.

363 "personal appearance in New York": *LAT*, Feb. 11, 1953.

363 "Jim gave me his word": Thomas F. Murray, quoted in *LAT*, Feb. 18, 1953.

EPILOGUE · 1953–1983

365   "There is no myth": Alessandra Stanley, *NYT*, June 6, 2009.

365   "The mortician won't touch": Quoted in letter from Jan Schroeder Iverson to author.

365   "devout baseball fan": Ibid.

366   "Mrs. Thorpe's screams": *LAT*, March 29, 1953.

366   "Mildred": *Columbus Citizen*, March 29, 1953.

366   "blasting it on all": Slim Harrison interview.

366   "recovered": Letter from Patsy Thorpe to John Steckbeck, n.d. [March 1953], P1-022-003, John S. Steckbeck Indian School Collection, CCHS.

366   Charlotte (married for the second time . . .): Charlotte Thorpe would marry a third time, to William Adler, and they had a son, John Adler.

367   "separate special memorial": "Mrs. Thorpe Rejects Oklahoma, Considers Carlisle for Jim's Rites," n.d. [1953], unattributed news clip, Jim Thorpe Drop File, CCHS.

367   "Jim was rather well fed up": Letter from Patricia Thorpe to John Steckbeck, May 9, 1953, P1-022-003, John S. Steckbeck Indian School Collection, CCHS.

367   "Thorpe's body has been more in demand": Rice, 236.

367   "To a whole generation": *NYT*, March 29, 1953.

367   "Jim never retaliated": *NYT*, March 31, 1953.

367   "makes Jim look bad": "Thorpe: As Good as He Had to Be; Mathias: Competitors Stepped Pace," *Chicago Daily News Service*, undated [1953], Jim Thorpe Drop File, CCHS.

368   "shock": Pop Warner, quoted in *Columbus Citizen*, March 29, 1953.

368   "a burly, simple wonderful gent": Red Smith, "Jim and His Baubles," reprinted in *The Best American Sports Writing of the Century*, ed. David Halberstam (Boston: Houghton Mifflin Company, 1999), 153.

368   "Let historians decide": *Los Angeles Examiner*, March 3, 1953.

368   HAIL AND FAREWELL: Telegram from Ernie Nevers to Patricia Thorpe, quoted in *Tulsa World*, April 10, 1953.

369   "weeping unashamedly": *NYT*, Apr.7, 1953.

369   "I learned with sorrow": Photocopy of telegram from President Dwight D. Eisenhower to Patricia Thorpe, April 9, 1953, RWWC.

370   Although such occasions are usually private: *Oklahoma City Times*, April 14, 1953.

370   "too cold": Patricia Thorpe, quoted in Grace Thorpe interview.

370   "Goodbye, dear!": "Thorpe Given Final Farewells," April 14, 1953, unattributed news clip, RWWC.

370   "Pat just wanted too much money": John B. Fowler, quoted in "The Regilding of a Legend."

371   "Where's Jim?": Patricia Thorpe, quoted in *Atlanta Journal and Constitution Magazine*, March 19, 1972.

371   "I don't see what authority": Governor Bill Murray, quoted in *Shawnee News Star*, Sept. 9, 1953.

371   "They hated each other": Richard Dugan, telephone interview. All subsequent quotations of Dugan's are taken from this source.

372   "to do *anything*": Rita Boyle Huggler, telephone interview.

373   "a remarkable contract": (Philadelphia) *Inquirer Magazine*, Aug. 8, 1982.

373   "are officially known and designated": Agreement made and executed May 19, 1954,

between Patricia G. Thorpe and the Borough of East Mauch Chunk and the Borough of Mauch Chunk, photocopy from RWWC. All quoted material from the agreement is taken from this source.

373   *Sports Illustrated* reported: McCallum, "The Regilding of a Legend."

373   Boyle said: Ibid.

373   "pure fiction": *Pittsburgh Post-Gazette*, Jan. 14, 2001.

373   "There was a plastic bag": Joseph L. Boyle, quoted in (Philadelphia) *Inquirer Magazine*, Aug. 8, 1982.

374   Nine days after the deadline passed: On October 11, 1956, *Requiem for a Heavyweight*, a teleplay by Rod Serling, was broadcast on *Playhouse 90* starring Jack Palance as a punch-drunk boxer at the end of his career. A film version would be released in 1962, starring Anthony Quinn. The final scene, indicating the boxer's ultimate humiliation, and an indication of an even further debasement of the stereotype, has him dressed in an Indian costume, faking an Indian dance around the ring, to the jeers and hoots of the audience.

374   none of the grand projects: One grand project, the Pro Football Hall of Fame, opened in Canton in 1963 with Jim one of four players elected unanimously to the seventeen-member charter group. The other three unanimous player votes were for Red Grange, Bronko Nagurski, and Sammy Baugh. *NYT*, Jan. 30, 1963.

374   "You mention you're from Jim Thorpe": Johnny H. Otto, quoted in *NYT*, July 22, 1964.

374   "All we got was a dead Indian": *Sports Illustrated*, Aug. 3, 1964.

375   "beyond dispute," "scapegoat": *Wall Street Journal*, Oct. 11, 1973. See also *Wall Street Journal*, Oct. 10, 1979.

376   "mascots": Billy Mills, quoted in *The Gazette* (Colorado Springs), Jan. 14, 2000.

377   "Simon ran with it": Robert W. Wheeler and Florence Ridlon interview. All subsequent quotations of Wheeler or Ridlon, unless otherwise noted, are taken from this source.

377   "impassioned plea": *NYT*, Oct. 17, 1982.

377   New medals would be cast: Hugo Wieslander had donated his decathlon gold medal to the Swedish Sports Museum in 1951; Ferdinand Bie's pentathlon medal had reportedly been stolen. According to Robert Wheeler, the IOC wanted to present "commemorative coins" to the family instead of duplicate medals, claiming the molds had been destroyed. Wheeler and Ridlon requested *Sports Illustrated* writer Jack McCallum to verify their existence, which he did, thereby removing the IOC's objection. Wolf Lyberg, currently Swedish Olympic historian, told the author he found the original molds.

377   "At long last": Letter from President Ronald Reagan to Charlotte Thorpe, Oct. 19, 1982. Facsimile in *Thorpe's Gold*, 242. Jim's children believed that working to reinstate their father was the chance to connect with the parent none of them had really known. "I missed my father all my life," said Charlotte (quoted in "A Legend Turns 100," Dennis Brown, *AAF—Olympian*, March 1988). Charlotte, sixty-three in 1982, told reporters in Phoenix, "You just don't know how I feel. You can't possibly know how I feel" (quoted in the *Massillon Independent*, Oct. 14, 1982). Dick, forty-eight, chief purchasing agent for the Oklahoma State Senate in Oklahoma City, said of his father, "He never felt he did anything wrong. It's a damn shame it took that long" (quoted in *Allentown* [Pa.] *Morning Call*, Oct. 14, 1982). Phil, fifty-five, a retired army lieutenant colonel (with tours of duty in World War II, the Korean War, and

Vietnam, holder of the Bronze Star and four Legion of Merit awards), working as an equal employment opportunity officer with the BIA in Washington, was "flab-bergasted" at the news. "I knew a great number of people have been working on this the past few months," he said. "I've had my fingers crossed, but I didn't expect this kind of action this soon. My God, this is just wonderful." He had lobbied hard on Capitol Hill for reinstatement and now admitted, "We were getting so tired" (quoted in the *Akron Beacon Journal*, n.d. [Oct. 1982], RWWC). Grace, almost sixty, living with her sister Gail, sixty-five, in Tahlequah, Oklahoma, both of them having become deeply involved in Indian affairs in their later lives, said, "We've worked all our lives to get the records restored" (quoted in *Philadelphia Inquirer*, n.d. [marked: Rec'd Nov. 24, 1982], RWWC). All of them felt complicated mixtures of shock, happiness, and disbelief, including Bill, fifty-four, the spare parts coordinator at Ling-Temco-Vought, who was living with his wife and son in Arlington, Texas, and the youngest, Jack, forty-five, in Shawnee, and the chief of the Sac and Fox nation.

377   "the name of James Thorpe": Press release, Comité International Olympique, Lausanne, 13 octobre 1982, copy faxed to author from the Olympic Museum, Lausanne, Sept. 25, 2001.

378   "The joy felt": *NYT*, Oct. 17, 1982.

378   "in the worst tradition": "The Regilding of a Legend."

378   "As this country's": Letter from Robert W. Wheeler and Florence Ridlon to President Juan Antonio Samaranch, Nov. 12, 1982, RWWC.

378   "This is simply outrageous": Robert W. Wheeler, quoted in Bob Oates, "Greatest Athlete of All?" *LAT*, n.d. [1983], Jim Thorpe Association, Oklahoma City.

379   "such a high value": Letter from Alain Coupat, private secretary to the IOC president, to Wolf Lyberg, secretary general, Swedish Olympic Committee, July 15, 1988, USOC Archives.

379   "Oh, what a stupid old business": Pierre de Coubertin quoted in Robert Pariente, "Jim Thorpe: What a Storybook Life!" *Olympic Review*, May 1983.

379   "No way": Mike Hickock, quoted in *Philadelphia Inquirer*, n.d. [marked: Rec'd Nov. 24, 1982], RWWC.

379   "an abandoned movie set": *Forbes*, Sept. 12, 1983.

380   "American Indians," wrote Selena Roberts: *NYT*, June 17, 2001.

381   "I think my dog": Hiram P. Thorp, quoted by Jim Thorpe in *Red Son*, 9. All the quoted material about this incident comes from Jim's recollections.

Selected Bibliography

Adams, David Wallace. *Education for Extinction: American Indians and the Boarding School Experience, 1875–1928*. Lawrence: University Press of Kansas, 1995.

Adelman, Melvin L. *A Sporting Time: New York City and the Rise of Modern Athletics, 1820–1970*. Urbana: University of Illinois Press, 1986.

Aleiss, Angela. *Making the White Man's Indian: Native Americans and Hollywood Movies*. Westport, Conn.: Praeger, 2005.

Alexander, Charles C. *John McGraw*. New York: Viking Penguin, 1988.

The Baseball Encyclopedia: The Complete and Definitive Record of Major League Baseball. New York: Macmillan, 1996.

Allen, Lee. *The American League Story*. New York: Hill & Wang, 1962.

———. *The National League Story*. New York: Hill & Wang, 1962.

Anderson, Dave. *The Story of Football*. New York: William Morrow, 1985.

Associated Press and Grolier. *The Olympic Story: Pursuit of Excellence*. Danbury, Conn.: Grolier, 1979.

Baird, W. David, and Danny Goble. *The Story of Oklahoma*. Norman: University of Oklahoma Press, 1994.

Bataille, Gretchen M., and Charles L. P. Silet. *The Pretend Indians: Images of Native Americans in the Movies*. Ames: Iowa State University Press, 1980.

Becker, Carl M. *Home and Away: The Rise and Fall of Professional Football on the Banks of the Ohio, 1919–1934*. Athens: Ohio University Press, 1998.

Bell, Genevieve. "Telling Stories Out of School: Remembering the Carlisle Indian Industrial School, 1879–1918." Ph.D. dissertation, Department of Anthropology, Stanford University, June 1998.

Benjey, Tom. *Doctors, Lawyers, Indian Chiefs*. Carlisle, Pa.: Tuxedo Press, 2008.

Bennett, Harry, as told to Paul Marcus. *We Never Called Him Henry*. New York: Fawcett, 1951.

Berkhofer, Robert F., Jr. *The White Man's Indian: Images of the American Indian from Columbus to the Present*. New York: Alfred A. Knopf, 1978.

Bernotas, Bob. *Jim Thorpe: Sac and Fox Athlete*. Philadelphia: Chelsea House, 1992.

Bernstein, Mark. F. *Football: The Ivy League Origins of an American Obsession*. Philadelphia: University of Pennsylvania Press, 2001.

Betts, John R. *America's Sporting Heritage, 1850–1950*. Reading, Mass.: Addison-Wesley, 1974.

Bird, S. Elizabeth, ed. *Dressing in Feathers: The Construction of the Indian in American Popular Culture*. Boulder, Colo.: Westview Press, 1996.

Bjarkman, Peter C., ed. *Encyclopedia of Major League Baseball Team Histories: The American League*. New York: Carroll & Graf, 1993.

———. *Encyclopedia of Major League Baseball Team Histories: The National League*. New York: Carroll & Graf, 1993.

Bloom, Harold. *Marianne Moore*. New York: Facts on File, 1986.

Bloom, John. *To Show What an Indian Can Do: Sports at Native American Boarding Schools.* Minneapolis: University of Minnesota Press, 2000.

Boda, Steve, Jr., and National Collegiate Sports Services. *College Football All-Time Record Book, 1869–1969.* New York: National Collegiate Athletic Association, 1969.

———. *Football's Finest: The NCAA's Career Statistics to Nearly 3,000 of the Finest Players and Coaches to Be Associated with Collegiate Football.* Indianapolis, Ind.: National Collegiate Athletic Association, 2002.

Brands, H. W. *The Reckless Decade: America in the 1890s.* Chicago: University of Chicago Press, 1995.

———. *Theodore Roosevelt: The Last Romantic.* New York: Basic Books, 1997.

Braudy, Leo. *The Frenzy of Renown: Fame and Its History.* New York: Oxford University Press, 1986.

Braunwart, Bob, and Bob Carroll. *The Alphabet Wars: The Birth of Professional Football, 1890–1892.* North Huntingdon, Pa.: PFRA (Professional Football Researchers Association), 1981.

Brinkley, Douglas. *Wheels for the World: Henry Ford, His Company, and a Century of Progress, 1903–2003.* New York: Viking Penguin, 2003.

Brown, Dee. *Bury My Heart at Wounded Knee: An Indian History of the American West.* New York: Holt, Rinehart and Winston, 1970.

Brownell, Susan, ed. *The 1904 Anthropology Days and Olympic Games: Sport, Race, and American Imperialism.* Lincoln: University of Nebraska Press, 2008.

Camp, Walter. *American Football.* New York: Arno Press, 1974. Reprint of 1891 edition.

———. *The Book of Football.* New York: Century Company, 1910.

Campbell, Jim. *Golden Years of Pro Football.* New York: Crescent Books, 1993.

Carlson, Lewis H., and John J. Fogarty, eds. *Tales of Gold: An Oral History of the Summer Olympic Games Told by America's Gold Medal Winners.* Chicago: Contemporary Books, 1987.

Carroll, Bob. *The Ohio League: 1910–1919.* North Huntingdon, Pa: PFRA (Professional Football Researchers Association), 1997.

———. *The Tigers Roar: Professional Football in Ohio, 1903–1909.* North Huntingdon, Pa.: PFRA (Professional Football Researchers Association), 1990.

Carroll, Bob, and Bob Braunwart. *Pro Football: From AAA to '03: The Origin and Development of Professional Football in Western Pennsylvania, 1890–1903.* North Huntingdon, Pa.: PFRA (Professional Football Researchers Association), 1991.

Carroll, Bob, and Bob Gill. *Bulldogs on Sunday 1919: Twilight of the Ohio League.* North Huntingdon, Pa.: PFRA (Professional Football Researchers Association), 1991.

Catlin, George. *Letters and Notes on the North American Indians.* Edited and with an introduction by Michael M. Mooney. New York: Clarkson N. Potter, 1975.

Cody, Iron Eyes, as told to Collin Perry. *Iron Eyes: My Life as a Hollywood Indian.* New York: Everest House, 1982.

Cohen, Richard M., Jordan A. Deutsch, Roland T. Johnson, and David S. Neft, comps. *The Scrapbook History of Pro Football, 1893–1979.* Indianapolis, Ind.: Bobbs-Merrill, 1976.

Collier, John. *Indians of the Americas.* New York: Signet, 1948.

Colton, Larry. *Counting Coup: A True Story of Basketball and Honor on the Little Big Horn.* New York: Warner Books, 2001.

Cook-Lynn, Elizabeth. *Why I Can't Read Wallace Stegner and Other Essays.* Madison: University of Wisconsin Press, 1996.

Cope, Myron. *The Game That Was: An Illustrated Account of the Tumultuous Early Days of Pro Football.* New York: Crowell, 1974.

Crawford, Bill. *All-American: The Rise and Fall of Jim Thorpe.* New York: John Wiley & Sons, 2005.

Cusack, Jack. *Pioneer in Pro Football.* Fort Worth, Tex.: n.p., 1963. Also reprinted in *PFRA* (Professional Football Researchers Association) *Annual 1987*, no. 8.

Daley, Arthur. *Pro Football's Hall of Fame.* Chicago: Quadrangle Books, 1963.

Daniels, George G. *The Olympic Century: The Official History of the Modern Olympic Movement.* Vol. 6, *The V and VI Olympiads: Stockholm 1912 Inter-Allied Games.* Los Angeles: World Sport Research & Publications, 2000.

Danzig, Allison. *The History of American Football.* Englewood Cliffs, N.J.: Prentice-Hall, 1955.

———, ed. *Oh, How They Played the Game: The Early Days of Football and the Heroes Who Made It Great.* New York: Macmillan, 1971.

Davis, Parke H. *Football: The American Intercollegiate Game.* New York: Charles Scribner's, 1911.

Debo, Angie. *And Still the Waters Run: The Betrayal of the Five Civilized Tribes.* Princeton, N.J.: Princeton University Press, 1991.

———. *Geronimo: The Man, His Time, His Place.* Norman: University of Oklahoma Press, 1976.

———. *A History of the Indians of the United States.* Norman: University of Oklahoma Press, 1970.

Deford, Frank. *The Old Ball Game: How John McGraw, Christy Mathewson, and the New York Giants Created Modern Baseball.* New York: Atlantic Monthly Press, 2005.

Deloria, Philip J. *Playing Indian.* New Haven, Conn.: Yale University Press, 1998.

Deloria, Vine, Jr., ed. *American Indian Policy in the 20th Century.* Norman: University of Oklahoma Press, 1992.

———. *Custer Died for Your Sins: An Indian Manifesto.* Norman: University of Oklahoma Press, 1988.

Dewey, Donald, and Nicholas Acocella. *The Ball Clubs: Every Franchise, Past and Present, Officially Recognized by Major League Baseball.* New York: Harper Perennial, 1996.

Dickson, Paul. *The Dickson Baseball Dictionary.* 3rd ed. New York: W. W. Norton, 2009.

Dietrich, Phil. *Down Payments: Professional Football 1896–1930 as Viewed from the Summit.* North Huntingdon, Pa.: PFRA (Professional Football Researchers Association), 1995.

Dulles, Foster Rhea. *American Learns to Play: A History of Popular Recreation, 1607–1940.* Gloucester, Mass.: Peter Smith Publisher, 1963.

Durso, Joseph. *The Days of Mr. McGraw: The Wild, Wacky, Wooly Era of John J. McGraw and His Baseball Giants.* Englewood Cliffs, N.J.: Prentice-Hall, 1969.

Dyreson, Mark. *Making the American Team: Sport, Culture, and the Olympic Experience.* Urbana and Chicago: University of Illinois Press, 1998.

Eastman, Elaine Goodale. *Pratt, the Red Man's Moses.* Norman: University of Oklahoma Press, 1935.

Eckert, Allan W. *Twilight of Empire.* New York: Little Brown, 1988.

Edmunds, David R. *The Potawatomis: Keepers of the Fire.* Norman: University of Oklahoma Press, 1978.

Eisenhower, Dwight D. *At Ease: Stories I Tell to Friends.* Garden City, N.Y.: Doubleday, 1967.

Elfers, James E. *The Tour to End All Tours: The Story of Major League Baseball's 1913–1914 World Tour.* Lincoln: University of Nebraska Press, 2003.

Eskenazi, Gerald. *There Were Giants in Those Days.* New York: Grosset & Dunlap, 1976.

Espy, Richard. *The Politics of the Olympic Games.* Berkeley: University of California Press, 1979.

Fear-Segal, Jacqueline. *White Man's Club: Schools, Race, and the Struggle of Indian Acculturation.* Lincoln: University of Nebraska Press, 2007.

Filichia, Peter. *Professional Baseball Franchises: From the Abbeville Athletics to the Zanesville Indians.* New York: Facts on File, 1993.

Fleder, Rob, ed. *Great Football Writing: Sports Illustrated, 1954–2006.* New York: Sports Illustrated Books, 2006.

Foreman, Grant. *Indian Removal: The Emigration of the Five Civilized Tribes of Indians.* Norman: University of Oklahoma Press, 1976.

Frazier, Ian. *Great Plains.* New York: Penguin Books, 1990.

Friar, Ralph E., and Natasha A. Friar. *The Only Good Indian . . . : The Hollywood Gospel.* New York: Drama Book Specialists, 1972.

Gavaler, Chris. *School for Tricksters.* Dallas: Southern Methodist University, 2011.

Gobrecht, Wilbur J. *Jim Thorpe—Carlisle Indian.* Carlisle, Pa.: Cumberland County Historical Society, 1969.

Graham, Frank. *McGraw of the Giants: An Informal Biography.* New York: Putnam's, 1944.

Grant, Madison. *The Conquest of a Continent; or, The Expansion of Races in America.* New York: Charles Scribner's Sons, 1933.

Guttmann, Allen. *From Ritual to Record: The Nature of Modern Sports.* New York: Columbia University Press, 1978.

———. *The Games Must Go On: Avery Brundage and the Olympic Movement.* New York: Columbia University Press, 1984.

———. *The Olympics: A History of the Modern Games.* Urbana: University of Illinois Press, 1992.

Hagan, William T. *The Sac and Fox Indians.* Norman: University of Oklahoma Press, 1958.

———. *Theodore Roosevelt and Six Friends of the Indian.* Norman: University of Oklahoma Press, 1997.

Hagenbuch, Mark O. "Richard Henry Pratt, the Carlisle Indian Industrial School, and U.S. Policies Related to American Indian Education, 1879 to 1904." Ph.D. dissertation. Pennsylvania State University, May 1998.

Halas, George, with Gwen Morgan and Arthur Veysey. *Halas by Halas: The Autobiography of George Halas.* New York: McGraw-Hill, 1979.

Heffelfinger, W. W. "Pudge," as told to John McCallum, *This Was Football.* New York: A. S. Barnes and Company, 1954.

Hertzberg, Hazel W. *The Search for an American Indian Identity: Modern Pan-Indian Movements.* Syracuse, N.Y.: Syracuse University Press, 1971.

Hilger, Michael. *The American Indian in Film.* Metuchen, N.J.: Scarecrow Press, 1986.

Hodge, F. W., ed. *The Handbook of American Indians North of Mexico,* Bulletin 30 of the Bureau of American Ethnology, Part 1, Washington, D.C.: 1907.

———. *The Handbook of American Indians North of Mexico,* Bulletin 30 of the Bureau of American Ethnology, Part 2, Washington, D.C.: 1910.

Hoxie, Frederick E., ed. *Encyclopedia of North American Indians.* Boston: Houghton Mifflin, 1996.

Hynd, Noel. *The Giants of the Polo Grounds: The Glorious Times of New York's Baseball Giants.* New York: Doubleday, 1988.

Jackson, Donald, ed. *Black Hawk: An Autobiography.* Urbana: University of Illinois Press, 1955.

Jackson, Helen Hunt. *A Century of Dishonor: A Sketch of the United States Government's Dealings with Some of the Indian Tribes.* Boston: Little, Brown, and Co., 1917. Originally published by Harper & Brothers, New York, 1881.

Jaimes, Annette, ed. *The State of Native America: Genocide, Colonization and Resistance.* Cambridge, Mass.: South End Press, 1992.

James, Bill. *The Bill James Guide to Baseball Managers from 1870 to Today.* New York: Scribner, 1997.

———. *The Bill James Historical Baseball Abstract.* New York: Villard, 1985.

———. *The New Bill James Historical Baseball Abstract.* Rev. ed. New York: Free Press, 2003.

Jenkins, Sally. *The Real All Americans: The Team That Changed a Game, a People, a Nation.* New York: Doubleday, 2007.

Jennings, Francis. *The Invasion of America: Indians, Colonialism, and the Cant of Conquest.* New York: W. W. Norton & Co., 1976.

Johnson, Tim, ed. *Spirit Capture: Photographs from the National Museum of the American Indian.* Washington, D.C.: Smithsonian Institution Press, 1998.

Josephy, Alvin M., Jr. *500 Nations: An Illustrated History of North American Indians.* New York: Alfred A. Knopf, 1994.

Kahn, Roger. *A Flame of Pure Fire: Jack Dempsey and the Roaring '20s.* New York: Harcourt, 1999.

Kilpatrick, Jacquelyn. *Celluloid Indians: Native Americans and Film.* Lincoln: University of Nebraska Press, 1999.

King, C. Richard, ed. *Native Athletes in Sport and Society: A Reader.* Lincoln: University of Nebraska Press, 2005.

Kirsch, George B. *The Creation of American Team Sports.* Urbana: University of Illinois Press, 1989.

Lawrence, D. H. *Mornings in Mexico.* New York: Alfred A. Knopf, 1927.

Levine, Peter. *A. G. Spalding and the Rise of Baseball: The Promise of American Sport.* New York: Oxford University Press, 1985.

Lewis, Guy M. "The American College Football Spectacle, 1869–1917." Ph.D. dissertation. University of Maryland, 1964.

Light, Jonathan Fraser, ed. *The Cultural Encyclopedia of Baseball.* Jefferson, N.C.: McFarland & Co. 1997.

Lipsyte, Robert. *Jim Thorpe: 20th-Century Jock.* New York: HarperCollins, 1995.

Lucas, John. *The Modern Olympic Games.* New York: A. S. Barnes & Co., 1980.

McClellan, Keith. *The Sunday Game: At the Dawn of Professional Football.* Akron, Ohio: University of Akron Press, 1998.

McCormick, Anita Louise. *Native America and the Reservation in American History.* Springfield, N.J.: Enslow Publishers, 1996.

McGraw, Blanche S. *The Real McGraw.* Ed. Arthur Mann. New York: David McKay, 1953.

McGraw, John J. *My Thirty Years in Baseball.* 1923. Reprint, Lincoln: University of Nebraska Press, 1995.

McNickle, D'Arcy. *The Surrounded.* Albuquerque: University of New Mexico Press, 1997.

Mallon, Bill, and Ture Widlund. *The 1912 Olympic Games: Results for All Competitors in All Events, with Commentary*. Jefferson, N.C.: McFarland & Co., 2002.

Maltby, Marc S. "The Origins and Early Development of Professional Football, 1890–1920." Ph.D. dissertation. Ohio University, 1987. Also published in book form, in the Garland Studies in American Popular History and Culture: Marc S. Maltby, *The Origins and Early Development of Professional Football, 1890–1920*. New York: Routledge, 1997.

March, Harry A. *Pro Football, Its "Ups" and "Downs:" A Lighthearted History of the Post-Graduate Game*. Albany, N.Y.: J. B. Lyon Company, 1934.

Meriam, Lewis. *The Problem of Indian Administration*. Baltimore: Johns Hopkins University Press, 1928.

Miner, H. Craig, and William E. Unrau, *The End of Indian Kansas: A Study of Cultural Revolution, 1854–1871*. Lawrence: University Press of Kansas, 1990.

Moore, Marianne. *Complete Poems*. New York: Penguin Classics, 1994.

Morris, John W., Charles R. Goins, and Edwin C. McReynolds. *Historical Atlas of Oklahoma*. Norman: University of Oklahoma Press, 1986.

Mrozek, Donald J. *Sport and American Mentality, 1880–1910*. Knoxville: University of Tennessee Press, 1983.

Murphy, Joseph F. *Potawatomi of the West: Origins of the Citizen Band*. Shawnee, Okla.: Citizen Band Potawatomi Tribe, 1994.

———. *Tenacious Monks: The Oklahoma Benedictines, 1875–1975: Indian Missionaries, Catholic Founders, Educators, Agriculturalists*. Shawnee, Okla.: Benedictine Color Press, 1974.

Nabokov, Peter. *Indian Running: Native-American History and Tradition*. Santa Barbara, Calif.: Capra Press, 1981.

———, ed. *Native American Testimony: A Chronicle of Indian White Relations from Prophecy to the Present, 1492–2000*. New York: Penguin, 1999.

National Association of Professional Baseball Leagues. *The Story of Minor League Baseball: A History of the Game of Professional Baseball in the United States with Particular Reference to Its Growth and Development in the Smaller Cities and Towns of the Nation—the Minor Leagues. The Record of Championship Performances from 1901 to 1952*. Columbus, Ohio: Stoneman Press, 1952.

Neft, David S., Michael L. Neft, and Richard M. Cohen. *The Sports Encyclopedia: Baseball 2007*. New York: St. Martin's, 2007.

Newcombe, Jack. *The Best of the Athletic Boys: The White Man's Impact on Jim Thorpe*. Garden City, N.Y.: Doubleday, 1975.

Oriard, Michael. *King Football: Spirit and Spectacle in the Golden Age of Radio and Newsreels, Movies and Magazines, the Weekly and Daily Press*. Chapel Hill: University of North Carolina Press, 2001.

———. *Reading Football: How the Popular Press Created an American Spectacle*. Chapel Hill: University of North Carolina Press, 1993.

Oxendine, Joseph B. *American Indian Sports Heritage*. Lincoln: University of Nebraska Press, 1995.

Pearce, Roy Harvey. *Savagism and Civilization*. Baltimore: Johns Hopkins University Press, 2001.

Penn, William S., ed. *As We Are Now: Mixblood Essays on Race and Identity*. Berkeley: University of California Press, 1997.

Peterson, Robert W. *Pigskin: The Early Years of Pro Football*. New York: Oxford University Press, 1997.

Philip, Kenneth R. *John Collier's Crusade for Indian Reform, 1920–1954.* Tucson: University of Arizona Press, 1977.

Pietrusza, David. *Major Leagues: The Formation, Sometimes Absorption and Mostly Inevitable Demise of 18 Professional Baseball Organizations, 1871 to Present.* Jefferson, N.C.: McFarland & Co., 2005.

Pope, Edwin. *Football's Greatest Coaches.* Atlanta: Tupper and Love, 1955.

Pope, S. W. *Patriotic Games: Sporting Traditions in the American Imagination, 1876–1926.* New York: Oxford University Press, 1997.

Porter, David L., ed. *Biographical Dictionary of American Sports: Baseball.* Westport, Conn.: Greenwood Press, 2000.

Porter, Joy. *To Be Indian: The Life of A. C. Parker.* Norman: University of Oklahoma Press, 2001.

Powers-Beck, Jeffrey. *The American Indian Integration of Baseball.* Lincoln: University of Nebraska Press, 2004.

Pratt, Richard Henry. *Battlefield and Classroom: Four Decades with the American Indian, 1867–1904.* Ed. Robert M. Utley. New Haven, Conn.: Yale University Press, 1987. Originally published by Yale University Press, 1964.

Professional Football Researchers Association. *Bulldogs on Sunday: 1920, 1921, 1922.* 3 vols. North Huntingdon, Pa.: PFRA, n.d.

Rampersand, Arnold. *Jackie Robinson: A Biography.* New York: Ballantine Books, 1997.

Reichler, Joseph L. *The Baseball Trade Register: Every Trade, Sale and Free Agent Signing from 1900 On.* New York: Macmillan, 1984.

Reinschmidt, Michael. *Ethnohistory of the Sauk, 1885–1985: A Socio-political Study on Continuity and Change.* Goettingen, Germany: Cuvillier Verlag, 1993.

Reising, Robert W. *Jim Thorpe: Tar Heel.* Rocky Mount, N.C.: Communique, 1974.

Remini, Robert V. *The Life of Andrew Jackson.* New York: Harper & Row, 1988.

Rice, Grantland. *The Tumult and the Shouting: My Life in Sport.* New York: A. S. Barnes & Co., 1954.

Riess, Steven A. *Touching Base: Professional Baseball and American Culture in the Progressive Era.* Westport, Conn.: Greenwood Press, 1980.

Ritter, Lawrence S. *The Glory of Their Times: The Story of the Early Days of Baseball Told by the Men Who Played It.* New York: Macmillan, 1966.

Roosevelt, Theodore. *The Strenuous Life: Essays and Addresses.* New York: Century Co., 1902.

Rosensweig, Sidney. *Casablanca and Other Major Films of Michael Curtiz.* Studies in Cinema, No. 14. Ann Arbor, Mich.: UMI Research Press, 1982.

Royce, Charles C., comp. *Indian Land Cessions in the United States, 18th Annual Report, Smithsonian Institution, Bureau of American Ethnology, for the Years 1896–1897, Part 2.* Washington, D.C.: Government Printing Office, 1899.

Savage, Howard, et al. *Current Developments in American College Athletics, with a Preface by Henry Suzallo, President of the Foundation.* Bulletin No. 26. New York: Carnegie Foundation for the Advancement of Teaching, 1931.

Savage, William W., Jr., ed. *Indian Life: Transforming an American Myth.* Norman: University of Oklahoma Press, 1977.

Schaap, Jeremy. *Triumph: The Untold Story of Jesse Owens and Hitler's Olympics.* New York: Houghton Mifflin, 2007.

Schaap, Richard. *An Illustrated History of the Olympics.* 2nd ed. New York: Alfred A. Knopf, 1967.

Seymour, Harold. *Baseball: The Early Years.* New York: Oxford University Press, 1960.

———. *Baseball: The Golden Age.* New York: Oxford University Press, 1971.

———. *Baseball: The People's Game.* New York: Oxford University Press, 1991.

Silko, Leslie Marmon. *Ceremony.* New York: Penguin Books, 1986.

Singer, Beverly R. *Wiping the War Paint Off the Lens: Native American Film and Video.* Minneapolis: University of Minnesota Press, 2001.

Smith, Donald B. *Chief Buffalo Long Lance: The Glorious Imposter.* Red Deer, Alberta, Canada: Red Deer Press, 1999.

Smith, Page. *America Enters the World: A People's History of the Progressive Era and World War I.* New York: McGraw-Hill, 1985.

———. *The Rise of Industrial America: A People's History of the Post-Reconstruction Era.* New York: McGraw-Hill, 1984.

Smith, Robert E. *Oklahoma's Forgotten Indians.* The Oklahoma Series, vol. 15, ed. Bob L. Blackburn. Oklahoma City: Oklahoma Historical Society, 1981.

Smith, Ronald A. *Sports and Freedom: The Rise of Big-Time College Athletics.* New York: Oxford University Press, 1988.

———, ed. *Big-Time Football at Harvard, 1905: The Diary of Coach Bill Reid.* Urbana: University of Illinois Press, 1994.

Smith, William E. "The Oregon Trail Through Pottawatomie County." In *Collections of the Kansas State Historical Society, Together with Addresses, Memorials and Miscellaneous Papers.* vol. 17, ed. William Elsey Connelley, Secretary. Topeka: Kansas State Printing Plant, 1928.

Spindel, Carol. *Dancing at Halftime: Sports and the Controversy over American Indian Mascots.* New York: New York University Press, 2000.

Stannard, David E. *American Holocaust: The Conquest of the New World.* New York: Oxford University Press, 1992.

Steckbeck, John S. *Fabulous Redmen: The Carlisle Indians and Their Famous Football Teams.* Harrisburg, Pa.: J. Horace McFarland Company, 1951.

Steiger, Brad, and Charlotte Thorpe. *Thorpe's Gold.* New York: Quicksilver Books, Inc., in association with Dell Publishing Co., Inc., 1984.

Stocking, George W. *Race, Culture, and Evolution: Essays in the History of Anthropology.* New York: Free Press, 1968.

Strickland, Rennard. *The Indians in Oklahoma (Newcomers to a New Land).* Norman: University of Oklahoma Press, 1981.

Sturtevant, William C., and Bruce G. Trigger, eds. *Handbook of North American Indians.* Vol. 15, *Northeast.* Washington, D.C.: Smithsonian Institution Scholarly Press, 1978.

Sullivan, James E., ed. *The Olympic Games Stockholm 1912*, Spalding "Red Cover" Series of Athletic Handbooks, No. 17R. New York: American Sports Publishing Co., 1912.

Tanner, Helen Hornbeck. *Atlas of Great Lakes Indian History.* Vol. 174, *Civilization of the American Indian.* Norman: University of Oklahoma Press, 1987.

Thompson, Stephen I. "The American Indian in the Major Leagues." *Baseball Research Journal* 12 (1983): 1–7.

Thorn, John, Peter Palmer, and Michael Gershman, eds. *Total Baseball: The Official Encyclopedia of Major League Baseball.* 5th ed. New York: Viking, 1997.

———, eds. *Total Baseball: The Official Encyclopedia of Major League Baseball.* 6th ed. New York: Total Sports, 1999.

Thornley, Stewart. *Land of the Giants: New York's Polo Grounds.* Philadelphia: Temple University Press, 2000.

Thorpe, Dagmar, ed. *People of the Seventh Fire*. Ithaca, N.Y.: Akwe:kon Press, 1996.

Thorpe, Jim, with Russell J. Birdwell. *The Red Son of Carlisle*. Unpublished movie treatment, 1930. *Jim Thorpe—All American* (1951) production file, Warner Bros. Collection, USC.

———, in collaboration with Thomas F. Collison. *Jim Thorpe's History of the Olympics*. Los Angeles: Wetzel, 1932.

U.S. Department of Health and Human Services. *Mental Health: Culture, Race, and Ethnicity—A Supplement to Mental Health: A Report of the Surgeon General*. Rockville, Md.: U.S. Department of Heath and Human Services, Substance Abuse and Mental Health Services Administration, Center for Mental Health Service, 2001.

United States Congress. *Carlisle Indian School. Hearings Before the Joint Commission of the Congress of the United States to Investigate Indian Affairs. February 6–8 and March 25, 1914*. 63rd Congress, 2nd Session, Part 2. Washington, D.C.: Government Printing Office, 1914.

Vecchione, Joseph J. *The New York Times Book of Sports Legends*. New York: Times Books, 1991.

Vogel, Virgil J. *This Country Was Ours: A Documentary History of the American Indian*. New York: Harper & Row, 1972.

Voigt, David. *American Baseball: From Gentleman's Sport to the Commissioner System*. Norman: University of Oklahoma Press, 1966.

———. *American Baseball: From the Commissioners to Continental Expansion*. Norman: University of Oklahoma Press, 1970.

Wallechinsky, David, and Jaime Loucky. *The Complete Book of the Olympics*. London: Aurum Press, 2008.

Walsh, Christy, and Glenn C. Whittle. *Intercollegiate Football: A Complete Pictorial and Statistical Review from 1869 to 1934*. New York: Doubleday, Doran & Co., for Intercollegiate Football, 1934.

Warner, Glenn Scobey. *Football for Coaches and Players*. Palo Alto, Calif.: Stanford University Press, 1927.

———. *Pop Warner: Football's Greatest Teacher: The Epic Autobiography of Major College Football's Winningest Coach, Glenn S. (Pop) Warner*, ed. Mike Bynum. Langhorne, Pa.: Gridiron Football Properties, 1993.

Washburn, Wilcomb E., ed. *The American Indian and the United States: A Documentary History*. New York: Random House, 1973.

Washburn, Wilcomb E., and William C. Sturtevant, eds. *Handbook of North American Indians*. Vol. 4, *History of Indian-White Relations*. Washington, D.C.: Smithsonian Institution Scholarly Press, 1989.

Watterson, John Sayle. *College Football: History, Spectacle, Controversy*. Baltimore: Johns Hopkins University Press, 2000.

Weyand, Alexander M. *Football Immortals*. New York: Macmillan, 1962.

———. *The Saga of American Football*. New York: Macmillan, 1955.

Wheeler, Robert W. *Jim Thorpe: World's Greatest Athlete*. Norman: University of Oklahoma Press, 1979.

Whitman, Robert L. *Jim Thorpe and the Oorang Indians: N.F.L.'s Most Colorful Franchise*. Defiance, Ohio: Hubbard Company, 1984.

———. *Jim Thorpe, Athlete of the Century: A Pictorial Biography*. Defiance, Ohio: Hubbard Company, 2002.

Whitney, Caspar W. *A Sporting Pilgrimage*. New York: Harper and Brothers, 1894.

Willard, Shirley, and Judy Cecrle, eds. *Trail of Death: 1838 Diary*. Rochester, Ind.: Fulton County Historical Society, 1988.

Williams, Ted, as told to John Underwood. *My Turn at Bat: The Story of My Life*. New York: Pocket Books, 1970.

Wilson, John. *The Earth Shall Weep: A History of Native America*. New York: Grove Press, 1998.

Wissler, Clark. *Indians of the United States: Four Centuries of Their History and Culture*. Rev. ed. New York: Bantam Dell, 1966.

Witmer, Linda F. *The Indian Industrial School: Carlisle, Pennsylvania, 1879–1918*. Carlisle, Pa.: Cumberland County Historical Society, 2000.

Wright, Muriel. *A Guide to the Indian Tribes of Oklahoma*. Norman: University of Oklahoma Press, 1951.

Young, David. C. *The Olympic Myth of Greek Amateur Athletics*. Chicago: Areas Publishers, 1984.

Index

Page numbers in *italics* refer to illustrations. Page numbers beginning with 390 refer to endnotes.

ILLUSTRATION CREDITS

2:
Smithsonian American Art Museum, Gift of Mrs. Joseph Harrison, Jr.
32:
Cumberland County Historical Society, Carlisle, Pennsylvania
56:
Cumberland County Historical Society, Carlisle, Pennsylvania
82:
Courtesy of Robert W. Reising
96:
Cumberland County Historical Society, Carlisle, Pennsylvania
118:
Cumberland County Historical Society, Carlisle, Pennsylvania
156:
Cumberland County Historical Society, Carlisle, Pennsylvania
192:
Robert W. Wheeler Collection
260:
Photofest
310:
From the collections of The Henry Ford
328:
Cumberland County Historical Society, Carlisle, Pennsylvania

CPSIA information can be obtained
at www.ICGtesting.com
Printed in the USA
LVHW050340061120
670868LV00002B/2